HERITAGE OF MUSIC

VOLUME I
CLASSICAL MUSIC
AND ITS ORIGINS

Sumer is icumen in · Lhude sing cuccu · Groweþ sed and bloweþ

Perspice xpicola · que dignacio · celicus · agrico-

med and springþ þe wde nu · Sing cuccu · Awe bleteþ after

la · pro uitis vicio · filio — non parcens exposu-

lomb lhouþ after calue cu · Bulluc sterteþ · bucke uerteþ

it · mortis exicio — qui captiuos semiuiuos

murie sing cuccu · Cuccu cuccu Wel singes þu cuccu ne swik

a supplicio — Vite donat et secum coronat · in ce-

Hanc rotam cantare possunt quatuor socij · a paucio-
ribus autem quam a tribus uel saltem duobus non debet
dici · preter eos qui dicunt pedem · Canitur autem sic · Tacen-
tibus ceteris unus inchoat cum hiis qui tenent pedem · Et cum uenerit
ad primam notam post crucem · inchoat alius · et sic de ceteris ·

þu nauer nu

li so li o ·

Singuli uero repausent ad pausaciones scriptas
et non alibi · spacio unius longe note ·

hoc repetit unus quociens opus est ·

Sing cuccu nu · Sing cuccu · faciens pausacionem in fine ·

Pes

Sing cuccu · Sing cuccu nu ·

hoc dicit alius · pausans in medio et non in
fine · sed immediate repetens principium

Heritage of Music

EDITED BY
MICHAEL RAEBURN AND ALAN KENDALL

VOLUME I
CLASSICAL MUSIC AND ITS ORIGINS

CONSULTANT EDITORS
ROGER BLANCHARD, DENIS ARNOLD
AND H. C. ROBBINS LANDON

OXFORD NEW YORK
OXFORD UNIVERSITY PRESS
1989

Oxford University Press, Walton Street, Oxford OX2 6DP

Oxford   New York   Toronto
Delhi   Bombay   Calcutta   Madras   Karachi
Petaling Jaya   Singapore   Hong Kong   Tokyo
Nairobi   Dar es Salaam   Cape Town
Melbourne   Auckland

and associated companies in
Berlin   Ibadan

Oxford is a trade mark of Oxford University Press

Published in the United States
by Oxford University Press

British Library Cataloguing in Publication Data
Heritage of music.
    1. Music—History and criticism   I. Raeburn, Michael,
1940-   .II. Kendall, Alan, 1939-
    780'.903   ML193
ISBN 0–19–520493–X (set)
    0–19–505370–2 (vol.1)

Library of Congress Cataloguing in Publication Data
Main entry under title:

Heritage of music.

    Includes index.
    Contents: 1. Classical music and its origins —
2. Romantic music — 3. Legacy of nineteenth-century
music — [etc.]
    1. Music—History and criticism.   I. Raeburn, Michael,
1940-   . II. Kendall, Alan, 1939-
ML160.H527   1988   780'.9   85-21429
ISBN 0–19–520493–X (set)
    0–19–505370–2 (vol.1)

Produced by Heritage of Music Ltd

Design and art direction: David Warner
Picture research: Julia Engelhardt, Lisa Agate,
Helen Ottaway, Robert Turnbull
Artwork: Roy Coombs
Translation from French: Derek McCulloch
Color origination: Scala, Florence

Printed in Hong Kong

CONTENTS

FOREWORD

Every writer on music must confront a paradox, since music is itself a language, but one that communicates its meaning without any use – or need – of words. Because this communication can be so immediate, words often seem to fail to grasp its essence, and indeed writing about music often has to be concerned with peripheral matters. Formal exposition, description of conditions of performance, or biographical information can help us get closer to the music, but the logic of a Bach fugue, a Haydn symphony or a Bartók quartet can only be grasped by listening to the music itself. The volumes of *Heritage of Music*, which use both words and pictures to inform the reader about the long western musical tradition, are designed principally as an accompaniment to listening. The plan and approach of the work take for granted that the reader will have an opportunity to listen to much of the music which is the subject of its pages, and the remarkable range of repertoire available in recordings makes this a quite realistic prospect.

This is, then, an approach to learning to understand musical language in many of its aspects. Music is at once more abstract and more sensual than any other artistic medium, and it is at the same time capable of both logical and expressive statement. In terms of the sheer pleasure of listening to music, no explanation is needed; indeed, many people fear that to understand how a composer achieves a particular effect may break the spell he has cast. Music's powers of physical arousal through rhythm, whether to war or love, go back to its very origins; but it also has an extraordinary ability to probe the memory, to evoke past experiences and emotions, comparable, as Proust showed, to the senses of smell or of taste. At different times very specific meanings have been attached to specific keys or modes, to the sound-colors of particular instruments or ranges of the human voice, and to harmonic, rhythmic or melodic patterns. In baroque music the connection of particular musical characteristics with specific emotions (*Affekte*) made it easy to evoke a pastoral or a heroic mood, a sense of quiet or contentment; and this could lead to the creation of elaborate musical pictures, Vivaldi's 'Four Seasons' concertos being the best known today. Music of that period developed a formal iconography, comparable to the allegorical significance of much baroque painting, sculpture

or architecture. Painting musical pictures continued through Haydn and Beethoven to the great Romantic tone-poems, many of them accompanied by elaborate programs – inevitably leading to a reaction and demands for a return to 'pure' music. But music has never been pure in that sense; at its most abstract and logical it still retains the overwhelming power to evoke emotions.

It is this that lends opera its extraordinary attraction. On the face of it the most artificial of art forms, opera at its best can display the emotional content of human situations with a vividness that words alone can seldom convey, and the range and subtlety of expression are quite extraordinary. It is a commonplace that opera libretti sometimes plumb the depths of absurdity, but even then the music of a Purcell, a Mozart or a Verdi can lend the most living and painful reality to a human situation; how much more is this the case when there is a true collaboration between composer and librettist – as Mozart and Verdi were to have, respectively, with da Ponte and Boito, and Richard Strauss with Hofmannsthal – or when, like Wagner, the composer writes his own words. However, faithful settings of the greatest poetry are seldom wholly successful in opera, perhaps because musical language is too powerful and inevitably dominates the words. Here the medium of the song offers a more even balance, and composers such as Schubert, Wolf and Debussy could do justice to Goethe, Mörike or Verlaine.

At the opposite pole to opera and song, music can express abstract thought with clarity and deep insight. In its most complex forms it may have a spiritual or metaphysical dimension, as in medieval polyphony, or the counterpoint of J. S. Bach, or Beethoven's string quartets. Here, the music can be described or analyzed, but what it expresses cannot be translated at all into verbal language.

It is for this reason, as well as to provide more vivid background to the composers and works discussed, that illustrations have been included in this work. Visual art, which also has its own language – a language that, like music, can be analyzed but not translated – is frequently concerned with a similar range of ideas, and its means of expression can often give an insight into the preoccupations of contemporary composers. Indeed, many of the commonest terms used in music criticism – color and line, foreground and background, the Baroque or Impressionism – are borrowed from the visual arts. However, with the notable exception of Edward Lockspeiser's pioneering *Music and Painting* (1973), there have been few detailed studies of the relationship and interpenetration between those arts at different periods. The insight that can be gained has been shown in a recent essay by Charles Rosen, one of the most brilliant living writers on both music and art, in which he discusses the 'fusion of color and line' achieved by both the painter Delacroix and his close friend Chopin; but in the absence of such detailed studies, supported by documentary evidence, a survey such as this can only offer more general parallels. We have, however, tried to choose pictures which match the musical foreground as closely as possible in both time and place. Most, of course, also illustrate more specific aspects of musical history – performances, musicians, instruments – but their style is an essential part of their content. If these books can help stimulate further comparative studies, they will have achieved one of their goals.

The plan of *Heritage of Music* derives from our intention to provide a many-layered background to listening to music, and it is related to the basic repertoire of music performed. The music of the past three hundred years is therefore discussed principally in terms of the major composers, while these accounts are complemented by chapters on general musical developments or, in the exceptional cases of Beethoven and Schubert, on the establishment of paradigmatic forms. These chapters which do not encompass the life and work of an individual composer are intended to go some way toward the kind of history of music called for by Carl Dahlhaus, in his chapter on Romantic Music in Volume II, in which the historical accounts should be primarily concerned with the 'problems that face composers.' These problems are presented here by the discussion and illustration of intellectual and cultural tendencies and social and political background as well as formal and technical musical developments. Thus, although specialist terminology has been avoided as far as possible and music examples are not given, the books are designed to give insights to the student of music as well as to the music-lover – both the *Kenner* and the *Liebhaber*, as the eighteenth century would have had it. While setting out basic patterns, we have not suggested that the authors of the individual essays should follow a unified approach, and the question, raised by Dahlhaus, of the validity of a biographical approach to a composer's music is answered in many different ways throughout these volumes.

In addition, each volume contains a number of 'interludes,' which describe with pictures and text a specific subject that falls outside the scope of the main chapters; these may be concerned with the evolution of musical instruments, developments in theater and ballet, composers outside the mainstream, or with other topics that can bring the main events of the history of music into sharper relief. At the end of each volume is a selective biographical dictionary of composers, designed to give essential information on the majority of musicians whose work may be heard in the current concert repertoire, thus freeing the authors of individual chapters of the need to account for every contemporary of the major composers.

In preparing the *Heritage of Music* over a number of years, we have incurred many debts of gratitude, and it would be impossible to mention all those who have contributed in their different ways. Our first thanks must be to the consultant editors and to the authors, who have shown great patience over the long period of preparation and have most helpfully accommodated our needs in matching text to illustrations. The searching out and selection of the pictures was principally in the hands of Julia Engelhardt, and the design in those of David Warner; the books themselves are a tribute to their work. Among those who have collaborated in the production of the work, special thanks are due to Alan Blackwood, Kathleen Blakistone, Ann Bridges, Thekla Clark, Joanne Downey, Dr Elizabeth Heine, Mara Puccini, Marianne Ryan and Victoria Wilson.

We have had patient support from Ed Barry, David Attwooll, Bill Mitchell, Bruce Phillips and Pam Coote of Oxford University Press, and, since the project was first underway, from Hiroshi Ishii, Ian Montrose, Robert Robinson and his client, and Marilyn McCully. The original plan of *Heritage of Music* was conceived by Alexander Mosley, and it is only through his unfailing help in every possible way that we have been able to complete the work. To him, to all those mentioned above, and to the many others who have worked with us we offer our most grateful thanks.

MICHAEL RAEBURN
ALAN KENDALL

INTRODUCTION

PAUL GRIFFITHS & ROLAND DE CANDÉ

The particular glory of western classical music is its heritage; it has a history, which is possible because it has a means of record: it has notation. This is what distinguishes the subject of these volumes from every other musical culture known to us and what has made possible the successive emergence within the western classical tradition of a Machaut, a Palestrina, a Bach, a Beethoven, a Wagner, each generation building on the experience of its predecessors.

Notation is not quite, however, the unique preserve of music in the West. We know that the ancient Greeks and the Chinese, among others, had ways of writing down musical sounds. But for them notation never seems to have developed beyond a rudimentary stage, and its importance lay in describing musical matters within the context of theoretical treatises, not in preserving music for future performance. Notation in this more practical sense appears to have arisen gradually in France around the year 1000, and to have developed as an *aide-mémoire* for choirs who had to deal with an ever-growing repertory of plainsong.

It is evident that notation is by no means the same thing as composition. A musician may be able to compose without having any idea as to how his composition might be written down. This is the case, for example, on the island of Bali, where a rich musical culture has developed on the basis of compositions which are taught and learned entirely by ear. It happens not infrequently, too, that composers of popular songs are musically illiterate, and rely on the services of others to note their compositions. So it should not be surprising that notation originated as an aid to performers, not composers. We may presume men and women to have composed songs and dances for themselves since prehistoric times, and to have handed on the music they learned from their elders, exactly as happens in folk and ritual music all over the world today. The significant change brought about by notation was that it gave people the opportunity to test out new ideas quickly and simply, and to make a permanent record of what they discovered.

The difference this caused can perhaps be explained by literary analogy; most music without notation has the features of legend, with fairly stable elements expressed anew by each generation and passed on to the next. In western classical music, however, the model is that of the novel, with emphasis on what is new and has never been expressed before. Hence the importance attached in highly sophisticated non-western musical cultures to subtleties of interpretation within a very narrow range of options, whereas the admirer of western classical music may well look for a whole new musical world in each work.

Naturally there are areas in which western classical music does not differ as fundamentally as all that. The *aficionado* of operatic sopranos, for example, shares with anyone who appreciates Indian music a taste that depends on fine judgment within a highly codified and conventional tradition. Moreover, the importance of tradition in western music should not be underestimated: tradition inculcated within families (the Bachs, the Mozarts), within nations, within genres (the symphony, the string quartet), or within musical culture as a whole. Nevertheless, it remains broadly true that the essence of non-western music is continuity whereas that of western music is change – a difference which could not have come about had it not been for notation, for change only becomes meaningful when one thing can be compared with another, and comparison demands some kind of record.

It is not to be wondered at, therefore, that the invention of notation, at first a purely mnemonic device, soon became an essential element of compositional activity. This transition was rapid; it is impossible to disentangle the early history of musical notation from the early history of polyphony. And here once more is a respect in which western tradition differs markedly from all others. Though the concept of two people singing different lines at the same time is a perfectly natural one, it is not an idea that has been much pursued in any non-European culture, probably because it is so much easier to remember one line than two. But once notation had relieved the burden on the memory, polyphony could flourish, as indeed it did from the early Middle Ages. In the twelfth century, almost as soon as conventions of musical notation had become established, one finds composers creating works for three or four voices on a grand scale, taking ecclesiastical chant and using it merely as a thread for imaginative exercises of their own devising.

Another essential difference springs to mind too. Throughout most of the world music is used with some purpose in view: to invoke a

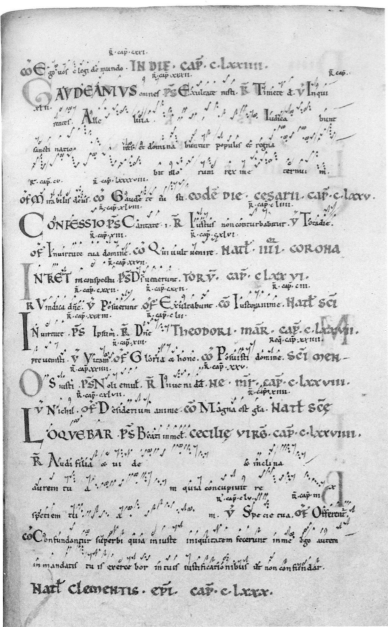

a continuation of these twelfth-century tendencies. It is a history of increasing standardization and also, paradoxically, increasing personality, for as the materials of music became ever more finely prescribed, so the individuality of any particular musical work could be more completely stated. Once again, it was notation that made such a development possible. Indeed, every stage in the evolution of western music is marked by change in notation, and from the twelfth century onwards it becomes quite impossible to conceive of western music existing without some written record.

• The keyboard •

Notation, however, is not the only unique feature responsible for the unparalleled development of music within the western tradition. Also to be considered is the invention of the keyboard instrument – first the organ, then the harpsichord and later the piano – which allowed a single performer to play many different notes at the same time. Certainly from the late sixteenth century onwards western music has been conditioned very much by keyboard instruments, and has to some extent been dependent on the ease with which a solo musician could study and perform music of a polyphonic nature. It would seem that keyboard instruments are quite unknown in other musical cultures; there is, indeed, no need of them. Only a musical culture of some polyphonic and harmonic sophistication could find a use for the keyboard, and it is worth noting that many outstanding innovatory composers of the western tradition, including Bach, Mozart, Beethoven, Chopin, Liszt and Debussy, were keyboard performers.

Without the keyboard it is unlikely that western music would have developed the equal-tempered chromatic scale, another of its integral features. In general terms the evolution of music is intimately linked with a gradual increase in

god, to celebrate a victory, to entertain a monarch. It is not primarily a means of personal expression for composer and performer. In the West, however, it is exactly that, beginning to take on this character from the twelfth century. Until that period western music had been no different from any other: it was monophonic, aurally transmitted, anonymous as to its composer, and related to some 'mode' or family of melodies. Then suddenly a great change took place. Since music could be notated, it could become polyphonic, and since it was polyphonic it necessarily began to extricate itself from the generalized concept of mode. As it was leaving behind such repositories of tradition, it was rapidly acquiring the profile of an individual. Listening to the music of Léonin or Pérotin we feel in contact with a particular human mind. Music begins to express not a tradition but a single intelligence.

The subsequent history of western music right up to the present day is hardly more than

the number of notes brought into play. The most primitive music is pentatonic, with five notes to the octave; modal music, represented for example by plainsong, generally needs seven. Western music, with twelve, has an unusually wide repertory of pitches and intervals, though only in the present century has music been written for all twelve notes at once. Not only can instruments designed for the chromatic system play in any of the twelve major and twelve minor keys, but music can also move freely from one key to another.

Such changes of key are hugely important. The rule outside the western tradition is that a piece of music begins in one particular mode and stays there. Indeed, in some cultures, to explore the possibilities within the constraints of the mode may be one of the principal musical points; Indian musicians, for instance, work in this way when improvising on ragas. By contrast, western music has developed on the basis of variety, and though a sitarist's improvisation may easily last as long as a symphony, western composers are able, by using different keys, to create works which are not only this long but decidedly progressive: one expects an improvisation to wander, a symphony to move in clear stages from its opening to its conclusion. And this progression is very simply achieved. The music moves forward from one key to another, with the expectation of an eventual return, which the composer may forcefully underline, hint at or conceal: this is the whole basis of sonata form, which dominated western music from Haydn to Mahler.

The symphonies of Mahler might almost be taken as exemplifying the most characteristic features of western music. They are all extensive and intended to be heard with complete concentration, so that the listener is drawn into the music. They show a perhaps unparalleled achievement of strong forward movement despite the vast range of ideas brought into play. Those ideas are, moreover, notated with great precision, so that although no two performances will be identical, there is little room for argument about the melodies, harmonies, rhythms, instrumentation, dynamic levels and phrasing intended by the composer. This makes each work unique but also repeatable, a peculiarly western concept.

Repeatability is an essential criterion for a piece of music to be considered a work of art, something to be studied, performed and heard over and over again in a progressive exercise of deeper understanding; it is an art of memory.

Four stages in the development of western musical notation.

Opposite top: Page from an early twelfth-century gradual from Noyons, France. The dots and strokes written above the words are neumes, a reminder of the melody to be sung rather than a truly notated record.

Opposite bottom: Part of a Mass by John Taverner of around 1525. This is true notation: the clef at the left of each line of music indicates the position of middle C, and each staff (or stave) line represents a particular pitch, with the notes placed on or between the staves; the shape of the notes indicates their relative duration. A drawing of the composer is worked into the initial letter.

Below: Martin Luther's famous chorale 'Ein feste Burg' (A Stronghold Sure), printed in 1533. Bars to define measures are now used.

Right: A century later, notation has quite a familiar appearance, as in this page of a *Royal Consort* by William Lawes of around 1635.

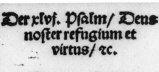

Non-western music exists for the moment and then is gone; the notion of repeating a piece twice, with no improvisatory attention, would be quite alien. As a tradition western music guards its past; music notated a thousand years ago is still being performed today.

Although western music is a clearly recognizable and self-contained tradition in itself, it has always looked outside for new ideas. Many of the standard orchestral instruments, for instance, developed out of prototypes from elsewhere; even the violin family has its ancestors in Islamic music. Folk music has also been thoroughly influential, certainly at all periods from Haydn and Beethoven to Bartók and Stravinsky. Meanwhile there have been injections from more exotic sources: the Turkish drums and cymbals that delighted the late eighteenth century with their crudity, the east Asian music that brought sympathetic vibrations from Debussy, the ritual music of Japan that has been so important to Stockhausen. Mahler too, though standing at

11

the apex of the symphonic tradition that is perhaps western music's greatest achievement, looks outside his own culture to folksong, popular dance and the pentatonic music of China. Western tradition has long been enhanced by these and other musical entities.

We are now in the privileged position of being able to observe that tradition as a whole. But no such viewpoint was available until quite recently. Anyone living in the time of Beethoven, for example, would have had little opportunity to hear any music more than a few years old. Nor was there much chance of hearing a major work like a symphony or a concerto twice, unless it was played for or by the listener as a piano version. In these respects, western music around 1800 was not so very different from music in other cultures: it was a thing of the moment, not a repository of masterpieces dating back several centuries.

There has been another remarkable change as well. In 1800 music was available to just a small minority. Only those in the largest cities – Vienna, London, Paris – would have been able to hear orchestral concerts or attend opera.

Above: Decorated page from an Italian lute book of 1517 – among the earliest examples of lute music to be set down on paper. The notation is a form of tablature, which instructs the player where to place his fingers to obtain the right notes. The lines across the page actually represent the strings of the lute, and the numbers indicate which frets on the fingerboard are to be touched. Time-values of the notes are indicated by the tails on the stems written above each line.

Above: The sixteenth-century Netherlandish artist Michiel van Coxcie's painting of St Cecilia, the patron saint of music, playing the virginal is a tribute to the growing importance of stringed keyboard instruments during the Renaissance period.

Below: A spinet of 1577 by the Italian instrument-maker Annibale dei Rossi. The main part of the decoration is ivory set with precious and semi-precious stones. The spinet was a small harpsichord similar to the virginal.

And only those with some financial means could have employed musicians or even bought instruments and music. Perhaps no more than a few thousand people heard Beethoven's Fifth Symphony during his lifetime, whether played in a concert hall or hammered out at the keyboard. In the two centuries since then the audience has grown immeasurably. Western music has spread beyond the cities of Europe to become the property of the world, and its repertory in almost constant performance has grown to embrace the finest products of a millennium.

• Music and primitive man •

Mankind has created music in order to suit not only its hearing, which is capable of observing all acoustic phenomena indiscriminately, but also its brain – and this takes us back to a fairly recent period in the evolution of our species. One might well associate it with the origins of language and communication, and this could go back as far as the end of the Middle Paleo-

lithic period, some 50,000 or 60,000 years. No doubt some rudimentary rhythmical organization could have appeared with the anthropoids of the Tertiary period, four or five million years ago: beating on fixed objects, shaking objects or knocking them together as a function of vital movements. Rather more certainly, the hominids of the Lower Paleolithic period (pithecanthropes), one or one and a half million years ago, could have imitated the rhythms or sounds of nature by means of their mouths and larynxes. A vocal cry would still, however, have been no more than a complicated muscular activity adapted to the conditions of the struggle for existence.

The earliest representatives of homo sapiens, in the Middle Paleolithic era, will have continued to use the sound possibilities of the mouth and the larynx in the same way. However, as emotion or expressive intent provoked variations in the pitch and timbre of their 'voices,' they must have tried to cultivate this phenomenon, so that the voice began to be adapted to deliberate variation. A 'homo musicus' emerged little by little as consciousness developed. Homo sapiens sapiens, coming later, possessed an apparent

Below left: A page from *Theorica Musicae* by the Italian composer and musical scholar Franchino Gafori (1451-1522), clearly relating the pipes of an organ to the pitched notes of a scale. Organs were the first keyboard instruments, and the introduction of the spring return key was a big advance on the huge and unwieldy systems of levers or sliders that had operated the earliest organs.

Below: Fifteenth-century Italian fresco of an organ and a set of chimes in the hands of a versatile musician.

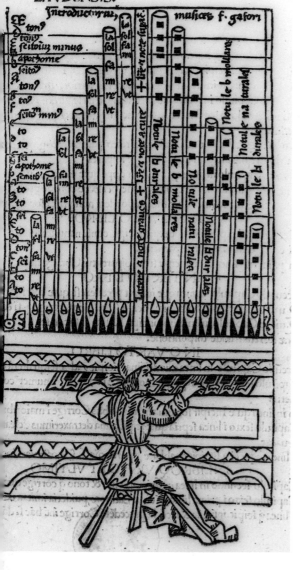

civilizations settled in fertile valleys: the Tigris and Euphrates (Mesopotamia), the Indus (India), the Nile (Egypt), and the Huâng-o (China). The most ancient musical traditions are certainly found in these countries. The timely appearance of metallurgy (copper, in Asia Minor, around 5000 BC) finally produced a means of creating new instruments of great refinement. Unfortunately, the catastrophic river floods and cataclysms which ravaged Mesopotamia and the neighboring countries (the biblical Deluge of about 3600 BC) destroyed virtually all vestiges of these ancient civilizations. The earliest musical evidence and the earliest extant cuneiform texts, whether from Egypt or from Western Asia, date from the period immediately following this disaster.

The means of making music have been similar the world over, but musical styles and traditions have varied enormously. The illustrations on these two pages represent the four basic categories of musical instrument (*see also* page 21), from very different times and places.

Above: Aerophone, where the sound is produced by a vibrating column of air – double-headed clay pan pipes from Peru of around 100 BC, the little figures themselves shown playing the pipes.

Right: Idiophone, an instrument which 'speaks' on its own when struck or shaken – bronze sistrum, or jingle, of around 2000 BC from Anatolia (Turkey), an instrument that was very widespread among the ancient civilizations of the Middle East.

musical consciousness (about 40,000 BC), alongside the development of abstract language. This man could manufacture sonorous objects which were more differentiated, more effective and capable of 'artistic' expression: stones and hollow trunks of trees, bones or reeds cut to measure. At the end of a slow encephalic and muscular adaptation, singing became possible, and then came the inspired idea of associating 'vocal' expression with 'instrumental' expression, thus divining their musical relationship.

The first real musical civilizations, however, could have appeared only in the Neolithic period, from 10,000 BC onwards, under the stimulus of the formation of social systems; an awareness of the future began to confer upon human action something of a purposive and considered character. It was only then that polished stone tools rendered it possible to manufacture, *according to a model*, sonorous objects tuned to a certain pitch – a prerequisite for the development of a musical civilization.

Music also called for a sufficiently structured social system for part of the population to take some time off from the procurement of food. Such a state of affairs was present, if not in the earliest agricultural villages (about 10,000 BC), at least in the walled cities (such as Jericho, between 8000 and 6000 BC, which probably had a population of three thousand); such urban concentrations favored the development of an economic organization and of a social system differentiated by division of labor. The progress of culture long remained peculiar to the rich

• Ancient civilizations •

In the lower valley of the Euphrates there was established a highly developed population, of unknown origin, the Sumerians. At the time of the earliest Semitic infiltrations, towards 2800 BC, they possessed a rich and ancient culture which the newcomers, the Akkadians, assimilated. Music played a major part in the solemn ceremonies and domestic rites of Sumer. The instruments found in the excavations of the cemetery of Ur, and also in the depictions of musical scenes, reveal a refined art making use of silver and reed flutes, harps, lyres (with from five to eleven strings), a long-necked lute, a timpan (Elamite harp with chords to be struck), and cymbals. A bas-relief in the Louvre in Paris, found in the ruins of Lagash, shows a kind of harp or zither with a supporting column, such as was not to be found elsewhere for another fifteen centuries.

Both Assur, on the Tigris, and Babylon, on the Euphrates, honored musicians more highly than the learned, placing them next after kings and gods. In the massacres following their conquests, the Assyrians always spared the enemies' musicians, whom they took back to Assur with their booty. Very soon bands were formed which at the height of Babylonian civilization grew to an enormous size.

The Sumero-Babylonian and Assyrian musical traditions spread over Syria and Phoenicia, whence they enriched the music of the Egyptians, Cretans and peoples of Asia Minor (Phrygians and Lydians). The Hebrews, whose history began when Abraham left Ur for Canaan towards 1800 BC, also inherited this musical patrimony, enriched by Egyptian influence, and brought by Moses' people into Canaan after the Exodus. It was only then that the union of the Twelve Tribes allowed the formation of a specifically Jewish musical tradition.

In India, the Indus civilization flourished between 2500 and 1500 BC just prior to the Aryan colonization, perhaps developed from the ethnic and cultural bases of Mesopotamian civilization. The absence, however, of precise evidence or reliable chronology prevents any hypothesis about the music of ancient India. All the same, the Vedic hymns (from 1300 BC onwards) make reference to an already distant cultural past and, according to legend, the god Shiva is supposed to have taught music to mankind six thousand years before our era.

The traditional account places the start of Chinese musical civilization as early as 4000 BC. According to the ancient theoreticians, the *k'in* has seven chords, and the *se* fifty chords; the *sheng* (an organ played by the mouth) would have dated from 3000 BC, as would have the system of *lyu* (standard pipes determining the scale and diapason, the basis of all Chinese music). Unfortunately, it is hard to check these traditional data, because an imperial decree in 212 BC ordered the destruction of the books, thus depriving us of most early written sources. Despite this catastrophic holocaust, Chinese

Above left: Chordophone, where the sound is produced by stretched strings vibrating – vertical-angled harp from Mesopotamia depicted on a clay tablet of around 1900 BC.

Above: Membranophone, where sound is produced by beating a stretched skin – a drum which accompanies the singing of a Nigerian musician.

musical culture never underwent the eclipses suffered by other civilizations. This continuity may be explained by the philosophical and political importance which the Chinese attributed to the perfection of music. Decisions relating to the system were always the acts of emperors, ministers and sages; and it was believed that if the determination of the *huan-tchong* (first *lyu*) was correct, there would be good government and a prosperous State.

The fundamental scale of the twelve *lyu*, determined by the cycle of fifths (sub-dominant, tonic, dominant, sub-mediant, super-dominant, mediant, leading note and so on) continues, even today, to constitute the pentatonic Chinese scales. In the same way the Chinese instruments of antiquity have continued in use to the present day in their original forms (except for certain refinements), and have infiltrated, under different names, other countries under Chinese cultural influence.

Egyptian musical civilization may go back as far as that of China and Mesopotamia. The oldest evidence known is a statuette of a dancer (about 4800 BC) and a schist copy of a plaque sculpted to show dancers, masked and playing flutes (3500 BC). A mural relief of the Old Empire

16

Different civilizations have developed musical styles that are as individual as their painting or architecture, despite the similar ways of actually making music. The long European musical tradition has developed one set of musical sounds, which are quite different, for instance, from the classical music of India or China.

Opposite top: Egyptian tomb painting of around 1400 BC, showing a musician playing a large bow-shaped harp. Her companion plays a long-necked lute.

Opposite bottom: Assyrian stone relief of around 700 BC of two horizontal-angled harps. The musicians have plectrums to pluck the strings.

Above: Chinese painting on silk from the T'ang dynasty (AD 618-906) of women flute players accompanied by a string player.

Left: Greek vase depicting (left to right) a kithara, harp and lyre. There is a strong link between classical Greek music and our western musical tradition, largely through the transmission of Greek musical theory by Roman and medieval writers. How the ancient Greeks actually performed their music is still largely a matter for speculation.

shows singers, a harpist and a flautist, playing a long flute, suggesting sweetness and refinement of music of a domestic rather than religious character. During this period, when the great pyramids were built, pharaonic musical tradition seems to have reached its classical stage. Under the Middle Empire (2544-2060 BC) there are many more documents, showing larger bands with harps, lutes, double-reeded flutes, trumpets, crotales, drums and other instruments. These instruments multiplied and came to perfection under the New Empire, the epoch of Ramses and Tutankhamen, from which period specimens in excellent condition have come to light. Unlike Mesopotamia and China, Egypt seems to have given lower rank to its musicians. They are rarely mentioned in documents and are very often represented as kneeling before their masters and dressed like slaves.

• Greek music •

Just when these ancient musical civilizations were beginning to decline, there appeared in the Greek world the earliest evidence of a musical culture which was to become our own. We know hardly anything about Greek music before the seventh century BC. According to ancient Creto-Mycenean tradition, music was cultivated in Ionian lands, enriched with contributions from Phrygia and Lydia, as well, perhaps, as Egyptian, Phoenician and Assyrio-Babylonian influences, and was finally re-imported into Greece, spreading, little by little, throughout the new colonized territories.

The first artists of Greek musical civilization were the Greeks of Asia Minor, descendants of those Achaean emigrants of Homeric legend. Drawn by the expansion of the towns of Attica and the Peloponnese as well as by the prestige of the new colonies in southern Italy, or perhaps wanting to escape from Persian domination, they set themselves up in a number of cities: Archilochus of Paros at Metapontum; Pythagoras of Samos at Croton; Anacreon of Teos in Athens; and in Sparta, Alcman of Sardis, Callinus of Ephesus, and Terpander, Sappho and Alcaeus, all from Lesbos. Under the influence of the three last named there opened in Sparta the first schools of Greek music, centers of Ionian song.

Lyric poetry called for unchanging music, as in the case of later songs: hence the static compositions known as *nomoi*. Inseparable from the poems or occasions which gave rise to them, these *nomoi* were probably inspired by popular dancing songs, if we take the rhythm of the verses as our guide. There were several varieties of these: zither *nomoi* (singer accompanying himself on the zither), aulodic (singer accompanied by a player of the *aulos* or flute), choradic (for choir), pythic (solo *aulos*). The entire history of Greek music was drawn from the musical forms and laws established by the lyric poets of the seventh and sixth centuries BC.

By the sixth century BC Pythagorean ideas were exerting a considerable influence on both thought and music, which had become closely connected; they encouraged the development of the musical ethics which Plato and Aristotle were to adopt as one of the foundations of their teachings. Music ceased to be a privilege or a constituent of some ritual; it became an indispensable element in the education of every free man and was the source of wisdom. There arose a numerous class of music-lovers who could join together in choirs; fashion favored the dithyramb, a danced chorus in honor of Dionysus. Polymnestus and Lasus, whose pupils constituted the Pythagorean sect of the 'harmonists,' represented philosophically and musically the more progressive tendency, which was resisted by the theoretician Pratinas, who condemned the excessive refinement of aulody and called for fidelity to the Spartan zither tradition.

Lasus was to have a considerable influence, not only by defining the *armoniai* and *tonoi*, but also by establishing a system of connections between 'harmonies,' types of poetry and circumstances. His pupil Pindar of Thebes, also liberal and progressive, perfected the art of chorody and was the first to put forward a theory of *mimesis* or imitation, one of the foundations of musical ethics. Athens, the center of Lasus's unifying work, became during the fifth

Left: Jewish music entered the western tradition as the medieval church took over many musical practices of the synagogue. The biblical King David, famed as a musician, is portrayed here with four other biblical musicians in a Christian manuscript which dates from the eleventh century.

Below: Title-page from a twelfth-century English manuscript copy of *De Musica* by the Roman scholar Anicius Manlius Severinus Boethius (470?-525). Through his translations of the work of earlier thinkers and by his own commentaries, Boethius helped to carry over into western medieval culture classical Greek and Roman musical systems and theories.

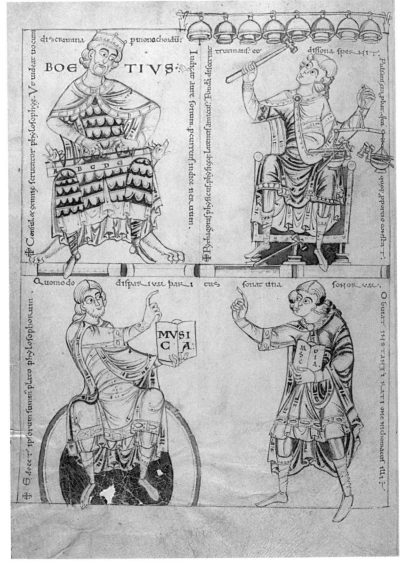

The Renaissance looked for a rebirth of the classical Greek spirit in music as in the other arts, but although the work of some theorists survived, there was no means of knowing what ancient music sounded like. However, the musical heroes of Greece were adopted, and their legends formed the subjects of many of the earliest operas – which were themselves attempts to revive the tradition of ancient Greek tragedy. Apollo is shown here (*right*, in a drawing of the early sixteenth century by Il Parmigianino) playing in his musical contest with the satyr Marsyas.

century the focal point of these new musical tendencies. This great century was dominated, as far as musical philosophy was concerned, by Damon of Athens, whose influence was at least as far-reaching as that of the disciples of Aristotle. Damon's pupils are believed to have included the musician Draco (Plato's master), as well as Socrates and Pericles. One famous speech by Damon on the Areopagus, around 450 BC, which dealt mainly with the subject of musical education, was referred to by many later writers from Plato down to Cicero. Above all, however, Damon was the most important source of inspiration for Plato's and Aristotle's dialogues on music, even if he was not quoted word for word. Following on from Lasus and Pindar, he was a major contributor to the definition of the famous 'ethos' of Greek music.

For the early Pythagoreans, *good* music was the perceptible expression of those same mathematical ratios which they believed governed the universe. In such music, the mind may recognize the universal harmony and the spirit become attuned to it: this means that music is not to be taken lightly. Having once gone deeply into its secrets, it remains for philosophers to define the ethos of the modes and rhythms by deter-

Above: The legend of the musician Orpheus and his tragic attempt to rescue his wife Eurydice from Hades was another favorite theme taken from Greek myth. (This drawing by Herman Weyer dates from the end of the sixteenth century.) As in the drawing of Apollo, the hero is shown playing a contemporary bowed stringed instrument.

mining precisely the arithmetical value of the intervals and time relations. But how is music (which must be good, rather than beautiful) to act as the intermediary between world order and the human soul? By *mimesis*, replies Damon: art is imitation, and the soul, in turn, imitates the representations of art. Now, in music, the models are not objects, but ideas. One can thus imitate the evil just as much as the good; this means a danger to the State, which therefore has a clear duty to ensure the good quality of musical education.

Plato, in his *Republic*, remains faithful to Damon's doctrines. In his *Laws*, however, he places the emphasis on musical pleasure, abandoning the principle of imitation. He does think though that music may serve to form the judgment of the child by connecting moral concepts and pleasure; it is thus for teaching to form tastes. To these ethical principles, Aristotle adds

the original doctrine of catharsis. This concerns a psychotherapeutic method, by which music gives rise to violent feelings which in turn create a kind of crisis which favors cure. Aristotle observes that catharsis does not act on the will; it must thus be understood that it sets off a kind of relaxation, a movement out of the self (e-motion).

During the second half of the fourth century a disciple of Aristotle's, Aristoxenus of Tarentum (*c.*370-300 BC), produced a complete theory of music. He was critical of the music of his own time, asserting the superiority of pre-Platonic classicism, and he blamed his contemporaries for their gross and perverted sense of hearing and for making judgments which were not controlled by reason.

The Greeks did evolve a fairly precise system of notation, but, as in other cultures, this was for the use of teachers and theoreticians rather than for the transmission of a musical heritage. A small number of 'compositions' have survived, but they are late and of little significance, the most interesting being two hymns in honor of Apollo (*c.*130 BC), found at Delphi. However, their well developed theory of music was preserved through the Roman period and widely diffused throughout the Mediterranean world. Practices changed, as did the vocabulary and, above all, the part played by music in society. It became more and more marginal and tended to be confined to a background of sound, or entertainment, for the wealthier classes. All the same, the main foundation of Greek musical theory and culture, enlivened by contact with the traditions of the early Christians of the East, left an important legacy to our Middle Ages, despite the intervening centuries of destruction, cruelty, anguish and barbarism, which preceded the splendors of Byzantine and medieval art.

The Basis of Western Music

Sound is energy, existing, like other forms of energy, as a kind of throbbing vibration. It can be transmitted, with varying degrees of effectiveness, through a number of media, including water and, of course, air. It moves relatively slowly (1,222 k.p.h. at sea level) compared with light or electricity, and its strength is soon exhausted; nevertheless, our ears are marvellously attuned, in conjunction with the brain, to those sounds we call music. Musical instruments, including the human voice, activate vibrations in the medium of the air. When these reach our ears, the eardrums vibrate in sympathy, and these vibrations, in turn, are interpreted by the brain as musical sounds.

For thousands of years, the function of musical instruments has been to mold

the physical properties of sound, much as a potter might shape his clay or a carpenter his wood. These basic properties can be measured scientifically in terms of waves, just like electricity or light. First, there is *pitch* (highness or lowness), determined by the rapidity of the vibrations and measured as *frequency*. The greater the wave frequency – the number of cycles per second – the

higher the pitch of the sound. The property of loudness is called *amplitude* and is measured in terms of the magnitude of the sound waves. The property of *tone*, or quality, is much more complicated to assess. It is based on the combined effect of many sound waves that go to make up practically all apparently 'individual' sounds, such as those of a violin, a clarinet or a trombone. When several of these individual instrumental sounds are themselves combined, as they usually are in music, the question of tone becomes very complex indeed.

Only in this century have totally new ways of producing sound been developed. The main instrument concerned is the synthesizer, which analyzes and then generates the properties of sound purely by electronics.

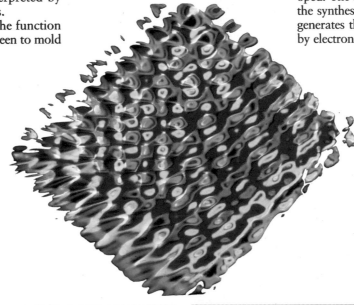

Sound waves are often likened to the ripples created on the surface of still water by a falling stone. Modern electronics and photography have made it possible to get impressions both of more complex turbulence on a liquid's surface (*right*, a Schlieren photograph) and of complex sound patterns (*bottom*).

Two nineteenth-century illustrations (*below*) of simpler sound patterns. A beam of light is deflected off the vibrating prongs of two tuning forks, then projected through a lens onto a screen. Depending on the interval between the notes, the interaction of the vibrations can create a range of patterns.

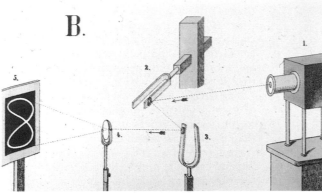

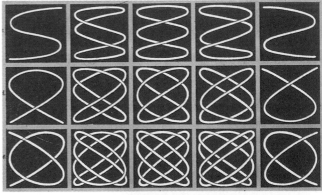

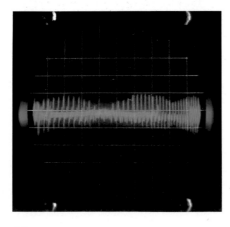

A cathode-ray oscilloscope (*left*) registers musical sounds. It converts the sounds into electrical voltages, which are recorded on the screen. Since musical sounds are a combination of many individual sound wave patterns, one use of the oscilloscope in recent music is as a control in a synthesizer.

One of the latest developments in recording technology is the compact disc. This is played not with a stylus, but with a laser beam (*right*). The absence of material contact with the disc, plus the hypersensitivity of the laser beam itself, eliminates the problem of all surface noise or distortion.

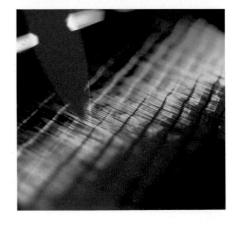

Musical instruments, except electronic ones, can be classified according to the source of their sound: idiophones (bells, gongs, cymbals, blocks), membranophones (drums), aerophones (wind instruments), chordophones (string instruments). A symphony orchestra classifies the sections differently, as strings, woodwind, brass and percussion. Most of these have their origins in the Middle Ages or earlier – the examples illustrated here are miniatures from the *Cantigas de Santa Maria* of Alfonso X of Castile (1221-84).

Stringed instruments are represented by (*top right*) a rebab and a type of lute, (*above*) two viols and (*right*) a psaltery. The strings are set vibrating either by plucking or by the action of a bow. The length of the string is the most common way of determining the pitch of the note it sounds – the shorter the length, the faster the vibrations and the higher the pitch. But its tautness and thickness are also important. The wooden bodies of stringed instruments act as resonators, vibrating in sympathy with the strings and amplifying their sound. The size and shape of the body have much to do with the tone quality of the instruments.

The two musicians (*left*) are playing whistles and beating small drums, or tabors. Instruments that are struck (percussive) include all those otherwise classed as idiophones and membrano-phones. In the case of idiophones – anything from a giant metal bell to a pair of wooden castanets – it is the whole fabric of the instrument that vibrates when struck. The vibrating agent in membranophones, or drums, by contrast, is a stretched skin or similar membrane. This is fitted over the frame of the instrument to enclose a body of air that vibrates in sympathy, so amplifying and giving tone to the sound. Depending on the area and degree of tautness of their skins, drums, unlike gongs and cymbals, can be tuned to sound notes of a particular pitch.

In wind instruments the sound is produced by a vibrating column of air inside the tube. In brass instruments, such as trumpets (*top left*), this motion is produced by the vibration of the player's own lips against one end of the tube. In some woodwind instruments, such as flutes (*above*), the vibrations are created by the way the player blows across the mouth of the tube. In others, such as shawms (*below*), they are created by the vibration of a thin piece of reed. In all wind instruments, length and diameter (*bore*) of the tube affect pitch and tone.

21

Scholars have for centuries been interested in the relationship between music and mathematics, particularly in what they once believed to be the connection between music and the proportions of the universe as expressed in the so-called 'harmony of the spheres.' One of the first to inquire into the mathematics of music was Pythagoras (c.580-500 BC). He demonstrated that the length of a vibrating string, or its tautness, and hence the frequency of its vibrations, is directly related to the pitch of the note it sounds. Here (*above*) Jubal and Pythagoras demonstrate the relationship between the size of hammers, bells and water tumblers, the tautness of strings, the length of pipes, and pitched notes.

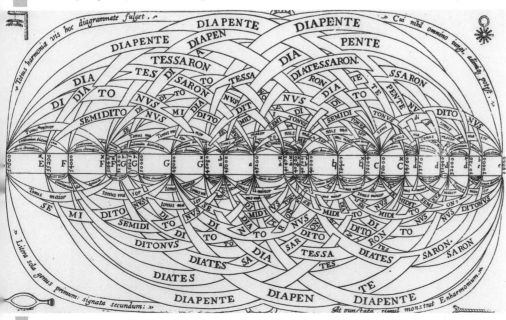

Pythagoras had concentrated on the intervals of the octave (1:2), the fifth (diapente – 2:3) and the fourth (diatessaron – 3:4), giving the series 4, 6, 8, 9, 12, 16, as shown in the first illustration (*left*). By introducing the additional intervals of major third (4:5), minor third (5:6), major tone (8:9), minor tone (9:10) and semitone (15:16), the Venetian composer Gioseffo Zarlino (1517-90) firmly established the diatonic system (the system of major and minor keys), which, with its underlying sense of resolution onto the fundamental keynote, has remained the basis of western harmony. The diagram, derived from Zarlino's *Istitutioni harmoniche* of 1558, shows that, unlike the 'equal temperament' of a modern keyboard, the scale is not made up of a series of equal semitones, but some notes (F sharp – G flat, for instance) have different values depending on their harmonic context.

From antiquity onwards, the notion that the mathematics of musical sound was an expression of some greater order haunted men's imaginations. Robert Fludd (1574-1643), a physician, astrologer and member of the order of Rosicrucians, tried to relate musical pitch and harmony to the shape and proportions of architecture and geometry in his extraordinary 'temple of music' (*opposite*), in which notation, the tonic sol-fa, clef signs and musical instruments lurk symbolically among the stonework, columns and arches. Although Fludd's structure is clearly symbolic, Palladio and other Italian architects of the late sixteenth century used the same harmonic ratios established by Zarlino in a quite practical way to define the proportions of the buildings they designed. The mathematical precision that underlies western architecture and music is one of their most striking characteristics.

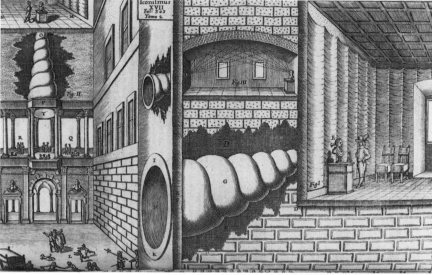

Another remarkable concept (*above*) is this so-called broadcasting system by Athanasius Kircher (1602-80). By means of the large spiral acoustic channels, sounds from the courtyard are picked up and conveyed to the surrounding rooms. Conversely, people in the rooms may address those in the courtyard through the 'microphones' such as the one marked 'E' in the illustration. Despite the fanciful nature of the scheme, Kircher's thinking was much more in line with the new scientific spirit than Fludd's.

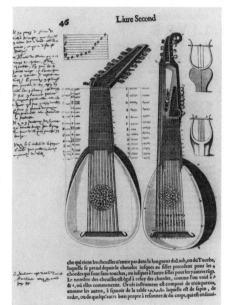

Among the instruments which appear in Mersenne's *Harmonie universelle* are the lute and theorbo (*left*) and the viol (*below*). Mersenne's illustrations show the component parts of the instruments and the tuning of their strings. Viols are bowed stringed instruments made to a variety of sizes and were predecessors of the modern violin family. The lute and theorbo were plucked stringed instruments very popular in the sixteenth and seventeenth centuries.

The other illustrations on this page are taken from a book entitled *Harmonie universelle* by the French philosopher, musical theorist and mathematician Marin Mersenne (1588-1648). Mersenne was a pioneer figure in the field of acoustics, being among the first to inquire into such phenomena as the speed of sound, echo and resonance. He was probably the first to make a truly accurate mathematical analysis of the pitch and tone of a vibrating string, based upon such variables as length, diameter or thickness, tautness or tension, and mass of the whole instrument. In his *Harmonie universelle* he described the sound properties and functions of various musical instruments, as well as explaining musical theory and discussing such matters as vocal ornamentation. Mersenne was a follower of Zarlino, but was also open to the new scientific, philosophical and musical ideas of his own day.

This illustration of the trumpet (*left*) includes its harmonic series (notated above the instrument itself). The harmonic series of wind instruments, produced by the column of air in the tube vibrating as a whole and in sections, is based on the same ratios as the harmonics of a vibrating string. In the case of wind instruments, notes in the series are obtained by the player changing the method of blowing into or across the tube. The illustration shows clearly how the pitch intervals get smaller as the harmonic series progresses up its scale. In what are called 'natural' brass wind instruments, such as the bugle and the hunting horn, the playing length of the tube is fixed and unalterable – hence such instruments are virtually limited to the notes of their own harmonic series. But nearly all wind instruments, woodwind and brass, now have either holes in the side of the tube or some system of valves which allows the player to alter the effective playing length of the tube and so obtain a wider range of pitched notes.

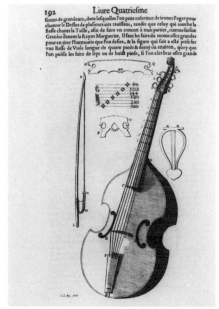

MEDIEVAL MUSIC

ALBERT SEAY & DENIS STEVENS

Opposite: The Minnesinger Heinrich von Meissen and fellow poet-musicians depicted in a manuscript of around 1320. The German Minnesingers (singers of love), French troubadours and trouvères, and English minstrels provided much of the secular music of the Middle Ages. Heinrich himself was known as 'Frauenlobe,' or 'Praiser of Women.' Instruments featured are (left to right) tabor, straight cornett, shawm, fiddles or vielles, psaltery and bagpipes.

The early history of music in Western Europe is almost entirely based on its use and development within the Roman Catholic Church, and the source from which the Church drew its basic liturgical organization was the Jewish set of services, primarily that of the synagogue, where stress on the singing of psalms and readings from sacred texts was of major importance. A central task for the early Church was the education of the Christian through the exposition of the Bible, both Old and New Testaments. To some extent the synagogue had set a precedent in its organized series of readings from the Torah (the first five books of the Bible) and the Prophets, all in a patterned annual cycle. The Catholic Church found it simple to give these practices a Christian atmosphere by adding, also in a yearly arrangement, material from the New Testament, while the practice of including psalms was also continued.

The major Christian addition to the Jewish service, with no roots in earlier rites, was the Eucharist, the Sacrament of the Lord's Supper. As a daily observance of the essence of Christian faith, it became the focus of the Mass, the principal service within the daily liturgy. Seasonal services on the Jewish model were also developed, but with new Christian significance, as at Christmas and Easter, and they extended to the periods before and after these great feasts.

With the emergence of the Church from persecution to a State-supported and encouraged religion under Constantine the Great (288?-337), and with the Council of Nicaea (325) acting to unify the western Church, the rise in complexity of the liturgy matched the Church's increasing intrusion into all facets of secular life – political, social and economic. The steady growth of the monastic movement, culminating in the founding of the monastery at Monte Cassino in 529 by St Benedict, led to the regularization of subsidiary daily services, many of which were already in existence, but which were now systematized into a standard scheme. With the rise of the Bishop of Rome to the position of Supreme Pontiff or Pope, these extra services became normal for the whole Church, in all areas, wherever the Roman rite was followed. This scheme covered the day, and its elements were: Matins (during the night before daybreak); Lauds (at cockcrow, 3am); Prime (6am); Tierce (9am); Mass (10am, or after Sext or None); Sext (noon); None (3pm); Vespers (6pm); Compline (at nightfall). The full program of services outlined here was observed mainly in monasteries, the parish churches for the laity normally celebrating only Mass and Vespers, but even the latter not consistently. As with the yearly pattern of services of greater and lesser importance, the daily series observed a hierarchy of solemnity, the Mass as the center of the liturgy and of the greatest complexity, the four services of Matins, Lauds, Vespers and Compline as Greater Hours, and the others as Lesser Hours.

In addition to its place in the liturgy, music played an important part within medieval education. For Greek philosophers, music had provided a way of understanding the world, through the numerical proportions from which musical sound derived, and their ideas were passed down to the Middle Ages, above all by Boethius (470?-525), whose *De Musica* established the mathematic ratios used in music, and whose work was still being referred to a thousand years later. Thus music became one of the group of four studies known as the *quadrivium*: arithmetic, geometry, music and astronomy. In them the student was taught the unity of the world and God's creations through the study of number and proportion. The progression was from the fundamentals of arithmetic and its definitions, through geometry, wherein proportions could be physically measured in space, to music, where proportions could be measured in sound, and finally to astronomy, where physical measurement was impossible but could be comprehended by analogy with the ratios seen and heard in music.

Boethius divided the field into three levels: instrumental (which included vocal) music, human music and worldly music. On the lowest level, the student was shown the ratios used to find the pitches of musical notes through their proportions; these were demonstrated on the one-stringed instrument known as the monochord. With human music, one was shown how these ratios, heard in sound, were also at the root of nature, as in the alternation of seasons, symmetry in human shapes, and so on, applying the concordance of musical proportions to the study of God's creations. In the final stage came the perception that these same ratios were found in the movements of the planets around the earth and their interaction with the sun, all of these proportions producing the 'Music of the Spheres' in their rational movement. Boethius's scheme, based on Greek neo-Platonism, saw music as a way of understanding and as a representation of greater truths. As explained by the writers of the time, music was a microcosm used as a mirror of the macrocosm that is the universe.

Why music should have held such a high place within the Church should now be apparent. Its significance was not just that of pleasant sounds heard during the performance of the liturgy, but in what the sound implied in its philosophical extensions, its necessity in understanding God's perfection as seen in His creations. It thus held a special place as a kind of language particularly appropriate when addressing God. Orthodoxy of music became as much a requisite within the Church as orthodoxy of belief. From medieval times to the present, the Church has kept a tight rein on its musicians, periodically reviewing innovations and ruling on their acceptance or refusal.

• Music in the Church •

Plainchant is the fundamental music of the Church. It is a functional music, designed to correspond to the nature and importance of the specific service or liturgical situation of which it is a part. In general terms, one may say that the nature and complexity of any piece of plainchant is determined by the importance of the particular day, particular service and particular part of that service. Since the center of the Catholic liturgy is the Mass, it must be treated first.

The Mass was formalized around the seventh century. Certain parts of it are constant, in that their texts are always the same; these parts are known as the Ordinary of the Mass and include the Kyrie, Gloria, Credo, Sanctus, Agnus Dei and Ite missa est. Originally performed by the congregation or by the celebrating priest, they were at first much simpler musically than chants assigned to the choir, normally made up of trained singers. The importance of the Ordinary sections comes only after the fourteenth century, when composers chose the first five as vehicles for polyphonic treatment, eventually unifying all five in a whole in which all of the parts were related. When one speaks of a Mass by Palestrina or by Mozart, it is in reference to a polyphonic setting of these five chant texts of the Ordinary.

None of the Ordinary chants uses a biblical text, and they are thus not associated with a particular feast. Chants of the second category, called the Propers of the Mass, normally do employ biblical texts, many of them from the Psalms, and they are tied to a particular celebration. These chants, designed in the main for professional singers, are the Introit, Gradual, Alleluia, Offertory and Communion. (The Alleluia, a song of rejoicing, is replaced by the Tract in penitential seasons, as in Lent.) All have texts which are more or less specific in terms of the particular celebration, and more or less elaborate musically as determined by the importance of the day. Only in a few chants, particularly in the

Gradual and the Alleluia, were musicians allowed to take the limelight, for all other chants were associated with liturgical acts centering on the celebrant. The Gradual, so named from being sung originally from the steps before the altar, had no accompanying priestly duty, nor did the Alleluia. As a result, these two chants seem to have been most attractive to composers.

The sections of the Mass confided to the celebrant are of least musical interest, for they are intoned, the voice beginning on a particular pitch, then rising to a note on which most of the text is sung and falling at the end, generally to

Right: Example of a long and elaborate melisma – a group of notes sung to a single word or syllable – written out as neumes, from an eleventh-century French collection of church sequences and tropes.

Below: An allegorical representation of the first of the four tones of the Gregorian chant on a capital from the monastery church of Cluny, France. The figure is King David.

the note on which it began. The method is particularly appropriate to the intonation of psalms, where line lengths are unequal, and for biblical readings.

The Hours also give a high place to the psalm, intoned in the usual manner but made more or less elaborate by the performance of a short introduction (antiphon), which is also used as an ending, while each of the Greater Hours is provided with a special excerpt from the Bible,

known as a canticle. The canticle for Matins, used only for occasions of rejoicing, is the *Te Deum*, for Vespers the *Magnificat*, for Lauds *Benedictus Dominus Deus*, and for Compline *Nunc dimittis*. In addition, one of four anthems in praise of the Virgin Mary, each for a season of the year, was added at Lauds and Compline. These texts later became of high importance as inspiration for composers of polyphonic settings.

The growth and definition of all these services and their outlines was a slow process. The great figures in the development of the liturgy and its music are Popes Leo the Great (440-461) and Gregory the Great (590-604). Plainchant is often called Gregorian chant because it was Gregory's work that established the idea of liturgical and musical unity within the whole body of the Church. He set up the practice of Rome as the standard to be followed, sending out legates to see to it that deviations were suppressed.

The process of unification was a long and difficult one, completed only in the sixteenth century by the decrees of the Council of Trent. The first area to conform was that under the control of the eighth-century rulers Pepin and Charlemagne. Gallican chant, as it is known, was so completely eradicated that we know almost nothing about it, for sources have disappeared. By the eleventh century, Roman rites had taken over in Spain, with the Mozarabic rite originally used in that country remaining only in certain churches in Toledo, and this by special dispensation. Milan in Italy still has a local variation, known as Ambrosian chant, from the importance of St Ambrose (333-397), patron saint of that city. In England most local variations were slowly rooted out, with the exception of that which originated at Salisbury, the Sarum rite. This also survived on the continent until the sixteenth century.

To describe the nature of plainchant is to show how much musical artistry can be achieved with the simplest of means. For its effect plainchant depends on but one line of music, unsupported by harmony and intended for male voices. Most chants are restricted in their overall range, with the average chant taking in no more than ten notes. Melodic movement is, for the most part, scalewise, from one note to its neighbor, up or down; interval skips are normally small ones. There is a feeling of rhythmic movement, although the notes are considered as equal in time length; there is a subtle connection in the most elaborate of chants between the accents in the Latin of the text and the rise and fall of the melodic line. At times there are long phrases on one syllable, to emphasize either an important part of the text or to make a musical difference through chant length for a day or service element of greater or lesser meaning. For minor feasts, the texts are usually set syllabically, with one note to a syllable; for the great days, particularly at Christmas and Easter, there are many long passages over one syllable.

We are today not completely sure how plainchant was performed in the Middle Ages. For some centuries chant was passed on from one

Left: Page from the thirteenth-century Beauvais Cathedral version of the *Play of Daniel.* As can be seen from the accompanying notation, the texts of such dramatic presentations were sung. Other contemporary records suggest that a certain amount of acting was also allowed, together with items of scenery.

Below: An earlier example of medieval church musical drama, an eleventh-century version of the Easter story, with an illustration of the three Marys being told by an angel that Jesus has risen from the tomb.

Below: Eleventh-century German ivory carving depicting the celebration of the Mass.

Below right: This group of entertainers with their instruments – cymbals, harps and an early type of lute – reflects the vigorous growth of secular music by the twelfth century alongside the dominant church music tradition.

generation to another by an oral tradition. much as folk music is handed on. Only when it was decided that there had to be musical uniformity in the Church were there attempts to provide a written music that would keep it unchanged. The first form of notation we have is one that merely recalls the shape of the melodic line for the singer who has already learned the chant; the scribe employed a set of symbols designed to suggest, but not define exactly, the rise and fall of the melody. Not until the ninth century did there begin the system of lines and spaces specifying the exact pitch of a note, an achievement contributed to by many musicians, but finally codified and disseminated through

the writings of Guido of Arezzo (c.992-1050). But he and many other writers on music say nothing about the manner of performance; practice was probably considered of such common knowledge that mention of it was unnecessary.

We have noted the general outlines of the liturgy as determined by Leo and Gregory. But throughout the Middle Ages there were efforts to add new elements to the old. The earliest of these additions to be accepted was the hymn, originally a popular melody but with its text changed to one of devotion and explanation of dogma. While the hymn began as a pre-existent melody with new words, a type exploited by St Ambrose, it soon became a recognized genre for which both musicians and poets could provide new material. Eventually hymns were considered significant enough to insert into many of the Hours, but they were never made part of the Mass.

This technique of adding words to an already existing melody, a process known as troping, was the inspiration for similar additions and extensions to other chants. One of the most important of these chants was the Alleluia, for, in its original form, it ended with a lengthy melisma or vocalization on one syllable, the *jubilus* or last syllable. As a way of helping to remember the melody and to comment on the following psalm verse, words were added to this given melody. As with the hymn, original music was later used for new texts. The sequence, as it is known, became such a popular form of expression that by the sixteenth century almost every day's Mass was supplied with one, and many churches were provided with sequences having meaning only to services given in that one place. With the reform of the liturgy by the Council of Trent only five sequences were retained as parts of the Mass. Perhaps the best-known is the *Dies irae* (Day of wrath), which is still part of the Requiem or Mass for the Dead. The process of troping reached its peak in the thirteenth century, but it lost its appeal for musicians as the novelties of polyphony became more and more exciting.

A final addition was the dramatization of an event on the particular day devoted to its celebration. This liturgical drama seems to have begun with the traditional division of the text of

the Passion according to St Matthew between three types of voices. The text of the evangelist was in a medium voice, the words of Christ in a low voice and the *turba* (crowd) in a high one. It was but a small step to add acting and scenery, with gradual provision of additional text and music. The best-known of these musical dramas came at Easter, with the scene at the tomb of Jesus and the visit of the three Marys as a starting point. From the eleventh century onwards subject-matter became ever more varied, with such works as *The Play of Daniel*, *The Conversion of St Paul*, and *The Last Judgment*.

All these additions had their origins in some part of the established liturgy, but one form developed outside the liturgy, the 'conductus' – music and text written for processional use. Although its forms were far freer, the music has the characteristics of chant, thus tying it in style to all the other music of the Church.

• Secular monophony •

One of the great frustrations of musical scholarship is to know that something existed, but to have almost no evidence as to its characteristics. Such is the case with the study of secular music in the Middle Ages. We do, however, have much secular Latin poetry from an early period, and there are indications that there was a popular poetry meant to be sung.

With the reign of Charlemagne there came a new interest in the classics, and one finds manuscripts of the time with primitive musical notation over the lines; there are copies of the *Aeneid* and of Boethius's *Consolation of Philosophy* so treated. Unfortunately, however, the notation is too indefinite for accurate interpretation. Also from this time there are many collections of poems, treating of love and similar subjects, that were obviously designed to be sung, but whose music was not written down.

The most noteworthy Latin secular songs are those coming from a group of poet-musicians known collectively as the Goliards. These were university students who wandered from one city to another, attending in each a different university. Compositions of the Goliards, many found in a manuscript known as the *Carmina Burana*, include both love lyrics and obscene drinking songs. Many of them are parodies of sacred texts, twisted to secular meanings.

Among the first areas to turn to the production of poetry and music within a completely non-religious framework was that part of southern France which used the *langue d'oc* or Provençal. In the more peaceful conditions of the eleventh century knights, deprived of the chance to win fame and a lady's heart in battle, became renowned as musician-poets, or troubadours, writing poems and singing them for the pleasure of their noble audience. The first great troubadour was William IX, Duke of Aquitaine (1071-1127), whose eleven preserved poems (we have but one fragment of his music) set the pattern for those who followed him. The major subject was love in its various forms, with emphasis on

Above left: Illustration from a twelfth-century Italian Exultet scroll. The Exultet was a special kind of Easter chant. The pictures on such scrolls were often placed upside down to the text, so that as the scroll was unfurled over the pulpit they appeared the right way up to the congregation.

Above: Page from a thirteenth-century Benedictine antiphon, with words and notation. This type of antiphon was a sung commentary on a psalm, the chant sometimes being linked to that of the psalm itself.

one's 'lady,' but other topics included poetic contests in dialogue, the Crusades and mourning songs. With the crushing of Provence and the social changes effected by the Albigensian Crusades in the years after 1209, the art and language of the troubadours disappeared; the last troubadour, Guiraut Riquier (1235?-92), died in exile in Spain. Some 2,500 troubadour texts have been preserved, of which about 250 are complete with melodies.

Northern France, from its contacts with the troubadours of the south, began early to imitate the art of its neighbors, first by the translation of texts in Provençal into the *langue d'oïl*, the vernacular of the north, then by turning to original compositions. The 'trouvères,' a literal translation of 'troubadours,' were active from the middle of the twelfth century through the thirteenth, with even more of their repertoire preserved, some 4,000 poems and 1,400 melodies. The rising importance of secular song can be noted in this evident concern for preservation.

It seems that troubadour and trouvère compositions were not normally performed by their creators. Instead, each poet-musician had with him as part of his retinue a professional performer, the *jongleur* or minstrel. The *jongleur* was not a noble and thus earned his livelihood by entertainment, not only before noble audiences but also for lower classes. While many

worked solely for a noble and traveled with him from castle to castle, others traveled about performing at fairs and in market-places. An important part of the *jongleur's* repertoire was the *chanson de geste*, the epic poem of the great deeds of the past; the *Song of Roland* was a great favorite. While the music is not preserved, it would seem that such poems were sung to a series of formulae.

The impact of this new secular art of France was great enough to spread rapidly, in succession to Italy, Spain, Germany and England. The largest number of preserved works come from Germany, where the Minnesingers produced compositions until the fourteenth century, and the tradition later spread to the middle classes, where societies of Meistersingers became numerous.

Secular monophony had a comparatively brief life, for polyphony as a new complication held greater interest for the musician. One must note that the contributions made by the troubadours and their successors were those of amateurs,

not professionals. With the increasing interest in polyphony, beginning in the thirteenth century in the Church and consequently spreading to noble circles, the amateur poet-musician received less and less attention. Many continued to write poetry, something not beyond the amateur's capabilities, but more and more they left the matter of musical setting to professional musicians. The last of the great amateurs is Guillaume de Machaut of the fourteenth century, who composed many monophonic secular songs. But his talents led him to the world of polyphony as well, a sphere in which he was the superior of most professionals.

• Polyphony •

The origins of the idea that music could consist of two or more different melodic lines sounding at the same time will probably never be known for sure. Regardless of how polyphony began, we do know that by the seventh and eighth centuries a form of note-against-note improvisation was fairly well spread. Travelers reporting from numerous countries mention its use and imply that it was a rather common practice. One of these writers, Bishop Aldhelm (640?-709), an Englishman, remarks that 'organum,' the term used to describe this note-against-note technique, was particularly apt for emphasis of major liturgical occasions. Polyphony, even with such simple procedures, was thus another way of stressing the importance of one feast over another.

In many ways the process of adding a new musical line to a pre-existing melody is like the process of troping, in which words are added to an untexted piece of chant. The added line is much like a musical commentary or gloss, as the trope is a textual one. Such a glossing, although improvised, could not be completely free, for the

Two examples of early notation, or near-notation, applied to organum singing.

Far left: A very interesting example, from a copy of the celebrated tenth-century *Musica enchiriadis*, of so-called Daseian (rough) notation. The letters indicating the pitch of the notes are written down the column on the left. The words and syllables to be sung are then strung out horizontally against them. The two lines of organum melody, treating the syllables of the same Latin text independently, can be clearly discerned.

Left: Part of an early twelfth-century manuscript from the St Martial monastery at Limoges, which exhibits some of the most elaborate use of organum up to that time.

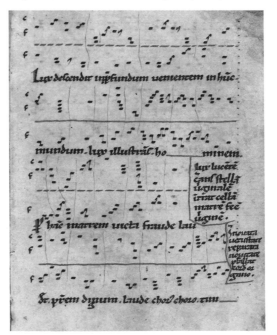

chant to which the new music was added had to remain unchanged, and the number of intervals that could be used against the given notes of that chant was tightly limited to those considered as perfect, the fourth and fifth.

This strictness is observable in the earliest surviving examples of polyphony, those contained in the *Musica enchiriadis* (Musical Manual) attributed to Hoger of Laon in the tenth century. To a given melody, one adds a new line below the chant at the distance of a perfect fifth or fourth; both these lines may be doubled at the octave above. This kind of parallel organum, where the counterpoint duplicates the given melody at a fixed interval, is given the name 'strict organum.'

The *Musica enchiriadis* also describes a 'free' style wherein the given chant and the added voice begin and end on the same note but use varying intervals at other points. The choice of intervals is small and the rules of choice are almost as limited as those in strict organum. The relaxation of some of these rules and an effort to provide more freedom may be seen in the eleventh-century *Micrologus* by Guido of Arezzo, whose importance in the history of notation has already been mentioned. The number of allowable intervals is expanded and more choices are given.

A treatise of about a century later, the *De musica* of John of Affligem, shows how much further musicians had come towards achieving genuine polyphonic composition. In John's

short discussion of counterpoint, strict organum is never mentioned, suggesting that it had declined in importance or even disappeared. For the principle of parallelism John substituted the idea that the given chant and its counterpoint should move by contrary motion where possible; that is, contrasting one against the other not only by the choice of interval but also in melodic direction. And, while before the given chant was always the uppermost voice, with John's approach the voices were allowed to cross the original melody on which the organum was built.

John remarks mainly on the nature of note-against-note counterpoint. In one or two sentences, however, he does admit that there is the possibility of making the added voice more interesting by using two or more notes in the added voice against one in the given chant. Unfortunately, he provides no examples. Such a concession – and it is an important one – indicates that singers were already feeling a sense of restriction and that they were anxious to go even further in the elevation of the added material to a place of primary importance. To make this shift, the use of counterpoint would require a change of locale, from the monastery church and its untrained choir to the popular church and cathedral, where soloists of professional ability were available.

Evidence of this shift comes with a pair of volumes known as the *Winchester Tropers*, English in their origin but showing influences from northern France. The repertoire consists of organum for two voices, totalling about 150 compositions, and they emphasize settings of chants from the Mass – Kyries and Alleluias in the main – with the major feasts having especially elborate organa. Although the notation is too primitive for accurate transcription, the desire for equality of the added voice, even almost a supremacy, is clear.

The culmination of all these developments comes in the late eleventh and early twelfth centuries at Limoges, with manuscripts from the monastery of St Martial that show the final stages before the artistic climax to be reached in Paris at the cathedral of Notre Dame. The emphasis here is upon the use of many notes in the added counterpoint, now called the 'duplum,' against only one of the given chant; since this technique means that the lower voice, the given melody, has each of its notes stretched longer in time, we speak of this line as the 'tenor' (from the latin *tenere*, to hold). This approach ensures that the attention is directed to the duplum, for the tenor, now in long notes, loses its coherence and shape.

• The Notre Dame school •

Paris during the twelfth century had become the most exciting city of its time. The University was the center of scholastic learning, and among its teachers were such great figures as Bernard of Clairvaux (1090-1153), founder of the Cistercian Order, Peter Abelard (1079-1142), the proponent of conceptualism, John of Salisbury (*c.*1115-80), historian and humanist, and Peter Lombard (*c.*1100-60), Bishop of Paris.

With Louis VII and Philip Augustus, whose reigns extended from 1137 to 1223, the monarchy in France became consolidated under a professional administration and steadily developed the concentration of power in Paris. Philip began the construction of the Louvre and continued that of the great cathedral of all France, Notre Dame, on which a start had been made in 1163, under Louis VII.

With such advantages, it is no wonder that Paris attracted the best minds and talents. Music as a traditional part of scholastic education was of importance within the University, but the practical side was not neglected. Peter Lombard encouraged the development of the choir school at the cathedral and integrated it into the University. This attention to music was not limited to Notre Dame alone, but extended to other churches of the area as well, so much so that it is certain that many of the innovations covered by the general heading, 'School of Notre Dame,' are in fact the products of other churches in the overall area of the Ile-de-France.

The first major contribution of the Notre Dame school was in the notation of rhythm. While it is possible and even probable that earlier music was performed in metrical patterns, the notation in the sources gives no clues as to how these patterns may have been applied. With Léonin, believed to have been master of the choir school at Notre Dame from around 1160, a system of six metrical patterns and a method of notating them were worked out.

The system was built around six different arrangements, or modes, of long and short notes, all tied to units of three; here one may

Right: Two facing pages from the so-called Montpellier Codex – a large manuscript collection of music now kept in the Montpellier Faculty of Medicine in southern France, but put together by the Notre Dame school of Paris between around 1280 and 1310. Many of the pieces are motets, such as the one shown here. The organum parts are written over the words to be sung, while the tenor part, perhaps intended to be played by an instrument, is written out on a separate line beneath.

see the dominance of speculative and theological thought, for three is the perfect number, which expressed the perfection of the Trinity. To show these modes and the variations within them, a system involving the grouping of single notes in units was devised, based on plainchant notation. By looking at these 'ligatures,' as the groupings were called because of their 'tying together' (from the Latin *ligare*), the singer could recognize and perform the correct mode.

Léonin's contribution to the history of polyphony is what a later writer describes as the *Magnus liber* (Great Book). It is a collection of forty-six organa, thirteen for the Hours and thirty-three for the Mass. That this music is designed for trained singers is evident from the part of the chant that is used for polyphonic treatment. The plainchant sections reserved for a solo voice are those given polyphony; those for the choir are left in plainchant. A typical organum by Léonin will thus have contrasting areas, some for soloists singing organum and others for the choir in normal chant.

Léonin's successor, Pérotin, whose career seems to have lasted from the last years of the twelfth century into the thirteenth, expanded upon the foundation laid down by his predecessor in almost every direction. His two organa for four voices, 'Viderunt' for Christmas and 'Sederunt' for St Stephen (26 December), are among the most important works of the period; their high place in the estimation of Pérotin's contemporaries is evidenced by their appearance on the opening pages of those manuscripts which include them. Pérotin is also given credit for the expansion of polyphony to conductus. But his most impotant innovation was the intro-

duction of 'clausulae,' substitute sections to replace long ones in organum style, which, it was felt by many ecclesiastics, were upsetting the balance of the service. Pérotin's clausulae replaced Léonin's tenors, which were in unmeasured long notes, with ones in rhythmic modes (in the so-called 'discantus' style), thus getting through the same part of the basic chant in much less time.

To provide some kind of individuality and interest, composers in the early thirteenth century turned to a technique already available, the process of troping. This led to the motet, from the French *mot* (word). The line originally labeled as 'duplum' is now called the 'motetus,' while the third line is known as the triplum. The earliest motets are those with Latin texts. If written for three voices, both the motetus and triplum will carry the same text. A second stage sees the beginning of double and triple motets, where each of the two or three upper voices carries a different text, all in Latin. In a third stage, French takes the place of Latin for the upper voices, which begin to lose their textual connection with the tenor.

Because of the texts and their relation of one note to one syllable in the upper voices, the older method of notation – the indication of proper rhythmic mode through the grouping of notes into ligatures – could not be used; each syllable had to have its own single note. By 1160, the process of shifting to a new notational method could be codified; this falls under the general name of Franconian notation, after Franco of Cologne, our best source of information. Franco defines the new system as one based on individual note shapes for particular

Above left: Interior of the Sainte Chapelle, Paris, consecrated in 1248, towards the end of the Notre Dame School period of Léonin and Pérotin. Many parallels can be drawn between High Gothic architecture and contemporary developments in church music, both in the evolution of much more complex structural systems and in the use of decorative elaboration dedicated to the glory of God.

Above right: French Bible illustration, dating from around 1250, showing musicians at a feast. All the characters are in contemporary dress and are playing contemporary instruments: (left to right) fiddle or vielle, hurdy-gurdy (also known as the *vielle à roue* or wheel fiddle), harp and psaltery.

Above: Commemorative tombstone to the blind organist Francesco Landini in the basilica of S. Lorenzo, Florence. Landini, the leading Italian composer at the end of the fourteenth century, is shown here playing a portative organ.

values, one for the long and another for the short, with rests made clear by the amount of vertical space taken by a line up and down. By the end of the century a third note shape had been added for the 'semibreve' or half-short.

In the course of the century the motet moved steadily away from its ecclesiastic roots, for its audience had more and more become a secular one, the noble court. To satisfy this audience, secular texts and secular melodies became part of the texture; in many there are excerpts taken from trouvère compositions. However, the only musician to form a consistent secular style based on the new developments was Adam de la Halle (1240?-88?) from Arras. He was the author of a pastoral play, *Le Jeu de Robin et de Marion*, in which he inserted many monophonic pieces, and he also composed a number of polyphonic works and a variety of pieces written in simple conductus style, with three voices working homophonically in the same rhythmic mode and with the same text.

From England comes one secular work of renown, 'Sumer is icumen in,' probably written in the last half of the century. It is for six voices, four in canon built on one melody taken up in succession by each voice; the two lower voices are also in canon, but on a short fragment that serves to set off the upper four. Polyphonic dance music was also part of the scene, but we have few extant examples. The bulk of this music was probably improvised.

• *Ars Nova* •

The end of the thirteenth century ushered in a time of troubles, with a divided papacy, wars, peasant revolts and the ravages of the Black Death. The Church no longer had control of its servants, for the abuse of privilege, the failure to observe vows, and a general attitude of worldliness became characteristic of the Church as a whole. In music, composers now began to look toward a secularized world for guidance. Nothing shows the change in music better than the content of a musical treatise by a major composer of the early part of the fourteenth century, Philippe de Vitry (1291-1361), a churchman in the service of the kings of France. In his book, Vitry condenses the new spirit of the age so effectively that its title, *Ars Nova* (The New Art), is now applied to the period as a whole. Written around 1322-3, the *Ars Nova* is a practical treatise, a handbook for modern practice in notation, setting the rules for the rhythmic complexities that characterize the period. This emphasis on *musica instrumentalis*, originally the lowest of the three levels of music, is an indication that it was now taking primary importance, with *musica humana* and *mundana* left to philosophers.

Vitry cites in the *Ars Nova* many of his own compositions as examples of the new methods. These works are evidence of an increased concentration on technical complexity, for, although clearly derived from the earlier motet, his motets are now governed by a new principle

of organization, one known as 'isorhythm' (i.e., same rhythm). Isorhythm is, in many ways, a large-scale extension of the ideas behind the rhythmic modes of a century or so earlier. The composer of an isorhythmic motet, the major *Ars Nova* form, begins by setting up a rhythmic pattern for the tenor. He will then decide upon a melody for that tenor, possibly using one borrowed from plainchant or a secular source, perhaps even free-composed. This tenor melody, called a 'color,' will then be laid out in the pre-set rhythmic shape. What makes the difference between this procedure and the practice of the thirteenth century is that the rhythmic pattern, or 'talea,' will normally be of a different number of notes from the color, so that when one of the two elements is repeated, the point of beginning again will not coincide with the point of repetition in the other. Over this foundation tenor, the composer adds two or three voices above, differentiated by relative speed.

While the isorhythmic motet remains at the center of the artistic repertoire, with the possibility of being either sacred or secular in its text, there is one new area of exploration that is purely sacred: the putting together of various parts of the Ordinary of the Mass to make a complete cycle. Four such Masses have survived from this period: three probably joined on the grounds of utility, with no conception of artistic unity, and one the work of a single composer, Guillaume de Machaut.

Machaut (*c.*1300-77) was distinguished both as a poet and musician, and, although he was a cleric, his work shows his marked preference for the secular. Of his twenty-three motets, which are in various forms and show his assimilation of the new styles and techniques, only two have a religious character. In other categories, he shows his indebtedness to the tradition of the trouvères in his monophonic compositions, particularly the 'lais,' but his special interest was clearly in polyphonic treatment, particularly of 'rondeaux' and 'ballades.' There is great variety in these settings, for two, three or four voices, though in most the attention is on a sung upper line with instrumental accompaniment. One of the most interesting is the rondeau 'Ma fin est ma Commencement' (My end is my beginning); in three voices, the music follows the text literally, for it proceeds to the middle and then takes what has been sung and repeats the notes backwards.

Machaut's *Messe de Notre Dame* is his best-known work, in which he added a setting of the 'Ite missa est' to the usual five parts of the Ordinary. The grandeur of the music is almost impossible to describe, particularly when it is heard in a performance where appropriate instruments, including brass, have been added as support. The vast intellectuality of the work and its demonstration of the ease with which Machaut handles the technical details disappear in the overall musical impression. There are few moments in the music of any period to rival the climax that comes when, in the Gloria, the rhythmic drive suddenly stops and the choir sings, in longer values than are used at any other time, the triumphant words, 'Jesu Christe.' Igor

34

Stravinsky's Mass for voices and winds shows just how much Machaut's masterpiece influenced him six hundred years later.

By the close of the fourteenth century French music, like society itself, had lost all sense of purpose and had become introverted, looking only at the intricacies and technicalities of its art, with little idea of meaning and even less of function. A breath of fresh air was needed, and it was from Burgundy and its dependencies that leadership of a new kind was to appear.

• Music outside France •

Although the term 'Ars Nova' is sometimes used to refer to Italy as well as to France in the fourteenth century, very little is known of any older art there that was superseded. There is evidence that suggests Italian musicians did practice polyphony before 1300, but that it was improvised. Certainly, in the fourteenth century Italian polyphonic compositions are overwhelmingly secular, for the trained singers in church choirs could provide what was needed by improvised polyphony.

The Italian tradition seems to begin with Marchetto of Padua, the composer of a double Latin motet probably written in 1305 for the dedication of a chapel there in honor of the Virgin. Marchetto's fame rests on his theoretical works, for his *Lucidarium* (1309-18) and *Pomerium* (1321-6) were the leading texts for Italian musicians for the next two centuries. Marchetto was a practical musician, choir director and teacher, as is reflected in his writings. The mathematical intricacies of speculative theorists, building on Boethius, were not for him. His audience was the singer, the performer.

For the true beginnings of Italian polyphonic music we must turn to Bologna. There, as early

as the second decade of the century, the new mensural music was popular for setting Italian poems of all kinds. None of these works has been preserved, but literature of the time reports on the musical activity that pervaded the city, much of it in this manner. Some idea of this production may be gained from the works of Jacopo da Bologna, whose first compositions came in the 1340s and whose fame spread rapidly throughout northern Italy, particularly in the courts of Verona and Milan. His texts, in the main, were in praise of courtly love, a clear survival of the influence of the troubadours and the Provençal poets.

A major form used by Jacopo and composers after him is the 'madrigal,' a form not to be confused with that of the same name so important in Renaissance Italy. The fourteenth-century madrigal was a rustic poem, singing of 'flowers, gardens, trees,' as one writer puts it. It was normally for two voices, the upper of which was florid and with long melismata, over an instrumental tenor that had no other function than that of support. Contrary to French practice, where one worked up from the

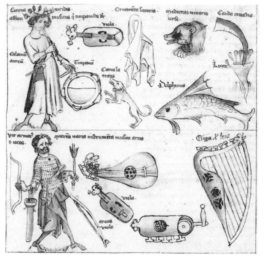

Bottom left: Early fifteenth-century keyboard intabulation (special arrangement) of a madrigal by Bartolino of Padua. The piece has been reduced to its top and tenor parts only.

Left: Instruments featured in an early fourteenth-century Dutch astrological treatise. The figure in the top panel is playing a shawm, and there are also pictures of a tambourine and a fiddle (called a viola). At the bottom are a cittern (a type of lute), a fiddle with bow, a hurdy-gurdy (or symphony) and a harp.

Below: Illustration of a wedding procession from an Italian manuscript of around 1380. The instruments featured (from left to right along the gallery and down the stairs) are: nakers (a small hand drum), bagpipes (flanked by two shawms), trumpets, portative organ and fiddle.

tenor, Italians worked down from the uppermost voice. The music is in two sections, the first part for the three-lined strophes and the second a ritornello for the closing two lines.

Two other forms utilized by Italian musicians were the 'ballata' and the 'caccia.' The ballata, in form the same as the French 'virelai,' was so named because it was originally both a song

and a piece to be danced to (*ballare*). The caccia, like the French 'chace' or 'chasse,' was a musical description of the hunt; hence its name. Not only is the text descriptive, complete with dogs and horses, but the music, for three voices, also involves a kind of chase; the opening voice is followed by a second singing the same material in canon. The third and lowest voice, as usual, is an instrumental support.

While the center of musical activity was in the north during the first half of the century, the second half saw the shift to Tuscany, where the major figure was Francesco Landini (*c.*1325-97). Blind from boyhood, he became renowned as an organist but was equally respected as a literary and philosophic figure. Many of the poems he set to music are his own. Such was his reputation that it is probable that almost all his musical production has survived, though it is thought that some religious works, including five motets, are lost. His extant compositions consist of 141 ballate, eleven madrigals and two caccie.

Boccaccio's *Decameron* gives an idea of the place of music in secular life, with its pictures of youth singing for sheer pleasure and the delight of others. Not only was the use of music an adornment of noble festivities but, from Boccaccio's description, it was also part of the social life of the bourgeoisie. Other writers make the same point, that Italian music was, in

Above: The power of music and poetry was a recurrent theme in medieval allegory. This late fourteenth-century French tapestry shows the seven angels with goblets filled with the wrath of God, and angels beneath singing God's praises to the accompaniment of harps, as described in the New Testament *Book of Revelation.*

Left: Secular allegorical scene on an ivory mirror case of the same period, showing a poet and lover being crowned for his deeds.

the larger cities, something for all levels of society. How far secular music had invaded religious circles is also shown by the complaint of a bishop of Florence that 'in the church musicians play ballate on the organ.'

Italian music at this period was already characterized by a closeness between the text and the music, with an almost intuitive feeling for the appropriate way to make one artistic unit out of the two elements. The complications of rhythm so beloved by the French were not for Italians such as Landini; their goal was the beauty of line, the pleasure in a lovely vocal sound, the imagery of the poetry, and the sensuousness of them all together.

The fourteenth century was a brief period of glory for Italian music; at the end of the century it was eclipsed by the swing of musicians' taste to French procedures as well as by the appearance in Italy of musicians from the north. The leader of this wave, Johannes Ciconia (*c*.1335-1411) from Liège, who worked in Padua and Venice, represents a new kind of musician, the professional composer who is not attached to any one locale but moves from place to place wherever his talents are demanded and paid for. The example set by Ciconia was to be followed by such great men as Dufay, Isaac, Josquin and many others.

There is ample evidence of the diffusion of the new style in other parts of Europe. For example, there is a manuscript, now in Turin, containing over two hundred works that come from the court of the Lusignans on Cyprus. The music, sacred and secular, using both Latin and French texts, shows the impact of French composers brought to the island in the early fifteenth century by the artistically inclined Charlotte of Boulogne.

Poland also reacted to the novelties issuing from France and Italy, for two sources now in Warsaw provide samples of works written for the royal establishment of Ladislas (*c*.1348-1434) at Kraków. Under this king, Poland was a major power in northern Europe, and its connections with the rest of the continent, particularly with Italy, were close and strong. Composers represented in these manuscripts are Polish, not imported foreigners, but they show an awareness of developments going on elsewhere.

Interchange between England and France had been close since the Norman Conquest. In the thirteenth century English music had already taken into account French innovations, for it seems from remarks made by an English visitor at the University of Paris towards the end of the century that a musical culture involving polyphony, like that of Paris, was flourishing in England under Henry III (1216-72).

While the thirteenth century saw a certain parallel development between English and French music, such was not the case in the fourteenth century. In France the novelties of the *Ars Nova* were rapidly exploited, while English composers failed to keep step with developments across the Channel. Nevertheless, the characteristics

Above: Illustration to the *pastourelle* (a type of dramatized poem with songs) *Le Jeu de Robin et de Marion* by Adam de la Halle. This miniature comes from the contemporary manuscript containing all his works – an extraordinary distinction for any poet or musician of his time.

Left: One of several allegorical miniatures concerning Guillaume de Machaut, considered the greatest figure of the *Ars Nova* period. Here the composer is visited by the person of Nature, who offers him three of her children – Sense, Rhetoric and Music – to inspire him in his work.

Coment nature voulant ordonoit plus · nature par qui tout est fourme

of English style which remained constant were powerful enough to influence continental composers when carried to Europe in the early fifteenth century.

The most important of these 'English' traits was a liking for a kind of parallelism in linear movement of polyphony in three voices; this is today called either English descant or *fauxbourdon* (false bass). It could be improvised or used in composed works and was a technique much like the earliest organum, where a particular interval was chosen at which the plainchant was accompanied by another voice. In English descant, the three voices moved in a series of full chords, with emphasis on a richness of sound achieved by harmony and not the contrast of lines one against the other.

The highest point in the English resurgence at the beginning of the fifteenth century is represented by John Dunstable (*c.*1390-1453), from whose music the great changes in the style of the Franco-Flemish school led by Guillaume Dufay are derived.

• High Middle Ages: the Franco-Flemish school •

If the scourge of the plague succeeded in closing down large areas of Europe in the fourteenth century, their gradual reopening in the fifteenth more happily coincided with improved conditions of travel and a noticeable upswing in the general economy. Music and musicians were strongly affected by these changes. They enjoyed

Right: Louis, Duke of Savoy – a region that in the fifteenth century covered much of southeast France and north Italy – portrayed by Jan van Eyck. Louis was one of Guillaume Dufay's most important patrons. The composer wrote the music for the colorful occasion of Louis's marriage to Anne of Cyprus in 1434.

greater freedom of movement from one court or cathedral to another, and their journeys became lengthier and more venturesome. The Church not only continued its patronage of composers and singers, it even increased the amount of money spent on the training and maintenance of first-rate choirs, following the lead of monarchs and nobles, among whom Philip the Good, Duke of Burgundy, was one of the most outstanding in his concern for the arts.

Prior to the sixteenth century, the careers of even the most famous composers can be reconstructed only with great difficulty. There is one exception, for the life and travels of Guillaume Dufay (*c.*1400-74) are fortunately reflected with often remarkable clarity by the documents of his time. It is even known that his personal library contained a bottle in the guise of a book, which he would fill with hot water to warm his hands in the chilly vastness of Cambrai Cathedral during the winter months. Dufay was without doubt the greatest composer of his century, yet he thought of himself primarily as a man of the Church (he was a priest who at various periods of his life held notable administrative positions), and only secondarily as a musician.

Dufay was born around 1400 in a village not far from Cambrai. He was a choirboy at the cathedral there, becoming a clerk (adult singer) by 1413. In the following year he apparently left Cambrai, probably in the retinue of Pierre D'Ailly, Bishop of the city, who attended the Council of Constance. Also present at this great ecclesiastical conclave were Carlo Malatesta, procurator of Pope Gregory XII, and his brother Pandolfo, archdeacon of Bologna and chancellor of the university. They took an avuncular interest in the young composer and provided him with one of his first commissions. By 1422 Dufay may already have settled in Bologna to study for a baccalaureate in canon law, which he completed before 1427. There he wrote two further works – a marriage song and the motet 'Apostolo glorioso' – for members of the Malatesta family and two works which seem to have been intended for performance in the church of S. Giacomo Maggiore on the via Zamboni: the motet in honor of St James the Great, 'Rite maiorem Jacobum' (We duly sing St James's praise) and the *Missa Sancti Jacobi*. Also dated 1426 is a delightful song, 'Adieu ces bons vins de Lannoys' (Farewell to these good wines of Laon), referring to a town famous for its white wines, situated about fifty miles south of Dufay's home town, which he may have revisited after completing his studies in Bologna.

In 1428 Dufay became a priest, a singer in the papal choir and a member of the curia in Rome. When Cardinal Condulmer was elected pope in 1431, taking the name of Eugene IV, it was Dufay who had the honor of writing a celebratory motet. In common with much of the composer's sacred and occasional music, this is in isorhythmic style, featuring three Latin texts sung simultaneously with two supporting instrumental parts. For all its complexity, the work sounds wonderfully robust and impressive, luminous in its intensity of musical feeling and

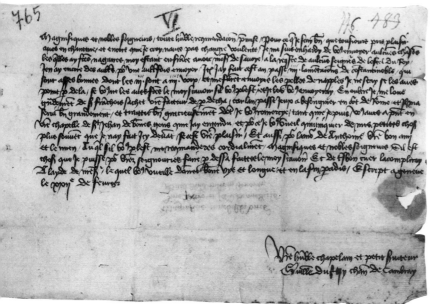

Above: Letter written by Dufay in 1456 to Piero and Giovanni de' Medici: 'Magnificent and Noble Sirs, Since I know full well that you have always been fond of songs (and since I also believe that you have not changed your preferences) I have felt encouraged to send you some songs which I composed recently when I was in France with the Duke of Savoy, at the request of some of the King's courtiers. I also have others which I will send you at a later date. In addition, I wrote last year four Lamentations for Constantinople which are quite good: three of them are for four voices and the texts were sent to me from Naples . . . I understand that you now have some good singers in your chapel at San Giovanni and in view of this – if it please you – I should like to send some of my little compositions more often than I have done in the past.'

Above right: Portrait of Dufay from his funeral monument.

imbued with an inner joy of consonant harmony. Two years later, Dufay was commissioned to supply another motet, this time to celebrate the meeting of King Sigismund with Eugene IV on 21 April 1433. Here he makes use of *fauxbourdon*, the smooth sonority of which contrasts powerfully and effectively with the main, isorhythmic, sections. Dufay's extensive travels included at least four spells in the service of the dukes of Savoy, the first in 1434. For the marriage of Duke Louis to Anne of Cyprus at Chambéry, Dufay was placed in charge of the music, and it may have been on that joyful occasion that he first met Gilles Binchois, one of the most famous from the brilliant chapel of Philip Duke of Burgundy.

However, he returned to the papal choir, which in 1435 went with Eugene to Florence and later to Bologna and Ferrara. From three highly attractive works dating from 1435-6, it appears that Florence exerted its influence upon the composer, for two are in praise of the city and her fair young ladies. Even more impressive, and understandably of more solemn character, was the motet commissioned for the consecration of the cathedral dome on 25 March 1436, the supreme pontiff being celebrant. The text, 'Nuper rosarum flores ex dono pontificis,' tells of the golden rose that had been blessed by the Pope and placed upon the high altar beneath Brunelleschi's great cupola. It has been suggested that there is much in common between the proportions of the cupola and the structure of Dufay's motet, and in view of the fact that architects of the time respected and used musical proportions to attain harmony in their buildings there may well be some truth in this theory.

Dufay returned to the service of Louis of Savoy for three more years (1437-9), passing his time at the court in Turin, on the pleasant shores of the Lake of Geneva, or at Basle, where he attended the council at which on 25 June 1439 Eugene, his former protector, was deposed. Dufay was now faced with a serious choice of patronage and loyalty, and after much deliber-

ation he returned to Cambrai, which was to be his principal residence for the next decade.

Although his extant works cannot be dated with certainty, it is very likely that Dufay composed some of his large-scale settings of the Ordinary of the Mass while he was at Cambrai; one may have been the Mass 'Se la face ay pale,' based on his own ballade with the same title: 'If my face is pale, the reason is love.' This free use of a love song to provide a structural basis for a sacred work implied no disrespect to the Church – on the contrary, a composer and priest such as Dufay would have looked upon it as a natural meeting of the sacred and the profane. The words of the ballade were not sung, nor was its principal melody heard. All that Dufay did was to borrow the textless tenor part of the song and set it out in various metrical patterns in such a way as to serve as a structural inner part without ever becoming too noticeable.

Dufay returned to the service of Louis of Savoy for a further six years (1452-8), during which time he traveled with the Duke to the court of King Charles VII of France and also sent some of his compositions to the Medicis in Florence. These included four 'Lamentations for Constantinople,' one of which has fortunately survived, a chanson-motet that demonstrates in music the universal sorrow felt at the fall of Constantinople in May 1453.

Dufay spent the last sixteen years of his life back in Cambrai, where he died on Sunday 27 November 1474. During this time he completed several new compositions in a recognizably mature musical style, characterized by the closely knit four-part texture and the equal sharing of polyphonic strands between all the voices. Today his music makes as powerful an impression as ever, ranging from the charm and lilt of the French and Italian songs to the noble dignity of the Mass settings and the splendor and variety of the motets and occasional pieces.

Gilles Binchois (*c*.1400-60), probably a native of Mons, began his professional life in the army and ended it in the Church. He composed music both sacred and secular and served the court of Burgundy for nearly thirty years. One of his best-known songs is 'Filles à marier': 'You girls thinking of marriage, don't ever get married unless you know what sort of a husband you'll have — for if jealousy should come into it, neither you nor he will have joy in your heart.' Two altos (or counter-tenors) declaim the words in a chattering, imitative fashion, with the unobtrusive support of two instrumental parts.

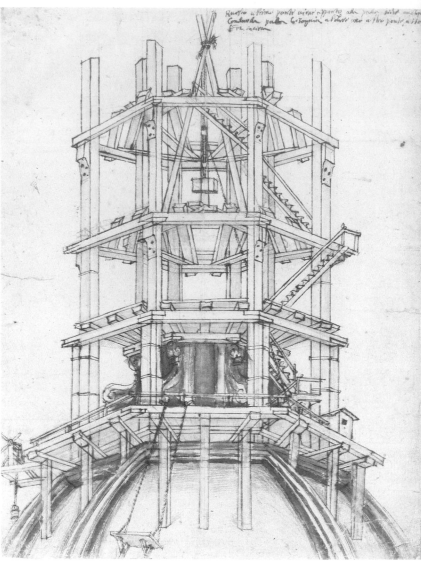

'Music,' said the theorist and composer Johannes Tinctoris, 'increases convivial pleasures.' It certainly did so for the lavish banquets at the Burgundian court in Binchois's time, at Lille (Feast of the Pheasant) in 1454 and at Bruges (wedding of Charles Duke of Burgundy and Margaret of York) in 1458. The entertainment at Lille, at which Philip the Good and the Knights of the Golden Fleece vowed to recover Constantinople from the Turks, did not in fact lead to a crusade, but a merry time was apparently had by all, and music played no small part in the elaborate scheme of events. In the banqueting hall one large table supported a model of a church with a bell and four singers inside, who sang and played the organ, while another table bore a huge pastry containing an orchestra of twenty-eight musicians. After the performance of a masque about the adventures of Jason (an altogether appropriate hero for the attendant knights), 'organs were played in the church for the length and extent of a motet, and shortly afterwards there was sung in the pastry, by three sweet voices, a song called "Sauvegarde de ma vie" [Guardian of my life]. Then, through the door, after those in the church and those in the pastry had each performed four times, there

Above left: Guillaume Dufay and Gilles Binchois portrayed in a miniature from the fifteenth-century manuscript *Le Champion des Dames.*

Above: Completion of the construction of Brunelleschi's dome to Florence Cathedral.

Right: Part of Dufay's motet *Nuper rosarum flores*, written for the consecration of the dome in 1436, which may echo in musical terms the mathematical proportions of the dome itself.

entered into the hall a wondrously great and beautiful stag: upon the stag was mounted a young lad, about twelve years old. The child held the two horns of the stag in his two hands. When he entered the hall, he began the upper part of the chanson, very high and clear: and the stag sang the tenor, without there being any other person except the child and the artifice of the said stag; and the song that they sang was called "Je ne vis oncques la pareille" [I never saw the likes of you]. While singing, as I have recounted to you, they made the rounds before the table, and then returned; and this interlude seemed good to me. After this interlude of the white stag and the child, the singers sang a motet in the church, and inside the pastry a lute was played with two good voices, and the church and the pastry always did something between the interludes.' Thanks to such descriptions by court chroniclers, who knew enough about music to record the way in which it was performed, much is now understood about the customs and traditions of the time.

Dance music, for instance, was created largely by means of improvisation over an existing melody, which might be taken from an earlier work or newly composed. This melody, played by a sackbut (trombone) in a series of notes equal in time-value, formed the basis for a two-part extemporization by shawm-players, and on

Right: The Hunt of Philip the Good (a sixteenth-century copy of the lost original attributed to Jan van Eyck), which shows how sumptuous were the festivities at the court of Duke Philip of Burgundy (1396-1467). His court was also one of the finest centers of music of its day, the musicians connected with it being known as 'the Burgundians.' The figure in black in the group by the table is thought to be Gilles Binchois.

occasion percussion instruments took part as well. One of the most popular of these dances was the *basse dance*, a slow and dignified affair which was usually followed by a *pas de Brabant* based on the same tune but played in a livelier tempo.

For many years the music of Johannes Ockeghem (*c.*1410-97) was considered to provide little more than intellectual treats for highly educated musicians. Now that most of his music is published, however, it can be performed and assessed in an entirely new light. Although he served as chaplain and composer to three kings of France, Ockeghem was, like many of his contemporaries, a great traveler, making use of every opportunity given him to improve his musical knowledge, whether of courtly songs or solemn Masses. In Spain he met Cornago and borrowed one of his songs, to which he added an extra voice-part; he spent two years at Cambrai, sharing pursuits both professional and convivial with Dufay; and he knew Binchois of Burgundy and mourned his passing in a lament of touching beauty. When he died, Josquin Despres wrote a 'Déploration' which

career. In the service of Cardinal Ascanio Sforza in Milan, Josquin found that his music was appreciated in every way other than the pecuniary. A story told by the Swiss theorist Heinrich Glarean suggests that the Cardinal was notorious for putting off requests for the payment of salary by saying: 'Lascia fare a me' (I'll see to it), which meant of course that nothing would be done at all. Josquin certainly wrote a Mass in the early 1490s based on a popular song with those words, and he followed the song in choosing a theme based on the notes 'La sol fa re mi.' Also from this time date a number of Italian 'frottole' (four-part songs for voices, or for solo voice and instruments), including 'In te Domine speravi' (In Thee O Lord have I trusted) and 'El grillo' (The cricket), which is amusingly imitative of the cricket's chirping.

Unable to find satisfaction in Milan, Josquin joined the papal choir in Rome in about 1486 and remained there, with short visits to Florence and Modena, until at least 1494. The Mass written for Ercole d'Este, Duke of Ferrara (*Hercules Dux Ferrariae*), may have been composed in the early 1480s, when Cardinal Ascanio, with

Below: Page from the 'La sol fa re mi' Mass by Josquin Despres. This copy, which dates from 1502, is one of the earliest examples of printed music.

IOSQVINVS PRATENSIS.

Above right: Portrait of Josquin in the form of a woodcut dated 1611 – that is, almost a century after the composer's death.

Right: View of Rome dated 1492, as Josquin would have known the city when he joined the papal choir. The Vatican (*palatium pape*) is at the upper right.

ranks as one of the most moving of all musical memorials. Ockeghem tempered the true steel of his technique in the white-hot inspiration of Dufay and Dunstable. Theirs was the model he followed, and if his mature work sounds richer than theirs, it is because instrumentally supported vocal lines were being gradually modifed in order to make way for sonorous choral harmony, and not because he invented (as is so often claimed) a polyphonic texture knit together by constant melodic imitation.

Of all the composers who left their homes in France, Flanders and Holland to journey southwards to Italy, Josquin Despres was indisputably the greatest of his generation. He was born in about 1440, and while still a youth sang in the company of older and more experienced musicians in the choir of Milan Cathedral. But as a composer he seems to have started comparatively late in life, and the bulk of his mature work belongs to the last thirty years of his

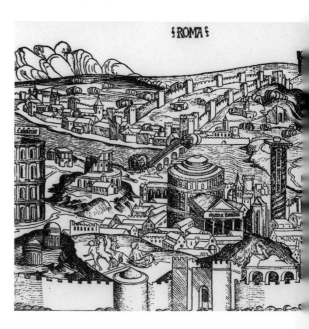

a large retinue, visited the court of Ferrara, and at a later date Josquin was approached by Duke Ercole's musical factotum with regard to an appointment. There was a rival, however, in Heinrich Isaac, who was reputed to get on with his colleagues better and compose more rapidly, whereas Josquin composed only when he felt inspired or in the right mood. Yet Josquin was nothing if not prolific, for aside from his twenty settings of the Mass he wrote at least ninety motets, and a further thirty (ascribed to him in various sources) may also be his. His later years were spent in Flanders, where he died in 1521, renowned throughout the courts and cathedrals of Europe as 'the prince of music.'

Cambrai long continued as a center for the training of first-class singers and composers. In 1484 the master of the choristers was Jacob Obrecht (c.1450-1505), who, like many of his fellows, traveled to Italy and was quickly accepted as a potential ornament to the court chapel of Ferrara. His comparatively short career saw the production of twenty-nine Masses, a number of motets and hymns, and settings of Dutch, Italian and French songs.

Antoine Brumel (c.1460-1515), a notable contemporary of Obrecht and Josquin, is mentioned by poets of the time in the same breath as those and other great names. His first important appointment was at Chartres Cathedral in 1483, and from there, after six years in Geneva, he went to Laon, later moving to Notre Dame, Paris, where he served as master of the choristers. After three years at Notre Dame, Brumel left for Ferrara, settling into a busy and productive musical life in an artistic community of such brilliance that it was almost without equal in the whole of northern Italy. His output was considerable by any standards, ranging over French songs of great charm, many motets, including fully-developed settings of complete psalms, and at least sixteen Masses, one of which was based on the much-revered popular song 'L'homme armé.' His setting, while exhibiting great contrapuntal skill, is nevertheless the work of a composer free in spirit.

• England •

The fifteenth century, for England, was one of turmoil and disruption. Much of its music remains anonymous (or is attributed here to one composer, there to another), and those musicians whose names have come down to us appear as shadowy, remote figures. There was also much willful destruction of manuscripts containing Latin liturgical music during the more violent years of the Reformation in the following century.

Many fine carols, some secular pieces and a quantity of church music have survived, however, to the lasting glory of a culture that was greatly admired by some of the foremost among continental composers. The carols, which are mostly anonymous, call for an unaccompanied

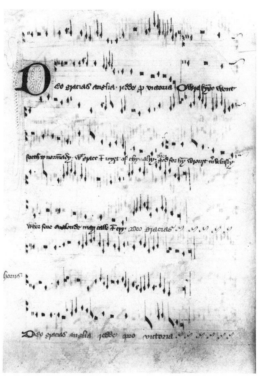

Left: Manuscript of the 'Agincourt Song' or 'Carol,' celebrating Henry v's famous victory over the French in 1415. The English King is said to have led his soldiers in the singing of it.

three-part choir, with soloists capable of doing full justice to the often subtle duets that serve as verses alternating with the choral refrains. Their texts are sometimes Latin, sometimes English, and not infrequently they mix the two languages, so that a carol beginning in the vernacular will end with a Latin tag, as often as not liturgical in origin. Although related to the liturgy, where they served as substitutes for the 'Benedicamus Domino' at Mass, carols could also be sung outside the church, so providing the first really large repertory of art music for use in stately homes and at court. A few compositions in carol form refer to topical events, such as the Battle of Agincourt, celebrated in 'Deo gracias Anglia: Our king went forth to Normandy.' This too could have been sung at the end of Mass, since its first two words form the response to 'Benedicamus Domino.'

Some of the earliest composers known today by name had their works copied into a large and beautifully written manuscript known as the Old Hall Manuscript. It was assembled in all probability for the Chapel Royal, or for the private chapel of Thomas Duke of Clarence, second son of Henry IV, and it seems to have been completed between 1415 and 1420. Although a few motets are included, the bulk of the repertory consists of settings of Gloria, Credo, Sanctus and Agnus Dei, grouped in four separate sections from which the director of music could assemble a complete polyphonic Mass. Their style ranges from the artlessly simple to the most devilishly abstruse, and if the earlier works belong to the late fourteenth century it is quite certain that the more modern settings were written in the first two decades of the fifteenth. French and Italian influences appear from time to time, but the greater part of the manuscript enshrines genuinely English production, of which the most mature pieces are by Chapel Royal composers such as John Burell, Robert Chirbury, John Cooke, Thomas Damett and Nicholas Sturgeon. One work by Dunstable appears, but his name is not mentioned.

The life of John Dunstable (*c*.1390-1453) is still very much a closed book, but it is highly probable that he was a member of the Duke of Bedford's chapel. Since the Duke was Regent of France from 1422 until his death in 1435, Dunstable may have accompanied him there, though not necessarily on a continuous basis. Prior to this he seems to have been active in England, for his motet 'Preco preheminencie' (Feast of John the Baptist) was chosen for performance at a solemn service of thanksgiving at Canterbury Cathedral in August 1416, just after the news had arrived that the Duke of Bedford had broken the Siege of Harfleur.

The composer and theorist Johannes Tinctoris stresses the suave character of Dunstable's music and mentions that the composer stands at the forefront of 'a new art whose fount and origin is held to be among the English.' This new art was in fact nothing more than a fusion of the harmonic factors inherent in English descant (smooth and flowing consonances caused by a succession of first-inversion chords) and the

Above: Page from the English *Old Hall Manuscript*, one of the most valuable musical sources to survive from the fifteenth century. The piece is a 'Gloria' by 'Roy Henry,' who may have been either Henry IV or Henry V.

Opposite: English drinking song of the fifteenth century, suitably illuminated.

tery of liturgical music, it is in his occasional motets that we find the most original ideas. One of the most brilliant of these was composed for a Venetian event – the installation of Michele Steno as Doge of Venice on 19 December 1400. It is written for two chorus lines in the treble range, doubtless sung by the choirboys of St Mark's, and an undesignated sustaining instrument, probably of the slide-trumpet type. One chorus sings of Venice as a shining example to Italy and to the whole world ('Venetia, mundi splendor'), while the other offers a euphonious eulogy of Steno and his illustrious family.

When Steno was followed by Tommaso Mocenigo in 1414, the motet for the installation ceremonies brought a new name to the fore – that of Antonio Romano, master of the choirboys since at least 1403, and a skilled composer of church music, of which two Gloria settings and one Credo are preserved. Once again there are two principal vocal lines, each having its own text, and it is very likely that the opposing voices were placed to the left and right of the two accompanying instruments to give the same kind of 'stereo' effect suggested by Ciconia's motet. Romano's four-part texture is richer,

contrapuntal ingenuities of the French school. The English contribution also featured melodies following the contour of the major common chord, while the French influence could be seen in the inexorable logic of the isorhythmic system. And it was precisely the marriage between suave harmony and flowing counterpoint that made Dunstable's work unique.

Only a handful of secular songs and instrumental pieces remain from a once vigorous tradition to prove that the English enjoyed music-making, but they are of sufficiently high quality to indicate that what has been lost may well have been superlative.

· Italy ·

Fifteenth-century Italy was full of seekers after outstanding musical talent. Not only the great cathedrals and churches, but also the private chapels of the powerful and wealthy rulers of city-states – above all the papal chapel – included among their staff men who were skilled at finding the best singers and composers. Notwithstanding the abundance of well-trained musicians of Italian origin, many tempting offers were made to northerners and they often accepted with alacrity. As far as can be ascertained, this new and foreign element was cheerfully absorbed, the high standards of the Franco-Flemish composers helping to encourage and inspire their Italian colleagues.

An early and specific example of this tendency may be seen in the music of Ciconia. Two of his songs with French texts survive and at least fourteen in Italian, showing how quickly he mastered the language within a musical context once he had arrived in Padua. Although his extant Mass sections indicate a certain mas-

Above: German woodcut entitled 'Music for a Banquet.' The music is supplied by pipe and drum, harp and lute.

Right: Fifteenth-century German engraving of a lady playing the lute.

Far right: The opening of one of Conrad Paumann's *Fundamenta organisandi*, a group of keyboard pieces. Note that the top 'voice' or part is in staff notation, while the lower parts are written in a form of alphabetic tablature. Paumann, born blind, was composer, organist and lutenist, and was considered the leading figure in fifteenth-century German instrumental music.

1433 with a slight change of text for another bishop, Francesco Malipiero. St Leonzio and St Carpoforo, the patron saints of Vicenza, are honored in the motet 'Martires Dei incliti' (Renowned martyrs of God) by another northerner, Johannes de Lymburgia, who is also the composer of works in honor of the city of Padua and of the patriarch of Venice, Giovanni Contarini.

The second pope after the schism, Eugene IV (1431-47), came from Venice, where he had observed the success of the choir school attached to St Mark's, and not surprisingly he strongly recommended that similar institutions should be developed in other Italian cities. He felt certain that if young boys were taught Latin and music in properly organized schools the resulting stream of singers would improve the size and quality of choirs throughout Italy. To some extent this improvement came about, although the emphasis on church music may have slightly reduced the production of secular vocal and instrumental music.

Nevertheless, we do have accounts of secular performances, and one virtuoso on the lute and lyre, Pietro Bono of Ferrara, achieved such fame that he was occasionally given permission to perform at rival courts, as in 1456 when he spent some time in the entourage of Francesco Sforza. The poet Antonio Cornazano describes how Pietro's heavenly singing and playing included several love stories, and how his last song was an unusual composition, apparently 'full of semitones' and much reliant upon metrical subtleties, imitative themes and a languid cadence. Mantua, in the early 1470s, witnessed an even more important recital, at which Angiolo Poliziano's *Orfeo* was given by a musician who apparently sang and played as Pietro Bono did. The music of these concerts has not survived, probably because it was extemporized, but it is sufficient to know that stories and legends were performed in musical settings and that they commanded popular attention as they had in medieval times.

however, and leads the way to a remarkable work by Christoforo de Monte, 'Plaude decus mundi' (Rejoice, ornament of the world), commissioned for Francesco Foscari (Doge, 1423-57), at the close of which the composer unleashes a series of brilliant fanfares. Foscari lived to a great age and had at least two further works written in his honor, one by Romano and the other by Hugo de Lantins, who also composed a sunny epithalamium in 1420 for Cleofe Malatesta of Rimini.

The Church was by no means forgotten amidst all these secular rites. A Dominican friar named Antonio, from the town of Cividale, wrote a bright congratulatory piece for Leonardo Dati, who in 1414 was elected superior-general of the Dominican order; he also wrote a complex motet with three texts, each one in honor of a saint of his order. When Pietro Emiliani was elected Bishop of Vicenza in 1409, the French composer Beltrame Feragut offered as a musical celebration 'Excelsa civitas Vincenzia' (O lofty city of Vicenza), which was reused in

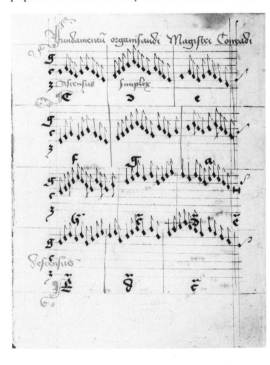

• Spanish music •

The general pattern of musical activity in Spain differs only slightly from that in Italy, with the Church as principal employer of composers and the royal court as a pinnacle of purposeful artistic creation. There was however one Spanish dominion outside the peninsula, the Neapolitan court of Alfonso the Magnanimous (1416-58), where the arts and letters flourished. Alfonso heard of a musically gifted Franciscan friar living in Rome, and sent for him in 1455 to join his chapel. Johannes Cornago, finding Naples to his liking, stayed on after the crown had passed to the King's son, spending his last years as a member of King Ferdinand's Aragonese chapel. Cornago left only one complete Mass, written shortly after 1480, but it is a work of unusual interest because of its all-pervading musical theme, taken from the song 'Ayo visto de la mappa mundi' (I have seen the map of the earth and the mariner's chart). It was obviously inspired by a map specially prepared by one of the King's artists, Giovanni di Giusto, at a time when the age of world discovery was dawning. Cornago's music must have been well known and admired, for songs of his were arranged both by his younger friend Juan Fernandez de Madrid and by Ockeghem.

Spain could boast of a highly gifted group of composers who came to their maturity as the century reached its close. Much of their music has been lost or destroyed, but its quality invites admiration, as with the unusually dark-hued 'Salve Regina,' for men's voices, by Fernand Pérez de Medina, a singer of Queen Isabella's chapel from 1477, though resident mainly in Seville. Also in Seville at that time was Juan de Triana, who held an appointment in the cathedral. Of his surviving eighteen works no less than fifteen are secular songs for three voices, the other three consisting of two settings of

'Benedicamus Domino' and one of the Lenten hymn 'Juste judex, Jesu Christe.'

Francisco de la Torre, a native of Seville, became a member of the Aragonese royal chapel in 1483 and almost certainly composed some of his sacred and secular songs before the close of the fifteenth century. Among his church music are three deeply moving responsories, one of which, the 'Libera me, Domine' (Deliver me, O Lord) from the Burial Service, is of such intensity and beauty that it has continued in use, at least in Toledo (where the original is still to be seen) until this century. De la Torre is better known, however, for his many secular songs and for the three-part dance entitled 'Alta,' referring to the band of loud instruments that would customarily perform it. The basic melody of this composition is the basse dance 'Il re di Spagna' (The King of Spain), possibly a direct compliment to the composer's royal patron.

One of the most outstanding among the Spanish masters, Juan de Anchieta (c.1462-1523) wrote much music early in the sixteenth century yet completed a considerable number of major works before 1500. Among them is his four-part setting of the romance 'En memoria d'Alixandre' (In memory of Alexander), which tells of the Spaniards' belief that their rulers would some day recapture the Holy Sepulcher, written at the time of Ferdinand's final campaign against the Moors in Andalusia in 1489.

• Germany and Austria •

Foreign influences were so extensive throughout the greater part of the fifteenth century in Germany that a relatively small repertoire of genuinely native works is all that remains. The presence of a German title or lyric with an undisputed attribution to a German or Austrian composer is no proof of authorship. The last of the aristocratic bards, or Minnesingers, was Oswald von Wolkenstein, whose accompanied song 'Der May mit lieber Zal' (May with its delightful throng) is really an arrangement of a French composition by Jean Vaillant. Some of his monophonic songs are original, however, as are the very numerous creations of the middle-class Meistersingers, for whom the art of song was closely bound by rules and customs.

A few secular songs and other pieces of German origin are found in the Lochamer collection (1455), in the anthology assembled by the Nuremberg doctor and historian Hartmann Schedel in the 1460s, and in the Glogau songbook from Upper Silesia (c.1477-88). Among the named composers are Conrad Paumann, Wenzel Nodler and Paulus de Broda; their contributions show a burgeoning national style despite the continuing influence of the Franco-Flemish musicians, who did, after all, dictate important matters of taste and style throughout the length and breadth of Europe. Instrumental music flourished mainly in the work of organists such as Paumann, whose composition treatise *Fundamentum organisandi* was a classic of its time.

Left: Page from the *Lochamer Liederbuch*, an important collection of German songs and keyboard pieces, copied down around 1455, probably by colleagues or students of Paumann.

Music at the court of the Emperor Maximilian

In the realm of music, one of the most colorful courts of Renaissance Europe was that of Maximilian I (1459-1519). He became King of Germany in 1486 and Holy Roman Emperor in 1493, thus beginning the ascendancy of the Hapsburg dynasty, which was to preside to a large extent over the fortunes of Europe until the First World War, and whose history is inextricably tied to the story of European music.

Maximilian was a transitional figure in the context of his time. In his conduct of affairs of state, in his taste for chivalry and pageantry, he looked back to the Middle Ages, while through his espousal of music and of the arts in general, he was very much a figure of the Renaissance. His marriages, to Mary of Burgundy in 1477, and to Bianca Maria Sforza in 1494, brought him into contact with the rich cultural life of the Burgundian court in the Netherlands and of Italy. He maintained at the Burgundian court, or invited to his own courts at Innsbruck and Vienna, some of the most eminent musicians of the age, including Antoine Busnois and Pierre de La Rue (protégés of Ockeghem), Heinrich Isaac, Ludwig Senfl, Paul Hofhaimer, Jacob Obrecht, and the Swiss humanist and musical theorist Heinrich Glarean. By so doing, he drew the German-speaking peoples into the mainstream of European music and laid the foundation of the great German musical tradition.

Maximilian (*above*) depicted in the Statute Book of the Order of the Golden Fleece. Founded by Philip the Good in 1429, this was the most famous order of chivalry and was later closely linked with the Hapsburgs. Maximilian himself was known as 'the last of the knights,' a comment upon his attachment to medieval chivalry and pageantry.

Stone plaque (*above*) of Maximilian with his wives, Mary of Burgundy (*right*) and Bianca Maria Sforza, now in the *Goldenes Dachl* (Golden Roof) house in Innsbruck, built in 1499-1500 to commemorate his marriage to Bianca Maria. The three of them are depicted watching the moresca dance.

A meeting (*below*) between the English King Henry VIII and Maximilian that took place at Guinegatte, near Lille, in 1513. Maximilian had been drawn into English, Netherlands and French politics by his marriage to Mary of Burgundy. Military musicians would have played a part in any such occasion.

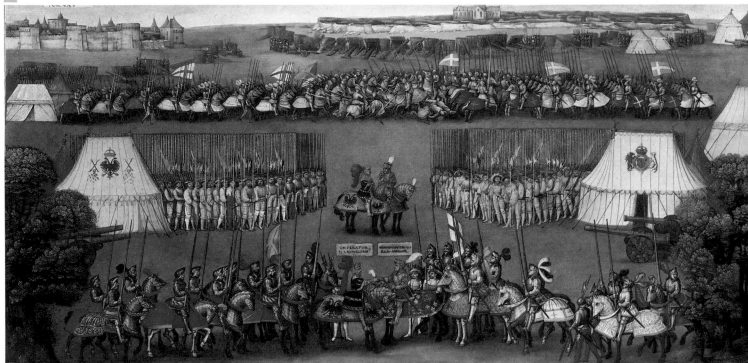

Maximilian produced a number of partly auto-biographical books, which showed him not only as a soldier and monarch, but also as a man of learning and a humanist in the new spirit of the Renaissance. In this woodcut (*below*) by Hans Burgkmair, the young 'Weisskunig,' as Maximilian called himself, joins a group of his musicians. He holds a conductor's staff, although there is no evidence that Maximilian was actually either an executant musician or a composer like his contemporary, Henry VIII of England. However, his enthusiastic patronage of music is well documented.

Prominent citizens of Augsburg (*above*) at the 'dance of the families' around 1520. This was the home town of the imperial bankers, the Fuggers, and also the scene of many of Maximilian's court festivals. His choir and instrumentalists would accompany him on such occasions, and he also sent his organist Hofhaimer to serve Fugger for ten years.

The moresca (*below*) watched by Maximilian and members of his court. This was an exotic Spanish dance with a strong Moorish element, as can be seen by the costumes and make-up in this picture. The traditional prize for the best dancer was a golden apple, seen in the hand of Bianca Maria Sforza, in the stone plaque (*opposite, top*).

Charles V (1500-58), portrayed here (*left*) by Titian, succeeded his grandfather Maximilian as Holy Roman Emperor and carried on the Hapsburg patronage of music in Spain, which, with its territories in America, was now added to the Empire. Charles V's reign ushered in a golden age of music.

After Maximilian's death, Austria was ruled by Ferdinand I (1503-64) (*right*), the youngest brother of Charles V and his successor as Emperor. His first court composer was the Fleming Arnold von Bruck (1490-1554), who confirmed the growing importance of Vienna as a musical center.

In another of the Emperor's allegorical publications, the *Triumphzug Kaiser Maximilians*, several of the splendid woodcuts (*top*) by Hans Burgkmair show the musicians of the imperial court taking part in a procession of chariots. Several of the leading musical figures of the court are individually featured: in the left-hand chariot is Bishop Slatkonia, seated with Senfl beside him at the rear of the court choir and the trombonist Johannes Steudel; the blind court organist Hofhaimer appears in the next one; then comes a group of wind-players led by the celebrated Nuremberg trombone-maker Hans Neuschel; and last a mixed ensemble of stringed and wind instruments with a drummer, entitled 'Musica sweet melody.'

The Renaissance in Germany is closely bound up with the Reformation, and several of the musicians and artists at Maximilian's court, notably Ludwig Senfl, later worked with Martin Luther, whose own chorales are a foundation stone of German music. The *Symphoniae Iucundae* (*right*) is a collection of pieces by various composers with a preface by Luther.

SYMPHONIÆ IV
CVNDAE ATQVE ADEO BREVI
QVATVOR VOCVM, AB OPTIMIS QVIBVSQVE MVSICIS COMP
sitæ, ac iuxta ordinem Tonorum dispositæ, quas vulgo mutetas appellare solemus,
Numero quinquaginta duo.

TENOR.

Vox ego sum simplex, tenuíq; canenda labore,
Hinc mea conueniens carmina nomen habent.
Vtq; ego, sic facili resonant modulamine cantus,
Qᴜos breuis hic omni parte libellus habet.
Hi tibi quisquis amas Musarum sacra placebunt,
Seu quia dulce canunt, seu quia sacra canunt.

Cum Præfatione D. Martini Lutheri.

Vitebergæ apud Georgium Rhau.
Anno XXXVIII.

Jacob Jonitke.

The Swiss-born composer Ludwig Senfl (*c.*1486-1542/3) (*above*) joined Maximilian's Vienna Hofmusikkapelle as a choirboy in 1496 and studied under Isaac, whom he succeeded as court composer. Senfl wrote Masses and motets for the court, a number of hymns for the Reformed Church, and many fine secular songs or *Lieder*. He also completed, after Isaac's death, a large collection of his Masses known as the *Choralis constantinus*.

Paul Hofhaimer (1459-1537), shown (*above*) in a drawing by Dürer, was Maximilian's chief organist. He was also a prolific composer of organ works and vocal pieces, though unfortunately only a fraction of his output has survived.

Memorial (*right*) to Georg von Slatkonia (1456-1522), who became first Bishop of Vienna in 1513. A humanist and gifted musician, Slatkonia was in charge of Maximilian's Hofmusikkapelle for over twenty years.

Heinrich Isaac (*c*.1450-1517), from Flanders, was one of the most highly regarded composers of his age, producing much church music and many songs. Shown here (*left*) is his setting of the well-loved song 'Isbruck, ich muss dich lassen.' Isaac was Maximilian's court composer from 1497 and Senfl was one of his pupils, but he also spent many years at the Medici court in Florence.

This drawing (*right*) by Urs Graf of 1523 shows four fashionably dressed mercenary soldiers playing what is described as a 'fluted serenade.' Alongside all the elaborate court and church music of Maximilian's time, there was also a good deal of military music-making, involving such instruments as the flutes or fifes in this picture, trumpets and a variety of drums.

Among Virdung's illustrations are a hurdy-gurdy (*above*) and (*below*) two shawms – double-reed woodwind instruments – and a pipe and transverse flute.

In 1511, Sebastian Virdung (b.1465), a prominent musician who had been employed at the cathedral of Konstanz, published his *Musica getutscht*, the first textbook in German on musical instruments. His main concern was with notation for the organ, the lute and other instruments, but he also published illustrations of many instruments, which would have been similar to those employed at Maximilian's court.

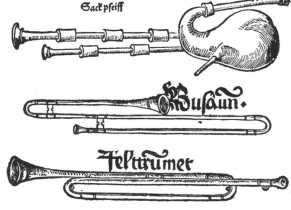

Above: Bagpipes, trombone and field trumpet from Virdung's book.

Albrecht Dürer, Renaissance Germany's greatest artist, was drawn into Maximilian's court circle. His peasant *Bagpiper* (*right*) plays an old folk instrument whose sound was often imitated by later composers to evoke the music of shepherds in 'pastorales.'

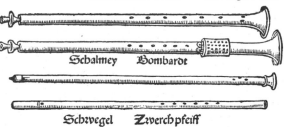

51

THE RENAISSANCE

ALEC HARMAN

The Renaissance was the first great secular period in Western history, for although the Catholic church was still a powerful religious and political force, albeit weakened by the Great Schism and assailed by the Reformation, and remained the principal patron of the arts, it could not stem the humanistic surge of imagination and intellect that swept with varying degrees of intensity right across Europe from its fountain-head in Italy. Humanism affected music later than the other arts for the simple reason that music, because it is the most abstract of the arts, cannot of itself express with any degree of precision the natural world or the thoughts, feelings or reactions of man. Hence it is not surprising that the predominant genre in the Renaissance, as in the Middle Ages, was vocal music, for only in the setting of words to music can a composer convey unequivocally what he wishes to express in his music.

The three main vocal types in Italy were the Mass, motet and madrigal. The Mass was that part called the Ordinary (Kyrie, Gloria, Credo, Sanctus, Agnus Dei), the words of which are invariable, whereas the motet could be based on any religious text. The madrigal was predominantly secular, ranging from the frivolous and pastoral to the serious and passionate.

Although music in both the Middle Ages and the Renaissance was almost wholly vocal, there were two significant stylistic differences. The first of these is that the medieval composer was not concerned with reflecting in his music the words he was setting, whether sacred or secular, whereas the Renaissance composer increasingly sought to underline or heighten certain evocative words or phrases in the text by various musical means, notably by procedures now called 'word-painting' and 'mood-expression.' In the latter the composer tried to convey through the character of the music the dominant mood or emotion of one or more lines of text; thus in a somber passage each voice might be in its lower register and moving slowly, or when dancing was mentioned the voices might change from the almost invariable duple meter of the period to triple meter and in a strongly rhythmic and chordal manner. In word-painting, however, the composer selected certain words and set them in such a way that their meaning would be 'painted' in sound. For example, the 'flight' of a bird would be set as a wavy melodic line, 'grief' as a short chromatic phrase, 'ascending' and 'descending' as up and down scales respectively. It should be noted that without words some of the musical figures used are ambiguous: for instance, a wavy line was also used to depict a stormy sea.

The second significant difference between medieval and Renaissance music concerns unity. As described in the previous chapter, medieval music consists of melodic lines, usually three, which are largely or wholly unrelated musically, and one or more of which are instrumental. Indeed, in the motet the vocal parts are also unconnected textually, singing different words simultaneously. Renaissance vocal music, on the other hand, which was usually for four or more voices, aimed at unifying a piece, by making it entirely vocal (that is, with no separate instrumental parts), by giving the same text to all the voices, and, most importantly, by relating the voices musically through a technique now called 'pervading imitation.' In this technique a composer divided the text into phrases, usually short, or even individual words, each of which made in effect, though not on paper, a section of the piece. He then devised an appropriate melodic idea or motif for each section, which was introduced and imitated by all or most of the voices one after the other; thus, although the imitative voices have the same text and motif within a section, they do not sing them at the same time. Pervading imitation may constitute an entire composition or it may be interspersed with chordal passages where all the voices sing the same words simultaneously.

Unlike medieval isorhythm, which can be regarded as an abstract means of unification in that it was not intended to be heard (a compositional device like the twentieth-century tone-row), pervading imitation was concrete, being clearly and intentionally audible to performers. In a modern score, of course, it would also be visually recognizable, but scores were extremely rare in the Renaissance, and performers sang or played either from part-books (as quartet players do today) or from books where the different parts were placed separately on facing pages or, for short pieces, even on the same page.

Renaissance secular music was mostly written for performers, not for listeners. There were no public concerts, although there were undoubtedly occasions when a selection from a madrigal book dedicated to a certain nobleman would be sung at his court before a small assembly. Much the same applies to church music, for which the presence or absence of a congregation was immaterial.

The fact that word-painting, mood-expression and pervading imitation became essential features of both sacred and secular music meant that there was no stylistic distinction between the two, but there was an important difference as regards performance, namely that church music was choral music (here defined as several singers per part), while secular music was sung by a solo ensemble. (The possible exceptions to this were those pieces written for a special occasion, such as the birth of a prince, when a choral rendition might have occurred.) The above distinction is important because, generally speaking, secular music reflects more intimately the nuances of the words, which soloists can convey more precisely than if there are several singers per part. Also, secular music was more prone than sacred to the practice of embellishing or ornamenting the written notes. Although only a handful of examples have survived, we know that the practice existed, especially in the later sixteenth century, and it clearly supposes one singer per part.

• The madrigal •

Of the three main types of vocal music the madrigal was unquestionably the most important, not so much in musical style, though it led the way as regards most of the developments that occurred during the century, but chiefly because it reflected the growing secularity of the period with its emphasis on man and his surroundings. Its beginnings and early development owed much to foreign influences and composers – in particular to a number of composers from north of the Alps who settled in Italy, of whom the most important were the Frenchman Philippe Verdelot (d. before 1552) and the Netherlanders Adrian Willaert (*c.*1490-1562) and Jacques Arcadelt (1505?-68); to these should be added the Italian Costanzo Festa (d. 1545).

The northerners brought with them a type of French chanson now called 'Parisian,' that owed something to the Italian frottola in the melodic importance of the top voice and clear-cut phrases, and which is a mixture of chordal and brief imitative writing, with word-painting infrequent, based on texts that are usually concerned with amorous complaints addressed to the loved one or to Cupid, the flavor of the whole being essentially light and diatonic – that is, added sharps and flats are rare except as required at cadences. This style, with Italian words, is that of the two earliest madrigalists, Verdelot and Festa, the main distinction between the two being that the former wrote more often in the richer texture of five or six voices (a typically north European trait), whereas Festa preferred the southern simplicity and clarity of three-part writing.

Important though these two composers were as exponents of the early madrigal, they were

Hor; che'l ciel, & la terra, e'l uento tace;
   Et le fiere, & gli augelli il sonno affrena;
   Notte'l carro stellato in giro meno;
   Et nel suo letto il mar senz'onda giace;
Vegghio, penso, ardo, piango; & chi mi sface,
   Sempre m'èi innanzi per mia dolce pena:
   Guerra è'l mio stato d'ira & di duol piena;
   Et sol di lei pensando ho qualche pace.
Cosi sol d'una chiara fonte uiua
   Moue'l dolce & l'amaro, ond'io mi pasco:
   Vna man sola mi risana & punge:
Et perche'l mio martir non giunga a riua;
   Mille uolte il di moro, & mille nasco;
   Tanto da la salute mia son lunge.

Left: A sonnet by Petrarch, from a sixteenth-century edition of his works. His sonnets were set as madrigals by many composers, this one by Monteverdi among others.

surpassed by Arcadelt and Willaert. Arcadelt, indeed, achieved considerable fame with his first book (1538?), which was reprinted nearly forty times, even as late as 1654. Most of his madrigals are for four voices, with smooth lyrical melodic lines, especially the top one, simple harmony and an avoidance of undue emotion.

If Arcadelt was the first famous madrigalist, Willaert was the more influential composer, for as music director of the basilica of St Mark's, Venice – possibly the most prestigious musical post in Europe – where he remained from 1527 to his death, he included among his pupils Nicola Vicentino (1511-*c.*1576), the first man to experiment in chromaticism, both theoretically and practically; Gioseffo Zarlino (1517-90), the greatest Italian theorist of his day, who castigated Vicentino's ideas; and the composers Cipriano de Rore (1515/16-65) and Andrea Gabrieli (*c.*1510-86). Willaert was also influential through his fecundity and versatility as a composer, for his considerable output included not only church music and madrigals but also chansons and frivolous pieces generically called 'villanelle.' These first appeared in print in 1541 and were of Neapolitan origin. They formed a marked contrast in every way to the madrigal and may indeed have been a reaction to it.

In his earlier madrigals Willaert follows the style already described, but in his later ones the voices increase in number and are more nearly equal in importance, the sections are dovetailed or overlapped, imitation predominates, and the accentual setting of the words, rather casual in earlier composers, is carefully matched to the music; he also occasionally employs chromaticism, a feature taken to extremes by Vicentino and most expressively used by Rore.

Rore followed Willaert as music director at St Mark's for a few years, but spent most of his life at the courts of Ferrara and Parma, the former being one of the principal cultural centers of the Renaissance. He was a man of serious disposition who set no frivolous texts and whose approach to the madrigal represents a turning point in its development. The single most significant feature of Rore's style is his use of mood-expression, a feature that can hardly be found before him but which in his hands reached

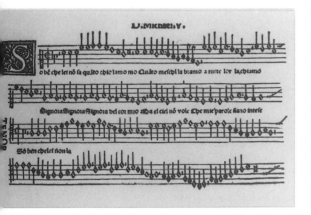

Far left: The cantus (or upper) and tenor parts of a frotolla by Don Michael of Vicenza, from an edition of 1518. The Italian frotolla was a forerunner of the madrigal.

taste during the latter half of the century, for while Petrarch's sonnets (*Canzoniere*), which deal with his love for the unknown Laura, were by far the most popular source of madrigalian texts throughout the entire period, with Ariosto's epic masterpiece *Orlando furioso* a long way behind, after around 1550 the passionate lyricism of Petrarch yielded some ground to Arcadian sentimentality, with shepherds and shepherdesses indulging in amorous sport. This trend was a natural outcome of the Renaissance emphasis on man's relationship with nature and the romantic longing for a simpler idealized past, and it is clearly seen in the pastoral poetry of Sannazaro, Tasso and Guarini.

a degree of intensity rarely equalled by later composers. Melody, harmony, rhythm, dissonance, chromaticism, and restrained word-painting, all are used to heighten the emotional content of the poems he chose, the great majority of which are set for five voices, which from this period on became the norm. With Rore what can be described as the classical purity of the madrigal began to crumble, as the balance between the textual and musical elements gave way to an increasing emphasis on the former, and for most composers after Rore the literary element became of paramount importance.

One major composer who was virtually unaffected by Rore was Giovanni Pierluigi da Palestrina (1525/6-94), whose style harks back to that of Arcadelt (who may have been his teacher), the main difference being that roughly half his output is for five voices and his word-painting is more frequent and slightly more graphic. But although he contributed nothing to the stylistic development of the genre, he established a new type, now called 'narrative madrigal,' in which two or more characters converse in a pastoral setting. The success of the narrative madrigal reflected a change in literary

Left: Study of a guitar player seated in a landscape; engraving by Marcantonio Raimondi of around 1480.

Left: Woodcut from the title-page of *Opera intitulata Fontegara* (1535), a treatise on the recorder. Its author, the Italian instrumentalist Sylvestro di Ganassi dal Fontego, also wrote a treatise on the viola da gamba. The players, who use instruments of different sizes, are shown performing from books of music with two singers. Families of instruments were developed in the Renaissance period to give a unified coloring over a wide compass; on the wall behind are three members of the viol family and a lute, and there are two cornetts in the foreground.

Above: French printing shop around 1530. Music printing, for which Paris became an important center, exerted a profound infuence on the diffusion of musical styles. Pierre Attaingnant, the first French music printer, who was active throughout the second quarter of the century, published 30 Masses, over 300 motets and more than 2,000 chansons, as well as collections of dances, lute tablatures and keyboard pieces.

Roughly contemporary with Palestrina was Andrea Gabrieli, a much more versatile composer who wrote a considerable number of the lighter kinds of music as well as instrumental pieces. His importance, so far as the madrigal is concerned, lies in the fact that he was one of the earliest composers to favor pastoral verse, which, in his later pieces, he sometimes clothed in a strongly rhythmic chordal style that inevitably highlights the top voice, and which is sometimes divided into two groups that alternate and combine. This division of the voices (polychoral writing) is found more often in sacred music than secular, and because it was essentially chordal in texture it was one of the late Renaissance features that heralded the rejection of imitative writing in the early Baroque.

Rore's influence on A. Gabrieli, as on Palestrina, was slight, but Rore and Palestrina had one thing in common, for both set Petrarch's 'Vergine bella,' a poem consisting of ten verses and a short concluding verse in praise of the Virgin. These 'spiritual madrigals,' as they were called, reflected the mood of the Catholic revival known as the Counter-Reformation, and almost every later madrigal composer of note wrote them, including Philippe de Monte (1521-1603) and Giaches de Wert (1535-96), the last two important madrigalists from northern Europe who worked wholly or mainly in Italy.

Although Monte was easily the most prolific madrigal composer, producing over 1,100 (including five books of spiritual madrigals), many of them of high quality, he failed to keep pace with the developments in Italy after his move to Vienna in 1568, where he remained till his death. Wert, on the other hand, was one of the most progressive composers of his day, for while his earlier madrigals, like Monte's, are clearly influenced by Rore, with Petrarch the preferred poet, his later ones show a pronounced predilection for Tasso and Guarini, both of whom he knew personally at the Ferrarese court, and are notable for their vivid word-painting, telling use of chromaticism, wide voice range, declamatory passages and a tendency to make the lower voices accompany the upper.

The work of Luca Marenzio (1553/4-99) has been described as 'the perfection of the madrigal style.' Every feature then in existence, except polychoral writing, he incorporated with an aptness and skill that is remarkable in its consistency. He can be as classically restrained and limpid in texture as Arcadelt, as serious as Rore and almost as passionate, and as declamatory and chromatic as Wert, but the one feature in which he excels is the frequency and graphicness of his word-painting, even indulging occasionally in so-called 'eye-music' (intelligible, be it noted, only to the performer), setting, for example, black half-notes and whole-notes to the words 'shady valley'! But despite his fondness for pictorial writing, potentially so fragmentative, he never lets it impair the flow and continuity of the music.

Chromaticism is the dominant feature in the madrigals of Carlo Gesualdo, Prince of Venosa (c.1561-1613), whose turbulent life reads like a nineteenth-century melodrama. His first four books of madrigals are completely up-to-date in style, with particular emphasis on word-painting but without Marenzio's unifying skill. His last two surviving books, however, which appeared in 1611, fifteen years after his fourth book, are full of the most audacious chromatic chord progressions. Never before had music so depended on words to give it meaning and coherence, for without them the violent changes in melody, harmony, rhythm and texture are largely incomprehensible. This was the *ne plus ultra* of the polyphonic madrigal, although the form had also been radically altered by an acquaintance of Gesualdo, Luzzasco Luzzaschi (1545?-1607), who published in 1601 (though certainly composed a good deal earlier) a remarkable collection of madrigals for one, two and three sopranos with a simple written-out keyboard accompaniment, the first of its kind. These madrigals were written for three highly talented ladies at the Ferrarese court, where Luzzaschi was also employed, and they demonstrate the kind of brilliantly virtuosic embellishment that was possible at this time. They also demonstrate in an extreme manner the growing tendency already mentioned of emphasizing the top voice. This was barely polyphony, but it was not yet baroque monody, and it was left to the last of the major Italian madrigalists to write in both styles – Claudio Monteverdi (1567-1643).

Of Monteverdi's eight books of madrigals, the last two belong to the baroque period, as they contain an obligatory *basso continuo* part, (a feature also present in some of the pieces in books five and six). In the Renaissance-type madrigals his style is not only thoroughly modern but also increasingly emphasizes rapid declamatory passages – some bordering on choral recitative and a freer treatment of dissonance.

The growing emphasis on chordal music by the late madrigalists reached its peak in the 'balletto,' the first collection of which, by Giovanni Giacomo Gastoldi (1550s-1622?), was published in 1591. Like the earlier types of light music, the balletto is not only basically chordal and strophic (with usually a 'fa la' refrain), but also pastoral in mood and strongly rhythmic and dance-like, as its name implies. Indeed, it is clear that instrumental participation and dancing were intended to accompany the singing, and it is likely that the whole was intended as a convivial musical entertainment, enjoyable to performers and listeners alike. A venue for this existed in the Academies that arose during the latter half of the century, where the cultured elite met from time to time to discuss various topics, artistic and intellectual, and where music was performed. This also included the so-called 'madrigal comedies,' which, though not acted, had plots that were often based on the immensely popular *commedia dell' arte*. The most famous of these pieces is *L'Amfiparnasso* (1594) by Orazio Vecchi (1550-1605), and they were one of the strands from which opera developed.

• Sacred music •

All the composers mentioned above wrote Church music, but few of them were as important in this sphere as in the secular. Unlike the style of the early madrigals, which differed markedly from Josquin's chansons, that of sacred music stemmed directly from his Masses and motets; thus the only major differences between Josquin and Willaert, the first notable composer of sacred music in Italy, are the latter's greater use of chordal texture and the concern that verbal and musical rhythms match. As music director of St Mark's, where there were two organs and several choir galleries, Willaert was presented with and took the opportunity of writing polychoral music, a technique that can be traced back to the early fifteenth century in Italy, where it may have originated.

Above: Dancing at the marriage festivities of the Duc de Joyeuse, favorite of Henry III, in 1581. The *Balet Comique de la Royne,* an allegorical glorification of the royal house, was performed on this occasion; while here the Duke and Duchess are leading the dance to the music of a lute band.

Left: French tapestry depicting the parable of the Prodigal Son. Music gives added pleasure to an amorous scene in a tavern.

The first examples by him were published in a collection of psalms (1550), where each choir sings alternate verses and both join in the 'Gloria Patri' or doxology.

Through his reputation as a composer and his influence as a teacher Willaert established the basic style of Catholic church music, a style that subsequently developed in two directions, which can be conveniently labeled conservative and progressive. The leading exponent of the former was Palestrina, who achieved a refinement of harmony, melody and rhythm that eschewed emotional extremes or dramatic contrasts but which is, nevertheless, beautifully expressive. The fervor of the Counter-Reformation encouraged a more subjective and emotional approach to the arts in general, which in sacred music could only be fully reflected in the motet, where any religious text, old or new, was permitted. However, Palestrina's motets are not only restrained, but their proportion to his total sacred output is also significantly smaller than that of other Italian composers. In only one respect was Palestrina 'modern' – namely, in his fondness for polychoral writing, which, as practiced, was essentially chordal and thus allowed the words to be clearly heard. Such clarity was strongly urged by the Council of Trent, which met at various times between 1545 and 1563 to consider ways of combatting the spread of Lutheranism, and at one stage the Council had serious reservations about contemporary church music, disliking the complexity that obscured the words. The composer who, more than any other, demonstrated that imitative polyphony need not destroy verbal clarity was the northerner

Jacobus de Kerle (1531/2-91), who dedicated to the Council a series of *Preces* or 'Prayers' (published in 1562) that were probably performed before each of the Council's sessions on music. These pieces are so written that textual intelligibility is retained, and they undoubtedly influenced the Council's decision not to ban polyphony from church music, provided that 'the words may be clearly understood by all.'

In Palestrina's day there were three main types of Mass: the Parody Mass – the most common type – in which a composer inserted into the movements of the Mass all or most of a previously composed sacred or secular polyphonic piece, either by himself or another, but changing the words of the original to those of the Mass; the *cantus firmus* Mass, in which a previously composed sacred or secular melody, usually paraphrased, or a series of hexachord notes, was placed in one or more of the voices, the melody sometimes keeping its original words; lastly, the freely composed Mass, including the 'Missa brevis,' which is self-explanatory. All three types were known in the previous century, but the third type was commoner in the Renaissance, especially the Missa brevis, in which brevity is achieved primarily through a preponderance of chordal writing.

Chordal writing reached its peak in the polychoral works of Giovanni Gabrieli (*c.*1555-1612), a nephew of Andrea and the principal church composer in Italy of the progressive development mentioned earlier. Giovanni not only increased the number of choirs to four and the total pitch range to over four octaves, but also juxtaposed passages of conventional

Below left: Part of a ricercare – a type of contrapuntal keyboard piece – for organ by the sixteenth-century Italian composer Marco Antonio Cavazzoni.

Below: A harpsichord of 1521 by Jerome of Bologna (Hieronymus Bononiensis).

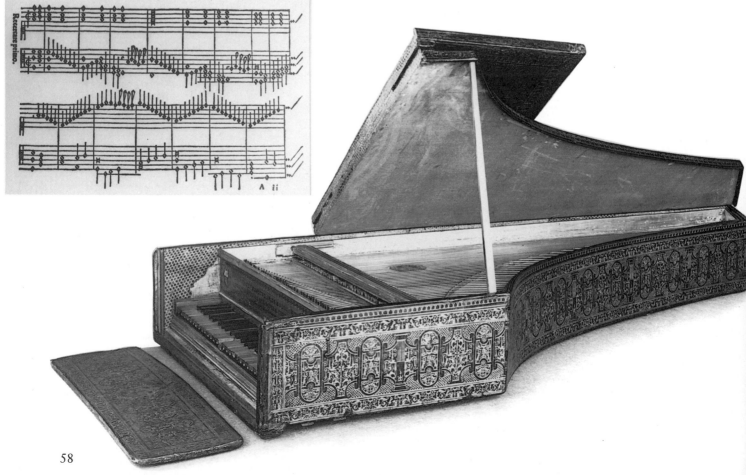

El SACROSANTO CONCILIO GENERAL DE TRENTO

CONCILIUM TRIDENTINUM

the ricercari in the simplicity of their motifs, the prevalence of chordal texture and the occurrence of some kind of repetition scheme; variations; dance music; and 'toccate', somewhat similar to the non-imitative ricercari but largely restricted to the keyboard and dominated by elaborately florid writing.

Ensemble music was the slowest to develop a distinctive style as it was easy for a 'consort' of recorders or viols (the most popular melody instruments) to play vocal music. And even when Willaert or A. Gabrieli wrote specifically for ensembles, the style was essentially imitative. G. Gabrieli, however, was both the first composer in Italy to write a substantial amount of ensemble music and one of the first to indicate exact instrumentation; he was also the first anywhere to explore contrasts of instrumental timbre. Thus in his *Sonata pian' e forte* (1597) – the earliest ensemble piece to include dynamics – he pits a cornett and three sackbuts against a viola and three sackbuts; an even greater contrast occurs in his motet *In ecclesiis*, where the two instrumental groups consist of three cornetts and a viola and two sackbuts respectively.

Above: Session of the Council of Trent in the mid-sixteenth century, at which the Catholic Church formulated many of the measures which made up the Counter-Reformation. Strict guidelines were laid down for church music, particularly for that performed during the celebration of the Mass.

Right: Title-page of Palestrina's *Missarum liber primus* (First Book of Masses) – music very much in the new, reformed church style. The composer is shown offering his work to the Pope.

rhythm with strikingly jagged syncopated motifs. These dramatic contrasts were further intensified by occasional chromatic harmony and unusual dissonances and, more significantly, by the use of instruments that alternated or combined with the voices.

The inclusion in some of Gabrieli's sacred pieces of specifically instrumental parts represented an important departure from the practice, fairly common in the late sixteenth century, of extemporizing a simple accompaniment on the organ from a bass part that merely consisted of the lowest vocal notes (hence called *basso seguente* or 'following bass'). This practice was taken a step further by Lodovico Grossi da Viadana (*c.*1560-1627), who in 1602 published a collection of motets with an organ bass that is frequently different from the lowest vocal part and is thus, unlike the *basso seguente*, essential to the harmony. This later became a fundamental feature of baroque music – the *basso continuo.*

• Instrumental music •

Both G. Gabrieli's and Viadana's works underline the growing importance during the Renaissance of instrumental music, which can be divided into three main classes – ensemble, lute and keyboard. The principal types of music were: transcriptions of vocal pieces; 'ricercari,' of which there were two kinds, imitative and non-imitative, the former similar to the motet in style, the latter, sometimes called 'fantasia,' more rhapsodic in character, combining chordal and short imitative sections with florid, sometimes sequential passages; 'canzone,' originally the counterpart of the French chansons and, although basically vocal in style, differing from

IOANNIS PETRI Loysij Praenestini in basilica S. Petri de urbe capellae Magistri. MISSARVM LIBER PRIMVS.

Because the lute is obviously unsuited to imitative polyphony, it developed a characteristic style much earlier than did ensemble music, beginning with Francesco Spinaccino and Joan Ambrosio Dalza (both fl. *c.*1500), whose ricercari were published by Petrucci in 1507/8. These short pieces consist largely of chords and scale passages, but as the skill of lutenists increased, transcriptions of vocal works appeared, as well as imitative ricercari, notable in the output of Francesco Canova da Milano (1497-1543).

all of whom published transcriptions, ricercari and canzone. Later composers included Claudio Merulo (1553-1604), whose toccatas are perhaps the most advanced technically and harmonically, and the two Gabrielis. Andrea is particularly important in that in some of his ricercari he uses only one motif throughout, instead of a succession of them (a type that led eventually to the baroque fugue), and in others he subjects a motif to lengthening or shortening of the original note values, or to inversion, learned procedures that were also used in the fugue. Compared to the lute repertoire, dance music was not nearly so prevalent, and it is significant that only stringed keyboards are specifically mentioned in two collections of dance music dated 1551 and 1592. On the other hand, only the organ was involved in a curious, indeed liturgically indefensible practice of replacing sections of the Mass or *Magnificat* with purely instrumental passages.

• Spain •

The amount of dance music that was published in Italy gives only some idea of the immense popularity of this pastime during the Renaissance, except, it seems, in Spain, where virtually no dance music was published during the period. Such a dearth underlines the fact that Spain was not only the one country apart from Italy that remained solidly Catholic, but also the country that gave birth to the organization

Dance music, too, flourished, the principal ones being the 'pavana' (slow, in duple meter), the 'saltarello' and 'gagliarda' (both quick, in triple meter) and the 'passamezzo' (moderate tempo, in duple meter). Some of the dances were joined to form a two- or three-movement suite, the most common being pavane-galliard, and in the last decade of the century some of these suites were unified by using the same basic chord progressions in each dance with partial melodic links.

Italian keyboard music did not achieve the same degree of idiomatic writing as the lute, because polyphony is better suited to the keyboard, whether stringed (harpsichord and clavichord) or organ – and only rarely was a distinction made in the music as to which keyboard was intended. The main problem with all three instruments was in tuning, for in the system then in use, 'mean-tone,' only a limited number of sharps and flats were in tune, whereas with the lute, viols and sackbuts any accidental was possible. Actually this problem did not become acute until towards the end of the century, when chromaticism became commoner, and various solutions were tried which, in the next century, led to our present 'equal temperament.'

The most popular types of keyboard music were the same as for the lute, and the first important composers were Marco Antonio Cavazzoni (*c*.1490-*c*.1560), his son Girolamo (*c*.1525-after 1577), and the latter's teacher, Willaert,

Above: St Ignatius Loyola, founder of the Society of Jesus (the Jesuits).

Opposite: One of the organs in Salamanca Cathedral; the horizontal pipes are a typical feature of Spanish organs.

Right: El Greco's *El Sueño de Felipe* II (Philip II's Dream) conveys the intensity of Spanish mysticism, which is also reflected in the music of Philip II's reign.

Opposite: St Theresa of Avila, reformer of the Carmelite movement. With St Ignatius she represents the deeply devotional and mystical nature of the Spanish Church.

which formed the militant spearhead of the Counter-Reformation, the Jesuits, founded in 1534 by the Spaniard Ignatius Loyola. It is thus not surprising that in Spain, unlike in Italy, secular music took a distinctly secondary place to sacred, a feature that is clearly revealed in the output of her three leading composers of church music, all of whom wrote an unusually high proportion of Masses and motets. The first of these composers was Cristóbal de Morales (*c.*1500-53), whose style is a curious mixture of old-fashioned and contemporary elements, the former evident in the bi-textualism of some of his Masses and motets, the latter in pervading imitation and parody. Although secular models form the basis of a third of his Masses, the overall flavor of his music is one of a rather austere devotion that is distinctly impressive.

Like Morales, Francisco Guerrero (1528-99) wrote very little secular music, and only two of his eighteen Masses are based on secular material. His style is akin to Palestrina's, and his best work lies in his motets, most of them Marian, which evince a lyricism and grace befitting their subject. The third Spanish master, Tomás Luis de Victoria (1548-1611), who can stand alongside Italy's finest composers, not only wrote no secular pieces, but only one of his twenty Masses is based on a secular song. This conservative trait is balanced by modest word-painting (virtually non-existent in Morales and Guerrero) and polychoral writing.

The almost exclusive concern of these three composers with church music was typical of other Spaniards, and there was, in effect, a dichotomy between sacred and secular composers

Right: Two facing pages of the opening Kyrie of a six-part Mass by Victoria, published in 1583.

Below: Title-page of an edition of Masses by Francisco Guerrero, published in Rome in 1582. By then he was choirmaster at Seville Cathedral.

and between the styles of the two genres. Thus while the Italian madrigal was imitated to a limited extent, the main type of secular music, as in the fifteenth century, was the 'villancico.' The preponderance of the native type is clearly shown in the work of Juan Vasquez (*c.*1510-*c.*1560), the only Spaniard who can be compared to his Italian counterparts. In his hands the villancico, while incorporating madrigalian features such as pervading imitation, is sharply differentiated in its lack of word-painting and in its use of refrain.

The dichotomy between sacred and secular music is even more apparent in the many solo songs with vihuela (lute) accompaniment, the character of which could hardly be further removed from that of contemporary church music. The importance of the accompaniments in these songs leads to their inclusion in any discussion of vihuela music, which, with keyboard music, formed one of the most distinctive contributions of Spain to the Renaissance.

The chief solo song writers were Luis de Milán (*c.*1500-*c.*1561), Alonso Mudarra (*c.*1510-80) and Miguel de Fuenllana (d. after 1568), all of whom wrote with great grace and refinement; indeed, they have been called the first composers of the art-song. Their principal publications appeared, respectively, in 1536, 1546 and 1554, and all include arrangements for vihuela of vocal pieces by both native and foreign composers, dances, romances (songs based on long poems dealing with historical or legendary subjects), and especially fantasias and 'tientos' (both similar to the ricercari), as well as villancicos.

Historically, the most important publication (in 1538) of vihuela music was by Luys de Narváez (fl.1530-50), for it contains, in addition to the various types already mentioned, probably the first fully fledged examples of the instrumen-

THOMAE LVDOVIC
A VICTORIA ABVLENSIS
MISSARVM LIBRI DVO
QVÆ PARTIM QVATERNIS, PARTIM
QVINIS, PARTIM SENIS.
CONCINVNTVR VOCIBVS.

Ad Philippum secundum Hispaniarum Regem Catholicum.

R O M Æ .
Ex Typographia Dominici Basæ.
M D LXXXIII.
CVM LICENTIA SVPERIORVM.

tal theme and variation, or 'diferencia.' The number of variations extends to as many as twenty-two, and while in most of them the theme is decorated, in a few it is merely implied through the harmony. This publication, together with Milán's, contains some of the earliest known indications of tempo.

Variation writing is also the most significant feature of the leading Spanish keyboard composer, Antonio de Cabezón (1510-66). The main collection of his works was published posthumously in 1578, and although its title implies that the music can be played on the 'tecla' (keyboard), harp and vihuela, there is little doubt from the character of the music that it best suits the organ. His fantasias are as complex as Fuenllana's, but the polyphony is more sustained and developed, a feature that can only be fully accomplished on the organ. The same feature is also evident in his diferencias, in some of which the variations, instead of being self-contained, are dove-tailed and so provide greater continuity.

•Germany and Austria •

One of the fundamental points in Martin Luther's attempt to 'reform' the Catholic Church was that the congregation should understand the service – hence his translation of the Bible and the increasing use of the vernacular in services. But he was unconcerned about the origins of the music, which to begin with was adapted from Catholic chants and previously composed Latin and German sacred and secular songs, some probably by Luther himself. The first major Protestant composer was Johann Walter (1496-1570), whose *Geistliche Gesang*

Büchlein (1524) consisted largely of 'spiritual songs' for from three to five voices. About half of them, following the style of Heinrich Isaac, had the tune, mostly in half-notes, in the tenor, the other parts being more florid and occasionally imitative; the remaining pieces also had the tune in the tenor, but the texture was basically chordal, anticipating the hymn-like character of the later chorale. It is not known to what extent the congregation participated in these songs, but they could have sung the tunes, a number of which were issued separately in the twenty or so years after Walter's book. It was now that the so-called 'Bar' form became common, in which the melody consists of two sections, the first of which is repeated to different words.

Walter's chorale collection was followed by many others, as well as simple psalm-settings, the only important development being the transference, near the end of the century, of the tune from the tenor to the top voice, where it subsequently remained. But inevitably the tide of imitative polyphony from the Netherlands affected Lutheran music as it had the Italian

Above left: Title-page of a Book of Masses (1544) by Cristóbal Morales, for some years a member of the papal choir in Rome. Compare it with the one on page 59. Both composer and pope are different, but otherwise the two title-pages are almost identical.

Above: Title-page to an edition of Victoria's Masses, published in Rome in 1583.

madrigal, and the Lutheran motet was the result. This differed from its Catholic counterpart only in its language; indeed, some composers wrote both kinds, notably the Protestants Hans Leo Hassler (1562-1612) and Johann Eccard (1553-1611) and the Catholic Ludwig Senfl (c.1486-c.1542/3).

Catholicism, despite Luther's success, was still a powerful force in Austria and southern Germany, where the principal composer, and one of the greatest in the Renaissance, was Roland de Lassus (1532-94). After spending some twelve years of his youth in Italy, Lassus settled in Munich in 1556 and remained there until his death. His enormous output was matched by his cosmopolitanism, for he was as much at home in French, German and Italian secular pieces as in Catholic music. It is in the last of these that his best music is found, especially the motets, which reveal a wide emotional range, vividly conveyed through word-painting and mood-expression, and sometimes in extreme chromaticism. The gradual decline of pervading imitation during the latter half of the century is shown in a feature that is more characteristic of Lassus than anyone else: a much less rigid form of imitation, in which only the melodic outline and rhythm of a motif is imitated. This feature underlines Lassus's concern with emotional expressiveness rather than with musical symmetry or orthodoxy, and he responded to the fervor of the Counter-Reformation more profoundly, perhaps, than did his contemporaries.

The principal composer in Vienna was Philippe de Monte, who also wrote copiously for the Catholic liturgy, but whose Masses are, on the whole, superior to his motets, which lack Lassus's emotional range and power of expression. However, although his style is more orthodox, the best of his church music, like his madrigals, ranks with the best of the period.

The style of secular song (*Lied*) remained tied to that of Isaac, described above, until, around the middle of the century, it was influenced by the polyphonic style of the Netherlands. The composer chiefly responsible was Senfl, whose style in both sacred and secular spheres reveals not only pervading imitation but also a new melodic gracefulness, with the principal melody not always in the tenor, but with little, if any, word-painting. Up to this point the great majority of *Lieder* were issued in anthologies, the main ones being by Johann Ott in 1534 and 1544, and Georg Forster between 1539 and 1556. In the second half of the century the influence of Italy was paramount, beginning with a book of villanelle by Antonio Scandello (1517-80), published in Nuremberg in 1566, which was succeeded by a number of similar books by, among others, Lassus, who set with equal ease both Italian and German words in a thoroughly madrigalian manner. Although Lassus's madrigalian style was non-progressive, its application to German secular music had a considerable impact, as can be seen in his first book of *Lieder* (1557); he, in fact, converted the *Lieder* into madrigals with German words, the only other difference being the frequent occurrence of a repetition scheme, such as Bar form.

The principal composers to follow Lassus were Leonhard Lechner (c.1553-1606), Jakob Regnart (1540/5-1599) and Hassler, a pupil of A. Gabrieli. The works of all three are thoroughly Italianate and comprise villanelle as

Above left: Roland de Lassus, aged twenty-eight, in a miniature by Hans Mielich.

Above: Lassus directing the chapel choir at the Munich court, where he served for nearly forty years, again in a miniature by Mielich, the court painter.

and secular part-songs, some, as in Spain, arranged for voice and lute accompaniment. The simplicity of the adaptations, compared to those in Italy and Spain, is probably explained by the greater popularity of the instrument with amateurs. Dance music also makes only modest technical demands and includes, in addition to foreign imports such as pavane, galliard, passamezzo and saltarello, two native dances, the 'Tanz' and 'Nachtanz', the former usually in duple meter, the latter in triple, clearly imitations of the pavane and galliard.

German keyboard music is similar to that for lute in its almost total dependence on vocal pieces, but dissimilar in that the transcriptions are much more ornate, sometimes grossly so, and the amount of dance music is considerably less, probably because the organ was the preferred instrument.

• The Netherlands and France •

The Netherlands could lay claim to being the most important musical region in the fifteenth and early sixteenth centuries, for it was the cradle of the polyphonic style which affected the whole of Europe. Most of the principal composers from Josquin on emigrated southwards, but there were three who did not — Nicholas Gombert (*c.*1495-*c.*1560), Clemens non Papa (1510/15-1555/6) and Jan Pieterszoon Sweelinck (1562-1621). The first two contributed substantially to both Catholic and secular music, and although they rarely left their native country, their Masses and motets were widely disseminated. Clemens is also important in that

well as German madrigals. The best of the three was Hassler, some of whose madrigals rank with the finest of the period and who also produced a book in 1601 that contains some typically Gastoldian balletti (very popular in Germany) and some instrumental ensemble pieces.

Although there are numerous references to ensembles in Germany, hardly any music has survived, and it seems likely that performances were largely restricted to renditions of vocal pieces. These last were, in fact, the prime source of lute music throughout the century, of which there is a considerable quantity, the bulk consisting of fairly simple adaptations of sacred

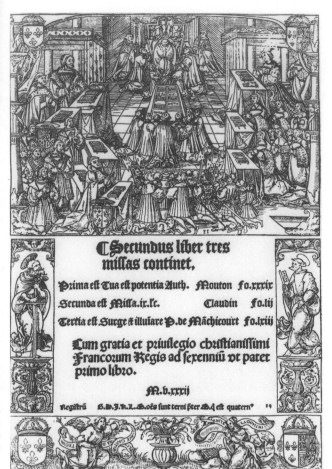

Left: Title-page from an edition of Masses, published by Pierre Attaingnant in Paris in 1532. Among the composers included are Jean Mouton, Claudin de Sermisy and Pierre de Manchicourt. The top scene shows Mass being celebrated at the court of François I.

Above: Title-page of Clément Marot's *Temple de Cupido*, a collection of his love poems, many of which were set by Janequin, Lassus, Sermisy and others.

*c.*1560), both of them published in 1547. Unlike Luther, Calvin objected strongly to part-music in church, but polyphonic settings of the psalms could not be gainsaid, and the two books by Bourgeois, in one of which the style is hymn-like, in the other more complex, were followed by many similar settings, notably by Claude Le Jeune (1528/30-1600) and Jacques Mauduit (1557-1627). Most of these were based on the original psalm-tunes, and while some of them were hymn-like, others were virtually motets in their use of imitation and even word-painting, the most influential being by Claude Goudimel (1514/20-1572). In some of his more ornate settings the tune, for the first time, is placed in the top voice.

Most of the leading composers contributed to both the Catholic and Protestant liturgies, some of them, like Goudimel, being converted to the latter faith, and all of them wrote the Parisian type of chanson. The first two composers of this genre were Clément Janequin (*c.*1485-1558) and Claudin de Sermisy (*c.*1490-1562), of whom the former owed his popularity largely to the enormous success of his 'program chansons,' in which such natural sounds as bird cries, and the sounds of battle are portrayed, sometimes by means of onomatopoeic syllables. His 'normal' chansons, like those of de Sermisy, reveal those features which affected the early Italian madrigal, although they are less polyphonic and imitative than those of their contemporaries Verdelot and Arcadelt.

The importance of the text in the madrigal has already been observed, but in France this literary emphasis reached a peak in the Académie de poésie et musique, founded in 1570 by Jean Antoine de Baïf. He was inspired by a group of poets, 'Le Pléiade,' of whom the most famous was Pierre de Ronsard, who attempted to emulate the dramatic and lyric verse of the Greeks and Romans, a thoroughly Renaissance ideal. Greek and Latin, unlike French, is based on metrical patterns of long and short syllables, and while Ronsard and most of the others in the group avoided imitating this aspect of classical poetry, de Baïf did not, producing what he called 'vers mesurée,' which Guillaume Costeley (*c.*1531-1606), Mauduit, Le Jeune and others set to long and short notes that matched the syllables. This 'musique mesurée' was basically chordal in texture and wholly irregular as to meter, depending entirely on the mensural construction of the verse, and largely because it was so shackled it soon fell into disfavor.

De Baïf's Academy also aimed at creating a unified spectacle in which music, poetry, dancing and scenery played an equal part; dancing, indeed, was probably more popular in France than anywhere else, as we might expect from the country that, via the late sixteenth-century *ballet de cour,* gave birth to modern ballet.

The same strong preference for the dance and the same overall simplicity occurs in French lute music, of which there was a considerable amount, including passamezzi, gavottes, courantes, pavanes and galliards – the last two, the most popular, usually paired. The bulk of this

he composed the only Protestant part-music in the Dutch language during the Renaissance, namely a setting for three voices of part of a psalter, the *Souterliedekens* (1540). This psalter, the melodies of which were mostly gleaned from folksongs, was so popular that it was reprinted over thirty times within the next seventy years, and unlike similar publications elsewhere, it was intended for use in the home, not the church.

The dearth of Protestant music was partly due to the almost fanatical opposition of the Spanish, especially during the reign of Philip II, to whom Charles V left this part of the Empire, and partly to the fact that the French (Geneva) psalter was adopted in the Netherlands in 1566. As a result, Sweelinck's predominantly Protestant music is almost wholly devoted to Calvin's Genevan psalter, the only significant exception being a fine book of Latin motets (1619).

The secular music of the two earlier composers consisted of French chansons, but by the last decades of the century, the influence of the Italian madrigal had grown so strong that the chanson, like the German *Lied,* had succumbed, and Sweelinck's examples are virtually French madrigals, apart from the strophic construction of some of them. While these pieces are thoroughly modern in their use of word-painting (including examples of 'eye-music'), this feature is strangely absent from his Italian madrigals.

Besides Sweelinck, there were many French composers who made polyphonic settings of the Geneva psalter during the Renaissance, the two earliest being by Louis Bourgeois (1510/15-

is contained in collections published by Attaingnant and Le Roy & Ballard; Le Roy was also a composer and distinguished performer, and the author of an important lute 'tutor.'

The difference, as regards dance music, between keyboard music on the one hand and lute and ensemble music on the other is even more evident than elsewhere, for in France keyboard music largely consisted of organ Masses and fairly elaborate transcriptions of vocal music, with original pieces such as fantasias remarkable for their rarity. Several large collections were issued, their contents, as was usual, making no distinction between organ and stringed keyboard and with the composers unnamed; indeed, the only keyboard composer of note was Jehan Titelouze (1562/3-1633), whose pieces are mostly variations on Catholic melodies, and who was the first Frenchman to advocate two manuals and a pedal keyboard, the latter rare outside Germany.

•England•

Protestantism in France was not officially recognized until 1598, after decades of bitter fighting. In the Netherlands recognition had to wait until, after several successful battles against Spain, independence was achieved in 1648. Compared to these two countries and to Germany itself, England's adoption of Protestantism was not only relatively bloodless but also the most radical, and from 1534, when Henry VIII formally rejected the Pope's authority, Catholicism was increasingly on the defensive, except for the years 1553-8, when Mary Tudor and her husband Philip II of Spain reigned.

In 1549, during Edward VI's reign, the first *Book of Common Prayer* was issued. This established the order of the three main Services in the, now official, English language – Morning Prayer (Matins), Evening Prayer (Evensong) and Communion, the last identical in structure to the Mass. This order of service has remained to the present day, and the sections set to music were and are the canticles – *Venite*, *Te Deum* and *Benedictus* at Matins, *Magnificat* and *Nunc dimittis* at Evensong – and the Communion service, all sung in English. In addition, there are anthems and psalms, the former being the equivalent of motets and, like them, an optional part

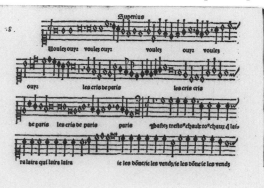

of the service, the latter first appearing in *Goostly psalmes* (c.1538) by Myles Coverdale (the translator of the 'Great Bible'), which contained among other spiritual songs fifteen psalms set to melodies culled from Lutheran and Catholic sources. This was banned by King Henry because of its Lutheran associations (he disliked the democratic structure of Lutheranism), and in about 1548 it was succeeded by the first edition of what became the most popular English psalter by far – *The Whole Book of Psalms* by Sternhold and Hopkins, which, despite its title, contained only nineteen psalms without music. The second and third expanded editions soon followed, the latter with tunes, and finally all 150 psalms were issued in 1562 together with sixty-five tunes.

The chaotic religious scene in England for most of the sixteenth century, exemplified by the switches from Roman Catholicism (under Henry VII and VIII) to Anglican Catholicism (under Henry VIII and Edward VI) to Roman Catholicism (under Mary) to Anglicanism (under Elizabeth I), must have been very confusing to composers, a confusion compounded by the edict in 1548 that not only must all liturgical music be sung in English, with no reference to

the Virgin or the saints, but that the settings must also be to 'a plain and distinct note, for every syllable one.' In other words, the traditional melismatic style so suited to the sonorous vowel-rich Latin language had to be replaced by a basically syllabic one, a style that, incidentally, reflected the greater prominence of consonants in the native tongue.

The first generation of church composers included John Taverner (c.1490-1545), Christopher Tye (c.1505-?1572) and Thomas Tallis (c.1505-85). All wrote for both Catholic and Anglican rites, the former richly melismatic, the latter simpler and more syllabic. Tye and

Above: Pierre de Ronsard, and facing him Cassandre de Salviati, the inspiration for his *Amours*. These poems, in turn, inspired many musical settings.

Left: Page from Clément Janequin's chanson *Les Cris de Paris*, noted, like many of his other songs, for its imitative effects.

Tallis are thoroughly contemporary in their use of pervading imitation, a technique largely absent from Taverner's work, which looks back to the previous century. As time passed, however, the same changes occurred in Anglican music as in the later settings of the Genevan psalter, and from the same sources, the motet and madrigal – namely, the greater use of melisma, with strongly contrasted chordal passages, and the introduction of word-painting, features that are clearly evident in the works of William Byrd (1543-1623), Thomas Weelkes (1576-1623), Orlando Gibbons (1583-1625) and Thomas Tomkins (1572-1656).

Byrd, one of the greatest composers of the Renaissance, remained a Catholic all his life, but was equally at home writing for the Anglican Church or for the Roman. Even more than those of his contemporaries abroad, his Catholic works show a strong predilection for the motet, the earlier ones (composed before 1591) revealing conservative traits in the occasional use of a borrowed melody (although his three Masses, *c.*1600, are all freely composed), infrequent

Right: Orlando Gibbons, who composed some of the best-known and most expressive English madrigals, in addition to church music and keyboard works.

Below: Page from the *Fitzwilliam Virginal Book*, a collection of nearly three hundred keyboard pieces of the sixteenth and early seventeenth centuries, mainly by English composers. The two works shown here are by the Dutch composer J. P. Sweelinck and by William Byrd.

word-painting and a preference, when writing for five or more voices, for doubling one of the lower voices. His later books (1605, 1607), published after a significant interval, during which most of the English madrigals had appeared, are more modern as regards pictorialism and in the emphasis on the top voice. In general his rhythm is more complex and his treatment of dissonance more unorthodox than that of his Continental counterparts.

Byrd's Anglican music comprises several settings of the Service (Matins, Evensong, Communion) and a considerable number of anthems, most of them contained in three collections of sacred and secular songs dated 1588, 1589 and 1611. The differences between his earlier and later motets are paralleled in his earlier anthems and those in the 1611 book, and the style is similar except for shorter and less frequent melismas. All three books contain two distinct types of anthem, the 'full' and 'verse.' The former is the true equivalent of the motet, while the latter, which Byrd may have been the first to introduce, is 'scored' for one or more solo singers, choir and a written-out instrumental accompaniment of viols and/or organ, an arrangement he also used in some of his Services. The verse anthem and Service can be regarded as

Below: Page from the Elizabethan *Mulliner Book*, another valuable collection of keyboard works, some original, some arranged. This example is an arrangement by Tallis. The compiler was Thomas Mulliner, himself a composer.

Below right: John Bull, who as organist of Antwerp Cathedral gave wider currency to the English keyboard style, particularly through his friendship with Sweelinck.

Bottom: Queen Elizabeth's virginal, made in Venice in 1570. The Tudor royal coat-of-arms is emblazoned on the left-hand panel.

the English equivalent of G. Gabrieli's motets such as *In ecclesiis*, except that they are less colorful but much more common, and the polychoral technique of Italy was matched by the practice, in full anthems and Services, of dividing the choir into *decani* and *cantoris*, representing the dean's side of the choirstalls and the cantor's side respectively.

Unlike Byrd, Weelkes, Gibbons and Tomkins composed only for the Anglican Church, a fact that reflects the increasingly anti-Catholic mood during Elizabeth's reign, which saw the return of those who had fled to the Continent to escape Mary's persecution and had been influenced by Calvinism. All three composers contributed proportionately more verse anthems and Services than Byrd, especially Gibbons, and all wrote in a similar style.

The quality of and range of mood in the Catholic and Anglican music produced in England during the Renaissance is fully comparable to that produced abroad, and in the Anglican Service the reformers devised a form of worship that was highly organized as to content, yet with some flexibility of choice, and which was strikingly different from any Protestant service on the Continent; yet hardly any anthems or Services were published for specific use in church, and the publication in 1560 and 1565 of John

Day's *Certain notes . . . to be sung at the Mornyng, Communion and Evening Praier*, which contained two Services and twenty anthems by mostly minor composers, remained the only such work for nearly eighty years.

The influence of the Italian madrigal on secular music north of the Alps was nowhere so strong or so fruitful as in England. For most of the century secular part-music was almost non-existent, the only exception being a collection by an amateur, Thomas Whythorne, published in 1571. However, books of Italian madrigals as well as manuscript copies began to circulate from the 1560s on, and this, plus the influence of a few immigrant Italian composers, notably Alfonso Ferrabosco the Elder (1543-88), led to an increasing interest in the genre, so much so that in 1588 the publisher Nicholas Yonge issued a selection with English translations entitled *Musica Transalpina*, which was followed by other 'Englished' collections. The year 1588 also saw the appearance of Byrd's *Psalms, Sonets & songs of sadness and pietie*, comprising arrangements by the composer, mostly for five voices, of the original versions for solo voice and an accompaniment of viols. The secular items are totally unmadrigalian, as they lack textural contrast and word-painting, and are harmonically very conservative. The 1589 book, and

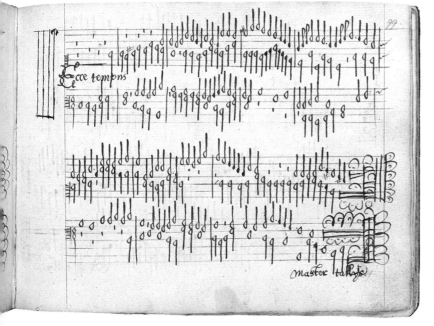

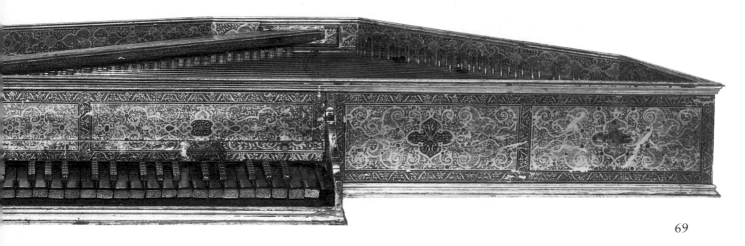

especially that of 1611, are more up-to-date, but in general Byrd's secular pieces do not match those of his contemporaries, of whom the chief among many were Thomas Morley (1557/8-1602), Weelkes and John Wilbye (1574-1638).

Morley was the first Englishman to publish an original book of madrigalian-like pieces, the canzonets for three voices (1593); this was followed by a book of madrigals (1594), and one of two-part canzonets and one of balletts, both in 1595, all issued before any other madrigal print. The balletts are thoroughly Gastoldian, even improving on their model by expanding the 'fa la' refrains and incorporating some imitation, thus providing a better contrast with the chordal verses. His canzonets and madrigals, however, look back to the pre-Rore type in their choice of lightly amorous and pastoral verse and in their restraint.

In 1601 there appeared *The Triumphs of Oriana*, an anthology of twenty-five madrigals by nearly all of Morley's contemporaries and edited by him, the most notable omission being Morley's teacher, Byrd, who may have declined to contribute. Perhaps the most striking piece in the book is by Weelkes, which, in its vivid word-painting and dramatic contrasts, is typical of his madrigalian style. Weelkes, who also wrote some balletts that match Morley's, represents, with Wilbye, the high watermark of the English madrigal, for he is pictorially as vivid, harmonically as daring and emotionally as wide in range as Wert, while Wilbye can be likened to Marenzio in the quality of the texts he chose and in the impeccable and sensitive way in which he set them.

Weelkes's book of madrigals of 1600 states in the title that it is 'apt for viols and voices,' and the practice of accompanying one or more voices with instruments seems to have been more popular in England than on the Continent. This preference is clearly evident in the 'ayre,' essentially a strophic song for solo voice with lute accompaniment. Unlike similar songs abroad, the ayre was not a transcription but an original composition, and among its many composers the chief were Thomas Campion (1567-1620), John Danyel (1564-c.1626) and John Dowland (1563-1626), the last named not only unquestionably the finest, but also one of the great song-writers of all time. His first book (1597) was immensely popular and contained two versions of each song, one for voice and lute on one page, the other for four voices on the facing page, an arrangement copied by later composers and unique to England. Dowland's emotional range is as wide as that of any madrigalist, and in his more serious through-composed songs he employs chromaticism and dissonance in a highly expressive way.

In ensemble music, more favored in England than abroad, the two chief types were the fantasia and the *In nomine*, the latter originally based on a passage from a Mass by Taverner, itself based on a plainsong, but later only the plainsong became the common factor in each *In nomine*. Nearly all the ensemble music was written for a consort of four or more viols, and the most important composers were Byrd, John Cooper (Coprario; c.1570/80-1626), Thomas Lupo (d.1628), Alfonso Ferrabosco the Younger (d.1628) and Gibbons. Of these Byrd is the most consistent in quality, Coprario the most prolific, Ferrabosco the most adventurous as regards chromaticism, and Gibbons the most forward-looking in the way he divided his fantasias into contrasting sections and in the distinctly instrumental character of much of his

Below left: A woodcut of 1568, showing madrigalists singing.

Below: A piece ('Come heavy sleep') from John Dowland's *Firste Booke of Songes or Ayres* of 1597. It is printed in 'table-book' form, designed for performance by the players or singers seated round a table. The lute accompaniment on the left-hand page is in tablature.

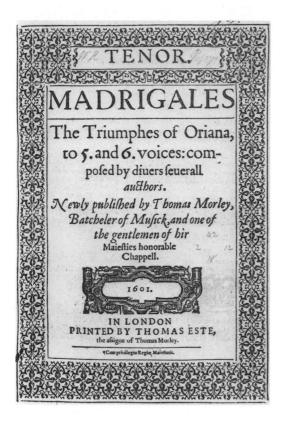

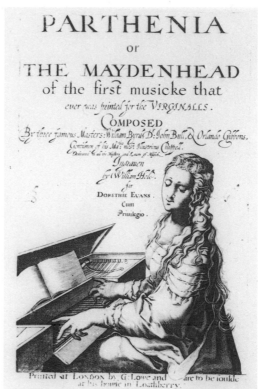

Title-pages of two of the most famous musical editions of Elizabethan England.

Far left: The Triumphs of Oriana, a collection of madrigals in honor of Queen Elizabeth, edited by Thomas Morley, himself one of the greatest composers of madrigals.

Left: Parthenia (the Greek word for 'Maidenhood'), the first printed edition of keyboard music in England. Published in 1611, it contains twenty-one pieces by Byrd, Bull and Gibbons. The word 'virginal' on the title page was at that time commonly used to described any stringed keyboard instrument.

writing (for example, large leaps and rapid repeated notes) and use of sequence.

Music for the lute was dominated by Dowland, although the instrument was not nearly so popular as on the Continent. Dances were the preferred type, with fantasias and transcriptions very much less frequent. The same preference is evident in keyboard literature, and while there was, as usual, no indication as to which instrument was intended, the character of most of the music in the second half of the century clearly implies the virginal. The earlier keyboard pieces were largely florid and rather uninspired arrangements of plainsongs, including the *In nomine*, and transcriptions, as shown in Thomas Mulliner's anthology of 121 compositions compiled between c.1545 and c.1585. However, the character of the writing and the types favored changed dramatically in the anthologies produced between 1590 and 1620, the most important being the *Fitzwilliam Virginal Book*, compiled by Francis Tregian between 1609 and 1619 and containing nearly 300 pieces by a host of composers. Its contents include dances, variations, fantasias, cantus-firmus arrangements, transcriptions of vocal music and pieces with descriptive titles, these last transferring the pictorialism of word-painting to the instrumental sphere, a type peculiar to England.

By far the most popular types were the first two listed above, and whereas the *Mulliner Book* contains only two dances and no variations, in the *Fitzwilliam Virginal Book* almost half the items are dances and nearly an eighth variations, while in most of the dances each section also has a varied repeat. The most common dances are the pavane and galliard, often paired and built on a 'ground,' that is, a short series of notes repeated several times in the bass, like the passamezzo. This is stylized dance music and, like the suites of Bach, not intended for dancing. The variations represent the peak of English keyboard music, for although there are instances of rather mechanical scale passages and routine figuration, the best of them combine a freshness of invention, effective contrasts between imitative and chordal textures, rapid arpeggios, broken chords and consecutive thirds in one hand, and a fascinating mixture of melodic and harmonic treatment of the theme.

The principal keyboard composers were Byrd, Gibbons, John Bull (1562/3-1628), Giles Farnaby (c.1563-1640) and Tomkins, of whom Byrd and Bull were the most prolific; the former is unequalled in the overall quality of his output, the latter – an acclaimed international performer – notable for his wide range of style, from charming simplicity to brilliant virtuosity. He is also important in the history of tuning, writing an extremely chromatic piece that would have sounded vile in mean-tone tuning; hence something like our 'equal temperament' must have been intended. Bull left England in 1613 and later became organist of Antwerp Cathedral, where he befriended and undoubtedly influenced Sweelinck, providing a direct link between the English keyboard style and that of Continental composers of the Baroque.

Instrumental music was also an important constituent of the masque, a musico-dramatic entertainment that was popular in aristocratic circles throughout the century and later, and which, during the reign of James I (1603-25), and influenced by the *ballet de cour*, reached a new level of excellence. It was the principal root of English opera and one of several links between the Renaissance and baroque periods.

MONTEVERDI, OPERA, AND ORATORIO

JOHN WHENHAM

Opera was created and first developed at two of the great Renaissance courts of northern Italy – Florence and Mantua – and for nearly forty years after the performance of the earliest operas in the years around 1600, the new form remained an occasional and almost exclusively courtly entertainment. From 1637, however, opera entered a new stage of development with the opening of the first commercial opera houses in Venice. From this date opera became a regular feature of Italian musical life. In addition to the annual opera seasons at Venice, touring companies were established and interest in the new form spread rapidly both within and outside Italy. These two stages in the early history of opera are linked by the work of Claudio Monteverdi (1567-1643), whose three surviving operas – *Orfeo* (1607), *Il ritorno d'Ulisse in patria* (1639/40) and *L'incoronazione di Poppea* (1642) – are generally considered the finest works in the early operatic repertoire.

Monteverdi arrived in Mantua probably in 1590. His appointment there as a viol player was part of a more general expansion of the Mantuan musical establishment begun by Duke Vincenzo Gonzaga soon after his accession in 1587. Vincenzo's aim was to create at Mantua a center of artistic excellence which would rival the achievements he had observed at the neighboring court of Alfonso d'Este, Duke of Ferrara, who had married his sister, Margherita, in 1579.

Margherita was passionately fond of music and dancing and her advent at Ferrara initiated a new and brilliant phase of activity at a court which had not only nurtured the talents of a number of able composers, but had also given employment to artists and to the poets Torquato Tasso and Giovanni Battista Guarini.

During the early 1580s, the Ferrarese court employed on a regular basis some forty professional musicians. Of these, twenty singers and fifteen instrumentalists were responsible for providing sacred music for the ducal chapel and also, under the direction of the composer and court organist Luzzasco Luzzaschi, for providing secular entertainments for the Duke and Duchess and their guests. For the most part, as was common practice at the courts of northern Italy, these entertainments took the form of large-scale concerts of madrigals and instrumental music, ballets and music to accompany such activities as banquets and tournaments. For the entertainment of his most privileged guests, however, Duke Alfonso introduced in the 1580s a special group of virtuoso lady singers – Laura Peverara, Anna Guarini (daughter of the poet), Livia d'Arco and, for a short time, Tarquinia Molza. This *concerto delle donne* specialized in singing madrigals composed by Luzzaschi for one, two and three voices with harpsichord accompaniment; they were characterized by the extraordinary difficulty of their ornamented vocal lines, in which the ornamentation was co-ordinated between the voices and thus had to be written and memorized rather than being improvised.

The singing of the Ferrarese *concerto* and of the rival *concerto delle donne* formed by Vincenzo Gonzaga at Mantua between 1587 and 1589 was described some years later by the Roman commentator Vincenzo Giustiniani. Giustiniani's description reveals not only the complex nature of the music that the ladies sang, but also the theatrical manner in which they projected the texts and sentiments of the madrigals to their audience: 'The ladies of Mantua and Ferrara were highly competent, and vied with each other not only in regard to the timbre and training of their voices, but also in the design of exquisite passages [ornamented lines] delivered at opportune points, but not in excess . . . Furthermore, they moderated or increased their voices, loud or soft, heavy or light, according to the demands of the piece they were singing; now slow, breaking off sometimes with a gentle sigh, now singing long passages *legato* or detached, now groups, now leaps, now with long trills, now with short, or again with sweet running passages sung softly, to which one sometimes heard an echo answer unexpectedly. They accompanied the music and the sentiment with appropriate facial expressions, glances and gestures, with no awkward movements of the mouth or hands or body which might not express the feeling of the song.'

From the early 1580s other composers, some of whom visited the Ferrarese court, began to compose polyphonic madrigals which included prominent soprano parts, rapidly running lines and written-out ornamentation. Among the first were Giaches de Wert, director of music at Mantua, with his seventh and eighth books of five-part madrigals (1581 and 1586), and Luca Marenzio, with his first book of six-part and second book of five-part madrigals (both 1581). Marenzio visited Ferrara in 1581, and the legacy of his visit can be heard in the opening and closing measures of his madrigal 'Occhi lucenti e belli' (Radiant, lovely eyes, 1582), where a sustained soprano line (the whole notes of which are a musical representation of 'eyes') is accompanied by the lower voices moving in faster, ornamented lines.

The type of virtuoso ornamentation cultivated by the *concerto delle donne* is heard even more clearly in the setting of the line 'Che non ten fuggi a volo' from the madrigal 'Mille volte il dí moro' by Carlo Gesualdo, Prince of Venosa, who married Leonora d'Este and stayed at the Ferrara court from 1594 to 1596. Many of his

Above: Pastoral, c. 1610, by the Dutch artist Abraham Bloemaert. It reflects the fashion for pastoral poems and plays that began in the late sixteenth century with such works as Guarini's Il pastor fido.

Right: Illustration from an early edition of Il pastor fido (The Faithful Shepherd). Guarini's pastoral play, with its choruses and songs, had a strong influence on early opera, and its verses also inspired many madrigals.

later madrigals contain passages of virtuoso writing, but their most striking feature is a mannerist use of extreme chromaticism and seemingly wayward and disjointed harmonic progressions serving a very personal interpretation of the dolorous texts which he favored.

With the example of Ferrara before him, Vincenzo Gonzaga created at Mantua a pleasure-loving court devoted to the pursuit of the latest musical and theatrical fashions, as can be seen in the changed nature and increased quantity of the secular music produced after Vincenzo's accession by the composers who had earlier served his father, Guglielmo. In 1588 both Giaches de Wert and Benedetto Pallavicino published books of serious virtuoso madrigals clearly influenced by the Mantuan *concerto delle donne*. New ground was also broken in the field of the lighter madrigal by the publication in 1591 of Giovanni Giacomo Gastoldi's *Balletti a cinque voci . . . per cantare, sonare, & ballare*, dance-songs written in a regular rhythm and often supplied with a 'fa-la' refrain, which were widely imitated.

• Monteverdi's madrigals •

Given the increased demand for new music at Mantua after 1587, the court authorities responsible for appointing Monteverdi can scarcely

have been unaware of his potential as a composer. His earliest published music, a volume of Latin motets (*Sacrae cantiunculae*) for three voices, had been published in 1582, when the composer was only fifteen years of age; and by 1590 he had no fewer than five volumes of music in print, including two books of five-part madrigals (1587 and 1590). The music of the second of these books shows that Monteverdi had thoroughly absorbed the techniques of counterpoint and word-painting found, for example, in Marenzio's lighter madrigals. He also exhibits assurance in his handling of a five-part texture, using contrasts of scoring to build satisfying large-scale designs. Ten of the settings are of texts by Torquato Tasso, texts full of concrete pictorial images of the kind which late sixteenth-century composers enjoyed translating into appropriate musical figurations. The best-known of the settings – 'Ecco mormorar l'onde' – is typical: the waves *murmur*; the leaves *tremble*; birds *sing* in the trees; the *high* mountains are gilded by the early-morning light; the *breeze* is the messenger of dawn, which restores each *burning* heart.

Madrigals of this kind, perhaps written for the amateur singers of his native Cremona, are also found in Monteverdi's third book, published in 1592, two years after his arrival at Mantua. They are outnumbered, however, by works which vividly reflect the new milieu in which the young composer was now working. Nine of the settings are of madrigals by Guarini, concise, often erotic texts which explore the depths of human emotion. Even the two Tasso settings in the book are drawn not from the

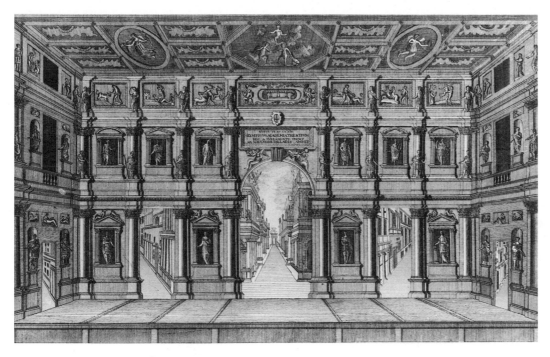

Left: Interior of the Teatro Olimpico, Vicenza, built by Palladio and Scamozzi and dating from around 1580. In a way that parallels Palladio's architecture, the art of opera originated in an attempt to revive the art and spirit of Greek theater.

poet's elegant pastoral madrigals, but from the more impassioned speeches of his epic poem *La Gerusalemme liberata* – texts which would perfectly display the theatrical talents of the Mantuan ensemble described by Giustiniani.

After his third book, Monteverdi published no further madrigals for eleven years. His fourth book appeared in 1603 and his fifth in 1605. It is unlikely that this gap in publication represents a break in Monteverdi's work as a composer. It suggests, rather, that during the intervening years he was consolidating his Mantuan experience, producing the refinements in style that we find in the madrigals of Book IV, and perhaps experimenting with the new modes of composition that we find in Book V.

Monteverdi's appointment as director of music at Mantua in 1601 may have provided the incentive to publish madrigals which had, so far, been available only in manuscript. Two madrigals – 'Anima mia, perdona' (1603) and 'Cruda Amarilli' (1605) – had certainly circulated in manuscript before 1600, for in that year they were criticized by the Bolognese theorist Giovanni Maria Artusi in a book entitled *L'Artusi, overo delle imperfettioni della moderna musica* (Venice, 1600). Monteverdi's answer to Artusi's criticism, set out by his brother in the preface to the *Scherzi musicali* (1607), declared that his madrigals did not belong to the tradition which Artusi espoused, but to a 'second practice' (*seconda prattica*), which 'turns on the perfection of the melody, that is, the one that considers harmony not commanding, but commanded, and makes the words the mistress of the harmony.' With this statement of the expressive power of music, Monteverdi allied himself not only with the modern generation of madrigalists schooled at Ferrara and Mantua, but also with the principles which lay behind the creation of operatic recitative.

The madrigals of Book IV represent a high point in Monteverdi's mastery both of musical technique and of the requirements of the court madrigal (that is, the madrigal to be performed by a virtuoso ensemble for an audience). The texture of the madrigals is uncluttered, their images drawn in broad, imaginative strokes, and each is provided with an extended point of focus, usually towards the end. This can be seen, for example, in 'Sfogava con le stelle' (text by Ottavio Rinuccini), in which the last two lines of the text occupy almost half of the setting, with bold dissonances underlying the word 'pietosa' (pitiful). The book also contains some of the most erotic of Monteverdi's settings, works like 'Ah, dolente partita' (Guarini), 'Ohimè, se tanto amate' (Guarini) and 'Sì, ch'io vorrei morire,' in which the words 'parting' and 'death' and the cry 'Ohimè' are used to suggest the sexual act.

Book IV was the last of Monteverdi's publications to be devoted wholly to the medium of the unaccompanied five-part madrigal. For although Book V does contain unaccompanied madrigals, the last six pieces in the book include extended solos and duets requiring an accompaniment played on harpsichord or lute. Since the vocal lines in these madrigals are also characterized by the use of virtuoso ornamentation, they could be seen as the Mantuan equivalent of Luzzaschi's accompanied madrigals for one, two and three sopranos. The type of accompaniment that Monteverdi employs is, however, quite different from Luzzaschi's. Instead of supplying a keyboard score which doubles the vocal lines, Monteverdi provides a bass line from which the instrumentalist has to improvise a simple chordal accompaniment. This accompaniment technique, known as *basso continuo*, was the technique used for the recitatives of the earliest operas, and its use for madrigals in Book V is our first indication that Monteverdi was looking to the new musical developments emanating from Florence in the years around 1600.

Above and below right:
Designs by Bernardo
Buontalenti for the
Florentine *intermedi* of
1589, which illustrate
the opulent and
extravagant character of
such entertainments.
Mercury, Apollo,
Jupiter and Astraea with
their appropriate
attributes (top left)
appeared in Intermedio
I, as also did Necessity
with the three Fates (top
right), while the scene in
which Apollo slays the
python (right) came in
Intermedio III.

•Florentine influence: the *intermedio* •

With its long history of artistic patronage and humanist scholarship, Florence was one of the most vibrant centers of cultural life in sixteenth-century Italy. Under the rule of the Medici family (created Dukes of Florence in 1537 and Grand Dukes of Tuscany in 1569), the musical establishment at the Florentine court became the equal of any in Italy. At Florence, as at Ferrara, musical patronage included the cultivation of virtuoso singing, and a *concerto delle donne* was formed there in 1584 under the direction of the singer Giulio Caccini.

The aspect of Florentine music-making which is most interesting in the present context is the tradition of associating music with drama in entertainments staged to celebrate such events in the life of the ruling family as births and marriages. For most of the sixteenth century these took the form of *intermedi* (interludes), self-contained dramatic musical scenes played between the courses of a banquet or between the acts of a spoken drama. Among the grandest of these were the *intermedi* staged to celebrate the marriage of Grand Duke Ferdinando I to Christine of Lorraine in 1589, and among the personnel involved in writing and staging them were some of the men later responsible for the creation of opera.

The Medici wedding of 1589 was a marriage of political convenience by which Ferdinando hoped to cement a new alliance with France to counterbalance the established Florentine links with Spain and the Hapsburg monarchy. Since the wedding was such an important political event, it was celebrated with a display of conspicuous spending designed to impress on the

many distinguished guests the wealth and importance of the Medici family. The celebrations lasted a little over a fortnight, the highlight being the presentation of a magnificent new set of *intermedi*, designed to accompany a five-act comedy, *La Pellegrina* (The Pilgrim), written for the occasion by Girolamo Bargagli. The *intermedi*, devised by Count Giovanni de' Bardi and directed by Emilio de' Cavalieri, superintendent of the artists, craftsmen and musicians at the Medici court, had been in preparation for more than a year.

There were six *intermedi* in all: four fairly short scenes to be played between the acts of the comedy and two longer scenes, one which preceded the comedy and one which formed and epilogue, culminating in a grand ballet. The entertainment (in effect two entertainments, since the plots of the *intermedi* and the comedy were unrelated) lasted for several hours without a break. Each *intermedio* forms a self-contained unit, either pursuing a single dramatic idea or presenting a single story drawn from classical mythology, but, unlike those of most later operas, the texts and music of the *intermedi* were the work of several hands; only numbers II and III have music by a single composer, Luca Marenzio. Although, in its plot, each *intermedio* is independent of the others, all are linked by a single theme – the power of music over gods and men. Giovanni de' Bardi, a humanist, philosopher and man of letters, had chosen scenes which allowed graceful homage to be paid to the newly married couple, and which also gave full rein to the scene designer, Bernardo Buontalenti, and his team of stage engineers to produce the most amazing scenery and stage effects of which they were capable.

A description of Intermedio IV will give some idea of the spectacle. The first part was played against the scenery for Act III of Bargagli's *La Pellegrina*. A sorceress flew across the stage in a chariot drawn by winged dragons. Stopping at center stage, she sang a solo madrigal to her lute, conjuring the scene to follow. (The music was composed by Giulio Caccini and sung by his wife, Lucia.) The sorceress's chariot left the stage and a fiery ball appeared in the air. It opened to reveal a chorus of heavenly spirits, who sang a madrigal (music by Cristofano Malvezzi, director of music at the Florentine court)

praising the married couple and prophesying the dawn of a new Golden Age. After a *sinfonia* by Malvezzi, the scene changed in an instant to a view of the flaming caverns of Hades. The floor opened and from it rose a statue of Lucifer, with a chorus of Furies and Demons seen tormenting the damned souls. The demons sang a madrigal composed by Giovanni de' Bardi in what he conceived to be the Greek Dorian mode.

The spectacular nature of this type of entertainment ensured its survival in courtly circles long after the creation of opera. Unlike opera, it consisted entirely of extended set pieces during which the audience could enjoy the marvels of the scenery and stage effects. What was lacking was a musical technique which would allow the characters on stage to converse at the speed necessary to allow a whole play to be set to music. By the time of the next major celebration in the Medici calendar, however, this technique – the technique of recitative – had been evolved, stimulated by Count Bardi's keen interest in the music of the Ancient Greeks.

Above: Painted panel commemorating the marriage of Grand Duke Ferdinando I de' Medici and Christine of Lorraine, the occasion for the *intermedi* illustrated here. The wedding ceremony is taking place in front of one of the triumphal arches painted with scenes glorifying the Medici that were erected for the ceremonial entry of Christine into Florence.

• Bardi, Galilei and Caccini •

Bardi's ideas about Greek music were derived from descriptions of its theory and practice given by classical authors. In studying these he was aided by Vincenzo Galilei (father of the astronomer Galileo Galilei), a lutenist and composer whose work on Greek music was sponsored by Bardi. Of Galilei's wide-ranging conclusions only two need be considered here: first, that Ancient Greek music had an ethical power, a power not only to move the emotions (affections) of the audience, but also to influence the moral and physical state of those who heard it; and second, that Ancient Greek music had been monodic – that is, sung by a solo voice. Bardi and Galilei discussed these ideas with a group of their Florentine colleagues who met informally at Bardi's house to talk and to make music. This group, which has come to be known as the Florentine 'Camerata' (salon), met irregularly from about 1573 until 1587. In 1592 Bardi left Florence to take up an appointment at Rome. The only known members of the Camerata are Bardi, Galilei, Giulio Caccini and Piero Strozzi, though it is possible that others attended their informal gatherings.

Bardi and Galilei both tried their hands at writing solo songs intended to recreate, in modern terms, the power of Ancient Greek music; but it was Caccini, the experienced virtuoso singer, who made the decisive breakthrough by adopting for his solo songs the technique of *basso continuo*. By restricting the accompaniment of his songs to a simple chordal framework, instead of the elaborate counterpoint typical of songs arranged from polyphonic madrigals, Caccini allowed the singer the rhythmic freedom to declaim the text in a rhetorical manner and to use all the artifices of the virtuoso singer – *rubato*, different methods of vocal attack, *crescendo* and *diminuendo* – to dramatize the emotions suggested by the text. The melodic outlines of his songs, though lyrical in nature, were shaped to support just such a rhetorical manner of delivery.

Caccini also sought to curb what he saw as excesses in the style and quantity of ornamentation customarily added to their songs by professional singers. To this end he wrote out the ornamentation that he considered appropriate to his songs, limiting its use to accented syllables in the text, so that the sense of the text would not be obscured. Caccini had evolved his new style of ornamentation certainly by 1592, when he visited Ferrara and instructed the Ferrarese *concerto delle donne* in the new art. His earliest continuo songs were also circulating in manuscript by this date, though they were published only in 1602, under the title *Le nuove musiche* (The New Music).

Le nuove musiche is an important and complex volume, at once a document of the ideas of Bardi's Camerata, a vocal method with instruction on ornamentation and attack, an exemplar of Caccini's own style of ornamentation, and a compendium of the musical forms and styles that were subsumed into the new manner of Florentine solo singing. For although the rhetorical manner of Caccini's songs and his technique of accompaniment were indeed new, the forms that he chose for his songs were not. The most serious songs in *Le nuove musiche* are madrigals – like their polyphonic counterparts,

through-composed settings of texts in a single stanza – and strophic variations – settings of texts in several stanzas, in which the music, though substantially the same for each stanza, is varied slightly to underline differences in the sense of the text. The last six songs, however, are light-hearted arias in which all the stanzas are sung to the same music.

The response to *Le nuove musiche* was at first slow and somewhat equivocal. Monteverdi, for example, first used the technique of *basso continuo* for accompanying polyphonic madrigals which included passages of solo and duet writing, and in this he was followed by a number of other north Italian composers working in the period to about 1650. By around 1610, however, volumes of solo songs, duets and trios with continuo were beginning to pour from the Italian presses. Notable among the earliest followers of Caccini was Sigismondo d'India, whose work illustrates admirably the poised, emotive style of Florentine solo song. Such was the popularity of the Florentine 'new music' that after about 1620 publishers virtually ceased to issue volumes of polyphonic madrigals without continuo accompaniment. By 1650 even polyphonic madrigals with continuo had given way to the fashion for solo songs and duets. In this respect, *Le nuove musiche* can be seen as an epoch-making publication and Caccini as a composer who changed the face of Italian chamber music.

• Jacopo Peri •

Caccini's song style also provided the technical basis for operatic recitative, though it was his rival at the Florentine court, the singer-composer Jacopo Peri, who was the first fully to realize its potential in this field. It is not certain whether Peri attended the meetings of Bardi's Camerata, but certainly the Camerata itself cannot, as was once supposed, have created opera, since the

Below: The second of the Florentine *intermedi* of 1589: the contest of the Muses and the Pierides (who are turned into magpies). The technical arrangements, which included the raising of Mount Parnassus from below stage, were directed by Jacopo Corsi.

PALAZZO DELLA FAMA INTERMEDIO PRIMO

Above: Stage design by Giulio Parigi for the first of six *intermedi* to celebrate the marriage in 1608 of Cosimo de' Medici and Princess Maria Magdalena of Austria. The illustration shows the Palace of Fame, made of mirror glass, which rose to receive the heroic ancestors of bride and groom.

Right: The first of three *intermedi* performed at the Uffizi Palace, Florence, in 1617, in honor of another wedding, this time between Ferdinando Gonzaga, Duke of Mantua, and Catarina de' Medici.

earliest operas were written only after Bardi's departure for Rome. Peri came to opera through the patronage of another Florentine nobleman, Jacopo Corsi, who, around 1594, had begun work on the opera *Dafne* in collaboration with the poet Ottavio Rinuccini. Peri completed the music for this opera, based on a story from Ovid's *Metamorphoses*, and it was first staged at Corsi's palace in Florence in 1598. Most of the music for *Dafne* is now lost, and our first clear picture of the nature of Peri's achievement comes from his second collaboration with Rinuccini, the opera *Euridice*, composed to celebrate the wedding of King Henri IV of France to Maria de' Medici and first performed at the Pitti Palace, Florence, on 6 October 1600.

The story that Rinuccini chose as the basis of his libretto was the myth of Orpheus, the semi-divine singer who, through the power of his singing, gains entrance to the underworld to rescue his bride, Eurydice. Rinuccini retained most of the main elements of the myth, but altered its ending in deference to the occasion for which the opera was written. In his version, no condition is put on Eurydice's release, so that, instead of Orpheus losing her and being torn to pieces by the Bacchantes, the two lovers are happily reunited at the end of the opera.

The libretto has affinities both with Guarini's pastoral play *Il pastor fido* and with the 1589 *intermedi*. Like *Il pastor fido*, it is cast in the form of a prologue and five actions, each ending with a chorus, and the Thracian scenes are set against a pastoral background, with shepherds and shepherdesses who act as the friends of Orpheus and Eurydice and also form the chorus. As in the 1589 *intermedi*, the work ends with a grand choral ballet, with instrumental music and passages for three singers punctuated by a choral refrain; and like the fourth *intermedio*, the opera, which was probably played without intervals, includes a spectacular scene change, from the Thracian fields to a vision of Hades.

The chief novelty of the opera was that the narrative and dialogue of the action, as well as the set-pieces, were set to music, for solo voices with continuo accompaniment. The style that Caccini had evolved for his songs, though appropriate for the more lyrical moments, was not adequate for rapid narration or for the more impassioned sections of the drama, passages like Orpheus's lament on the loss of Eurydice. For these, Peri created an unornamented style which he described as 'lying between the slow and suspended movements of song and the swift and rapid movements of speech.' By using a slower-moving bass line than Caccini, Peri was able to adopt a more *parlando* style of declamation, occasionally allowing the vocal line to clash with the bass to create moments of particular poignancy or anguish.

The preparation and performance of *Euridice* provoked what amounted to a war of words between the composers associated with the Florentine court. Caccini rushed his own setting of the opera into print late in 1600, prefacing it with the claim that he had been the first to compose in the new style. And Emilio de' Cavalieri anticipated the Florentine performance by presenting his own opera, *La rappresentatione di anima et di corpo*, in the oratory of the Chiesa Nuova at Rome in February 1600, and publishing the score just as the Florentine celebrations were beginning.

The *Rappresentatione*, a musical morality play in which Soul, Body, and allegorical figures such as Time, Intellect and Worldly Life contrast the transience of earthly pleasure with the enduring riches of Heaven, does contain passages of recitative, though its main musical attractions are the ensembles, choruses and dances. Cavalieri's main concern was to create an entertaining piece of theater, including a variety of musical idioms and telling stage effects. Unlike Peri and Rinuccini, he was not concerned to recreate the ethos of Greek tragedy.

79

by the aria 'Possente spirto,' in which Orpheus attempts to persuade the boatman Charon to ferry him across the River Styx. Eventually Charon falls asleep, Orpheus steals his boat and crosses to the infernal city. His singing, though it failed to persuade Charon, has profoundly moved Proserpina, the consort of Pluto, and in Act IV she persuades Pluto to release Eurydice. This he does, on condition that Orpheus does not look back as he leads Eurydice from the underworld. Orpheus weakens, looks back and loses Eurydice again. The act ends as a chorus of infernal spirits point the moral: 'Orpheus conquered Hades, but was then conquered by his own emotions.' Act V, set again in Thrace, begins with an extended lament for the loss of Eurydice, sung by Orpheus in recitative. After this, the opera originally ended (as can be seen from the published libretto) with a chorus for the Bacchantes who, in the myth, tore Orpheus to pieces. The published score of *Orfeo*, however, conforms with the tradition of the *lieto fine* (happy ending), by having Orpheus ascend to the heavens in the company of his father, the

• *Orfeo* and its followers •

In the atmosphere of cultural rivalry that existed between the courts of northern Italy, it was almost inevitable that the early Florentine experiments in opera would soon be imitated at Mantua. It seems likely that Monteverdi had access to a score of Peri's *Euridice* soon after its publication in 1601, for the first of the continuo madrigals in his fifth book – 'Ahi, com' a un vago sol' – is cast in the form of a duet with choral refrain, a structure similar to that used in the refrain choruses of *Euridice*. His first opportunity to write a full-scale opera came in 1606-7 when he collaborated with the Mantuan courtier Alessandro Striggio to produce the opera *Orfeo*, which was first performed on 24 February 1607.

The choice of subject matter, the treatment of some details of the text and the style of recitative developed by Monteverdi are clearly indebted to Peri's *Euridice*. Nevertheless, *Orfeo* represents a considerable advance, both dramatically and musically. Striggio, though a lesser poet than Rinuccini, proved a better librettist; his text is more concise, allowing for briefer, more intense recitatives, and he seems to have collaborated closely with the composer in providing ample opportunity for musical variety.

Where the action of *Euridice* can be seen to fall into five scenes, that of *Orfeo* has an explicit five-act structure, preceded by a prologue in which Music herself introduces the story of Orpheus. In Act I, we are introduced to Orpheus and Eurydice on their wedding day, which is celebrated in choral songs and dances rather in the manner of an *intermedio*. Act II begins with the same atmosphere of rejoicing, but turns to tragedy as the messenger, Sylvia, relates the news of Eurydice's death, and Orpheus and his companions lament her loss. Act III, the central act of the drama, is set in Hades and is dominated

Above: Orpheus taming the wild beasts with his music, shown in a painting of the early seventeenth century by Roelandt Savery, court painter to Emperor Rudolph II. The myth of Orpheus and Eurydice, with its celebration of the magic power of music, provided the material for several of the first operas, from Peri's *Euridice* to Monteverdi's *Orfeo*.

Opposite top: Echo and Narcissus, c.1628-30, by Nicolas Poussin, the French painter who was part of the intellectual circle in Rome in the 1630s. The myth of the nymph Echo, whose punishment was to be able only to repeat the last syllable she had heard, gave rise to the echo effects which are heard in so many seventeenth-century operas, starting with Monteverdi's *Orfeo* at the opening of Act V.

Opposite: Apollo and Daphne (1622-5) by Bernini. The myth of Daphne, transformed into a laurel to escape the attentions of Apollo, was one of the first opera subjects used by Florentine composers, and was also taken for the first German opera, Schütz's *Daphne* (1627).

god Apollo. The music of the opera develops and heightens the tragedy primarily by portraying the emotional responses of the characters to the unfolding of events. Monteverdi's skill in composing emotive and quasi-dramatic madrigals for Mantua served him well in the new medium and many of the devices he uses in his recitatives are madrigalian in origin.

The opportunity to write a second opera followed quickly. After protracted negotiations, Prince Francesco Gonzaga was betrothed to Margaret of Savoy, and the date for the wedding in Mantua set for the end of the carnival period in 1608 (in other words, before 19 February). Late in 1607 Monteverdi, tired, unwell and depressed by the death of his wife, was ordered to prepare a new opera, *Arianna*, as well as a ballet and the prologue to a set of *intermedi* for Guarini's comedy *La idropica*. In the event, political considerations caused the wedding celebrations to be postponed until May. To entertain the guests who had assembled, two stage works were mounted shortly before the end of the carnival season. One of these cannot now be identified. The other was the opera *Dafne*, a revised and expanded version of Rinuccini's first opera libretto, set to music by another Florentine, Marco da Gagliano, with contributions from Prince Ferdinando Gonzaga.

Gagliano's opera is a work of great charm, though its musical attractions lie mainly in the writing for chorus. Its libretto is rather loosely constructed, encompassing as it does two episodes from Ovid's *Metamorphoses*. In the first, allowing opportunities for stage spectacle, the god Apollo slays the python which, according to Ovid, had 'struck terror into the new-born race of men.' In the second, Apollo, enamored of the nymph Daphne, pursues her, only to find that she has been transformed into a tree. The work contains a number of the ingredients which, by this time, were becoming commonplace in operatic composition – a lament for

Apollo on the loss of Daphne and refrain choruses, for example – but the recitative, which contains the emotional heart of the work, is more melodious, less powerful than that written by Peri and Monteverdi.

Monteverdi's own major contributions to the 1608 celebrations were the opera *Arianna* and *Il ballo delle ingrate* (Ballet of the ungrateful women). The texts for both were written by Ottavio Rinuccini. The music for *Arianna* is almost entirely lost, but its centerpiece, Ariadne's lament on being abandoned by Theseus (which, according to contemporary commentators, moved the audience to tears), survives in three separate sources. It was arranged by Monteverdi as a five-part madrigal and published in his sixth book of madrigals (1614); the original version for solo voice and continuo was published in 1623; and a more extended solo version survives in manuscript. The fame which this piece enjoyed seems to have stimulated other composers, Sigismondo d'India among them, to include lament settings in their published songbooks, and it may well have been the source of the tradition of operatic laments in later Venetian opera.

• Opera in Rome •

The next major group of surviving operas represents the work of Roman composers. The first two operas of this group – Stefano Landi's *La morte d'Orfeo* (1619) and Filippo Vitali's *Aretusa* (1620) – are settings of libretti which develop themes found in the earliest operas. *La morte d'Orfeo* presents a (sometimes unintentionally) humorous variation of the myth in which Orpheus, having omitted to invite Bacchus to his birthday banquet, is dismembered by Bacchus's followers. His soul descends to the underworld; Eurydice fails to recognize him and

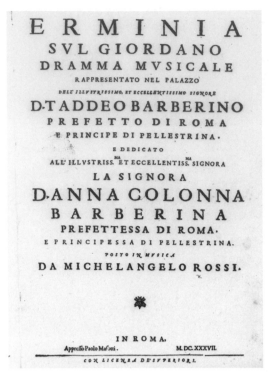

ERMINIA
SVL GIORDANO
DRAMMA MVSICALE
RAPPRESENTATO NEL PALAZZO
DELL' ILLVSTRISSIMO, ET ECCELLENTISSIMO SIGNORE
D. TADDEO BARBERINO
PREFETTO DI ROMA
E PRINCIPE DI PELLESTRINA.
E DEDICATO
ALL' ILLVSTRISS.ᴹᴬ ET ECCELLENTISS.ᴹᴬ SIGNORA
LA SIGNORA
D. ANNA COLONNA
BARBERINA
PREFETTESSA DI ROMA·
E PRINCIPESSA DI PELLESTRINA.
POSTO IN MVSICA
DA MICHELANGELO ROSSI.

IN ROMA.
Appreſſo Paolo Maſotti.   M.DC.XXXVII.
CON LICENZA DE' SVPERIORI.

often became simply the means for moving as quickly as possible from one set-piece to the next. Domenico Mazzocchi, though an able writer of recitative, wrote in the preface to *La catena d'Adone* that, in addition to arias and ensembles, he had included 'many other *mezz' Arie* scattered throughout the work to relieve the tedium of the recitative.' The concept of the 'semi-aria,' a short lyrical passage introduced into, or rounding off a passage of recitative, was not in itself new, for even Florentine recitative had been a flexible mixture of the dramatic and the lyrical. What was new, however, was that the 'semi-arias,' with their regular pulse and faster-moving bass-lines, form quite distinct sections within the recitative.

After the death of Urban VIII in 1644 his successor, Innocent X (Pamphili), instituted an investigation into the misappropriation of funds during Urban's reign. As a result, the Barberini theater, constructed in 1632 especially for the performance of opera, was closed, and the cardinal-nephews took refuge in France, an accident of history which, as shall be seen, was to be significant for the establishment of opera in that country. With the reconciliation of the Barberini and Pamphili families in 1653, the Barberini family returned to Rome and their theater reopened with a performance of the comic opera *Dal male il bene*, jointly composed by Marazzoli and Abbatini. Meanwhile, however, the future of opera had been even more securely established by the opening of the first commercial opera houses at Venice.

• Opera in Venice •

Monteverdi took up the appointment of director of music at St Mark's, Venice, in 1613, just over a year after he had been summarily dismissed from Mantua by the new Duke, Francesco Gonzaga. The city to which he came enjoyed a cultural life quite unlike that of Mantua, for Venice was a trading republic ruled not by an autocratic prince but by an elected Doge and a Council of Ten. The role of the state in musical affairs was limited to ordering the music at St Mark's (the Doge's chapel) and to commissioning new works for such ceremonial occasions as state banquets or the annual wedding of

he is translated to the heavens as a demigod. *Aretusa*, like *Dafne*, is a transformation opera: the nymph Aretusa is pursued by the huntsman Alfeo and is saved from his amorous embraces by being transformed into a stream.

But the first significant departure from the patterns established at Florence and Mantua came with the series of operas presented at Rome during the reign of the Barberini Pope Urban VIII (1623-44). Urban and his cardinal-nephews, Francesco and Antonio, were considerable patrons of music and under their rule, opera became the major form of theatrical presentation at Rome.

Under the Barberini, the range of subject matter treated in opera was expanded to include plots drawn not only from pastoral mythology (Vittori's *Galatea*, 1639), but also from the epic romances of Marino, Tasso and Ariosto (Domenico Mazzocchi's *La catena d'Adone*, 1626; Michelangelo Rossi's *Erminia sul Giordano*, 1633; Luigi Rossi's *Il palazzo incantato*, 1642), from the lives of the saints (Landi's *Sant'Alessio*, 1632) and from popular comedy (Virgilio Mazzocchi and Marco Marazzoli's *Chi soffre speri*, 1637, revived as *Il falcone*, 1639). This expansion in the range of plots effectively marks the emancipation of opera as a theatrical medium, for its heroes were no longer confined to those figures, like Apollo and Orpheus, who were traditionally associated with singing.

By comparison with the early Florentine and Mantuan operas, Roman opera relied much more heavily for its effect on stage spectacle (including magical transformation scenes) and musical diversity, with a concentration on large-scale choruses. In early opera, too, the most profound moments of the drama had been set in recitative. Strophic arias, ensembles and choruses were reserved for the more static parts of the plot. In Roman opera, recitative all too

Left: Engraving of 1622 by Antonio Tempesta, showing musicians encouraging nightingales to sing. Instruments in the foreground include trombone, viol, cornett, harp, lute, bass viol and virginal or harpsichord. In the background are more musicians, playing shawms of various sizes.

Venice to the sea. Secular music on a smaller scale was patronized by the literary Academies and by private individuals – the wealthier merchants, foreign ambassadors and the visitors who flocked to the city to enjoy the pleasures of the carnival season.

During his early years at Venice, much of Monteverdi's time must have been given over to directing and composing music for the choir of St Mark's. His sixth book of madrigals, published in 1614, was the product of his last years at Mantua, and his seventh book of madrigals (1619) also contains music which seems Mantuan in style. The majority of its contents are, however, madrigals and arias for two voices

and continuo, works of a kind admirably suited to the small-scale musical soirées held at private houses in Venice.

Monteverdi's first dramatic work for Venice was a large-scale dialogue setting, *Il combattimento di Tancredi e Clorinda* (1624). The text is drawn from the twelfth *canto* of Tasso's epic *La Gerusalemme liberata* and depicts a combat between the Christian knight Tancred and the Saracen maiden Clorinda, who is disguised by her armor. After a strenuous fight, Tancred mortally wounds Clorinda, removes her helmet and is horrified to discover that he has been doing battle with a woman. He baptizes Clorinda, and she dies in his arms.

When Monteverdi published *Il combatti-mento* in his eighth book of madrigals (1638), he described it as a *madrigale con gesto* (an acted madrigal), and it is clear from his account of the first performance that the work was staged in a stylized manner, with Tancred riding in on a hobby horse and miming his sword-play in time with the music. The music itself, which requires a body of string players in addition to the harpsichord, paints a vivid picture of the action, with passages representing the gallop-ing of a horse, trumpet calls, the two warriors circling each other and the clash of their swords. Its chief *raison d'être*, however, is the *stile con-citato*, a musical style which Monteverdi used to convey the agitated passions engendered by war. The essence of this style is the use of rapid repeated notes, a stylized extension of the pro-cess found in operatic recitative, where the

citizens, or perhaps because they were unwilling to finance so ephemeral an art form.

The solution to this problem was typically Venetian: to make opera pay for itself in the commercial theater. Paradoxically, though, the pioneers of Venetian commercial opera were two Roman musicians, Francesco Manelli and Benedetto Ferrari. Manelli (1594-1667), a com-poser and bass singer, had worked as director of music at Tivoli Cathedral from 1627 to 1629 before taking up residence in Rome. Ferrari (1603/4-81), composer, theorbo player and poet, had trained as a choirboy at the German College in Rome and during the early 1620s was a musician at the Farnese court at Parma.

Encouraged by a group of Venetian noble-men, who, presumably, invested in the project, Manelli and Ferrari rented the newly refur-bished Teatro San Cassiano at Venice during

Opposite: Street life in Venice around 1620 is vividly brought to life in Fetti's modern-dress painting of the parable of the 'Pearl of Great Price.'

Left: Scene from the ballet *Il carnevale languente*, produced in Turin in 1647. Baroque operas and ballets revelled in such spectacular scenes of destruction and disaster.

Opposite: Painted plan of Venice in the seventeenth century: the Grand Canal winds its way through the city; the Piazza San Marco is in the center of the picture; the Doge's state barge is shown on the right.

pace of the music naturally speeds up as a char-acter becomes agitated. *Stile concitato* is em-ployed in a number of the madrigals in Book VIII, which has for its title *Madrigali guerrieri et amorosi* (Madrigals of war and love), and it may well have served Monteverdi in the comic opera *La finta pazza Licori* (Licoris's Feigned Mad-ness), to a libretto by Giulio Strozzi, which he began to write for performance at Mantua in 1627, though the work was never played and both libretto and music are now lost.

In 1630 Monteverdi worked once again with Strozzi to prepare the opera *Proserpina rapita* for the wedding of Giustiniana Mocenigo, the daughter of a Venetian senator. Only the trio 'Come dolce hoggi l'auretta spira' (published in a posthumous collection of Monteverdi's music) survives, but Mocenigo's commission is our first evidence of an awakening of interest in opera at Venice. For seven years, however, it remained an isolated event, perhaps because the expense of commissioning and staging an opera was beyond the means of most Venetian

the carnival season of 1637 and presented their opera *Andromeda* to the paying public. The plot was based on the Greek myth in which the maiden Andromeda is rescued from the ravages of a sea monster by the hero Perseus. The pro-duction seems to have been largely a family affair. Ferrari wrote the libretto, acted as im-presario and played theorbo in the orchestra. Manelli wrote the music and sang two roles, those of Neptune and Astarco. His wife, Mad-dalena, sang the prologue and the title role. Whatever money may have been saved by the expedient of doubling roles, however, no ex-pense was spared to ensure that the costumes and staging were as spectacular as possible. The stage effects included having Aurora descend in a cloud, the magician Astarco appear suddenly from under the stage, the sky open to reveal Jupiter and Juno enthroned and, finally, having the sea monster appear from the waves, with Perseus flying in on the winged horse Pegasus.

The venture was a great success, and Manelli and Ferrari returned to the Teatro San Cassiano for the carnival of 1638 with a new opera, *La maga fulminata* (The sorceress thunderstruck). The mixture was much as before, although the opera produced one innovation in the figure of Scarabea, the sorceress's old nurse, a comic figure played by a man. The aged nurse, cynical, full of worldly wisdom and as unfeminine as possible, became a lasting and endearing figure in Venetian opera; in Monteverdi's *Poppea*, for example, there are two such characters.

So popular did these early operas become that within four years of Manelli and Ferrari's production no fewer than three further opera houses opened their doors in Venice: the Teatro Santi Giovanni e Paolo in 1639, with a production of Manelli's *Delia* (libretto by Giulio Strozzi); the Teatro San Moisè in 1640, with a revival of Monteverdi's *Arianna*; and the Teatro Novissimo in 1641, with Sacrati's *La finta pazza* (libretto by Giulio Strozzi).

Monteverdi, by now in his seventies, wrote three new operas for the Venetian commercial theaters, of which two have survived. *Il ritorno d'Ulisse in patria* (*The return of Ulysses to his homeland*) was first performed probably in 1639 or 1640, since in the latter year it was taken on tour to Bologna. In many respects it is typical of early Venetian opera. Its libretto (by Giacomo Badoaro) is in three acts and rather loosely constructed to accommodate the ingredients which Venetian audiences had come to expect.

Spectacle is provided in Act I by the appearance on stage of a Phoenician ship; choruses of Nereids and Sirens sing; and there is a dialogue between Neptune, who rises from the waves, and Jupiter, who descends from the heavens. Comedy is provided in Act II by the fat suitor Iro, endowed with a stutter, who fights with Ulysses, affording Monteverdi an opportunity to employ the *stile concitato*. Ample provision is made for laments: in Act I, for example, Ulysses and his wife Penelope each sing a lament characterized by the powerful recitative style which Monteverdi evolved for *Orfeo*.

The undoubted masterpiece of Monteverdi's Venetian period, however, is *L'incoronazione di Poppea* (The Coronation of Poppea), with libretto by Giovanni Francesco Busenello, which survives in two manuscripts dating from the early 1650s, with cuts and additions made by the touring companies who used the manuscripts.

The opera was first performed at the Teatro Santi Giovanni e Paolo in 1642. In several respects it breaks new ground. It is the first Venetian opera to be based on historical rather than mythological sources, and it gives relatively few opportunities for spectacular stage effects. At the same time, it is dramatically much more mature than other contemporary operas. The substance of the plot remains faithful to its source – the *Annals* of Tacitus – and inverts the formula of good triumphing over evil.

The plot concerns Poppea's ambition to gain the crown of Rome. In pursuing this ambition she quite ruthlessly abandons her husband, Ottone, and persuades the Emperor Nero to abandon his wife, Ottavia, and to sentence his adviser, Seneca, to death. Ottavia plots with Ottone to have Poppea killed. Through the intervention of Cupid, the plot fails. Ottavia and Ottone are banished, and, in the original version, the opera ends with Poppea's coronation and with a chorus of cupids who descend

to celebrate the love of Nero and Poppea, his new empress.

The character of Poppea clearly fascinated Monteverdi and presented him with a considerable challenge: how to portray a woman who is ruthlessly ambitious and yet so attractive that she can hold Nero helpless under her spell. Her charms are conveyed through particularly seductive recitative writing interspersed with numerous semi-arias written in a ravishing triple-meter style.

Unique though it is in many respects, *L'incoronazione di Poppea* also retains some of the more familiar features of Venetian opera. At the outset of the opera two comic characters – soldiers on guard duty outside Poppea's house – are cleverly used by Busenello to set the background to the story, so that the action can begin without further preamble. Towards the end of Act III there is a fine lament for Ottavia, now

banished from Rome; and this is pointedly contrasted with a comic scene played by Poppea's nurse, who envisages her new social status as servant to the Empress of Rome.

Poppea, like all the surviving early Venetian operas, is essentially a play set to music. Its flexible mixture of recitative and arioso styles allows considerable latitude in pacing and interpretation, and its success depends on intimate contact between the actor-singer and the continuo player, who provides a discreet and spontaneous accompaniment. The orchestra (mainly of strings) plays only a limited role: to provide ritornellos between the stanzas of arias and introductory sinfonias for the grander scenes.

The history of Venetian opera from the death of Monteverdi in 1643 until the early 1660s has to be constructed largely from the evidence of the printed libretti, which were sold in the theaters prior to the performance. For, unlike the court operas, whose scores were published to commemorate the occasions for which they were written, Venetian operas were as ephemeral as the carnival seasons in which they were presented. The scores which have survived from this period are the work of two composers: Francesco Cavalli (1602-76) and his younger contemporary and rival, Antonio Cesti (1623-69).

Between 1639 and his death, Cavalli wrote over thirty operas for the Venetian theaters and for the theaters which opened in other Italian cities. The scores of twenty-six of his operas survive today. His early works can appear experimental in character, but his collaboration with the librettist Giovanni Faustini, from *Ormindo* (1644) to *Eritrea* (1652), saw a consolidation of his style and works of greater maturity, among them *Calisto* (1651-2), which was

Above: Four German curtain designs by Joseph Furttenbach, dating from 1640. They are all Italian in spirit; the bottom right-hand one depicts the main square in Siena.

Left: Engraving of 'The Burning of the City of Argos' from Francesco Cavalli's opera *Hipermestra*, produced in Florence in 1658 – a scene of disaster that called on all the resources of baroque stage machinery.

performed at the Teatro San Apollinare, the sixth opera theater to open in Venice.

The Faustini-Cavalli collaboration also spans the years in which Venetian opera developed a distinctive character, with fast-paced plots involving a high degree of intrigue and humor. During the 1650s, the large choral scenes which had dominated Roman opera, and which are still found in the early Venetian repertoire, largely disappeared, and an orchestra of only modest proportions was used. Those elements which had proved successful in the early operas – laments, slumber scenes and invocations – were, however, retained.

Throughout this period of development, Cavalli maintained an approach to operatic composition which was essentially the same as that of his mentor, Monteverdi. That is, he employed a fluid succession of recitatives, arias and semi-arias subordinated to the requirements of the drama. Even during his lifetime, however, this approach to opera was going out of fashion, as greater provision was made for favorite singers to display their voices in arias. This change in fashion can be detected as early as 1649 in *Orontea*, the first opera written by Cesti for the Venetian stage. Very few scenes are set simply in recitative, and in some sections of the opera arias appear on almost every page of the score. Moreover, the recitatives themselves are more rapid in diction than those of Monteverdi and Cavalli, so that one often has the impression of being carried quickly from one aria to the next.

Only four of Cesti's Venetian operas survive. Most of his later operas were written for Innsbruck, where he served the Archduke Ferdinand Karl of Austria from 1652, and Vienna, where he served the Emperor Leopold I from 1666. His best-known opera, *Il pomo d'oro* (The Golden Apple, 1668), is not a Venetian work at all, but a full-blown five-act court opera.

• The spread of opera •

The operas that Cesti wrote for Innsbruck and Vienna represent part of a more widespread dissemination of opera both within and outside Italy during the second half of the seventeenth century. Following the establishment of opera at Venice, Manelli and Ferrari were themselves involved in a touring company; in 1640 they took Manelli's *Delia* and Monteverdi's *Il ritorno d'Ulisse* to Bologna; and they returned to the same city in 1641 with revivals of *La maga fulminata* and *Il pastor regio* (The Shepherd King).

After their early successes at Venice, both Manelli and Ferrari took up court appointments, at Parma and Modena respectively, and their later dramatic works were written mainly for court occasions. The activities of Venetian touring companies did not, however, cease with their departure. Companies like the Febiarmonici and the Accademici Discordati took operas to such cities as Florence, Naples, Genoa, Lucca and Piacenza, seeking financial support from local patrons in the cities where they played.

Naples, which had seen a performance of the Roman opera *Galatea* in 1644, witnessed renewed activity in 1650 and 1651 with the performance of Venetian operas, including Cavalli's *Didone* and Monteverdi's *L'incoronazione di Poppea*. A permanent home for opera at Naples was established around 1654 at the Teatro San Bartolomeo and two years later a similar theater – the Teatro della Pergola – was opened at Florence with a production of Jacopo Melani's *Il potestà di Colognole*.

The reverberations of this intense operatic activity were felt as far afield as England. One of Cavalli's operas, *Erismena*, found its way to England, where it survives in a manuscript score with an English singing translation. An attempt to create a native English opera was made with *The Siege of Rhodes* (1656), with libretto by Sir William Davenant and music by Henry Lawes, Matthew Locke and others, but this engendered few successors. Purcell's *Dido and Aeneas* (1689) is an almost unique landmark, and its recitative owes more to the style of mid-seventeenth-century Venice than to contemporary developments in Italian opera.

Though opera failed to take root in England, its importation into the Austro-German Empire and France was more successful. Vienna was essentially a center of Italian culture, whose leading figures were Cesti and, later, Antonio Draghi (c.1635-1700), who composed some 170 operatic works. In the German states, an early attempt to establish opera was made at Torgau where Heinrich Schütz's opera *Dafne*, to a German translation of Rinuccini's libretto, was performed in 1627 to celebrate the wedding of the daughter of the Elector of Saxony. The establishment of German opera was hindered by the Thirty Years' War (1617-48), but the 1650s and 1660s saw performances of operas by Johann Jakob Loewe and Johann Kaspar Kerll. The first permanent opera house devoted to German opera, the Gänsemarkt Theater in the free city of Hamburg, opened in January 1678 with a performance of Johann Theile's *Der erschaffene,*

Below: Engraving of the elaborate ballet sequence for a German production in 1693 of the Italian opera *Camillo generoso.*

Above: Trumpeters and a bass player in the service of the Doge of Venice.

Left: Organ loft in the church of the Ospedale della Pietà, Venice, with singers and instrumentalists assembled behind the grill.

gefallene und aufgerichtete Mensch, based on the story of Adam and Eve.

In France Cardinal Mazarin, who had worked in the Barberini household at Rome during the 1630s, introduced Italian opera apparently to divert attention from his own political machinations. In the carnival of 1645 an (unidentified) Italian opera was given for the entertainment of the French court, and later in the same year Sacrati's *La finta pazza* was performed with magnificent stage machines and with ballets added at the end of each act to conform with French taste.

In January 1646 the exiled Barberini family arrived in France, lending further impetus to the cultivation there of Italian opera. The opera *Egisto* (possibly in Cavalli's setting) was performed in February 1646 to celebrate their arrival. In June of the same year the Roman composer Luigi Rossi, who had earlier written for the Barberini theater, was brought to Paris to work on a new opera, *Orfeo*. The libretto was written by Francesco Buti, secretary to Antonio Barberini and later, under Mazarin, superintendent of Italian artists at the French court. Buti's treatment of the Orpheus myth contains numerous digressions from the original story, providing scope for ballets featuring, among other things, owls, tortoises and snails. The result is a loosely wrought entertainment, which lasted some six hours in performance.

Rossi's opera was a great success, though further operatic ventures in France were precluded for some years by anti-royalist feeling. In 1659 Cavalli was invited to compose the opera *Ercole amante* for the wedding of King Louis XIV to the Infanta of Spain. In the event, the theater in which the opera was to have been performed remained unfinished at the time of the wedding celebrations in 1660, and

an existing opera by Cavalli, *Xerse*, was hastily re-arranged in five acts and presented in a temporary theater. *Ercole amante* was finally performed in 1662. Contemporary reports suggest that the theater was so badly designed that the words of the opera were scarcely audible. In any case, the music which attracted most attention was that for the ballets, in which the King and Queen danced. The music for the ballets was written, not by Cavalli, but by Jean-Baptiste Lully, a composer of Florentine birth who had settled in France in 1646 and, by 1662, had risen to the position of master of music to the French royal family. With the decline in the fortunes of Italian opera that followed Mazarin's death in 1661, it was Lully who created, for France, the only tradition of opera which seriously challenged the domination of Italian musical culture during the baroque period.

• Church music •

The introduction of the *basso continuo* technique in secular music at the end of the sixteenth century also had an impact on church music, for it provided an elegant solution to the problem of furnishing an accompaniment for choral music — an everyday problem for the hosts of organists employed to provide music for Italy's churches. Although we tend to think of the sixteenth century as the Golden Age of *a cappella* — that is, unaccompanied — choral music, it is quite clear that such music was often accompanied by the organ or by other instruments. A very few choirs — the papal choir at Rome was one — specialized in singing unaccompanied music. Other professional choirs

mixed *a cappella* with accompanied singing. At St Mark's, Venice, for example, the great ceremonial motets of Giovanni Gabrieli often included parts for wind and stringed instruments, the instrumental sonorities contributing to the grandeur of the effect of this music. For the average church organist with limited choral resources, an organ accompaniment was essential, if for nothing else than to keep the choir in tune.

There were several alternatives open to the organist who had to provide an accompaniment for choral music. He could prepare a full score from the vocal parts and play from this; he could produce a short score, either limiting himself to writing out the top and bottom parts and improvising an accompaniment from these, or reducing the counterpoint to the essential entries which the choir would need as cues; or he could write out the bass part alone, and improvise from this.

The inclusion of organ scores in church music published during the 1590s, however, opened the way to compositions in which a *basso continuo* was provided to accompany music for a few voices rather than the usual complement of four or more. The earliest published music of this kind is found in the *Cento concerti ecclesiastici*

Above left: Title-page of a 1587 edition of choral and instrumental works by Andrea Gabrieli and his nephew Giovanni, both organists at St Mark's basilica.

Above: Transport of the Body of St Mark (1562-6) by Jacopo Tintoretto. This work, painted for the Scuola di San Marco by one of the greatest Venetian artists of the Renaissance, reflects the equally intense and dramatic character of the city's religious music of that time.

(One Hundred Ecclesiastical Concertos – *concerto* in this case meaning music for voice with instrumental accompaniment) issued at Venice in 1602 by Lodovico Grossi da Viadana, director of music at Mantua Cathedral from 1594 to 1597.

Viadana offered motets specifically composed for two, three and four voices with continuo accompaniment. His motets retain the restrained, mellifluous lines of late sixteenth-century sacred music, enlivened occasionally by passages of word-painting or vocal ornamentation, or with a short refrain in triple time to unify the composition. In the music for solo voice the continuo bass usually imitates the vocal line, so that it could have the text added and be sung as well as played. In the pieces for two and more voices the instrumental bass usually follows the lowest voice.

Encouraged by Viadana's example, a number of choirmasters in northern Italy, especially those working for lesser musical foundations, began to turn their attention to composing for voice and continuo, and from 1605 a steady stream of their publications issued from the musical presses. Not surprisingly, since these composers rarely had virtuoso singers at their disposal, few wrote for solo voice. They were more interested in writing music for ensembles of two, three and four

Antonio Cifra, who worked at Rome and at the Holy House of Loreto and published nine books of small-scale motets between 1609 and 1619.

The publication of such small-scale continuo motets is not the only evidence of changing musical fashion at Rome in the early seventeenth century. Agazzari and Anerio, for example, were both active in publishing motets for four and more voices with continuo and in cultivating the polychoral idiom, that is, writing music in which a large choir is divided into two or more groups which sing in alternation as well as joining to form a single ensemble. Polychoral music, which is so often associated only with Venice and, in particular, with the work of Giovanni Gabrieli, had been cultivated at Rome during the lifetime of Palestrina, whose eight-part, double choir setting of the *Stabat Mater* was a prized possession of the papal choir. During the seventeenth century it became one of the most characteristic idioms of Roman music, culminating in the work of Orazio Benevoli (1605-72), director of music at St Peter's from 1646 until his death. Benevoli composed settings of the Mass for up to sixteen voices, and of the *Magnificat* for up to twenty-four voices, as well as smaller-scale motets with continuo.

Although Roman motets of the early and mid-seventeenth century embody many of the newer elements of baroque style and technique, Mass settings of the same period, particularly those written for the greater Roman churches and the papal chapel, are often more conservative in style and continue the tradition of *a cappella* polyphonic music represented by the Masses of Palestrina. This was due partly to a lingering reverence for Palestrina himself on the part of his pupils and successors, and partly to the feeling that his restrained and dignified style was more appropriate to the devotional celebration of the liturgy than the more colorful secular idioms of the continuo style.

Below: Page from the printed score of Cavalieri's sacred opera *La rappresentatione di anima e di corpo* (The Representation of Soul and Body), first performed in Rome in 1600 and an important step in the development of oratorio.

Right: Title-page of an early edition of sacred pieces by Domenico Mazzocchi, one of the pioneer figures in the development of oratorio. He was, incidentally, one of the earliest to add dynamic markings (indications of loudness and softness) to some of his scores.

voices in which imitative writing could be used to maintain interest and to build extended musical structures. For the most part, like Viadana, they restricted themselves to setting motet texts.

The impact of Viadana's work was felt not only in northern Italy, but also at Rome. The earliest surviving Roman publication to contain continuo motets dates from 1606 and its contents seem to have been composed in 1603. This publication was the *Sacrarum cantionum, liber quartus* of Agostino Agazzari, then choirmaster of the Jesuit German College at Rome. Agazzari's lead was soon followed by other Roman composers: by Giovanni Francesco Anerio, a pupil of Palestrina, and by the prolific

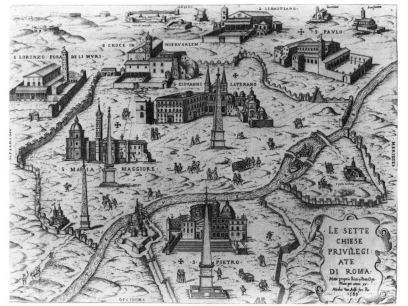

the duet 'Pulchra es' and the six-voice motet 'Audi coelum,' which begins with an extended solo, are written in the new style of Florentine declamatory recitative, with harmonic and melodic gestures closely related to the emotions and the meaning of the words. 'Audi coelum' also uses the technique of having one voice echo the other, a device which Monteverdi had used in the last act of his opera *Orfeo*.

When Monteverdi went to Venice as director of music at St Mark's in 1613, where Giovanni Croce (d. 1609) had recently held the same post and Giovanni Gabrieli (d. 1612) that of first organist, he inherited a musical establishment in which indiscipline and dissension were rife. During his early years at Venice he was, therefore, largely occupied with reorganizing and rebuilding the choir, with bringing its repertoire up to date, and with writing his own church music. As the years went by, however, he was able to appoint to his staff other composers of great ability: Alessandro Grandi, who became

The distinction between Mass settings in an *a cappella* style and motets with continuo, which is evident at Rome in the first decade of the seventeenth century, marks the beginning of a split in church music between the *stile antico* (the old style) and the *stile moderno* (the modern style) which was to persist throughout the baroque era.

The dichotomy between the old and the new styles is evident in Monteverdi's first major publication of church music – *Sanctissimae virgini missa senis vocibus ad ecclesiarum choros ac vespere pluribus decantandae cum nonnullis sacris concentibus* – which was issued in 1610 while Monteverdi was still working as choirmaster at Mantua. The first item in the book is an *a cappella* Mass setting for six voices. In a letter to Cardinal Ferdinando Gonzaga, dated 16 July 1610, one of Monteverdi's Mantuan colleagues, Bassano Casola, commented that the composition of the Mass had cost Monteverdi a great deal of study and labor. At Mantua, Monteverdi had had little opportunity to gain experience in writing large-scale polyphonic church music, and this lack of experience undoubtedly contributed to the 'great study and labor' required to master the style.

The remainder of Monteverdi's 1610 publication is devoted to a setting of the service of Vespers. This Vespers setting – the *Vespro della Beata Vergine*, appropriate to feasts of the Virgin Mary – with its diversity of styles and rich tapestry of vocal and instrumental colors, has become one of Monteverdi's best-known and most widely admired works.

The title-page of Monteverdi's *Vespers* advertises the setting as 'composed on *cantus firmi*.' The use of a *cantus firmus* is traditional enough, but the rhythmic vitality and rich sonority of Monteverdi's settings bears less relation to the music of Palestrina than to the music of northern Italian composers like Giovanni Gabrieli. The continuo motets are unashamedly written in the *stile moderno*, or the 'second practice' as Monteverdi himself called it. Both

Top left: Map of the principal churches of Rome in 1589 – the time and place of the birth of oratorio.

Above: Autograph page from the manuscript of a Mass by Orazio Benevoli, choirmaster at St Peter's, Rome. Benevoli's church music is in the polychoral tradition of Palestrina.

his assistant in 1620, Giovanni Rovetta, who succeeded Grandi in 1627; and Francesco Cavalli, who became second organist in 1639.

The earliest of Monteverdi's Venetian church music to appear in print was a series of motets published in various anthologies between 1615 and 1629. These include a few motets for five and six voices, like the fine miniatures 'Cantate Domino' and 'Christe, adoramus te,' which appeared in Giulio Cesare Bianchi's *Libro primo de motetti* of 1620; but most are scored for only one or two voices and continuo. Some of these, like 'Salve, o Regina' (1624) for solo tenor, continue to use the essentially Florentine style of declamation found in the motets of Monteverdi's 1610 publication. Others, however, perhaps following the path opened up by Alessandro Grandi, exhibit a new tunefulness. Among these are the solo motet 'Currite populi' (1625), and the duet 'Cantate Domino' (1615) in which a broad triple-time refrain is contrasted with passages written in a more florid style.

Although it was only his small-scale motets that found their way into print during the first twenty-five years of Monteverdi's work at Venice, it is clear that from the outset he was also engaged in writing larger musical settings. In a letter of 29 December 1616, for example, he mentions that he had spent the whole month writing a Mass for Christmas Eve. A later letter (2 February 1634) shows that it was part of Monteverdi's duties to write a new Mass each year for Christmas. If so, then the two complete *a cappella* settings which are all that survive from Monteverdi's years at Venice must form only a very small proportion of his total output.

The Mass settings survive in two large published collections. The first, the *Selva morale e spirituale*, was published in 1641. The second, the *Messa a quattro voci, et Salmi*, was collected after Monteverdi's death by the publisher Alessandro Vincenti and issued in 1650. Apart from the Mass settings, the two collections are devoted mainly to settings of psalms for Vespers, the other principal musical service at St Mark's. These represent a wide variety of musical styles, from rather severe *a cappella* settings for double choir, like 'Credidi propter quod locutus sum' (1640) to a work like 'Beatus vir' (1640), for six voices, two violins and three trombones (or lower strings), whose lively and attractive melodies are constructed above the same ostinato bass that Monteverdi used for his secular duet 'Chiome d'oro' (1619). In whichever style Monteverdi was working, however, his technique is much freer than in the 1610 Vespers. Occasionally he hints at a psalm tone, as at the beginning of the first setting of 'Dixit Dominus' in the 1650 collection; but the psalm tones are never used consistently as *cantus firmi* as they were in 1610. The madrigalian technique of word-painting, on the other hand, is used frequently, occasionally leading to some striking musical imagery, as in the six-voice setting of 'Nisi Dominus' from the 1650 book, which includes a passage in the *concitato* style and a splendid display of vocal pyrotechnics for the phrase 'Like as arrows in the hand of a giant: even so are the young children.'

The publications of sacred music by Monteverdi's younger colleagues – Grandi, Rovetta and Cavalli – follow a similar pattern in containing Masses, Vesper psalms and *Magnificats*, and motets which could be used as antiphon-substitutes in the celebration of Vespers. In one respect, however, these composers differ from Monteverdi in that each published a complete *concertato* Mass setting, that is, a Mass with orchestral as well as continuo accompaniment. A rare glimpse of Monteverdi's work in this field is afforded by the splendid but isolated setting of the Gloria, for seven voices, two violins and four lower strings (or trombones), which he published in the *Selva morale*, and which seems to have been composed for a service held at St Mark's in 1631 to celebrate the end of an outbreak of plague.

The most grandiose of these Mass settings by the younger generation of Venetian composers is Cavalli's *Messa concertata*, published in

1656. It is a huge work, scored for double choir, strings, trombones and continuo, and may have been written as early as 1644 to celebrate the peace negotiated between the Pope and the Duke of Parma. As well as massive double-choir sonorities which look back to Giovanni Gabrieli, Cavalli introduces expressive solo and duet writing and orchestral passages which are strongly reminiscent of his operatic writing.

Twenty years later, shortly before his death in 1676 he made a final setting of the Mass, a Requiem for double choir, which is a powerful and deeply felt work and one of his finest compositions. Parodoxically, though, for a composer whose reputation had been secured in the most modern of art forms – opera – it is a work written in the *stile antico*.

• Oratorio •

The discussion has so far centered on music written for the regular liturgical celebrations of the Church; but performances of sacred music were by no means limited to this function. Monteverdi's *Vespers* of 1610, for example, are

Above: Bernini's representation of St Theresa and the Angel (*c.* 1647-52) in the church of S. Maria della Vittoria, Rome. The powerful theatricality of baroque art was also a notable feature of the early oratorios.

advertised on the title-page of the publication as being suitable for princely chapels or chambers, and the small-scale *concerti*, in particular, are suited to chamber performance. Numerous collections of Italian madrigals, too, including music written in the new continuo style, contain or are wholly devoted to *madrigali spirituali*, settings of devotional texts in the vernacular.

By far the most important extra-liturgical function served by sacred music during the seventeenth century was as an adjunct to the spiritual exercises conducted in the oratories (prayer halls) of Rome and other major Italian cities. One particular type of musical setting – the setting of dialogue texts in which two or more characters converse with each other – became so closely associated with this function that before 1700 it had acquired the name of its place of performance – the oratorio.

The Oratorian movement, an evangelical movement within the Catholic Church, was founded in the early 1550s by the priest and mystic Filippo Neri (1515-95). In its early stages the movement consisted of nothing more than an informal gathering of laymen who met at Neri's quarters at the church of San Girolamo della Carità, Rome, for religious discussions and prayer. Such was Neri's personal magnetism, however, and so attractive the informal nature of his 'spiritual exercises,' that by 1554 the movement had grown to the extent that it was necessary to hold its meetings in a converted loft over one of the aisles of San Girolamo. This loft, then, was the earliest of the oratories, but it was superseded in 1575 when Pope Gregory XIII granted the Oratorians their own church – Santa Maria in Vallicella – and recognized them as a religious community,

though one organized on a much less formal basis than older religious communities.

Neri and his followers had the old church of Santa Maria demolished and a new one built in its place. Work on the rebuilding was largely finished by 1577, though the permanent oratory attached to the church was not completed until 1640. Santa Maria in Vallicella, or the Chiesa Nuova as it is more commonly known, remains even today the spiritual home of the Oratorian movement.

Music had played a part in the daily spiritual exercises of the Oratorians from the early days

Above: St Cecilia and Singers, painted in the first quarter of the seventeenth century by Domenichino and showing the patron saint of musicians playing a violin.

Left: The Sacrifice of Jephthah (*c.* 1660) by the Venetian painter Sebastiano Mazzoni; this tragic Old Testament story was also the subject of one of Giacomo Carissimi's best-known oratorios, written some ten years earlier.

Above: Angel blowing a labyrinthine trumpet appearing to St Jerome, an engraving (*c.* 1621) by the Spanish painter Ribera, who worked in Naples. In music, too, Spanish influence reached Italy through Naples, which was governed by Spanish viceroys throughout the seventeenth century.

been reduced to one, and the pattern was set for the usual outline of the oratorio as a musical form in the late seventeenth century – a work in two parts, with a sermon preached between the first and the second part.

Although dialogue *laude* were being sung in the oratories well before the end of the sixteenth century, the evolution of dialogue settings using the new styles of continuo-accompanied solo song seems to have taken place independently of the oratories, and it is not clear exactly when such dialogue settings were first introduced into the *oratorio vespertino*. Dialogue texts in Latin and Italian had been set to music during the sixteenth century as polyphonic motets and spiritual madrigals, and their composers occasionally attempted to differentiate between the characters of the dialogue by, for example, setting the words of one character for the higher voices of the ensemble and the words of the other for the lower voices. With the coming of continuo song and operatic recitative, however, it became possible to set such dialogue texts as though they were small-scale operatic scenes to be performed without stage action. Numerous examples can be cited, though none seems to have been specifically written for the oratories. Viadana's *Cento concerti ecclesiastici*, for example, includes a dialogue setting for three voices – 'Fili, quid fecisti?' – on the finding of Jesus in the temple, and the *lauda* 'Anima mia, che pensi?' was set for tenor, bass and *basso continuo* by another north Italian composer, Lodovico Bellanda, and published in his *Le musiche* of 1610.

The performance of Cavalieri's *La rappresentatione di anima et di corpo* at the Oratory of the Chiesa Nuova in 1600 undoubtedly alerted the Oratorians to the potential of the new idioms of dramatic music for drawing large congregations, although the first volume containing spiritual dialogues in the new style specifically intended for performance at an oratory was published only in 1619. This was the *Teatro armonico spirituale di madrigali* (Rome, 1619) by Giovanni Francesco Anerio.

The music of Anerio's *Teatro* was intended for use during the winter *oratorio vespertino* at the oratory of San Girolamo della Carità, though a copy of his publication was also used at the Chiesa Nuova. The book contains ninety-four spiritual madrigals, and its list of contents indicates the Sundays and feast days for which each was appropriate. Eighteen of the madrigals are settings of dialogue texts in a single section, ranging in length of performance from about six to about twenty minutes. They include dramatizations for soloists and chorus of the stories of the Prodigal Son, David and Goliath, and of the conversion of St Paul.

The papacy of Urban VIII (1623-44), the period during which opera became firmly established at Rome, also saw a considerable expansion of musical activity at the oratories, including the performance of extended dialogue settings. The composers involved in writing music for the Roman oratories during Urban's reign included several, like Domenico

of the movement. At first the principal form was the *lauda*, a simple devotional song in several stanzas, usually set for three or four voices. Initially the *laude* were presumably sung by the congregation, though towards the end of the sixteenth century more complex settings are found which may have been performed by professional singers. By the late 1570s, however, another type of exercise had been added, and one which was to be much more important for the development of oratorio as a musical form. This was the *oratorio vespertino*, a service which was held after Vespers on Sundays and feast days and which was open to the general public. The *oratorio vespertino* consisted not only of sermons by Oratorians, but also of brief sermons delivered from memory by young boys and interspersed with performances of *laude*. These latter elements were designed to attract large congregations, and people of every class of society thronged to the services, particularly when, in the summer months, they were held out of doors.

During the winter, from All Saints' Day (1 November) to Easter, the *oratorio vespertino* was held indoors with more elaborate music, including motets as well as *laude*. By the end of the sixteenth century the number of sermons preached in the winter *oratorio vespertino* had

Mazzocchi, Luigi Rossi and Marco Marazzoli, who were also actively involved in writing opera. Among them, however, was one who made no contribution to opera, but whose oratorios are of the first importance, Giacomo Carissimi (1605-74). After holding posts at Tivoli Cathedral and at Assisi, in 1629 he was appointed director of music at the German College in Rome, a position he held until his death.

Carissimi's surviving works include two Italian and possibly thirteen Latin oratorios, the latter of which were probably written for performance at the Oratorio del Santissimo Crocifisso. The most famous of his Latin oratorios is *Jephte*, which was written before 1650. The libretto is based on an Old Testament story and consists of a mixture of direct quotation from the Bible and newly-invented dialogue. The first part of the oratorio is taken over almost literally from the biblical account. Jephthah, captain of the Israelites, is about to make war on the Amorites. As he goes out to battle he vows that if he is given victory he will offer as a sacrifice on his return 'whatsoever first cometh forth of the doors of my house to meet me.' He returns home victorious and is met by his only daughter. Thus the seeds of tragedy are sown.

The scene is set in a simple recitative sung by a narrator – Historicus (alto) – and followed by a short solo passage in which Jephthah (tenor) makes his vow. The narrative is then taken up by a six-part chorus, who paint a vivid picture of Jephthah's going out to war and defeating the Amorites. On his return home, Jephthah is greeted joyfully by his daughter (soprano), who sings an extended aria. The chorus then give thanks for Israel's victory.

As the tragic consequences of Jephthah's vow become apparent, the music changes suddenly and dramatically from major to minor, and the second part of the oratorio is largely given over to two laments, the first for Jephthah, the second for his daughter, both of which are written in a passionate operatic style of recitative. The setting is completed by an extremely powerful six-part chorus, 'Plorate filii Israel,' which was later reworked by Handel for the chorus 'Hear Jacob's God' in his own oratorio *Samson* (1741). With its scenes of rejoicing followed immediately by a tragic blow of fate, Carissimi's oratorio follows a scheme similar to that of the first two acts of Monteverdi's opera *Orfeo*. The musical means used to convey the sense of tragedy – the change from major to minor mode and the laments, the second of which employs an echo – also parallel operatic technique. The essential difference is, of course, that Carissimi's oratorio was not a stage work. Its plot is conveyed through narrative rather than through stage action.

By the last decade of Carissimi's life the oratorio had, to all intents and purposes, become the sacred counterpart of opera, a dramatic entertainment to be enjoyed especially during Lent, when the public opera houses were closed. It was, moreover, a musical form which was by no means restricted to Rome. In

Right: Sketch from Bernini's workshop for an organ for the church of S. Maria del Popolo, Rome. The design was done shortly after the election in 1655 of Agostino Chigi as Pope Alexander VII and refers to the Chigi family emblem – the oak tree.

Below: A landmark in the history of oratorio – the new church of S. Maria in Vallicella, where Cavalieri's *La rappresentatione di anima e di corpo* was first performed in 1600. Beside it is the Oratory of St Philip Neri, built in 1637 by Borromini, Rome's greatest baroque architect.

other Italian cities where oratories had been founded – Florence, Bologna, Naples and Venice – and in centers of Italianate culture like Vienna, the cultivation of the oratorio both complemented and paralleled the development and dissemination of opera during the mid- and late seventeenth century. Carissimi was himself influential in France and Germany through the work of pupils such as Marc-Antoine Charpentier (?1645/50-1704) and Christoph Bernhard (1628-92). It is worth remembering, though, that the tradition of setting sacred dialogues in the new continuo-accompanied styles had begun independently of the oratories and that the settings of such texts found in French, German and English sources during the seventeenth century should not necessarily be linked with the Oratorian movement.

GERMANY BEFORE BACH

FREDERICK HUDSON

The emergence of German music in its own right may conveniently be pinpointed by three events, each a century apart – the births of Martin Luther (1483), Heinrich Schütz (1585) and J. S. Bach (1685). Luther's writings show that he had a great love for music and an understanding of its value in worship, and the growing treasury of chorale hymns and tunes inspired by Luther and his followers formed a basis for composition in every art form except that of opera, from organ chorale preludes and variations to works such as Bach's *St Matthew Passion.*

To the second event, the birth of Schütz, the so-called 'father of German music,' must be linked the births of his contemporaries, Johann H. Schein (1586) and Samuel Scheidt (1587), with each of whom he had a personal friendship. The works of these three exhibit the mainstream transmigration of modern Italian – chiefly Venetian – ideas to Germany, this stream merging with Flemish, English, and French influences (though to a lesser extent), until all were absorbed and adapted into German music.

The long-standing commercial relationship between the south German cities and Venice, where there was a German 'college' or hostelry to accommodate travelers who regularly crossed the Alps, inevitably affected musical style. There existed a strong friendship between Giovanni Gabrieli and members of the great Augsburg commercial house of Fugger – wealthy music-lovers and patrons of music and the sister arts. This connection was maintained by Gabrieli's pupils and followers, and it is significant that there are more original and early sources of his works in Augsburg State and City Library than in the whole of Italy.

The first German of importance to receive an Italian training was the Lutheran Hans Leo Hassler (1562-1612), who was sent from Nuremberg to study with Giovanni's uncle Andrea Gabrieli in 1584, after which he was appointed private organist to Octavian II Fugger at Augsburg, later filling similar posts at Nuremberg, Ulm and the Electoral Chapel at Dresden. Venetian influence is apparent in his secular music, and his Latin Masses and motets have the sonority of Andrea's style. His *Lustgarten neuer teutscher Gesäng* of 1601 (thirty-two German songs and eleven instrumental ballet *intradas*), includes the tune which we know as the 'Passion Chorale,' 'O Haupt voll Blut und Wunden.'

The most influential of the pioneers of modern Italian music in Germany, however, was Michael Praetorius (?1571-1621), who paradoxically never had the opportunity of visiting Italy or the benefit of instruction from one of the Italian masters. This outstanding composer and scholar gained his remarkable insight through study of modern Italian works and the treatises on style, instrumentation, performance, embellishments and other features published in Venice and Rome by G. dalla Casa, Bassano, Bovicelli, Conforti and others between 1584 and 1607 – and by a life-long correspondence with Italian masters and German court musicians who had assimilated Giulio Caccini's *Le nuove musiche* of 1602. Such was his reputation that he was commissioned to reorganize the musical constitution of several German courts on modern Italian lines – at Dresden in collaboration with the newly appointed Schütz and elsewhere with Scheidt. He was also in demand throughout Germany to compose polychoral works and organize their performance for princely occasions – weddings, baptisms, conferences of rulers, jubilees and the like.

Praetorius was trained in the Flemish contrapuntal style as is apparent in his *Musae Sioniae*, nine volumes containing 1,244 Lutheran liturgical works for two to twelve voices, published between 1605 and 1610. He was so captivated by the new Venetian *concertato* styles of solo voices, multi-choirs and instrumental ritornelli and accompaniment, however, that he considered making a complete redraft of *Musae Sioniae* in the new, colorful style, before rejecting the scheme as impracticable. Instead, he threw himself into the composition of magnificent polychoral settings which reflect the pomp and splendor of Venice under the Gabrielis. These he published in 1619 under the title of *Polyhymnia caduceatrix et panegyrica.* Several are completely new workings of pieces from *Musae Sioniae* – for example, 'Vom Himmel hoch' from the fifth volume. The 1607 version is a four-voice setting of Luther's chorale text, while that of 1619 includes opening and intermediate instrumental ritornelli and colorful contrasts of several choirs of voices and instruments, all on the foundation of a *basso continuo.* The transformation of 'Puer natus in Bethlehem' from the 1610 version is even more striking.

In 1612 Praetorius published *Terpsichore*, a collection of 312 dances in four to six parts drawn from the musicians and dancing-masters of the court of Henri IV of France, which also illustrates the rich variety of instruments in use at that time. The three volumes of his *Syntagma Musicum* (1614-19) detail fully the whole art of composition and performing practice in the new Italian style, grafted on to those of Italy and Germany of the sixteenth century.

•Heinrich Schütz•

Schütz is now recognized as the outstanding figure in seventeenth-century German musical and intellectual life. He began law studies at

and was always receptive to changing styles in neighboring lands, which he could adapt to German tradition and development.

The years 1618-48 saw Europe engaged in the Thirty Years' War, during which Germans suffered more than others from the cruelty and deprivation inflicted by the opposing forces. Schütz's new employer, the Elector of Saxony, was a weak, bigoted and unintellectual man, who nevertheless was gratified to have a musician of growing fame in charge of his Kapelle. Dresden was little affected by the early years of the war and, in his *Psalms of David* (1619), Schütz reflects the magnificence of the Venetian polychoral motet with contrasts of *soli/tutti* and rich instrumentation. Psalm 24 ('Domini est terra') is a later example of this style. This was followed in 1623 by the *Resurrection Story*, Schütz's first narrative composition, intended for Easter Day Vespers. He is traditional in giving the evangelist's part to a tenor, but adds a new dimension by providing an accompaniment for four viole da gamba. The words of Christ, the disciples, Mary Magdalene and other participants in the drama are accompanied

Above: Schütz directing the Dresden court chapel choir. In fact, the engraving shows the chapel as it had been restored in 1662, after Schütz's time as Kapellmeister.

Left: The palace at Dresden, from an engraving of 1679.

Below: Autograph page from Schütz's *Resurrection Story* of 1623.

Marburg University in 1608 but, the following year, the enlightened Landgrave Moritz of Hesse-Kassel, at whose Collegium Mauritianum at Kassel Schütz had studied from the age of fourteen, gave him a generous allowance to study in Venice with Giovanni Gabrieli, where he remained until 1613, the year after Giovanni's death. The first fruit of this study was the publication of Schütz's five-voice *Italian Madrigals* in 1611. The madrigal form at this period was no longer the most fashionable stylistically, but Giovanni used the severe discipline of contrapuntal writing, the expression of the text and the development of a personal style, culminating in publication, as a sort of 'passing-out' exercise – many such publications by his pupils are extant. Schütz's madrigals show a command of style in voice figuration, motivic and rhythmic contrast, expression and harmonic individuality, and are by no means copies of Italian models. He used these means of expressing the text in both church and secular works throughout his life,

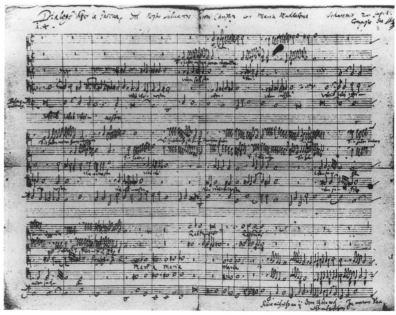

for the first time in the history of the Passion and Easter story by an organ *basso continuo*. This Easter oratorio is historically important also because of its descriptive power and reflections on the gospel events, prophetic of Bach's *St John Passion* a century later. Two years after this came the *Cantiones sacrae*, a collection of forty Latin motets for four voices, some in the old style of imitative counterpoint and others in the new Italian style of text expression, while for the wedding celebrations at Torgau of one of the Elector's daughters in 1627, Schütz composed *Dafne* – the first opera by a German composer – altough only the libretto by Martin Opitz survives, in part translated from Rinuccini's text of 1594.

Above: Engraving of 1643 entitled 'The Grand European War Ballet' – a political allegory about the Thirty Years' War, which brought such havoc and devastation to Germany.

Schütz made a second visit to Italy in 1628-9, to gain first-hand experience of Monteverdi's new style of expressive composition (*stile moderno* or *seconda prattica*). There is no record that Schütz sought lessons from him, but his reputation would assure him of a personal approach to and frequent contacts with this great master. He became aware of the *stile concitato* ('exited' or 'agitated' style), including the new tremolo effect Monteverdi had used in *Il combattimento* of 1624. Schütz partially applied his new experience in *Symphoniae sacrae I* (1629), a collection of twenty Latin works for one to three solo voices of varying ranges, and one to four instruments in a variety of combinations – violins, recorders, shawms, cornetti, trumpets and trombones, all with organ continuo. A classic example from this set is 'Fili mi, Absalon,' a setting of David's lament for his son, for bass solo, four trombones and organ continuo, in which he shows great depth of feeling and poignant interpretation.

Meanwhile, the Elector of Saxony had vacillated in his allegiance to Protestant and then to imperial forces, with the result that both armies wrought vengeance in turn and laid Saxony waste. Conditions became intolerable and Schütz now made the first of his visits to Christian IV's court at Copenhagen in September 1633, where he worked as Kapellmeister until 1635. His

works there have been lost, but surviving libretti show that he composed an opera-ballet and other stage works.

Back in Dresden, Schütz composed the first so-called German Requiem, his *Musikalische Exequien* (1636), for the funeral of Prince Heinrich of Gera, a patron of the arts and a personal friend. He uses the Venetian divided-choir principle, each choir with its own organ continuo. The same year he also published his first set of *Kleine geistliche Concerten* (Little Spiritual Concertos), followed by a second set in 1639. This was the worst period of the war, and Schütz's works reflect this in his meager scoring; the pieces in these two sets are for one to five voices with a continuo for organ and string bass – in the rare pieces where instruments are included he does not specify them but leaves the choice to the performers. The pieces are intended for church or domestic use, and one is given the impression that Schütz had in mind a few people gathered together for solace and brief forgetfullness of the misery surrounding them. Between the publication of these two sets Schütz may again have fled to the Copenhagen court, from August 1637 to 1638. He certainly returned on one last occasion, when he composed his *Symphoniae sacrae II*, which he presented in manuscript to Crown Prince Christian. These are settings of scriptural texts in German (unlike his first set) for one to three solo voices with two instruments and continuo. In the late 1640s, Schütz composed his best-known Passion setting, *The Seven Words from the Cross*, a deeply meditative work which reflects the composer's life-long personal faith and devotion as well as giving a moving portrayal of the events of the crucifixion.

The Peace of Westphalia, 1648, disintegrated the Holy Roman Empire into 360 secular and ecclesiastical principalities, 1,500 small independent states and 100 free towns and cities. The proliferation of independent German states worked in due time towards the ascendancy of German music, in that each state, no matter how small, established its own group of musicians, though these varied greatly in quality and numbers according to financial resources and ambition for prestige. In addition to official court duties at Dresden – and elsewhere when accompanying electoral visits – Schütz's advice and services were in demand at other courts and cities, and, because of his reputation, pupils came to him from far and near.

In the year of the Peace Schütz published his *Geistliche Chor Musik* (Sacred Choral Music), dedicated to Leipzig city council and St Thomas's choir. This marks the point where the pupil of Gabrieli and the admirer of Monteverdi became German again. It was his intention to revert to the *a cappella* principle of older counterpoint, but, as in his *Cantiones sacrae* of 1625, he says it was his publisher who persuaded him to add a *basso continuo*. These twenty-nine motets are in five, six and seven parts, some in the old choir-motet style, and others for solo voices with instruments. In 1650 he published his *Symphoniae sacrae III*, a collection of twenty-

Left: A fine portrait of Jan Pieterszoon Sweelinck, painted by his brother in 1606.

Below: A seventeenth-century Dutch interior. The instruments are a virginal made in Antwerp and a theorbo-lute.

had now reached the age of eighty-six, composed his last works in 1671 – his settings of Psalms 119 and 100, and his *Deutsches Magnificat*. With the last work, Schütz returns after sixty years to Gabrieli's Venetian organ galleries with his two spaced choirs (*cori spezzati*). In his dedication to the Elector, he says that this *Magnificat*, a canticle dear to his heart, should be sung 'by eight voices with two organs, by two musical choirs placed opposite one another above the organs.'

• Cantors of St Thomas's •

It is significant that Saxony played a major role in the development of German music before Bach, musical culture at Leipzig waxing parallel with that at Dresden and then surpassing it. Originally an Augustinian foundation, St Thomas's Church formed a choir school in 1212, providing boys and youths with a sound musical and general education, followed by the

one German compositions for three to six voices and two instruments, frequently with optional supplementary vocal and instrumental choirs.

In 1651 Schütz was so dissatisfied with the state of music at the Dresden court that he addressed a letter to the privy secretary in terms such as no musician would have dared to use to his employer up to that time. Conditions began to improve, and so started the 'Golden Age' of Dresden court music. The Elector died in 1657 and was succeeded by Johan Georg II, who combined his princely chapel, consisting mainly of young Italian musicians, with the existing court music establishment. He relieved Schütz, now aged seventy-two, of his more onerous duties; though active to his death, he seems to have spent his last fifteen years in semi-retirement.

At the request of the new Elector, Schütz composed the *Christmas Story* (1664), a work that has delightful characterizations of Mary, Joseph, angels, shepherds, high priests, Herod, and the Magi, and uses a colorful variety of *obbligato* instruments. To this period also belong the three settings of the *Passion* – according to *St Luke* (*c.*1653), *St Matthew* (1666), and *St John* (*c.*1666). These are liturgical works which mark the highest point in the development of the ancient choral Passion, in which the parts of the Evangelist, Christ and other participants were sung by three priests at the high altar, with the *turbae* (crowd parts) sung by the choir. They are *not* concert hall works – indeed, they achieve full significance only when performed in the appropriate liturgical office as an act of devotion by a congregation which understands the gospel narrative in German, otherwise the long, unaccompanied, plainsong recitatives become dull and largely meaningless. Schütz, who

opportunity to matriculate at Leipzig University. The cantor of St Thomas's also held the directorship of music at St Nicholas's, had the oversight of music in the other three Leipzig churches and, in addition to singing, taught Latin and other subjects in St Thomas's School. In due time this appointment, like that at the Marienkirche, Lübeck, became one of the most coveted musical posts in Germany. In 1519 Luther had made his famous Disputation in Leipzig, which thereafter became a bastion of Lutheran biblical and Augustinian theology, with the founding of a tradition of elaborate church music to support it. The succession of cantors before Bach all contributed to this development.

Sethus Calvisius (1556-1615), the first of these, was widely cultured – composer, teacher, astronomer and chronologist; he was also, like his friend Michael Praetorius, a theoretician who influenced musical and intellectual life in Saxony and beyond. In 1597 he published his *Harmonia cantionum ...*, the first Leipzig hymn book, which contained 115 four-part chorales with the melody in the top part (instead of in the tenor, as formerly).

His successor, Johann Hermann Schein (1586-1630), gifted both as musician and poet, prolific in his output of church, secular and instrumental music, was one of Bach's most illustrious predecessors. Like Praetorius, he did not study in Italy – indeed, he never left Saxony – but he was fully acquainted with the works of the Gabrielis, Viadana, Monteverdi and other exponents of modern Italian styles.

In 1616 Schein took up his appointment as cantor at Leipzig. He had just published his first collection of church music, *Cymbalum Sionium* (1615), thirty motets equally to Latin and German texts, mostly biblical, and a single canzona. These settings, for five to twelve voices, show his assimilation of the Venetian polychoral antiphonal style. Schein's most important pioneer work in Germany was the publication of the first part of his *Opella Nova* (1618). His title continues, 'composed in the current style of Italian invention,' and these thirty motets, for three to five voices, reflect Viadana's sacred concertos of 1602, reprinted in Germany in 1609. This is Schein's first use of *basso continuo* – he refers users to Viadana's manner of realizing the bass, and provides a part for organ, harpsichord or theorbo, as well as one for trombone, bassoon, or bass viol. Like most German composers, he founds these pieces on Lutheran chorales. The second part of his *Opella Nova* (1626), twenty-seven motets to German texts and five to Latin, goes much further. Though mostly settings of biblical texts, only about a third are chorale-based, and his three- to six-part texture with *basso continuo* includes *obbligato* instruments and solo voices, and *soli/tutti* antiphonal contrasts. His poetic instinct shows in a heightened text interpretation, developed over the intervening eight years, and in an enriched scoring. Between the two parts of *Opella Nova* he had published his *Fontana d'Israel* (*Israelis Brünnlein*, 1623), composed 'in the specially graceful manner of the Italian madrigal.' In

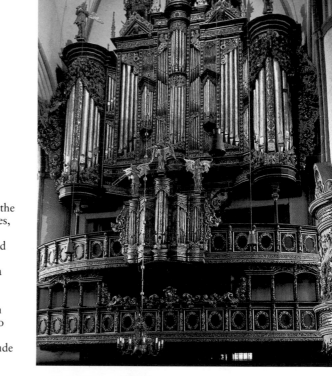

Right: The organ in the church of St Johannes, Lüneburg, built by Heinrich Niehoff and dating from 1553. Niehoff was one of a famous family of German and Netherlandish organ builders. He was also responsible for the instrument in the Oude Kerk, Amsterdam.

Left: The celebrated organ in Frederiksborg Castle, Denmark, the work of Esaias Compenius, member of another family of German organ builders.

these twenty-six settings of German biblical texts for five to six voices and continuo he explores all possibilities of word-painting and emotional expression of the new Italian madrigal, using great freedom and boldness in melodic and harmonic resources, frequently with subtle chromaticisms. Other publications to be noted are *Banchetto Musicale* (1617) – twenty instrumental suites; *Musica Boscareccia* (1621, 1626 and 1628) – fifty settings of Schein's own poems in Italian villanella ('rustic part-song')

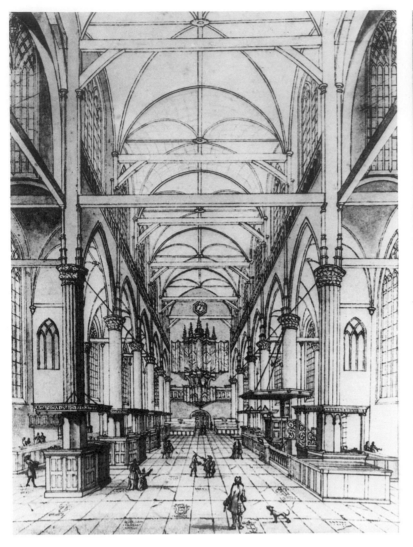

suites in his *Neue Clavier-Übung* of 1689, adding a first section of keyboard sonatas to this and publishing a second section in 1692. These sonata publications proved popular and he followed them with a further set of seven in *Frische Clavier Früchte* (1696). Four years later he published his *Biblical Sonatas*, a set of six descriptive keyboard pieces which are famed as early examples of program music.

Above: Drawing of the Oude Kerk (Old Church) in Amsterdam, where J. P. Sweelinck was organist. His father before him, and then his son, held the post from around 1564 to 1652 – an unbroken span of nearly a century.

Above right: Samuel Scheidt, one of Bach's most important German predecessors in the field of organ music. He was a pupil of Sweelinck in Amsterdam.

style, apt for voices or instruments; and his *Cantional* (1627) – over 200 chorales, including about 80 original melodies.

Schein's successor, Tobias Michael, published eighty works from 1634/5 to his death in 1657, including many fine examples of the early cantata type. With his successors Sebastian Knüpfer and Johann Schelle, a high point is reached in the development of concerted church music on the basis of the Lutheran chorale. Bach's immediate predecessor Johann Kuhnau, appointed organist of St Thomas's in 1684 and founder of the Leipzig Collegium Musicum in 1688, was the most progressive of Leipzig musicians before Bach. Though he wrote many chorale-based cantatas, he realized that further attempts at development of this structure would result in stagnation, and his great contribution was in his reconciliation of these traditional forms with the operatic elements of recitative and the *da capo* aria, binding these diverse elements into a coherent setting of the complete text. The 'motor-energy' of his rhythms and instrumentally conceived thematic material place him in the period of the late-baroque – a small step before Bach. Kuhnau was also progressive in his keyboard writing, effectively translating the form of the Italian chamber sonata to the keyboard. He published sets of dance-derived

• Organ and keyboard music •

Samuel Scheidt (1587-1654), like Handel a century later, was born in Halle, Saxony, and from 1603/4 until 1607/8 occupied the same post as organist of the Moritzkirche that Handel held for a year. His church works show that he, like Schütz and Schein, was quick to adopt new Italian trends and adapt them to Lutheran traditions, but it is in his organ works that he takes the lead in Germany, sharing this honor with Holstein composers. In about 1608 he journeyed to Amsterdam and spent the next three or four years studying under Jan P. Sweelinck (1562-1621), the greatest organist and organ teacher of his time.

Scheidt's *Cantiones sacrae* (1620), is a set of thirty-nine *a cappella* (unaccompanied, or with organ 'shadowing' the voices) double-choir motets, some to Latin texts, others on German psalms and chorales. These are attributable to Flemish-English models rather than Venetian; only in one does he add instruments. His next set, *Concertus sacri I* (1622), owes something more to Venice; it contains three settings of the *Magnificat*, a Lutheran Mass, and six Latin and one German bible-text settings for two to twelve voices, with instruments which accompany and provide interludes or 'symphonies'. Four further sets are extant – *Newe geistliche Concerten*, 1631, 1634, 1635 and 1640. They belong to the period of Swedish occupation of Saxony, and the rigors of war forced him to reduce his scoring to a minimum. His setting of Psalm 103, 'Nun lob, mein Seel, den Herren,' for solo alto, tenor and bass, double choir, instruments and *continuo* is an example of the lavish, polychoral settings he was seldom able to realize.

Scheidt's three-section *Tabulatura nova* (1624) for organ set new standards and marked out new paths in German keyboard composition. Up to this time German keyboard writing had consisted largely of *Coloriren* (coloring), basically the embellishment of melodies with seemingly aimless running passages. Scheidt rejected this in favor of organic development of subject material and motivic imitation within the texture. The first section of *Tabulatura nova* contains sets of variations on Latin hymns, Lutheran chorales and secular songs and dances, and the second consists of fugues, canons, echo toccatas and so on, both sections aimed at the virtuoso player. The third section, aimed at the serious, 'musically-minded' player, contains settings of the Mass, *Magnificat*, psalms and other pieces, in which the organ expounds on the plainsong in alternate verses, an early Renaissance technique greatly developed by Scheidt. Scheidt's work is valuable also for his innovations in notation, his detailed registration and his extensive use of the pedals.

In Germany the organ, with its potential for contrapuntal texture, had taken precedence over the harpsichord – indeed, over all instruments. The first German keyboard composer of rank is Johann Jacob Froberger (1616-67), who was court organist at Vienna from 1637 to 1657, spending his first four years studying under Frescobaldi in Rome. He journeyed to England and was befriended by Christopher Gibbons, and

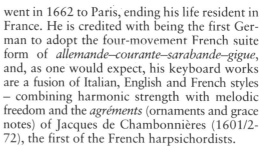

Top: Engraved title-page of an edition of Johann Kuhnau's *Neue Clavier-Übung* (New Keyboard Exercise), published in 1689. Kuhnau was Bach's immediate predecessor as cantor of St Thomas's in Leipzig.

Below: Title-page of Johann Rist's *Hausmusik*. Rist was a clergyman-poet, many of whose verses, secular and sacred, were set to music and became popular songs of the period.

went in 1662 to Paris, ending his life resident in France. He is credited with being the first German to adopt the four-movement French suite form of *allemande–courante–sarabande–gigue*, and, as one would expect, his keyboard works are a fusion of Italian, English and French styles – combining harmonic strength with melodic freedom and the *agréments* (ornaments and grace notes) of Jacques de Chambonnières (1601/2-72), the first of the French harpsichordists.

Johann Pachelbel (1653-1706), a disciple of J. Kaspar Kerll in Vienna and organist in turn at Stuttgart, Gotha and Nuremberg, bridged the Austrian/south German virtuoso style of organ playing and the more able, developed style of middle and north Germany. His organ toccatas, often built on long pedal points, rely more on virtuosic *Coloriren* and are mostly lacking in the harmonic strength and fugal development associated with Buxtehude, Bruhns, and others of the north Elbe school. Bach's indebtedness to him lies in his organ chorale partitas (suites, or variations), fugues (with the chorale opening treated as the subject) and chorale preludes (in which the melody was either decorated or accompanied by rhythmic figuration). Georg Böhm (1661-1733) was organist at Lüneburg and also influenced the young Bach – his chorale partitas are notable for using French *agréments*. Pachelbel and Böhm, like Kuhnau, stand at the threshold of the high Baroque.

• Music in the north •

The close ties between Germany and Denmark make it important also to consider the musical life of that country, in particular during the reign of King Christian IV (1588-1648), which marked a new epoch in Danish cultural life. The King was an architect, building and rebuilding many castles and palaces, but his main interest was music. He established a larger *cappella* than either Queen Elizabeth or James I of England (by 1640 employing thirty-one singers and forty-six players), importing musicians from England, Italy, Poland, Germany and Flanders, and, from 1599, sending his most promising native musi-

Left: An ingenious painting on a ceiling in Rosenborg Castle, Denmark, showing musicians at the court of Christian v (1670-99). Going round it (clockwise) there are cornetts, trombones or sackbuts, lutes and viols.

Below left: Guitar, inlaid with tortoiseshell and ivory, made in Hamburg in 1693 by Joachim Tielke.

Below: An elaborately framed portrait of the Hamburg organist and composer Johann Adam Reincken (1623-1722) by Gottfried Kneller.

cians to study under Giovanni Gabrieli. Among these were Hans Nielsen (Giovanni Fonteio) and Mogens Pedersøn (Magno Petreo), each publishing sets of madrigals in Venice before returning to Copenhagen – Nielsen's set of 1606 is the first known madrigal publication by a pupil of Gabrieli. John Dowland was court lutenist from 1598 to 1606; the famed English violists William and Christian Brade served there during three periods; and Sweelinck's pupil, Melchior Schildt, was court organist between 1626 and 1629. A peak was reached during Schütz's first visit, in 1633-5, when he composed and directed the music for Crown Prince Christian's wedding celebrations in 1634. Among many famed instruments, mention must be made of the 27-stop organ built by Esaias Compenius for Christian IV in 1612 – so noteworthy for its time that Praetorius described it in detail in his *Syntagma Musicum*. The remarkable flowering began to wither from 1640 due to economic decline, although Denmark had withdrawn from the war in 1629.

Holstein, or the north Elbe region, which is bounded by the River Elbe to the south and the border with Denmark to the north, included three important musical centers – the Hanseatic cities of Hamburg and Lübeck, and Gottorf, where the grand dukes of Gottorf-Holstein had their main seat. Close cultural, economic and political relations existed between Holstein and Denmark with complete freedom of movement. Similar cultural relations existed with Flanders, especially Amsterdam, whence spread the influence of Sweelinck, his pupils and followers. Characteristics of the Holstein region which differentiate it from the rest of Germany

are that the organist achieved a position of supremacy over the cantor, that the city musicians of the Hanseatic ports became of great importance, and that a public concert organization developed at an early date. Musicians there were versatile and, in addition to taking the lead in organ composition, established the region's progressiveness in three other areas – the sacred aria, the church cantata and music for strings.

Franz Tunder (1614-67) was appointed at the age of eighteen to the key position of court organist at Gottorf, a flourishing musical foundation which attracted leading musicians such as William Brade and his sons, Englishmen who established the region's ascendancy in string writing. In 1640 Tunder obtained the key post of organist at the Marienkirche, Lübeck, where his new association with the wealthy, culturally-minded business community gave him new freedom and opportunity. His predecessor, Peter Hasse, had introduced Thursday morning concerts at the city council's request, held before the assembly of the Stock Exchange, and Tunder inherited this custom. In January 1646 he broached a plan to extend these concerts to include vocal and instrumental participation, and the city agreed. These evening concerts began the long tradition of the famed *Abendmusiken*, which played a major role in establishing and developing the forms of the church cantata and oratorio.

Only fifteen of Tunder's organ compositions survive, but, given their virtuosity and structure, as well as the constant demands of concert recitals and church services, they must represent but a fraction of his total output. His chorale fantasias show his great virtuosity, the cumulative

Below: A painting of 1675, believed to show three of the major figures in North German music of the time: Johann Theile (playing bass viol), J. A. Reincken (at the keyboard) and Dietrich Buxtehude (head resting on hand).

interest being maintained, for example, throughout the 257 measures of 'Was kann uns kommen an für Not' – this may be compared with Scheidt's *tour de force* in his longer fantasia on 'Ich ruf zu Dir' from his *Tabulatura nova*. Tunder's surviving *Praeludia* are historically important; each consists of a four-voice fugue preceded by a free toccata and followed by a shorter toccata in which there is often a thematic link with the fugue subject. This is the beginning of the two-movement 'prelude and fugue,' 'toccata and fugue' and 'fantasia and fugue' taken over from Tunder by Buxtehude, Bruhns and Reincken, and finally developed by Bach.

Tunder's sacred arias, solo motets and cantatas are among the most progressive and satisfying of their kind in Germany at that time; the solo works, with three to five solo strings, were probably intended for the limited space of the organ loft, while the cantatas, with their rich texture of five vocal and five string parts, were performed in the choir gallery under the direction of his son-in-law, the cantor Samuel Franck. The soprano aria, 'An Wasserflüssen Babylon,' 'con 5 viole,' illustrates the *Vorimitation* technique he used as an emotional as well as a structural principle (the string *ritornello* introducing the theme in diminution and close imitation before each section) – a technique used by Bach up to his last work, the organ prelude 'Wenn wir in höchsten Nöthen sein.' Tunder's typically expressive use of chromatic sequence suggests an intimate knowledge of Carissimi's oratorio style. His choir-gallery works are equally expressive, full of rythmical vivacity and élan, and show a complete absorption of Italian sacred concerto style. This is evident in his settings of German as well as Latin texts, for example, in 'Hosanna dem Sohne Davids' (*soli, tutti* and strings, each in five parts), and the Vespers Psalm 127, 'Nisi Dominus' (same scoring), capturing the *concitato* style of Monteverdi's 1610 *Vespers* and later madrigals.

As with Lübeck, the growing mercantile prosperity of Hamburg was reflected in its cultural progressiveness and the attraction such conditions had for musicians both native and foreign to Holstein – conditions which nurtured excellence in church music, virtuoso organ playing and composition, aria and song writing, a corps of city musicians, public concerts and a public opera house. William Brade served there during three different periods, his pupil Johann Schop founded a violin school there, and Heinrich Scheidemann (*c.*1595-1663) brought Sweelinck's style to Hamburg and north Germany when he succeeded his father as organist of the Catharinenkirche in about 1625. The musical dynasties of the Baltzar, Ebel and Hasse families worked to the advantage of music in Lübeck, and the same is true of the Praetorius family in Hamburg, among them Jacob Praetorius II, organist of St Peter. Schütz's pupil Matthias Weckmann (1619-74) was sent to Hamburg to study under Jacob Praetorius II and, from 1655, was organist of St Jacob and St Gertrude. Christoph Bernhard (1628-92) arrived from Dresden and, in 1660, collaborated with Weckmann in founding the Collegium Musicum, a public concert organization which performed regularly in the refectory of St Mary's Cathedral. This lasted until Weckmann's death, when Bernhard returned to Dresden.

Johann Adam Reincken was a pupil of Scheidemann and succeeded him at the Catharinenkirche in 1663, holding the post until his death. He was famed throughout Germany and beyond as a virtuoso performer (visited by Bach on several occasions between 1700 and 1720), and his compositions display rhythmic vitality, dexterity in pedal as well as manual writing, and original – even ingenious – registration.

Below: The autograph of a keyboard piece by Johann Froberger, dated 1656; it is a lament for Ferdinand, son of Emperor Ferdinand III, who had died two years earlier at the age of twenty-one.

Below right: Title-page of a 1637 edition of Frescobaldi's keyboard compositions. Frescobaldi's works had a strong influence on German keyboard music of the period, mainly through his pupil Froberger.

The hiatus left by the end of the Collegium Musicum was filled, to a certain extent, by his founding, together with Johann Theile, Hamburg's burgher-promoted Opera. It opened on 2 January 1678 with Theile's *Adam und Eva*, a *Singspiel* on a biblical subject which set the style for several years; his *Die Geburt Christi* (Birth of Christ) was produced in 1681.

It is highly significant that the twenty-year-old Bach should have specially chosen to make an extended visit to this region. After obtaining four weeks' leave of absence from Arnstadt, he began his 300-mile trek to Lübeck in October 1705 to arrive in time for Buxtehude's *Abendmusiken* concerts, remaining there for some four months enthralled by what he heard.

Dietrich Buxtehude (c.1637-1707) was probably born in Oldesloe, half-way between Hamburg and Lübeck, and must have received his early musical training from his father, who held an organist's post at Helsingør, where Dietrich was himself appointed organist of the Marienkirche. Buxtehude and Tunder almost certainly had personal connections, for, during Tunder's last years there seems to have been an understanding that Buxtehude would become his son-in-law, and on this basis Tunder recommended him to Lübeck city council as his successor. He was elected organist on 11 April 1668 and married Anna Margaretha on 3 August. He completely reorganized the Thursday public concerts, concentrating them on the last two Sundays after Trinity and the second, third and fourth Sundays in Advent; they followed the afternoon Vespers service and lasted about an hour. Elaborate figural vocal and instrumental music featured more prominently than usual in the morning and afternoon services of the first Sunday in Advent. He received financial and moral support from the burghers and built galleries left and right of the organ loft to accommodate some twenty-four singers and twelve to fourteen players, with room for a portative regal (small chamber organ) as needed. As with

Tunder's concerts, admission was free. At first his performances were of shorter choral and orchestral works, but they moved on to the stage where each concert was devoted to a single, full-length oratorical work. During Bach's 1705-6 visit two major oratorical works were performed – *Castrum Doloris* (*in memoriam* Emperor Leopold II) and *Templum honoris* (for the accession of Emperor Joseph I), though the music is lost.

Buxtehude was one of the most prolific composers of his time, his scope including liturgical music, cantatas and oratorical works for services and concerts, solo arias and cantatas, organ preludes, fugues, toccatas, chorale variations and fantasias, and chamber music including nineteen keyboard suites. Some 150 cantatas and 100 organ works of his are extant, but it is certain that this represents but a small part of his output; in the surviving libretti for the five Advent concerts of 1700, not one work corresponds with any available today.

Judging from features common to both, Buxtehude's cantata *Jesu, meine Freude* may well have served as Bach's model for his five-part motet on the same chorale (BWV227), and Bach's 'St Anne' Organ Fugue (BWV552) is built on the principle of Buxtehude's two- and three-section fugues in which each section develops the same subject but in a different rhythm. The first composer named in the quotation from Bach's *Nekrolog* is Nicolaus Bruhns (1665-97), Buxtehude's most brilliant pupil. His chorale fantasia on 'Nun komm der Heiden Heiland,' shows the finest paraphrase technique of any composer before Bach, who must have known very many more such works. Though it is arguable that Buxtehude was Bach's greatest precursor, it would be foolish to think of his vast output merely as a preparation for Bach. Buxtehude's music deserves to stand at the summit of his age in its own right.

Below: Title-page of the 1699 edition of the *Hexachordum Apollinis* by Johann Pachelbel – six sets of airs and variations for organ or harpsichord.

Below right: Autograph of the soprano solo part of an aria by Franz Tunder, organist at the Marienkirche, Lübeck. He was succeeded there by his son-in-law Buxtehude.

THE ITALIAN BAROQUE

ARTHUR HUTCHINGS & ERIC CROSS

Opposite: An Italian violinist of the early eighteenth century, painted by a Bolognese artist. Although he has sometimes been identified as Vivaldi (or Corelli), the subject is unknown.

Although the period loosely defined as the Baroque enables us to recognize the ascendance of sounds which increasingly expressed the common humanity of listeners beyond natural frontiers, these were born and nurtured in Italy. Pre-eminent among them were the sounds of instruments of violin shape accompanied by chord-playing instruments; indeed, the baroque period could as well be called the continuo period. With few exceptions, vocal or instrumental ensembles of the seventeenth and eighteenth centuries involved at least one accompanying instrument reinforcing the bass and sounding the harmonies above it. To perform a *concerto grosso* or one of Bach's Passions without such an instrument, or with such an instrument inaudible, is to falsify the composer's intentions. A trio-sonata is not usually well served as a duet for two violins and keyboard with no fourth instrument – for example cello or bassoon – reinforcing the bass. On manuscripts and scores the continuo was normally indicated only as a single-line bass, with figures below the stave where other harmonies than common chords in root position were required. Corelli's op.1 Trio-Sonatas of 1681 specify 'col basso per l'organo,' which indicates that they were intended for church use. However, they were not thought desecrated if they were heard in concert rooms where there was no organ. His op.2 Chamber Sonatas are for two violins 'e violone o cembalo,' and his op.3, for the same string instruments, mentions archlute and organ as possible continuo chord players.

The sonata and concerto were the two most important instrumental forms ascendant in Italy during the seventeenth and eighteenth centuries. Although the term sonata was used to distinguish an instrumental piece from a cantata or vocal one, its form was at first that of a French chanson, in sections which included polyphonic texture; hence the alternative title, canzona. Until about 1650 a vast number of 'canzone,' 'canzone da sonar' or 'sonate' defy any other distinction than that of their titles. Moreover, many of them belong not to the ascendance of the trio-sonata but of the orchestral sound in concertos, suites and overtures. The best-known of Giovanni Gabrieli's sumptuous instrumental works, the *Sonata pian' e forte* of 1597, comes from a set entitled *Sacrae Symphoniae*. Among his later *Canzoni e Sonate*, issued posthumously in 1615, no distinct differences of structure mark the differing titles. The impressive feature is *concertato* – a term still used to designate antiphony or interplay between groups, which were called *cori* by Gabrieli's contemporaries, whether the groups were vocal or instrumental.

Concertato suggested sequences and 'echoes,' and punctuation between passages by cadences at various pitches, leading to the ternary and binary key-schemes of late baroque and classical sonatas and quartets. These features were especially advanced as sonatas reflected changes of taste in vocal music. When madrigals were accompanied, the voices had no need to supply the bass or other essentials of harmony. Madrigals became solos, duets or trios with continuo; so did sonatas.

The trio-sonata made most progress in northern parts of Italy. Bologna, Modena, Venice, Rome and several other northern Italian cities either contained or were near the residences of a music-loving aristocracy and wealthy cardinals, and the music at some of the greater churches was under aristocratic as well as ecclesiastical patronage. Limiting mention to outstanding composers from only three cities – Modena, Venice and Bologna – historical preference must be given to those associated with Modena in surveying the development of the sonata. Uccellini, Stradella and G. M. Bononcini extended violin technique both in *sonate da camera* – suites including dance forms – and in *sonate da chiesa* – of alternating fast and slow movements, some of which would not have sounded incongruous in chamber sonatas but were not actually entitled 'sarabanda,' 'gavotta' or 'giga.' With the Modenese School the polyphony of the old canzona is retained, especially in the first or second movements of some of their church sonatas, but the trio-sonata, church or chamber, is consolidated as a clear form of four or five movements (not sections), destined to be known by no other name.

Yet the composers of the Modenese School were outshone by Giovanni Legrenzi (1626-90), *maestro di coro* of the Ospedale dei Mendicanti, Venice, and later director of music at St Mark's, whose operas and choral works also attest to his characteristic vigor and clarity in composition. The earlier overtures and incidental music for operas in Venice – for example, those of Cavalli – often resembled sonatas with extra violins, but Legrenzi's church sonatas, the last set of which was published in 1685, show a contrapuntal interest – even in the lovely 'sarabandes' – which was hardly bettered for its assurance before Bach, who paid tribute to Legrenzi by using one of his themes as the subject of an organ fugue.

Until the end of the century, however, Bologna claimed pre-eminence as a training ground for string composition. Bologna had no famous opera theater or opera composers; its atmosphere was hieratic, and there was a huge demand for both church and chamber sonatas. The orchestra at the basilica of San Petronio,

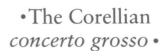

Below: Arcangelo Corelli (1653-1713).

Bottom: The center of Bologna, where from 1666 Corelli studied the violin with Giovanni Benvenuti and Leonardo Brugnoli. In 1670 he was admitted to the Accademia Filarmonica in the city.

• The Corellian *concerto grosso* •

Michael Praetorius in his *Syntagma musicum*, Part 3 (1619) derived concerto from *concertare* (to compete); he could as validly have derived it from *conserere* (to consort or participate). He certainly stated that Italians sometimes used concerto and symphonia as equivalents – a point already noted with reference to Giovanni Gabrieli. In 1602 Viadana issued the first part of his *Cento concerti ecclesiastici*, often cited because, though they use one, two, three or four singers, the accompaniment is indicated by an unfigured organ bass with directions about its interpretation. The only connection between this music and the later concerto lies in the contrast (*concertato*) of vocal and instrumental sound.

This contrast could also be purely instrumental in pieces which, although not called concertos, nonetheless anticipate salient features of later works known by no other name. Thus, during the 1670s, Alessandro Stradella (1638/9-82) composed pieces which have been called 'incipient *concerti grossi*' because they conspicuously employed contrasts of *tutti* and *concertino*. They may have been used as overtures to operas or cantatas, and it is clear that Stradella thought his contrasts of *tutti* and *concertino* unfamiliar enough to warrant explanation.

Some of Stradella's works are designated 'concerto grosso', by which it seems he meant simply 'full ensemble'. It was the violinist and composer Arcangelo Corelli (1653-1713), however, who first used the term as the title of a specific musical genre. Corelli traveled in Germany and France, but for most of his creative life he lived in Rome, where he remained under the princely patronage of Cardinal Ottoboni. He is said to have been meek and highly self-critical, an observation supported by the meticulous preparation of his published works and the fact that they only reached op.6. They comprise four sets of trio-sonatas (opp.1-4), the enormously popular twelve sonatas with only

which was patronized by the Este family of Modena and included virtuoso players from the Modenese court, began its most splendid period after the appointment in 1657 of Maurizio Cazzati (*c*.1620-77).

Cazzati's pupil G. B. Vitali (1632-92) was renowned as a violinist-composer, and it is widely believed that the 1684 set of Vitali's sonatas provided models for Purcell; certainly the sonata entitled *La Graziani* supports the belief. Vitali's many publications between 1666 and his death show the gradual acceptance of *sonate da camera* instead of correnti, balletti, gighe and so on, and similar titles were used when *sonate* designated the church type. Late in life (1689) he published *Artifici musicali*, a pre-Bachian demonstration of contrapuntal skill. His son, Tommaso, who edited some of his father's sonatas, brought the music at the Modenese court to a peak of fame.

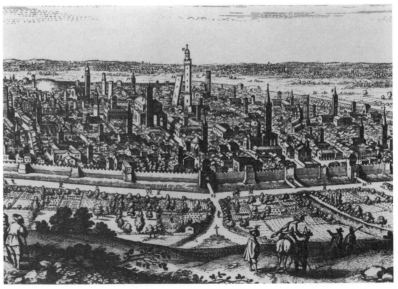

Above: Title-page of *Harmonia d'Affetti Devoti*, 1655, a collection of motets and psalm settings by Giovanni Legrenzi. They were his first published work in a long career, in the course of which he did much to establish the forms and structures of the baroque sonata, as well as contributing to the development of opera and oratorio in Venice.

Below: Opening of a *sonata di viole* by Alessandro Stradella, in effect a *concerto grosso*, a form he helped bring into being. The score clearly shows the antiphonal treatment of the three *concertino* instruments (two violins and lute) and the *concerto grosso* of viols.

one violin and continuo (op.5), and the twelve *concerti grossi* (op.6). Although these were first published posthumously in 1714, Corelli's pupil Georg Muffat declared that he heard at least some of them during the 1680s in Rome. It has been suggested that Corelli did not want them to be played inadequately by those unfamiliar with his own standards or that, intimidated by his own success, especially with op.5, he withheld them until he had often used and revised them.

The instruments specified by Corelli on the title-pages of his twelve *concerti grossi* are a necessary minimum. Muffat describes a splendid performance of Corelli's concertos in Rome, given by a 'large ensemble,' and Corelli's title and demand of no more than nine players – if the unmentioned keyboard continuo is included – ends with the words 'che si potranno radoppiare' – 'which may be augmented.' But it is essential to have two violins and cello for the *concertino*, as well as two other violins, viola and 'basso.' We assume that only one organ or harpsichord accompanied both *concertino* and *tutti*, but we know that sometimes, with larger forces, each had its own keyboard continuo. All twelve of Corelli's *concerti grossi* use a *concertino* comprising the constituent instruments of the trio-sonata.

The term *concerto grosso* has been loosely applied to other baroque concertos than the Corellian form, for even in the great twelve which Handel purposely entitled op.6 to honor Corelli we find several which are like suites (Corelli himself did not keep to a fixed number of movements) and some often called *ripieno* (meaning 'full') concertos, without *concertino*, their texture formed from groupings of the full orchestra. Moreover Handel normally began his movements *tutti*, and his *concertino* brought thematic contrast, its entries being therefore less frequent but more arresting than in Corelli's concertos.

Although Corelli's conception of concerto design hardly survived his death in his native Italy, and was prolonged only by some of his pupils, such as Geminiani, the influence of his musical vocabulary and style was enormous.

He was admired as a performer whose facial expression reflected intense emotion and was the supreme stylist of his period, expressing the emotions and ideals of his age as no one else.

• Bologna and Venice •

If Corelli had not existed, the transition from the canzona sonata to the late baroque three-movement concerto could be completely documented by works heard during meetings of the Bologna Accademia Filarmonica and in the basilica of San Petronio. Well-kept registers of players reveal that on ferial days the church used only between six and twelve instrumentalists, apart from the organists. There are still two organs with similar cases facing each other across the chancel. One of them still contains fifteenth-century ranks; the other, less heavy but with bright stops, was called the 'organo del concertino' and was used to accompany solos or small vocal or instrumental ensembles. Their functions are confirmed by the fact that works requiring the augmented orchestra for high festivals, and what are termed 'occasioni' and 'funzioni,' have figured bases under both organ parts. One can believe that sonatas by Cazzati, dall'Abaco, Corelli, Vitali and others were often played with more than one instrument to each part, and that, as the leader may have been expected to introduce ornamentation in slow movements and cadenzas in others, the treatment of sonatas at Bologna led to solo concertos. As early as 1665 Cazzati published church sonatas with solo trumpet, which could hardly have been widely used if he had not directed that 'a solo violin may be used where no trumpet is available.'

The extra players for special occasions increased until 1695. They came from Modena and the university, and also included fine performers like Count Albergati called 'dilettanti' – a term which at the time referred to 'delighters' in music of professional standard who were not dependent upon their talents for a livelihood. The minutes reveal that the regular orchestra at San Petronio was reduced in 1695, having become too costly. But from that year the special augmented orchestra rose to maximum brilliance. The archives begin to include works for one, two, three or even four trumpets, the finest being by Torelli and Perti. Some are called 'sinfonie,' others 'concerti,' but the titles do not reliably distinguish their designs. Some of them resemble the Venetian 'sinfonia avanti l'opera,' a form of overture noted for its trumpets; but in others the solo trumpets are given regular dialogue and interplay with the strings, as is the solo violin of Torelli's op.8 *concerti grossi*.

Venice had long had strong artistic connections with Vienna and was much visited, as Europe's chief pleasure resort, by the princelings of the German states, accompanied by members of their musical establishments. The four Venetian concertists most admired and most influential in the subsequent development of music in Germany and the rest of Europe were Antonio Vivaldi (1678-1741), Tomaso Albinoni (1671-1751), Alessandro Marcello (1684-1750) and Benedetto Marcello (1686-1739). All composed operas and cantatas, including an enormous number of arias for solo voice, each preceded by an orchestral prelude ending in the tonic key. This was called the 'ritornello' because it returned, in full or compressed form, to frame the main solo sections, which often had short rests punctuated by the return or echo of short ideas from the ritornello. The importance of ritornello technique lay in providing a method of constructing extended movements which were at the same time diversified and satisfactorily unified. Although sometimes, as in some of Vivaldi's concertos speedily written to fulfill a commission, too few ideas are too often repeated, or the music makes too few excursions to other keys than tonic and dominant, usually ritornello technique ensures more diversity. The solo may enter with fresh music or recall

Left: Benedetto Marcello, a noble Venetian who became a member of the city-state's governing Council of Forty. His concertos have many similarities with those of Vivaldi.

Left: Title-page of the L'Estro armonico concertos (op.3) by Vivaldi, dedicated to Ferdinando de' Medici and published in Amsterdam in 1711. They were soon widely disseminated and did much to spread Vivaldi's fame abroad. The arrangements of them by J.S.Bach were probably made as early as 1713/14.

death, he let his younger brother direct the family business, dropped the term 'dilettante' on his title-pages, and substituted 'musico di violino.' He was some seven years older than Vivaldi, yet his ten volumes, each of twelve works, achieve adventure and length by their cycle of tonality. Some in op.5 (1707) and in op.7 (1715) are so similar to specimens in Vivaldi's famous op.3 (1711) that some authorities believe Vivaldi's set to have been published earlier in Venice, and admired by Albinoni. The last and finest of Albinoni's concertos, however, follow in their outer movements the ritornello principle and design that can be regarded as the established form.

The pulsating vigor of Albinoni's sets of *Balletti* was continued in the fast movements of his magnificent *Concerti a cinque con 1 e 2 oboi*, op.9 (1722) and *Concerti a cinque*, op.10 (1737) for strings with solo violin. His extrovert clarity has been mistaken for shallowness, and his slow movements – especially those in the chaconne form of which he was fond – sound less romantic than those of the impassioned Vivaldi, whose ebullient vein is chiefly to the fore in solo parts. Albinoni rarely favors solo parts in high relief but anticipates Bach in maintaining a balance of dialogue. Indeed he was greatly admired by Bach, who used parts from his textures as exercises to be continued or completed by pupils.

Alessandro and Benedetto Marcello were privileged and well educated, holding government positions and composing little for public performance – unless more has yet to be discovered. The younger brother, Benedetto, was the better known outside Italy because of his satirical booklet, *Il teatro alla moda* and his fifty psalms of *Estro Poetico-Armonico* – versified paraphrases, some with continuo only, some with strings. Several of his sonatas are to be found in northern libraries, but only six concertos by him, published in 1708, are known. Since he died at the age of fifty-two, these comparatively early works should not be regarded as proving him

the orchestral gambit, but new material must follow during progress towards the dominant or relative major, which key is immediately confirmed by a full ritornello. Even a simple binary form imposes further invention during the 'unwinding' return to tonic, but the most admired models presage the classical development and reprise, with solo-tutti interplay. The final orchestral ritornello, full or compressed, may accommodate a solo cadenza.

Although Albinoni's family owned paper mills, young Tomaso's devotion to music led him to serve with the Duke of Mantua's chamber players. Returning to Venice after his father's

Above: Interior of St Mark's Basilica in Venice in the eighteenth century. It shows a new Doge addressing the Venetian people.

Below: Musical party at a private house in Venice in the early eighteenth century.

an inferior concertist to his brother, whose best work may have been contemporary with Bach's. Benedetto's solo parts are exceptionally brilliant, his adagios passionate and his textures similar to Vivaldi's, with unison and tremolo effects.

There is no proof that Alessandro's music was performed except in his own house or among other members of the select Arcadian Academy. His six elaborately printed concertos entitled *La Cetra* (The Lyre) do not bear his own name, but his Arcadian one – *Eterio Stinfalico,*

Academia Arcade. The preface to *La Cetra* requests flutes, oboes and bassoons as well as the strings and forbids 'alterations and additions,' which may mean embellishments or cadenzas. Four of the works are in minor keys, and few of them can be called concertos for this or that solo instrument, since solo instruments and groups may vary or change between movements, which do not keep to the normal sequence of three. The third (in B minor), for instance, opens with a long and somber slow movement, without soloist, but is varied by angry loud passages. Chromatic and deliberately dissonant harmonies, abrupt key changes, asymmetrical rhapsody amid neatly balanced phrases – these features were for select hearers. Rarely showing freakish contrivance, these concertos still delight connoisseurs of baroque expression; yet it is the conventionally planned oboe concerto transcribed by Bach and perhaps composed earlier than the others which still seems Alessandro Marcello's most beautiful known work.

•The concertos of Vivaldi•

One of the best violinists at St Mark's in Venice was known as G. B. Rossi – for the unusual reddish-fair hair which earned for his famous son the sobriquet of *il prete rosso* (the red priest). The future priest, Antonio Vivaldi, was

113

Right: Antonio Vivaldi (1678-1741), the red priest, drawn in Rome in 1723 by P. L. Ghezzi. It is the only authenticated portrait of the composer.

Opposite top: Claude Lorrain's print (1662) of Apollo leading the dance of the four seasons to the music of time – a well-known subject (Poussin's painting is the most famous version) for which Vivaldi's 'Four Seasons' Concertos provide a musical counterpart.

Right: Allemanda from one of Vivaldi's op.2 violin sonatas, printed in Venice in 1709. The form of printing is much more primitive than the later Amsterdam editions of Vivaldi's works (*see opposite*).

sections in some of those in Germany), while after 1700 several European cities instituted public concerts, which had already been pioneered in Germany and in London. Above all, no good Italian singer or player lacked prospects as Italian opera became an export industry.

Vivaldi's vast output, which included many commissions from German princes and Kapellmeister, gives him overwhelming pre-eminence in what is today called the Venetian concerto, a three-movement work with ritornelli framing either solo or contrasted sections. It was the favorite baroque form in Germany and the immediate ancestor of the classical concerto.

It is regrettable that the witticism 'Vivaldi wrote not 447 concertos, but the same concerto 447 times' is quoted every time one of his less inventive commissions is sampled. When in poor health and pressed for time (and always glad to receive a fee!), he was capable of filling

a sickly child, not known to have been taught outside his native Venice, where he often deputized for his father. One can understand, however, the unproven belief that he had lessons from Corelli and Legrenzi if an examination is made of his somewhat neglected early trio-sonatas (1705). All sonatas by Vivaldi deserve more frequent performance, if only to counterbalance the impression of rapid procedure and shallow construction in concertos more numerous than a genius should be expected to produce during a life of ill-health and over-work.

Yet it was the concertos of op.3 (1711) and op.4 (c.1714) which first blazed Vivaldi's genius outside Italy, and we are justified in supposing that some were composed before the dates of publication, and most of them for the famous public concerts at the Ospedale della Pietà, an orphanage or foundling hospital for females, where Vivaldi was appointed to the teaching staff in his twenty-fifth year and rapidly rose to an important position.

The municipality also promoted music in three other foundling charities, and it is known that tuition there was sought by some who were not orphans, nor always youthful. Private as well as public money was forthcoming to maintain the many actually or virtually fatherless children in a Venice of vast maritime commerce and frequent naval engagements with the Turks. Encouragement of musical talent by curators of the Ospedali or Conservatori was particularly wise at the time, since a well trained Italian musician could be sure to find employment. Between 1650 and 1750 church and court musical establishments all over Europe were greatly increased (with excellent wind

the three-movement design for this or that performer on a wind or plucked instrument, unaware that posterity would collect the parts and charge him with facility. With notable exceptions, the finest of Vivaldi's concertos are those for string soloists (he was particularly fond of the cello) and are found among nine printed sets from op.3 to op.12, but it must be added that Vivaldi was well acquainted with the technique of wind instruments – hence his admiration of the Dresden and other German orchestras – and that, although printed parts are lacking, oboes, flutes, horns, organs and plucked instruments were seen amplifying the orchestral *tutti* in his Pietà concerts.

There is little need here to examine one tenth of those 447 or other recently alleged total of Vivaldi's concertos. Even if the 'Four Seasons' Concertos of Vivaldi's op.8 had not survived, his artistic and historical importance would have been established by his op.3 *L'Estro armonico* of 1711 and op.4 *La Stravaganza* of *c.*1714. *L'Estro* has been translated as 'whim' or 'fancy,' but a contemporary English phrase is better, 'the divine afflatus,' defining inspiration, like Beethoven's, which could transcend convention. J. S. Bach transcribed and arranged the splendid Venetian models, but the one concerto in *L'Estro* most worthy of Bach himself is no.11, opening with an amalgam of allegro and adagio, with a splendid fugue, followed by a movement labeled *largo e spiccato.*

• Italian opera •

The opening of the first public opera house in Venice in 1637 was one of the most decisive events in seventeenth-century musical history.

Above: Vivaldi's manuscript of the concerto (for 'flute or violin') entitled 'La Notte' (The Night), which was published *c.*1728 as part of op.10. Like the 'Four Seasons,' the work contains descriptive music to match its title.

Left: Early printed edition (Amsterdam, 1725) of the solo violin part for the first of the 'Four Seasons,' 'Spring,' from Vivaldi's op.8 concertos. The program for the work is printed on the score together with the lines of a descriptive poem: 'A. Spring is at hand . . . B. Song of the birds . . . C. The streams run . . . D. Thunder . . . .

Opera, the dominant art form of the baroque period, which began life in the courtly circles of the Florentine nobility, suddenly became available to the general public, and the unique power of music to heighten the emotional content of a drama rapidly caught audiences' imagination. Very soon two further theaters had begun producing musical dramas, and by 1700 nearly four hundred productions had been mounted in seventeen theaters, with as many as seven being open at one time. Venice soon became the leading center for opera, a position which it was to hold well into the eighteenth century.

There were several opera seasons, but the most important was at carnival time. This lasted from 26 December to Shrove Tuesday (theaters were closed during Lent) and was a period when, according to several accounts by foreign visitors, the whole of Venice went mad. It was a time of masking, a custom which broke down social barriers as everyone dressed up; the most popular garb was a black cloak and hood with a white mask, a costume which appears in many Venetian paintings of the time. Though some theaters restricted themselves to low-brow comedies (with 'the most filthy double meanings imaginable,' as Joseph Addison noted with disgust), others put on two or three operas each. The theaters, which were owned by leading families from the Venetian nobility and took their names from the parishes in which they were situated, were normally leased on short-term contracts to a manager or independent entrepreneur. Each contained several tiers of boxes built in a horseshoe shape around the stage, and many of the local noblemen would hire their own personal box, complete with key, for the season. The floor of the theater was reserved for the less exalted members of the audience, and gondoliers were frequently admitted free.

An evening at the opera at the turn of the eighteenth century was a far cry from a visit to Covent Garden, La Scala or the Metropolitan Opera today. People would eat, talk and play cards while the music was in progress. Gambling was a favorite Venetian pastime, and some theaters even had *ridotti*, or gambling salons,

Above: Entrance of Cardinal Ottoboni into Rome. The nephew of Pope Alexander VIII, who acceded in 1689, Pietro Ottoboni became the most important patron of music in Rome. He showed particular favor to Corelli, making him his first violin and director of music and giving him a lodging in his palace. He was a great patron of Roman opera and is also supposed to have written an opera himself – which was not a success – about Columbus's discovery of America.

the use of filters, in the form of bowls of colored water, and of powerful reflectors enabled designers to achieve impressive effects.

One further visual element was that of ballet. Many operas had ballets between the acts, though the music for these was not regarded as an integral part of the main work. Connected to some extent with the art of ballet was a whole code of gestures and actions by which the baroque actor could portray his emotions by the simple movement of an arm or a hand.

Whereas nowadays opera companies produce mainly revivals of repertory works, and a new work is an unusual event, in the seventeenth and eighteenth centuries the opposite was the case. The public demand was for novelty; operas were rarely repeated and, if they were revived, they were usually rearranged. This being so, it is not surprising that the overworked composer often fell back on reusing material from an earlier work that had already proved its popularity. This was a perfectly acceptable practice which can be seen in the works of all the leading musicians of the age, including Bach, Handel and Vivaldi. Sometimes the material borrowed was by another composer (there were no copyright laws), and this is seen at its most blatant in the genre known as the *pasticcio*.

The *pasticcio* (literally 'pie') was a piece involving music by several different composers. It was often put together by an independent impresario using popular arias from various recent operas, thereby creating with very little effort a work whose success was almost guaranteed. As with self-borrowings, it was a practice followed by many famous composers, though artists such as Handel or Vivaldi only resorted to the *pasticcio* when they were acting as their own impresario. Although such a work could just be thrown together with little artistic consideration, the best *pasticci* were dramatically convincing, and Handel's production of *Catone*, assembled from the music of several composers for London in 1732, was even mistaken for his original work.

During the seventeenth century the status of the individual singer gradually rose. By the 1660s and 1670s operatic composers were expected more and more to provide arias with opportunities for vocal display, and the virtuoso singer rapidly came to dominate the genre of *opera seria*. Not surprisingly, the most sought-after singers for Italian opera were Italians themselves, and this held true not only for performances in their native country but also for those in Germany, Austria or even London. The training of young would-be virtuosi was taken very seriously and involved an intensive course covering varied aspects of musical education, with the result that many Italian singers developed phenomenal voices and became star attractions. The composer was expected to tailor all the roles specifically to the abilities (and to hide any failings) of his singers.

Opera seria was dominated by the high voice, and it was, especially, the age of the castrato. This was a singer who, as a young child, underwent castration so that, as he grew older, his lungs developed normally, giving him the power

attached to them. Others provided small anterooms behind each box for eating and socializing, while some proprietors were thoughtful enough to supply the boxes with shutters so that complete privacy could be enjoyed. Thus the opera house was a popular place for political or amorous assignations, aided by the anonymity of the custom of masking. As many of the audience went to the theater several nights a week, they would often see the same opera half a dozen times, so that after a couple of hearings they would pay attention only to their favorite songs or singers. There was also no need to worry about missing a vital element in the plot, as copies of the complete libretto were sold, along with wax candles, at the theater door.

The most important type of baroque opera was the *opera seria* (literally 'serious opera'). This involved various conventions, many of which are foreign to us today, and one vital element was that of spectacular scenery. In the seventeenth century there were countless extravagant sets involving elaborate machines which enabled gods or goddesses to appear or disappear, generally seated on a cloud; scenes to be transformed suddenly from one location to another as if by magic; or battles to be waged on land or sea. Many leading architects were stage designers (a parallel can be seen here with the importance of Inigo Jones in the English masque), and sets were particularly designed to employ effects of perspective.

The enormous expense of complex and elaborate scenery was offset by the fact that it could be used over and over again. Most theaters had about a dozen stock scenes, such as temples, palaces, gardens, dungeons, caves and quaysides, which reappeared regularly from opera to opera. The singers' costumes – sumptuous and fanciful, but with no attempt at historical accuracy – were also an important consideration and could make a valuable contribution to an opera's success.

Stage lighting, too, was often surprisingly elaborate, for although it relied on candle power,

Above: Pannini's painting of the sumptuous musical celebration given in the house of the French ambassador in Rome in honor of the birth of the Dauphin in 1729. The music (which set a text by Metastasio) was by the operatic composer Leonardo Vinci.

Left: Musicians at the court of Prince Ferdinando de' Medici. The Prince was himself a brilliant keyboard player, a patron of Cristofori (the inventor of the pianoforte) and of Alessandro Scarlatti; he was also the dedicatee of Vivaldi's 'L'Estro Armonico' concertos and Handel's first patron in Italy.

117

and breath control of an adult, while his vocal chords retained the flexibility and range of a boy's. This produced a unique combination of a strong, penetrating tone coupled with excellent agility; a first-rate castrato was a great draw and could guarantee a full house. As a result the leading castrati, along with their female colleagues, could command exorbitant fees.

Castrati almost always took the leading male roles. While some visitors, such as Joseph Addison, found it difficult to 'endure to hear one of the rough old Romans, squeaking through the mouth of a eunuch,' most opera-goers quite happily accepted seeing castrati in heroic parts like Julius Caesar or Tamburlaine, and indeed probably enjoyed the occasional resulting double meanings which also stemmed from the frequent travesty roles, both male and female. (In Rome, where there was a papal ban on women performing on stage, all female parts were played by castrati.) Tenors and basses were generally relegated to playing unimportant characters — faithful servants, old men, messengers and so on.

The importance of vocal display in music at this time extended beyond simply singing the notes which the composer had written and into the realm of improvisation. All singers were expected to add ornaments to a melody at sight, and not just any ornaments but ones suitable to the mood of the music, so that a sad, gentle aria was not distorted with flashy exhibitions of unrestrained virtuosity. Many musicians, indeed, felt that a mediocre singer with a flair for extemporization was worth more than a brilliant performer with poor invention. This emphasis on improvisation is reflected in the dominant aria form in late baroque opera, the *da capo* aria. This was simply an aria in three sections. The second section, shorter than the first, contrasted with it to some extent with different keys and sometimes even a complete change of mood, speed and time. The aria was then rounded off by a repeat of the first section, giving the over-

all structure ABA. This was not, however, an exact repeat, for the singer was expected to reveal his or her artistry by ornamenting the original vocal line, and the audience, having already heard the melody in its simple form, was in an excellent position to judge.

The importance and size of the opera orchestra varied considerably during the late baroque period. From the 1650s it was reduced to a few continuo instruments (harpsichords and plucked string instruments such as lutes) and a four- or five-part string group. The strings were largely used for short independent pieces (called 'sinfonias') and for instrumental sections (called 'ritornellos') which recurred between the vocal phrases of some arias; the voice itself was generally accompanied by the continuo alone, and the majority of arias did not use strings at all.

Gradually during the latter part of the century the instruments became more important, and the strings took over from the continuo as the commonest form of accompaniment in the arias. In addition to the strings, around 1670 there was a vogue for arias involving the trumpet (which also became important in instrumental music about this time), and a few years later other wind instruments began to appear. By the eighteenth century the string group had become the basis for the opera orchestra, with individual or pairs of wind instruments (recorders, flutes, oboes, horns or trumpets) being added now and again for extra color. The orchestra was generally directed from the first harpsichord (there were usually two), placed in the center of the pit facing the stage, and this was frequently played by the composer himself.

• The libretto •

Baroque opera is notorious for the complexity of the plots, which are full of intrigues, disguises and mistaken identities, with frequent travesty roles adding to the confusion. The subject-matter of these operas was generally based on mythology or ancient history, but beyond the employment of famous names such as Cleopatra or Pompey there was no attempt at historical accuracy; the names were merely used as a peg on which to hang a plot of amorous intrigues. Contemporary events were sometimes reflected in the opera house, and libretti frequently contained political overtones: Venice was often linked with that other great republic, Rome, and the long-standing war with Turkey led to many operas being set in that country. Other works were set further afield, in Africa, America or even China, as was fitting in an age of world exploration. There was a strict form of censorship, and all libretti had to be approved by the authorities before performance was allowed.

The opera libretto was regarded as the leading literary form in Italy, and it was here, at the end of the seventeenth century, that many writers sought to reform Italian literature. Arcadian Academies were formed in many Italian cities, the most important in Rome, centered on Queen

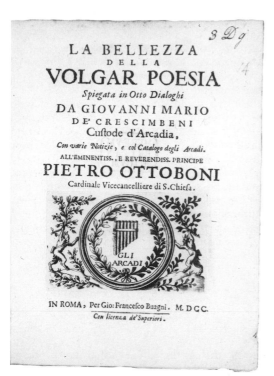

Far left: Arcadian treatise written in 1700 by G. M. Crescimbeni, in which he calls for a new lofty operatic style with no mixture of comic elements and also advocates a reduction in the excessive number of arias.

Left: Caricature of G. B. Pergolesi by P. L. Ghezzi. Pergolesi's greatest successes in Rome were his comic operatic works, which besides *La Serva Padrona* and *Livietta e Tracollo* (each originally an *intermezzo* in an *opera seria*) included the Neapolitan dialect opera *Lo Frate 'nnamurato*, first performed in 1732.

Christina of Sweden. These groups of intellectuals, who adopted pastoral pseudonyms and met regularly to read their works to one another for mutual criticism, aimed at a return to the classical ideals of Aristotle in preference to the baroque excesses of some contemporary dramatists. They felt that the main thrust of the action, with its heroic characters and its ideals of honor and glory, should not be debased by frivolous interruptions, and so attempted to purge all serious operas of comic characters.

One of the leading members of this reform was Apostolo Zeno (1668-1750). He helped found the Venetian branch of Arcadia before becoming court poet at Vienna and, along with Nicolò Minato, Domenico David and Silvio Stampiglia, did much to improve the literary value of the libretto. Under his influence emphasis was placed on historical rather than mythological subjects, and the number of arias per opera was reduced, as was the number of scenes (a 'scene' in opera of this period indicated not a change of set but merely the departure or arrival on stage of a character). With fewer arias, the characterization within each one could be more profound, and the composer was allowed more time in which to develop his musical ideas. Zeno also attempted to lessen the importance of love as the motivating force, stressing as well the ideals of duty, virtue and renunciation.

By 1700 the libretto was clearly laid out in two separate styles. The main part, containing all the action of the plot, was written in lines of seven or eleven syllables and was designed to be set as recitative, a kind of heightened speech in which the text was declaimed to music. The composer set most of this text as 'simple recitative' – that is, the voice was accompanied simply by the continuo instruments, generally harpsichord and cello; but at moments of great importance or emotion he would break into 'accompanied recitative' (using the full string group to accompany the singer). Every now and then this type of text was interrupted by stricter verse with a regular rhyme scheme, normally laid out in two stanzas; here a character stood back and reflected on his or her situation, and this was designed to be set as an aria, the two stanzas forming the 'A' and 'B' sections of the ABA *da capo* aria.

The positioning of the aria became regularized; it gravitated towards the ends of scenes and culminated in the singer's exit. This convention of the 'exit aria' was particularly popular with singers, since sweeping off the stage after a display of virtuosity was an obvious stimulus for applause. Recitative and aria accounted for the major part of the opera; there were occasional ensembles – normally a duet or a trio – but rarely any chorus (this, according to many contemporaries, belonged to the oratorio). Most operas ended with a very brief piece in which all the soloists came together to sing a closing stanza.

Following Zeno as court poet at Vienna in 1730 came the most important eighteenth-century librettist, Pietro Metastasio (1698-1782). His work more than any other reflected the new philosophy of rationalism and the ideals and attitudes of the Age of Enlightenment. His clear, ordered language, following his predecessor's neo-classical style, ideally suited contemporary Italian composers, and it is no coincidence that Metastasio trained as a singer and a composer. His early years were spent largely in Rome and Venice, though many of his works were first performed in Naples; after moving to Vienna he was encouraged to write opera and oratorio texts by Emperor Charles VI. Although most of his major works were produced by the time of Charles's death in 1740, they were set over eight hundred times during the eighteenth and early nineteenth centuries.

Above: Title-page of Pierfrancesco Tosi's *Observations on Florid Song*, published in Bologna in 1723, in which the author objects to the growing practice of writing out ornaments for singers, on the grounds that 'whoever accustoms himself to have Things put in his Mouth, will have no Invention, and becomes a Slave to his Memory.'

Below: Operatic scene in a royal palace by Ferdinando Galli da Bibiena (1657-1743), one of a family whose members combined illusionist architectural painting with the design and construction of theaters, several of which still survive, notably at Bayreuth, Verona and Bologna.

Bottom: Set by one of the Bibienas. The use of diagonal perspective with elaborate staircases and vistas seen through balconies and balustrades was begun by Ferdinando and is often seen in the work of his son Giuseppe.

Metastasio largely continued the stylistic trends established by Zeno, adding his own contributions. Usually he reduced the number of characters to around six or seven (all of them serious), but nevertheless explored a wide range of personalities, being particularly interested in psychological conflicts, especially the conflict of love and duty in heroic figures. He experimented with tragic endings in a few works, despite the fact that a happy dénouement was a long-standing convention, and he drew inspiration, especially in some of his oratorios, from French tragedy. Although Metastasio attempted to apply the rules of classical tragedy to opera, he retained many of the customary moral dilemmas and amorous intrigues, disguises, mistaken identities and so on from earlier times.

It was up to the librettist (or the arranger of the text if, as was often the case, an old libretto was being revised) to present the composer with a varied selection of aria texts appropriate for settings in various styles. One of the commonest types of text was the so-called 'simile aria,' in which the singer likened his situation to some

natural phenomenon such as a ship tossed by a storm, a bird flying home to the nest or a moth fluttering round a candle. These were designed to give the composer an opportunity for pictorial writing and became enormously popular during the eighteenth century.

Another convention closely connected with these different classes of aria was the 'system of affections,' which involved the allocation of a single mood, or 'affection,' to each aria. These affections usually reflected the passions aroused by love — jealousy, rage, desire for revenge, despair, hope, joy, and so on — and it was up to the librettist to make sure that the overall layout of the arias allowed for sufficient contrast and that two pieces in the same mood never followed each other.

• The *intermezzo* and comic opera •

During the seventeenth century many operas contained a mixture of heroic and comic elements. Cavalli's works, for example, employ characters derived from the traditional commedia dell'arte, and his later operas frequently include a nurse sung by a tenor. Gradually, comic scenes gravitated toward the end of an act, providing light relief from and sometimes a parody of the main serious action. As the Arcadian reforms attempted to rid heroic opera of comedy, these sections became entirely separate from the main work and were given the name '*intermezzo*'. Thus the *intermezzo* was a comic work in two or three short parts which fitted in between the acts of a serious opera.

In Venice early *intermezzi* were generally written by the composer of the main work, as was the case with Albinoni's famous *Vespetta e Pimpinone* of 1708. The most popular center for these pieces, however, soon became Naples, where they became customary during the first

Right: Garden pavilion as the centerpiece of an operatic scene, designed by one of the later Bibienas.

Above: Group portrait, *c.*1751, by Jacopo Amigoni, showing the great castrato Farinelli in the center with his friends the soprano Teresa Castellini and Pietro Metastasio, the librettist of countless operas, in many of which Farinelli sang. The painter stands behind Farinelli, and on the right are the singer's dog and his page, while in his hand he holds a favorite song he himself composed.

few decades of the eighteenth century and were frequently added by local composers to works first heard elsewhere. They generally involved two singing parts (though additional mute roles were common), and, like *opera seria*, were divided into recitative and aria, each section commonly ending in a duet.

The plots, normally very simple, often poke fun at the foolish love of an old man or woman for a younger partner and have a strong *commedia dell'arte* influence. Disguises play an important part in the action, along with an element of slapstick and the use of dialect and foreign languages.

As in *opera seria*, the two or three arias which, along with recitative and the closing duet, made up each section of the *intermezzo* were in *da capo* form, and the recitative itself was largely 'simple' apart from the occasional passage with orchestral accompaniment, frequently treated as a parody of the heroic style. Its musical style, however, was quite unlike that of its serious counterpart. With its simple harmonies, uncomplicated accompaniments, and emphasis on melody with evenly-balanced phrases, it looked forward to the new 'classical' style of the later eighteenth century. The music aimed at reflecting the text as closely as possible, and there were frequently changes of speed and style within individual arias. Some arias were really vocal dances (like the minuet or gavotte); others attempted to imitate natural sounds such as laughter, stuttering, crying or sneezing. A lively melodic style was cultivated involving rapid repetitions of

words to a single note (a kind of patter singing later found in nineteenth-century operetta), frequent reiterations of whole phrases, and, in the duets, short interjections and interruptions of one character by the other – all in all a vigorous, naturalistic style far removed from the heroic, stately reserve of *opera seria*.

A further artificiality from the world of serious opera was also firmly rejected: the castrato. This voice had no place in the *intermezzo* or in any other form of musical comedy; the most common vocal combination was that of bass and soprano. The importance of vocal display, too, was greatly reduced. Many singers specialized entirely in these comic roles, touring cities in Italy and abroad, but by 1750, the *intermezzo* was past its peak, its place as interval music in the opera-house largely being taken by ballet.

Full-length *opera buffa* (comic opera) was also developing. There had certainly been comic operas in seventeenth-century Italy, but more common, as we have seen, was a mixture of comic and serious characters, and it was in the next century, following the Arcadian reforms, that *opera buffa* really became popular. Unlike the *intermezzo*, opera buffa involved a sizeable cast of some six to ten characters, but it was similar to the *intermezzo* in its constitution of recitatives, arias and ensembles; all the text was set to music, unlike its eighteenth-century counterparts elsewhere in Europe – the *Singspiel* in Germany, the *opéra comique* in France, and the ballad opera in England – all of which contained spoken dialogue.

Above: Title-page of Domenico Scarlatti's harpsichord 'Exercises' (London, 1738). During his years in Portugal and Spain, Scarlatti absorbed into his own works much of the native music of the peninsula.

Below: Portuguese 'words for a minuet, composed by two very unlucky Frenchwomen, who for lack of money are not going to see the bulls.'

The growing popularity of comic opera in Europe reflected the sweeping social changes at this time with the rise of the bourgeoisie, and in Italy the libretti generally involved a strong moral lesson. Misers were cheated of their hard-earned savings; lecherous old men were tricked into giving up the young girl, often their own ward, who was the object of their affections; and bragging military men were exposed as cowards at heart. As in serious opera, love was central to the plot, but as well as pairs of young lovers there were the stock *commedia dell'arte* characters of Pantaloon, the elderly man, or Dr Graziano with his fake medical knowledge. The characters were invariably taken from the common people; this was no place for heroes and famous historical figures.

During the first decade of the eighteenth century the earliest comedies written in Neapolitan dialect were produced as entertainment for the aristocracy, and a three-act comic opera in dialect put on at the Fiorentini theater in Naples in 1709 was such a success that the city rapidly became a flourishing centre for comic opera. The vogue swiftly spread to Rome, Venice, and other Italian cities, and by 1750 works were being performed in other European centres, including Paris and London. While the early operas relied on caricature and low comedy, the style soon became more refined, and serious characters were included to add variety and to raise the tone. Later in the century there was a strong influence from the sentimental style prevalent in literature and drama, and one of the most famous eighteenth-century comic operas, Piccinni's *La Cecchina, ossia La buona figliuola* (Cecchina, or The good girl), was based on Samuel Richardson's novel *Pamela*. With its receptiveness to general artistic and social trends, comic opera was a much more sensitive medium in which to reflect the mood of the times than was the stylized *opera seria*, and it was also the place for new musical developments. Gradually the *da capo* aria decreased in popularity and

was replaced by other forms, while the greater interaction of characters within comic works encouraged the growth of the ensemble finale, a continuous musical number at the end of an act in which characters come and go, the resulting dramatic events being reflected by internal changes of musical style.

• Opera after 1650 •

The second half of the seventeenth century was in some ways a transitional period, during which the free, fluid structure of opera – based on the ideals of the early Florentine composers that music should reflect the text as naturally as possible – solidified into the more rigid, stylized mold of Metastasian *opera seria*. The polarization of recitative and aria increased, with musical interest becoming concentrated in the latter, which by 1680 was most commonly in the *da capo* form. The lighter music of the 1660s and 70s, with its emphasis on dance rhythms, gave way to a more serious, weighty style, and vocal virtuosity gained increasing importance, as did the role of the orchestral accompaniment.

Among the leading composers in the 1660s and 70s were Sartorio, Legrenzi, Pallavicino and P. A. Ziani. Antonio Sartorio (1630-80) divided his career between Venice and the court at Hanover. His best known opera, *L'Adelaide* (1672), is typical in its large number of very short arias, many of which involve continuously moving bass lines with repeated melodic patterns, and its inclusion of a dungeon scene, something very common in operas throughout the baroque era. His setting of *L'Orfeo* (1672) might seem to hark back to the very first mythological operas, yet the libretto reflects the changes which had taken place since the beginning of the century. Extra sub-plots, by now regarded as essential, are added to the basic story; Orpheus is given a step-brother, Aristeus, of whom he becomes jealous, and he even tries at one point to kill Eurydice. The third act contains another very popular type of scene, a lament, in which the strings are used to echo the vocal phrases, and harsh dissonances portray Orpheus's unhappiness. Another interesting work by Sartorio is his double opera *La Prosperità d'Elio Seiano* and *La Caduta d'Elio Seiano* (The Rise and Fall of Aelius Sejanus), in which the two halves were intended by the librettist Nicolò Minato to be performed on successive nights, thus providing a fascinating precursor to Wagner's *Ring*.

Legrenzi was important not only as a composer of stage, church and instrumental music but also as a teacher of the following generation. His operas include both heroic and comic elements, with the emphasis often on light-hearted music based on folk rhythms and dances. His numerous short arias (anything up to eighty per opera) are basically either fast, common-time pieces with lively rhythms and clear melodies or slower, more emotional, lyrical pieces in triple time. *Giustino* (1683) was one of the most successful seventeenth-century operas. Its libretto

Right: Caricature by P. L. Ghezzi (which was owned by the composer Niccolò Jommelli) of two virtuosi from Brescia: one plays a 'colascionino,' a type of two-stringed lute, while the other accompanies him on the guitar.

by Nicolò Beregan, later set by Albinoni, Vivaldi and Handel, deals with a representative of the common people, Justin, who is first seen singing as he ploughs, but soon takes on a more heroic role in support of the Roman Emperor Anastasius.

Carlo Pallavicino (d.1688) was influential in encouraging the spread of Venetian opera, as he was employed at the court of Dresden for some years; his last opera, *La Gerusalemme liberata* (Jerusalem Freed) was commissioned for a gala celebration at Dresden in 1687 and so involves splendid scenic effects. His smaller-scale arias are frequently in a simple, popular style, while his larger arias employ more florid vocal writing and orchestral passages. His flair for comic scenes was also shared by Pietro Andrea Ziani (*c.*1616-84), who again visited Dresden, as well as Innsbruck, Vienna and Naples. In his preference for lightweight libretti, even the leading characters are sometimes comic figures, and many scenes involve an element of parody, while his interest in using particular musical ideas to characterize people or situations prefigures nineteenth-century operatic ideas.

Stradella also worked outside Venice. His comic opera *Il Trespolo tutore*, performed at Genoa in about 1677, is one of the earliest works to have a comic bass in the leading role; Trespolo, the guardian in love with his ward, is a forerunner of later comic basses such as Don Pasquale. His music makes much use of rapid repeated notes and often parodies operatic conventions, occasionally using falsetto and nonsense language. There are comic mad scenes, dream sequences and a 'simile aria' in which he compares his body to a kitchen in which the fire of love is roasting his heart on a trivet. Stradella's recitatives follow the natural flow of

speech rhythms and often expand into arioso at the end of sections. His orchestra, generally comprising two violins and continuo, either alternates with the voice or provides a continuous accompaniment.

• Alessandro Scarlatti •

Among the generation of composers preceding the great names of baroque music – Bach, Handel, Vivaldi and Rameau – the outstanding figure is undoubtedly Alessandro Scarlatti (1660-1725). Father of Domenico Scarlatti, whose keyboard sonatas have made him familiar to today's concert-going public, Alessandro was a prolific composer of operas, cantatas, oratorios, Masses and instrumental music. For a long time he was regarded as the founder of a 'Neapolitan School' of opera, which supposedly replaced that of Venice as the center of operatic developments, and as the inventor of a new style of vocal writing which culminated in the works of Handel. Although recent research has shown that composers working in both Naples and Venice developed similar new styles at much the same time and that Scarlatti did not invent a whole genre but merely adapted existing styles, he is nevertheless a key figure in the history of opera.

Following his move from his native Sicily to Rome in 1672, Alessandro Scarlatti would doubtless have relished the city's flourishing musical life. In 1679 he composed his first opera, *Gli Equivoci nel sembiante* (Mistaken Identities), a successful small-scale pastorale in three acts, in which a shepherdess and her sister fall in love with twin brothers, requiring a cast of four (two sopranos and two tenors), a small string orchestra and simple staging.

Though some of Scarlatti's earliest works are comparatively lightweight affairs, *Il Pompeo*, first performed privately in Rome in 1683, is a full-scale serious drama without comic characters, although the servant class is represented by the slave girl Harpalia (at least until Act II, when she is murdered). The confused libretto by Nicolò Minato, which had already been set by

Cavalli for Venice in 1666 (*Pompeo Magno*), deals with Pompey's triumphal entry into Rome, though this is as far as historical accuracy goes, the plot comprising the usual amorous intrigues, confused identities and unexpected magnanimous gestures. It is typical of Scarlatti's Roman operas in that several scenes – even the final scenes of the first two acts – end with recitative rather than an aria (the 'exit aria' not yet being a strict convention). There is, nevertheless, a clear separation between the two styles, and the size of

Right: Alessandro Scarlatti with the manuscript of one of his cantatas.

Below: Battle with a centaur, scene from an opera performance at the Teatro San Carlo in Naples, which was built next to the royal palace in 1737. It was by far the largest opera house in Europe, a sign of the dominance of Naples during the first half of the eighteenth century.

the arias varies depending on the dramatic significance of the scene. Many arias are still strophic, with the same music repeated for two verses of text, while others are in *da capo* form. Several use a 'motto' opening, a device popular in arias of this period: the voice enters with its initial phrase but then breaks off; only after a short instrumental passage does the aria proper begin, frequently starting with a repeat of the opening 'motto' phrase.

The next period of Scarlatti's career, spent in Naples, was a very busy one, for he was not only writing works for the new city, but his old patrons from Rome still kept him supplied with commissions. Naples began its interest in opera in the early 1650s, when visiting singers performed works from the Venetian repertory by composers including Monteverdi and Cavalli. For many years Naples depended on Venetian works, which were often rearranged by local composers, but from the 1680s onwards it became more independent, with many operas specially written for its stages. The Viceroy of Naples had his own private theater, while the Teatro San Bartolomeo, reconstructed in 1653, put on regular opera seasons for the public. In 1683 the San Bartolomeo's permanent company of nine singers, five instrumentalists and a music copyist were under Scarlatti's direction. The Viceroy between 1696 and 1702, the Duke of Medinaceli, was a great opera-lover and made considerable improvements to the stage machinery at the San Bartolomeo; under his encouragement, Scarlatti's output during his years at Naples included around seventy operas.

Above: Scene from Act III of the *pasticcio* opera *Giunio Bruto* at its first performance at the Teatro Ottoboni, Rome, in 1709. The music was written by Carlo Cesarini (Act I), Antonio Caldara (Act II) and Alessandro Scarlatti (Act III), while the setting was designed by Filippo Juvarra.

Right: Judith with the head of Holofernes, painted by the Neapolitan artist Francesco Solimena (1697-1768). This violent biblical story was a favorite subject for oratorio, and was used by both Alessandro Scarlatti (two versions of *La Giuditta*) and Vivaldi – *Juditha triumphans*, first performed in Venice in 1716, with symbolic reference to Venice's recent victories over the Turks.

Il Pirro e Demetrio was first performed at the San Bartolomeo in January 1694. It proved a tremendous success and was soon performed in Rome, Milan, Florence, Brunswick and even London, where excerpts were printed under the title *Pyrrhus and Demetrius*. The opera, like Scarlatti's Roman works, contains a large number of very short arias, many of which are accompanied by the continuo instruments alone, but by now the *da capo* aria was the dominant form. In some arias with two stanzas, the second verse is sung by a different character, turning the piece into a kind of duet. Other features of Scarlatti's arias around this time include frequent 'motto' openings, short orchestral passages to round off pieces accompanied by continuo alone, and unusual harmonic progressions. This last trait is often caused by introducing an unexpected note in the melody, generally near the end of a phrase and on a particularly emotional word; the most important chord produced in this way is known as the 'Neapolitan sixth,' because of its popularity with Neapolitan composers at this time. In Scarlatti's work this harmony often appears in a type of aria known as a 'siciliano,' a gentle lilting song based on the rhythm of a Sicilian dance.

La Caduta de' Decemviri (The Fall of the Decemvirate, 1697), like so many operas of this time, mixes history with the intrigues and misunderstandings of star-crossed lovers. It contains one scene where the heroine is found asleep and another scene in which the decemvir Appius Claudius is haunted by evil specters, both very popular operatic devices. There are, however, two other particularly interesting features of this work. The overture, instead of opening in the traditional Venetian fashion with a solemn slow introduction, is in three movements. Two lively allegros, the second in dance rhythm and in two sections, sandwich a slow, reflective piece, the outer movements providing textural contrast by using two solo violins. This type of overture in three sections – fast, slow, fast – rapidly became established and is now known as the 'Italian overture.' The other point of special

Above: The theater of S. Giovanni Grisostomo in Venice, founded by the Grimani family in 1674, which became the home of *opera seria*. It was one of some eighteen theaters in the city around 1700, seven of which were given over to opera.

Below: Two of the great stars of opera, the prima donna Francesca Cuzzoni (*c.*1698-1790) and the castrato Nicolini (Nicolò Grimaldi, 1673-1732), caricatured by A. M. Zanetti. Nicolini was particularly associated with Scarlatti's operas at the start of his career, and both singers had superb parts written for them by Handel.

interest in this opera is its inclusion of a pair of comic servants, a bass and a soprano, who have scenes to themselves in all three acts – a direct forerunner of the *intermezzo*.

In the beginning of the eighteenth century Naples saw three kinds of comic opera: *intermezzi*, of which Scarlatti wrote several; the more earthy dialect comedies, which in their early days tended to be by relatively unknown local composers; and full-length *commedie in musica* (musical comedies), such as Scarlatti's *Il Trionfo dell' onore* (The Triumph of Honor, 1718). In the last the ensemble played a more important part than in *opera seria*, for the greater movement and interaction of the characters in comedy required more than just the static solo aria.

Many of Scarlatti's later operas, mainly written for Neapolitan or the more conservative Roman stages, show features typical of early eighteenth-century opera. *La Griselda*, produced in Rome in 1721, had probably been performed privately the previous month. In any case, the arrival of the talented castrato Carestini, who made his début as Costanza, caused the composer to alter his score, adding probably three new arias and rewriting two others so that they included more virtuosic singing. The typical accompaniment for a late Scarlatti aria is full strings rather than continuo alone. The accompanying parts often have a degree of thematic independence, and sometimes extra instruments are added to the basic string group. *Il Mitridate Eupatore*, written, though without a great deal of success, for Venice in 1707, has considerable orchestral variety, with important solos for oboe, trumpet, violins and two cellos.

A further feature of Scarlatti's later operas for Rome is their emphasis on spectacle. Visual splendor was provided by extremely elaborate sets and the use of ensembles, choruses (Rome having a strong choral tradition), ballets and processions, while aural interest was supplied by a particularly full orchestra including oboes, bassoons, trumpets and horns.

As well as being a prolific opera composer, Scarlatti also wrote an astonishing number of cantatas, some six hundred of which have

survived. The cantata, along with opera and oratorio the most popular form of baroque vocal music, was a work for one or more voices with instrumental accompaniment. In the seventeenth century it was generally a secular work providing an opportunity for members of the aristocracy to show off their favorite singers even during periods such as Lent when theaters were closed. As the cantata developed in the second half of the century, differentiation between recitative and aria increased, while the number of such sections decreased. As in operatic music, musical interest became concentrated in the arias, in which *da capo* structure became increasingly frequent. The commonest type of accompaniment was continuo, which provided introductions and ritornellos between the vocal sections of arias just as in opera.

Of Scarlatti's cantatas, more than five hundred are for a solo voice (mainly soprano) and continuo. Some early texts deal with historical or mythological subjects, but the most popular topic is love. The Arcadian reforms which swept opera at the end of the seventeenth century (Scarlatti himself became a member of Arcadia in 1706) also applied to the cantata, which became just like a small section of an opera. The unrequited love of a shepherd or shepherdess became the favorite subject and, again, the form of the cantata became more regular, reflecting the approach of the Age of Reason. It comprised alternating sections of unrhymed lines of seven or eleven syllables to be set as recitative, and more regular rhymed verses to be set as arias. *Da capo* structure took over as the dominant aria form, and the number of contrasting sections was gradually reduced, the commonest structure for the eighteenth-century cantata being recitative, aria, recitative, aria. The two aria texts involved contrasting moods to allow the composer musical variety.

•Scarlatti's contemporaries•

Although Carlo Francesco Pollarolo (*c*.1653-1723) spent much of his life on the staff of St Mark's, Venice, it was his thirteen oratorios and more than eighty operas that made him more famous in his own time than even Scarlatti. His early operas show a wide range of recitative styles, from slow, expressive sections to faster, more declamatory passages and sections involving florid vocal writing; by 1700 the recitative is standardized in the faster style. One of Pollarolo's most interesting features is his orchestration. As well as increasing the use of the orchestra (including the oboe) in the aria, he also favored a texture of four solo violins or violins in unison with the voice instead of the more normal continuo accompaniment. In *Onorio in Roma* (1692) he employs the *concerto grosso* principle (also found in oratorios and instrumental music at this time), using a small *concertino* group in three parts offstage and a full five-part group onstage.

Antonio Lotti (*c*.1667-1740), Francesco Gasparini (1668-1727) and M. A. Ziani (*c*.1653-1715), as well as Albinoni, were all leading figures in the Venetian operatic scene at the turn of the century. Lotti, who studied with Legrenzi, wrote at least sixteen new operas for Venice between 1706 and his departure for Dresden in 1717. The reputation of Francesco Gasparini, possibly another of Legrenzi's pupils and Vivaldi's colleague at the Ospedale della Pietà for many years before his move to Rome, reached as far as London, where his *Ambleto* (Hamlet) proved a great success in 1712. He was also famous for his comic *intermezzi*, especially *Melissa e Serpillo*, in which a soldier swindles an elderly woman and spends his ill-gotten gains on her younger rival. Marc' Antonio Ziani, the nephew of P. A. Ziani, inherited his uncle's lightweight style and was extremely popular in Venice in the 1690s. He, like Pollarolo, was interested in orchestration, and his varied instrumentation includes solo parts for such rarities as bassoon, viola da gamba, chalumeau (a predecessor of the clarinet) and lute. Albinoni wrote over fifty known operas, as well as numerous solo cantatas and other works. Although not a great dramatist, he had a talent for melodic writing and a strong feeling for formal balance. He, too, wrote *intermezzi*, his most well-known being *Vespetta e Pimpinone* (1708), a libretto later set by Telemann.

The varied career of Giovanni Bononcini (1670-1747) took him to Rome, Berlin, Vienna, London, Paris and Lisbon. During his early Italian period he collaborated with the leading poet Silvio Stampiglia on operas, serenatas (a cross between a cantata and an opera written to celebrate a particular event) and an oratorio; one of the operas, *Il Trionfo di Camilla* (Camilla's Triumph, 1696) helped to establish his reputation in London and led to his appointment as one of the composers, alongside Handel, for the Royal Academy of Music in the 1720s. Many Englishmen found his gentle, graceful and

Above: Caffarelli (Gaetano Majorano, 1710-83), one of the most extravagant and arrogant of the castrato singers, but a superb artist, who for twenty years was attached to the royal court in Naples (though this did not prevent many very highly paid appearances elsewhere). At the conclusion of his career he was able to purchase an estate in Calabria, a palace in Naples and the dukedom of San Donato.

Left: Farinelli (Carlo Broschi, 1705-82), the greatest of the castrati, seen here playing a female role in Rome in 1724 in a caricature by P. L. Ghezzi. He had made his début at the age of fifteen in a Porpora *serenata*, forming a lifelong friendship with its librettist Metastasio. By eighteen he was a principal singer, and for nearly twenty years he toured extensively in Europe, retiring in 1737 to become private musician to Philip v of Spain, where he became a friend of Domenico Scarlatti. A superb artist with unusual agility and beauty of sound, he did much to spread the new florid, ornamental vocal style.

Right: Venetian painting of the performance of an *intermezzo*, the short comic operatic work inserted between two parts of an *opera seria*.

Right: Portrait of a musician, said to be Pergolesi, although it bears a striking resemblance to another painting believed to represent the young Alessandro Scarlatti.

elegant style, with its expressive text setting, preferable to Handel's more vigorous heroism, and his music was also popular in France.

• Vivaldi's operatic music •

Although the name of Antonio Vivaldi is generally linked with the development of the instrumental concerto, he also devoted much of his time to stage music. As with most baroque composers, the exact number of his operas is uncertain, but he himself claimed ninety-four in a letter of 1739 (though it must be remembered that Vivaldi was somewhat prone to exaggeration). Only about twenty scores, however, have survived.

Although Vivaldi was an ordained priest, the eighteenth century saw nothing unusual in his devotion to the secular world of the opera house. And despite a congenital respiratory ailment which he claimed stopped him from saying Mass, he had the energy not only to compose operas rapidly (*Tito Manlio* claims on its title-page to have been composed in five days!) but also to direct first nights from the leader's desk and frequently to act as impresario, hiring the theater, booking the singers and – one of his favorite activities – quibbling over money. Vivaldi's relationship with his prima donna Anna Girò, however, did raise a few eyebrows and led to his being banned from Ferrara in the late 1730s by the strict Cardinal Ruffo.

In many ways Vivaldi is typical of the early eighteenth-century operatic composer. He was happy to accept the conventions of *opera seria* with little more than a murmur (unlike Handel,

who delighted in flouting them for dramatic effect), and he began writing in much the same style as his Venetian contemporaries. During his career, however, fashions changed; Metastasio came to dominate the opera libretto, and a new generation of composers, several of whom were centered on Naples, encouraged new styles and ideas.

Vivaldi's early operas were mainly written for the smaller Venetian theaters. They are not dissimilar to some of Scarlatti's works of the 1710s in their fresh melodic ideas and thematic independence of the accompanying instruments. Those familiar with Vivaldi's instrumental music

will recognize the same infectious rhythmic vitality, as well as an interest in experimentation with orchestral colour, varying the basic string texture with effects such as muting or *pizzicato* and adding extra instruments, including such rarities as a psaltery (a type of dulcimer) and a viola all' inglese, a kind of silvery-toned viola.

Tito Manlio, written in 1719 for the court at Mantua, where Vivaldi worked for three years, is a good example. Its story deals with the Roman consul Titus Manlius who, according to Livy, had his son executed for disobedience. This would have been too much for Venetian audiences, and the librettist Matteo Noris provides a customary happy ending in which the younger Manlius is saved by a military revolt, something philosophically accepted by his father. Around these basic events are entwined sub-plots which provide numerous opportunities for conflict between love, duty, friendship and honor. There is also a rather outdated element (the libretto was first set in 1697), a comic servant who comments facetiously on the problems of the other characters; Vivaldi's music reflects the different nature of this character, with rapid repeated notes, short phrases and patter singing that would not be out of place in an *intermezzo*.

In the late 1720s and 30s Vivaldi's musical style changed. The emphasis was placed almost entirely on the voice; the orchestral accompaniment generally contained little of interest, often comprising short repeated figures, so that all the listener's attention could be devoted to the singer's displays of virtuosity. Indeed, the emphasis on florid writing has led some modern commentators to use the term 'aria-concerto' for this kind of operatic writing. Both the concerto and the aria require a virtuoso soloist and orchestra; both use the 'ritornello form,' in which the sections for the soloists are framed by orchestral passages which return several times within the piece; and both often draw on the pictorial powers of music, whether it be to portray the rushing of the wind in one of the 'Four Seasons' or to depict the storm of indecision within the mind of an operatic hero. In view of these similarities, it is not surprising that Vivaldi sometimes borrowed material from one genre for use in another; it is quite common to find an orchestral passage from a concerto movement being reused as an introduction to an aria.

A typical late Vivaldi opera is *Griselda*, written for Venice in 1735. Zeno's text was one of the most popular eighteenth-century libretti, and for Vivaldi's work it was revised by Carlo Goldoni. The story is taken from Boccaccio's *Decameron*. The Marquis of Saluzzo decides to put his low-born wife Griselda through a series of tests in order to prove her worth to the people. He pretends to take another wife (in fact his own daughter Costanza, whom everyone else believes to have been killed as a child); Griselda's unswerving loyalty and devotion to her husband in the face of such cruelty moves the people,

Below: Antonio Caldara (1670-1736), a prolific composer of opera, who did much to bring the Italian style to Vienna, where he was attached to the court from 1716 until his death.

Above: Portrait of a young opera singer in Venice in the mid-century painted by Francesco Zugno.

Left: Giovanni Bononcini (1670-1747), who worked in both Vienna (1698-1712) and London (1720-32), where he became Handel's chief rival as a composer of Italian operas.

Above: Johann Joseph Fux (1660-1741), principal Kapellmeister in Vienna from 1715 and a composer of some twenty Italian operas, as well as his celebrated treatise on composition, the *Gradus ad Parnassum.*

who are delighted when the Marquis relents and recalls his former wife to his side. As usual, this basic story is filled out by Zeno: Costanza is given a weak-willed lover, Roberto, and Griselda in turn is the object of the unwanted attentions of a nobleman, Ottone, the villain of the piece.

By now Vivaldi had turned away from the very colorful instrumentation of his earlier years, and the orchestra consists simply of strings with continuo plus two horns. The title-role, written for Vivaldi's protégée Anna Girò, concentrates on her predilection for largely syllabic text-setting (exploiting her acting abilities), but in contrast the part of Ottone, a castrato role, involves elaborate vocal pyrotechnics over the whole of the singer's range. The vast majority of arias are fast and in major keys, a feature typical of Italian opera around the 1730s, though for moments of extreme emotion, as at the end of Act I when Griselda gives vent to her true feelings of despair, minor tonality is used very effectively.

It may well be that Vivaldi was unhappy with the modern style of the 1730s, for during this decade he frequently turned to the *pasticcio,* taking arias from several other composers and linking them with fresh recitatives to form a hybrid work. Certainly, his music was no longer in fashion by the end of the decade; the Venetians, in their incessant pursuit of novelty, were now looking to younger composers.

Operas, although important, were by no means the only vocal music in Vivaldi's output. Much of his church music was written for the Ospedale della Pietà, and this is reflected in his motets scored for soprano or alto voice, strings and continuo. These sacred cantatas consist of two arias (generally *da capo*), separated by recitative, and a concluding 'alleluia'; with their contrasting moods and virtuosity they too resemble vocal concertos.

Vivaldi's only surviving oratorio, *Juditha triumphans,* provided a showcase not only for the Pietà's best girl singers but also for its instrumentalists, with a large orchestra including, in addition to the normal strings and continuo, two recorders, two oboes, a chalumeau, two clarinets, two trumpets, drums, mandolin, four theorbos (a type of lute), organ, viola d'amore and a consort of viole all'inglese. The biblical story of Judith, who beheads the sleeping barbarian Holophernes, was regarded as an allegory of Venice's struggle against the Turks. This 'sacred military oratorio' is very close to Vivaldi's operas, comprising a series of recitatives and *da capo* arias with very little for the chorus and no ensembles.

•Vivaldi's contemporaries •

The newer style apparent in some of Vivaldi's later works can be seen clearly in the music of many composers writing during the second quarter of the eighteenth century, a time when Bach and Handel were largely happy to continue in the heavy traditional baroque idiom.

Leonardo Leo (1694-1744) wrote *opere serie* for many Italian cities, including Rome and Venice, as well as numerous comedies and *intermezzi* for Naples. The latter, generally in Neapolitan dialect, were musically superior to most other works in this genre, and the dialogue often involved the type of rapid exchange between characters typical of later comic opera. As well as emphasizing the role of the chorus in his later works, Leo expanded the use of the orchestra with powerful accompanied recitatives and modern dynamic contrasts and crescendos, which parallel if not precede the developments in this field of the symphonic composers at Mannheim.

Leonardo Vinci (*c.*1690-1730) was a prolific composer of operas during the 1720s. His output varies from pieces in Neapolitan dialect to many settings of Metastasio texts, his most famous being *Artaserse* (1730). Like many composers at this time, his accompaniments are simply chordal rather than having any thematic importance, and his melodies are built out of several short fragments. According to the famous eighteenth-century historian Charles Burney, Vinci was 'the friend, though not the slave to poetry, by simplifying and polishing melody, and calling the attention of the audience chiefly to the voice part, by distinguishing it from fugue, complication and laboured contrivance.'

Along with Vivaldi, the most familiar name from opera of this period is that of Giovanni Battista Pergolesi (1710-36). Though many works have been incorrectly attributed to Pergolesi over the years, in his short life he composed in all the different operatic styles, from religious opera (with comic scenes) and *opera seria* to comedies of various types. His setting of Metastasio's most famous libretto, *L'Olimpiade* (1735), shows his gift for gentle, expressive melodies in the new sentimental idiom; this was not, apparently, enough for its audience, for Pergolesi was hit on the head by an orange aimed by an unimpressed spectator. Two years previously another serious opera, *Il Prigionier superbo* (The Proud Prisoner) had been performed at Naples with, in the intervals, the *intermezzo La Serva padrona* (The Maid-Mistress), whose libretto was by the leading Neapolitan comedy-writer Federico. The story of the old man outwitted by his young servant girl was that of Albinoni's *Pimpinone,* but Pergolesi's simple musical style with its lively melodies and vigorous characterization was more forward-looking. The *intermezzo* was performed largely unnoticed in Paris in 1746, but at a revival in 1752 it caused a sensation; it became the symbol of the straightforward comic style prized by many French artists, including Jean-Jacques Rousseau, as opposed to the more weighty, tragic idiom. The involved debate thus aroused, known as the 'Querelle des Bouffons,' proved a strong influence on French comic opera.

The main operas of Nicola Porpora (1686-1768) were written in the 1720s and 1730s; and, as well as writing for the stages of Naples, Rome, Venice and Vienna, he wrote five works for London's Opera of the Nobility, the company

Left: Model of the opera house (Teatro Communale) at Bologna built in 1756-63 by Antonio Galli da Bibiena.

which rivaled Handel's in the 1730s. His style, particularly in his operas for Italy, emphasizes the vocal melody and its embellishment, something not too surprising as Porpora was an important singing teacher, his pupils including the famous castrati Farinelli and Caffarelli. Although his operatic output declined in later years, his influence continued through his contact with his pupil Haydn.

Johann Adolf Hasse (1699-1783) studied with Porpora in Naples. He was the first composer to set many of Metastasio's texts and his music reflected the neo-classical ideal of Metastasio's style. A powerful dramatist, he was particularly renowned for his careful use of accompanied recitative. Hasse's long career covered the period around the middle of the eighteenth century when composers were seeking to depart from baroque aesthetics, and his later works reveal attempts at overall unity by means of tonal

planning and a reaction against the *da capo* aria like those in the later works of Gluck. As well as being one of the most successful opera composers in Naples, Hasse became a leading figure at Dresden from the 1730s and at Vienna in the 1760s, both courts which had for many years been centers of Italian opera.

During the seventeenth century, as has been seen, Italian opera spread throughout much of Europe. By the 1640s it had been introduced to Paris and it also appeared at many other courts, generally to celebrate particular events such as the birthday or wedding of a prominent member of the nobility. Traveling troupes circulated the Venetian repertory throughout Italy and abroad, and Vienna and the German courts such as Dresden, Hamburg and Munich attracted poets and musicians from Italy.

The leading composer at Vienna in the second half of the seventeenth century was Antonio Draghi (*c.*1635-1700), who wrote numerous operas, oratorios and other stage works, especially to libretti by Nicolò Minato. The celebratory nature of many Viennese court works led to elaborate effects, with the frequent use of choruses, ballets and thicker wind scoring in the orchestra, reflecting the influence of French music. This grandiose style particularly suited the old-fashioned, massive approach of J. J. Fux (1660-1741), who served three different Hapsburg emperors; his deputy Antonio Caldara (*c.*1670-1736) set many texts by his colleague Zeno and adapted his native Venetian style, dependent on public support, to the grander approach popular with the emperor.

The success of Italian opera, then, was by no means limited to the southern side of the Alps. Composers and poets traveled widely, and Italian opera became an international language in the major European countries with the exception of France. For more than a century it dominated the musical scene, adapting itself from a restrained courtly entertainment to an immediately appreciable showcase for its virtuoso singers, always mindful of its new patron, the public.

Below: Johann Adolf Hasse (1699-1783), who studied with Porpora and Scarlatti in Naples and for many years was associated with the Ospedale degli Incurabili in Venice, during which time he married the singer Faustina Bordoni. In 1734 he became composer to the court of Dresden, where he stayed nearly thirty years, becoming one of the most powerful exponents of the Italian operatic style in Germany.

Left: Faustina Bordoni (1700-81) playing the title-role in Hasse's *Attilia Regolo*, written in 1750 to a libretto by Metastasio.

131

Baroque stage machinery

Opera's origins in Renaissance court festivals meant that elaborate scenic effects were at least as much a part of the form as was the music. Flying machines had been used as early as 1589 by Buontalenti at the Medici court, while effects of fire and smoke were much used – and resulted in frequent fires in opera houses. Transformation scenes too were popular, and the choice of Torquato

Tasso's Gerusalemme liberata (written in 1575) as a source of countless opera libretti was no doubt due to the possibilities provided by the magic powers of the central figure of Armida.

The most extravagant of all the baroque stage designers was Lodovico Burnacini (1636-1707), who worked at the Viennese court and whose last work, *La Monarchia Latina Trionfante*, remained unsurpassed. The action of the opera was entirely allegorical, with personifications of Peace and Religion, Abundance and Earth set against Idle-

ness, Ambition, Hate and Confusion, appearances by the Olympian gods, contests between the great rulers of antiquity – all to pay homage to the peaceful ruler Emperor Leopold I. In the illustration (*above*), a flying figure lifts the curtain painted with the battle of the Titans against the Olympian gods to reveal the army of Queen Semiramis marching to war.

In a scene from another Burnacini opera, *Il pomo d'oro* (*below*), produced in 1666 with music by Cesti for the wedding of Leopold I to Infanta Margarita of Spain, the whole stage is transformed into the mouth of hell, through which a burning city is seen in the distance across the waters of the River Styx.

At the French court the most brilliant decorator was the elder Jean Bérain (1637-1711). In Campra's *Hésione* the final scene is a hall of clouds (*below*), in which Venus is escorted by cupids. In earlier scenes an earthquake had destroyed a temple, and a desert was transformed into a 'pleasant garden.'

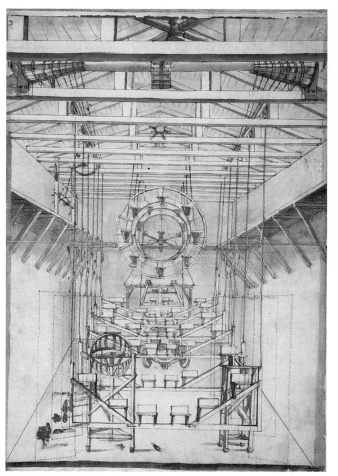

The two drawings above (for Legrenzi's opera *Germanico sul Reno*, produced in Venice in 1675) demonstrate the kind of machinery used to produce the spectacular effects in baroque opera. Virtually everything is controlled by winches, gears and ropes, while the whole central structure on wheels is able to move slowly from the back to the front of the stage, though the horses were probably painted. The circle of cloud also revolves, and there are seats or stands on which some eighty people could have perched.

Above: A model of the stage area of the first opera house in the Palais Royal, Paris, opened in 1673. It gives some idea of the structure necessary to hold the machines used for scenic effects, to the sides of, above and below the space actually occupied by the stage itself.

Right and above right: Backcloth designed by J. O. Harms for the storm-at-sea scene in *Heinrich der Löwe*, produced in Hamburg in 1696. The lower drawing shows the squaring-up which enabled the scene-painter to enlarge the artist's original design.

The cross-section (*below*) of the Stuttgart opera house, rebuilt in 1758-9 to a design by Philippe de la Guêpière, shows the elaborate interior decoration covering a very simple structure. Long after the end of the baroque period, a setting of this kind was felt to be demanded for the performance of opera, so that even into the present century, baroque decoration has characterized the design of opera houses.

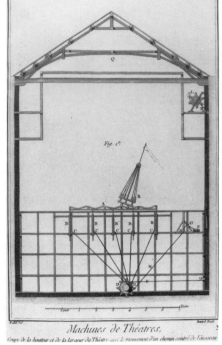

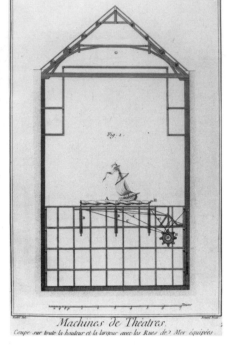

Machines de Théatres.

Machines de Théatres.

Two diagrams (*above*) showing the machinery used to create the effect of a ship pitching and rolling. In one (*right*) the movement of the waves is suggested by revolving the twisted cylinder on which the ship rests.

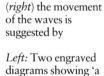

Left: Two engraved diagrams showing 'a desert with a mountain composed of rocks assembled by the Giants to destroy Jupiter' and 'a spring in the rocks with its roller to make it move.' These and other illustrations are taken from the volume of plates published as a supplement to Diderot and d'Alembert's *Encyclopédie*. Although these date from 1772, they represent techniques and practices that had been current for at least a century at the Paris Opéra.

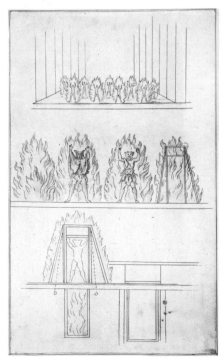

Drawings by Jean Bérain for a ballet of fiery devils for the Paris Opéra, with a diagram of the trap-door mechanism for their appearance out of the flames and their disappearance.

A new opera house, the Salles des Machines, was opened in the Tuileries in 1662, with a stage 40 meters deep and fully equipped with machinery. In 1738 the stage was enlarged by the architect G. N. Servandoni, principal decorator at the Paris Opéra from 1727 to 1746, whose cross-section drawing of the backstage area is shown below. There were eighteen sets of wings on each side, and the scale can be judged by the height of the columns of the proscenium arch (at the right).

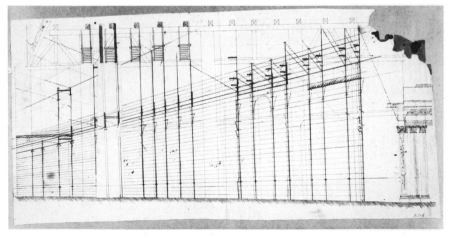

Left: Jean Bérain's design for the destruction of Armide's palace at the end of Lully's opera (Paris, 1686).

Above: Underwater scene in which Theseus battles with creatures, from *Fedra incoronata* (Munich, 1662).

Right and below: Five engravings from the *Encyclopédie* showing various scenic effects which had been in use at the Paris Opéra: Medea riding through the clouds in her chariot; the appearance of Juno with her peacock in a fiery nimbus above a garden with flowing fountains; the demolition of a tomb in flames, showing the torchbearers who set it alight; an erupting volcano; and a flaming dragon that crossed the stage carrying off any heroes that were brave enough to challenge it.

The plan (*right*) of the new Stuttgart opera house (the cross-section is opposite, top left), which was one of many plans carried out by Carl Eugen, Duke of Württemberg. It dates from the time when Niccolò Jommelli was in charge of opera and music, and it is remarkable how small a space is occupied by the auditorium. The space on the extreme right was intended to be used for a circular concert hall.

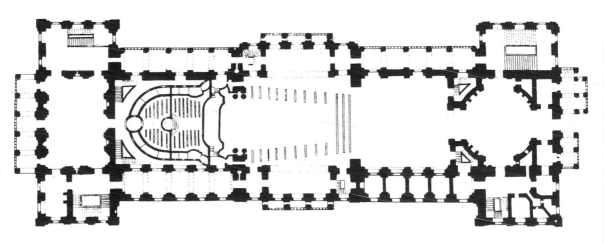

135

Juder galantre Jucus

MUSIC IN FRANCE IN THE SEVENTEENTH AND EIGHTEENTH CENTURIES

ROGER BLANCHARD & WILFRID MELLERS

Opposite: Costume drawing by N. Bocquet for Rameau's third opera-ballet, *Les Indes galantes*, first produced at the Opéra in Paris on 23 August 1735.

Within less than a century, between the creation in 1581 of the first Court Ballet, the *Balet comique de la Royne*, and the foundation of the Académie Royale de Musique in 1672, a lyrical art form emerged in France. This art form reflected the influence of Italy, and also French culture dating back to the Middle Ages. The *Balet comique de la Royne* was a collective opus involving the collaboration of musicians, poets, actors, choreographers and producers, based on the story of Circe the Sorceress. Its successful fusion of the arts bears witness to the influence of the ideas of the poet Jean Antoine de Baïf, leader of a group known as the Pléiade, which envisaged a revival of the drama of the ancient Greeks, combining the 'measured music in the ancient style' and dramatic action.

From 1581 to 1610 a number of ballets were presented in Paris, in the Grande Salle des Fêtes du Louvre, at the Arsenal or at the residence of Queen Margaret of Valois, and also in certain provincial towns. It is unfortunate that the libretti have not been preserved, but from the titles known to us it seems that most of these ballets were of a burlesque nature. Beginning with the *Ballet d'Alcine* or *Ballet de Monsieur Vendôme* (1610), however, it became customary to publish the libretti, and from then on we can distinguish between two types of ballet – the melodrama with continuous action and the *ballet à entrées*, a survival from the masquerades – which foreshadowed the later distinction between *tragédie lyrique* and *opéra-ballet*.

Among the most important *tragédies lyriques* were *La Délivrance de Renaud* (1617), derived from an episode in *Gerusalemme liberata* by Torquato Tasso (also the source of Lully's opera *Armide*), and the *Ballet de l'aventure de Tancrède en la forêt enchantée* (1619), another of Tasso's episodes, taken up by Campra in 1702. For these ballets, dance music was by Belleville and the *airs* by Pierre Guédron, Surintendant de la Musique. The numbers involved were considerable: sixty-four voices, twenty-eight viols and fourteen lutes. The Musicians of the King's Chamber were joined by those from the Chapelle and from the Grande Ecurie; some of the dancers were court noblemen, supported by professional players. The *mise-en-scène* was sumptuous, with complicated machinery, and some idea of the lighting may be formed when we remember that for the *Ballet de Minerve* in 1615, twelve hundred torches were lit and, in order to heighten the effect, the costumes and decorations required scintillating fabrics, embroidered with gold and silver.

After 1620 the *ballet à entrées* took the place of the melodrama, and allegorical subjects became less popular than picturesque, burlesque and scenic marvels. All such ballets were in a sense collective, hybrid works, including either an instrumental overture, foreshadowing what was later to be known as the 'French overture,' or an introductory chorus, followed by accompanied recitatives alternated with polyphonic airs in the style of the *Airs de Cour*, all interspersed with dances of simple structure.

As the popularity of such sumptuous entertainment spread from the French court to the colleges and wealthier merchants' houses, the beginnings of opera itself were being nurtured in Italy. Although the French royal house had been closely linked with the Medici of Florence since the time of Henri II, and Italian composers, librettists and singers had been frequent visitors to the French court, it was Cardinal Mazarin, successor to Cardinal Richelieu as the First Minister of State, who, for both political and artistic reasons, introduced opera to the French public by promoting the introduction of Italian opera companies into France.

In 1645 *La finta pazza* with verses by Giulio Strozzi and music by Francesco Sacrati was performed before the Court. This piece, although of mediocre quality, was a success, partly on account of the astounding machinery invented by the 'sorcerer' Giacomo Torelli. In 1646 a performance at the Palais Royal, of *Egisto* by Francesco Cavalli, bored the audience to tears – but Mazarin nonetheless commissioned an opera from Luigi Rossi to be given in Paris in 1647. This was *Orfeo*, with a libretto by Francesco Buti, Cardinal Barberini's secretary; the production was entrusted to Torelli. Not only was the composer brought to France, but also a company of Italian singers including two famous castrati, Marc-Antonio Pasqualini and Panfilo Miccinello. To the French public this opera was a revelation, but its reception was somewhat mixed; the audience failed to respond to the recitatives, which they found tiresome, but did appreciate the 'symphonies,' the blend of tragedy and comedy, the choreography and, above all, the machinery.

In 1659 festivals were being organized to accompany the marriage of the young Louis XIV

137

Jean Baptiste Lully.
Sur-intendant de la Musique du Roy.

Top left: Jean-Baptiste Lully.

Above: Decree of April 1672 giving Lully control of the Académie de Musique, established three years earlier by the poet Pierre Perrin.

with Maria-Theresa of Spain. Mazarin had commissioned an opera from Cavalli with libretto by Francesco Buti, but the First Minister died in 1661, and it was only in the following year, in the new Salle des Tuileries, that Cavalli's *Ercole amante* was performed. It was a heterogeneous work, which included at the end of each act a ballet interval to music by the young composer Lully, as a concession to French tastes. To judge from the contemporary periodicals, all that the public noticed in this spectacle was the rich décor, the ingenious stage machinery and the agreeable interludes. In other words, this was a disappointment for Cavalli and a success for Lully, who already enjoyed royal protection. Other triumphs were those of the production magicians, Vigarani and Torelli.

•The Académie Royale de Musique •

Spectacles such as *La Grande journée des machines* or *Le Mariage d'Orphée et d'Eurydice* in 1648; the tragedy *Andromède* by Corneille, with music by Dassoucy and machinery by Torelli (1650); the *Comédie sans comédie* by Quinault

(1654), including in the fourth act the fable of Armide and Renaud; and Boyer's tragedy *Les Amours de Jupiter et de Sémélé*, with music by the lutenist Mollier (1666); all prepared the way for the birth of French opera. Another factor was that the poetical themes of the 'pastorale' on mythological subjects, which had always been popular with the French public, were now being used again in opera.

It is to the poet and musician Charles Coypeau, Sieur Dassoucy, that we owe *Les Amours d'Apollon et de Daphné* (1650), a pastoral in three acts preceded by a prologue in praise of the King, the music to which has, alas, been lost. In 1655 Michel de La Guerre, organist at the Sainte Chapelle, produced at the Louvre *Le Triomphe de l'Amour*. The original feature of this work was the inclusion of a sung dialogue in the form of songs for one or more voices, the work being sung throughout.

Of more significance were the endeavors of Pierre Perrin and Robert Cambert. Perrin had supplied verses for a number of musicians including Moulinié, Lambert, Boësset, Cambefort and Bacilly. Cambert, an organist and harpsichordist, was a gifted composer, who had already made a name for himself when in 1659 he presented, together with Perrin, *La Pastorale d'Issy*. This success brought them to the attention of Mazarin and of the King, who had the work produced at Vincennes. Perrin then had the idea of establishing an Académie de Musique to promote operatic works. In 1669, with the support of the Minister Colbert, he was granted letters patent for twelve years for 'the establishment of academies for opera, or performances of music with French verses, in Paris or other towns within the kingdom.' Perrin accordingly founded a company with Cambert exclusively in charge of the music, the Marquis de Sourdéac

J. Berin delt.

Above: Presentation of Lully's opera *Roland* at the Académie Royale in 1685.

Right: Indian costume designed by Bérain for Lully's *ballet de cour Le Triomphe de l'Amour* (1681). Jean Bérain (1637-1711) was the King's official set designer, contributing to the operas performed before the court from 1674 on.

Opposite top right: Page from the score of Lully's *Armide* (1686). This five-act opera was written to a text by Quinault after Tasso's *Gerusalemme liberata*, which was also the subject of some forty other operas including Gluck's *Armide* (1777). Lully's interpretation of the poem is regarded as one of the most beautiful works in the repertoire of French opera.

in charge of machinery and décors, and Bersac de Champeron, a dubious financier, in charge of finance. Beauchamp, the King's Maître de Ballet, was responsible for the dancing, and La Grille, a singer from the Comédie Française, was the Régisseur Général. The partners chose their site, the Salle du 'Jeu de Paume de la Bouteille,' taken on a seven-year lease. Within five months, Guichard, the Intendant des Bâtiments of the Duke of Orléans, had the first Paris Opera House constructed there.

The first work to be presented by this new Académie was Cambert's *Pomone* (1671), which was a success. During the earlier part of 1672 they gave *Les Peines et les plaisirs de l'amour*, an heroic pastoral with libretto by Gabriel Gilbert, which was also successful. Disagreement, however, broke out among the partners. Perrin was heavily in debt, and Lully, Surintendant de la Musique since 1661 by favor of the King and enjoying every kind of official support, took advantage of the circumstances, offering to buy Perrin's letters-patent from him so as to satisfy his creditors. Once dispossessed, Perrin and Cambert had to go into exile in England. King Charles II appointed Cambert Master of the King's Music, an appointment he retained until his death in 1677.

Once installed, Lully ruled with a rod of iron. When Molière died in 1673, he hastened to obtain the King's permission to set up at the Palais Royal, in the place of the Comédiens Français. He was thus able to obtain a monopoly of musical theater in France, any fresh undertaking having first to pay him a heavy royalty. Lully also enjoyed another monopoly, that of composing operas. The principal victims of this monopoly were the unfortunate Cambert, as well as Marc-Antoine Charpentier, who had to wait until Lully's death in order to make a start in opera with his *Médée*. Thus if, administratively speaking, Perrin and Cambert were the founders of the first operatic theater in France, the credit for having created French opera falls to Lully.

• Jean-Baptiste Lully •

Born in Florence in 1632, Giovanni Battista Lulli (1632-87) came to France at the age of fifteen as a page to Mademoiselle de Montpensier. He was already a dancer and violinist. Following the Fronde disturbances in 1652, Mademoiselle de Montpensier had to go into exile at her castle of Saint Fargeau, and she gave Lully permission to leave her service. In Paris Lully, a born plotter, soon made his way among the young King's courtiers. He took part in the Court Ballet and quickly attracted the King's notice and became his semi-official companion. In addition to his ability as a dancer, he gained favor by his talent as a fiddler, and he was allowed to form the orchestra of the Petits Violons alongside the band of the twenty-four fiddlers of the Chapelle Royale. Then he completed his musical education with the organists Gigault and Roberday.

Soon Lully enjoyed a triple reputation, as dancer, violinist and composer. With ballet coming back into favor after the Fronde, he composed his *Alcidiane* (1658), *La Raillerie* (1659), *Les Saisons* (1661), and the *divertissements* for Cavalli's operas. In 1661 he was appointed as Surintendant de la Musique and wrote further ballets: *Les Arts* (1663), *La Naissance de Vénus* (1665), *Les Muses* (1666) and *Flore* (1669).

Lully also collaborated with Molière, composing most of the *divertissements* for the Comédiens Français. The peak of this output was *Le Bourgeois gentilhomme* and his well-known

Cérémonie turque (1670). In 1672 he took over the Académie Royale de Musique which, under his stern rule, was to become an institute of the highest prestige. He undertook the conducting of the orchestra and the recruitment and training of singers and became the true creator of a school of lyric declamation based on the style of the Comédiens Français.

The operas' published libretti provide some general information on the detail of the casts, from which we may estimate that a chorus of between twenty and thirty and about twenty dancers took part in performances. The orchestra is believed to have consisted of some thirty musicians, a third of these playing wind instruments (flutes, oboes and bassoons). However, documents from the archives dating from 1704 make it possible to form a more specific idea of the composition of the orchestra, which was then divided into two groups, the Petit Choeur and the Grand Choeur. The former was responsible for the bass continuo and had two treble violins and two bass violins, two bass viols, two theorbos and a harpsichord; the second group included eight woodwinds (recorders and flutes, oboes and bassoons, some musicians doubling flute or oboe) and twenty-five stringed instruments, together with a timpanist.

For décor and machinery, Lully's first collaborator was the famous Vigarani, followed by the no less brilliant Jean Bérain, who continued to work with the Académie long after Lully's death. Working with Quinault, Lully produced an impressive series of tragic operas, from *Cadmus et Hermione* (1673) to *Armide* (1686), including *Alceste, Thésée, Atys, Isis, Proserpine, Persée, Phaëton, Amadis* and *Roland*, establishing an art form which lasted beyond the middle of the eighteenth century.

The great novelty within Lully's operas is that the tragedy is sung throughout, thanks to the adoption of a new style of recitative. As distinct from airs of regular structure, Lully allows his recitatives a great freedom in tempo by the alternation of duple and triple time, and, by the use of expressive pauses or the introduction of more song-like passages, he lends diversity to the discourse. In short, such a recitative is intensely alive while still observing the requirements of the prosody. All the later composers of opera, from Lully to Rameau, were to remain faithful to this style. Such recitatives are generally not supported except by a bass. Where, however, the action so requires, at the moment of keenest feeling, Lully does use his orchestra, and this becomes the grand dramatic recitative, distinguished from the aria by its freedom and,

Left: Van der Meulen's painting of Versailles in 1669, showing the park of what was still a country residence, rather than the permanent home of the French court, which it became in 1682.

Right: Jean Garnier's picture shows a portrait of Louis XIV surrounded by various symbols of art. The man to become known as the Sun King presided over a golden age of French literature and art, which flowered at the royal court, soon in permanent residence at Versailles. The King's love of music and dancing gave the most gifted musicians the opportunity to practice their talents at court.

Above: Jean-Antoine Watteau's painting *Assemblée dans un parc.* Watteau (1684-1721) painted many figures from the Comédie Française and Comédie Italienne, and it is the mood of these and of his pastoral works which allies him with many contemporary French musicians in the period which saw lyric tragedy eclipsed by the new genre of opera-ballet.

Left: Harpsichord made by court instrument-maker Antoine Vaudry in Paris in 1681. The orientalist decoration on the lid dates from the following century.

sometimes, by its vehemence. Lully's arias contribute less novelty: some retain the form and spirit of the old *Airs de Cour*; others are more fully developed with a richer harmonic support, mostly in rondo form.

In instrumental music, Lully adopted what was known as the French overture in two or three parts – a slow introduction in pointed style followed by a lively movement in fugal style, the slow movement sometimes being repeated to conclude. This type of overture offers a majestic opening, bearing no particular relation to the drama which follows it, and not indicating any of the principal themes of the setting.

Lully also added many descriptive 'symphonies,' underlining the successive scenery of each tragedy: pastoral scenes, in which he excelled, scenes of war, of the underworld, or funeral scenes, and of course scenes of great spectacle. Lyric tragedy thus provided a total spectacle that was varied and sumptuous, traditionally preceded by a long prologue to the glory of the King and faithfully reflecting the splendor of the Sun King's court.

• Lully's successors •

After Lully's death in 1687 the King, under the influence of Mme de Maintenon, turned to piety. Music and dance left Versailles for the smaller, princely courts and the rich bourgeois houses

and it was in this context that the rise of opera-ballet occurred. Historians have taken 1697 as marking the birth of this new genre, the year of the creation of *L'Europe galante* by André Campra, to a libretto by Houdar de la Motte.

Opera-ballet is distinct from lyric tragedy in that it presents no unity of action. Under some quite comprehensive title such as *Les Saisons*, *Les Ages*, *Les Eléments* or *Les Fêtes* come independent plots or episodes as mere pretexts for *divertissements*, the music and the dancing taking precedence over the drama. This formula allowed for any reworking, additions or cuts, just as the writers pleased and to the chagrin of the publishers.

Thus, *L'Europe galante* has four acts and a prologue titled *Les Forges de l'amour*. The first act, devoted to France, consists of an idyllic pastoral scene. The second act is set in Spain and depicts the rivalry of two lords serenading a beauty under her balcony. The third act takes place in Venice where, during a ball, Octavio, the rejected lover, expresses his hatred and his desire for vengeance; and the last act is set in a fantastic Turkey and tells a tale of the harem. All credibility is sacrificed to exoticism and to the picturesque.

André Campra (1660-1744), the most important composer between Lully and Rameau, began his career as a church musician in the schools of the French Midi. In 1694 he became Maître de Musique at the cathedral of Notre Dame, Paris, resigning in 1700. He then became conductor of the orchestra and, in a way, musical director of the Académie Royale, presiding over revivals of Lully's operas while also presenting a fresh work each year. By comparison with Lully, Campra's style appears more melodic and more polyphonic. His harmonic structure is more modulatory, and above all, he never renounced Italianism.

Campra's pupil André Cardinal Destouches (1672-1749) was one of the King's musketeers before beginning his studies. In the same year as *L'Europe galante* (1697) Destouches gave his pastorale *Issé* at Versailles. It was a flattering success in that Louis XIV declared to the young composer that 'since Lully no music had given him so much pleasure.' Destouches's talents were his spontaneity, his freshness and his sensitivity; at times he displays a harmonic felicity, but his technique in the composition of polyphonic ensemble is often clumsy. Unlike Campra, he rejected the Italian style, adopting Italianism only by way of parody.

Jean-Joseph Mouret (1682-1738) entered the service of the Duchesse du Maine, and was director of the pageants given at the Château de Sceaux, which became celebrated under the name of Grandes Nuits de Sceaux. It was there that in 1714 he had great success with a little comedy in three acts, the ancestor of *opéra-bouffe*, *Les Amours de Ragonde*, to a libretto by Néricault Destouches based on folk culture. In the same year, Mouret made his début at the Opéra with *Les Fêtes ou Le Triomphe de Thalie*, an opera-ballet which buttressed his reputation. In 1722 he added to that work a fresh act, 'La Provençale,' in which, for the first time, couplets were sung in the Provençal dialect. Mouret's muse was a lightweight one, and his tunes were always amiable, fresh and such as to carry the public along with them. Further, having been appointed the official composer to the Comédie Italienne in 1717, he wrote a number of *divertissements* which render him one of the creators of French comic opera.

Along with these prolific writers mention should be made of certain operatic works by musicians who made their names in other fields. Marc-Antoine Charpentier (?1645/50-1704), a pupil of Carissimi in Rome and talented composer of sacred music, made a start in opera with his *Médée*, written to a libretto by Thomas Corneille (1693). Michel-Richard de Lalande, the creator of the French grand motet, composed a number of ballets, while collaborating with Destouches for *Les Eléments*.

Above: Rameau and Voltaire. Besides writing on all manner of subjects, including music, François-Marie Voltaire (1694-1778) wrote a number of libretti for operas, both comic and tragic. His most important collaboration in this field was with Rameau, for whom he wrote the text of *Samson* (1732) – which was banned because its religious subject matter was considered unsuited to the profane stage – as well as the comedy-ballet *La Princesse de Navarre* (1745). In the era of the *Querelle des Bouffons*, Voltaire sided with Rameau and the French music tradition, whereas writers such as Jean-Jacques Rousseau and the Encyclopedists favored the Italian Bouffon style.

Top left: Madeleine Sophie Arnould as Thelaïre in *Castor et Pollux*. This tragic opera by Rameau was first produced in Paris on 24 October 1737 and performed in a revised version in 1754. *Castor et Pollux* is regarded as one of Rameau's best operas and contains some fine solo passages besides well-known choruses.

Among Lully's immediate disciples was Pascal Collasse (1649-1709), who composed *Thétis et Pélée* (1689) and *Ballet des saisons* (1695), and the viol virtuoso Marin Marais (1656-1728), who composed four operas including *Alcione* (1706), long remembered for its tempest scene. The dramatic symphonies embodied in operas by Marin Marais are evidence of a feeling for instrumental coloring upon which Rameau was to draw. Lastly, Henry Desmarets (1661-1741) collaborated in productions given at the Collège des Jésuites, where he succeeded Charpentier. At the Académie Royale he had a number of tragedies performed, the most notable of them being *Didon* (1693) and *Iphigénie en Tauride* (1704), with its setting completed by Campra.

Finally there was a biblical opera, *Jephté* by Michel Pignolet de Montéclair (1667-1737), a bass fiddler in the Opéra orchestra, composer of cantatas and of theoretical works. The libretto for *Jephté* was by the Abbé Pellegrin, and it is said that this marvellously constructed work, written in 1733, inspired Rameau and determined his artistic vocation. It is worth noting that while the Italians devoted themselves more and more to the search for pure vocal virtuosity, the French clung, above all, to expressiveness. Lully's teaching, based on the example of actors' declamation, was thus never lost from sight.

• Jean-Philippe Rameau •

A contemporary, within a couple of years, of J.S. Bach, Handel and Domenico Scarlatti, Rameau (1683-1764) was the greatest French musician of the eighteenth century and the most outstanding exponent of French classic

Left: Allegorical representation of Rameau and Gluck. The German composer came to Paris in 1774, at the age of sixty, to produce his opera *Iphigénie en Aulide* (ten years, in fact, after Rameau's death). Gluck built on the French operatic tradition, even adapting some of Lully's libretti, and created a new form of French classicism in the late eighteenth century. In this picture the figure of the messenger carries a scroll entitled *Iphigénie*, whilst Rameau's *Castor et Pollux* can be seen in the bottom left-hand corner.

style. Born in Dijon, he spent the first part of his life as an organist, harpsichordist and Maître de Chapelle, successively in Avignon, Clermont, Dijon and Lyons, before settling in Paris in 1722. In 1727 he met the Fermier-Général, or head tax-collector, Le Riche de la Pouplinière, a wealthy patron, who was to support him for nearly twenty-five years.

La Pouplinière kept an orchestra, the direction of which he entrusted to Rameau. His town house was a kind of shrine frequented by leading spirits of the time including Voltaire and the Abbé Pellegrin, who were to provide Rameau with his first libretti. Thus, at the age of fifty, Rameau began his operatic career with his first tragedy *Hippolyte et Aricie*, presented first in concert form at La Pouplinière's house and then at the Académie Royale de Musique on 1 October 1733. This first attempt proved to be a masterpiece. The aged Campra declared to the Prince de Conti: 'Monseigneur, there is enough music in this opera for ten operas and this is a man who will eclipse us all!'

At this time Rameau was producing some of his finest works, such as the second *Trio des Parques* and the monumental choruses *Puissant maître des flots* or *Que ce rivage retentisse*. He supplied spectacles for both the Opéra and for the Court of Versailles: opera-ballet, tragedy, heroic pastoral, comic opera, and a number of works in one act known as *actes de ballet*. Lully's faithful followers were so perturbed by his success that a conflict arose between the Lullistes and the Ramistes – a confrontation between ancient and modern. The reign of the great Rameau had begun.

Rameau's recitative is not especially novel when compared with Lully's. Nevertheless, his concern for expressiveness and his melodic facility can lead us, imperceptibly, from recitative

PIERRE JELIOTE

Left: Pierre de Jélyotte. This celebrated French singer was appointed principal counter-tenor at the Opéra in Paris in 1732. He made his début the following year and subsequently performed several of Rameau's greatest roles with the soprano Marie Fel. He retired from the stage at the height of his fame when he was forty-two, but continued to sing in society concerts and at the French court. He also wrote and sang (to his own accompaniment) many songs and composed one opera-ballet, *Zelisca*.

Above: Jean-Philippe Rameau, in a copy of the portrait by Chardin.

the clowning of the liveliest pages of *Platée*. It is the bringing together of so many differing elements, and the often abrupt change from one to another, which gives Rameau's operas their vivid intensity.

• *Querelle des Bouffons* •

In 1752 a small Italian company playing in Paris performed a few Neapolitan *intermezzi*, including *La Serva padrona* by Pergolesi, which had attracted virtually no notice on its first presentation in 1746. This time, however, the cognoscenti were really excited. A few months earlier, Baron Grimm in his *Lettre sur Omphale* had denigrated the entire French repertory, sparing only Rameau (because of his *Platée*) and praising the Italians to the skies. The familiar style of the Italian Bouffons, their vivacity and the simplicity of their tunes was what enchanted the encyclopedists and their supporters. A chasm opened between the two schools of opera-lovers, the French Party and the Italian Party, known at the Opéra respectively as the 'King's corner,' favoring the French side with Mme de Pompadour, Rameau and certain chauvinists, and the 'Queen's corner,' favoring the Italians, along with Baron Grimm, the encyclopedists and Jean-Jacques Rousseau. The quarrel became ever more venomous, with invective being exchanged in the theaters, pamphlets being circulated and even duels being fought.

In that same year, 1752, Jean-Jacques Rousseau presented *Le Devin du village* before the court at Fontainebleau, a dull tale of country folk, comprising a suite of slight and facile airs, not without their own charm but which would have attracted little attention had they not appeared under the name of one of the 'thinkers' of the century.

The year 1752 also saw the re-opening of the Théâtre de la Foire by Jean Monnet (1703-85), supported by a fresh grant of royal privilege. This was a favorable situation for the development of lyrical drama of a lighter form, and for the continued evolution of French *opéra comique*, the history of which can be traced back to the end of the seventeenth century. Two pleasure-grounds – St Laurent and St Germain, one on either side of the Seine – put on popular entertainments, which were originally more closely related to circus than to theater. These inspired some jealousy on the part of the official theaters, the Comédie Française and the Académie Royale de Musique. Some way had to be found between comedy and opera, and this turned out to be a light-hearted mixture of comedy and music; the music descended from the popular or folk tradition (vaudevilles), whether original or parodied. At the beginning of the reign of Louis xv the Théâtre de la Foire enjoyed its hour of glory under Lesage and Orneval, and later under Favart, with such musicians as Villiers, Mouret and Saint-Sévin. Following a long decline, the Théâtre de la Foire was beginning to recover its impetus when

to aria and vice versa. The harmonic support, moreover, is infinitely fuller, with certain daring effects which stunned his contemporaries. His arias offer much more diversity than any before, and he initiated the ariette, simple vocalization with no direct relation to the action, as a concession to virtuosity and to Italian style. In composing for choruses and ensembles, Rameau had the benefit of his experience as a choirmaster; he handled fugal style with ease, and some of his grand ensembles rival even those of Handel.

It was, however, in the field of instrumentation that Rameau showed the greatest originality. His overtures were no longer a mere decorative introduction; they gained real dramatic power and took their inspiration (in *Zoroastre*, for instance) from the subject-matter of the tragedy. In his symphonies he uses sparkling instrumental combinations to emphasize the events in the action. He was a real musician of the theater and one of the first to make the orchestra participate in the drama.

Finally there is in the genius of Rameau a breadth and an impetus exemplified by the fact that in opera-ballet nobody had ever achieved the expressive power which is admired in *La Fête du soleil* in the Incas' act in *Les Indes galantes*. And in comic opera he displayed an unprecedented fertility of imagination – as in

the Comédie Française forced it to close down in 1745. Seven years later, by sheer obstinacy, Jean Monnet brought it to life again, and, right in the middle of the *Querelle des Bouffons*, he had the idea of commissioning Antoine Dauvergne (1713-97) to produce a score in the Italian style. Dauvergne wrote *Les Troqueurs*, which was presented in 1753. The work was announced as having been composed by a Milanese residing in Vienna but well acquainted with the French language. The Bouffonistes fell into the trap and Monnet soon had everybody laughing on his side by revealing the name of the real composer.

Alongside the Théâtre de la Foire there had existed in France, from the end of the fourteenth century onwards, troupes of Italian actors. Given official recognition by the Regent, Philippe d'Orléans, in 1723 the company, led by Luigi Riccoboni, assumed the title of Comédiens Italiens Ordinaires du Roi; Mouret continued for many years to be the official composer. The *divertissements* by the Italian comedians rivalled those of the Théâtre de la Foire. Both companies had their alternating periods of success and failure, and by 1762 they were amalgamated. This date marks the official birth of a French comic opera theater; from now on 'to go to the Italians' meant 'to go to the Opéra Comique.'

• Rameau's contemporaries •

Jean-Joseph de Mondonville (1711-72) began his career in Lille, where he was engaged as first violin in the town orchestra. It was also at Lille that he had his first grand motets performed. In Paris he played at the *Concert Spirituel* as a solo violinist, and was soon noticed; in 1738 that same *Concert Spirituel* accepted his motets, which met with immense success. After coming to the attention of the Marquise de Pompadour, who engaged him as first violin in her theater orchestra, he finally made his start in the theater in 1742, with the pastoral *Isbé*. For the Marquise's theater he also composed some ballets: *Bacchus et Erigone* (1747) and *Vénus et Adonis* (1752), which he later combined with *Psyché*

Left: Drawing by N. Bocquet of a costume for *Les Indes galantes*. Rameau's most successful opera, to a text by Louis Fuzelier, was produced in Paris on 23 August 1735, though not until the following year was it performed in its completed version. This consists of a prologue and four entrées, which relate four different tales of love in different regions of the world.

Left: Scene from Rameau's comedy ballet *La Princesse de Navarre*, which was staged with designs by Cochin at Versailles in 1745. The composer brought to French opera and ballet music a new richness of style, which caused a great deal of controversy in musical circles. In this ballet the orchestra was of necessity large, being composed of at least fifty-six players. These could not be directed, as had been the practice in earlier years, from the harpsichord, but had to be kept in order by the conductor, wielding a roll of music.

in order to form the vast ensemble of *Les Fêtes de Paphos*; and in 1749 *Le Carnaval du Parnasse*, an opera-ballet to a libretto by Fuzelier, dedicated to Mme de Pompadour at the Académie Royale.

Once the *Querelle des Bouffons* broke out, he was an ardent defender of the French cause and its official 'champion.' In 1754 he surprised everyone, his supporters as well as his detractors, by putting on a pastoral in Provençal, for which he wrote all the words and music (except for a prologue in French by the Abbé Voisenon). This 'Gascon opera,' as it became known, *Daphnis et Alcimadure*, was perhaps Mondonville's answer to Jean-Jacques Rousseau and to the partisans of the Bouffons.

Of the artists who enlivened the Académie Royale de Musique in the time of Rameau, the names of Marie Fel and Pierre de Jélyotte frequently recur. Marie Fel (1713-94), soprano, made her début at the Opéra in 1734 and immediately took leading roles. The darling of Paris, courted and adulated, she enjoyed the friendship of Voltaire among others. Pierre de Jélyotte (1713-97) was primarily a counter-tenor but also a guitarist, organist, harpsichordist, violinist and even composer – the complete musician. He came to the Opéra in 1733, but his real success dates from *Les Indes galantes* (1735). His career is inseparable from that of Rameau, and he interpreted all the master's works as well as operas by Mondonville, Boismortier and Leclair and revivals of the works of Lully, Mouret and Destouches. He also created the role of Colin in Rousseau's *Le Devin du village*. Jélyotte left the Opéra in 1755 but continued to take part in spectacles at the court at Versailles and at Fontainebleau. He did not really retire until 1765, and even then he was seen at the château of the Prince de Conti, where he accompanied the infant Mozart.

Among the female dancers the names of Mesdemoiselles Françoise Prévost (1680-1744), Marie-Anne Camargo (1710-70) and Marie Sallé (1707-56), deserve mention. Mlle Sallé was brought to England by Handel for Covent Garden, but returned to Paris for *Les Indes galantes*. Of the male dancers the most famous were Louis Dupré (*c*.1697-1774), Jean-Georges Noverre (1727-1810) and Gaetano Vestris (1729-1808), who began at the Opéra in 1749 and was recognized as the best dancer of his time until his own son, Auguste, captured the favor of the public. Thanks to the patronage of Queen Marie-Antoinette, Noverre was appointed Maître de Ballet of the Académie Royale in 1776 and it was he who commissioned from Mozart in 1778 the ballet *Les petits riens*.

• The Harpsichord •

Each of the three great European cultures that dominate the Heroic Age of the seventeenth and eighteenth centuries has a distinctive instrument associated with it. In Italy the development of the violin reached its apex at this time, emulating the

lyricism and expressivity of the human voice while attaining a greater agility and brilliance than that of which the voice is capable. In Germany the distinctive instrument was the organ, which was capable of true polyphony in three, four, five or even six voices, thereby establishing links with the past; but was also superbly adapted to the performance of dissonances, since the sounds, however harsh or lacerating, are sustained as long as the keys are depressed. The quintessential instrument of France was the harpsichord, which was, of course, the basic domestic keyboard instrument all over Europe, but which in France became associated with a mature 'school' of composers for whom it was a major, if not exclusive, medium. In order to understand how this happened, it is necessary to look at the harpsichord's relationship to the lute, which in the hands of the leading musical representatives of the salons – Denis Gautier (1603-72), Jaques Gallot (d. *c*.1690) and Charles Mouton (1626-1710) – had become an instrument of high sophistication.

The tone color of the lute – especially the kind of lute played in the seventeenth-century French salons – is rarefied and exquisite. Though soft, it is capable of an infinite variety of nuance; moreover, since the strings are directly under the control of the player's fingers it speaks with intimate humanity. The harpsichord resembles the lute in being a plucked string instrument. It differs from the lute in that the strings are plucked not by the fingers, but by quills operated by mechanical jacks. Inevitably, the harpsichord tended to take over from the lute as music became less intimate and more the servant of baroque court ceremony. Even so, French harpsichord composers were reluctant to sacrifice the lute's sensitivity to the harpsichord's potential brilliance. The Italians built harpsichords which were well adapted to dance music, since, although the tone is often sweet as well as full, their action produces an initially explosive 'pop,' which soon decays. The French harpsichord, based on Flemish models, lacks the sharp ictus which marks the start of every note on an Italian instrument, and the tone, being gentler, more subtly colored and more sustained, was responsive to the *mignardise* (delicacy) and sensibility favored by the French court. There is a parallel

Above: The French town of Chaumes-en-Brie, where the Couperin dynasty of musicians originated.

Above: André Campra depicted on a commemorative medal dated 1730; the inscription reads, 'He knows how to sing the glory of saints and heroes,' referring to his excellence in church music and in opera.

La Salle du Bal donné dans le petit Parc de Versailles. IV. Aula frondibus et virgultis septa, ad saltationes et choreas ducendas parata, Jn Hortis Versalianis.

Right: A ball given in a temporary pavilion in the gardens of Versailles in 1678.

Above: Elisabeth-Claude Jacquet de la Guerre (1666/7-1729), commemorated on a medal. A youthful prodigy, who performed at court before Louis XIV when only fifteen, she became a famous harpsichord teacher in Paris. In 1707 she published a set of her compositions for harpsichord, and among her other works the lyric tragedy *Céphale et Procris* (1694) was the first piece by a woman composer to be given a performance at the Académie Royale de Musique.

between the richness of Italian harpsichords and that of Italian *bel canto* singing and of Corellian violin style, whereas the French harpsichord 'spoke' intimately and defined line meticulously, as did the French *petite voix* — the head-voice technique favored in the singing of ariettes and much church music — and French fiddling. French harpsichord building reached its apex in the work of the Blanchet family and their successors, the Taskins, who survived long enough to build fortepianos as an alternative to, not as a substitute for, harpsichords.

• Chambonnières •

Jacques de Chambonnières (1601/2-72), was the first harpsichordist composer of the great tradition. Of aristocratic birth, he was a leading musical representative of the Hôtel de Rambouillet, a member of *précieux* society, and a friend of Louis XIV as well as his court clavecinist. His father had been an amateur harpsichordist of distinction and his ancestors included several lutenists. He divided his time between the court and his country estate; but although he was, like his father, in the best sense an amateur, he was universally admired for the skill and sensitivity both of his harpsichord playing and of his compositions.

Given Chambonnières's ancestral lineage, it is not surprising that much of his finest music is elegiac in tone. The contrapuntal entries, the rhythmic flexibilities and the dissonant false relations (the simultaneous or near-simultaneous sounding of the major and minor third), for instance in his three large-scale G minor Pavanes,

hark back to the noble polyphony of the old organ school while contrapuntal survivals are evident in the 'simulated polyphony' which he adapted directly from the lutenists — from whom he also took over his forms. His works begin with a prelude, usually written in unmeasured notation, to be interpreted by the performer — a more organized development of the preliminary flourishes in arpeggios which a player might improvise to a song, or employ as loosening-up exercises before a solo performance. This prelude is succeeded by a sequence of dances — pavane (later replaced by allemande), courante, sarabande, gigue — all of which preserve the features of the court dance as originally performed by the nobility, though the character of the dance may be submerged in the melodic and figurative extensions. Court dances were not merely entertainment, but were related to patterns of behavior and psychological states: pavanes were noble, allemandes grave but tougher, courantes more animated, sarabandes lyrically tender or alternatively grand, being love-dances that were also sacramental. The slighter dances that were often incorporated — bourrés, canaris, branles, passepieds, etc. — tend to preserve their 'popular' character as occasional music, though Chambonnières, being a real composer, transmutes them into music of a personal savor.

But the most beautiful and personal of Chambonnières's pieces are the most aristocratically valedictory, in particular the sarabandes. These combine diatonically innocent melodies which sound like civilized reincarnations of French folksong, or the fragrant if more sophisticated monody of the medieval troubadours, with a harmonic texture wherein inner parts come

147

Right: Portrait of Charles Mouton by François de Troy the Elder. Mouton had been a pupil of Denis Gautier before becoming lutenist at the court of Turin from 1670 to 1678. After that he settled in Paris, where he gained fame as a virtuoso player and a teacher, with such pupils as Le Sage de Richée and Milleran, lutenist to the King. Of Mouton's compositions for the lute two books, published in 1699, survive. Other works, in manuscript, include lute transcriptions of extracts from operas by Lully.

Opposite: Charles Couperin (1638-79) painted by Claude Fèbvre, shown with the painter's daughter. Charles was a brother of Louis and François. At the age of twenty-one he was given a post as viol player at the French court, and when Louis Couperin died in 1661, Charles took over his post as organist at Saint-Gervais in Paris.

and go, with the improvisatory delicacy of lute music. The idiom sounds as though it is being composed *ad hoc*; augmented and diminished intervals, created by suspensions in the inner parts, give poignancy to the graceful melodies, while complementarily the symmetrical proportions – the balance of phrase against phrase – disciplines any tendency to self-indulgence. The fragile ornamentation introduced into inner parts as well as the main melody attempts to imbue the relatively mechancial harpsichord with the subtle immediacy of the lute; most of the ornaments, especially the port de voix and the mordent, have vocal origins, being means of rendering a melodic line more *humanly* expressive. Significantly, the most intimate of Chambonnières's pieces tend to be the best; we may

mention in particular the exquisite sarabandes in G, D and F majors. He is a *grand seigneur* of the old world, whose grandeur remains chivalrously discreet.

• Louis Couperin •

Chambonnières's estate was near Chaumes-en-Brie, the little town where the Couperin family had lived for generations. It was he who 'spotted' the talent of Louis Couperin (1626-61), took him to court and fostered his gifts both as harpsichordist and as composer. The quasi-improvisatory quality in Chambonnières's music is foreign to Louis Couperin's – except of course

Right top: The actor-dramatist Jean-Baptiste Molière, who, starting in 1664, collaborated with Lully to create comedy-ballets (*divertissements*) for the Comédie Française; after his rift with Lully in 1672, Molière worked with the composer Marc-Antoine Charpentier.

Right center: Pierre Corneille (1606-84), considered by many to be the founder of French classical theater.

Right bottom: Jean Racine (1639-99), whose involvement with the musical world was established only toward the end of his life, mainly in collaboration with Jean-Baptiste Moreau, the Master of the King's Music, who provided the music for his *Cantiques spirituels*.

in the Preludes deliberately written in unmeasured notation. For the most part his technical assurance is as potent as his imagination; when, as in the G minor Allemande (no. 92), he employs a contrapuntal technique harking back to the old organ school, he does so with a toughness very different from Chambonnières's consciously archaistic polyphony. Similarly his nobly expressive sarabandes, such as the D major (no. 60), substitute for Chambonnières's old-world fragrance a lyrically warm but tightly organized *bel canto* style almost prophetic of Handel. The E minor Sarabande (no. 65) is especially rich in powerful, sometimes unprepared dissonances; while his famous funeral tribute to the lutenist Blancrocher revives the resplendently decorated, dissonantly improvisatory *tombeau* convention of the lutenists, but intensifies it to a pitch of passion that is almost operatic. A comparable piece is the magnificent Pavane in F sharp minor – a key known to the lutenists as *le ton de la chèvre* because it was notoriously tricky in mean-tone tuning. The 'bad' – that is, out of tune – intervals that cannot be avoided in mean-tone F sharp minor may be exploited for emotive effect. Certainly the chromatic alterations in Louis Couperin's piece give it remarkable pathos, though again the sensuality of the dissonances is disciplined by the classically elegant proportions.

149

The most impressive of Louis Couperin's pieces, as well as the most 'modern' in effect, are those using the transitional technique of the chaconne or passacaglia – originally a dance in triple tempo, built over an ostinato bass. The recurrent bass auralizes the formality and control without which civilization is impossible; but it both supports and stimulates melodic variations which grow progressively more exciting. French chaconnes and Italian passacaglias lent themselves to development on an extensive scale and were used for the climacteric moments in Lully's operas. A related convention was the chaconne-rondeau, a rondeau being a symmetrical dance tune intermittently repeated, each recurrence being separated by a 'couplet' or episode which changes the melody but not usually the rhythm; the changes may or may not affect the original tune's recurrences.

Especially remarkable in Louis Couperin's output are the spiky D minor Chaconne (no.55) and the powerful G minor Passacaille (no.99), his biggest piece in every sense. Built over a falling scale bass, it employs every device later to be used by Couperin le Grand to build a climax – dissonant suspensions, flowing scale passages in parallel and contrary motion, increasing rhythmic complexity. A near sublime sense of release is created by a modulation into the major, incorporating richly spaced suspensions and a chromatically modified version of the bass, counteracted by a soaring diatonic scale. The final couplet keeps the chromatic base but returns somberly to the minor.

• Chambonnières's pupils •

Chambonnières was also the teacher of Jean-Henri d'Anglebert, who was born in Paris in 1635 and became organist to the Duc d'Orléans in about 1660. With Chambonnières's support he became a court musician in 1662 and published his harpsichord pieces in 1689, two years before his death. He is perhaps the greatest and certainly the grandest of the French harpsichord composers before Couperin le Grand, for he transfers to the instrument much of the contrapuntal sinew and harmonic luxuriance that distinguish his superb organ fugues (1660), creating a darkly passionate music that is often strenuous, and seldom characterized by the 'charm' that is supposed to be the hallmark of French music of most periods. This is obviously the case in an austerely wrought movement like the G minor Allemande or any of the harmonically audacious unmeasured preludes. But even his positively 'affirmative' pieces have a glowing incandescence that disturbs even as it elevates; one may mention the brillantly expansive variations on *La Folia*, or the chaconne-rondeaux in G major and D major.

Gaspard le Roux (1660-1705) may count as a late representative of the *grand goût* of the mid-century. Less of an amateur than Chambonnières, less of a modernist than Louis Couperin, he combines a nobly balanced lyricism with richly sequential harmonic writing. His personality is more sober, even somber, than that of d'Anglebert – not surprisingly, his music seems to have been much appreciated in Germany. The Suite in the 'dangerous' key of F sharp minor from the 1705 edition of his harpsichord pieces is especially beautiful, while the D minor Chaconne deserves to keep company with the grandest pieces in this grandest of contemporary forms. The long Sarabande with variations in G minor – in effect also a chaconne – is remarkable for being, unlike most of Le Roux's music, 'progressive' in its keyboard technique. Its use of arpeggio and scale figurations almost suggests the Handel of the harpsichord passacaglias.

There is also a distinguished woman composer among Couperin's immediate predecessors – Elisabeth-Claude Jacquet de la Guerre. Born in 1666 or 1667, she came of a family of musicians, her father and brother both being organists, and

Below left: Jean-Henri d'Anglebert, composer, harpsichord player and organist. The pupil and successor of Jacques de Chambonnières, he held several posts as organist before being appointed harpsichord player to the King in 1662.

Below: Frontispiece of d'Anglebert's book of compositions published under the title *Pièces de Clavecin* in 1689, two years before his death. It included sixty pieces for harpsichord, five organ fugues and a quartet on the Kyrie theme.

Louis XIV greatly admired her ability as harpsichordist and as improviser. Like Couperin, she is a linear composer, who thinks in terms of two polyphonic voices, one for each hand; their interplay creates surprisingly dense harmonic implications. Especially lovely in the D minor Suite (published in 1707) is *La Flamande* and its double; the tender sarabande, which shifts dreamily between the major and the minor; the chromatically witty gigue; and the grandly pathetic chaconne-rondeau. Her range is more limited than Couperin's; her music lives and breathes in her aristocratic salon and does not, like his, evoke a multifarious world. Nonetheless, within her salon live and breathe she certainly does; and the parallel between her and Couperin suggests how inseparably, in this society, masculine and feminine elements of the psyche were intertwined.

•Couperin le Grand•

François Couperin (1668-1733) – known as le Grand to indicate his pre-eminence among his colleagues as well as his family – came from a dynasty of musicians exceeded in distinction and longevity only by the Bach family. After Louis Couperin was introduced to court by Chambonnières the Couperins officiated as organists at Saint-Gervais in Paris. Louis was succeeded in that post by Charles (1638-79), and Charles's son François took over while still in his teens. François's earliest music – certainly his earliest publication – were his organ Masses, in the old French Catholic liturgical tradition; and he continued to compose motets and elevations after he had become an official court composer in the last years of the seventeenth century. Exquisite and often profound though these works may be, the heart of Couperin's music lies in the harpsichord pieces which he wrote for himself and his friends and pupils. For although Couperin was born into a world which had illusions, if not delusions, of grandeur, he himself was a private rather than a public composer.

His harpsichord pieces – which he published himself, in exquisitely engraved calligraphy, in four volumes dated 1713, 1716-17, 1722 and 1730 – stretch over his working life. Their self-enclosed character is manifest in the formality of the conventions, of which there are really only two. One is the binary dance movement, such as was employed by all Couperin's predecessors. Basically this consists of a (usually sixteen-measure) tune modulating from tonic to dominant, returning in the second 'half' to the tonic, usually in another sixteen measures. The dances themselves – by Couperin's day established as allemande, courante, sarabande, gigue, with a miscellany of lighter, more popular dances – derive from the court dances as originally performed by the King and nobility, though as private feeling modifies public assumptions, so the dances cease to be music for dancing to and become 'mood' pieces existing in their own right. Each dance acquires a specific emotional characteristic, just as each key comes to have a psychological symbolic import. Masque dances were an emblem of human perfectability; the dancers, graciously civilized beings, created the Golden Age as they moved in concordant solidarity. The mirror-like quality of binary form reflects this; phrase echoes phrase just as the windows of Versailles symmetrically answer one another.

Much the same is true of the other basic formal convention Couperin employs. That is the rondeau – a symmetrical, usually eight- or sixteen-measure tune recurrently repeated but interspersed with episodes or 'couplets' of related material – wherein the repetitions imply habituation and conformity while the episodes comment on and suggest alternative possibilities. Rondeaux thus effect a compromise between the private and the public life, while always assuring us that the whole is more important than the parts.

An extraordinary range of private feelings is evident in Couperin's harpsichord pieces. He intersperses simple dance pieces with 'portraits' of the people who made up his world, along with soundscapes of the places wherein they lived. Often the subject of these portraits is easily recognizable: the first piece in the first book, a noble allemande called *L'Auguste*, is a portrait of Louis-Auguste, Duc de Maine, a close friend and patron of the composer; *La Majestueuse* would seem to be a portrait of the King himself (the feminine gender in this title implies 'la pièce majestueuse'). At the opposite pole to these intimately grand portraits is a witty sketch like *La Milordine*, a portrait of an English lordling who was living, in exile from the English court, at the palace at St Germain-en-Laye. Many princesses figure in the gallery (*La Princesse de Sens*, *La Princesse de Chabeuil*), but so do simple peasant or servant girls (*La Nanette*, *La Fleurie tendre*), and many girls connected with the theater who may or may not also have had associations with high life through being mistresses of the nobility. Even when it is impossible to identify Couperin's 'subject,' the

Above: Title-page of Chambonnières's first book of harpsichord compositions, published in 1670.

Above: Watteau's painting of Gilles (*c.*1718-20) parallels Couperin's observation, in his harpsichord piece entitled *L'Arlequin*, of the strange and lonely harlequin figure of the *commedia dell'arte*.

music usually has a particularity which indicates that the portrait is specific, not generalized. The famous *Soeur Monique*, for instance, is certainly an adolescent nun but is also a flesh-and-blood young woman, virginally innocent yet sensuously subtle, even a bit of a minx. Couperin must have known her well; she may even have been his daughter who entered the cloisters.

Couperin also makes his listeners aware, from time to time, of the world outside the shuttered salon; portraits merge into a soundscape of the Parisian streets below his window in the Rue Neuve des Bon Enfants – the martial glitter of soldiers (*La Marche des gris-vêtus*), the whine of beggars' hurdy-gurdies, the bleat of bagpipes and the squawk of pipes and fifes, accompanying the antics of monkeys and dancing bears. (The most justly celebrated of these descriptive pieces is the brilliant *Les Fastes de la grande et ancienne ménestrandise*, a cycle of pieces deliberately confusing the trivial and the sublime.) Many pieces tell of his youth in the Arcadian gentleness of La Croulli (the piece of that title, the *Musètes de Choisy* and *de Taverni* – both places in Couperin country). The sundry pieces about birds are also redolent of the open air, even though 'bird' had a human as well as avian sense in Couperin's day, as it does now. *Le Rossignol en amour*, for instance, is liquidly lovely enough to sound like a real nightingale in the silence of the night; at the same time the caressing convolutions of its ornamentation

evoke the young woman who, lovelorn, primps herself in the solitude of her salon.

The numinous may be manifest in what seem the simplest of Couperin's evocations of the external world. For instance in that sophisticated evocation of rusticity *Les Vergers fleuris*, from Book III, he is probably depicting the delights of the orchard at his country house at St Germain-en-Laye; but the tenderly ornamented lines create, over the bagpipe drone, intertwining dissonant suspensions that imbue the music with another dimension. The elegant symmetry of the form dissolves into a summer-haze of dream; much as in the *fêtes champêtres* of Watteau, the architectural gravity of the figures is absorbed into glowingly idealized hues of nature.

The equivocation between the public world and the private dream takes a different form in the pieces associated with the *commedia dell'arte*, whose players Couperin, like Watteau, met and knew, probably quite well, on their sojourns in Paris. These pieces are most prevalent in the later books and in the last volume most profoundly reveal the impulses behind this obsession with theatrical illusion. *L'Arlequin*, for instance, is balanced between simplicity and sophisticated sensitivity, like Watteau's miraculous portrait of Gilles. Both Watteau and Couperin seem to be transmuting a personal loneliness into the world of the *commedia* precisely because the theater can mythologize the crudities and indignities of life into 'something rich and strange.' Couperin's harlequin is grotesque and foolish but magically dreams through his sequential chromatics. The scaramouche from another piece from the last book, *La pantomime*, moves puppet-like through the *grande précision* of his dotted rhythmed gestures, which tightly control the pain of the dissonant ninths and sevenths. The piece is not so much disillusioned as illusionless; from which it draws its nervous pride and sinewy strength.

Couperin's harpsichord music is properly regarded as intimate, witty and sensitive, rather than impassioned; he himself recommended a delicate approach to the harpsichord and said he preferred to be touched rather than surprised. Yet his pastoral arcadias may hide a profound melancholy, and the witty audacity of his *commedia dell'arte* pieces may plumb unexpected depths. The gloomy, viscid texture of *La Ténébreuse* and *La Lugubre* is certainly exceptional in Couperin's work; and the fact that some of the major-keyed pieces in the suite are unwontedly, even farcically, frivolous only reinforces the intensity, as though facetiousness were an escape valve but for which the anguish would be insupportable. Similar feelings are evoked in the famous B minor Suite from Book II, in which all the pieces are at once grave and richly impassioned, complex in texture, until they culminate in the tremendous *Passacaille en rondeau*, wherein each couplet adds to the intensity until a shattering climax is attained in the seventh couplet's anguished triple suspensions, percussively exploiting the entire range of the keyboard. Although the passion increases cumulatively, the unaltered repetition of the opening clause, demanded by the chaconne-rondeau convention, gives to the music an implacably fateful, Racinian quality. Significantly, Couperin does not end the Ordre there, at its climax, but appends a modest little Corellian gigue, *La Morinète*, to bring the listeners back safe and sound, if precariously so, to the social world in which they habitually exist.

The climax of the thirteenth Ordre in B minor, *Les Folies françoises ou les dominos*, depicts in the sequence of its variations a masqued ball. Couperin's music, like Watteau's painting, presents the ball in ideality, each variation being a different-colored mask which enshrines psychological truth even as it propagates illusion. The moods range from pristine innocence (*La Virginité, couleur d'invisible*) to impudent wit (*La Coquéterie, sous differens dominos*), from sinister taciturnity (*Domino gris de maure*) to a frenzied despair (*Sous le domino noir*). So Couperin has revealed the blackest horrors behind the masking dominos and the ball's frivolous façade and he appends as an epilogue his most concentratedly tragic utterance, *L'Âme en peine*, a piece as violent as *La Passacaille* but covering only one page. Again Couperin's irony and his melancholy are interdependent, and that *Les Folies françoises* is riddled with witty japes only makes this epilogue the more agonizing.

For a distillation of what one might call Couperin's civilized wisdom, however, it is

Right: Page from François Couperin's second book of harpsichord pieces. The composer's harpsichord compositions numbered some two hundred and forty works, arranged in four books. The first of these was published in 1713, the second in 1717, the third in 1722 and the fourth in 1730.

Right: This anonymous portrait (*c.*1695) is presumed to be of François Couperin le Grand and shows the composer as a young man of about twenty-seven, when he had already assumed the role of organist to the King and had composed several works for both organ and harpsichord.

necessary to return to the first book and specifically to the chaconne-rondeau which resolves the turbulence of the C minor Suite. Published in 1713, this was perhaps inspired by the events, calamitous for the French nobility, of 1712. Though the piece may well be entitled *La Favorite* as a tribute to the dead Dauphin, its gravity and grace define a disinterested passion that amounts to an 'attitude to life' rather than a particularized portrait. The melancholy of the dissonances is given stability not only by the symmetrical structure, but also by being absorbed

into a dialogue between treble and bass. The drooping scale figure of the melody, its falling sequences, and the declining chromaticism of the harmony are answered, mirror-wise, by the upward scale figure in the *cantabile* bass line. Moreover, the 'positive' elements grow stronger throughout the piece; when we hear the theme for the last time we can understand why its tone should be, though elegiac, also noble.

• Couperin's *Art* •

Couperin's book *L'Art de toucher le clavecin* is conversational in tone, addressed to friends and colleagues rather than to the general public; nonetheless, he offers his experience as a touchstone, and most of what he says is relevant not merely to his own music, but also to the work of the French harpsichord school in general. The essence of the French style, Couperin suggests, derives from the harpsichord, whereas Italian style derives from the violin. The distinction is most evident in the approach to rhythm. The Italians for the most part play the note values as they are written, the French do not; and the reason is that the French, thinking in terms of the mechanized lute which is the harpsichord, are always trying to make it capable of emotional gradations – as was noted above with regard to the style of Chambonnières. This is why rhythmic inequalities are common practice in France, but comparatively unfamiliar in Italy. Such inequalities are not notated because they could not be notated. If they could be written out, they would not have the expressive fluidity which is the reason for their existence. The commonest type of inequality occurs in progressions of four or more eighth notes or sixteenth notes moving by step; except in fast tempo, the first note of each pair is played longer than the second. Hardly less common is the reverse process: in eighth notes slurred in pairs, the first note is slightly shorter than the second. Both kinds of inequality can occur, in different lines, in the same bar, possibly combined with other lines played equally. Precisely where the inequalities are introduced, and the proportional relationship of long to short notes, depends not on rigid rules but on the context, and ultimately on 'le bon goût.'

Ornamentation in French harpsichord music is inseparable from these subtleties of rhythm. Of course, the basic ornaments – the long appoggiatura, the trill and the mordent – are common to all baroque music; if there are more of them in Couperin's harpsichord music than in, say, Handel's, this is because Couperin is revealing the soul of the instrument, whereas Handel is usually writing dance music, influenced by string idiom, for keyboard. The weaving garlands of appoggiaturas and passing notes in a piece like *Les Langueurs tendres* indicate how closely Couperin's ornamentation is related to his rhythmic flexibility; passing notes become suaver when the first note of each pair is slightly longer than the second, appoggiaturas become more caressing when the first eighth note of each pair is slightly the shorter. Some of Couperin's ornaments are not common property in baroque music, but are direct adaptations of lute techniques. The 'suspension' and the 'aspiration' effect a momentary catch in the breath, a quivering silence before or after a note respectively. Earlier and other French harpsichord composers probably employed them spontaneously, but it is Couperin, as the classical master, who codifies them. He explicitly says that their purpose is to make the instrument speak more intimately, and adds that they can be used only by persons 'susceptible de sentiment.'

• Clérambault and Rameau •

Louis-Nicolas Clérambault (1676-1749) came from a family of musicians who had served the French court since the late fifteenth century. Like Couperin, he had no instinct for public ceremonial and composed no operas. He was most renowned for his chamber cantatas on classical themes and for his organ music, which, like Couperin's, absorbed the galanteries of aristocratic dance and *Air de Cour* into an austerely ecclesiastical polyphony. Unlike Couperin, however, he devoted little attention to the harpsichord. Such harpsichord music as he did produce has a gentle distinction collateral with that of his beautiful cantatas; refinement of line co-exists with harmonic voluptuousness, so that his harpsichord music has a paradoxically sensuous chastity.

Certainly Clérambault is closer to Couperin than is Rameau, the greatest composer of the next generation. Rameau's harpsichord music is for the most part early, composed during Couperin's lifetime, though its manner is very different – more harmonic, less linear in layout, more virtuosic and theatrical in treatment. It is more brilliant, and more immediately emotional, than Couperin's work – but not more profound. Perhaps Rameau's very finest pieces, such as the superb A minor Allemande and in quieter vein *Les Tendres plaintes*, are an exception to this, having much of Couperin's gravity. But they are less characteristic of Rameau than an audaciously imaginative 'coloristic' piece like *Le Rappel des oiseaux*; a grand Handelian piece like the Gavotte with variations or the A major Sarabande; or expansive virtuoso pieces such as *Les Tourbillons*, *Les Cyclopes*, with its nonmelodic Alberti bass, *La Dauphine*, *La Triomphante*, or the exciting rondeau *Les Niais de Sologne*.

Rameau looks forward rather than backward. There are passages in his harpsichord music which, although contemporary with Couperin, already give intimation of eighteenth-century sonata style. *La Poule* is a genuine harpsichord piece in the classical baroque tradition; yet towards the end, just before the coda, there is a passage, harping on the chord of the diminished seventh, which has in miniature the structural and harmonic effect of the cadenza to a Mozart concerto. There is nothing at all comparable with this in Couperin. Similarly one of the most remarkable of Rameau's pieces, *L'Enharmonique*, is, as its title indicates, a study in tonal relationships. It has a diminished seventh cadence which is not produced by linear movement but is harmonic in its own right, marking a rhetorical or dramatic point in the structure, as do the cadences in an eighteenth-century sonata. Rameau's delightful *Pièces de clavecin*

Top: Page of the original manuscript of Rameau's harpsichord piece *La Dauphine*. Most of Rameau's keyboard works were composed in Couperin's lifetime, but they were in general much more theatrical in style, looking forward to Rameau's later career as a composer of opera and ballet.

Above: Title-page of one of Jacques Duphly's four books of harpsichord pieces. Duphly (1715-89) composed nearly fifty keyboard pieces, which were published towards the end of the golden age of French harpsichord music.

en concert, cast in the three-movement Italian concerto form of allegro–andante–allegro, illustrate this progressive modernism even more clearly. Their harpsichord part is not a continuo part like that of Couperin's trio sonatas, nor a piece of polyphonic writing like that of Bach's sonatas. The keyboard is treated as a virtuoso solo instrument in a way that suggests Haydn's and Mozart's use of piano with strings.

Jacques Duphly was born in 1715 (by which date some of Couperin's first volumes of harpsichord pieces were already published), and did not die until 1789. Four volumes of his clavecin works were published in 1755; starting in the first, the allemandes, courantes and some of the rondeaux preserve the linear dignity of the classical style as manifest in Couperin, and some of them – for instance, the D minor Allemande and Courante – are exceptionally beautiful. But there are pieces in the fourth book, such as *La de Sartine* and *La de Juigne*, which are fully fledged rococo movements relying on simple chordal progressions rather than on line, with tunes and fill-in scales and arpeggiated Alberti basses that would sound as well on the fortepiano as

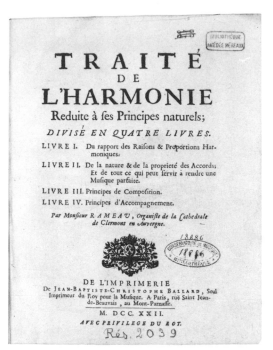

Left: Title-page of the first edition of Rameau's *Traité de l'harmonie*. Rameau's theoretical works on music were as notable as his compositions. The *Traité*, published in 1722, was the first of them. Rameau worked out a coherent harmonic system and believed that certain tonalities had psychological as well as harmonic effects.

Left: Plate from the *Encyclopédie* of Diderot and d'Alembert illustrating one of the articles on instrument-making with diagrams of a spinet, a psaltery, and two parts of the mechanism of a two-manual harpsichord.

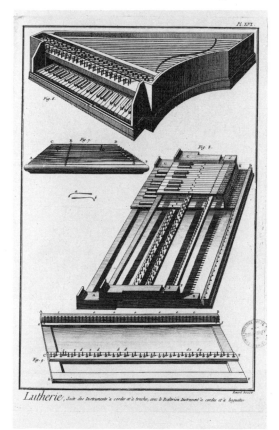

Scarlatti. Still more dazzling is a piece appropriately titled *La Victoire*.

Duphly's 'modern' and/or 'decadent' characteristics should not necessarily be regarded as loss. He is a real composer who profited from, rather than being inhibited by, his transitional position; if he surrenders some of Couperin's civilized elegance, he is alertly responsive to a mutable world.

It is clear that Couperin stood for something from which the modern world was to turn away. His influence survived in France for barely twenty-five years after his death. The architectural symmetry of the classical tradition had perished; along with it went much of the human expressivity which Couperin supremely represents.

Two daughters of Couperin, Marie-Madeleine (1690-1742) and Marguerite-Antoinette (1705-78), became professional musicians, the former being organist of the convent she entered, the latter succeeding to some of her father's court appointments as harpsichordist. Nicolas Couperin (1680-1748) and Armand-Louis Couperin (1727-89) succeeded to the organ loft at Saint-Gervais, and the latter composed copiously in several media. But the great tradition of French harpsichord composers was by now moribund; its influence was felt only in Germany, which, perhaps as a result of the time-lag occasioned by the Thirty Years' War, tended to be valedictory, even anti-modernist, in its culture. In 1757 Bach's son, Carl Philipp Emanuel, was producing keyboard pieces for harpsichord or fortepiano with French titles, including such familiar ones as *L'Auguste* and *Les Langueurs tendres*. The composer adapts the binary structure, the staccato arpeggio figurations and the sequential passage-work typical of Couperin's lighter pieces, but the form is now harmonically and metrically dictated, in a manner that suggests Haydn and the early symphony.

on the harpsichord – perhaps better. Somewhat paradoxically, Duphly exploits these modern techniques even in the old-fashioned convention of the chaconne, for he has a very long Chaconne in F which is riddled with Alberti figurations, a device which Couperin, as a linear composer, regarded with suspicion and used, if at all, satirically, as in *Le Tic-toc-choc* or *Les Tricoteuses*. Even in the first book Duphly includes a piece, *La Cozamajor*, which uses scale and arpeggio figurations that in virtuosity, if not in intensity, rival Rameau and even

Children of the Chappell.

Gentlemen of the Chappell.

Henry Purcell and English stage music

The great flowering of English music during the Renaissance faded in the early seventeenth century, and, apart from Purcell, there were no native composers of international stature for almost three hundred years. The Puritan movement, especially when it held power during the Commonwealth (1649-60), certainly inhibited musical development, but its dampening effect on English theater was short-lived, and it seems that it was the strength of the spoken theatrical tradition that held at bay the new art of opera, perpetuating the same mixture of speech and music found in Elizabethan plays and in court masques. The latter contained songs and dances but did not adopt Italian operatic recitative; such musical setting of speech was felt to be inappropriate on stage.

During the first part of Purcell's career, he composed mainly for the church, but his last ten years were largely devoted to theater music. However, only *Dido and Aeneas* written for amateur performance in a girls' school in 1689, can be counted an opera, although he wrote five 'semioperas.' These embody many features of the court masque, and the problems of staging for modern audiences mean that England's finest dramatic composer is known, *Dido* apart, largely by his songs, anthems and instrumental music.

Top: Henry Purcell (1659-95), a portrait after Kneller.

The Chapel Royal, whose function was to perform divine service for the royal family and which comprised some thirty-two men and a dozen boys, had been a principal training-ground for English musicians since the fifteenth century, and it remained virtually unaltered through all the upheavals of the Reformation. Some of its members are shown (*above*) in the procession at Queen Elizabeth's funeral in 1603.

Below: The self-portrait (*c.*1650) of Peter Lely with his family (including his wife in four different mythological guises) evokes the intimate nature of family

The Chapel Royal was reconstituted by Charles II after the Commonwealth, and Purcell's father and uncle sang at his coronation in 1661. Soon after, Henry himself became a chorister there, and in 1682 he was appointed organist. Perhaps his finest sacred music is found in the verse anthems he composed in the years 1682-5, with strings providing overtures, *obbligato* parts and accompaniment to the voices.

chamber music – an important field for composers. Purcell wrote fantasias in the old style for viol consort as well as trio-sonatas in the new Italian style.

Below: One of the royal violins used by the band of violinists formed by Charles II in imitation of Louis XIV's *Violons du Roi*. In 1677 Purcell was appointed composer in ordinary to the King's Violins.

Purcell contributed music for over forty stage pieces, working with many of the foremost playwrights of his day, including John Dryden. One of his last works for the theater was Thomas D'Urfey's *Don Quixote* (1694), based on Cervantes' novel, on which he collaborated with John Eccles (*c*.1668-1735), supplying songs, duets, choruses and ensembles. Here (*right*), the song 'Let the dreadful Engines' from the play is seen in Purcell's manuscript collection of solo songs and duos with *basso continuo*.

Above: Players at a wedding masque (*c*.1595) for Sir Henry Unton, Queen Elizabeth's special envoy to Henri IV of France. English masques, which combined dancing, speech and song, were clearly derived from the Italian *intermedi* and French *ballets de cour* and reached their high point in the reign of James I (1603-25). Among the most notable later masques were *Comus* (1634) by John Milton, with music by Henry Lawes (1596-1662), and James Shirley's *Cupid and Death* (1653), with music by Matthew Locke (1621/2-77) and Christopher Gibbons (1615-76).

Right: As in France and Italy, designers of masques were at least as important as poets or composers. In England the master of the art was Inigo Jones, an architect dedicated to the new classical style of Palladio. The figures of a transformed statue and a fiery spirit (*right above and below*) are costume designs by Jones for *The Lord's Masque*, put on for a royal wedding in 1613. The poet was Thomas Campion (1567-1620), one of the most prolific of English lute-song writers, who also wrote songs for the masque, while the dance music was written by John Coprario (d.1626).

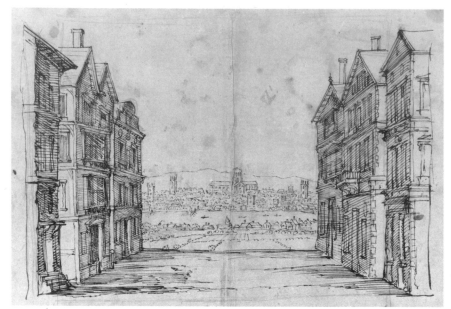

The cast of *Britannia Triumphans* was a typical mixture, including emblematic figures, court personages, figures of order and discord, as well as ordinary people. The scene (*left*) shows 'English houses of the old and newer formes . . . and farre off a prospect of the Citie of London and the River of Thames,' with old St Paul's in the center; while the figures (*below*) represent the peasant rebel leader Jack Straw (*left*) and a 'crier of mouse-traps' (*right*).

During the 1680s the commemoration of St Cecilia, patron saint of music, became established practice, and Purcell wrote several odes for her saint's day. The declamatory solo (*right*) with its elaborate ornaments, which were sung by Purcell himself, comes from *Hail, bright Cecilia* (1692). These odes, like those he wrote to welcome the monarch's return to London or to celebrate a royal birthday, were in essence cantatas for solo voices, chorus and orchestra.

Above and right: Another of Jones's masques, *Britannia Triumphans* (1638), had a text by Sir William Davenant, who later, during the Commonwealth, put on the first English opera, *The Siege of Rhodes*, with music by Locke, Henry Lawes and others.

Below: The Thames at Westminster in 1647. Whitehall Palace – extending down river from Westminster Hall – which housed the Chapel Royal, and Westminster Abbey provided the background to much of Purcell's career.

A Venetian visitor to London twenty years earlier described the 'gay and burlesque scenes' which were interspersed with the action of a masque, but the music 'did not strike us as very fine, spoiled as we are by the beautiful and harmonious music of Italy.'

After his voice had broken, he was employed as an organ-tuner at the Abbey, and he was appointed organist there in succession to John Blow (1649-1708) in 1679. His house was in St Ann's Lane, behind the Parliament House.

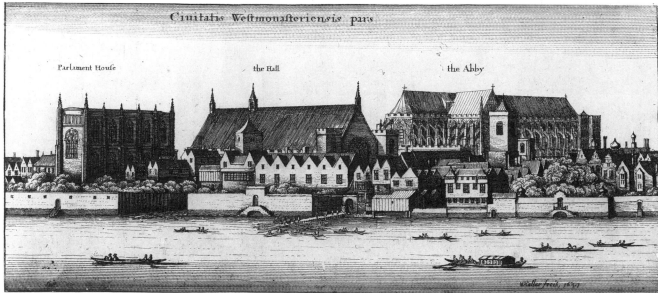

Civitatis Westmonasteriensis pars

Parliament House   the Hall   the Abby

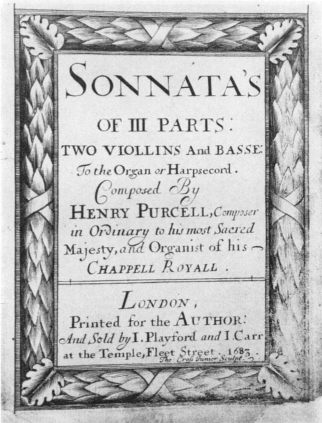

Right: 'Celia has a thousand charms' is one of the three songs Purcell set in the year of his death to be performed in Gould's play *The Rival Sisters, or The Violence of Love*. The fact that it was reprinted in the collection *Orpheus Britannicus*, issued at the turn of the century, is testimony to the continuing popularity of Purcell's music after his death, despite the growing fashion for Italian opera, which was beginning to be introduced in the years around the turn of the century and became the rage after Handel's *Rinaldo* in 1711.

John Playford (1623-86) was the foremost music-publisher in Commonwealth and Restoration England, issuing many works by Purcell's older contemporaries and by the composer himself. Purcell commemorated his death with the elegy 'Gentle shepherds' (1687). The trio-sonatas (*top*) were Purcell's 'just imitation of the most fam'd Italian masters' (meaning Corelli above all), and they were written in concerted style with *basso continuo*. However, they still share many features with his earlier fantasias written for viol consort. *Music's Hand-maide* (*above*) followed Playford's first successful anthology issued in 1651, *A Musicall Banquet*, containing 'rounds, catches and pieces for viols.' The second volume of *Music's Hand-maide*, published in 1689 by Playford's son Henry, includes several keyboard pieces and arrangements by Purcell.

JOHANN SEBASTIAN BACH

BASIL LAM

Opposite: J. S. Bach
(1685-1750), the
portrait painted in 1746
by E. G. Haussmann for
presentation to the
Mizler Society, in which
the composer holds a
Canon triplex.

Between 1678 and 1703 ten members of the
Bach clan were educated at the Eisenach Gymnasium. They were the sons either of Johann
Christoph Bach (1642-1703) or of his cousin
Johann Ambrosius (1645-95), the father of
Sebastian, who was born on 21 March 1685. Of
the eight who survived childhood, only one did
not become a professional musician; Johann
Sebastian's cousin Johann Michael, his junior
by a few months, became an organ-builder.
While Johann Sebastian was evidently a clever
child – his class position was above that of his
brother Johann Jakob who was three years his
senior – nothing, either at Eisenach or at Ohrdruf, where he completed his education, suggested that he would surpass the rest of his
family. Although more distant lines of the family
had produced several distinguished composers,
Sebastian's father was an amiable person whose
genuine talent remained untroubled by any
touch of genius. His son learned from him the
rudiments of string playing, and had his father
lived, yet another Bach would probably have
taken his place among the Eisenach town musicians. However, when Sebastian was ten years
old both his parents died, and he was sent with
Johann Jakob to live with their eldest brother
Johann Christoph, who since 1690 had been
organist at the Michaeliskirche in Ohrdruf.
Sebastian excelled at the local school, and his
musical studies over the next five years with
Johann Christoph laid the foundations of his
keyboard technique.

From Ohrdruf Johann Sebastian went to
Lüneburg, where, thanks to his fine treble voice,
he received a scholarship to the choir of the
Michaeliskirche. With his schoolfellow Georg
Erdmann he arrived in Lüneburg towards the
end of March 1700. As part of his duties Bach
sang with the Mettenchor at the Ritterakademie,
a boarding school for the sons of noblemen
connected with St Michael's Convent, and when
his voice broke he continued to be of use as a
violinist and organist. There was also in Lüneburg at that time a Thuringian musician, Georg
Böhm, known to posterity for his chorales and
keyboard suites, who was organist of the Johanniskirche. Bach may well have been in contact
with Böhm, and it is known from the *Obituary*,
by his son Emanuel and pupil J. F. Agricola, that
he went on more than one occasion on foot to
Hamburg, to hear Johann Adam Reincken play
at the Catharinenkirche. In this way, and by

studying the works of other composers, Bach
became a highly accomplished musician.

In the summer of 1702 Bach left Lüneburg
and applied for the post of organist at the Jacobi-
kirche at Sangerhausen. The seventeen-year-
old Sebastian won the appointment, only to be
disappointed when Duke Johann Georg of
Sachsen-Weissenfels, lord of Sangerhausen,
chose to set aside the election in favor of a
somewhat older candidate. This was in November; from March to September 1703 the
'Laquey Bach' was on the payroll of Duke Johann Ernst of Weimar, brother of the reigning
duke, perhaps on the recommendation of the
lord who had deprived him of the much more
valuable position at Sangerhausen. Johann
Ernst had a chamber ensemble in which Bach
doubtless played violin or viola. He would have
worn livery and performed various menial tasks
when not occupied with music, and it is not
surprising that he took the earliest opportunity
of winning a measure of independence.

In September 1703, Bach was offered the post
of organist at the Bonifatiuskirche in Arnstadt,
known as the New Church after the rebuilding
of 1683. The organ, the work of the Mühlhausen builder Wender, was completed by July
1703, and the post offered to Bach was of
course a new one.

His contract specified that he should be present at the organ, for the care of which he was
responsible, on Sundays, feasts and other services, but mentioned no further obligations.
However, the church had no choirmaster and
Bach soon found he was in fact expected to take
charge of an undisciplined gang from the high
school. According to a complaint made before
the council in 1706, 'the boys fight, play games
in class and even in church, drink, gamble and
roam the streets at night shouting.' When Bach
insisted on airing his grievance over the choir-
training, however, he was reminded of his obligation to assist in all the music, not merely
with what concerned the organ. His duties
were not, in fact, over-exacting. Apart from the
Sunday morning *Hauptgottesdienst*, there were
services with hymns on Mondays and Thurs-
days. The consistory's rejection (19 August
1705) of their organist's complaint about his
duties shows that 'musicalische Stücke' were
expected, besides the hymns, but Bach seemingly wrote nothing apart from keyboard music.
The cantata *Denn du wirst meine Seele nicht in*

161

der Hölle lassen (BWV15), formerly cited as Bach's composition for Easter 1704, is by the 'Meiningen Bach,' his distant cousin Johann Ludwig. It was one of eighteen of his cantatas performed at Leipzig in 1736 from copies made by Sebastian, whence the misattribution, though various crudities in part-writing, left intact in the transcript, ought to have raised doubts long ago.

When, in October 1705, Bach asked for a month's leave of absence, the consistory may well have felt that a deputy, probably his cousin Johann Ernst, might make a welcome contrast to the tiresome young genius, who, apparently, gave no reason for his request. On his return, possibly as late as February 1706, he was asked why he had overstayed his leave, and where he had spent it. The *Obituary* is specific on the matter: '. . . he set out, and on foot at that, to Lübeck, in order to listen undetected to Buxtehude.' Where he stayed, how he paid for his subsistence, what he did with the long hours when he was not sitting in a corner of the Marienkirche, are questions beyond answer. The church had a splendid library, accessible surely to a visiting organist, and if Bach took his violin in his pack he may have found employment as an extra for the series of *Abendmusiken* that took place in November and December. These sacred concerts, established at Lübeck under Buxtehude's predecessor Franz Tunder, were given under the patronage of the city merchants. In Buxtehude's day the town band was augmented to an orchestra of about sixteeen players, while the choir numbered some two dozen.

Bach's defense to the consistory of the Lübeck visit – that he had gone to broaden his grasp of his art – was minuted without comment, but he was taxed with faults in his work as organist: he had hitherto made many strange *variationes* in the hymns, to the confusion of the congregation. The rest of the indictment – rather obscurely – refers to the introduction of a *tonus peregrinus*, or even of a *tonus contrarius*, meaning perhaps that Bach harmonized a melody in the 'wrong' mode or key, as he was to do with sublime result at the beginning of the *St Matthew Passion*, where the major mode 'O Lamm Gottes' is drawn into the prevailing relative minor.

Bach was given a week to think over his position, and a truce seems to have held until November, when the unresolved dispute over his duties rose once again. By now Bach's evidently prodigious skill as a virtuoso must have become widely known and the pride natural to a young genius was probably an element in his obstinate refusal to take choir practice. Hence the remark in the minute of 11 November 1706: 'If he thinks it no shame to attend church and take his salary, he ought not to be ashamed of making music with the choir.'

• First compositions •

Only a very few autographs are extant from the earliest years, so the authenticity of practically everything assigned to the decade 1703-13 must be judged by the methods of stylistic criticism. Probably the earliest datable autograph is that of the Prelude and Fugue in G minor (BWV535a) in the version found in the 'Möller' manuscript of 1705-7, or the fantasia (not so designated) on *Wie schön leuchtet der Morgenstern* (BWV 739), inspired perhaps by Buxtehude's extensive working of Nicolai's hymn.

Various compositions both for harpsichord and for organ have been placed by some scholars in Bach's schooldays. Quite apart from questions of authenticity, these pieces show a bewildering variety of styles and techniques hard to associate with a single creative personality. The E major Capriccio (BWV993) is a rambling, energetic, barely coherent display of boyish virtuosity, full of invention, but plainly the work of an absolute beginner. Most of the Sonata in D (BWV963) is similar in its mixture of imagination and immaturity. Of the partitas on chorales, *Ach, was soll ich Sünder machen?* (BWV770) – if it is indeed by Bach – must be the earliest, and, in spite of the indications *Oberwerk* and *Rückpositiv* in the manuscript, is evidently written, not for organ, but for the pedal harpsichord used in the Capriccio and Sonata. The three partitas generally accepted as authentic (BWV 766, 767 and 770) show quite different qualities from the works in other forms; although they betray technical inadequacy, they are astonishingly, almost impossibly, clean and 'correct' in partwriting and grammatical in harmony, if really the product of the youth who, in the fugue of the Prelude and Fugue in A minor (BWV551), came close to boring inepitude.

Bottom left: The Latin school in his home town of Eisenach, in Thuringia, which Sebastian Bach entered at the age of seven.

Bottom right: The little town of Ohrdruf, some twenty-five miles east of Eisenach, where after the death of their parents Sebastian and his brother Jakob went to live with their eldest brother Johann Christoph.

Left: Receipt signed by Bach for his salary for the period to 15 June 1707 paid by the consistory of Arnstadt. Bach had been appointed organist of the Bonifatiuskirche in the town in September 1703 after he had tested the new organ there.

From those early works it seems clear that the young Bach could write skillfully in established forms, using the vocabulary of figurations to be found in the masters he studied, but remained for a surprisingly long time rather tentative in his free preludes and fugues. It is indeed difficult to make any reasoned assessment of his early development. For example, while the three versions of the C minor Fugue (BWV574) are evidence for his 'study of the most famous composers,' the other C minor Fugue (BWV575) is a far better piece, showing 'the fruits of his own reflection on them,' though both works may well have been written at about the same time – that is *c.*1702-3. The raciness of the very original theme that is the making of BWV575 is carried over into the eminently memorable subject of the G minor Fugue (BWV578). This is a self-portrait, surely, of one side of the cheerful and irrepressible young man whose charm must have tempered his ill-concealed impatience with elders and betters.

These, with the earlier Preludes and Fugues in C major (BWV531) and D minor (BWV549a), must have provided the repertoire with which Bach made such a name for himself in Thuringia that he was called in to 'prove' the new organ at Langewiesen, near Ilmenau, in November 1706, and at Easter the following year made such an impression by his playing at St Blasius, Mühlhausen, that he was later offered the vacant post last held by the distinguished J. G. Ahle, who had died in the previous December. Bach therefore sought his release from Arnstadt; a minute merely records that he presented himself before the consistory to report that he had accepted the 'vocation' to Mühlhausen, but he seems to have left on perfectly good terms with his employers.

Bach was twenty-two, already a known virtuoso of organ and clavier and a gifted composer

for both instruments, but he had not yet written a line of vocal music. Even if the first version of *Christ lag in Todes Banden* (BWV4) was given at that same Easter, perhaps as a test piece for Mühlhausen, the profound expressiveness of Bach's rhetoric is matched neither by structural mastery nor by much grasp of a genuinely vocal style – many textures seem near to those of the chorale partitas themselves. Fine though it is, *Christ lag* is equalled in merit by the cantatas of Bruhns and excelled by some of those by Buxtehude. The obscure beginnings of Bach's art are exemplified by the acceptance as his work, until recent times, of another Easter cantata (no.15) composed by his distant cousin Johann Ludwig, a gifted musician, but certainly no genius.

• Bach at Mühlhausen •

After Arnstadt all things must have seemed to work together for good in Bach's life. A legacy worth more than half a year's salary from his Uncle Tobias, who died in August, helped towards marriage to his cousin Maria Barbara on 17 October, and within a few months of his arrival at Mühlhausen he was given the first real commission of his professional life. The city council, as was the German custom, made a

Top left: Johann Adam Reincken (1623-1722), organist at the Catharinenkirche in Hamburg since 1663. While living in Lüneburg from 1700 to 1702 Bach went several times to Hamburg to hear Reincken's improvisations.

Above: The figured part for the aria 'Ich bin nun achtzig Jahr' in the cantata *Gott ist mein König* (BWV 71), written for the service on 4 February 1708 to mark the town council election in Mühlhausen. Bach had taken up the appointment as organist at the Blasiuskirche there the previous year, and the town council had this celebratory cantata printed – his first published work.

grand civic occasion out of its annual election, and for 1708 the pastor of the Marienkirche, Georg Christian Eilmar, handed over to the new organist of the Blasiuskirche the libretto he may have written, to be set, it seems, for the largest array of voices and instruments that could be assembled. Furthermore, the music was printed in parts as well as the text, which bore the words, in rather small type at the foot of the page, 'by Johann Sebastian Bach Organist of St Blaise.'

Bach made the most of his resources, inspired perhaps by the recollection of the Lübeck *Abendmusiken* at their most splendid. He was to have a comparable wealth of instruments only once more in the whole of his career, for the *Ratswahl* (council election) at Leipzig in 1723. As in Schütz's then long forgotten *Psalms of David* of 1619, the various forces are grouped in the Venetian manner, and Bach even uses the words 'diviso in quatuor chori' for the orchestra, and distinguishes between full choir and solo quartet. The young composer's musical inspiration is less remarkable than his astonishing inventions in matters of tone color; in fact only the chorus 'Du wollest dem Feinde nicht geben' and the fugue in the final section rise above the level of superb craftsmanship applied to unmemorable material.

If BWV71 effectively disposes of the judgment that Bach was indifferent to tone color, we must look to the other Mühlhausen cantatas for music that shows the imaginative qualities proper to the highest genius. Both *Aus der Tiefen* (BWV 131) and *Gottes Zeit* (BWV106) are placed in

of the cantatas is directed towards consolation for a premature death: 'God's time is the best of all. We live in Him . . . we die in Him at the proper time, as He wills.' With *Gottes Zeit* Bach rose far above even the best of his contemporaries, showing for the first time unmistakable evidence of profound imaginative genius.

• Weimar •

Bach was twenty-three when, in the autumn of 1708, he entered the service of Duke Wilhelm Ernst of Sachsen-Weimar, a post he accepted, according to his letter of resignation at Mühlhausen, in the hope of attaining a better living and 'to further a well-regulated church music to the glory of God.' His position in the ducal establishment was that of court organist; it was not until 1714 that he became Konzertmeister, and he never succeeded to the chief post of Kapellmeister. The Duke, a stern but paternalistic ruler, prescribed for his domain a life of puritanical seriousness (lights out at eight in winter, at nine in summer) tempered by music, the art so much favored by Martin Luther himself. In earlier years he had even allowed opera and drama in the castle, and when such mundane pleasures incurred banishment, instrumental music was retained, the players being clad in the then fashionable Hussar (Heyduk) uniform. On Sundays instrumentalists and singers (there were twelve voices available) performed in the

Below left: Johann Ambrosius Bach (1645-95), Sebastian's father, who in 1671 had been appointed a town musician in Eisenach. An older cousin of his was already a respected musician in the town, and throughout this period there were few important towns in Thuringia (the region of central Germany north of Bavaria and west of Saxony, now part of the German Democratic Republic) where one of the extensive Bach family did not hold a musical post.

Below: The earliest surviving autograph by Bach, his organ chorale *Wie schön leuchtet der Morgenstern* (BWV 739), based on the celebrated Advent hymn and written while he was organist in Arnstadt, around 1705.

1707 by most scholars, though as recently as 1970 evidence has been brought forward suggesting that *Gottes Zeit*, plainly a funeral piece, was written on the death of the sister of Pastor Eilmar in June 1708 and not, as generally supposed, for the funeral of Tobias Lämmerhirt in the previous August. Bach's uncle attained the then ripe age of sixty-eight, whereas Dorothea Tilesius died in her thirty-fifth year. There is much to be said for the argument that the text

Above: Interior of the Michaeliskirche in Lüneburg, painted in the early eighteenth century. In 1700 Bach had left Ohrdruf to join the choir school attached to this church in the north German city. The organist of the Johanniskirche there was Georg Böhm, and it seems likely that Bach not only studied the organ with Böhm, but may well also have gained from him much of his knowledge of organ construction, tuning and testing.

ducal chapel, a fantastically baroque building dating from 1658. Known as the Himmelsburg (Heavenly City), it was lavishly decorated with blue sky, clouds and cherubs.

Bach wrote no cantatas, nor indeed any other liturgical music, for at least five years after his move from Mühlhausen. The first certain date is Palm Sunday 1714, when he produced *Himmelskönig, sei willkommen* (BWV182). The solo cantata BWV54 may have preceded BWV182 by three weeks. The explanation may be that he was given no such opportunity before his promotion to Konzertmeister, and even then he remained inferior in rank to the younger Drese, son of the aging Kapellmeister. The *Obituary* stated that Bach composed most of his organ music at Weimar, encouraged by the Duke's admiration for his playing, and it is possible that such famous works as the Passacaglia (BWV582) and the 'Dorian' Toccata and Fugue (BWV538) were produced by – to quote again from the *Obituary* – the wish 'to have at command and explore all the possibilities of the organist's art.' The *Orgelbüchlein* collection of short chorale preludes, though it was left only one third complete, dates from no later than 1716, and some of its forty-five extant pieces may belong to the first Weimar years.

When Bach became Konzertmeister, he relinquished his position as Kammermusicus to the palace steward. It is unlikely he would have been content merely to perform chamber music without composing any of his own, and some of the works assigned to Cöthen (*c*.1720) may have been based on earlier versions for the Weimar court. Certainly a number of the Weimar church cantatas are close to chamber music, but for certain feasts, such as Christmas and Pentecost, Bach could assemble forces comparable with those of Leipzig. *Christen, ätzet diesen Tag* (BWV63) requires, besides the usual strings and organ, no less than four trumpets with drums, three oboes and bassoon, as well as chorus and four soloists; *Der Himmel lacht!* (BWV31), first performed on Easter Day 1715, has the same scoring. At the opposite extreme, *Nun komm, der Heiden Heiland* (BWV61), given on the first Sunday in Advent 1714, though a full-scale work with chorus, uses only strings, while BWV54 and BWV199 (also 1714) are for solo voice with strings, perhaps one player per part.

For almost three years Bach wrote and performed (with some gaps in the sequence) a monthly cantata in the Himmelsburg chapel, most of the texts being by Salomo Franck, Duke Ernst's court poet and chief 'consistorial secretary,' who had provided such material since 1694. Although his poetry is full of sentiment, with imagery often drawn from the biblical *Song of Songs*, the avoidance of personal feeling made him acceptable to even the most severe orthodox Lutherans, including, we must suppose, Bach himself, though he would have had little choice in the matter. The Weimar cantatas are in no sense to be regarded as immature, however. Until recent times, the most reputable Bach scholars happily assigned to his later, Leipzig, period cantatas which were in fact written as much as twenty years earlier, simply on grounds of their accomplishment, although the chronology was made more obscure by Bach's practice of reviving earlier cantatas on suitable occasions.

The last Weimar cantata, *Herz und Mund und Tat und Leben* (BWV147), was the third for successive Sundays in Advent, this being the first time Bach had departed from the monthly interval. The long-inactive Kapellmeister Samuel Drese had died on 1 December, and Bach must have thought it certain he would succeed to the senior post, since Drese's son, who had deputized for his ailing father, was in no way distinguished. In its extant form BWV147 belongs to Leipzig; the accompanied chorale famous in the English-speaking world as 'Jesu, joy of man's desiring' was not in the original version, and it is not even certain that the work was completed. What is certain is that when Bach heard that he had been passed over in favor of Drese he at once gave up composing cantatas for the ducal chapel. By 1716 he was not merely better than the Dreses, he had become incomparably the finest composer in Germany, with the single exception of Handel, who had already made his way to London.

Perhaps Wilhelm Ernst – who was, after all, bound to respect the hereditary principle – saw

Above: Title-page of a collection of poems by the Weimar court poet Salomo Franck (1659-1725), including the libretto of Bach's hunting cantata *Was nur behagt* (BWV 208) written for the birthday of Duke Christian of Weissenfels in 1713; this includes the famous 'Sheep may safely graze.' Bach had taken up an appointment at the Ducal court in Weimar in 1708, and Franck was to provide the texts for some twenty of his cantatas.

Right: Duke Wilhelm Ernst, Bach's employer at Weimar, with (below) a view of the city, including, on the left, the Ducal residence in the Wilhelmsburg.

no reason for refusing to confirm Vicekapell-meister Drese, not envisaging that Bach would break his 1714 contract with its obligation to provide a new four-weekly cantata, especially as his salary had been increased in March 1715 to match those of the two Dreses. It has been suggested that Bach's cordial relationship with Duke Wilhelm Ernst's co-regent Ernst August may have hindered his promotion, as uncle and nephew were not on the best of terms. Ernst August's wife was sister to Prince Leopold of Cöthen, and doubtless provided the influence that helped Bach to his new post. By August 1717 Maria Barbara and the four children were installed at Cöthen, but the severe (though paternal) Wilhelm Ernst refused to release his retainer; from 6 November to 2 December, Bach was imprisoned on account of his too-insistent demand for his dismisal.

When Bach left Weimar he was thirty-two. Had he lived no longer than Schubert he would still have shown himself as one of the greatest composers, although his major achievements lay in the future. There are wonderful things in the Weimar cantatas, but it could be argued that they were surpassed by some from the Leipzig period. In organ music a list of the Weimar compositions comprises a catalogue of un-equalled masterpieces of the instrument's literature. To the Passacaglia and 'Dorian' Toccata and Fugue already mentioned may be added the Fantasia and Fugue in C minor (BWV537), the Toccata and Fugue in F (BWV540), and the Fantasia and Fugue in G minor (BWV542).

• Cöthen •

Supporters of the traditional view that Bach was a devoted servant of his Lutheran Church have always been disconcerted by the seeming eagerness with which he abandoned his mission 'to further a well-regulated church music' to become Kapellmeister to a Calvinist prince.

Admittedly the change of employment brought a doubling of salary, and the twenty-three-year-old Leopold was deeply fond of music. Besides playing violin, gamba and harpsichord with decent skill, he maintained a large Kapelle that provided Bach with nearly twenty players, plus such extras as, for instance, the pair of horns mentioned in June 1722. Nevertheless, Calvin, after scrutinizing the Old Testament with a legalistic eye, had ruled that only psalms in plain settings without instruments could be allowed in the churches, and Bach, a keen ama-teur of theology, must have realized that his vocation as church composer, if not broken, was severely bent. The only type of cantata demanded of him at Cöthen was the celebra-tory ode for such occasions as the Prince's birthday. As for the organ, he had no chapel duties, so the matchless skill that alone had already brought him fame remained unused apart from occasional recitals in other centers.

It may be assumed that the years 1718-20 were a time of happiness and creative freedom. Court duties must have been not so much de-manding as stimulating to a great composer in his prime. Besides the concertos and suites that formed the public repertoire, there was scope for chamber music of all kinds, so that the lack of Bach's works in these categories is puzzling, particularly the absence of trio-sonatas. In the baroque era, music for two melody instruments with accompanying keyboard and string bass was the equivalent of the string quartet in the classical period, yet there are precisely two trios (BWV1039 and *Musical Offering* BWV1079) of undoubted authenticity among the thousand or so works listed in Schmieder's catalogue. There is a similar lack of overtures, or suites for orchestra 'à la Française,' of which at least one would have been needed to open each concert in the great hall of the castle at Cöthen. Even if it is assumed that all four of Bach's overtures were in fact written *c.*1721, where are the others? Tele-mann claimed to have produced more than two hundred suites, most of them during two years when he worked at the Sorau court. No doubt some of Bach's works have been lost and others reworked for later church cantatas. Trio-sonata movements are not far from the vocal duet (their origins are closely connected); the overture – the first movement – of the fourth suite became the opening chorus of the 'Christmas' cantata *Unser Mund sei voll Lachens* (BWV110), and there are arias certainly derived from concerto or sonata movements.

If these years produced few – if any – organ compositions, the major part of Bach's keyboard music dates from Cöthen, though no certain chronology can be established in some cases. The list includes the French and English Suites, the Chromatic Fantasia and Fugue, Two- and Three-part Inventions, and the Twenty-four Preludes and Fugues in all the keys that Bach called *Das wohltemperierte Klavier* (dated 1722). Of these works, not one was published, though Bach's most eminent contemporaries – Handel, Cou-perin and Rameau – all had their harpsichord suites engraved and sold to the public.

Above: Rehearsal of a cantata in the Collegium Musicum of the German university in Zürich in 1713.

Top right: Erdmann Neumeister (1671-1756), who was pastor of the Jakobikirche in Hamburg for forty years, in 1717. He wrote nine cycles of cantata texts, introducing a more operatic form made up chiefly of recitatives and *da capo* arias, with or without ensembles and choruses. Although Bach set only five of Neumeister's texts, this form was adopted by Franck and other poets whose work he used extensively.

It was not until 1726 that Bach published the first of the six Partitas, the others following yearly until, in 1731, all six appeared as op.1. The Twenty-four Preludes and Fugues in all the keys were not innovatory; perhaps as many as twenty years before Bach, J. K. F. Fischer had written his *Ariadne Musica* of twenty preludes and fugues to exemplify the tuning temperament promoted by the famous theoretician and organist Andreas Werckmeister. So long as European music remained within a narrow harmonic framework, intonation – that is, the blending of intervals in chords – presented no problem, but once the keyboard had become standardized with twelve semitones to the octave, the question arose as to how the black notes were to be tuned, for example, the one above C having to serve both for C sharp and D flat. If keys with more than a few sharps or flats were avoided, however, the adjustments of relative pitches could favor the generally required notes.

Such matters were much discussed in the baroque period, and by favoring the systems that made all possible keys usable, Bach placed himself on the side of the 'progressives.' When, after his death, the *Well-tempered Clavier* became celebrated throughout Europe, equal temperament was universally accepted, and the great work was valued for its marvelous combination of inspiration and learning. The preludes range from the plainest chord progressions, as in no.1, to profound studies in combining themes as in no.19, and no two fugues are alike either in structure or expression. Bach's absolute mastery of fugal style shows itself in imaginative freedom, not in the display of ingenuities, though in these also he is supreme – when he chooses.

• The 'Brandenburg' Concertos •

In May 1718 Prince Leopold traveled to the spa at Carlsbad, taking with him six of his musicians, and he repeated the trip the following year. Bach was present on both journeys, and it may have been on one or other of the occasions that he encountered the music-loving Christian Ludwig of Brandenburg, to whom Bach dedicated the six concertos that bear his name, with the customary apologies for 'their inadequacy.'

When Bach had performed before the Margrave is not on record, but it is known that he was twice in Berlin, having been sent first to order, then to collect, a new harpsichord for his master. It was in his Berlin town house that Brandenburg maintained his musical establishment, and Prince Leopold had probably praised to the skies his genius of a Kapellmeister. Bach never claimed that the concertos 'avec plusieurs instruments' were specifically written for their dedicatee, and there can, in fact, be little doubt that all six were heard at Cöthen, and some may in fact even have been composed at Weimar, where Bach had become acquainted with the Italian concerto style. Soon, perhaps, after his appointment in 1708 Bach needed a model for instrumental music, which he found in the concertos of Vivaldi, whose op.3 *L'Estro armonico* was published in 1711 and rapidly

indeed, frequently enhances the powerful thrust and drive of Vivaldi's allegros. Bach, however, possessed a mind vastly more subtle, and from the somewhat primitive paradigm offered to him made formal structures marvelously complex, yet lucid and balanced in their proportions.

The first movement of the Second 'Brandenburg' Concerto, for instance, has to provide solos for the unique *concertino* group of trumpet, recorder (sometimes flute in modern performances), violin and oboe. A double theme of melody and accompaniment is so devised that all four can be displayed, after which they can combine with the main body of strings in an endless variety of textures and thematic developments, anticipating at times the methods of the Viennese classics, as when the opening phrase is made into a motif passing from key to key, sometimes in a unison of the upper strings marked *p* or *pp*. With no.5, Bach virtually invents the harpsichord concerto.

Bach's solo concertos stand alone, although only three – the two for violin and the double violin concerto – have reached us in their original form. Bach was an accomplished violinist (his son Emanuel said he continued to play until his last years in a decisive and pure style), but these concertos do not exploit the virtuoso techniques developed surprisingly early in the history of the instrument. If the allegro movements of the Concertos in A minor and E major are comparatively straightforward examples of baroque forms, the slow movements make the violin the medium of a lyricism scarcely equalled for beauty and depth in the whole of music.

As noted earlier, Bach left scarcely any triosonatas for two instruments and continuo, but a number of works by him – all of the highest quality – represent the genre in what may be called trios for two players (and later he was to

Above: The Ducal chapel, known as the Himmelsburg, in Weimar, from a mid-seventeenth-century painting. Bach played the two-manual organ here, reconstructed shortly after he arrived in Weimar, and his early cantatas were also performed in the chapel.

Right: Portrait, believed to show Bach after his promotion to Konzertmeister at Weimar, around 1715.

became celebrated all over Europe. Of these twelve works Bach arranged no fewer than six – nos.3, 9 and 12 for solo harpsichord, nos.8 and 11 for organ, and no.10 for four harpsichords and strings. However, the authenticity of the solo transcriptions has been questioned. Further transcriptions were from Vivaldi's op.7. In some cases Bach evidently had access to manuscript copies, as his texts differ from the printed versions.

Another Italian Bach is said to have especially admired was Albinoni, who had published concertos as early as 1700. From the Venetian masters (he seems to have taken little note of Corelli) Bach learned the craft of constructing concertos. The plan is essentially simple, with a main theme (ritornello) appearing several times – not always complete – in the main key and its close neighbors, these returns being interspersed with 'episodes' for the soloist or group of solo instruments. Even in the finest of Vivaldi's concertos the solo episodes are apt to run into formulas of broken-chord figurations rarely connected thematically with the ritornello, which itself is not often developed, tending rather to appear somewhat literally transposed to the appropriate key. This directness is not necessarily a defect and,

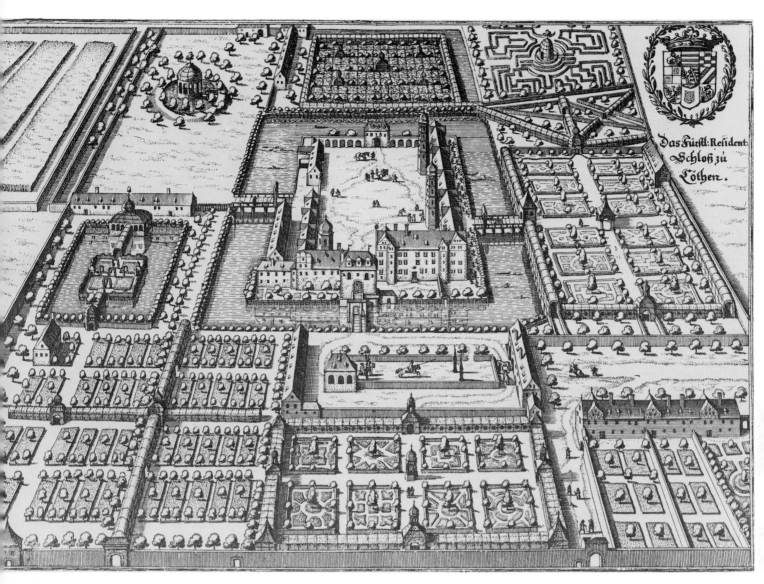

Das Fürstl: Resident Schloß zu Cöthen.

compose six trios for a single performer). The seeming contradiction is readily explained: for baroque music theory the trio was a composition for two *obbligato* parts over a supporting bass. In his sonatas for violin and harpsichord (as in three for viola da gamba and two for flute), Bach allocated two parts to the keyboard, following a method dating back to the previous century. One of these 'trios' (BWV1027) is Bach's transcription of the Sonata for two flutes and continuo (BWV1039), and some of the others may well have had similar origins in trio-sonatas of the usual kind. These sonatas, especially those with violin, are almost unrealizable in performance because of the difficulty of giving equal prominence to all three essential parts in the texture. Nevertheless, they contain some of the greatest chamber music, not surpassed by the string quartets of the classical period.

Solo music for violin without accompaniment had been composed long before Bach's time; a suite 'pour le violon seul sans basse' by J. P. von Westhoff is dated 1683. Bach's three each of sonatas and suites were written at Cöthen, as were the six suites for cello, doubtless for the excellent players of the Court, though Bach

himself may have performed the violin works, and neither set could have been written except by one who had a master's knowledge of both instruments. These wonderful paradigms of economy and suggestion were long regarded as teaching material and were so little understood that even such great masters as Mendelssohn and Schumann wrote piano accompaniments to complete them and make them 'suited' to performance. These futile exercises were confined to the violin works, however; the cello suites remained forgotten until the young Casals rediscovered them early in the present century.

• Leaving Cöthen •

So far as we know Bach's life at Cöthen was, until the summer of 1720, happy as well as marvellously creative. In May of that year Prince Leopold, taking, as before, a group of his favorite musicians, went to Carlsbad, where he stayed for some weeks. During Bach's absence Maria Barbara fell ill, died and was buried several weeks before his return. Many years later Emanuel, only six years old at the time,

Above: The castle and park of the Princes of Anhalt-Cöthen, where Bach was appointed Kapellmeister to Prince Leopold in August 1717. He remained at Cöthen, much attached to the music-loving Prince Leopold, until 1723.

wrote how his father 'after thirteen years of blissful married life' heard the tragic news only when he entered the family house. Bach kept no diary, wrote no personal letters, left no record of private, as distinct from professional, friendships. Therefore nothing whatever is known of his response to the shattering of his domestic life, leaving him with four children, the eldest a girl of twelve.

A few months after his bereavement Bach went to Hamburg in circumstances that have been much discussed by scholars. Heinrich Friese, organist of the Jakobikirche, had died in September and Bach was listed as one of the applicants for the vacancy. However, before the day fixed for auditions, a minute of the Hamburg selection committee recorded: 'Nov. 23 Mr Bach had to return to his Prince.' The post was still vacant in December, but it seems Bach rejected an offer from the selectors, having evidently changed his mind about renouncing the many advantages of his position as Kapellmeister for the humbler rewards of the church organist. Various contemporaries noted the memorable recital at the Catharinenkirche during which Bach improvised with such magisterial power of invention that the celebrated Johann Adam Reincken (then in his hundredth year) declared he had thought the art dead, but saw that it lived again.

Just a year later, Bach married Anna Magdalena Wülcken, the youngest daughter of a trumpeter in the service of the Prince of Saxe-Weissenfels and herself a trained musician described as 'Fürstliche Sängerin.' This second marriage was no less happy than the first, and the remaining two years at Cöthen saw the completion of the 'Brandenburg' Concertos, the first part of the *Well-tempered Clavier* and two church cantatas, BWV23 and BWV22. Several Cöthen birthday or celebratory cantatas have been identified in their sacred 'parody' forms, but the two mentioned above were the first of their kind since the abrupt termination of the Weimar series. They were the result of Bach's decision to apply for the post of cantor at Leipzig, a vacancy caused by the death on 5 June 1722 of Johann Kuhnau. It has been argued that life at Cöthen had become less agreeable after Prince Leopold's marriage (only a week after Bach's own) to his cousin Friederica, a pleasure-loving girl whom Bach, in a letter, called an *Amusa*. The letter, though, was written seven years later and does not specifically say that the Prince's loss of interest in music was the reason for the move to Leipzig, and it was in fact not until a year after the new Princess had appeared that Bach's name was put forward. In fact the Leipzig councillors at first hoped to secure Telemann, then recently settled at Hamburg.

The post actually involved school teaching, but the condition was waived to meet Telemann's objection, and he was appointed in August. By October it was plain he had no intention of leaving Hamburg, thanks to an increase in salary, so the Leipzigers had to look elsewhere, and just before Christmas the council

considered five names, including Bach and the Darmstadt Kapellmeister, Graupner, who became the preferred candidate after he had performed his Latin *Magnificat* on Christmas Day. However, he too was suspected of having used the vacancy to improve his own position. After prolonged exchanges he finally withdrew, recommending Bach as a worthy substitute. Meanwhile the other competitors carried out their trial performances; Bach probably presented both cantatas mentioned, *Du wahrer Gott und Davids Sohn* and *Jesus nahm zu sich die Zwölfe.*

• Leipzig •

It is clear from the minutes of the meeting that Bach's appointment to the post was regarded as *faute de mieux* by most of the Leipzig worthies, who have been much derided by posterity for their philistinism. This is not altogether fair; the man they were appointing was known as an unequalled virtuoso organist and authority on instruments, whom few – if any – recognized as the most profound musical genius of the age.

Composing music was far from being the main function of the cantor. Bach was responsible not only for musical instruction but also for duties we would associate with a housemaster in a boarding school. As one of the four principal senior staff he took his turn as 'inspector of the week,' presiding over morning and evening prayers, supervising meals, visiting the sanatorium, and ensuring that the boys returned sober and in good order from weddings and funerals. Senior scholars might be in their twentieth year.

The school provided choirs for four churches, the first choir serving alternately at the Nikolaikirche and the Thomaskirche, while less expert and junior singers, supervised by a prefect, sang at the Neukirche and Peterskirche. Leipzig was among the most devout communities in Thuringia, following the strict Lutheran orthodoxy; on Sundays the town gates were closed and chains across the main streets silenced traffic during the hours of church services. Whatever may be argued about Bach's sense of vocation, the move from Cöthen could hardly be seen as an emancipation from feudal servitude; one clause in his contract forbade him to leave town without permission from the Bürgermeister.

On 30 May 1723, the first Sunday after Trinity, 'the new Cantor and Collegii Musici Direct.[or] Hr. Joh. Sebastian Bach who came

Above: Johann Kuhnau (1660-1722), Bach's predecessor as cantor at the Thomasschule in Leipzig with (*left*) the title-page of his *Fresh Clavier Fruits* (1696).

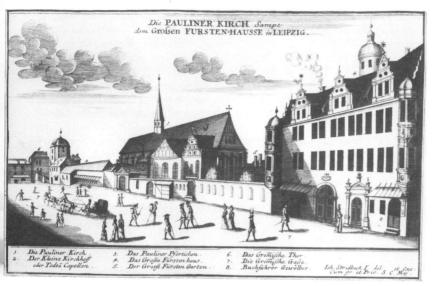

Die PAULINER KIRCH Sampt dem Groſsen FURSTEN-HAUSSE in LEIPZIG.

1. Die Pauliner Kirch. 3. Das Pauliner Pförtichen. 6. Das Grimische Thor.
2. Der kleine Kirchhoff 4. Das Groſse Fürsten haus. 7. Die Grimische Gaſse.
   oder Todte Capellen.   5. Der Groſse Fürsten Garten. 8. Buchführer Gewölber.

Ich Stridbeck J. del et Exc
Cum gr. et Priv. S.C. Maj.

Left: The University church in Leipzig. Bach's first brush with the city authorities arose from his responsibilities for the music for the services here, some of which in the time of his predecessor had been handed over (together with the salary) to another musician; Bach had to petition the Elector in Dresden to get the case settled. His ode on the death of the Electress, *Lass, Fürstin, lass noch* (BWV 198) was performed here — after further difficulties – in October 1727.

Below: Bird's-eye view of the city of Leipzig in 1712. After Kuhnau's death in June 1722, Bach applied for and was appointed to the post of cantor at the Thomasschule, but only after it had already been offered to Telemann and another candidate. On 22 May 1723 the Bach family moved to Leipzig. This view is taken from a point close to the Thomasschule (off the picture, bottom right) looking into the market square with the University ('Pauliner Collegium') at top right.

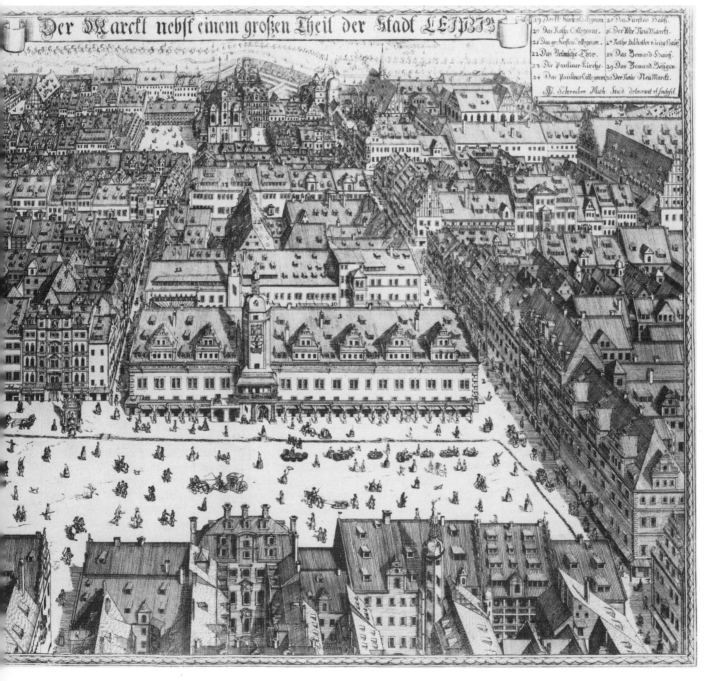

here from the princely Court at Cöthen performed his first music with good *applausu*.' The work was *Die Elenden sollen essen* (BWV75), a grandly spacious piece in two sections, each as large as a cantata of average proportions. The second cantata, performed a week later, is also in two parts and follows an identical scheme.

When these two masterpieces were composed is not precisely known; the formalities surrounding Bach's appointment were not completed until 13 May, but three weeks earlier the assurance that he would be released from Cöthen removed the only possible impediment to the council's selection, so work on the first cantata following the 'test pieces' may have begun before the end of April. Having set out on the cruelly exigent task of composing, rehearsing and performing a weekly cantata, by the third Sunday after Trinity Bach resorted to an earlier composition. *Ich hatte viel Bekümmernis* (BWV21) belongs originally to the Weimar period and may have been written in 1713 for performance at Halle. It was revised while Bach was at Cöthen, possibly for Hamburg and, it seems, several times at Leipzig.

The next great work after the first two Leipzig cantatas was of a different kind. Vespers on 18 July 1723 was a memorial service for the wife of the postmaster, and for the customary funeral motet Bach wrote *Jesu meine Freude* (BWV227), a work of majestic dimensions in eleven movements. Doubtless the hymn *Jesu meine Freude* had been a favorite of Frau Kees, and by combining it with verses from the same Pauline Epistle Bach was able to create his own profound sermon in music. Only a week later, the congregation heard *Herr, gehe nicht ins Gericht mit deinem Knecht* (BWV105), a work of somber power, mitigated only by the last aria. The cantatas in the following weeks were also mostly severe or penitential in tone, cheerfulness breaking in only with the first of Bach's celebrations of the council elections (BWV119).

The Christmas of 1723 brought (in its first version) Bach's only setting of the *Magnificat* (BWV243a). Like his predecessor Kuhnau, he included four interludes, sung and played at the crib (the representation of the Holy Child in its cradle). As in *Jesu meine Freude*, the sublime is mingled with the traditional art of the unlearned.

In the New Year the weekly cantata continued to appear without interval until the beginning of Lent when, surely to Bach's immense relief, music fell silent, except for the Feast of the Annunciation, for which he revived a Weimar work (BWV182). Until recently it was thought that the *St John Passion* was first performed on Good Friday 1723, having been prepared before Bach left Cöthen, but expert opinion places it in the following year, in which case the several weeks' respite would have made its composition, by Bach's standards, comparatively unhurried.

What Passion music was given in 1723 is not known, but Bach's predecessor, Johann Kuhnau, had performed his *St Mark Passion* only a few weeks before his death in June 1722, and this work was perhaps repeated in his memory.

During the seventeenth century two distinct traditions had developed in Passion music: the liturgical settings of Schütz, for example, and the oratorio. In the strict style only the prescribed biblical words were admitted, at least as far as the dramatis personae were concerned. The freer type, adopted by Handel, Telemann, Keiser and others, gave arias and dramatic reflections to Christ, Peter and other figures. To Bach's severely orthodox Leipzigers, the notion of a duet between the Crucified and his Mother was not to be tolerated, though present in the text by the Hamburg councillor Brockes set by

a number of composers including Handel. Bach drew on this libretto for his *St John Passion*, using six of the meditative and commenting verses, but totally rejecting anything put into the mouth of a biblical character. Brockes's often deplorable poetry is somewhat modified, perhaps by Bach himself, who must have chosen the eleven hymns which, according to tradition, were set into the narrative. Bach possessed a score of Handel's *Brockes Passion*, which may have been his source for the aria texts.

In planning his first Passion (suggestions that he wrote one at Weimar remain unsupported), Bach had no model, and the defects of formal structure in the *St John Passion* are obvious enough, though their effect is negligible against the greatness of the music in all other respects. For instance, after the somber and massive opening chorus, the action proceeds rapidly

Above: Bach's letter seal, an intertwined monogram of his initials, which he began to use in 1722.

Right: Ceramic crucifix made in the famous Saxon pottery at Meissen by the Dresden sculptor Benjamin Thomae around 1715.

through the capture of Jesus to his appearing bound before the High Priest. The alto sings of the bondage of sin, and the Evangelist has a brief sentence: 'Simon Peter followed Jesus with another disciple.' Next comes a second aria, 'I follow You likewise with joyful steps.' Besides the long break in the narration, this second aria seems inapposite; Peter follows Jesus not joyfully, but with apprehension. A much larger question concerns the repetition of certain choruses with music identical, or only slightly modified, set to different texts. When it was thought that the work had been prepared for 1723, some commentators argued that these repetitions were the result of Bach's haste to complete his score, but it is clear that he had some positive intent. Apart from this strange feature, the choruses – all representing the *turba* or mob – are marvellously vivid, far exceeding in dramatic force anything in baroque or classical opera. As chapters 18 and 19 of St John's Gospel make no reference to the Last Supper, the part of Jesus offers no scope for arioso as in the *St Matthew Passion* and consists entirely of recitative accompanied – like that of the other participants – by the continuo. Bach performed the work several times in his later years, making a number of revisions to the score; evidently he did not regard it as superseded by the *St Matthew Passion*.

Above: View to the west of Leipzig in 1740 taken from a point close to Bach's lodgings. Beyond the River Pleisse can be seen the newly laid-out garden of the merchant Andreas Dietrich Apel, where on the night of 12 May 1727 Bach's birthday cantata for King Augustus II of Saxony, *Entfernet Euch, Ihr heitern Sterne* (BWV Anh.9) is said to have been performed by the university students.

Left: Bach's manuscript of the opening of the *St John Passion* (BWV 245), which was first performed in the Nikolaikirche in Leipzig on 7 April 1724 and repeated at the Thomaskirche the following year.

• The Leipzig cantatas •

Right: List of the
members of the orchestra
in the Leipzig Concert
Society in 1746-8. The
orchestra was directed
by C. G. Gerlach, who
had been a pupil of
Bach's and had for a
time taken over from the
composer as director of
his Collegium Musicum.
This was a body Bach
had assembled which
gave public concerts in
Zimmermann's coffee-
house and was the
forerunner of the
Concert Society – and
the later Gewandhaus.

For two years, that is from his appointment at
Leipzig until Trinity Sunday 1725, Bach produced weekly fresh cantatas, most of which
were newly composed. Such a feat of sustained
creative energy at the highest level is nowhere
else approached in the history of music, or
perhaps of any art. To regard these 120 or so
compositions as masterpieces of equal distinction is to dehumanize Bach, making him in the
critic's mind a divinely programmed computer.
What is true is that his technique never failed to
produce structures at once more complex and
more cogently organized than those of his contemporaries; Brahms said that something could
be learned from every piece Bach wrote.

In this sense, there are no weak cantatas, but
if, as Stravinsky recommended, 'the Bach cantatas were to form the basis of our repertoire,'
quite a number would receive only occasional
performance. This is not to say that even the
least inspired, the most aridly didactic, is without interest, but the constructive energies of
music's greatest mind seem to have functioned
sometimes in the absence of what we would
call inspiration, notably in certain arias where
the return of the whole first part – according to
the convenient *da capo* scheme – can be welcomed by few hearers. What has to be remembered is that the cantatas were intended to
edify, to instruct the faithful through the power
of art. There is plenty of evidence that Bach
regarded all music as holy in a broad sense, and
made no distinction between sacred and secular

styles, though it is significant that he would
never adapt church works to profane use, while
often resorting to the opposite procedure.

In the course of the first Leipzig year's cycle,
Bach arrived before long at what might be called
a standard form for the weekly cantata: 1a
Orchestral introduction leading to 1b Chorus;
2 Recitative; 3 Aria; 4 Recitative; 5 Aria; 6 Four-
part Chorale. After the three bipartite works 75,
76 and 21, with their considerable demands on
the performers, came three cantatas for solo
voices, followed by a further two in bipartite
form. It was not until the eighth Sunday after
Trinity that Bach, with BWV136, adopted
anything approaching a routine in planning the
weekly music. What has here been called the
'standard' form appears in 136, 105, 46, 179,
(199 was a Weimar work), 69, 77 and 25. The
Viennese classics, no less inexhaustibly creative
than Bach, were willing to repeat, in quartet or
symphony, the broadly stereotyped scheme of
four movements, varied only by slow introduction or changed order of the middle movements.
One might reasonably suppose that Bach, con-
fronted with the unremitting demands of his
churches, would have maintained unbroken a
similarly useful convention. Not at all: no.119
for the *Ratswahl* (council election) begins with
a splendid French overture; no.138, based on a
hymn text, alternates chorus with recitative
and attains unity by featuring the hymn melody
throughout. A week later no.95 incorporates
three different chorale melodies in a complex
design.

As the cycle proceeds the variety of types
increases, some cantatas including chorale
verses as well as arias, while others are dialogues
for solo voices. No.194, composed to celebrate
the inauguration of a new organ at Störmthal,
a small town near Leipzig, is a cantata in the
form of a complete orchestral suite or overture.
By the New Year the 'standard' type is becoming
the exception, and the second half of the cycle
contains nine Weimar works. For the three
successive days of Pentecost four cantatas were
needed, plus two for Trinity Sunday a few days

Right: Student concert
or serenade. Bach's
Collegium Musicum
was largely made up of
students, and they gave
many performances out
of doors, most notably
those in the market
square sung outside the
house of the merchant
Apel, where the Elector
always stayed on his
visits to Leipzig. On the
occasion in October
1734 which proved too
much for Gottfried
Reiche (see p.177), they
performed the Homage
Cantata *Preise dein
Glücke, gesegnetes
Sachsen* (BWV 215),
after a torchlight
procession in which six
hundred students took
part.

Ein Theil der Cather Strasse.
1. Das Hohmännische 2. Örtelische
3. Schacherische Haus.

later. Nothing new was composed, as may be noted: day 1, 172 and 59 (both Weimar); day 2, 173 (originally Cöthen Birthday Ode); day 3, 184 (probably Cöthen New Year Ode); Trinity, 194 (written for Störmthal) and 165 (Weimar). Evidently the year-long prodigious creative effort had brought even Bach to a standstill, with the imperative need for reflection before embarking on a second cantata marathon. During those few weeks (21 May to 11 June), he seems to have decided that in future the Lutheran chorale, with its hymn text, should be the basis of every cantata. The opening chorus would be constructed round the hymn melody, placed (with a few exceptions) in the soprano, where it would be most readily audible to the congregation. Besides thus dominating the most important movement, the chorale henceforth often recurs in the course of the work, apart from its now invariable appearance as conclusion.

After Palm Sunday 1725, Bach gave up writing chorale-based cantatas. The year's cycle was completed with nine compositions to texts by his young Leipzig contemporary Mariane von Ziegler (1695-1760), but the continuous creation of two incomparable years was at an end. For two months from Trinity no performances are traceable, and in the whole of the third church year no more than a dozen new cantatas were produced. As six of these are for soloists, it seems possible that Bach was having trouble with his choral forces, though there is no evidence of this; nor, indeed, of any reason for the drastic change in his professional activity.

Easter Sunday also had nothing by J. S. Bach; BWV15, supposedly written in Arnstadt in 1704, is certainly the work of the 'Meiningen' Bach, his cousin Johann Ludwig. Six more cantatas by this solid if uninspired musician provided the *Musik* for the weeks after Easter, and he had already been drawn upon in the period from the Purification to the Sunday before Holy Week. *Denn du wirst meine Seele* (BWV15) was accepted as genuine Bach by everyone until 1955, when its authenticity was challenged, so it is unlikely that the Leipzig congregations noticed how the standard of their Sunday music had declined. There is no record of complaint, and such indifference must have increased Bach's ebbing enthusiasm for his 'well-regulated church music.' It is significant that he should have left unamended the minor solecisms he found in his cousin's scores.

The run of J. L. Bach cantatas was succeeded by only two bearing BWV numbers (146 and 43). The first must be regarded as at least in part of doubtful authenticity, and the work for Ascension Day, *Gott fähret auf*, shows a strange laboriousness of invention with its stereotyped themes and mechanical procedures, even in the heavily jubilant opening chorus. Later, in 1726, the beginning of a further cycle was marked by a masterwork, BWV39, indicating that whatever had troubled Bach (perhaps ordinary human exhaustion) had been overcome. A splendid fugal chorus – maintained a few weeks later in BWV187 and 102 – shows renewed confidence in the Thomaschor, though awkward word-setting in arias (also in 187) betrays the adaptation of music – perhaps instrumental – composed for some other purpose.

Little is recorded of Bach's life in these years. He was involved in a dispute over fees for providing music at university functions. The matter was settled in Bach's favor during 1727, and a year later he stubbornly resisted attempts to deprive him of his prerogative of choosing the hymns for *Gottesdienst*. Bach, though totally without vanity or self-regard, reacted angrily to any slight on his professional dignity and pride.

• The *St Matthew Passion* •

With a sequence of solo cantatas in the later months of 1726, Bach seems to have ended the commitment to church music begun at Weimar only twelve years earlier, and interrupted by the wonderfully creative period at Cöthen. Although the two masterpieces of religious music were composed later, the *Passion* stands apart from the cantatas, and the Mass was not intended for Leipzig at all, but for the Catholic court at Dresden. After performing his own *St John Passion* in 1724 and 1725, Bach resorted in 1726 to Keiser's *St Mark Passion*; it is not known what Passion music was given in the next two years, but in 1729 Bach gave his *St Matthew Passion* on Good Friday in the Thomaskirche, the text of the non-liturgical portions being taken mainly from a collection of *Serious, Entertaining and Satirical Poems* by 'Picander,' the pen-name of C. F. Henrici (b.1700), a prolific and not entirely reputable author who had already worked with Bach.

As in the *St John Passion*, the Gospel text is that prescribed in the Catholic liturgy, where, however, it belongs to Palm Sunday. Picander's madrigalian verses sometimes seem excessive in their emotionalism, but it must be remembered that modern taste is very unlike that of the German baroque age.

Left: The house of Peter Hohmann on the Catherstrasse, leading off the market place, built in 1708-14. Here, on 27 November 1725, Bach's Wedding Cantata *Auf! süss entzückende Gewalt* (which has not survived) was performed to celebrate the marriage of Hohmann's son. Both Hohmann and his neighbor, the architect Theodor Örtel, were councillors who had supported Bach's appointment to the Thomasschule.

With its division into two 'Choruses' the *Passion* demanded not only first and second choirs at full strength but also two orchestras, each containing the full resources normally used for cantatas. For later performances, the continuo group of organ and string bass was duplicated as well. Soloists – who were, of course, members of the choir – came either from Coro I or Coro II, a feature lost in modern versions. Psalm settings 'in due cori' were written by Vivaldi, late examples of a tradition going back to sixteenth-century Venice, and Bach himself had already composed double-choir motets; but the two groups, each complete in itself, are deployed in the service of a characteristically logical formal plan. In medieval plainsong settings the Gospel text is divided between Christus, Chronista (narrator) and 'others,' and Bach follows the ancient tradition. In the *St Matthew Passion* the choral forces have various functions: Coro I represents the disciples, Coro II the *Gläubigen* (believers) and, in one instance, 'those that stood by.' The crowd (the *turba* of early Passions) comprises both choirs, but in the opening chorus Bach sets chorally for Coro I the words allocated by Picander to the Daughter of Zion. All hymns (chorales) are sung by the united voices and instruments (not by the congregation), representing the Church in history. The Daughter of Zion sings from Coro I, so her dialogues with the *Gläubigen* (Coro II) are antiphonal in effect. When Bach accompanies the *Vox Christi* with strings he is not an innovator; but who else would have withdrawn this sign of Godhead for the last words from the Cross?

The work has been called a drama, but though the events in it are presented with a realism almost beyond that of the stage, there is no continuity of time or action, and the primary purpose is to involve the Christian community at all levels in the solemn restatement of the sacred words which everyone knew by heart. The treatment of the Gospel text is far nearer to a sermon on the Passion than to any conceivable drama, and indeed Bach's contract of employment bound him to exclude operatic elements from the music in the Leipzig churches.

Whether the 1729 performance was the first remains a matter for scholarly argument; ten movements were used by Bach for the state funeral of his friend and master Prince Leopold at Cöthen, three weeks before Good Friday, and it seems he was away from Leipzig for most of the month of March. While it is possible that the *Passion* was completed six or seven weeks before it was required, Bach's virtually invariable practice was to write to meet the immediate need, composing movement by movement in sequence.

About the time of the 1729 *Passion*, Bach became director of the Collegium Musicum, which had been founded by Telemann in 1702. These Collegia were originally private gatherings of professionals, but later became more comprehensive, including as members students and non-performers who provided audiences. The importance of the 'Telemann' Collegium in the musical life of the city can be gauged from the fact that it was able to invite Bach to conduct it. Though denied the wider celebrity of Telemann, Vivaldi or Handel, he was recognized in his own country as an unrivalled organist and musician of majestic authority and knowledge of art. The notion that he was unappreciated and neglected is a romantic invention. What is true is that, whether from choice or lack of opportunity, Bach published scarcely

Below: Frontispiece and title-page of the 'Dresden Hymn Book,' which was used in Leipzig. This was one of the causes of the dispute over the choice of hymns to be sung at church services that Bach had in 1728 with Gottlieb Gaudlitz, subdeacon at the Nikolaikirche and later pastor of the Thomaskirche.

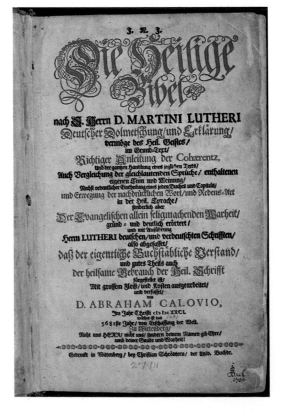

Far right: Bach's own copy of Luther's Bible, one of an edition printed in 1681, that he acquired in 1733. At the foot of the page can be seen the composer's signature (enlargement, *right*), and there are many of his notes and annotations in the Bible itself.

any of his works, in contrast with his contemporaries, who seem to have found a ready market among amateurs with instrumental music of various kinds. When Bach offered to the public the first of the six partitas for harpsichord (BWV825) in 1726, the announcement said that the *Autor* would be his own publisher, adding that the issues would continue until the opus was completed.

• Disillusionment at Leipzig •

How much organ music Bach wrote at Leipzig is uncertain; several of the great fugues and preludes may be late works (BWV544 or BWV548, for example). The six trio-sonatas (BWV525-530) are placed in the period 1727-9, and the only published collection, the chorale preludes framed by the E flat Prelude and Fugue, which Bach called *Clavierübung* III, appeared in 1739 (undated), though it is not known when these pieces were written. Eight or nine years later, the Canonic Variations on the Christmas Hymn 'Vom Himmel hoch' were engraved. Although the other set of chorale preludes known as 'The Eighteen' was set down in a fair copy at the end of Bach's life, he was not composing so much as revising music from his years at Weimar. Besides the partitas, other late harpsichord works were the Italian Concerto and French Overture (published in 1735), and the 'Goldberg' Variations (*c*.1742).

In August 1730 Bach's employers discussed his conduct in harsh terms. He neglected the singing classes for which he was responsible and had taken unauthorized leave of absence. As a result of these criticisms the Bürgermeister reported that he had 'spoken with the cantor, but he shows no disposition to work.' In October Bach wrote the often-quoted letter to his old school companion Georg Erdmann, in which he expressed, not without wry humor, the wish to quit Leipzig in the hope of being better paid and appreciated. Could Erdmann use his influence at Danzig (Gdansk), where he was Russian consul?

That Bach stayed at Leipzig was probably due in part to the fact that the rector, J. H. Ernesti, who died in October 1729, was succeeded by Johann Matthias Gesner, who had been corector of the high school at Weimar and remained a life-long friend and admirer of his old colleague. Ernesti had been no less well disposed, but in his later years – he was rector for nearly half a century – discipline had lapsed, and he was little regarded by the authorities. No doubt Gesner restored at least formal peace between Bach and the council, but after only four years he accepted a professorship at Göttingen University, to be succeeded by a second Ernesti, very unlike the first. Johann August Ernesti was only twenty-seven, a scholar of some distinction, but with no interest in music.

Neither Gesner's support nor Ernesti's indifference and later hostility seems to have much affected Bach's change of direction after 1730.

Composing scarcely anything for the church, he busied himself with his Collegium, for which he produced, in revised versions, instrumental works from the Cöthen years, favoring especially concertos for two or more harpsichords based on originals for the violin, and, occasionally, perhaps for wind. The only work among these which is not a transcription is the splendid Concerto in C (BWV1061). Presumably these concertos were played in the Collegium concerts by the Bach family. On purely musical grounds, it would be hard to justify the damage done to music conceived originally for the violin by transferring it to the inexpressive harpsichord.

Although several cantatas were composed in the early 1730s (including one masterpiece, BWV140), the period between the *St Matthew Passion* and the first two parts of what was to become the Mass in B minor can be seen as a creative pause; the *St Mark Passion* of 1731 was made up of earlier works, mainly the *Funeral Ode* (BWV198). This year saw the publication of a set of the six partitas, which, though comment was rightly made on the technical demands of many pieces, won appreciation from all connoisseurs: 'Such excellent clavier compositions had never before been heard or seen.'

Above: Portrait by F. G. Haussmann (who later painted Bach himself) of the trumpeter Gottfried Reiche (1667-1734), who had become senior city musician in Leipzig in 1719. The high virtuoso trumpet parts in Bach's works of this period were written for Reiche, but when he took part in the performance of a cantata in homage to the Elector on the night of 5 October 1734 in the market place, the smoke and exertion proved too much for him, and he collapsed and died in the street the following day.

•The Mass in B minor •

As has been seen, Bach was no longer content with his official post at Leipzig, and must have been much disappointed when his appeal to Erdmann brought no result. The way to regain his lost status – 'It seemed at first far from proper to change from Kapellmeister to cantor' – was clearly to obtain a court appointment, and Dresden, besides being the royal establishment, had attracted many of Europe's most successful musicians of all kinds. King Augustus II died on 1 February, and his son ordered a period of public mourning lasting more than four months, during which all concerted music was prohibited. Taking advantage, as is generally supposed, of this unexpected relief from what had become a weekly burden, Bach decided to do homage to the new monarch with a Missa, that is, the Greek Kyrie and Latin Gloria of the Roman Mass – Augustus III, like his father, was a Catholic convert. These were the only parts of the Mass retained in the Lutheran Church, but there are many settings by Italian composers, so Bach's offering would have had a dual use.

Bach's dedicatory letter to his sovereign is dated 27 July, from Dresden itself. The set of

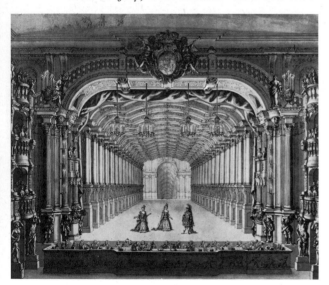

parts presented had been copied by the Bach household, but no score was provided. Perhaps the composer hoped he would be asked to direct a performance? In the event he seems never to have heard the work. Besides requesting the royal protection and a court appointment, the letter reiterates more emphatically than to Erdmann the earlier complaints against the Leipzig authorities. Augustus had more important matters to consider than the grievances of a cantor. Besides being Elector of Saxony, he was also King of the Poles, who in May 1733 declared their intention of choosing a native ruler, Stanislaus Leszczynski, who was finally defeated at Danzig in June 1734. Not surprisingly, Bach's priceless offering remained unacknowledged, but he produced for the royal nameday, soon after his return from Dresden, a slightly refurbished version of the cantata with

which he had marked the reopening of the Thomasschule in 1732, on completion of building works. For a long time it was thought the Mass in B minor was completed in the period immediately following the composing of the Kyrie and Gloria. As more recently established, the dates for the work should be: Sanctus 1724, Missa 1733, remainder c.1748.

As in other large works, Bach resorted to 'parody' in composing the Missa. Music written for some secular occasion was later wasted unless recycled for further use. Apart from the opening measures, models are known for only two of the eleven movements – both, as it happens, church cantatas – but it has been argued that other things in the Kyrie and Gloria were recomposed from originals now lost. When in his later years Bach completed the setting of the Latin Mass, he made much more use of music written long before. The Crucifixus is, in all essentials, taken from a cantata (BWV12), written at Weimar in 1714; other movements were derived from cantatas of the earlier Leipzig years and, in the case of the Osanna, from a secular work written in 1732.

Some scholars and critics have denied that Bach intended to compile a single work comprising the four sections of his score, which he entitled 'Missa; Symbolum Nicenum; Sanctus; and Osanna, Benedictus, Agnus Dei et Dona nobis pacem.' However, J. F. Agricola, who at one time was Bach's pupil, wrote in 1775 of 'a Credo from a great (or "large") Mass by the late J. S. Bach,' and about the same time C. P. E. Bach referred to his father's 'Messe.' Copies of the complete score were circulated; we know that Haydn possessed one.

When choirs began to perform the Mass, it was assumed that so sublime a work must have been designed for large forces, and for more than a century music composed with consummate art for a modest-sized all-male chorus has been – and continues to be – misrepresented by being treated as repertoire for choral societies. A similar fate befell the two Passions; when Mendelssohn revived the *St Matthew Passion* in 1829 the choir numbered around 158. The objection to large choirs is not pedantic; Bach's

Left: Interior of the new opera house in Dresden, directed, from 1734, by J. A. Hasse, who was court Kapellmeister. It is reported that Hasse and his wife, the singer Faustina Bordoni, used to visit Bach in Leipzig, and that when Bach was in Dresden he went several times with his son to the opera.

Below: The Zwinger in Dresden, the great royal parade-ground which was completed in 1736 by the architect M. D. Pöppelmann. Bach would have witnessed the transformation in the face of the city, as the schemes embarked upon by the extravagant Elector Augustus 'the Strong' were all under way at this time.

Bach's loyal devotion to his sovereign in 1733 bordered on the fulsome. In August the Collegium celebrated the royal nameday, followed a month later by the birthday of the infant Prince, and in December by that of the Queen. No church cantatas were written during the year, and in 1734 only one (BWV97), of which the uncouth word-setting strongly suggests that it was not newly composed. Besides two royal celebrations, the Collegium welcomed the new rector in November. At first relations were friendly enough, despite Ernesti's anti-musical intentions. He stood godfather to two of the Bach children in 1733 and 1735, and it was in the summer of 1736 that a disagreement on delegation of responsibility in the school became a bitter dispute from which neither the rector nor cantor was to emerge with much credit, and which dragged on until Easter 1737, when a compromise was reached.

• The 'Christmas' Oratorio •

As we have seen, Bach wrote very little church music after 1730, apart from the Missa for Dresden, so it is not surprising that when he produced for Christmas 1734 an 'Oratorio' in six parts he adapted much of it from earlier compositions, mostly secular odes. Recitatives and chorale settings were of course new, but otherwise all but one of the arias and nearly all the choruses were 'parodies.' The incongruity of secular and sacred texts in some cases has

Above: Interior of the Protestant Frauenkirche in Dresden with the organ by the great Gottfried Silbermann which was dedicated on 25 November 1736. Six days later Bach gave a recital on it attended by the Russian ambassador and members of the electoral court.

Top right: Opening of the Kyrie from the B minor Mass (BWV 232) in Bach's original manuscript. This section and the Gloria were sent with his unsuccessful petition for the title of Court Composer in 1733. It was probably completed without any performance in mind and was not given final form until the very end of the composer's life.

writing for voices and instruments is based on the equal audibility of both, as may be seen in the opening chorus of the Mass (the largest he ever wrote), where soft-toned flutes and oboi d'amore are given independent lines of melody no less essential to the design than those of the five-part choir. The mighty Sanctus is written for what the Venetians would have called four choirs – three trumpets with drums; three oboes; two violins and viola; and six vocal parts, plus continuo of cellos, double bass, bassoon and organ.

Although the Mass can be understood only with some regard to Bach's interpretation of the Lutheran theology of which he was a keen student, his purely musical intention seems to have been to include outstanding examples of all the styles in which he composed and so feature every type of instrument except the obsolescent recorder. The unity of the work is to be sought not in imaginary thematic relations, but in the ordering of sometimes bold contrasts, as for instance in the Kyrie: Kyrie I, baroque expressionism at its most intense; Christe eleison, the perfection of Italian lyricism in Bach's most personal melodic style; Kyrie II, the severe polyphony of the *stile antico*.

179

distressed devout Bach-lovers and has prompted one or two scholars to argue that the composer first planned the oratorio with the intent of using the same music for the secular cantatas, Picander writing parallel texts in the same meters. This would have been contrary to everything known of the many other parodies in Bach's work. The six cantatas of the 'Christmas' Oratorio are designed to be performed on separate days from Christmas Day to Epiphany, but it does not necessarily follow that they are unconnected. Bach must have composed the work continuously, and there are many, sometimes obvious, sometimes subtle, connections between the separate parts. For instance, the first chorale heard in Part I also ends the whole oratorio.

One of the most beautiful arias, the lullaby for the Holy Child, was originally addressed to the infant Hercules (that is, the baby Prince of Bach's *Birthday Ode*, BWV213) by Wollust (Pleasure). Somewhat less provocatively, the splendid 'Grosser Herr und starker König' flattered the Queen-Electress on her birthday. Bach's practice in such matters was consistent with baroque theory of the *Affekten*. Music could arouse certain responses in the hearer, but could not make these specific.

The 'Christmas' Oratorio was virtually the last of Bach's major contributions to the music of his church, later works being almost exclusively either parodies or revisions of cantatas written in former times, when he was still devoted to the maintenance of 'a well-regulated church-music.' In addition to the Missa that grew into the B minor Mass, four other Kyrie-plus-Gloria settings were assembled from cantata movements (BWV233-236), frequently with a disregard for aesthetic values. 'False dissemblers are like Sodom's apples' declares

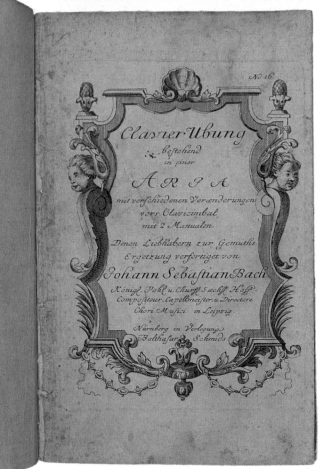

Above: Title-page of the first part of Bach's *Clavierübung*, published in 1741-2, containing the 'Goldberg' Variations (BWV988) which were commissioned by the Russian ambassador at the Dresden court, Count Keyserlingk, for his harpsichordist J. G. Goldberg to play.

Above: View of Dresden in 1748, painted by Bernardo Bellotto. The court church is on the right, while the great dome of the Protestant Frauenkirche (built in 1722-43) is seen behind the new Augustus Bridge. Bach had been seeking closer ties with Dresden since the early 1730s, with visits to the city and celebratory cantatas for events in the Elector's family, and in 1736 he was finally rewarded with the title of Court Composer.

the tenor in cantata no.179; Bach has no scruple about using the music for 'Quoniam Tu solus sanctus' in the G major Missa. Besides such incongruities of text and sentiment the Latin declamation – admirably just in the B minor Mass – is often clumsy. It is hard to dismiss the reflection that the fading of the impulse to compose sacred music and the almost cynical casualness of these adaptations suggest a deep disillusionment that impelled Bach in his last years to an ever-growing concentration on the most esoteric and abstract elements in his incomparable art.

In 1731 the six partitas had been collected to form the first part of the *Clavierübung*; four years later Part II appeared, comprising the Seventh Partita, or 'Overture in the French Manner,' and one of Bach's most familiar masterpieces, the Italian Concerto. Part III of the *Clavierübung* was published in 1739, with the description: 'comprising diverse preludes on the Catechism, and other hymns, for the organ.' The chorale preludes are framed by the tremendous Prelude and Fugue in E flat (BWV552). How many of these pieces were newly composed cannot be established. By composing the first prelude ('Kyrie, Gott Vater') in the *stile antico* on the Gregorian 'Kyrie fons bonitatis,' Bach showed how his highest art was rooted in tradition. The collection includes trios, fughettas (short fugues based on the chorale melody) and – one of the *stile antico* pieces – the monumental 'Aus tiefer Not' in six parts with double pedal. Theorists of the post-Bach generation analyzed the complex interaction of the modal scales found in some of the chorales with the 'modern' harmony of major and minor key tonality. Other commentators have sought to unravel the symbolism, both theological and philosophical, they claim to find in, for example, the fantastically elaborate canonic setting of 'Vater unser im Himmelreich' – the Lord's Prayer.

• The 'Goldberg' Variations •

When, three years after presenting the Missa to his sovereign, Bach received his appointment to the Dresden Court, the intermediary was Count Keyserlingk (or Kayserling), the Russian ambassador, a noted patron of music. In 1737 the Count entrusted to Bach the ten-year-old Johann

Gottlieb Goldberg, already a remarkable harpsichordist, who before long became private virtuoso to the Keyserlingk household. Bach was a guest of his admiring patron in 1741 and, according to Forkel, was asked to write some pieces for Goldberg to play at night to his master, who suffered from insomnia. This was not quite a commission – the 'Goldberg' Variations bear no dedication – but Bach was rewarded handsomely, and Keyserlingk used to call them 'his' variations.

The work, while more accessible to the unlearned than the *Musical Offering* and *Art of Fugue*, shows Bach's preoccupation with large-scale constructions unified by some basic theme. Here it is not the melody of the sarabande – perhaps by another composer – heard before the thirty variations, but its bass and harmony that are the subject, thus making a vast *passacaglia*, or what Purcell might have called 'Variations on a Ground.' The most rigorous contrapuntal form is the canon – a special kind of fugue where one part follows another exactly note for note (or rather interval for interval) after a time interval. From the earliest flowering of music in the Middle Ages down to Schoenberg, the fabricating of canons has fascinated composers; in the 'Goldberg' every third variation is a canon for two parts over the ever-present bass pattern. The answering voice is one note higher in successive canons, beginning at the unison. Thus in canon No. 5 (variation 15) the first note g is answered by d above. To make things more complicated, Bach has the answering melodic line going in the opposite direction, rising where the leader descends, and vice versa. It is significant of a change in Bach's outlook that he should have published these late instrumental works, whereas he showed no interest in the destiny of his church music.

Bach's frequent journeys to Dresden and to towns where his advice was wanted on matters of organ design or repair must have emphasized his withdrawal from the community he was to continue to serve to the end of his life. Even the Collegium Musicum lost its appeal for him as his sons left home, Friedemann in 1733, Emanuel five years later. However, it would be wrong to imagine his life as one of unrelieved gloom. The 'Peasant' Cantata, a work full of warmth and uncondescending humor, was composed for an occasion in August 1742. The versatile librettist of the *St Matthew Passion*

Below: Frederick the Great, King of Prussia, whom Bach visited in his new palace of Sanssouci at Potsdam in 1747 and for whom he composed the *Musical Offering* (BWV 1079).

Bottom: Dedication of the *Musical Offering* to the King: ' . . . With respectful pleasure I still remember your quite especial royal grace, when . . . Your Majesty yourself condescended to play a theme for a fugue on the clavier, and at the same time graciously obliged me to execute this in your presence. . . . I soon realized that through lack of adequate preparation the execution could not match the demands of so excellent a theme. I therefore decided, and immediately undertook to elaborate this right Royal theme more perfectly and then make it known to the world. . . .'

supplied the not entirely decorous text. Of the very few church cantatas performed after 1740, none is certainly newly composed, and Bach's last known appearance as cantor was to direct in August 1749 *Wir danken dir, Gott* (BWV29). By this time his failing sight was already troubling him, having, according to Forkel, weakened over several years.

The first book of *The Well-tempered Clavier* had never been printed, but its fame had spread through many copies, and in the period following the appearance of the 'Goldberg' Variations Bach prepared a second set of twenty-four preludes and fugues, which he completed in 1744. A few of these exist in less developed earlier versions, and it is not known how many were newly composed for the collection. What is certain is that *The Well-tempered Clavier* provided Bach with teaching material, and the devoted enthusiasm he inspired in his pupils may have prompted the composition of new examples, supplemented by material from the Cöthen period. The fugues of Book II tend to be longer; to take an arbitrary example, fugues of fifty or more measures number nine in Book I, and seventeen in Book II. It can be said of both sets that had all Bach's other music vanished, his immense genius would be evident in these preludes and fugues. The publication in 1746 of the six 'Schübler' Chorales gives further evidence of Bach's reluctance to compose in later years. Of these organ pieces, five are transcriptions of cantata movements with minimal alterations.

•*The Musical Offering*•

In 1738 C. P. E. Bach had entered the service of the Crown Prince of Prussia, and on Frederick's accession two years later he became a favorite musician of the Potsdam Court, composing for the royal flute – the instrument on which Frederick had early become expert – and playing the harpsichord.

Perhaps on account of the war between Prussia and Silesia, Emanuel had not seen his father for several years, and when peace returned it was the elder Bach, always fond of traveling, who went to Berlin in May 1747. The King, a thorough musician with a respectable ability as composer, was naturally eager to meet 'old Bach.' His son Friedemann related that his father had been summoned by the royal enthusiast. When Bach arrived at the palace a concert was in progress, but was immediately abandoned as Frederick escorted his visitor to a piano. The then new instrument was much favored by the progressive monarch, who demanded an instant improvisation. How many of the dozen or more Silbermann pianos Bach was made to try is not known, but he had a professional audience as the members of the orchestra followed their master from room to room. An organ recital followed the next day, with a second visit to the palace in the evening, and the King doubtless turned his attention to other matters; but Bach, back in Leipzig, decided to consolidate his tenuous hold on the favor of so important a patron. For the improvisations Frederick had provided a fugue-subject – a very good one – of his own invention, but when asked to make a six-part fugue on it, Bach had declined the challenge, preferring to choose his own theme. However, he composed the magnificent Ricercar à 6, which became known as the 'Prussian Fugue.' Struck by further possibilities of the royal theme, he made it the basis of a collection called: 'Musical Offering to His Majesty . . . most respectfully dedicated by J. S. Bach.'

The accompanying dedicatory epistle is in the obsequious style demanded of artists addressing their betters, but makes no specific request. When the work was engraved the pages were left unnumbered, so the order of the two ricercars (the first surely representing Bach's first improvisation), trio-sonata and various canons remains a matter of argument. Some of the canons are remarkable more for ingenuity than for beauty, but the trio is a splendid example of a genre little cultivated by Bach, and the great ricercar, composed for harpsichord, has been much transcribed, the most famous – or notorious – version being that for orchestra by Anton Webern.

Most of the canons are set down in the conventional notation, with no hint at the manner in which they were intended to be performed. The devising of canons was regarded as a pastime for expert musicians; only one part was written down and the 'solution' had to be discovered from the presence of several clefs and/or an enigmatic motto. Sometimes more than one solution is possible.

Canon, used by Bach as an artistic resource throughout his life, is the basis of another work composed in 1747. A Bach pupil in the 1730s, Lorenz Mizler had founded the Leipzig Society for Musical Science. Handel, Telemann and the then famous C. H. Graun had become members, but Bach, who was known to take little interest in theory, did not respond to Mizler's presumed invitation until a month after his return from Potsdam. Every new member had to submit his portrait and a piece of music, the more learned the better. A year earlier, Bach had written a canon for the society. His composition was entitled: 'Some [or a few] Canonic Variations on the Christmas Hymn "Vom Himmel hoch da komm' ich her," for organ with two manuals and pedal.' In each of the five movements one part has the hymn melody, while the others weave round it strict canons at various intervals – as in the 'Goldberg' Variations. For his distinguished colleagues Bach presented the work incomplete, leaving it to the performer to 'read' the missing parts according to the canon, or rule. In what was perhaps intended as the climax of ingenuity (the order is uncertain) one variation combines with overlapping figures all four lines of the hymn. Others might have matched Bach's mere cleverness in such things; what gives this work its stamp of the highest genius is the beauty of melody and harmony achieved by rigorous adherence to predetermined schemes.

Above: 'Contrapunctus 1,' the opening four-part fugue of the *Art of Fugue* in Bach's manuscript.

·*The Art of Fugue*·

By 1747, or perhaps even before that date, Bach began to work on what was to be his last composition. *The Art of Fugue* (*Die Kunst der Fuge* – the title is not Bach's) may well have begun as a didactic work, demonstrating the techniques of various types of fugue, but it became a masterpiece of creative imagination as well as of supreme skill in resolving deliberately invented problems in counterpoint. *The Art of Fugue* consists of fourteen fugues and four canons, all based on the same theme; in one sense the work can be seen as a vast set of variations. In many of these pieces Bach explores – for purposes purely artistic – the possibilities of invertible counterpoint. This technique simply involves writing combined melodies in such a way that they make good harmony regardless of which is above or below another. Other fugues show melodic inversion also; here Bach devises pairs of fugues in which the second reverses all the steps in the first one. Upward scale figures go down, a falling interval of three or six notes becomes an ascent. Augmentation (giving the theme in longer notes) and diminution (the opposite) are demonstrated with fabulous ease and smoothness; the main subject in what are the finest things in the collection is combined with new themes.

When Bach died, the engraving of the work was incomplete, and the publication, though supervised by Bach pupils, was unsatisfactory; the 'Berlin autograph' is not comprehensive and leaves some questions unanswered, especially concerning the final fugue. This wonderful composition, the greatest of all Bach's fugues, breaks off in the autograph shortly after the introduction of the theme B A C H (H in German nomenclature = B natural, B being B flat), and a few measures earlier in the original edition. It does not include the *Art of Fugue* subject, though its first theme can be regarded as a variant of this, but the Beethoven scholar Gustav Nottebohm discovered that the three themes already present will in fact combine with the subject, making a four-part fugue. It has been proposed that Bach had completed this last fugue, though those close to him were clear that it was left a fragment. Some, including the present writer, believe Bach decided that the fourfold combination was unsatisfactory on account of the close resemblance between two of the themes, a feature found nowhere else in his work. Various attempts have been made to work out the closing section, but none has proved convincing.

Far more serious has been the absurd misunderstanding of the whole nature of *The Art of Fugue* that has arisen from the fact that it was published in score, with a line of music to each part. This was by no means unusual for elaborate keyboard music, and all eighteenth-century musicians realized that *The Art of Fugue* was a clavier work, like *The Well-tempered Clavier*. However, in 1923 the young German polymath Wolfgang Graeser declared that the work was purely abstract and not intended for performance unless 'realized' by orchestration. His own version won the attention of famous conductors and gave a precedent for many such arrangements, some still widely current, though they are without exception totally alien to Bach's whole aesthetic; a similar fate has befallen the six-part ricercar in the *Musical Offering* – also

Right: The Johanniskirche at Leipzig with its graveyard where Bach was buried.

Below: The incomplete final fugue in the *Art of Fugue* with the note in Emanuel Bach's handwriting: 'While working on this fugue, where the name BACH is introduced as a countersubject, the author died.' Although this cannot be taken literally (Bach's blindness would have prevented his working so shortly before his death), the reason for this unfinished fugue remains a mystery.

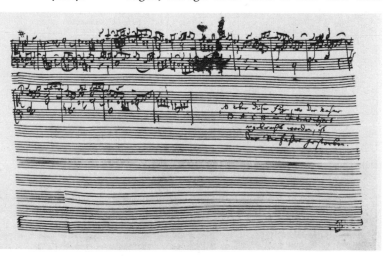

S. Johannis Kirche mit dem neu gebauten Thurn.

published in score, though it is, of course, the six-part harpsichord fugue Bach declined to improvise for Frederick of Prussia. Now that *The Art of Fugue* has once more been recognized in its true nature, performances on harpsichord and organ are revealing the work as the consummation of Bach's keyboard music.

By the summer of 1749 Bach must have been seriously ill; the insignificant Gottlob Harrer was brought forward as the new cantor 'in the event of the demise of Herr Bach' and even went so far as to perform one of his works in public. However, Bach recovered to some degree, only to become completely blind. According to the *Obituary* an unsuccessful attempt to restore his sight left him much weakened, and he died on 28 July 1750.

The Baroque Organ

The two most important schools of baroque organ music were in Protestant northern Europe and in Catholic Spain. The founder of the northern school was the Dutchman J. P. Sweelinck (1562-1621) – the instrument in the drawing above is the seventeenth-century organ in St Martin's church in Utrecht – and the heirs to his tradition were Buxtehude, Reincken and Bach. In Spain the tradition of Cabezón (1500-66) was carried on in the seventeenth century by Correa de Arauxo and Cabanilles, whose works made use of the horizontal pipes characteristic of Spanish organs.

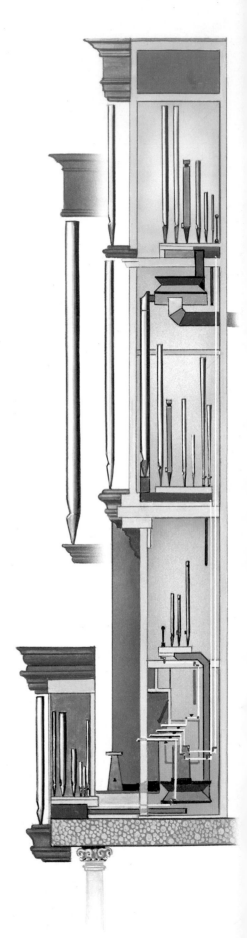

Eighteenth-century organ in the gallery of the Gothic church of S. Martin at Trujillo, in western Spain.

One of the two eighteenth-century organs on either side of the nave of the cathedral in Mondoñedo.

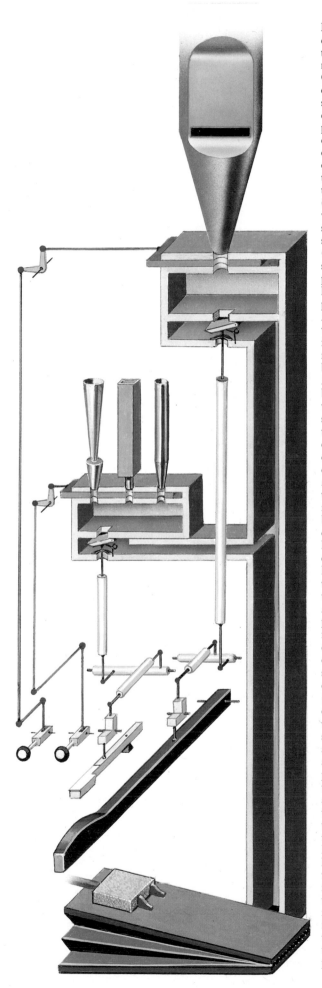

Diagrams (*left and opposite*) showing the structure and mechanism of a German baroque organ. The cross-section shows the different groups of pipes, each of which corresponds to one of the four manuals on the keyboard: the top manual controls the *Brustwerk* (marked in green), with short reeds and stopped pipes; the second controls the *Oberwerk*, with flute stops and long reed pipes; the third, linked with the pedals, the *Hauptwerk* (blue), with principals, flutes and some reeds; and the bottom manual the *Rückpositiv* (olive) behind the organist, with a mixture of stops; the pipes on the outside of the case are for decoration only. The diagram of the mechanism shows the air passage on the right filled by a bellows, which is opened with a long lever, while the air is expressed by the large weight and then distributed to the ranks of pipes. Access to any rank is possible when the inlet between channel and pipes is opened by aligning a slider operated by one of the stops (left). The depression of the key (or pedal) then opens the springed pallet, allowing the air access to the pipe or pipes corresponding to the note. Smooth action is ensured by the system of trackers and rollers: the depression of the key is converted into horizontal motion by the square, and the first connecting tracker causes the roller to rotate forwards, so moving the vertical tracker which opens the pallet.

The tone color and volume of each stop is dictated by a variety of factors, the main distinction being between flue pipes and reed pipes, which use a different means to produce the sound: in the one the pipe contains a vibrating column of air, in the other it acts as a resonator for the vibrating reed. There is also the ratio of the diameter of a flue pipe to its length, the shape (conical or cylindrical) whether the end is open, stopped or half-stopped – factors similar to those that give the character-istic timbre to wind instruments.

The foot of a reed stop (*left*) is similar to the mouthpiece of a clarinet (*above*): a thin metal tongue (whose length affects the pitch and can be adjusted by the tuning wire) is made to vibrate by the action of the wind.

The foot of a flue pipe (*below*) is constructed to direct the pressure of wind against the thin edge of the upper lip, as in the mouthpiece of a recorder (*right*), creating eddies that set in motion the column of air in the pipe.

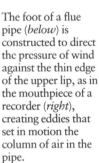

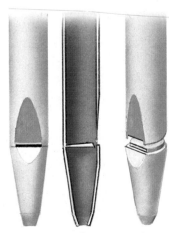

The diagram at the bottom right shows flue pipes of various shapes, all of which would produce the same note. The five pipes on the left are open, and it can be seen that a narrower diameter requires a slightly longer pipe to reach the same pitch, although this is not the case with a pipe where the shape is conical rather than cylindrical. The first three pipes give a variety of flute tones, the fourth, a narrower cylindrical pipe, produces a sound closer to string timbre, while the fifth, called the principal, is the most characteristic of the open flue pipes, often providing the main body of organ sound.

Volume is dependent not only on wind pressure but also on the width of the lip. Next to the principal is the half-stopped Rohrflöte, whose end is closed but pierced with a pipe, while the other three pipes have closed ends – like the flute among woodwind instruments; in this case the pitch of the pipe is approximately an octave below the pitch of an open pipe of corresponding length and shape. The two diagrams (*right and opposite*) from eighteenth-century books show the basic system of an English church organ and the arrangement of pipes in a large French instrument.

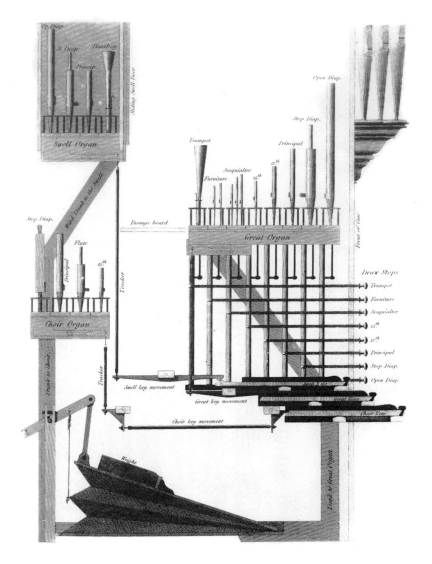

Left: The Jesuit theorist Athanasius Kircher (1601-80) used the six stops of a celestial organ to symbolize the six days of creation.

Below: Two organs built in the same period in the Jesuit school in Munich.

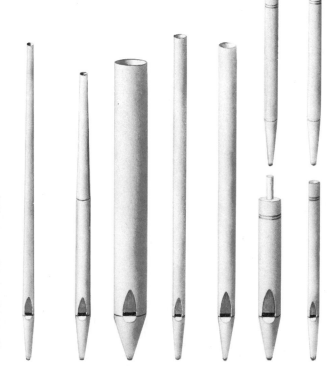

Vue perspective de l'intérieur d'une Orgue de 16 pieds.

The diagram at the bottom left shows a selection of reed pipes, the first four with the tongue and its housing enclosed in its 'boot,' the others exposed. With these the pipe acts as a resonator for the reed tongue, and the pitch of the note is dictated by the length of the tongue rather than by that of the pipe, though the two must have a correct relationship if the note is to speak at all; tone is also affected by the width and thickness of the tongue. This is generally made of brass, while the best material for organ pipes was found to be an alloy of lead and tin, malleable enough to be worked to a very high degree of accuracy and sufficiently strong not to deform even in very large pipes. Reed pipes are mostly named after the wind instrument whose tone they resemble. Thus the pipes below correspond to trumpet, bassoon, oboe, clarinet, trumpet, crumhorn, shawm, sordun, cornett, racket and regal.

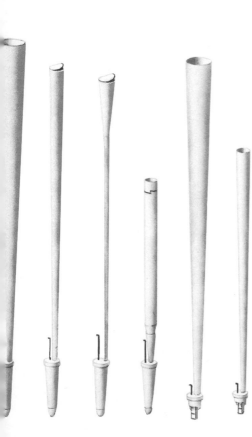

Right: Specification of the stops of the organ built in 1716 by Johann Scheibe (*c.*1680-1748) for the university church in Leipzig, which was tested and approved the following year by J. S. Bach, who submitted a detailed report.

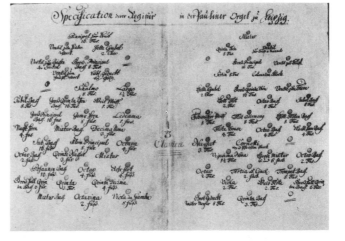

Top: Page from Bach's *Orgelbüchlein*, a collection of chorale settings for organ. In several cases, as here, lack of space led the composer to complete the piece in tablature at the bottom of the page rather than use notation on staves.

GEORGE FRIDERIC HANDEL

ANTHONY FORD

Opposite: George Frideric Handel (1685-1759) in middle years; portrait by Philippe Mercier.

Georg Friederich Händel (as he was christened) or George Frideric Handel (as he styled himself in his English naturalization petition of 1727) was born on 23 February 1685 in Halle, Magdeburg. He was the son of Georg Händel, a celebrated barber-surgeon, and Dorothea Taust, daughter of a Lutheran pastor. His first significant musical experiences were probably at the Lutheran Liebfrauenkirche, whose organist was the talented composer Friedrich Wilhelm Zachow (1663-1712). According to Johann Gottfried Walther's *Musicalisches Lexicon* (Leipzig, 1732), Handel began serious studies with Zachow, in composition and performance on organ and other major instruments, in about 1694. He composed for the services and, as he later put it, 'wrote like the devil' for the oboe. His first extant works are six sonatas for two oboes and continuo (*c.*1696). He also had access to Zachow's valuable collection of music.

In February 1702 Handel registered as a student at Halle University, but he followed no particular course of study, and in March became organist of Halle Cathedral. This Calvinist foundation offered few opportunities to a musician of his talents, so it is not surprising that on 12 September 1703 the post was re-advertised. Handel had gone to Hamburg in July, perhaps to look for an organist's position. The singer, keyboard player and composer Johann Mattheson (1681-1764) relates that in August both he and Handel visited Lübeck to audition for the post occupied by the ailing Dietrich Buxtehude. But with the job went also the master's daughter, an offer they both refused.

Mattheson claimed to have first introduced Handel to the management of the Theater am Gänsemarkt, the most celebrated public opera house in Germany, the orchestra of which Handel joined in autumn 1703 as a second violinist. The musical director was Reinhard Keiser (1674-1739), who had been primarily responsible for establishing the fame of the opera house. He was a fine composer whose music, notably his colorful use of wind instruments, was to leave a lasting impression on Handel. For the 1704/5 season Handel was promoted to the harpsichord, then, on 8 January 1705, came the first night of his first, and only extant, Hamburg opera, *Almira*. This, like most contemporary Hamburg operas, has several arias in Italian and makes effective use of ballet. Its success, although not matched by his second

opera, *Nero*, apparently caused a rift at the theater; Handel appears to have been forced to resign, and the jealous Keiser deliberately set both subjects anew in 1705/6. Keiser's triumph was short-lived. He fled Hamburg to escape his creditors and Handel was asked to write another opera, *Florindo and Daphne.* This long work was produced in 1708 in two parts on consecutive nights, but by then its composer was in Italy.

One of Handel's Hamburg patrons was Prince Gian Gastone de' Medici, younger son of the Grand Duke of Tuscany. He and his elder brother Prince Ferdinando invited Handel to Florence, where he arrived in the autumn of 1706. Handel was in Italy for three and a half years, spending each autumn until 1709 at Florence. There, in about October 1707, his opera *Rodrigo* was produced under a moralizing title, a common practice at the time: *Vincer se stesso è la maggior vittoria* (To conquer oneself is the greatest victory).

Handel also paid two visits to Venice (in late 1707 and in the winter of 1709/10), and one to Naples (in July 1708), but the rest of the time he was at Rome. Opera there was temporarily banned, but music was encouraged by Church and nobility, particularly by the Cardinals Ottoboni, Pamphili and Colonna, and the Marquis Ruspoli, to whose household Handel was attached. While in Rome he worked with Arcangelo Corelli and Alessandro Scarlatti, the second of whom had also worked for the Florentine court and may well have provided Handel with his introduction to Rome's musical life.

Handel also attended meetings of the important Arcadians' Academy, where opera had been much discussed in the years preceding his visit. In *La Bellezza della Volgar Poesia* (Rome, 1700) Giovanni Maria Crescimbeni, a founder of the Academy, indicated his dislike of supernatural libretti and of the tragi-comedies mixing low-life and noble personages favored by the Venetians. The 'heroic' style of *opera seria*, in which the stupendous technique of contemporary singers could be fully exploited, was thus gradually emerging. Crescimbeni had also noted a desire that in the recitative room be left 'for the passions' and that the 'exorbitant number of ariettas' (often over fifty) be reduced. As an extension of this principle, long soliloquies (or *scene*), in which accompanied recitative and song elements were combined, began to appear in Handel's later operas.

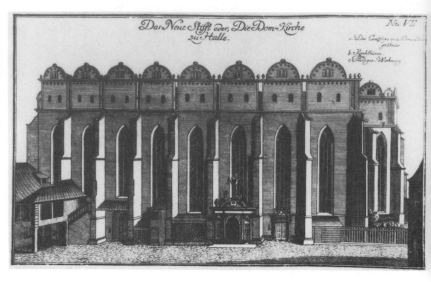

Top left: The organ in the Lutheran Lieb-frauenkirche in Halle, Handel's birthplace, where the composer received his first lessons from the church organist Friedrich Wilhelm Zachow. By the age of eleven Handel was able to substitute for his master when necessary.

Top right: The Calvinist Cathedral in Halle, where Handel was organist in 1702-3.

Above: Miniature of Handel at the age of about twenty-five by Christopher Platzer.

The origins of the *scena* undoubtedly lie in the cantata. Partly because Ruspoli required cantatas every Sunday, Handel wrote many of these multi-movement solo songs, cast in alternating recitative and, normally, *da capo* aria, and with pastoral love as their subject. Many of these mirror the questing spirit of the Academies in their daring chromatic harmonies, wide-ranging melodies and unexpected turns to avoid cadences. Others are more extended than usual, less 'formal' in their design and more dramatic in their subject-matter, like Handel's superb quasi-operatic scena *Lucrezia* for soprano and continuo, an intensely moving portrayal of the distraught agony of a raped woman.

Another outgrowth of the cantata was the *serenata*, a quasi-operatic conversation piece of about an hour's duration. A fine example is *Apollo e Dafne*, a light-hearted retelling of Ovid's tale concerning the origins of the laurel. Its typically colorful scoring is exemplified in the aria in which Apollo pursues Dafne. The concerto-like accompaniment uses solo violin (Dafne) and bassoon (Apollo). As the lustful god embraces the fleeing nymph she is suddenly metamorphosed, leaving everyone bewildered, for Handel breaks off in mid-beat in the middle of a measure. Such dramatic interruptions are typical of his music.

Another *serenata* of the Italian period is *Aci, Galatea e Polifemo* (Naples, 1708). There are also two oratorios: the allegorical *Il Trionfo del Tempo e del Disinganno* for Ottoboni (1707), and *La Resurrezione* for Ruspoli (Easter Day 1708), which was given a spectacular performance with scenery. Handel's output of Latin church music includes pieces for Vespers on the feast of the Madonna del Carmine (Rome, 16 July 1707). Of these, *Dixit Dominus* is an outstanding choral work, demanding in its brilliance, miraculous in its contrapuntal virtuosity, terrifying in its musical imagery.

On 26 December 1709 *Agrippina*, Handel's first dramatic masterpiece, was produced in Venice, the homeland of opera. It was a triumph. The theater echoed to shouts of 'Viva il caro Sassone' and the opera received no less than twenty-seven performances.

Handel had gone to Italy a comparatively unknown composer and left as one of the most celebrated composers of Europe. All were eager to engage him for their musical establishments. Handel hedged his bets. He accepted the offer of a Kapellmeistership at Hanover from 16 June 1710, provided that he was given immediate leave to visit England. The Elector of Hanover was heir to the British throne, and Handel was angling for an eventual English court post.

• First London works •

Regular opera performances were new to London. They had begun with the *pasticcio Arsinoe* in 1705, but the work that established opera firmly in England was *Camilla* (1706), an English version of Giovanni Bononcini's *Il Trionfo di Camilla*. Handel was the first composer to write an Italian opera specifically for London. *Rinaldo*, written in a fortnight, was produced on 24 February 1711 at the Queen's (later King's) Theatre, Haymarket, the major London opera house. Its enormous success resulted as much from the singing of the castrato Nicolò Grimaldi and Handel's harpsichord improvisations as from the work itself. Its spectacular staging would have appealed to those who hankered after the days of Purcell's semi-operas, for, like them, *Rinaldo* and most of Handel's early London operas have magic elements. One scene also spectacularly – but unwisely – introduced sparrows and chaffinches into the auditorium.

As soon as the season ended Handel returned to Hanover, but by November 1712 he was back in London for good. He wrote four more operas between 1712 and 1716: the pastoral *Il Pastor fido* and 'magical' *Teseo* (1712-13), the 'magical' *Amadigi* (May 1715), and *Silla*, a modern-style heroic opera presented on 2 June 1713, probably at Burlington House, Piccadilly, home of Handel's new patron.

Lord Burlington was an enthusiastic Italophile, who gathered around him some of the finest minds of the age. His mother served Queen Anne, and it is probably due to her that Handel received his first court commissions in 1713, the *Ode for the Birthday of Queen Anne* (6 February), the *Te Deum* and the *Jubilate* celebrating the Peace of Utrecht (both first performed 7 July). In these first major settings of English, Handel imitated closely the style of Purcell's court odes and of his festal *Te Deum* and *Jubilate* in D. The Queen granted Handel a pension of £200 a year. Anne died in August 1714, to be succeeded by Handel's Hanoverian master, who doubled his pension. A further £200 was later added for teaching Queen Caroline's children the harpsichord.

During these years Handel composed his only Passion, a setting of a text by Heinrich Brockes. It was given in 1719, in Hamburg Cathedral, but may have been performed in 1716. It differs from Bach's Passions in that its text paraphrases the Gospel narrative. It includes chorales but, unlike Bach, Handel treats them rather perfunctorily. His operatic approach ideally suits dramatic scenes, but may seem to Bach lovers less satisfactory for the many meditative sections.

•The Royal Academy of Music•

Handel visited Hanover with the King in 1716, returning at the end of the year. In the following summer he went to live at Cannons, near Edgware, residence of the Earl of Carnarvon (later Duke of Chandos), where he stayed until 1720. During this time he composed the celebrated Chandos Anthems and two masques, *Acis and Galatea* and the first version of *Esther*. *Acis*, Handel's first English dramatic work, has a libretto by John Gay, writer of *The Beggar's Opera*. Short though it is (it lasts about one and a half hours), this wonderful *serenata* was justly to become one of Handel's most popular works.

The composer's absence from London was probably a result of the decline of public interest

Right: Johann Mattheson (1681-1764), who became a close friend of Handel's after his arrival in Hamburg in 1703. He learned counterpoint from Handel, while the younger composer began to practice his melodic gifts under the influence of Mattheson and of the operatic music he heard in the city. When Handel went to Italy, Mattheson stayed in Hamburg as a composer, critic, tenor at the opera and diplomat, later also becoming one of the outstanding theorists of music in the eighteenth century.

Below: The Exchange in Hamburg, financial hub of the most important port and commercial city in Germany.

in Italian opera. The King's Theatre's 1716/17 season did not begin until December. By then the rival Lincoln's Inn Fields Theatre, under Carnarvon's director of music Johann Christoph Pepusch (1667-1752), was ready to produce three competing English-language operas, including *Camilla* in an improved translation, and while no more were produced at the King's until 1720, English operas continued at Lincoln's Inn for one more season.

The 'English' thus gained a brief victory over the 'Italians.' Handel's Cannons masques may reflect this change of taste. *Acis* certainly owes

IOANNES MATTHESON
Celsitudinis Imperialis Magni Russiæ Principi Supremi Holsatiæ Ducis Legationum Consiliarius.
æt.
nat. Hamburg d. 28. Sept. A. 1681.

much to English masques by Pepusch and others performed in London theaters in 1715-18. But the Italian party, backed by King and nobility, with Handel's patrons Burlington and Chandos in the vanguard, fought back. They launched an opera company called The Royal Academy of Music. Handel was ordered to 'procure proper Voices to Sing in the Opera' and 'engage Senezino' (the castrato Francesco Bernardi). Setting out in May 1719, Handel went via Halle to Dresden. There he booked Senesino and other virtuosi, including Margherita Durastanti, the first Agrippina. On 30 November 1719 the directors minuted that Handel be 'Ma[ste]r of the Orchestra with Sallary' and that 'Seignr Bona Cini be writ to, to know his Terms for composing & performing in the Orchestra.' Bononcini left for London in the summer of 1720, remaining until about 1733. The stage was set to make London briefly the opera center of Europe.

The Academy, aiming to provide each year fresh works by different composers, first opened

at the King's on 2 April 1720 with *Numitore* by Giovanni Porta (*c.*1690-1755), continuing with Handel's *Radamisto* and Domenico Scarlatti's *Narciso*. The 1720/1 season opened with Bononcini's *Astarto*, whose librettist Paolo Antonio Rolli had been invited to London in 1715, after its first performance in Rome had so impressed Burlington. Bononcini's music immediately conquered all opposition: of fifty-eight performances that season, thirty-two were by Bononcini and only seven by Handel (another ten were shared). In 1721/2 there were forty Bononcini performances compared with nineteen by Handel. As a result, Handel for a time avoided the rich instrumentation he had used in *Radamisto*, favoring Bononcini's simple style.

One unusual opera in 1720/1, which, probably unintentionally, encouraged the growing partisanship of the audience, was *Muzio Scevola*, for which Filippo Amadei (fl. 1690-1730) wrote Act I, Bononcini Act II and Handel Act III, each act having an overture. Each act was also longer than the preceding one, Handel's being the longest — not, as was usual, the shortest. He was, after all, music director. The work, like most Academy operas, is an *opera seria*. It presents the Romans (that is, Italians) in a truly heroic light, fighting for freedom from their Etruscan oppressors. Each act features a great deed of bravery, and the librettist Rolli quotes directly from Livy. These operas occupy a different world from those of the popular pastoral theater or the extravagant magic operas with their amazing transformation scenes and ballet. Gone too are the comic servants whose antics so amused *Camilla*'s audiences. Spectacle is rationalized; plot, not setting, dominates.

In 1721/2 *Floridante* was the only new Handel opera. For the 1722/3 season another com-

poser, Attilio Ariosti (1666-1729) joined the Academy. The aim was apparently to present two new works by each composer per year. Handel's offerings were the heroic *Ottone* and an anti-heroic opera, *Flavio*, in which the noble characters find themselves in far from heroic situations. *Ottone* marked the London début of the soprano Francesca Cuzzoni. She refused at first to perform her wonderful first aria, but Handel threatened to throw her out of the window – she sang it!

In 1723/4 Handel wrote only one opera to Bononcini's two, but Handel's opera was *Giulio Cesare*, one of his finest works. This returned

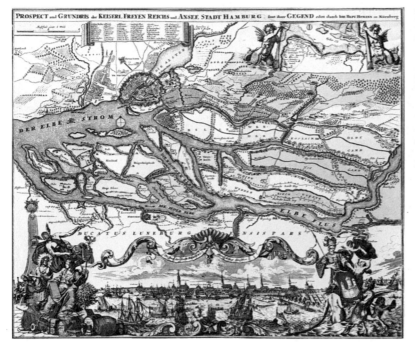

to a richer orchestration. Cleopatra's Act II aria 'V'adoro pupille,' for example, requires a pit orchestra of muted four-part strings and continuo and a stage orchestra of oboe, viola da gamba, bassoon and four-part strings, with theorbo and harp.

At the end of the season, after a period of wrangling within the management of the Academy, Bononcini was dismissed and joined the private music of the Duchess of Marlborough. Handel thus lost his most dangerous competitor. His two operas in the 1724/5 season included fine roles for the tenor voice (often ignored in contemporary Italian opera), notably Bajazet in *Tamerlano*, whose great death scene ranks amongst the finest in all opera. These were written for the company's new tenor, Francesco Borosini. *Rodelinda* also contains a powerful role for the heroine, who attempts to rescue her husband from the clutches of a tyrant.

Handel's new works for the following season were *Scipione* and *Alessandro*. In the latter the mezzo-soprano Faustina Bordoni made her London début. Her arrival heralded an increasingly violent rivalry with Cuzzoni, which culminated in a scandalous public brawl on 6 June 1727. However, Faustina and Cuzzoni did appear as Alceste and Antigona in Handel's new opera

Admeto, a superb work in which the Alkestis myth is used to study the conflict in Admeto's mind between constancy to the dead Alceste and love for Antigona.

On 29 January 1728 the Lincoln's Inn Fields Theatre presented John Gay's ballad opera *The Beggar's Opera*, a political satire and parody of Italian opera in general, and the 6 June scandal in particular. Handel's friend, Mrs Pendarves (later Delany) noted that it 'entirely triumphs over the Italian one.' So despite a reasonably successful autumn, with the performance of Handel's patriotic *Riccardo Primo* (given one month after George II's coronation), and the introduction of his new operas *Siroe* and *Tolomeo* later in the season, the Academy had entered its last year. The rival attraction proved the last straw for an organization plagued with financial problems and disturbed by internal wrangling. The main singers departed for Italy, and London was without an Italian opera for a year. In that year Handel too went to Italy to find more singers, while a new Academy was formed under the joint control of Handel and John Jacob Heidegger, manager of the King's Theatre.

• Operas of the early 1730s •

The new arrangement lasted from autumn 1729 until summer 1734, a crucial period in Handel's career. He was much more his own master now, but his operas had to compete with ballad operas at Lincoln's Inn Fields, Drury Lane, and the nearby Little (later 'New') Theatre in the Haymarket. In December 1732 yet another competing theater opened, Covent Garden.

In this period Handel composed seven Italian operas (*Lotario* and *Partenope* for 1729/30,

Poro and *Ezio* for 1730/1, *Sosarme* for 1731/2, *Orlando* for 1733 and *Arianna in Creta* for 1734) and one *serenata, Il Parnasso in Festa* (1734). He presented music by other composers but, with revivals, his own music easily predominated. This, together with the tight control he kept on his singers, were the probable reasons for increasing tensions within his company. Possibly pressure from them lay behind revivals of Ariosti's first Academy opera, *Coriolano*, in 1732 and of Bononcini's *Griselda* in 1733.

From January 1733 the Italian party, headed by Rolli and Senesino, met with certain members of the nobility, led by the Prince of Wales (who was at loggerheads with his father, Handel's patron), with the apparent object of deposing Handel upon the expiry of his five-year lease. They formed the Opera of the Nobility, to which Senesino, with most of Handel's singers,

departed, leaving him without a company. Nicola Porpora (1686-1768), who later taught Joseph Haydn, was the new company's musical director.

Having rapidly hired singers, Handel planned for January 1734 his *Arianna in Creta*. Porpora spiked Handel's guns by producing at Lincoln's Inn Fields his own *Arianna in Nasso*, surely no coincidence. And significantly, in view of the 1733 revival of *Griselda*, the Nobility's second opera was Bononcini's *Astarto*. Handel's opponents rapidly established themselves, and at the expiry of his lease of the King's in 1734 moved in, thus obtaining the state opera subsidy.

Most of Handel's operas of these years were heroic. *Poro* and *Ezio* are based on libretti by Pietro Metastasio, the foremost exponent of *opera seria*. Handel had set only one other Metastasian libretto, *Siroe*, in 1728, and was to set no more. His sympathetic understanding of the joys and sufferings of humanity, so wonderfully expressed in the bitter-sweetness of the love duet 'Per le porte del tormento' in *Sosarme*, was an uneasy partner to Metastasio's political dramas, and he goes out of his way to instill some warmth into the poet's cool characters.

Most of Handel's heroic operas are set in classical or medieval times, but *Arianna in Creta*, like *Admeto* before it, is based on a Greek myth, Theseus and the Minotaur. This new approach was to be continued in the two English-language 'musical dramas,' *Semele* and *Hercules*. The interest in classical mythology probably stemmed from the growing impact of French opera plots on Italian opera and was to increase as the century progressed. Classical myth, like 'magic' operas, provided Handel with the possibility of spectacular staging and

Below: Old London Bridge, drawn by Canaletto in 1746. Handel arrived in London in the autumn of 1710, and although he returned to Hanover for a year in 1711-12, the rest of his life was spent with the English capital as his home.

Right: Title-page of the first edition of Handel's *Water Music*, probably performed originally by a group of musicians under the composer's direction on a barge on the Thames at a royal water-party in 1717.

Far right: Title-page of a collection of arias from Handel's opera *Rinaldo*, commissioned shortly after his arrival in London and completed in two weeks at the beginning of 1711, much of the music being taken from earlier works. The opera was an immediate success and established Handel's reputation in England.

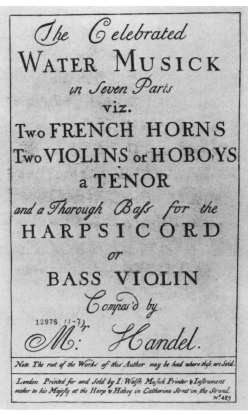

balletic elements, as for example in Hercules's harrowing of Hell in *Admeto*, or in the exciting scene in *Arianna* in which Theseus kills the Minotaur, where Handel uses the orchestral accompaniment of Theseus's aria to reflect the battle between man and monster.

Of the remaining operas, *Partenope* is another anti-heroic work, whilst *Orlando* marks a return to 'magic' opera, but with elements of the heroic, anti-heroic and pastoral. Instead of the evil sorceress of many 'magic' operas, *Orlando*'s Zoroastro is a benign magician, watching over the hero who has abandoned Duty for Love. Orlando's love is unrequited, and jealousy leads him in a fit of madness to attempt the destruction of his beloved Angelica, of her husband Medoro and of himself, but Zoroastro averts the calamity and restores his sanity. The experience teaches him that it is not enough to conquer one's enemies; one must learn to conquer oneself.

The opera requires colorful scenery and spectacular staging (exploding caves, flying chariots, visions). Handel's score is equally colorful. A memorable piece is the wonderful sleep aria sung by the exhausted Orlando in Act III, which Handel, always on the search for new effects, accompanied with two violette marini (instruments like the viola d'amore).

If this superb score has a highlight, it is the magnificent *scena* which ends Act II, where Orlando has a vision of Angelica in Hades. It is always quoted for Handel's brief use of 5/8 time (for three measures), but this is only one element in a telling translation into musical terms of the unbalanced mind. Changing tempi and the disruption of regular rhythms, notably

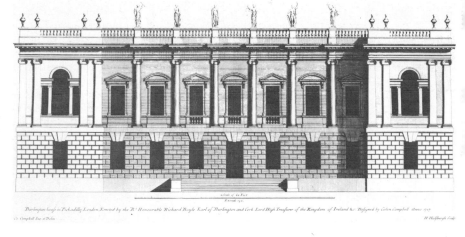

Burlington house in Picadilly London, Erected by the R.t Honourable Richard Boyle Earl of Burlington and Cork Lord High Treasurer of the Kingdom of Ireland &c. Designed by Colen Campbell Anno 1717

by triplets, also play their part. But a masterstroke is the inclusion, as a refrain, of a gavotte, whose simple tune suggests, in the context of its anguished surroundings, the simpleton. Gavotte rhythm and triplets once more appear in Orlando's mad aria in Act III, demonstrating Handel's concern to maintain consistency of characterization throughout an opera.

• First oratorios •

In February 1732 Bernard Gates (1685-1773), Master of the Children of the Chapel Royal, revived with Handel's blessing the Cannons masque *Esther*. The work, at the Crown and Anchor Tavern, was probably staged and was in costume. The choir (from Westminster Abbey and the Chapel Royal) was placed 'between the

this revision, and that, together with the seven-part choral writing, introduced a wholly new sound into the theater.

Esther's plot is based on a play by Racine, whose aim was to apply the principles of Greek tragedy to Old Testament subjects. In this sense the work is in the same tradition as *Arianna in Creta*. Its use of chorus within the action is also classical, but musically stems from French opera. Handel's grafting on to this of a *ceremonial* choral style is, however, unique. *Esther*'s popularity established the Handelian oratorio form, and a genre, conceived accidentally to fit the circumstances of one particular performance, produced some of the finest masterpieces in the history of music.

The other Cannons masque, *Acis*, was given one performance in March 1731 at Lincoln's Inn Fields. The following year saw an unauthorized revival under Arne. As in the case of *Esther*, Handel in June 1732 responded with a new version, an extraordinary bilingual combination of *Acis* with his 1708 *serenata Aci, Galatea e Polifemo*. *Acis* is essentially a static plot, and the advertisement apologizes for this: 'There will be no action . . . but the Scene will represent . . . a rural Prospect, with Rocks, Groves, Fountains and Grotto's; amongst which will be disposed a Chorus of Nymphs and Shepherds, Habits and every other Decoration suited to the Subject.'

Although *Acis* became exceedingly popular, Handel showed little interest in either the English pastoral or in oratorio, treating the latter solely as a means of extending his opera season into Lent, when opera was forbidden. In 1733 came *Deborah*, a *pasticcio* which included passages from the coronation Anthems once more and from the Chandos anthems. *Athalia* was Handel's first newly composed oratorio. It was not, however, written for London, but for a

Above: John Jacob Heidegger (*c.* 1659-1749), the Swiss opera manager whom Handel had met on his first visit to London. When the Royal Academy of Music, an opera company backed by the King, Lord Burlington and Lord Chandos, was formed in 1719, Handel became music director and Heidegger the manager. Later they formed a new opera company, which lasted from 1729 until 1734 and for which Handel wrote seven operas.

Above left: Title-page of an English edition of Handel's *Giulio Cesare*, composed for the Royal Academy's 1723/4 season. An outstanding opera, written at the time of Handel's rivalry with Bononcini, it was performed by a cast led by the castrato Senesino, the soprano Cuzzoni and the bass Boschi, and gave Handel clear supremacy, for the time being at least.

Left: Funerary monument to James Brydges, first Duke of Chandos (1673-1744), in the church at Little Stanmore, where Handel often played the organ. While attached to the Duke's court at Cannons, from 1716 to 1720, Handel composed the Chandos Anthems and two masques as well as instrumental works, including, in all probability, the op.3 Oboe Concertos.

stage and the orchestra,' suggesting its non-involvement in the action, perhaps because the stage was small or because they sang from music.

An unauthorized performance of *Esther* at York Buildings in April encouraged Handel to act on the suggestion of his pupil Princess Anne and perform the work himself on 2 May 1732. The advertisement contained the following: 'N.B. There will be no Action on the Stage, but the House will be fitted up in a decent Manner . . . The Musick to be disposed after the Manner of the Coronation Service.'

The reason why a work which was called 'Oratorio or Sacred Opera' or 'Oratorio or Sacred Drama' was not staged is uncertain. It is generally thought that the Bishop of London, who was Dean of the Chapel Royal, refused permission for his boys, whom Handel was using, to appear as actors in the theater. This may have been for moral reasons or because he felt that to introduce Handel's popular anthems written for the coronation of George II in 1727 in a staged work would be inappropriate. Whatever the reason, the performance was, as the anonymous writer of *See and Seem Blind* commented, 'a mere Consort.' Handel was 'plac'd in a Pulpit,' beside him the soloists 'in their own habits,' and before him the choir. The introduction of the coronation anthems would have made staging difficult, for they were essentially static and they demanded large resources (in 1727, 160 in the orchestra and 47 in the choir). Whatever its precise size, Handel used a huge orchestra in

Left: Aeneas prostrates himself before Dido, while in heaven Venus pleads with Jupiter to avert the lovers' tragic fate. The painting, by the foremost English artist of the period, Sir James Thornhill (1675-1734), recalls the less heroic treatment of the same subject by the great English composer Henry Purcell in 1689. It is probably a sketch for one of the paintings Thornhill executed in 1715-25 at Cannons for Lord Chandos, perhaps on the great staircase there.

visit to Oxford in the summer of 1733. Like *Esther*, it is based on a play by Racine. It again features the ceremonial style of the coronation anthems. Another feature of the work is the close integration of solo and chorus in some numbers. Despite its deserved success Handel did not perform it in London in 1734, preferring *Deborah*.

• The late 1730s •

For the 1734/5 season Handel moved to Covent Garden. His opponents had engaged the most famous castrato of all time, Farinelli. Handel had one asset, however: Covent Garden's French ballet troupe, led by Marie Sallé. He revived *Il Pastor fido*, with a prologue aptly named *Terpsicore*, and introduced short ballets with great effect into his new operas, the heroic *Ariodante* and the 'magic' *Alcina*.

Ariodante, into which the ballet scenes are introduced with apparent ease – no mean feat in an heroic opera – is an exciting story of intrigue, in which the hero's betrothed, Ginevra, is falsely accused of infidelity. The King, her father, beautifully characterized, has to choose between his royal duty to uphold the law and his love for his daughter. If Ginevra is in the same tradition as the patiently suffering heroine of Bononcini's *Griselda*, Alcina is a very different sort of woman. An evil enchantress who has the nasty habit of transforming her lovers into anything she pleases, she wields regal power, but even then cannot force the one she loves to love her. At last, stripped of her magic, both she and her island disappear. Handel's music raises her to the status of a tragic heroine. She is one of his finest female roles, subtly drawn in all her varied moods.

In *Athalia*'s first London performance that season Handel introduced a new element: organ concertos, with himself as soloist. Concertos were to become thereafter a feature of his oratorio performances. He had already composed works in the form, notably his *concerti grossi*

for wind and strings, op.3, and he was to write a series of organ concertos, most of which were published as op.4 and op.7. To follow too were his great set of twelve 'Grand Concertos' for strings, op.6. His concertos generally follow the multi-movement Corellian pattern rather than the three-movement Vivaldian one favored by Bach. However, like his *Suites de pièces* for keyboard, they show a bewildering variety of design. In everything Handel was a dramatist, and surprise is of the essence in his art. His concertos are large-scale public works; the delicate chamber-like interplay of Bach's 'Brandenburg' Concertos has little place in them. Not that Handel was averse to the instrumental chamber idiom, as his trio sonatas op.2 and op.5, with their imaginative counterpoint, bear out. But in these too, as in his great set of solo sonatas op.1, dramatic surprise is paramount.

Handel's next opera was not performed until the spring of 1736; Covent Garden was awaiting a new castrato singer, so the season opened in February with a non-operatic work for the first time; not an oratorio, but a setting of John Dryden's St Cecilia's Day ode, *Alexander's Feast*, which justly became very popular. The new opera, a pastoral called *Atalanta*, was a patriotic work written for the wedding of the Prince of Wales, patron of the Nobility Opera, which also presented a work for the occasion, but theirs was eclipsed by Handel's spectacular presentation including chorus and a firework display.

For 1736/7 Handel presented a particularly ambitious program, which gives some idea of his almost superhuman energy. Between 14 August 1736 and 13 April 1737 he wrote and produced three new operas: *Giustino*, *Arminio* and *Berenice*. He also completed the cantata *Cecilia volgi* and a revision of *Il Trionfo del Tempo e del Disinganno* – all this in addition to the production of other works throughout the season including *Alcina*, *Poro*, *Partenope* and performances of *Alexander's Feast*. The night of 13 April saw the opening of *Didone abbandonata* by Leonardo Vinci, with Handel's recitatives, but the pressure proved too great. That morning, 13 April 1737, Handel had a stroke, which paralysed his right arm and affected his mind. After treatment at Aachen, he made a miraculous recovery; his company, however, had disbanded, as had his operatic rivals; but Heidegger formed a new company, for which in the 1737/8 season Handel wrote the heroic opera *Faramondo* and the tragicomic *Serse*.

Serse is Handel's only opera apart from *Armida* to use a *buffo* character, Elviro, who in one scene parodies the traditional bridge collapse by using it as an excuse for a drinking song. The appearance of a comic servant points to the libretto's origins in Nicolò Minato's text, set by Cavalli for Venice in 1654. In 1694 this was very considerably altered by Silvio Stampiglia (librettist of *Camilla*) and set by Bononcini. Handel apparently obtained the work from Bononcini's score, for, although there are some changes in the libretto, Handel's setting uses

Below: Caricature probably showing Senesino, Cuzzoni and Berenstadt in Handel's anti-heroic opera *Flavio*, composed for the Royal Academy of Music in 1723.

THE BEGGARS OPERA

et cantare pares et respondere parati

*Brittons attend — view this harmonious Stage
And listen to those notes which charm the age
Thus shall your tastes in Sounds & Sense be shown
And Beggars Opras ever be your own*

Printed for John Bowles at the Black horse in Cornhill

Below: John Gay (1685-1732), author of *The Beggar's Opera.*

Mr Gay Author of the Beggars Opera.

Above: Poster for *The Beggar's Opera* (1728), the satirical work written by John Gay with music assembled by J. C. Pepusch, whose attack on the Italian opera led to the dissolution of the Academy. Swift wrote: 'This comedy . . . exposes that unnatural taste for Italian music among us which is wholly unsuitable to our northern climate, and the genius of the people, whereby we are overrun with Italian effeminacy and Italian nonsense.'

Right: Ticket designed by Hogarth for a performance of *The Beggar's Opera* at Covent Garden for the benefit of Thomas Walker, the actor who first played Macheath, the anti-hero of the piece.

some of Bononcini's musical ideas. There are remarkable resemblances, for example, between the two settings of Serse's opening aria 'Ombra mai fù,' now unfortunately better known as 'Handel's Largo,' although it is marked *larghetto*. It has no solemn connotations, being the praises of a self-indulgent monarch for the plane tree under which he is taking his siesta. *Serse* is a subtle mixture of the serious and the comic, full of confusions and misunderstandings. It seems incredible that it was a total failure.

• *Saul* and *Israel in Egypt* •

FOR THE BENEFIT OF Mr WALKER.

THEATRE ROYAL COVENT GARDEN.

On 28 March 1738 Handel gave 'An Oratorio,' which consisted of a Chandos Anthem, a coronation anthem and, in between, arias from *Deborah*. From this concert perhaps originated the great choral work *Israel in Egypt*. Another work of this year, Queen Caroline's funeral anthem, also plays a part in the *Israel* story.

Charles Jennens had as early as 1735 sent Handel a libretto, probably *Saul*. He laid it aside, and began work on *Imeneo*, only to return again to *Saul*. In January 1739 he began an oratorio season, including *Saul* and *Israel in Egypt*. All performances included concertos 'for various instruments' or 'for organ.' *Saul*'s overture also employs solo organ and includes far more internal orchestral numbers than was

usual, all linked with the dramatic design, and colorfully scored.

One amazing piece represents the 'joyful dance with instruments of musick' which, starting alone, eventually accompanies the women's 'thousand praises' to Saul and 'ten thousand praises' to David — an acclamation which plants in Saul the seed of envy that eventually leads to his destruction. Handel's brilliant treatment of the scene takes us gradually from the real world of the opening, with its bright tinkling bells and women's voices, into the nightmarish world of Saul's mind, in which the phrase 'ten thousand praises' hammers at his brain with terrifying loudness: full four-part chorus and a huge orchestra including trombones, trumpets and timpani. Another instrumental number is the famous 'Dead March,' in which Handel used to wonderful effect the massive timpani he had borrowed from the Tower of London, contrasting them with quiet flutes and solemn trombones.

One of *Saul*'s most impressive scenes is that between Saul and the aged Witch of Endor (a tenor role). As she raises Samuel's ghost, oboes and bassoons play slow chords in three quarter notes per measure, while weird string figures in four quarter notes per measure completely disorient the listener. The considerable choral element includes, as well as internal numbers commenting on or participating in the action, a huge coronation-style sequence at the beginning of the work and a concluding section setting David's 'Lament for Saul and Jonathan' in anthem style.

Perhaps with the intention of giving an 'oratorio' concert as in 1738, Handel had set the *Song of Moses* (now Part II of *Israel in Egypt*). But he was inspired by the story of the plagues of Egypt and the escape of the Israelites to set this under the title of *Exodus* (now Part I of *Israel*). Before this he placed Queen Caroline's funeral anthem, under the title 'Lamentations of the Israelites for the death of Joseph,' which explains the apparent absence of an overture. *Israel*, which requires double chorus, has a tremendous range of styles, varying from choral recitative to complex contrapuntal structures, from unaccompanied writing to pieces with large orchestra. The tone pictures in *Exodus* have an amazing intensity, which effectively makes the choir participants in the scenes they describe. Yet *Israel* was unsuccessful. It used

only scriptural texts, had few solo numbers, and could have disturbed some by its very vividness.

In 1739/40 Handel moved to Lincoln's Inn Fields. Possibly in response to Arne's *Comus*, his major new work was *L'Allegro, il Penseroso ed il Moderato*, Parts I and II of which are a combination, in the dialogue style of *Il Trionfo*, of two poems by Milton. In Part III Jennens (the compiler) himself advocates 'a middle way' between the previous excesses. *L'Allegro* is one of the greatest evocations of the English spirit in countryside and town. The aria and chorus 'Haste thee, nymph' is justly famous; Handel takes Milton's phrase 'laughter holding both his sides' and, by repetition of the syllables in italics, fills the stage with infectious laughter.

Although Handel seemed to be moving towards the English camp, his new works for his second and final season at Lincoln's Inn Fields in 1740/1 were Italian operas: *Imeneo* and *Deidamia*. Both are anti-heroic, in the tradition of *Serse*, although neither contains a comic servant. *Imeneo* was shorter than usual and was advertised as 'an operetta.' It includes an exceedingly funny mock mad scene. Neither work was successful. Although he made no deliberate decision to cease opera production Handel had in fact written his last London opera.

• *Messiah* •

It was rumored in 1741 that Handel would leave England for good. However, a tempting opportunity to escape from the stress of London's theatrical scene presented itself: Handel

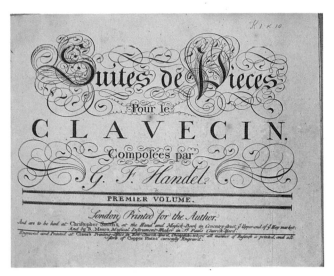

Above: Bust of Handel in 1739 by the French sculptor Roubiliac. The full-figure statue of the composer playing a lyre made for Vauxhall Gardens two years earlier had established Roubiliac's fame in England.

Right: Harpsichord built around 1612 by Hans Ruckers of Antwerp, which Handel owned when he lived in England. It was left in his will, with his house organ, the Roubiliac bust and his scores, to John Christopher Smith the Elder, passed to his son and then to King George III, an ardent Handelian.

was invited by the Duke of Devonshire, Lord Lieutenant of Ireland, to visit Dublin and give a season at the New Music Hall, which was due to open in October 1741. He accepted, and in the summer began two new oratorios: *Messiah*, for charity performances at Dublin and *Samson*, presumably also intended for Dublin, but, in the event, not given there.

Handel composed *Messiah* in twenty-four days from 22 August to 14 September. One reason for his haste in composing *Messiah* must have been his need to begin as soon as

possible the composition of *Samson*. When under pressure Handel frequently borrowed material. In *Messiah* the choruses inevitably posed the greatest problem, and it is surely no coincidence that most of the longest, and indeed some others, were based on pre-existent material. Four incorporate movements from recently composed Italian chamber duets, whose soloistic texture affords an excellent contrast to coronation anthem-type choruses such as 'Hallelujah.' One of the remaining three choruses in each of Parts I and III is a choral continuation of

Above: George Philipp Telemann (1681-1767), a lifelong friend of Handel's and a composer whose music Handel borrowed on a number of occasions (though he repaid this by sending Telemann rare tulip bulbs for his garden).

Top right: Telemann's autograph of the Pastoral from his *Christmas Music* of 1759.

a solo movement. In Part II 'Let all the angels' is based on a keyboard canzona by Johann Kaspar Kerll (1627-93). 'Let us break' also started off as an arrangement of this piece, but its material was changed, keeping only the contrapuntal procedures of the original. Three other choruses are similar short contrapuntal movements which would have posed no difficulty to an improviser of Handel's stature, while 'And with his stripes' looks remarkably like an organ ricercar, although there exists no proof of this.

Borrowing was a common feature of eighteenth-century music. But while Bach's borrowings generally remained close to the originals, Handel, in *Messiah*, *Israel in Egypt* (a particularly famous case of borrowing) and elsewhere, tended to rework his material. He sometimes borrowed only a few measures, for he delighted in discovering possibilities in other composers' material which they had not seen. Even when he borrowed directly the fine last chorus of the miniature oratorio *Jephte* by Giacomo Carissimi, he so transformed it in rhythm and orchestration that it is almost unrecognizable. However, when he saw in the *Postillons* from the *Musique de Table* of his lifelong friend Georg Philipp Telemann an ideal orchestral movement for the gathering together of *Belshazzar*'s Wise Men, he used it without alteration.

Messiah is really a gigantic anthem using a compilation of texts – a common feature, seen also in Handel's recent funeral anthem. There are no characters in Jennens's superb libretto.

It is a meditation, with the 'story' told principally through Old Testament prophecy and the Epistles. Although a casual glance at a late baroque score may suggest that it consists solely of a string of separate numbers, in Handel's operas and oratorios the work is always greater than the sum of its constituent parts. This is never more true than in *Messiah*, and in the sublime sweep of Act III of *Saul*, from its opening at Endor to its close in David's proclamation as king. It is no accident that trumpets and drums first appear properly in *Messiah* in 'Hallelujah.' In 'Glory to God' the angels had played their trumpets (only) 'da lontano' (from afar). Now trumpets and drums proclaim Christ's rule here on earth.

• *Samson* and *Semele* •

Samson capitalized on the popularity of *L'Allegro*, for Newburgh Hamilton (arranger of *Alexander's Feast*) based it on Milton's tragedy *Samson Agonistes*. Its classical style has affinities with Racinian oratorios like *Athalia*, and it features the pagan/Jewish conflict of that work, portraying the hedonistic Philistines and serious-minded Jews in beautifully contrasted solos and choruses. It also owes much to *Saul*, concluding in an anthem of mourning with a 'Dead March' (originally newly composed, but from the first performance probably the march in *Saul*). *Samson*, however, has only three instrumental numbers. Like *Saul* it contains a large number of movements (sixty-four compared with sixty-two), far more than the forty-two of *Athalia* and forty-three of *Deborah*. It has the largest number of choruses in Handel's dramatic oratorios, although some of these twenty-two pieces are repeats, and some short. One renowned solo number is Samson's 'Total eclipse, no sun, no moon,' which movingly uses unaccompanied voice and silence, a feature Handel understood better than any other composer. Micah's 'Return, oh God of hosts' is a splendid example of the possibilities of using the solo voice in close conjunction with chorus.

Opera opened at the King's on 31 October, but Handel left four days later for Dublin. As well as odes and oratorios he included in his highly successful season a concert version of *Imeneo*, the last opera he directed. *Messiah* was first given publicly on 13 April 1742 'for Support of Hospitals and other pious Uses.' Handel intended to return in 1743, but when he left Dublin in August 1742 it was for good.

He returned to an uncertain future. It was rumoured that he might direct the Opera, but the plan failed. After more uncertainty he eventually gave a subscription series of oratorios at which *Samson* was performed with success. Handel gave *Messiah* under the anonymous title *A New Sacred Oratorio*. He was right in expecting criticism. Four days before the London début, one 'Philalethes,' in the *Universal Spectator*, had asked whether, if an oratorio were an '*Act of Religion*, the *Playhouse* is a fit *Temple* to perform it in, or a Company of *Players* fit *Ministers* of *God's Word*.' Nevertheless the season as a whole triumphed over the rival Opera.

That summer George II scored a resounding victory over the French at Dettingen. Handel wrote a *Te Deum* and anthem for the King's return in November 1743. By November the battered Italians had also re-opened with *Rossane*, a new name for Handel's *Alessandro*. Handel struck back with *Semele*, which he presented 'After the Manner of an Oratorio.' William Congreve had published the text of *Semele* as 'An Opera' in 1710 and it had first been set in 1706 by John Eccles (*c*.1668-1735). Handel's choice of it clearly indicated his conversion to the English opera camp. Extra choruses were added to the original in order to fit the work for 'oratorio' performance, but only ten out of fifty-eight numbers are choruses, and some of these are short.

Below: Last page of Handel's *Messiah*, which he completed on 14 September 1741.

Bottom: View of Dublin, where *Messiah* received its first performance on 13 April 1742.

Based on a classical myth, *Semele* was undoubtedly the finest English full-length opera yet produced. It mingles romanticism, humor, infectious gaiety and intense drama: romanticism in Act II's wonderful love scene (which includes such famous numbers as 'Oh, Sleep' and 'Where'er you walk'); humor in the person of Somnus the god of Sleep; gaiety in the Purcellian dance choruses; and drama in the great action choruses in the opening scene and in Jupiter's final scene with Semele, when, to his horror, she forces him to swear to appear to her as the god of Thunder. His disturbed response, the stunning brilliance of her reply ('No, no! I'll take no less'), the tenderness of her death scene and the effect of the wonderful chorus which follows, with its powerful use of silence and unaccompanied singing, long remain in the memory. That this piece, with its detailed stage directions (including transformation scenes), should not have been in some way staged seems incredible, but that is what is implied by 'After the Manner of an Oratorio.'

Joseph and his Brethren, the new oratorio, had, like *Semele*, only ten choruses. It also

marked Handel's return for good to a total of under fifty numbers, while the chorus do not enter until Scene III of Act I. English opera and dramatic oratorio were drawing closer together.

· The late 1740s ·

In November 1744 Handel hired the King's Theatre for the first complete English oratorio season, organized by subscription. (The Opera moved to the New Theatre.) Handel's new compositions were a classical 'Musical Drama,' *Hercules*, and a dramatic oratorio, *Belshazzar*.

Hercules is the tragedy of the hero's wife Dejanira as much as his own. Believing, falsely, that Hercules is unfaithful to her, she is desperately driven by her mounting jealousy to try

A perspective View of the CITY of DUBLIN, from Phœnix Park.

Left: Procession of the Order of the Bath outside Westminster Abbey on 26 June 1749, painted by Canaletto. Three days before his death (ten years after these festivities) Handel added a codicil to his will asking to be buried in Westminster Abbey in a private manner and requesting that a monument should be erected for him there.

Below: Fireworks display on the Thames at Whitehall on 15 May 1749 in the presence of the King. It was part of the same celebration – of the Peace of Aix-la-Chapelle – for which Handel wrote his *Music for the Royal Fireworks*, though that was performed at an earlier, and near-disastrous, display in Green Park on 26 April. The music was repeated with other celebratory works at a great benefit concert in the chapel of the Foundling Hospital on 27 May in the presence of the Prince and Princess of Wales.

and force his love with the aid of the magic robe given her by his enemy. It is poisoned, and Hercules dies in agony. Overcome by remorse, Dejanira believes herself to be pursued by the Furies – one of the finest mad scenes in opera, at least the equal of that in *Orlando*. There is scarcely a weak number in this powerful tragedy, which has claims to be the greatest of all English operas.

The tragedy of Belshazzar in the work of that name is as much Babylon's as his, a universalizing of the subject typical of oratorio. Handel's approach to setting the ghostly Writing on the Wall is subtle. He writes a recitative, but for violins (it is writing, not speech) and unaccompanied (it is disembodied), slow and staccato (deliberate and emphatic), high, and unusual in its chromatic opening (inhuman, ghostly), and its ending includes hidden in it (for only Daniel can unravel the message) more usual recitative clichés which exactly fit the words MENE MENE TEKEL UPHARSIN. That Handel's imagination was stimulated by Jennens's libretto is demonstrated in a series of letters to the latter, and it was at Jennens's suggestion that Handel concluded with movements from the Chandos Anthems.

The enthusiasm bestowed on the composition of these two works, however, was to prove fruitless: first *Hercules*, then *Belshazzar* failed. A nervous breakdown ensued, Handel's second relapse since 1737.

In July 1745 Charles Edward Stuart landed in Scotland, and the Jacobites marched on London. By December they had reached Derby, but then retreated. There was no theater in London while the threat existed, but to celebrate the 'victory' the King's reopened in January 1746 with a performance of *La Caduta de' giganti* by Christoph Willibald Gluck, who had just arrived in the capital. The work belonged to the ultra-patriotic traditions of Arne's *Alfred* (containing the well-known 'Rule, Britannia'), performed at Drury Lane in 1745.

Handel, presumably because of his illness, aimed to make up only the eight remaining concerts of the previous year's disastrous subscription series. But three performances alone were given – at Covent Garden – of the *Occasional Oratorio*, an extended anthem celebrating the Jacobites' defeat.

Henceforward Handel limited his seasons to after Christmas, perhaps because his health would not permit him to undertake a full season. The 1747 offering was *Judas Maccabaeus*, an allegory of Cumberland's final rout of the Scots at Culloden in April 1746. Its simple, direct style was an immediate success, and its appeal rightly continues. Handel had written better music, and he knew it, but he and his librettist, the Revd Thomas Morell, had accurately judged the public mood. *Judas* proved a money-spinner.

Morell provided the two new libretti for 1748, *Alexander Balus* and *Joshua. Alexander Balus* is a sequel to *Judas*, but is more obviously operatic, with only eight choruses to *Judas*'s fifteen. Cleopatra's colorful aria, 'Hark, he strikes the golden lyre,' for flutes, bassoons, harp and mandolin, with strings (including divided cellos, sometimes pizzicato) and continuo, reminds one of 'V'adoro pupille' in *Giulio Cesare*. Did the name Cleopatra remind Handel of that piece?

Joshua is an unduly neglected work. A warlike piece, like *Judas*, it contains two unforgettable scenes: the fall of the walls of Jericho and the halting of sun and moon. Here also, as in *Judas*, is the famous march 'See, the conqu'ring hero comes,' which the Victorians used *ad nauseam* to open new public works. It occurs in almost exactly the same position in Act III as the purely orchestral 'Dead Marches' in *Saul* and *Samson*.

• Last Oratorios •

The war ended in October 1748 and celebrations heightened the already patriotic atmosphere. *Solomon* (1749) reflected this, portraying a country of peace and plenty, ruled by a just, wise and powerful monarch. Uniquely, *Solomon* is a series of separate tableaux.

It is exceedingly varied, contrasting the coronation style of the opening with the serene tenderness of Act I's choral finale, which evokes the nightingale and the evening breeze – the world of *L'Allegro*. Act III echoes *Alexander's*

Feast in its short choruses depicting the changing moods of a pageant. The many double choruses recall *Israel*, whilst the Judgment Scene is operatic.

Susanna, 1749's other oratorio, although a biblical story, resembles *Semele* rather than *Solomon*. Like *Alexander Balus* it has only eight choruses, the lowest proportion in the oratorios, while it has a higher proportion of *da capo* arias than any English work since the Cannons masques. In Handel's oratorios the number of *da capo* arias is linked in inverse proportion to the number of choruses, for the more choruses there are the shorter must the

Below: Roubiliac's model for the monument to Handel in Westminster Abbey.

Above: Admission ticket to a performance of Handel's *Hercules*, a 'musical drama' first performed at the King's Theatre in 1745 and revived more than once, including performances at Covent Garden in February 1752 (when this ticket was used), at the time of Handel's oncoming blindness.

Above right: Caricature (1754) variously entitled 'The Charming Brute' or the 'Harmonious Boar,' ridiculing Handel's gluttony and musical extravagance. It was drawn by Joseph Goupy, who had been a close friend and associate of the composer in the days of the Royal Academy of Music, when he had designed the sets for several of his operas.

arias become. *Da capo* arias also imply greater singing technique, for they generally require decoration. The impact of the introduction of choruses was to simplify the plots as compared with contemporary opera. However, *Susanna* is nearer to contemporary opera than any other Handel oratorio. Two elders, espying Susanna bathing, each desire her. When she spurns them they accuse her of adultery, an offence punishable by death. But the prophet Daniel proves her innocence, and her accusers are themselves executed. The quite risqué plot of this delightful pastoral opera stands at the opposite pole to *Messiah* and later puzzled the Victorians, with their narrow vision of Handel's art.

Handel revived *Messiah* in 1749, an Eastertide performance which was to continue annually thereafter. It now ended his season and, from 1750, was repeated for charity in the chapel of the Foundling Hospital, of which Handel was a great benefactor. These charity performances established *Messiah*'s popularity, gradually changing Handel's image from that of a secular to a sacred composer. The first Foundlings' charity concert was in May 1749. It included excerpts from *Solomon*, the *Peace Anthem* and the *Foundling Hospital Anthem*. One month before, Green Park had heard his *Music for the Royal Fireworks* in celebration of the Peace. The hundred players, in a downpour of rain, saw one of the pavilions set on fire and the designer arrested for drawing his sword on the event's organizer.

Early 1750 saw Handel writing incidental music for the first time since he had provided pieces for Ben Jonson's *The Alchemist* (Drury Lane, 1732). The play was Tobias Smollett's *Alceste*, which for some reason was never performed. Its music was used in a short conversation piece, *The Choice of Hercules*, given with Handel's revival of *Alexander's Feast* in 1751.

Theodora, 1751's new oratorio, is Handel's only dramatic oratorio with a non-Jewish background. It is based on a story of a Christian saint. She refuses to make pagan offerings on Diocletian's birthday and is arrested and condemned to be a prostitute. Her beloved Didimus, a Roman soldier and a Christian convert, breaks with his oath of loyalty and rescues her, with the tacit approval of another soldier, his friend Septimius. Didimus is arrested and sentenced to death. Theodora offers her life for his, but both are led to execution. Handel warmed to this plot's study of conflicting loyalties. Some of his finest music concerns freedom, and the spectacle of two young people physically crushed by, but morally triumphant over, the might of the Roman Empire drew from him a magnificent score. Earth tremors had already necessitated a shortened season; now *Theodora*, his favorite oratorio, was a failure. He bitterly commented: 'The Jews will not come to it because it is a Christian story, and the Ladies will not because it [is] a virtuous one.'

• *Jephtha* •

On 21 January 1751 Handel began *Jephtha*. On 13 February, at the end of the first section of the last chorus of Act II ('How dark, O Lord, are thy decrees!'), he wrote: 'unable to continue owing to the weakening of the sight of my left eye.' On 23 February he noted: 'feeling rather better, began again,' but it took him four days to conclude this mighty chorus. He resumed composition again only on 18 June, and it took until 30 August, over two months, to complete the work. It was not given until 1752, by which time he had lost the sight of one eye and was losing that of the other. An operation was unsuccessful. By 27 January 1753 he was reported to have 'quite lost his sight.'

Jephtha, Handel's last work, is again concerned with conflicting loyalties. Jephtha takes an oath that, should he be successful in battle, he will sacrifice the first living creature he meets on his return home. He is successful. His daughter meets him. Torn between his love for her and honoring his oath, the agonized Jephtha chooses the latter. Only the intervention of an angel saves his daughter's life, provided she is dedicated to God in eternal virginity.

Although *Jephtha*'s general design is similar to *Theodora*'s (just over twice as many solos or ensembles as choruses, and near-equal division of arias between *da capo* and non-*da capo*), its more static plot gives greater scope for dramatic soliloquies. There are seven accompanied recitatives, more than usual in Handel's operas, more than in any dramatic oratorio since *Belshazzar*, but still far short of *Semele*'s staggering thirteen. There are two magnificent ensembles: the Act II quartet in which Jephtha's wife and friends vainly attempt to persuade him to break his oath, and the quintet in Act III in which the daughter and her beloved resign one another to Heaven, while their elders look on. Morell's text has 'freely ... resign,' but Handel, knowing what it is like to be separated from one's loved ones, belied the glib text, just as he had in *Theodora*'s finale.

Blindness almost totally halted Handel's composing career, but did not stop him performing organ concertos from memory, or directing, with the aid of J. C. Smith Junior, his oratorio seasons. Instead of new works he offered a greater number of pieces each season, and seems to have set out to perform all his odes, oratorios and 'musical dramas.' On his death only the *Ode for St Cecilia's Day* and *Semele* had not been revived. The core of his repertoire in these years was *Judas*, *Messiah* and *Samson*. The tenor John Beard's performance of that blind hero's 'Total eclipse' moved composer and audience alike. But, as throughout Handel's life, the fickle London public often deserted him; in 1755 and 1756 only *Messiah* truly succeeded.

An apparent new work of the period is *The Triumph of Time and Truth* (1757), but this is essentially an English version of *Il Trionfo del Tempo* of 1737, with no new music. Handel did however compose some new pieces, largely arias for insertion into his oratorios and a new chorus for *Esther*. J. C. Smith Senior acted as his amanuensis.

Handel, though in failing health, was active almost to the end. After revivals of *Samson* and *Judas* he gave two performances of *Messiah* on 4 and 6 April 1759. Already ill at the last performance, he took to his bed. He died, aged seventy-four, on 14 April 1759, the day after the anniversary of both his first stroke and *Messiah*'s première. He left nearly £20,000, a huge fortune at that time, unheard of for a musician.

His life had been a continual struggle in a blaze of publicity. Rarely had he compromised his art, but, by responding to the changing taste of his public, he had created an immense variety of different forms in opera, ode, oratorio and English 'musical drama.' Although forced, by financial and other difficulties, to give up Italian opera for the yet unestablished oratorio, he still maintained interest in revivals of his operas until only five years before his death. As much through his dynamic personality as by his music (some of the best of which was unsuccessful) he dominated the English musical scene for fifty years during his lifetime, and for well over a hundred years after his death. He was also a major influence on later composers, notably Haydn, Mozart, Mendelssohn and, in particular, Beethoven, who is reported to have exclaimed of Handel's music, 'There is the Truth.'

Left: Print depicting the performance of an oratorio in a church; frontispiece of a collection issued by John Walsh, Handel's publisher in London since *Rinaldo* in 1711.

Far left: John Christopher Smith the Younger (1712-95), organist from 1754 at the Foundling Hospital, who, after Handel had become blind, helped him direct performances of his oratorios and took down his last compositions from the composer's dictation.

Left: The Revd Thomas Morell (1703-84), Handel's librettist for several of his late oratorios and his favorite poet in these years.

THE CLASSICAL STYLE

DAVID WYN JONES

Johann Sebastian Bach died in 1750, George Frideric Handel in 1759. In the same year a comparatively unknown composer named Franz Joseph Haydn entered the service of Count Morzin, a minor aristocrat in Bohemia. The twenty-seven-year-old Haydn was already a skilled composer, with trios, quartets, concertos, harpsichord works, sacred choral works and German operas to his credit. During that same year, the three-year-old Wolgang Amadeus Mozart was amusing himself and astonishing his family by continually striking the same consonant interval on the harpsichord and showing great pleasure in its sound. Of course, Handel would have known nothing of Haydn and Mozart, but, more surprising to modern minds, Haydn and the Mozarts at that date were equally ignorant of the music of Handel and Bach.

There was a gulf in musical style to match this mutual ignorance. A traveler lucky enough to be in England and Austria in the same year would have been amazed at the difference in style between, say, Handel's last oratorio, *The Triumph of Time and Truth*, and Haydn's First Symphony (D major); the first representative of what is often termed the 'high Baroque,' the second of the early classical style. Although the differences are strikingly apparent to us, the new classical style was not a sudden conscious revolt against the grandeur of the Baroque initiated by one composer in the mid-century. Rather, it had been a continually evolving process, whose origins can be traced back to the first decades of the century and which did not gain maturity and universal acceptance until the 1770s. In reality, therefore, there was a period of overlap between the achievements of Bach and Handel and the beginning of the new style that was to lead to the masterpieces of Haydn, Mozart, Beethoven and Schubert.

The differences in kind between the two eras cover every aspect of music; its form, its style, the way it reached the public, as well as the status of the composer himself. New concepts governed the grammar and syntax of music, new genres came into being, commercial practices increasingly determined a composer's reputation (particularly in places beyond his immediate neighbourhood) and, by the end of the century, the public's view of the composer had changed substantially.

Even before the listener hears a single note of music from the classical period, the number of entirely new titles given to works is striking. In orchestral music the *concerto grosso* of the Baroque is displaced by the symphony, in chamber music the trio-sonata by the string quartet, and in keyboard music the suite by the sonata. Other genres to be created included the string trio, string quintet, piano trio, piano quartet, piano quintet and *symphonie concertante*. The only instrumental genre to survive the change in style from baroque to classical was the concerto for soloist and orchestra which in Mozart's hands became one of the subtlest formal creations in the entire history of music.

Italian *opera seria* came to be regarded as stultified in its attitudes and unreal, occasionally absurd, in its impact. During the century it was slowly but surely being replaced by *opera buffa*. Dramatic realism in serious opera was given much-needed respectability by Gluck in a series of 'reform' operas produced in Paris. Both these trends reached their apogee in the operas of Mozart. While opera in the Italian language continued to be regarded as the most fashionable, opera in other languages with different conventions began to establish itself. In German-speaking countries the *Singspiel* with its alternation of spoken dialogue and music grew in stature and popularity. In France a similar process was apparent; *opéra comique* is the French equivalent of German *Singspiel*.

Oratorio, cantata, Mass and other related genres retained their status but changed their accent so as not to seem old-fashioned in the company of the new symphony and opera. For some severe-minded observers, Haydn, Mozart and others were too accommodating, and their church music was criticized for being inappropriately elaborate or joyful. Solo song (*Lied*) attracted the attention of many composers, and there are several beautiful individual examples by Haydn, Mozart and C. P. E. Bach, but the genre was not to acquire pre-eminence until the arrival of Schubert.

None of these profound changes in genres would have occurred without changes in the style itself, the grammar and syntax of music, and indeed it was the continuous interreaction of genre and style — a new stylistic feature suggesting new formal procedures and the expansion of the genre, which in turn produced further stylistic innovations — that produced the musical transformations in the middle of the eighteenth century.

A comparison of the openings of a Bach 'Brandenburg' concerto and a Mozart symphony would reveal fundamentally diverging attitudes to the business of creating a coherent musical language. The Mozart symphony begins with a statement of a thematic idea that has an innate sense of completeness – a proposition, hence the frequent use of the term 'subject.' It may be overtly melodious, even tuneful in a folk music manner. A Bach theme, however, is likely to be rhythmic with much immediate repetition of a compact pattern in a self-perpetuating manner and with a less obvious sense of a con-

tained proposition. In the classical period there is a clear distinction between theme and accompaniment – that is, between the foreground and the background of the music; typically, the melody is on top and the accompaniment underneath, but a similar relationship can be set up at any level of the texture. In order to make this distinction as clear as possible, classical composers often employed certain stock accompaniment patterns. The Alberti bass, so named after the Italian composer Domenico Alberti who made frequent use of it, consists of the oscillation of the constituent notes of a chord; though at its most idiomatic when played by the left hand on a keyboard, it found its way into string and wind writing too. *Trommelbass* (drum-bass) is more typically orchestral and consists, as the term implies, of a repetition of a single note in a pulsating rhythm. These accompaniment patterns give an impetus to classical music which compensates for the absence of the energetic driving forward of a baroque work. In a second-rate composer the impetus can disguise the paucity of thematic and harmonic invention, but in Haydn, Mozart and Beethoven it is only one of several factors that give direction and atmosphere to a work. Similarly, every aspect of the accompaniment in the hands of a resourceful composer, though clearly subordinate, plays an important part in pointing up the foreground of the music.

Increased emphasis on a texture of theme and accompaniment during the century led naturally to the virtual exclusion of a texture consisting of several equally important voices: the polyphony of the high Baroque gave way to the homophony of the classical period. Themes are recognizable as such because of their frequent presentation as the musical equivalents of phrases and sentences, which in turn are ordered in a logical flow to form paragraphs and chapters.

Left: Title-page of one of the sets of string quartets written by Luigi Boccherini, who was court composer in Madrid to the heir to the Spanish throne. Boccherini was, with Haydn, one of the creators of the classical string quartet, writing some hundred works in the form – and as many string quintets, for two violins, viola and two cellos.

Left: String quartet made up of players at the court of the ardent musical patron Prince Krafft Ernst Oettingen-Wallerstein in 1791: Joseph Reicha, Ignaz von Beecke, Franz Anton Rosetti and Anton Janitsch. Haydn had successfully canvassed the Prince's subscription in 1781 for his op.33 quartets.

Right: Two *symphonies concertantes*, op.18, by Carl Stamitz, issued in Paris around 1776. The *symphonie concertante*, though its movements were constructed in sonata form, harked back to the baroque *concerto grosso* with a group of soloists and a small ensemble. It was a form made popular in Paris, where Stamitz had settled in 1770.

Music from the classical period also has more explicit instructions for the performer. Whereas in earlier times changes of dynamic tended to occur from one section to the next and were often left to the performer to judge, the later style encouraged the use of contrasting dynamics, the alternation of *forte* and *piano*, the differentiation (always clear in Haydn and Beethoven) between degrees of loudness and softness (*forte, fortissimo, piano, pianissimo*) and the invention of the 'average' dynamic, the *mezzo forte. Crescendo* and *diminuendo*, exaggerated accentuation of a note (*sforzando*) and indication of the type of tone quality required,

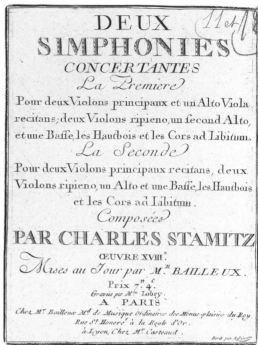

DEUX SIMPHONIES CONCERTANTES

La Premiere

Pour deux Violons principaux et un Alto Viola recitans, deux Violons ripieno, un second Alto, et une Basse, les Hautbois et les Cors ad Libitum.

La Seconde

Pour deux Violons principaux recitans, deux Violons ripieno, un Alto et une Basse, les Hautbois et les Cors ad Libitum.

Composées

PAR CHARLES STAMITZ

ŒUVRE XVIII.

Mises au Jour par M.R BAILLEUX.

Prix 7.#4.

Gravées par M.me Lobry.

A PARIS

Chez M.r Bailleux M.d de Musique Ordinaire des Menus-plaisirs du Roy Rue St Honoré à la Regle d'Or. à Lyon, Chez M.r Castcaud.

Above: Duet on a fortepiano; illustration from the title-page of an album of sonatas for four hands published in 1781. The keyboard sonata was another of the most important new classical forms, and several composers, including Mozart, wrote duo as well as solo sonatas.

such as *sotto voce* (whispered), all play a vital part in shading the music. It would be naïve to assume that all these aspects of performance were unknown before the middle of the eighteenth century, but the very act of notation in an increasingly precise way demonstrated that such matters were now an integral part of the composer's thought process. Likewise, instrumental sonority came to be more closely attuned to the changing moods of the music from one moment to the next; themes are readily associated with particular instruments to the extent that they are unimaginable on other instruments, an association that Bach, for instance, would have found alien, even indulgent.

All these differences are apparent within a few minutes of listening to a Bach 'Brandenburg' concerto and a Mozart symphony. Less noticeable, but no less crucial to the working of the new style, is the revised attitude to harmonic rhythm. Harmonic rhythm is simply the frequency of the change of chord; in a normal hymn-tune it is one chord per beat. In the baroque period harmonic rhythm is usually very regular and emphasizes the pulse of the music. In classical music the rate of change of harmony

is generally slower and – more crucial to the impact of a movement – more varied, playing a determining role in the ebb and flow of the music. Many of the most sensationally climactic moments in Haydn, Mozart, Beethoven and later composers as diverse as Wagner and Tchaikovsky are the result of confident manipulation of harmonic rhythm.

Harmonic practice in the baroque period was inextricably bound up with thorough bass (*basso continuo*). This, 'the most perfect foundation of music' as Bach called it, had started as a short-hand means of indicating harmonies above a written-out bass line, but by the high Baroque it had become a principle of composition; everything was built upon and related to the thorough bass, and the instruments that played that line (the continuo) were a standard feature of all music involving more than one performer. With the increased emphasis in the new style on melody, the thorough bass as a principle of composition weakened and then disappeared.

For all these stylistic changes, which took some fifty years from 1720 onwards to accomplish, greater simplicity was the dominant precept. Simplicity of melody, harmony and structure at first resulted in music that, to the modern ear, sounds simplistic; an easy-going, elegant, but emotionally superficial idiom that was described as 'galant.' Later composers appreciated that the new style was capable of a more profound emotional content. The disposition of this emotional content, however, was very different from that operating in the Baroque.

Most music in the earlier period, particularly that from northern Europe, was composed, performed and listened to according to the well-understood doctrine of *Affekt*; one movement (vocal or instrumental) would convey a consistent mood throughout, such as joy, sorrow, love, fortitude, and so on. Consistency of expression in this manner is rare in classical

211

Right: The Village Bride (1761) by J. B. Greuze. The complex interplay of feelings represented in the painting — an attempt to follow the esthetic of sentiment advocated by Diderot — stands comparison with the construction of a novel (the new literary form of the period) or the contrast of mood and texture in classical music.

Above: Archduchess Maria Antonia (1755-93) as a young girl. She was the daughter of Empress Maria Theresa and sister of the future enlightened Emperor Joseph II, a pupil of Gluck and extremely musical, like many of her family. Later, as Marie Antoinette, Dauphine of France, she used her influence to have Gluck's reforming operas staged at the Paris Opéra.

Above: Jean-Jacques Rousseau (1712-78) by Houdon. Rousseau was a talented composer, and both his views on music and his political philosophy were guided by an appeal to reason and to nature.

music. There is more variety within movements, one mood will be juxtaposed with another, and the music will seek to balance or reconcile the differing emotions. Whereas in Handel, Rameau, Vivaldi and Bach the emotion accumulates as the movement progresses, there is in Haydn, Mozart and others a stronger sense of narrative and drama; contrasting moods are created, tension alternates with relaxation and the pacing of climaxes and their dénouement assumes cardinal importance.

• The orchestra •

Discussion of the evolution of the classical style cannot be divorced from the development of instruments and the orchestra, the one nourishing the other. The greatest single musical invention of the eighteenth century – many would say of the entire history of music – was that of the piano. In the first decade of the century a harpsichord-maker in Florence named Bartolomeo Cristofori produced the result of several years of experiment, a *gravicembalo col piano e forte* (large harpsichord with soft and loud). The harpsichord had always had the expressive limitation that, however aggressively or gently the key was depressed, the intensity of the sound remained the same and, as on the contemporary organ, volume and tone color could only be varied by changing stops. On the clavichord it was possible to grade the volume, but the instrument lacked the penetration of the harpsichord and was confined to domestic use. The new pianoforte combined the virtues of the two instruments, the full sound of the harpsichord with the expressive quality of the clavichord. J. S. Bach tried out a piano during his visit to the court of Frederick the Great in 1747, but in general the instrument did not become popular until the 1760s and even then co-existed with its predecessors for several decades. The new piano also replaced the organ and, in the same way that Buxtehude, Bach and Handel had established reputations as virtuoso organists, many composers from the late eighteenth century onwards were renowned as pianists. Mozart and the young Beethoven are the obvious early examples, but in their day Clementi, J. L. Dussek and Hummel were equally renowned.

The piano was not the only new instrument to come to the fore with the change in style. The clarinet was known and used by several baroque composers, but it too did not establish itself until the second half of the eighteenth century. Its invention is attributed to Johann and Jacob Denner (father and son) who were woodwind-makers at Nuremberg, and the first clarinet appeared in the same decade as Cristofori's piano. At first many players specialized in one of the two distinct registers of the clarinet, the bright soprano register from which the instrument got its name (*clarinette* means 'little

trumpet') or the rich, low register, the *chalumeau*; but as the instrument gained wider acceptance players were expected to be skilled throughout the entire compass. At first, too, the clarinet was seen as an alternative to the flute and/or oboe, but composers gradually realized that its unique properties complemented those of these instruments rather than duplicated them. The range of the clarinet from low tenor to highest soprano (wider than that of the flute and oboe), its creamy, liquid sound and the ease with which it responded to *crescendo* and *diminuendo* markings soon stimulated the imagination of composers.

By and large, however, classical composers had the same instruments at their disposal as composers of the late baroque: flutes, oboes, bassoons, horns, trumpets, trombones, timpani and strings. For these instruments standards of manufacture and playing improved steadily during the century, with one curious exception. Trumpet-players in the Baroque had acquired a high degree of expertise and social prestige through their playing of the florid high-sounding parts composers required of them in works such as Vivaldi's *Gloria*, Handel's *Music for the Royal Fireworks* and Bach's Second 'Brandenburg' Concerto. During the century this 'clarino' technique died, so that trumpet parts in Mozart, Haydn and Beethoven confine themselves to the fewer notes available in the middle and lower registers of the contemporary instrument. In themselves, the parts may be less interesting than in the Baroque, but the entry of trumpets, usually in association with timpani, can still be highly evocative in classical music.

A transformation occurred in the playing technique of the horn too, but with more spectacular results. Florid writing in the high register gave way to the cultivation of the lower and middle registers but in an equally florid manner. This was made possible by the growing use from the 1750s onwards of hand-stopping, the alteration of the pitch of the notes by careful placing of the right hand in the bell of the instrument. Orchestral writing restricted itself in the main to the natural notes of the harmonic series, but works with solo horn, such as the well-known Mozart concertos, made extensive use of hand-stopped notes. Virtuoso horn players, highly skilled in this technique, toured Europe dazzling audiences with their expertise.

It was during the classical period that the modern orchestra was founded, much later acquiring in English-speaking countries the appropriate appellation 'symphony orchestra'. Theoretically, the full orchestra can be said to consist of two each of flutes, oboes, clarinets, bassoons, horns and trumpets; three trombones; timpani: and strings divided into first and second violins, violas, cellos and double-basses. In practice, however, Haydn and Mozart employed this full orchestra very rarely, almost exclusively in opera and large-scale choral works and never in symphonies, where trombones were not used until Beethoven's time. Up to the 1780s it is therefore better to think of the standard classical orchestra as consisting of two oboes,

Left: Denis Diderot by Fragonard. Diderot (1713-84) was the most influential of the *philosophes* – whose system was built on the Enlightenment concept of natural reason. He was a founder of the *Encyclopédie*, a systematic compendium of knowledge and ideas in which J J Rousseau wrote the article on 'Music' and he himself wrote the article on 'Art.' Diderot joined Rousseau in attacking the artificial conventions of French opera, advocating the simplicity, melodic independence and natural development that are basic features of the classical style.

two horns, two bassoons and strings, with other instruments as extras.

Although the thorough bass had become redundant as a principle of composition, the keyboard continuo (harpsichord, then piano) was still an important member of the classical orchestra. The player, seated in a central position facing his colleagues, was responsible for directing the performance even if, apart from recitatives, he did not actually play very much. The progressive trend during the period was for the leader of the first violins to assume more and more responsibility by gesturing with his body and with the bow of his violin. From here it was one short step to the introduction of the conductor with a baton in the nineteenth century.

For performances of large-scale works with choral forces, where the performers might be widely separated, an additional director was employed, another rudimentary conductor who marked time with a rolled piece of paper. In February 1788 Mozart did exactly this in a performance of C. P. E. Bach's oratorio *Die Auferstehung und Himmelfahrt Jesu*, and thirty-six years later the deaf Beethoven threatened to ruin the first partial performance of his *Missa Solemnis* by undertaking this unnecessary duty.

The numerical size of orchestras in courts, churches, concert halls and theatres varied as much as their internal composition, and for any traveling musician orchestral resources were largely unpredictable. Mozart, for instance, in his home town of Salzburg could muster an orchestra of about forty players, but no clarinets; for the first performance of his 'Paris' Symphony in that city in 1778 the orchestra numbered some fifty-nine players. In Vienna in 1781 for a performance of another symphony Mozart reports that 'there were forty violins, the wind instruments were all doubled, there were ten violas, ten double-basses, eight violoncellos and six

bassoons' – a total of close on ninety; but in Prague six years later, for the first performance of *Don Giovanni*, Mozart seems to have had an orchestra of only twenty-six players at his disposal, containing a meager six violins.

The style, *per se*, of classical music, together with the revised instrumental techniques, ensured that the orchestra of Haydn and Mozart sounded very different from that of Bach and Handel. But the craft of orchestration also changed, in a manner which complemented the stylistic changes. In the high Baroque individual lines of a composition are often literally doubled by all available instruments. This duplicating procedure is to be found in the classical period too, but it is one type of orchestration among many. There is from measure to measure greater variety in weight and sonority, helping to articulate the foreground and background of the music. Generally, wind instruments have a background role, their presence being more effective because of surrounding rests, but on occasion they will assume leading roles. One of the many marvels of Haydn's 'Representation of Chaos' from *The Creation* is the constantly shifting perspective produced by the large classical orchestra, here as varied in shade and depth as Chaos itself.

• Composer and public •

Most composers in the second half of the eighteenth century continued to be employed by a patron, whether a royal court, a local aristocrat, a church, cathedral or monastery. Unsympathetic commentators often imply a moral judgment when they state that the composer was only one rung up the social ladder from the servant, but there is no doubt that, by and large, the system worked to the mutual satisfaction of

Below: P. A. Caron de Beaumarchais (1732-99), author of *Le Barbier de Seville* (1775), set by Paisiello in 1782 and later by Rossini, and of *Le Mariage de Figaro* (first publicly performed in 1784), on which Mozart's opera was based. Once music teacher to the daughter of Louis xv, he later became an outspoken critic of the corruption of the *ancien régime*, and *Figaro* was banned by the King for several years because of its attacks on aristocratic privilege.

Left: The Foire Saint-Germain, revived in 1752 for playing French comic opera. For a decade the Théâtre de la Foire and the company of Italian Comedians were rivals, before they amalgamated, providing a firm foundation for the French tradition of *opéra comique*.

Right: Plate from the *Encyclopédie*, edited by Diderot and d'Alembert and published between 1751 and 1780, showing instrument-makers at work.

Right: Title-page of a posthumous collection of vocal pieces by J. J. Rousseau, published in 1781 under the title *The Consolations of the Miseries of my Life*. The illustration reflects this title, while the inscription beneath the bust of the composer is from the sixteenth-century philosopher Montaigne: 'Nature is a gentle guide. Everywhere I seek her path: we have confused it with artificial tracks.'

Although music printing had followed soon after the invention of printing itself, it was not until the late seventeenth or early eighteenth centuries that it became a powerful force in the dissemination of music, and even then its impact was variable: Corelli and Vivaldi achieved a degree of international fame through their published music, but very few of J. S. Bach's compositions were available in print. With the greater use of engraving rather than movable type in the middle years of the eighteenth century, music publishing took a huge leap forward. Paris was the center of this development; a review of its musical activities that appeared in *L'Almanach musical* in 1783 stated that forty-four music publishers were to be found in the city. Some of these firms were small, with an insignificant output, but many had an international outlook, printing music by composers not resident in Paris and distributing it widely. The most important Parisian publishers were Huberty, who moved to Vienna in 1777, de la Chevardière, Sieber, le Menu et Boyer, and Venier.

Without the stringent copyright laws of the twentieth century, business ethics varied considerably. Composers who lived in Paris could usually expect their work to be printed honestly and to receive a reasonable fee. The work of other composers was frequently published without their knowledge; was altered (minuet movements were often omitted and instrumentation of symphonies reduced); and the names of popular composers sometimes substituted for unknown ones to improve sales. Most of the actual engraving was done by women.

Europe's other cities had fewer publishers, but among the most important were Haffner in Nuremberg, Bremner and Longman & Broderip in London, Hummel in Amsterdam and Berlin, and Breitkopf in Leipzig. Although music by many Austrian composers was printed in Paris and elsewhere, and many of these prints were available in Viennese bookshops, music printing established itself comparatively late in that

composer and master. Composers were paid in cash and in kind, the latter consisting of board and lodging and annual allowances of wine, firewood, candles, rye, wheat and other foodstuffs. Composers and their fellow-musicians could be, and often were, summarily dismissed and some did die in poverty, but there were numerous instances of personal kindnesses too. The cumulative effect of successive wars and increased taxation meant that many courts were forced to reduce or disband their musical retinue in the second half of the eighteenth century, but to compensate for this the increasing role of the public opera house and concert hall, and the ever more pervasive presence of music publication, offered new opportunities to the composer.

country, the first firm being Artaria, regular publishers of Mozart's and Haydn's music. Within Austria and Italy music was distributed as handwritten copies, a system affected by the same ethical vagaries as publishing. It was with considerable justice that Mozart advised his father to beware of pirated manuscript copies, which seem to have been as prevalent in the eighteenth century as the illegal taping of records today.

In the Austria and Italy that Mozart knew, opera houses and churches provided the venues for regular public performances, in the sense that concerts of music elsewhere were either organized on an *ad hoc* basis with no consistent promotional identity or were played to an exclusive audience. In the remainder of Europe there was a recognizable pattern of establishing concert series under a general title; regular concerts of music were played by a reasonably stable body of musicians where the public was a large and paying one. Paris was once again at the forefront of these developments.

The *Concert Spirituel* was founded in 1725 and dominated Paris concert life until 1790. Concerts were held throughout the year at the Palais des Tuileries, with a concentration of activity at Easter time. At first 'spirituel' music featured prominently in the programs but, by the 1770s, secular music, especially symphonies and *symphonies concertantes*, came to dominate.

Other cities in Europe also established regular concert life. In Leipzig the *Grosses Conzert* had been formed in 1743 to become in 1781 the concert series of the Leipzig Gewandhaus Orchestra, a series and an orchestra that over two centuries later still exist, making them the oldest in Europe. In London in 1765 Johann Christian Bach, together with another immigrant composer, Carl Friedrich Abel, established a regular subscription concert series, known as the Bach-Abel concerts, which dominated musical life in London for over fifteen years and inspired the organization of similar enterprises.

The Bach-Abel, the Gewandhaus, the *Concert Spirituel* and all other concerts had a similar approach to program content. An evening's entertainment consisted of contemporary music with, typically, a first performance of a new work; the playing of older music was an aspect of concert life that was not to become prominent until the following century. A typical program would contain between five and ten items and include orchestral, chamber, solo and vocal music. A third trend may be discerned in the tendency for concerts to become longer towards the turn of the century. When one couples that with the fact that most were given after only one rehearsal one wonders what the standard of performance was like. This state of affairs certainly vexed Mozart when his 'Paris' Symphony was given its first performance at the *Concert Spirituel* on 18 June 1778; after a disastrous rehearsal he went to the concert 'determined that if my symphony went as badly as it did at the rehearsal, I would certainly make my way into the orchestra, snatch the fiddle out of the hands of Lahoussaye, the first violin, and myself conduct.'

The printing of music and the increase in concert life ensured that the composer's public was becoming a widespread and knowledgeable one. With this knowledge came the desire for more information and understanding. Until the middle of the eighteenth century written commentary on music had been in the hands of theorists who often took several years to produce their *magnum opus* and couched it in abstract, philosophical terms, but during the eighteenth century writing on music became copious, vigorous, informative and occasionally gossipy. The most controversial writing of the period occurred in Paris in the 1750s when some forty writers waged a paper war on the relative merits of French and Italian music — the celebrated *Querelle des Bouffons*.

Accounts of concerts and operas in the daily press at first restricted themselves to a general description of how successful they had been in social terms; gradually correspondents became more critical of the performance itself. Biographical accounts of composers and performers and reviews of music could be found in the pages

Above: C. F. Abel (1723-87), painted in 1777 by his friend Thomas Gainsborough. A virtuoso and composer for the viola da gamba, Abel had possibly been a pupil of J. S. Bach in Leipzig and was closely associated with Bach's son Johann Christian in London, particularly in the subscription concerts they jointly organized. One of his symphonies in E flat (op.7 no.6) was transcribed by the eight-year-old Mozart while he was in London (and was at one time attributed to him as K.18).

Right: Drawing by Rowlandson of a concert at the Vauxhall Gardens in 1784 in the presence of the Prince of Wales (at right) and (seated in the box on the left) James Boswell, Samuel Johnson, Mrs Thrale and Oliver Goldsmith, champions of the Enlightenment in English literature; the singer, Mrs Weichsel, who had been famous for her Vauxhall songs since the 1760s, is accompanied by a large orchestra. The pleasure-gardens played an important part in London's musical life; J. C. Bach wrote music for performance here, and they were visited by the Mozarts in 1764 and by Haydn in 1792.

Above: Ticket for one of the Bach-Abel concerts, engraved by Francesco Bartolozzi.

Right: Gainsborough's portrait of J. C. Bach, another of his musical friends, which was commissioned by Padre Martini and completed in 1776. Two years later it was taken out to Bologna by the castrato singer Francesco Roncaglia.

of periodicals such as the *European Magazine* and *Analytical Review* of London and more specialist publications such as the *Magazin der Musik* of Hamburg and *Allgemeine musikalische Zeitung* of Leipzig.

Many musicians were increasingly inquisitive about the relationship of their music to that of the past, and the century witnessed the first histories of music. The most eminent author was the Italian, Padre Giovanni Battista Martini, a competent composer and respected theorist whose opinion on musical matters was sought by the Mozart family and J. C. Bach among many others. Padre Martini never left his native Bologna and devoted most of his life to assembling material for a history of music, but at his death in 1784 at the age of seventy-eight he had completed only three volumes out of five of the *Storia della Musica*.

If Padre Martini was the most eminent author of the day, the most famous history was that prepared by the Englishman Dr Charles Burney. *A General History of Music from the Earliest Ages to the Present Period* appeared in four volumes between 1776 and 1789. Naturally, many of the facts and opinions offered by the volumes have been superseded by the more rigorous work of later scholars, but in the breadth of its conception and the range of its sympathies Burney's *History* continues to command respect; it is one of the most enduring products of the Age of Enlightenment.

To gather material for his *History*, Burney in the early 1770s had made two journeys to Europe. His immediate impressions were published in two volumes: the first, entitled *The Present State of Music in France and Italy*, was published in 1771; the second, *The Present State of Music in Germany, the Netherlands and the United Provinces*, appeared in 1773. More informal than the *History*, they contain observations on local performance practice and pen portraits of composers, singers and librettists, in addition to vivid descriptions of some of the difficulties of travelling across Europe.

The increase in learned and casual discourse on music, the spread of public concerts and the new momentum of published music meant that by the end of the century the relationship between the composer and his public was very different from that which had existed at its beginning. For the composer there was greater independence; he could exercise control over his affairs without continual deference to his employer. For the public, composers began to assume the status of celebrities. Out of these twin aspects of the composer's position grew the nineteenth-century Romantic notion that the creative artist and his art were omnipotent and that all obligations were to the art itself and none to society. But all that was in the future.

• The eighteenth-century view •

In his own lifetime J. S. Bach was recognized as being out of step with the times. In 1737 – that is, when Bach was fifty-two and Haydn a five-year-old at Rohrau – the north German musician Johann Adolph Scheibe offered a critical assessment of Bach's music. It included the following sentences: 'This great man would be the admiration of whole nations, if he were more agreeable, and if he did not deprive his pieces of their naturalness by giving them a bombastic and confused style, and obscure their beauty by an excessive application of artifice . . . In short, he is in music what formerly Herr von Lohenstein was in poetry. Bombast has led both of them from the natural to the artificial, and from the noble to the obscure; and one admires in both the onerous labor and an exceptional effort, which, however, is vainly employed if it conflicts with Nature.'

Scheibe's observations were the thoughts of a man who could perceive the irreversible changes that were taking place in music and who did not have the modern advantage of being able to embrace the greatness of J. S. Bach as well as the potential of the newer style. Not surprisingly, given the presence of Bach and Handel, the regions that swam against the tide the longest were north Germany and England. In 1764 Charles Avison, a composer from Newcastle, had his Six Sonatas for harpsichord, two violins and cello (op.8) published in London. As a composer of the old school he took the opportunity of issuing a preface denouncing what was in England a recent enthusiasm for the new symphony. The difficulties faced by contemporaries in trying to be objective about their art is demonstrated by Avison's choice of vocabulary; he regards the new style as confused and unnatural, the very qualities that Scheibe saw in the music of Bach: 'Sorry am I to instance the new foreign overtures now pouring in upon us every season, which are all involved in the same confusion of style, instead of displaying the fine varieties of air and design. Should this torrent of confused sounds, which is still increasing, overpower the public ear, we must in time prefer a false and distracted art to the happy efforts of unforced nature.'

Notwithstanding Avison, 'naturalness' and 'freedom from artifice' soon became bywords of the new style, and they do serve to differentiate the high Baroque from the *galant*, but to apply them without amplification to the mature classical style would be to ignore its profundity; the esthetic of the mature style balances apparent simplicity with more personal and enduring qualities. Haydn defined the essence of the style in his appraisal of Mozart. '[He] is the greatest composer known to me either in person or by

Opposite: Cross-section of the Teatro San Carlo in Naples, which had opened in 1737, with capacity for an audience of 3,500, and had become the center of Neapolitan musical life and of the whole world of opera.

Above: Opening of one of the arias in J. C. Bach's first opera, *Artaserse*, which was first performed in December 1760 at the Teatro Regio in Turin.

Right: Milan Cathedral in the 1720s. Musical life in Milan was for many years dominated by G. B. Sammartini (1700-75), who specialized in instrumental music, and through whose influence many features of Italian music were passed on to classical composers in Austria and Germany. J. C. Bach was organist at Milan Cathedral from 1760 to 1762.

VEDUTA DEL FIANCO   DEL DUOMO DI MILANO

name. He has taste and, moreover, the most profound knowledge of composition.' Taste and knowledge (eighteenth-century English speakers would have said 'science') are the twin pillars of the style; taste, not in the nineteenth-century sense of mere propriety but as indicative of the balance between subjective and objective qualities, between sense and sensibility, avoiding the dangers of effete simplicity in one direction or redundant exaggeration in the other. This judicious balance gives the music its tension and is the product of Haydn's second element, 'knowledge of composition.' Haydn and especially Mozart were most scathing of their contemporaries when criticizing some particular point of compositional technique such as a weak melody, misjudged scoring or ineffectual conclusion. Sound craftsmanship, the ability to put down on paper the seething sounds of the imagination, is one quality that separates Haydn and Mozart from their contemporaries.

Dr Charles Burney mentions over a hundred composers in the two volumes of tours which were the immediate result of his two European journeys to investigate 'all that was curious' in contemporary music. Every country, district and city had its own popular composer and, even if two hundred years later the majority of these together with their music have been forgotten, the sheer number of composers is a sharp reminder that classical music did not mean only Haydn and Mozart.

• Italy •

Italy had contributed with great distinction to the history of music during the baroque period, Monteverdi and Vivaldi being only two of the major composers of Italian origin. At first glance its contribution to the classical period is less obvious – after all, none of the major figures was an Italian – but Italy provided the main sources of the style itself, the beginnings of at least two major genres, the keyboard sonata and the symphony, and throughout the century its overwhelming predilection for opera meant that the country was always feeding the mainstream of stylistic development.

The solo keyboard sonata can be viewed as arising logically from the baroque sonata for violin and continuo, keyboard players quite naturally wanting to play sonatas on their own rather than be relegated to an accompanying role. But though interest in complete independence for the keyboard was undeniably important, the main factor that encouraged the growth of the solo keyboard sonata throughout Europe was a social one. It became very fashionable for amateurs, particularly ladies, to while away their leisure hours playing the clavichord, harpsichord and, later, piano, and throughout the century, and well into the next, keyboard sonatas were composed mainly with the amateur performer in mind. Indeed many of the finest keyboard works of the century were inspired by the musical gifts of these lay players.

If social fashion encouraged the cultivation of the genre, its continued popularity was ensured by its up-to-date musical language. For this composers went to contemporary opera, so that the new keyboard sonata flourished in the wake of the popularity of Italian opera. Within Italy itself many of the opera composers based in Venice, Rome and Naples composed sonatas in the same pleasant, light idiom that they used in their stage works. The output of Baldassare Galuppi is typical of dozens of Italian composers of the time.

Galuppi composed over eighty operas and was noted in particular for his comic operas, most of which were produced in his native Venice. Although opera composition was undoubtedly his main preoccupation, he also composed over ninety keyboard sonatas. There are only a few reminders of the Baroque, mainly in movements that have the rhythmic characteristics of the minuet or gigue. Opera is a much more tangible influence. The melodic lines are extremely singable with plenty of long notes followed by a gentle emphasis on a strong beat. The left hand, meanwhile, concentrates on providing a steady accompaniment that allows the listener to focus attention on the melody. The steady accompaniment also, of course, has the merit of being easy to play, much easier than the average left hand of a baroque harpsichord work. Any dramatic or more forceful content is usually restricted to a mock-pathetic temporary shift to a minor key, sometimes complemented by filling out the texture from the basic two parts. These movements in a moderately fast tempo have acquired the highly appropriate label 'singing allegro.' The general style which Galuppi and his contemporaries called *galant* corresponds perfectly to that composer's undemanding definition of good music: 'vaghezza, chiarezza e buona modulazione' (gracefulness, clarity and good modulation).

These early sonatas by Galuppi and his compatriots were all written with the harpsichord

Above: Frontispiece of Metastasio's libretto for *L'Alessandro nell'Indie.* This was set by J. C. Bach, whose first three Italian operas (the last two written for San Carlo in Naples) were all based on libretti by Metastasio. They followed the traditional pattern of *opera seria,* the action being carried forward in a succession of set-piece arias separated by recitative.

in mind. Despite the fact that the piano had been invented in Italy and that the first set of sonatas to imply the use of the instrument had been published in the same country in 1732 (Giustini's twelve sonatas 'di piano, e forte'), the piano displaced the harpsichord much later in Italy than elsewhere in Europe, and Italian composers did not respond so readily to the challenges offered by the new instrument. In this aspect of musical development as in many others Italy occupies a vital but unfulfilled role; it provided the source and impetus for many of the century's most important developments but it was never to see them to fruition.

This is particularly true of the symphony. The genre had its origins in the overture preceding the opera, the *sinfonia avanti l'opera*. At the beginning of the eighteenth century in the hands of composers such as Alessandro Scarlatti, Leonardo Leo and Giovanni Battista Pergolesi the *sinfonia* had crystallized into a three-movement pattern (fast, slow, fast). Usually the overtures had no particular dramatic relevance to the succeeding opera and were

often reused for other operas. Their general language, however, was undeniably that of the opera house, and when they were performed in concerts they provided a whiff of greasepaint to contrast with the different pleasures of a Vivaldi concerto or a Scarlatti cantata. Their popularity encouraged the composition of independent *sinfonie*, works in the same style but having no connections with any stage work, and as soon as the *sinfonia* gained this independence, it was free to become more elaborate than its original function as a curtain-raiser permitted. The fact that, unlike the keyboard sonata, it was performed by professional musicians in public helped to stimulate the imagination of composers. Thus, as the century progressed, the concert symphony became more and more sophisticated, leaving the opera overture more or less unchanged.

Although the Italian opera had provided the movement pattern and the style for the early symphony, few Italian composers made any notable contributions to the subsequent development of the genre. An honorable exception is Giovanni Battista Sammartini (1700/1-75). He was probably born in Milan, an exceptional city in eighteenth-century Italy in that its musical life was directed towards instrumental music rather than opera. Sammartini composed only three operas but seventy-seven symphonies, ten concertos and some twenty-five sacred compositions (Masses, settings of the *Te Deum*, etc.). Because opera featured minimally in Sammartini's career, his symphonies often have features derived from other instrumental genres, in particular the baroque trio-sonata and the baroque concerto.

Up to the 1740s most of his symphonies were written for a three-part string orchestra, two violins and bass, which encouraged the performance of these works as chamber music with one player per part as well as the normal orchestral performance. The progressive trend was towards a four-part texture, and later in his career Sammartini revised some of these early trio-sonata-type symphonies and, by adding a viola part, turned them into four-part symphonies. Only a handful of Sammartini's symphonies have parts for wind instruments, a reflection of the Italian baroque concerto, an association made more telling by the many passages of demonstrative string writing that could have been transplanted directly from a Vivaldi concerto.

Above: Bakery mold from the second half of the eighteenth century. Most of the instruments have molds for both front and back (and occasionally a middle piece as well), so that the cakes made could be fully three-dimensional models. This and the other illustrations on these pages show how far music had penetrated the popular culture of the period.

Opposite: St Cecilia and biblical musicians praise the Trinity; a painting behind glass from a Protestant church in Bavaria.

Left: Octave clavichord built into a life-size figure of a woman; made in southern Germany around 1775.

Above: Illustration from a Nuremberg album of 1772 showing a young couple dancing to the music of a hurdy-gurdy.

Sammartini achieved a very deliberate fusion of elements from the opera house and the instrumental tradition of the time. The composer was quite explicit that the result was to be called a *sinfonia*, but the diverse influences on the independent symphony and the flexible attitude of eighteenth-century performers is demonstrated by the profusion of titles under which these works often circulated. A popular early symphony in F major by Sammartini was labelled an 'Overtura' in Paris, a Sonata for 'Two Violins with a Thorough-Bass for the Harpsicord [sic]

or Violoncello' in London, and a 'Sinfonia a Violino 1mo violino 2do Viola con Basso' in Stockholm.

Admirers noted his skill in writing interesting parts for every instrument; a contemporary wrote that it was possible to hear 'the separate play of the violas . . . and the continual movement of the second violins, which flowed with a beautiful novelty in a completely different way from that of the first violins.' Given his interest in creating a four-part texture with lively interplay, it is not surprising that towards the end of his life Sammartini composed five works that may be regarded as genuine string quartets. The composer's own title for them was *concertino*, an indication of his attitude to the scoring – an ensemble concerto.

It was left to another Italian, Luigi Boccherini (1743-1805) to become a leading composer of quartets. Boccherini's quartets, quintets, symphonies and concertos are almost without exception polished works with a winning charm and melodiousness, qualities that ensured his position as one of the most popular composers of the second half of the century.

Although born in Italy, Boccherini spent most of his working life in Spain as court composer and cellist to the Infante, Don Luis. The musical facilities of the court gave rise to the

THERESIENS LEZTER TAG.

Above: Maria Theresa's Last Day, in November 1780 – attended by the priest, the doctor and her children, including her son Joseph, co-regent since his father's death in 1765, who kneels beside her. The influence of the imperial court, which did much to foster music, was felt in many institutions and also at courts abroad, where the Empress's daughters had married.

Right: Eating and dancing in Vienna to a small musical ensemble in the late eighteenth century.

invention of the string quintet for two violins, viola and two cellos, of which Boccherini was to compose over a hundred. The court included an excellent quartet ensemble made up of members of the Font family, a father and three sons. Boccherini, a virtuoso cellist himself, did not wish to disrupt the existing ensemble and so, in addition to quartets, he composed quintets in which he could be the second cellist.

• Austria •

Eighteenth-century Austria had close links with Italy. Large areas of northern Italy were part of the extensive lands governed by Austria, and the coming and going of artists, sculptors and musicians across the Alps was continual. The strongest bond between the two countries was Italian opera; the public of large cities such as Vienna, Prague and Pressburg (Bratislava) clamored for the latest Italian opera with an enthusiasm equal to that of audiences in Naples, Rome and Venice.

Austrian-born composers understood that their musical apprenticeship was not complete or their subsequent career fulfilled unless they had traveled to Italy, and a composer like Joseph Haydn, who never visited the country, was very much the exception. Though the classical style was to reach its apotheosis in Austria, its origins and progress must be viewed against this Italian background; it is equally crucial to realize that the great figures of the high Baroque, Bach and Handel, played little part in this process – a few manuscript copies of individual works (especially harpsichord works) found their way to Austria and were known to *conoscitori*, but by and large their works were unplayed and unknown. When they did become familiar to Mozart and Haydn in the 1780s and 1790s, the classical style had been fully formulated.

A telling factor favoring the development of the classical style in Austria was that the country's music-making, unlike that of Italy, maintained an equitable balance between instrumental, operatic and sacred music. The imperial court in Vienna supported an orchestra that played the latest symphonies and chamber music, but the real life-blood of Austrian music was to be found in the music establishments of the aristocrats. The names of the Erdödy, Lobkowitz, Schaffgotsch, Schwarzenberg and Esterházy families recur regularly in the musical life of eighteenth-century Austria. This network of princely palaces, which vied with each other to secure the best Kapellmeister, the best singers, the best orchestra, was complemented by that of the Austrian monasteries, many of which maintained equally active musical establishments; abbeys such as Göttweig, Melk and Kremsmünster were as interested in collecting secular as sacred music – a distinction they would have regarded as sophistry.

One of the earliest composers to gain international prominence was Georg Christoph Wagenseil (1715-77). His output included more than sixty symphonies; over ninety keyboard concertos, as well as a dozen concertos for various other solo instruments; over ninety string trios; two hundred works for the keyboard; ten operas; and three oratorios. By his fortieth birthday he was so successful that he was able to negotiate the publication of his music directly with firms in Paris, from where his fame extended to the rest of Europe.

The tradition of performing opera overtures outside the theater was strong in Austria, and at least eight of Wagenseil's earliest symphonies started life as operatic overtures. As in Sammartini's symphonies, the standard three-movement pattern shows the influence of the Italian concerto, particularly in the use of authoritative repeated chords to begin an allegro (often aptly termed 'hammerstrokes') and the empty bustle of the string writing. Wagenseil's instrumentation, however, is more colorful than Sammartini's, the standard orchestra of two oboes, two horns and strings often being supplemented in C and D major works by trumpets and timpani to produce a brilliant festive sound; these works are the immediate forerunners of the many joyous symphonies in C and D major by Haydn and Mozart.

The Wagenseil three-movement symphony has a natural balance, two fast movements surrounding a central slow movement. First movements soon became the most closely argued, based on a thematic style that was tightly rhythmic and instrumental rather than generously melodic and operatic. The slow movement provided some repose. The finale, usually a *tempo di menuetto* or rondo, ensured a lighthearted conclusion. Haydn had to look no further for a model for his early symphonies.

Wagenseil was also a leading composer of concertos. Although J. S. Bach, in the early decades of the century, is usually credited with composing the first concerto for keyboard, within Austria Wagenseil, who was a notable solo harpsichordist, was a leading participant in a trend that replaced the violin with the keyboard as the favored solo instrument.

Many of these early keyboard concertos were closer in conception to chamber music than to the symphony. The accompaniment, in Wagenseil's case, often consisted of two violins and a bass, which permitted it to be played by either a string orchestra or an ensemble of three soloists; on occasions the orchestral sections were incorporated into the keyboard part enabling the player to play the entire work himself. Even as late as 1784 Mozart indicated that a recent piano concerto (K.449) could be accompanied by a full orchestra of strings, two oboes and two horns or by four string players only.

Wagenseil's harpsichord sonatas reveal both the conservative and the progressive in the composer. Most are in three movements, but included among the sonatas are many movements that reveal the tangible influence of older styles. There are preludes consisting of arpeggiated chords (like the familiar C major prelude from Book I of Bach's *Forty-eight*), pompous French overture movements and gigues. Most of the sonatas were given the title 'divertimento,' the term 'sonata' not becoming common in Austria until the last quarter of the century. In that country 'divertimento' was applied to a wide variety of genres that later acquired different names, but its usage was quite specific. It was hardly ever applied to orchestral music but to what was later to be called chamber music; and it arose to describe music that was to be played without a continuo to distinguish it from the tradition of chamber music based on the continuo. Although individual works may have been lightweight in tone, the divertimento did not habitually carry such a connotation.

Wagenseil was seventeen years older than Haydn, and by the time of his death in 1777 his music was already regarded as outmoded. Apart

Above: Michael Haydn (1737-1806), who from 1762/3 until his death was in the service of the Prince-Archbishops of Salzburg.

Left: Title-page of three of Michael Haydn's symphonies.

from the birth of Joseph Haydn, the decade 1729-39 saw the births of six influential composers who were to make a distinctive contribution to Austrian music. Gassmann was born in 1729, Ordonez in 1734, Michael Haydn in 1737, Hofmann in 1738, Dittersdorf and Vanhal in 1739. As individuals, each one of these composers came to be associated with a particular genre of composition – Gassmann with comic opera, Dittersdorf with *Singspiel* and Michael Haydn, Vanhal and Hofmann with church music – but all shared an equal enthusiasm for the symphony, as a parade of statistics will show. Gassmann composed thirty-three, Dittersdorf approximately one hundred and twenty, Michael Haydn over forty, Vanhal seventy-six and Ordonez over seventy. Wagenseil's symphonies were all in three movements, and despite the solitary example of a single four-movement work (fast, slow, minuet, fast) dated 1740 by Matthias Georg Monn, the larger scheme did not really become fashionable until the 1760s, when it was favored by Hofmann. Even then, many composers, Michael Haydn, Ordonez and Vanhal in particular, continued to compose three- as well as four-movement symphonies; indeed the four-movement scheme cannot be said to have become the norm until the very last decade of the century.

In the meantime, however, some of Joseph Haydn's symphonies had featured a four-movement scheme in which the first movement is slow rather than fast. A legacy of the baroque *sonata da chiesa*, it is a pattern also encountered in several symphonies by Ordonez. Slow introductions – as opposed to complete first movements – became more common from the 1760s onwards, and many examples can be found in the symphonies of Hofmann, Ordonez, Vanhal and Michael Haydn.

Above: Carl Theodor (1724-99), the Elector Palatine, who made his court at Mannheim the most celebrated musical center in Europe. In 1778, following the death of the Elector of Bavaria, he took over that title as well and moved his court, including the orchestra, to Munich.

Three composers in particular, Haydn, Ordonez and Michael Haydn, show an interest in nourishing the potentially anemic textures of the early classical style by the occasional use of fugal procedures. Also indicative of a desire to make the music more emotive is the new interest in the minor key. Only two out of over sixty symphonies by Wagenseil were in a minor key; the proportion rose dramatically in the symphonies of the second generation of Viennese composers. For Vanhal and Gassmann, like Joseph Haydn, this interest was concentrated in the late 1760s and early 1770s, when they produced a series of vigorous and agitated symphonies in the minor. Often dubbed *Sturm und Drang* by modern commentators, after a play by Klinger of that title (1776), the idiom ruffles the neat world of the *galant* and marks a significant stage in the development of the classical style.

In the more withdrawn, private world of the string quartet Austrian composers of the second generation contributed with equal distinction. In a way the invention of the string quartet was inevitable, a logical outcome of the frequent practice of performing orchestral music with one player per part and, in Austria, a similarly logical outgrowth of the divertimento tradition. The string quartet could not have happened until the move from three-part to four-part string writing in symphonies had been achieved, but even so it is mildly surprising that it was not until the late 1750s, with the appearance of Joseph Haydn's ten divertimenti, that the genre began to flourish, making it by several decades the youngest of the major new genres produced by the classical style.

The new genre was habitually termed 'divertimento' up to the 1780s when, because of the usual trend by printers towards uniformity and the wider dissemination of music, 'quartet' became the standard term ('string quartet' and its German, French and Italian equivalents did not come into use until the early nineteenth century). Although the progressive tendency led by Vanhal, Haydn and later Pleyel was towards a four-movement scheme similar to that of the symphony, several well established alternatives were used in the period 1760-80. There were composers like Albrechtsberger and F. X. Dussek, who followed Haydn's lead in his early quartets and composed works in five movements; others such as Gassmann, Ordonez and (again) Albrechtsberger continued an older tradition, writing three- and four-movement schemes with fugal movements and slow first movements. At first the forces were not always the standard two violins, viola and cello; the last-named was frequently replaced by a violone, an instrument similar to the modern double-bass but lighter and more nimble.

• Mannheim •

Mannheim was the court city of the Elector Palatine and in the eighteenth century it rose to pre-eminence as a center for all manner of cultural activities. There were flourishing academies of art and literature and well-known collections of engravings and antiquities. As a center for music, its contemporary fame was soon legendary and far eclipsed that of any other single court, including the various royal courts.

Carl Theodor was only eighteen when he became Elector Palatine on 1 January 1743, but within a few years he transformed the music establishment of the court. The first violinist, Johann Stamitz, already an experienced composer, became head of instrumental music, and other composer-players were thus enticed to the thriving court. Franz Xaver Richter, at the age of thirty-nine, left his post as Vicekapellmeister to the Reichlin-Meldegg family in Kempten to become responsible for church music, and Ignaz Holzbauer, aged forty-two, left his position as Kapellmeister to the Duke of Württemberg at Stuttgart to supervise opera. Other eminent musicians who became part of a retinue of some eighty instrumentalists and singers included Anton Filtz, Joseph Toeschi, Christian Cannabich and Johann Stamitz's son, Carl.

For the court, the opera house was the main center of activity, but the wider reputation of

Left: The concert hall in Mannheim seen during a medical lecture in 1793. The hall was incorporated in the plans of the new National Theater, built some ten years earlier, and was designed specifically for musical performances – the spectators occupying the galleries and the spaces beneath them – although it could serve other purposes as well.

Mannheim was based on the virtuosity of its orchestra. In 1777 it numbered some fifty players with a full complement of wind instruments. As individuals, their equals could probably be found elsewhere, but as members of a drilled ensemble they were peerless. Instrumental composition at Mannheim was, not surprisingly, directed towards exploiting the resources of this orchestra; the Mannheim contribution to the development of the keyboard sonata and the string quartet was, by comparison, neglible.

The Mannheimers were prodigious composers of concertos. Their model was not the old-fashioned *concerto grosso* for a group of soloists and an orchestra but the concerto for one soloist and orchestra pioneered by the Italians, especially Vivaldi. Johann Stamitz, the violinist, wrote seventeen concertos for his own instrument in addition to thirteen for other instruments; Wendling, the first flute player, composed some nine flute concertos, and Anton Filtz, a cellist, five concertos for that instrument. As with Wagenseil in Austria the number of movements follows the usual Vivaldi pattern (fast, slow, fast), a feature that was to remain standard, apart from idiosyncratic examples, until the towering example of Brahms's Second Piano Concerto; even then the four-movement concerto remained a rarity. Within movements, the Mannheim composers, like their contemporaries throughout Europe, were content to follow well-established formal patterns: ritornello structures in the outer movements and, typically, a relaxed 'aria' for soloist over a persistent accompaniment for the slow movement. In the solo concerto the spotlight was naturally on the individual, but Mannheim's greatest claim to fame rested on the already-mentioned corporate virtuosity of its instrumentalists, best demonstrated in symphonies.

Left: Abbé Georg Joseph Vogler (1749-1814), chaplain and Vicekapellmeister at Carl Theodor's court at Mannheim and an important musical theorist and teacher.

Johann Stamitz composed symphonies in four movements as early as the 1740s – that is, a decade before Hofmann in Vienna. His symphonies, like those of Sammartini and Wagenseil, show a mixture of influences from the concerto and opera overture. The operas of Jommelli were particularly well-known in the courts of southern Germany, and Stamitz seems to have appropriated some techniques from their overtures and developed them into a highly characteristic style. Most typical is the opening gesture of repeated *forte* chords followed by a long, steady crescendo from a *pianissimo* during which all the instruments gradually enter and the music climbs up the scale, an effect calculated to thrill the audience. This feature was used, to a greater or lesser extent, by most of the resident composers and has acquired the name 'Mannheim crescendo.' Indeed, in Stamitz's symphonies players and listeners recognized their appearances as landmarks in the structure of the movement; three appearances became the norm, marking the beginnings of major sections.

Here, *in nuce*, were the seeds of the decline of the Mannheim composers from the 1760s onwards, for the very factors that had been its strengths – the excellence of the orchestra and the closely knit community – explain why the court never nurtured a Haydn or Mozart. Towards the 1770s the symphonies of the Mannheim composers became more and more predictable in language and dated in outlook (there are, for instance, very few symphonies in a minor key). Demonstrating the virtuosity of the orchestra for its own sake became a dominant concern, and features such as the Mannheim crescendo became tedious party tricks; the medium had become more important than the message.

•North Germany•

The number of composers active in north Germany in the mid-eighteenth century was equal to that in any other part of Europe. The Graun brothers, the Benda brothers, Johann Friedrich Klöffler, J. C. F. Bach, Johann Gottfried Müthel and Johann Philipp Kirnberger were all prominent in the musical life of the area. Some of these were pupils of the great Johann Sebastian Bach, and their outlook on musical development was a conservative one; generally they accepted the new symphony and keyboard sonata, but in chamber music they still clung to the old

continuo-based sonata rather than embracing the string quartet.

One of the most original and idiosyncratic talents of the eighteenth century was Carl Philipp Emanuel Bach (1714-88), the second surviving son of Johann Sebastian. At the age of twenty-four he joined the court of Prince Frederick and when in 1740 the Prince became the new King of Prussia, C. P. E. Bach became the court's keyboard player. Frederick the Great was a skilled flautist and a competent composer, but, though only two years older than Emanuel Bach, he never warmed to the personality of the young man. Accompanying the King in private flute recitals remained Bach's principal duty for the next twenty-eight years and he was never promoted. In 1768 he finally moved away to Hamburg to succeed Telemann as cantor of the Johanneum and director of music in the five main churches.

His first compositions to receive widespread recognition were two sets of keyboard sonatas, the first dedicated to the King of Prussia (1742), the second to the Duke of Württemberg (1744). In three movements, they are far more concentrated in emotion and varied in style and structure than most contemporary keyboard sonatas; these were qualities that captivated the

Above: Performance in Paris of a solo work for bassoon, accompanied on a pyramid piano.

Left: C. P. E. Bach, a composer who made a unique contribution to the development of music for the new piano, and who in his 'private' music probed deep into the emotional content of his art.

Right: Chamber performance of a cantata – still in the baroque manner – in which the singer is accompanied by three violins, with continuo provided by cello and harpsichord. The engraving of 1769 by Daniel Chodowiecki is designed as an allegory of social harmony.

Above: Poster for a *Concert Spirituel* – the first important series of public concerts, which had been founded in Paris in 1725. The huge program (the concert began at six) included a *symphonie concertante*, concertos for oboe and harpsichord, an orchestral symphony, ten arias of various kinds and 'The hunt of the fifteen-year-old in love.'

young Joseph Haydn for one: 'I did not leave my clavier till I had played them through,' he declared to a biographer.

Even more influential was his treatise published in two parts in 1753 and 1762 and entitled *Essay on the True Art of Playing Keyboard Instruments*. Like many treatises of the time it contains paragraphs on technical matters such as the execution of ornaments and the realization of figured bass, but what makes the treatise something more than a pedantic manual are the observations on the emotional commitment required from a performer. 'Play from the soul, not like a trained bird,' he exhorts the keyboard player.

Emanuel Bach practiced what he preached. Dr Burney visited him in October 1772 and wrote the following vivid account of his playing: 'After dinner, which was elegantly served, and cheerfully eaten, I prevailed upon him to sit down again to a clavichord, and he played, with little intermission till near eleven o'clock at night. During this time, he grew so animated and *possessed* that he not only played, but looked like one inspired. His eyes were fixed, his under lip fell, and drops of effervescence distilled from his countenance.'

This picture seems more that of the typical Romantic artist than the reserved eighteenth-century figure. C. P. E. Bach's music, too, is strongly characterized and, on occasions, eccentric. The flow of the music is interrupted by pauses; there are abrupt changes of direction that momentarily disorient the listener, and there are violent changes of mood with agonizing use of the minor key. In his fantasias for keyboard (C. P. E. Bach advocated the clavichord or the new piano) harmonies are present as much for their evocative color as for forward momentum – anticipating Debussy by over a century – and he recommends the removal of bars so that the music has an inner compulsion that is not circumscribed by a regular meter. Twentieth-century musicians were to refer to the 'tyranny of the bar.'

Many of his symphonies and concertos have an unnerving, quixotic air about them. Some of the rhetorical gestures recall J. S. Bach, others anticipate Beethoven. Sometimes the imagination is given too much rein and there is a lack of discipline; the music is always fascinating but on occasion it sounds like a series of events with no coherent overall plan or sense of wholeness.

Right: Dancing at the Madrid festival of San Antonio de la Florida, to the traditional accompaniment of guitars and clapping, in a tapestry cartoon of 1777 by Goya. Boccherini, the leading composer in Spain, who incorporated many Spanish elements in his works (including the celebrated *Fandango* attributed to Soler in one of his guitar quintets), got to know Goya around this time through the Benavente-Osuña family, where both were able to hear performances of many works by Haydn.

Below right: Gainsborough's portrait (1758-9) of the amateur flautist Sir William Wollaston.

This *empfindsam* (sensitive) style, as contemporaries labeled it, demonstrated that symphonies and sonatas need not restrict themselves to the emotional scope of, say, the music of the Mannheim school. Bach's music acted as a catalyst to the more orderly imaginations of Haydn and Mozart.

• Paris •

With its active concert life and busy publishers Paris could claim to be the musical capital of Europe. The music of many of the composers mentioned so far provided much of the fare: Boccherini's quartets and quintets, Wagenseil's symphonies and sonatas, the symphonies and quartets of Haydn and Vanhal, the concertos and symphonies of Cannabich and Stamitz — all were popular in Paris. But this interest in the new classical style, the *avant garde* of the day, occurred late in the century compared with other parts of Europe.

Before the 1760s Parisian enthusiasm for music was directed towards French opera and the dated instrumental music of Couperin and Rameau. There are no French figures of the importance of Sammartini, Stamitz or Wagenseil in the early development of the classical style. The change in taste occurred swiftly in the 1760s, a state of affairs commented upon by Leopold Mozart in a letter dated 1 February

Right: Boucher's *Summer Pastorale* (1749) combines the artificiality and the charm of the French pastoral, played out to the accompaniment of the bagpipes. Diderot, in his review of the Salon of 1765, compared Boucher's shepherdesses to a performance by the *opéra comique* star Marie Favart in Monsigny's pastoral opera *Rose et Colas*, which had had its first performance the year before.

1764 to Maria Theresia Hagenauer in Salzburg: 'There is a perpetual war here between the Italian and the French music. The whole of French music is not worth a sou. But the French are now starting to make drastic changes, for they are beginning to waver very much; and in ten to fifteen years the present French taste, I hope, will have completely disappeared. The Germans are taking the lead in the publication of their compositions. Amongst these Schobert, Eckhardt, Honauer for the keyboard, and Hochbrucker and Mayr for the harp are the favorites. M. Le Grand, a French clavier-player, has abandoned his own style completely and his sonatas are now in our style.'

Leopold Mozart's estimate of the time-scale proved accurate. Within fifteen years Paris and the remainder of France were fully converted to 'our style' and native and resident composers were playing a full part in its cultivation. In such a musically cosmopolitan atmosphere, Parisian audiences were acquainted with all the latest trends and fashions from abroad, but they did create a few of their own too.

Johann Schobert was born *c.*1735 in Silesia and arrived in Paris in the early 1760s, where he soon established a reputation as a harpsichord player. His brilliant career was brought to an abrupt end (he died through eating poisonous mushrooms), but not before he had published nineteen sets of works in Paris. All involve the keyboard. Some are concertos, one is a set of solo harpsichord sonatas and the others are harpsichord sonatas with the optional accom-

Above: The King's Theatre in the Haymarket, London, for which J. C. Bach composed many of the Italian operas that he wrote in England.

Above: Giovanna Baccelli (*c.*1753-1801), the leading dancer at the King's Theatre from 1774 to 1782. In 1778 she appeared in a *divertissement* in Bach's *La Clemenza di Scipione*, his last opera for the theater, and she is seen here in *Les Amans surpris*, in which she partnered Auguste Vestris in 1780-1.

paniment of one or more string instruments (one violin, a violin and cello or two violins and cello). Like the contemporary keyboard sonata proper, these accompanied sonatas catered mainly for the amateur market; the parts were not vital to a performance but allowed unskilled string players to play the most modern music. From these humble circumstances grew the classical violin sonata, the piano trio, piano quartet and piano quintet, the string parts gradually contributing more to the texture until, at last, their presence became absolutely essential.

Schobert's keyboard music, whether solo or accompanied, is much fuller in sonority than that of most of his contemporaries. He was obviously acquainted with Italian opera overtures and Mannheim symphonies, and Burney in his *History* commented that 'the novelty and merit of Schobert's compositions seem to consist in the introduction of the symphonic, or modern overture style, upon the harpsichord, and by light and shade, alternate agitation and tranquillity, imitating the effects of an orchestra.'

Paris, apart from being an ever-hungry market for the quartets of Haydn, Boccherini and Vanhal, had its own distinctive attitude to the medium. The Italian-born Giuseppe Cambini, who lived in Paris most of his life, composed nearly 150 quartets, most of which set out to exploit the virtuosity of the first violinist in the most dazzling manner. In terms of musical content they are often trifling, but they represent a strand woven into the general development of the genre that was to encourage Haydn, for one, to make his quartets more demonstrative in the last decade of the century.

Ostentation too played a large part in explaining the rise in Paris of a new orchestral genre, the *symphonie concertante*. When Mozart visited the city in 1764 it had not been invented; by the time of his visit in 1778 it dominated public concerts and publishers' lists, and threatened to usurp the position of the symphony. As the term implies, it is essentially an orchestral work with parts for several soloists; two violins were a standard combination, but on occasion as many as five or six soloists were employed. In a way, it was an up-dated version of the old *concerto grosso*, but slighter in musical content than the old genre and indeed than the contemporary symphony. Two movements rather than the three or four of the symphony were standard: an opening allegro and a lighthearted rondo.

• London •

In the development of the classical style London had many features in common with Paris. A strong native baroque tradition, personified by the revered Handel, meant that the classical style came late, but from the moment of its arrival in the 1760s it flourished in the energetic commercial and artistic life of the city.

Handel at the beginning of the century had brought all that was new in music into the country. Two other Germans accomplished a similar feat in the years immediately after Handel's death in 1759. Carl Friedrich Abel, who was born in 1723 and had possibly been a pupil of J. S. Bach at Leipzig, had traveled through Germany and France before arriving in London early in 1759. Three years later he was followed by Johann Christian Bach, the youngest son of J. S., who had traveled even more extensively in Europe and had even lived for eight years in Italy. Through the Bach-Abel subscription concerts, these two composers were soon the leading figures in propagating the new style in England. Of the two, J. C. Bach is the more significant, and he exerted a decisive influence on the young Mozart when he lived in London for fifteen months in 1764-5.

J. C. Bach's symphonies, concertos and keyboard sonatas, like those of Mozart, are never far removed in spirit from the opera house. The term 'singing allegro' can be applied to countless movements, and his music in general has a cultured elegance, an easy fluency and an intuitive feel for balancing the lyrical and the dramatic, the decorative and the structural; only Mozart's emotional commitment is lacking.

Of special interest to Mozart was J. C. Bach's experimental attitude to the solo concerto. Although this genre maintained its position as one of the most popular of the day, most concertos by Austrian and Mannheim composers lacked the creative spark that characterized their symphonies. They continued to use the formal patterns of the baroque period with little modification, finding it more exciting to explore the potential of the developing sonata form in the new symphony than to adapt and refine the old ritornello form of the concerto to the new style. J. C. Bach was more acutely aware of the problem than most composers before Mozart.

In his op.1 harpsichord concertos, published in London in March 1763 and dedicated to Queen Charlotte, four of the six works are in two movements (allegro and a minuet) and employ structural procedures which would have been familiar to the London public. But two works, op.1, nos.4 and 6, are titled 'Concerto o Sinfonia' (Concerto or Symphony) and are altogether more experimental. The 'sinfonia' element is shown by the three-movement structure, the more expansive 'theatrical' language of the music from measure to measure and, in the first movements, the novel idea of composing the movement in sonata form (with central double bar and repeat marks) rather than the customary ritornello form. J. C. Bach is forcing himself to reconsider the relationship between style and structure in the concerto, and though he was never to repeat this particular experiment, all his later keyboard concertos show an understanding synthesis of the principles of the concerto and the symphony.

Apart from their own compositions J.C. Bach and Abel introduced those of the Mannheim composers and, towards the end of the 1770s, the music of Vanhal and Haydn from Austria. The French taste for the *symphonie concertante* was also introduced to London, and it was in this city rather than Paris that Haydn became familiar with the genre in the 1790s.

In one particular aspect musical life in London in the reign of George III differed from that of most European capitals. The popularity of the classical style did not result in the gradual demise of the Baroque, but rather the new style flourished alongside the continued performances of older music. Handel had died in 1759, but the devotion to his oratorios and, to a lesser

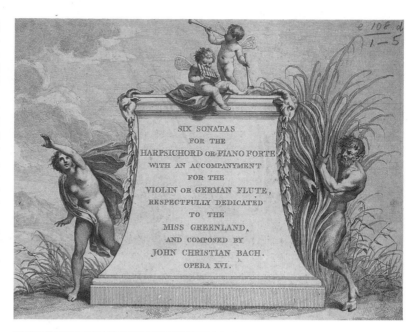

Above: Title-page of six keyboard sonatas with accompanying violin or flute part, op.16, by J. C. Bach. Bach was chiefly responsible for the introduction of the piano to England, and these simple sonatas (typically described as 'for the harpsichord or pianoforte'), dedicated to the daughter of a friend, were written in 1779, but published some four years later, after his death.

Left: Memorial print to J. C. Bach, engraved by Francesco Bartolozzi, who had designed title-pages for Bach's works as well as the decorative tickets for the Bach-Abel concerts.

extent, his instrumental music was never to wane, and the music of Corelli, Geminiani and others was still played; indeed, a few native composers still adhered to the old idiom. Some musicians felt the need to dispute the rival merits of the old and the new, but most, like Dr Burney, were able to enjoy both. The significance of this state of affairs — what is now called 'museum culture' — was not for the origins of the classical style but for its expansion from the late eighteenth century onwards. Without the English interest in Handel, Haydn's *Creation* would not have been composed, and a small but distinct element of Beethoven's musical personality would be absent too.

The Orchestra in the eighteenth century

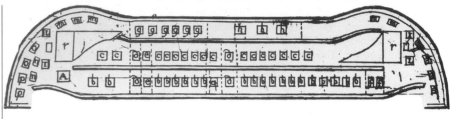

Before 1750 the categories and distinctions of types of music and the occasions for musical performances were rather different from those of today: bodies of musicians could have a variety of employers – courts, churches, city councils – and music was written for performance in a variety of contexts – the theater, at outdoor festivals and ceremonies, in an intimate setting at court (at meals, or with members of the noble family taking part themselves), in church (as part of the Catholic or Protestant liturgy or for special occasions), and so on. A local composer would generally write appropriate music for the resources that were available. However, wherever there was a larger body of musicians, a similar pattern would be found: a group of string players, using violins (divided), violas, cellos and contrabasses to provide the basic four-part harmony, a keyboard player (the Kapellmeister or maestro di cappella), some woodwinds (oboes and bassoons, and sometimes flutes – which might also be played by the oboe players), and perhaps horns, trumpets and drums.

Bodies of this kind would generally be attached to a court, to one of the great churches, or to a theater or opera house, and it was their very existence, together with the often seasonal nature of their work, that encouraged composers to write symphonic music and promoters to put on public concerts. The symphony and the orchestra thus have a parallel development.

The detail from a painting (c.1740) and the plan (c.1790) above show the arrangement of the orchestra at the Royal Theater in Turin. The continuo group on the left includes the maestro di cappella (by 1790 no longer playing, but on a raised podium – A), one cello (I), and one contrabass (L), while the main continuo group is on the right. The woodwinds are interspersed with the strings – only two oboes and two bassoons in 1740, but by 1790 four oboes (d), two clarinets (e) and three bassoons (h), while brass instruments – in 1790 trumpets (p) with drums (o) as well as horns (n,f) – are mainly on the extreme left. The string players (b,q,c,g,I,L,m) now number fifty-six, as against the twenty-four in 1740. The Turin orchestra contrasts with the caricature of a more intimate concert in a salon in eighteenth-century Paris (right), where the players are vigorously conducted by the singer they accompany.

The painting (left) of 1772 by J. P. Horemans shows a musician with some of the instruments of the Munich court orchestra, at a date before Elector Carl Theodor had transferred his famed Mannheim orchestra to the Bavarian capital. There are violins, a viola, cello and contrabass; flute, oboe, bassoon and horns; a lute and a viola d'amore; and, at bottom right, trombones and kettle-drums.

Above: F. X. Richter, Kapell-meister at Strasbourg Cathedral, directing his singers and instrumentalists, using the traditional roll of music paper.

Below: A group of eighteenth-century wind instruments, all but the clarinet made in England: the ivory flute (*left*), fitted with six keys, dates from the end of the period, in contrast to the simpler wooden flute (*second from right*); the oboe dates from around 1775, the boxwood recorder from around 1725, while the five-keyed clarinet, made in Belgium, dates from the latter part of the century.

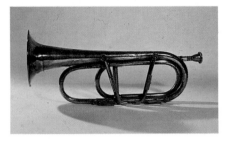

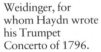

Above: A Viennese keyed trumpet of the kind devised in 1793 by Anton Weidinger, for whom Haydn wrote his Trumpet Concerto of 1796.

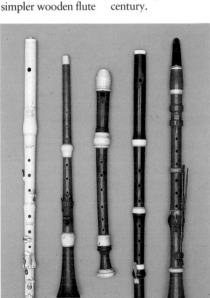

Of the instruments shown on this page only the violin, cello and oboe would have been regular members of an eighteenth-century orchestra. Flutes were more often used as solo instruments, although versatile oboists might change over to a flute; recorders had virtually disappeared from use by the mid-century. Clarinets were increasingly found after 1770 – initially also often played by oboists – once improvements had modified their strident tone and had made their intonation surer. Trumpets were used in conjunction with kettle-drums to give a festive or martial character to music, though trumpeters and drummers were generally members of a separate court establishment.

The violin above was made in 1758 by J. B. Guadagnini, an outstanding instrument-maker who was a younger contemporary of Stradivari and Guarneri in Cremona.

Above: A cello (about fifty survive in addition to some six hundred violins) made by Antonio Stradivari of Cremona (*c.*1644-1737).

Left: Leopold Mozart, who for over forty years was a member of the court orchestra of the Prince-Archbishops of Salzburg, reaching the position of Vicekapellmeister.

Right: Map showing the location of the principal orchestras in Germany and Austria in the early 1780s.

The remarkable development during the eighteenth century of symphonic orchestral music owes much to the constitutional system of Germany and Austria with their numerous princely courts. The most powerful families had made the great offices of Empire – Emperor, the three Spiritual Electors and six Secular Electors – virtually hereditary, while other ruling princes and the principal independent cities tried to rival the electoral courts. Vienna, which was the seat of the Emperor, had by far the most extensive musical forces, including a court orchestra, several theater orchestras and a number of private bands in the great noble houses. The three spiritual electors had their courts at Bonn, Koblenz and Mainz. At Koblenz the Archbishop of Trier's orchestra, though second in size only to that of Mannheim, concentrated on playing church music, but this was no longer the case at Mainz, nor at Bonn, where the Archbishop of Cologne, Elector Clemens August, took part in operatic performances and music with his relations; in 1732 he was one of ten players in a family concert in Munich, and in 1752 he played trios with the Elector of Bavaria and the Elector Palatine. Beethoven's grandfather was for a time conductor of the Electoral orchestra at Bonn. The other electors had their seats in Hanover, Berlin, Dresden, Mannheim and Munich. After the Elector of Hanover had moved to London in 1714 to become King of England, the court there diminished, although a small court orchestra was maintained.

Dresden (*below*) was the seat of the Elector of Saxony (at that time also King of Poland). Its great orchestra had been built up under the Konzertmeister J. F. Pisendel (d.1755) and J. A. Hasse, Kapellmeister from 1734 to 1764, but after the near-destruction of the city in 1760 in the Seven Years' War, many members left for positions elsewhere. There was something of a revival under J. G. Naumann, director of the orchestra in 1776 and again from 1786 to 1801, who also encouraged subscription concerts in Dresden.

Mannheim (*below*), seat of the Elector Palatine, had the most celebrated orchestra of all with a wealth of players and composers attached to the court of Elector Carl Theodor, including Johann Stamitz, Konzertmeister from 1745 until his death in 1757, and his pupil and successor Christian Cannabich.

In 1778, following the death of the Elector of Bavaria, his electorate was combined with that of Carl Theodor, who then moved his court to Munich (*below*), taking many members of his orchestra with him. However, despite the invigorating effect on Munich's musical life, the achievements of the orchestra's Mannheim years were never equalled.

The orchestra in Berlin (the Royal Palace is seen above) was considerably enlarged by Frederick the Great, who became King of Prussia (and Elector of Brandenburg) in 1740. He employed many distinguished musicians including C. P. E. Bach, the flautist J. J. Quantz, C. H. and J. G. Graun, the Benda brothers and J. F. Agricola. The King's tastes were conservative, and the orchestra's best years were in the early part of his reign, but his Kapellmeister from 1776, J.F.Reichardt, (who continued to serve for a time under his cello-playing successor Frederick William II), was an important innovator, both in abolishing the keyboard from the orchestra and introducing baton conducting, and in establishing series of public concerts in Berlin performed by professional musicians.

Size and composition of orchestras around 1780*

	Total	strings (violins)		woodwind	horns
Vienna (opera orchestra)	34	22	(12)	8	4
Bonn	28	17	(11)	7	4
Koblenz	37	22	(13)	11	4
Mainz	23	15	(10)	6	2
Hanover	21				
Berlin	37	24	(13)	11	2
Dresden	43	28	(17)	12	3
Mannheim	54	33	(23)	15	6
Munich	35	23	(17)	8	4
Kassel	24	16	(11)	6	2
Gotha	21	13	(9)	4	4
Ansbach	39	24	(12)	11	4
Stuttgart	34	25	(13)	7	2
Wallerstein	24	16	(10)	6	4
Regensburg	30	18	(12)	8	4
Salzburg	22	14	(10)	5	3
Eszterháza	23	17	(11)	4	2
Hamburg (opera, 1738)	33	15	(8)	14	4
Leipzig	28	19	(12)	7	2

* The figures are necessarily approximate, as records are frequently incomplete or ambiguous. They omit any keyboard instrument that the Kapellmeister would have played, and also any trumpets and drums, which were generally maintained as a separate corps. In every case, all of these instruments should be added to give a more complete picture.

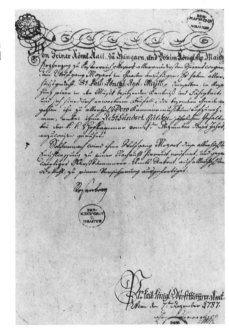

Layout of the orchestra and choir for the Handel festival in Westminster Abbey in 1784.

Kassel, Gotha, Ansbach, Stuttgart, Wallerstein and Regensburg were all seats of princely houses – almost all connected with the electoral houses and with each other by marriage. Often the orchestras had been formed to play Italian opera, and many Italian Kapellmeister were employed, most notably Niccolò Jommelli at Stuttgart. In the Hapsburg territories, Vienna (the Burgtheater, where Italian opera was performed is shown *below*) was without rival, and while many of the great landowners had private bands, the Esterházys were the only ones to have an orchestra on the scale of those of the German princes, although the Prince-Archbishop of Salzburg always had a good musical establishment.

Finally, Hamburg and Leipzig were the two most important places where an orchestra was maintained by the city itself, and both did much to establish public concerts in Germany. In Hamburg, Telemann had been active early in the century, while subscription concerts were inaugurated in 1761 in the new Konzertsaal auf dem Kamp, directed from 1768 C. P. E. Bach. In Leipzig, regular concerts had been held in the Gewandhaus (Cloth Hall) since 1743; but the city was severely hit by the Seven Years' War, and the series was re-established by J. A. Hiller, who conducted the inaugural concert in the new hall in 1781.

Left: Certificate of Mozart's appointment as chamber musician to the court in 1787; his career shows the difficulty of survival without such a post.

Above: Salary list of the Bologna Accademia Filarmonica orchestra, 1770, the best paid being the maestro di cappella, first violin, oboe, cello and a singer.

Right: The Archbishop of Salzburg's musical establishment in 1775. The two Kapellmeister are both Italians, Leopold Mozart is Vicekapellmeister, while his son and Michael Haydn are the Konzertmeister. There are eight male singers plus choirboys and three organists. The orchestra has a further twelve string players, two bassoons and three oboes and horns.

J. S. Duplessis
pinx parisis 1772

C. W. GLUCK AND THE REFORM OF OPERA

JULIAN RUSHTON

Opposite: Christoph Willibald Gluck (1714-87), a portrait painted in Paris in 1775 by J. S. Duplessis.

Certain periods in musical history stand out as possessing a general significance, for reasons both historical and symbolic. The decade leading to Monteverdi's *Orfeo* of 1607 was one such; so was the decade leading to Gluck's *Orfeo* of 1762. Monteverdi's work, itself a product of the Renaissance, marks the beginning of baroque opera as a mature art form. Gluck's marks a new approach to the dramatic construction and meaning of serious operas, and was to remain a potent influence at least until Wagner.

Gluck's early musical output gave little clue as to his later operatic achievement, though opera was his chosen field from the start. Musical studies in Prague, Vienna and Milan culminated in 1745 in an invitation to work for the Italian opera in England and the first publication of his work: a set of trio-sonatas (his only instrumental opus apart from ballets) and several arias recycled from his compositions to date – eight operas written in Italy between 1741 and 1745. The next few years saw Gluck traveling round Europe, doubtless seeking regular employment, and producing several successful operas for various musical centers, none of which resulted in a permanent post. The mid-1750s found him settled in Vienna, established as a competent and successful composer of traditional *opera seria* (several of his operas had libretti by Metastasio). His work at this stage shows outstanding inventiveness but no involvement in operatic reform.

Gluck never wrote an *opera buffa*. It was, however, in the comic genre that the liveliest developments in Italian opera were to be found during the 1750s, building on a considerable foundation of comedies including *intermezzi*. The principal librettist of this period, Carlo Goldoni, who was also a major playwright, introduced serious characters into works that were frequently subtitled *dramma giocoso* – the designation later given by da Ponte to Mozart's *Don Giovanni* and *Così fan tutte* – and his more elaborate comedies provide the main link with the early *buffo* works, themselves not far removed in plot from the improvised theater, although more highly developed musically. Goldoni collaborated with Baldassare Galuppi in a series of comic operas throughout the 1750s, and the vivid realism, recalling Goldoni's comic plays, the ingenious twists of plot and variety of action make those works more than significant forerunners.

One of the main achievements of the Goldoni-Galuppi collaboration was the development of the extended concerted finale. The last stages of plot are organized into a loosely constructed musical number in several sections of varying speeds (but showing a propensity to accelerate). By the time Mozart composed the greatest examples of this genre it was almost outdated. After Galuppi it had been developed by others such as Niccolò Piccinni, one of the principal composers of the generation born in the 1720s. Piccinni turned his hand to serious opera as well, but his greatest triumph, and one of the most successful operas of the later eighteenth century, was a comedy based on Richardson's *Pamela*. La Cecchina, ossia La Buona figliuola* was first performed at Rome in 1760; the libretto, by Goldoni, had already been used by Egidio Duni. Piccinni is sometimes credited with the creation of the *buffo* finale; but the credit really belongs to the librettist.

The rapid development of *opera buffa* into a complex art-form capable of appeal to all types and nations was paralleled by the development of an indigenous form of musical comedy in France. French comic opera had hitherto existed mainly in the fairground, and even so it was repeatedly banned because the Académie Royale de Musique had a monopoly of musical theater. At this time, however, the comedy found its Goldoni in Charles-Simon Favart (after whom the Opéra Comique in Paris is still named), whose libretti turned a popular, largely improvised theater into a minor literary genre. At the same time a clutch of good composers took an interest in *opéra comique*. Among them was Duni, who came to France in 1756, the year of his setting of Goldoni's *La Cecchina*. His collaboration with Favart included *Ninette à la cour* (1756); *La Fille mal gardée* (1758); and *Les Moissonneurs* (1768). The last-named, based on the biblical story of Ruth, considerably widened the scope of *opéra comique* towards the serious and tearful – the *comédie larmoyante* fashionable at the time under the influence of the Encyclopedist Denis Diderot.

French composers were quick to take up the challenge. At the forefront was François-André Danican Philidor, whose brilliant one-act opera, *Blaise le savetier*, was performed in one of the fairground theaters in 1759. Few composers before Philidor could so convincingly combine disparate feelings into a lucid confusion. Most

237

Right: Count Durazzo (1714-87), director of court spectacles and chamber music at the Viennese court for ten years from 1754. He favored the *opéras comiques* and *opéras ballets* popularized by Favart in Paris, and brought Gluck to Vienna where, as director of the Court Theater, he composed eight *opéras comiques* as well as Italian operas.

J. COMTE DE DURAZZO
Noble Genois
Ambassadeur Imperial a Venise

Below: Carlo Goldoni (1707-93), the Venetian dramatist, whose collaboration, from 1749, with Baldassare Galuppi laid the foundation for *opera buffa* in the second half of the century. The first opera based on one of his works was, in fact, Gluck's *Tigrane* (1743).

CARL GOLDONI.

of his works contain excellent quartets, quintets or even septets, as well as duets and arias both vigorous and sentimental. The tearful element creeps into the mostly boisterous *Tom Jones* (1765), and the musical techniques are those of modern Italian serious opera, such as had not yet been heard on the French stage (although it was enjoyed in concerts). When his heroine is left alone in a hostile environment, she sings an impressive orchestrated recitative, in which the solo wind is deployed with a skill anticipating Mozart, and a full-length Italian aria. Small wonder that Philidor's next work, *Ernelinde*, was a new kind of tragedy-opera, in which the musical idiom of Italy, particularly the full-length arias, at last reached the stage of the Académie Royale.

Curiously enough, comic opera in French was being developed on similar lines, at the same time, by Gluck in Vienna. Although for most of the eighteenth century Vienna was more receptive to Italian than to any other kind of opera, there were periodic flirtations, usually centered around the court, with opera in other languages. French became fashionable in the early 1750s, and Gluck was engaged by Count Durazzo in 1754 to nourish this interest, alongside Favart. He produced eight original *opéras comiques*, varying in character from mythological fantasy or rollicking humor to oriental farce. The last of them, *La Rencontre imprévue* (The Pilgrims to Mecca), was Gluck's most often performed work and, in German translation, played a part in the revival of German-language opera. The music of these works was straightforward at first; it was here that Gluck learned the virtues of directness and simplicity of expression. By *La Rencontre*, however, without sacrificing these qualities, he was also able to incorporate scenes approaching the measured grandeur of *opera seria*. The increasing vocal and instrumental elaboration parallels that of native French *opéra comique*.

• Italian operatic reform •

The condition of Italian opera in the 1750s was rather more complicated than is usually realized. It was not simply divided between a lively and developing *buffo* genre and a creaking tragic genre founded on the libretti of Metastasio and his imitators. New ways of writing serious opera did not appear from nowhere; nor did they banish the old. Gluck did not reform *Italian* opera; he participated in a reforming movement in the Austrian capital, where opera was usually in Italian. He did not thrust himself forward as a reformer; he was chosen. Only later did he take the initiative in reforming movements, and then mainly in his association with Paris.

The type of operatic entertainment cultivated in any large city would depend on the demand. If that were for a dignified spectacle full of fine singing, *opera seria* would suffice; but if something shorter, more varied, or more suited to celebration was required, other forms were called into play such as the rather neutral *azione teatrale* or, more suited to a special occasion, *festa teatrale*. Metastasio contributed to these types of entertainment, as befitted a court poet; Gluck's earlier Metastasian works included *La Contesa de' numi* and *Le Cinesi*. He later set Metastasio's *serenata, Il Parnasso confuso*. After 1760 the Viennese court turned mainly to Metastasio's favorite composer, Hasse. Gluck was by then firmly in the reformist camp. Nevertheless *Orfeo* belongs to this genre, its subtitle *azione teatrale* reflecting its complete distinctness from *opera seria*, with which, in truth, it has no connection. The characteristics of *feste teatrali* which distinguished them from the *dramma per musica* (the usual title for *opera seria*) included the use of mythological subject-matter, whereas traditional music-drama was based mostly on historical palace intrigue. Mythology's supernatural beings needed complicated stage machinery, and it therefore follows that *feste* were the prerogative of court, rather than public theaters.

In France the general rift between the *ancien régime* and the brilliant Encyclopedists who took the *bouffon* side in the famous *Querelle des Bouffons* of 1752 was symbolized by the lively Italian *intermezzo* and the *opéra comique* sniping at the grandiose lyric tragedy at court and Académie. It is therefore a curious paradox that the unregenerate French *tragédie lyrique* should contribute to the reforming movements in Italian opera, and that the first masterpiece in which the main reform is manifested should be in the courtly genre of *azione teatrale*; for Gluck's *Orfeo* is also a product of intellectual enlightenment.

There was considerable dissatisfaction with the form of Metastasian *dramma per musica* even among those who cultivated its musical style. By the 1750s, however, that style was changing. The structure – plot in recitative and exploration of feeling in aria – served well the musical language of the early eighteenth century (the 'late Baroque'), as represented by such

Right: Pietro Metastasio (1698-1782), court poet in Vienna since 1730 and the grey eminence of *opera seria* throughout its last flowering.

masters as Handel, Bach (in cantatas and Passions) and Hasse. But a change in musical idiom emanated from Italy itself. From the Neapolitan *intermezzo* there emerged a new style. The baroque counterpoint of a singing voice against a driving, melodically independent bass gave way to a melodic line supported by simple chords and rhythmic propulsion; elegantly ornate melody, and in faster pieces the repartee of short motifs, came to dominate musical forms. The classical orchestra was born when the fixed instrumentation of the late Baroque, with selected forces almost continuously in play, was replaced by a larger group deployed in varied combinations.

The change of musical style was slower to affect vocal music. At first the internal style of the aria was modified, without affecting the increasingly swollen dimensions of the *da capo* form. Yet a modification of musical style should create a new framework; such new forms were being developed in comedy, and the artificiality which, properly speaking, is one of the virtues of *opera seria*, became dangerous. The later works in the *opera seria* tradition are often strikingly beautiful; among the loveliest, and best-known, are two early works written for Milan by Mozart in his teens, *Mitridate* and *Lucio Silla* (1770 and 1772). But like some of Gluck's, Haydn's or Jommelli's works in this form, they strain the patience of the listener because the potency of the musical language is scarcely accommodated to the stiffness of the forms.

The Encyclopedists understood this; in criticizing the French opera and praising Italian music, d'Alembert, for example (*De la liberté de la musique*, 1759), proposed adapting the Italian musical idiom to French dramatic forms. The Italian *philosophe* Francesco Algarotti, who imbibed French ideas at the court of Frederick II at Potsdam in the early 1750s, returned to Italy and in 1755 published his *Saggio sopra l'opera in musica*, in which he insisted upon the primacy of drama in opera, to which singing,

PIETRO METASTASIO
Poeta Cesareo

staging, even poetry itself, must be subordinated. He concluded with a libretto in French, *Iphigénie en Aulide*, based on Racine's *Iphigénie* and thus indirectly on Euripides; it is likely that Gluck had this example in mind when he chose this subject for his first venture into French serious opera in the early 1770s. Algarotti found a place for chorus, ballet and spectacle in an integrated drama, thus recognizing the original intentions of the founders of French opera of creating a reunion of the arts.

At the same period, French opera came to influence Italian by the most direct means, the translation of libretti and their new setting in Italian. The culmination of this movement was certainly Mozart's *Idomeneo*, written for the Munich court in 1781; but the tendency goes back to the 1750s and centered at first on Parma, where the duchy was in the hands of the Bourbons and the theatrical intendant was a Frenchman, Guillaume du Tillot. Tommaso Traetta was appointed court composer in 1758, when he was just over thirty and had served his apprenticeship composing operas to libretti by Metastasio. The Parmesan court poet Frugoni translated the libretto of Rameau's first opera, and Traetta's *Ippolito ed Aricia* was performed in Parma in 1759, followed the next year by *I Tintaridi* (after Rameau's *Castor et Pollux*). Traetta included some of Rameau's dance music, but he brought to the solo vocal writing a mature Italian idiom which extended certain scenes beyond the scale of the original conception, and so altered the balance of the structure. Nor did he entirely renounce ornament in favor of that simplicity which Gluck, in similar circumstances, was to cultivate. In 1761 Traetta's setting of an

Below: Frontispiece and list of characters for Metastasio's *La Semiramide Riconosciuta*. Gluck's early Italian operas were mostly based on libretti by Metastasio; *Semiramide*, his twelfth opera, written for Vienna in 1748, marks his coming of age as an operatic composer.

PERSONAGGI.

SEMIRAMIDE *in abito virile sotto nome di Nino Re degli Assiri, Amante di Scitalce, conosciuto, ed amato da lei antecedentemente nella Corte d'Egitto come Idreno.*

MIRTEO *Principe Reale di Egitto fratello di Semiramide da lui non conosciuta, ed Amante di Tamiri.*

IRCANO *Principe Scita amante di Tamiri.*

SCITALCE *Principe Reale di una parte dell'Indie, creduto Idreno da Semiramide, pretensore di Tamiri, ed Amante di Semiramide.*

TAMIRI *Principessa Reale de' Battriani, Amante di Scitalce.*

SIBARI *Confidente, ed Amante occulto di Semiramide.*

DEL-

Italian version of Quinault's *Armide* was produced in Vienna; one of the translators was none other than Count Durazzo.

The connection of the Parmesan with the Viennese reform is thus clearly established. Durazzo, who had fostered Gluck's production of French works, was set on a course of deliberate opposition to Metastasio which had manifested itself as early as 1755. Some commentators have even dated the Gluck reform as far back as the production that year of *L'Innocenza giustificata*, a *festa teatrale* with aria texts by Metastasio and recitative by Durazzo. *L'Innocenza* is not, however, a strong enough work to bear the weight of reform or polemic. It consists mainly of conventional recitatives and elaborate arias. At the end, though, something of that directness of expression was introduced which Gluck was to cultivate in greater works.

Whether Gluck or Traetta, or indeed Algarotti or Durazzo, played the major role in operatic reform is not a question of much interest. What matters is that certain ideas were widely

current in the 1750s, and the leading spirits were usually poets or impresarios rather than musicians. Gluck's next works after *L'Innocenza* used popular libretti by Metastasio; they were *Antigono*, for Rome, and *Il Rè pastore*, for Vienna, both 1756. Mozart, who was born that year, set the latter text in 1775.

It needed a librettist to decree new operatic forms, and fortunately there were a number about this time who were willing to try. One such was Mattia Verazi, who in 1762 adapted *Sofonisba*, a libretto of Metastasio's predecessor, Zeno, for Traetta. Verazi also wrote for Niccolò Jommelli, who produced a series of remarkable Italian operas for the court of Stuttgart between 1753 and 1768 using libretti by Metastasio, but also a number of new texts, in which French influence is more apparent in the use of mythological subjects, spectacle, chorus and dances. The last opera of the German period, Jommelli's *Fetonte* (1768), has a libretto by Verazi. This work shows some consciousness of what Gluck had already done. Its overture is left incomplete, going straight into the first number, which also challenges convention by combining aria with chorus. However, despite the almost continuous music of the finale, nothing

in *Fetonte* challenges the Italianate conventions so clearly as do the libretti of Marco Coltellini, set by Traetta and Gluck. Traetta's *Ifigenia in Tauride* (Vienna, 1763) is virtually a reformed tragic opera, and it precedes the first reformist tragedy of Gluck by four years. Gluck set one Coltellini libretto, *Telemaco*. But the librettist who counts for most in this reform collaborated mainly with Gluck; he was Raniero da Calzabigi, who had previously edited a fine edition of Metastasio with a flattering preface, but who now joined Durazzo's faction in opposing the influence of the court poet.

• *Don Juan* and *Orfeo* •

One more element needs to be discerned before *Orfeo* itself is considered: the importance of gesture, acting, dance and mime. In this period the traditional dancing-master, who devised steps for formalized meters, was being challenged by choreographers who aimed by dancing, gesture and mime to convey powerful emotions; and they required appropriately vivid music which did not necessarily fall into the customary dance meters. Thus while we may attribute to French influence the presence of dancing in these reformed operas, the manner in which it was used, at least before the final celebratory scenes, was quite new. Gluck had already tried his hand at an 'action ballet,' as the new genre came to be called. His *Don Juan*, choreographed and danced by Gasparo Angiolini, was given at the Viennese court in October 1761.

Angiolini was one of the great dancers of the age. His intention, which he formulated simultaneously with his more successful rival Noverre, was to return to the art of pantomime the dramatic force it was believed to have had in ancient times. The courtly symmetry of dance was abandoned for a stylized realism, even expressionism,

Above and opposite top: Il Parnasso confuso, a *serenata* by Metastasio set by Gluck and performed for the Viennese court at the palace of Schönbrunn in 1765 by the Empress's children as a surprise celebration of their brother Joseph II's second marriage, to Princess Josepha of Bavaria. Archduke Leopold played and conducted the orchestra, the youngest children danced, while on stage here are the Archduchesses Marianna, Maria Christina, Elisabeth and Maria Carolina.

Left: Victory and Reward of German Music, an allegorical print by Hieronymus Löschenkohl, published on Gluck's death in 1787. The composer left Vienna for Paris in 1772 and composed no more operas during his retirement back in Vienna after 1780. Despite this, and the fact that he wrote no operas to German libretti, his *La Rencontre imprévue*, 1764, was frequently performed in German, as *Die Pilgrime von Mekka*, and he was seen by contemporaries as one of the founders of a national style.

Angiolini's ideals bear some resemblance to those of David Garrick in the spoken theater; Garrick actually coached Gaetano Guadagni, Gluck's first Orpheus.

Directness, emotional intensity, freedom from mere ornament, and eschewal of conventional formulae in the interests of penetrating to the emotional heart of a subject, are ideals shared and manifest in works earlier than the masterpiece which united the reformers' efforts, *Orfeo*. In some senses this *azione teatrale* is not the beginning of a reform, but a culmination. Performed for the Emperor's birthday in 1762, it was designed, as was *Don Juan*, by one of the ubiquitous Quaglio family, choreographed by Angiolini, sung and acted by Guadagni and promoted by Durazzo; these contributions, all irretrievably lost, combined with what survives, Calzabigi's poetry and Gluck's music, make *Orfeo* one of the theatrical events of the century.

Our understanding of *Orfeo*, despite growing knowledge of contemporary stagecraft, dance and spectacle, is of a fusion of poetry and music; and there is no doubt that, in this collaboration, the poet was the leader. Even in Paris, when Gluck certainly assumed a dominating role in collaboration with librettists, and was a veritable tyrant in the opera house itself, he acknowledged Calzabigi's leading role in their first collaboration. Calzabigi later claimed some of the credit for the music itself, but this need hardly be taken seriously. A certain rivalry was to develop between the two men, but in fact Calzabigi needed Gluck as much as Gluck needed Calzabigi; the latter had only a mediocre success in collaboration even with such a talented composer as Paisiello (*L'Elfrida* and *Elvira*, both performed at Naples in 1792 and 1794 respectively), in spite of the fact that without doubt he was one of the best poets for music of his time; his verses have a clarity and polish worthy of Metastasio, but without the artificiality of the older poet. Without him and Durazzo, as well as Angiolini, Gluck would probably have remained among the more original composers of a conventional genre, a less fluent, more rugged version of Jommelli. Since *Orfeo* is an *azione teatrale*, not an *opera seria*, the presence of spectacle, ballet and chorus can have occasioned little surprise. What is so striking is the manner in which they are used, and while the musician rose superbly to the occasion, it must have been the poet who conceived the new pattern and put it into execution; doubtless French dramatic forms played an influential part.

The subject matter of *Orfeo* in no way tallies with the celebratory nature of its first performance, and the opera has been roundly abused for its spirited overture, which matches the happy ending of the finale but fails to set the tragic mood of the work in general and the opening scene in particular, which has often been compared to the tomb scene in Rameau's *Castor et Pollux*. The first act, and indeed the second, are highly unified schemes, yet they rely for dramatic and musical effect on contrast: the

conveying the violent passions of characters in a drama. Particularly in *Semiramis* (1765), the other surviving Gluck-Angiolini ballet score, the dramatic force is reflected in the incompleteness of musical numbers, which run into each other with abrupt, almost perverse, discontinuities of speed and mood.

Don Juan is the more balanced and artistically successful work. The contrast between social elegance and tragic action was superbly expressed through Gluck's sensitive and dramatic score, culminating at the end of the ballet in the immense dance of demons (later to be re-used in the French version of *Orfeo*), excelling even the most impressive orchestral effects of French opera.

Don Juan was accompanied by a manifesto in which Angiolini set out his intentions clearly; it is probable that Calzabigi had a hand in it, as he

Right: Le Triomphe de l'amour (still with Gluck's music) was the younger children's chance to perform for their brother's wedding: Ferdinand and Maxmilian and their sister Antonia (Marie Antoinette) were attended by members of the noble families of Clary, Fürstenberg and Auersperg.

isolation of the individual against the expressive ritualistic forces of the chorus; the richness of the orchestral texture enhanced by contrast with Gluck's habitual austerity. Act III is more conventional in its musical gestures, but this is precisely because the drama now takes place on a purely human level. Orpheus, the demigod, who has conquered the Underworld, fails to command the emotions of his wife. Although the happy ending appears contrived, Gluck's music for most of this act is no less powerful than for the first two; and it sets the tone for the operas that followed, all of which, despite occasional divine intervention, are essentially human dramas.

• After *Orfeo* •

Orfeo itself was widely played, but it did not exactly take Europe by storm, and its publication passed almost unnoticed. Gluck then undertook various commissions, including his last and finest French comedy, *La Rencontre imprévue*, and *Il Trionfo di Clelia* (text by Metastasio; Bologna, 1763), a festive piece, in which Gluck made some alterations to the text and followed up his practice in *Orfeo* by accompanying much of

Below: Orpheus leading his wife Eurydice back from the Underworld – a scene from Act II of Gluck's *Orfeo*, from the first edition published in Paris in 1764.

Euridice amor ti rende.   atto II Sce II.

C. Monnet inv. del. 1764.   N. le Mire Sculp.

the recitative with the orchestra. The same applies to his collaboration with Coltellini, *Telemaco* (Vienna, 1765), in which the principal character is the sorceress Circe; it includes much orchestral recitative and some ensembles, as well as grouped movements involving chorus, solo and dance. These bring *Telemaco* into line with one principle of reform, the flexibility of forms, characteristic of French opera rather than Italian throughout the eighteenth century but now, with Traetta and Gluck, given a quite different flavor.

The Italianate musical idiom, both in Traetta's *Ifigenia* and Gluck's *Telemaco*, is adapted to serve a new kind of design. The vocal parts are still profusely ornamented, but the lengthy arias are fewer, and there are several shorter arias or fragments of aria interspersed into the recitative. Even Traetta's finest works, however, such as his *Sofonisba* (libretto by Verazi; Mannheim, 1762) and *Antigone* (Coltellini; St Petersburg, 1772), do not attain that piercing simplicity of which Gluck was increasingly the master. Their beauties are softer, suited to the type of magical subject which Gluck tackled in *Telemaco* and *Armide* rather than to the complex passions of Greek tragedy.

Gluck produced a few occasional one-act works, and a work in the tradition of French opera-ballet, *Le Feste d'Apollo*. Such pieces may seem retrogressive within the genre of *festa teatrale* but they have nothing to do with tragic opera and still less to do with *opera seria*; Gluck's last work properly so called dates from 1756. But in 1767 he and Calzabigi produced a work whose very nature challenged *opera seria* directly: *Alceste*, the final watershed of Gluck's career. In its publication, in 1769, was included the famous manifesto in which Gluck wrote: 'I have striven to restrict music to its true office of serving poetry by means of expression and by following the situation of the story, without interrupting the action or stifling it with a useless superfluity of ornaments; and I believe that it should do this in the same way as telling colors affect a correct and well-ordered drawing, by a well-assorted contrast of light and shade, which serves to animate the figures without altering their contours.'

What is most obviously new about *Alceste* is its uncompromising tragic coloring. This time the overture does not anticipate the happy ending; it begins with sounds of impending doom, a severe striding figure in the basses followed by plaintive cries from the wind. In the manifesto it is stated that the overture should prepare the minds of the spectators for what is to come, and 'so to speak, unveil the plot.' The innovation of having the overture linked to the first scene was improved on by Gluck in *Iphigénie en Aulide*. There the curtain rises as the opening phrase returns, actually sung. Gluck's reform of the overture was among the most readily acceptable of his ideas; with Mozart's *Don Giovanni* it even entered the realm of *opera buffa*.

Alceste employs similar means to *Orfeo* – the mingling of chorus, solo and dance into

reforming gesture it must be accounted a failure, for it would be impossible to imitate its formal and dramatic innovations other than by copying them or watering them down; they are already carried out to an extreme degree. Gluck himself recognized that *Alceste* went too far when he adapted it for Paris, and it is the later version, in which the sheer monumentality of the original is diluted, which has nearly always been used in performance. *Alceste* was certainly influential. The orchestral forces are Gluck's largest; even in later works he seldom wrote for oboes and clarinets in the same movements or wrote such extensive parts for trombones. *Alceste* gave impetus to the development of larger orchestras around the turn of the century. More important than weight of scoring, however, is its expressiveness; the orchestra goes beyond its function in *Orfeo*, echoing accents of mourning or painting a scene, and now seems to have a voice of its own in the drama, expressing what the characters cannot see or say. This is particularly so in the infernal scenes; the Wagnerian orchestra seems to begin here.

Left: Title-page of the libretto of *Orphée*, the later amplified version of Gluck's opera, published for its first Paris performance in 1774 – on which the original librettist Calzabigi's name does not appear. It is dedicated to the composer's former pupil, Marie Antoinette, now Queen of France.

Left: Gluck's autograph for the first scene of Act II of *Orphée*: Orpheus at the entrance to Hades calms the demons and furies. In Paris in 1774 the title-role was sung by Joseph Legros while Madeleine Sophie Arnould sang Eurydice and Rosalie Levasseur L'Amour.

tableaux – to create a totally different atmosphere. The principal character is no longer a demigod, but a wife and mother who is also a queen; the subject may be mythological, and supernatural elements are indispensable to it, but the setting is no longer Arcadian. The chorus represents ordinary people in a political setting recognizably modern; they are only too human, which is why the work challenges *opera seria* on its own level and shows it to be almost irredeemably frivolous in its approach to major human issues.

Alcestis herself is poignantly real. Her famous aria 'Ombre, larve' illustrates a crucial aspect of Gluck's reform. Gluck declared that he wanted to get rid of superfluous ornament, and also to avoid hurrying over the middle section of an aria, which is often the most expressive. The reference is specifically to the *da capo* aria, in which an eloquent middle section is indeed often rather cursory, so that it is lost between the two statements of the huge main section. Gluck departs from the *da capo* form altogether, and his form is devised specifically for the occasion. The main idea comes three times, separated by two tender episodes and, before the last return, a sudden faster section in which Alcestis feels the new strength her resolution to die has given her. The musical language is dangerously simple and, especially in this section, more reminiscent of *opéra comique* than *opera seria*. Gluck was occasionally criticized, by those who went to the opera to be soothed and entertained, for the crudity of his musical language; but those willing to experience harrowing emotions in the theater can perceive the rightness of his solution. He lays bare the flesh of feeling, which the slightest elegance would have covered.

Alone among Gluck's operas of the 1760s, *Alceste* was not written for a special occasion, nor to fit any conventional framework. As a

That Gluck and Calzabigi now felt they had reached the end of a road is suggested by their last collaboration, *Paride ed Elena*. This is a remarkable dramatic experiment, for its action is nearly all psychological. Gluck pointed with pride to the differentiation of national types, the rugged Spartans and effete Trojans, but this is merely the backcloth to the wooing of Helen, from her courteous reception of Paris as a stranger, through her indignant refusal of his advances and her growing fascination with him, to her yielding and elopement.

The work is in five acts, with a good deal of recitative, and Gluck reverts to his practice in *Orfeo* of orchestrating all of it. The advantages of expressiveness and depth of musical response meant that orchestral recitative soon became

Paride, and numerous French comedies, had prepared him to meet French expectations half-way. What Gluck certainly did was to demonstrate the obsolete nature of French musical style; he obliterated the watered-down Rameau practiced by several French composers of his own generation or even younger. And in this he merely succeeded in doing what had already been tried by Philidor in *Ernelinde*; the French dramatic form, with its blend of solo and chorus in short and flexible units, its integrated ballet and spectacle, remained unchanged in essence. Gluck fulfilled the prescription of d'Alembert: retain the French form while modernizing the music.

Gluck succeeded because he worked gradually, and in some sense backwards. Among the most evidently French in character of his last operas is *Iphigénie en Aulide*; the least French of them, though possibly the greatest, is *Iphigénie en Tauride*, in which his lifelong habit of

the norm. But its virtues are diminished by abundance, and both *Paride* and *Iphigénie en Aulide* suffer from this.

Nevertheless *Paride* gave Gluck the opportunity for some of his most penetrating and truly dramatic music. Paris, a character with one aim, sings in a direct and melodious style; some of his songs are among Gluck's loveliest inspirations. Helen's greater complexity is revealed in her arias. The dances, removed from *Paride* to the French *Alceste*, seem a little out of place; it appears that Gluck did not fully appreciate the integrity of his last Italian opera, or at least, practical man of the theater as he was, could see no way of accommodating it to French taste. His thoughts were already turning to the French capital; in 1772 Burney visited Gluck and reported that he was given a complete rendering of *Iphigénie en Aulide*.

· Gluck in France ·

With hindsight, it may seem that Gluck's whole career from the 1750s onwards constituted a preparation for his final and greatest achievement, the conquest of Paris. With the support of his former pupil, the Dauphine (soon Queen Marie-Antoinette), he was able to gain the consent of the management of the Paris Opéra to mount his *Iphigénie en Aulide*; in their turn, the directors, quickly seeing that such a work would kill the old French operatic style once and for all, insisted upon his producing at least six operas for them. In fact Lully's *Thésée* lingered on until 1779, and Rameau's *Castor et Pollux* was revived in 1781, but they were the last flickering embers of a once-great fire, and both soon suffered the indignity of having one or two favorite numbers used within what was otherwise an entirely new setting of their libretti (*Thésée*, by Gossec, 1782; *Castor*, by Candeille, 1791).

Yet Gluck did not revolutionize French opera. He reformed it; but he was only able to do so because his experience in *Orfeo*, *Alceste*, and

Top left: Finale of Act I from Gluck's autograph score of *Armide*, with its powerful writing for soloists and chorus. They call for merciless pursuit of the enemy ('poursuivons jusqu'au trépas l'ennemi qui nous offense').

Above: Portrait of Pierre Alexandre Monsigny (1729-1817) by Charles Thévenin. Monsigny's sentimental *opéras comiques* written in the sixties and seventies continued to be popular in Paris in the years following the Revolution.

Opposite: Miniature of the operatic composer André-Ernest-Modeste Grétry (1741-1813) in 1790. His *Mémoires*, or essays, on music, published the previous year, show his strong support for Gluck's ideas on lyric theater.

Above: Madame Favart in Gilbert's opera *Les Trois sultanes* (1761). Marie Duronceray (1727-72) was the wife of Charles Favart, director of the Opéra Comique of the Foire, and she fiercely opposed the Italian musicians in Paris. She appeared in many operas by Grétry, Monsigny and Philidor, for all of whom her husband wrote libretti.

Above right: Costume design for Philidor's pioneering opera *Ernelinde, princesse de Norvège*, performed at the Paris Opéra in 1767.

reusing older music is triumphantly vindicated in a work whose flexibility of musical form accommodates Italianate arias as well as much of the ballet *Semiramis*.

Gluck did not attempt to transfer the monumentality of the Italian *Alceste* to French opera. He continued to use flexible aria forms, in several tempi, disregarding the criticism of Rousseau that 'this is not an air, but a suite of several airs'; and he devised within the confines of his own musical language a very French blend of declamatory music, neither recitative nor aria, in which lyrical and dramatic utterances can flow spontaneously into each other as the sense of a character's thought dictates. His comic operas, rather than the Calzabigi ones, prepared the way for the precise characterization which is so remarkable a feature of the *Iphigénie* operas, and of *Armide*. In the latter Gluck justifiably claimed that the listener could tell who was

singing, Armida or one of her servants, by the musical style alone. Equally, Iphigenia, the young, affectionate, and courageous heroine, is sharply distinguished from her anguished and ferocious mother Clytemnestra; while the hot-headed Achilles is contrasted with the arrogant but guilt-ridden Agamemnon. This is a new type of opera, closer to the spirit and complexity of spoken drama, Greek or Racinian, than opera had ever been before.

Perhaps because of the very energy of the characterizaton, and the dramatic potency of the flexible forms, the traditionalist party received *Iphigénie en Aulide* coolly, and particularly criticized Gluck for neglecting the ballet. Gluck's most remarkable achievement – getting the French chorus to move about naturally rather than standing in rigid lines – was probably not seen as a choreographic element, although it derived from his work with Angiolini.

So well, however, did Gluck adapt himself to French taste that he was soon opposed by an Italian party. In 1774 he produced *Iphigénie en Aulide* with great success and also *Orphée*, an undisputed triumph. The following year his comedy *Cythère assiégée*, fleshed out into a full-length entertainment, failed to please; and in 1776 *Alceste*, fully revised to a form approaching that of *Aulide*, was at first deemed too dismal to be borne. At this point a journalistic war, which had begun as a mild affray between Gluck and the traditionalists in 1774, broke out in earnest. The anti-Gluck party included severe traditionalists, who argued that tragedy was the business of spoken drama and that

Above: Design by Pierre Adrien Paris for the prison of Orestes and Pylades in the original production of Gluck's last great tragic opera, *Iphigénie en Tauride,* first performed at the Paris Opéra in 1779.

opera was intended for the type of magical drama which united poetry, music and spectacle on an equal footing. This objection Gluck soon met by setting Quinault's *Armide* (1777), with scarcely any alteration to the original poem; the production is said to have used the same sets as that of 1686. It is astonishing how, in what is perhaps his most sensuous opera, Gluck accommodates the characteristic movement of eighteenth-century music to a seventeenth-century conception. The musical style, while remaining close to the spirit of Lully's setting, reveals complex and dramatic passions, and the work culminates in a furious symphonic catharsis.

Armide is certainly a great work, but it provided Gluck's enemies with the ammunition they required. It was obvious that he now belonged to the traditional party, and those who objected to him, because they considered opera to be entertainment which should not harrow their feelings, were brushed aside. The line of attack became purely musical. Gluck, it was argued, was pretending to reform French music on Italian lines; but he was no Italian, his music was uncouth, without melody, and he depended for effect on the braying of an outsize orchestra. Jean-François Marmontel was at least consistent with his Encyclopedist principles; he wanted to keep French forms, but to use a real Italian composer. Accordingly he rewrote several libretti by Quinault, retaining the spectacular and dance elements without mitigating their seriousness; indeed he made of *Atys* a more somber work than Quinault had. His alterations were intended to leave space for full-length Italianate arias and an occasional ensemble, for which he generally wrote new words. His party persuaded Niccolò Piccinni to come to Paris; the Italian composer arrived at the very end of 1776 (by which time *Alceste* had established itself) and witnessed the controversy surrounding *Armide* while composing his first opera in the French language, which he hardly understood. *Roland* was produced early in 1778.

In retrospect it is clear that Marmontel would have done better to send for Traetta; but the latter's fortunes were in decline. Piccinni, on the other hand, was at the height of his powers and probably the most successful composer in Italy. He showed himself, in his French works, able to rise to occasional dramatic heights; he was even, from time to time, considered to be imitating Gluck, for whom he felt a sincere admiration. *Roland* is a patchy work in which, curiously enough, the Italianate elements are the least successful, for their conventionality is too apparent. Only the title-role, composed for Larrivée (Gluck's Agamemnon and Orestes), breaks free of prettiness. One cannot but sympathize with Piccinni, who was out of his depth, and he deserves credit for some very good scenes, especially when the hero is mad.

Gluck had started to compose *Roland,* but destroyed his work when he heard that the opera management had commissioned Piccinni as well. In the event direct rivalry was arranged with *Iphigénie en Tauride,* but Piccinni's work was not produced until two years after Gluck's (although it was promised the first production), and direct comparisons, although many may be made, are affected by the different libretti (whereas in *Roland* both composers might have been setting the same words). One spectator at *Roland* was Mozart, on his second visit to Paris. *Idomeneo*, while evidently indebted to Gluck (as was Piccinni), is remarkably close to Piccinni's type of French opera, for it retains for their own sake the full-length arias and luscious orchestration that Gluck so rigorously eschewed.

• Last years •

After *Iphigénie en Tauride* Gluck wrote one more French opera, *Echo et Narcisse*, which was a disaster. Angry at its failure, he returned to Vienna to pass his declining years as court composer with a good salary but no duties. He later adapted *Tauride* as a German opera for Vienna; and this is the real culmination of his career. Many critics consider it, all round, to be his greatest work. Certainly it combines his powers of musical invention and development with a complete control of dramatic structure, to form a drama by turns exciting, frightening and touching. The background, in barbaric Scythia, is set by applying local color to the ballet and choral music: not only did Gluck use 'Turkish' instruments – cymbal, triangle and bass drum – he also devised a savagely angular musical idiom. The barbaric scene is integral to the drama, and the fierce, superstitious Scythian king is unerringly etched in a short aria. Nature, too, plays its part. The opera has no overture; it begins with the depiction of a calm sunrise, followed by a storm. Musically Gluck's storm may seem slight beside Beethoven's, but Wagner himself need not have been ashamed of the dramatic power this music has in the theater, especially when the voices of Iphigenia and her priestesses are raised in prayer against the tempest.

Some of the most effective touches in the libretto are attributable directly to Gluck himself. He was no longer the servant of his poet; the willing supporter of Calzabigi, the composer self-effacing enough to set an ancient libretto without alteration, is now the dramatist who not only tells his poet (N. F. Guillard) to rearrange certain scenes, but even dictates the meter of the verse. This is partly because he wished to set it to music which already existed; but that reinforces Gluck's dominance, for he planned the opera on the basis of its scenario, conceiving it as a musical-dramatic entity, and caused the poet to adjust his work to fit his musical scheme. Mozart was occasionally to do the same.

Little is now left of the monumental character of the Viennese 'reform' operas. The structure is varied to include longer arias within a flexible scheme in which lyrical recitative, lyrical utterance and short choruses can be combined in a virtually continuous unfolding. The orchestral recitative is kept from monotony by such devices as choral exclamations, as well as variation of accompanimental texture; along with that of *Armide*, it is Gluck's subtlest. The arias stand out as major dramatic statements, as they do in *Alceste*.

Once in Vienna Gluck wrote little more and, apart from the adaptation of *Iphigénie*, no more operas. He began to suffer strokes, and when Salieri departed for Paris to capitalize on the success there of his *Les Danaïdes*, Gluck bade him farewell in a mixture of three languages. He died in 1787, and Piccinni proposed, without success, the creation of a permanent memorial in Paris. Just before his death the greatest tribute to the power of the bodeful opening of *Alceste* was heard in Prague: the statue music in *Don Giovanni*. Mozart succeeded Gluck as court composer, on a fraction of his salary, and died only four years later.

Gluck's achievement may be summarized not as that of a successful reformer, but as that of a composer of outstanding individual works which contributed more than any others to the currents of change then flowing. He broke the established pattern whereby numerous operas could be composed to a single blueprint; his treatment of a subject became definitive, just as Goethe's *Faust* is definitive.

Above all, Gluck must be seen not as a harbinger of the nineteenth century, but as a man of his time, in whom certain tendencies took shape and reached fruition. His is the supreme achievement of neo-classicism in musical drama, a century after its climax in the spoken theater of Racine. It is appropriate that his first French work is based on Racine, while his last masterpiece shares the subject and indeed the date (1779) of Goethe's exercise in neo-classicism, *Iphigenia auf Tauris*.

Above: Rosalie Levasseur (1749-1826), leading soprano at the Paris Opéra from 1766 to 1785, who from 1776 took over all the leading roles in Gluck's operas, creating Alceste, Armide and Iphigénie en Tauride. She became a close friend of the composer and his leading interpreter.

Left: Madeleine Sophie Arnould (1744-1802), in the title-role of *Iphigénie en Aulide*, which she created with great success in 1774. Her Eurydice the same year was apparently not so well received.

247

The Keyboard Concerto

Harpsichord (*above*) built in Paris in 1786 by Pascal Taskin, probably for a child. Taskin made many improvements to the harpsichord – particularly the 'buff' stop using leather 'quills' and a mechanism to change register using the knees. Towards the end of his life he also began to manufacture pianos.

The triple concerto performed (*below*) at the court of Johann Theodor, Cardinal-Bishop of Liège, in 1753 would have been in the old baroque style, with passages for the soloists (including Johann Theodor himself playing the cello) alternating with *tutti* passages.

Mozart's piano concertos, some of the most perfect and most prophetic music of the classical age, were the result not only of the composer's individual genius, but also of parallel developments in musical style and in the technology of keyboard instruments. While the harmonic rhythm of a baroque concerto, underpinned by the continuo, was consistent through both *solo* and *tutti* passages, with the contrast evident principally in the texture and virtuosity of the solos, the classical concerto, depending on melodic development and harmonic modulation within sonata form, no longer had any need for a keyboard continuo, and soloist and orchestra were able to develop the thematic material in different ways. This more dramatic plan of the concerto – which could not have been realized with the limited dynamic scope of the harpsichord – was most fully carried out in the piano concerto, since the new instrument was not only harmonically self-sufficient, but also had a wide and expressive range of dynamics. It was this coincidence between the needs of the music and the characteristics of the instrument that led to the pianoforte's overwhelming success.

Above: Harpsichord built in London in 1777 by Jacob and Abraham Kirckman. By now all makers were looking for ways to make the instrument hold its own with the new piano: the compass was extended beyond five octaves and a variety of new stops were incorporated. Here the pedal on the right engages the 'nag's head swell,' a flap in the lid that produces a gradual crescendo.

Left: Mozart's concert piano, made by Anton Walter in Vienna, which the composer bought in 1784. In that and the following two years Mozart wrote twelve (all but the last two) of his mature piano concertos, most of which he himself performed on this instrument, which was transported to the concert hall wherever he was playing.

In 1795 Haydn brought back from England a piano by Longman and Broderip (*right*). English pianos tended to be more sturdily built and their action was heavier; this meant that they were less likely to go out of tune, but their tone was also less even; however, their damping action, *sopra una corda*, was much subtler.

The invention of the pianoforte was due to Bartolomeo Cristofori (1655-1731), who in 1698 in Florence produced an instrument he called 'gravicembalo col piano e forte.' Rather than plucking the strings, as in a harpsichord, or striking them by the direct action of a lever, as in a clavichord, hammers were used, and an escapement action was built into the mechanism, making it possible to control the force with which a hammer hit the string, but allowing it to fall straight back without the key having to be released (*see Volume II, p.49*).

The instrument below, made in 1720, is believed to be the earliest surviving Cristofori pianoforte. Although the invention was taken up by Gottfried Silbermann in Germany at the end of the 1720s, it was not until after 1750, when one of his apprentices, C. E. Friederici, started to make smaller instruments – and musical taste called for a keyboard instrument with both a powerful sound and the ability to interpret an expressive melodic line – that the new instrument began to gain general acceptance.

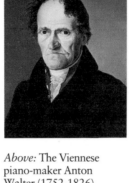

Above: The Viennese piano-maker Anton Walter (1752-1826), whose instruments were used by Mozart, although Haydn wrote to Frau von Genzinger in 1790 that only one instrument in ten could be described as good and that they were, in addition, very expensive.

Above: One of the finest surviving Walter pianos, built *c.* 1785. Mozart's Walter piano had a shallow fall of key, facilitating rapid playing, and he achieved his celebrated singing tone with sparing use of the pedal.

Right: A beautifully decorated upright piano made in the 1790s by Leopold Sauer in Prague.

Johann Christoph Zumpe was an apprentice of Gottfried Silbermann's who moved to England in 1760 with eleven other instrument-makers. Like Friederici, Zumpe concentrated on smaller instruments, 'square' pianos, in which the strings were laid out in a pattern similar to that used in the clavichord. He was extremely successful, doing much to oust the older types of instrument; the example above dates from 1767. J. C. Bach was an enthusiast for the new pianoforte, and played some of his op.5 Sonatas on a Zumpe instrument at a benefit concert given for the German oboist and composer J. C. Fischer in London in June 1768, apparently to a good reception. He also designated his op.7 Keyboard Concertos as being 'per il cembalo o Piano e Forte,' although the music shows no sign of his having really appreciated the musical possibilities offered by the new instrument.

Above: Performance of a harpsichord concerto, no doubt in the old-fashioned style, at a Zürich subscription concert in 1777. The four-part accompaniment is provided by pairs of flutes, violins, horns and a cello.

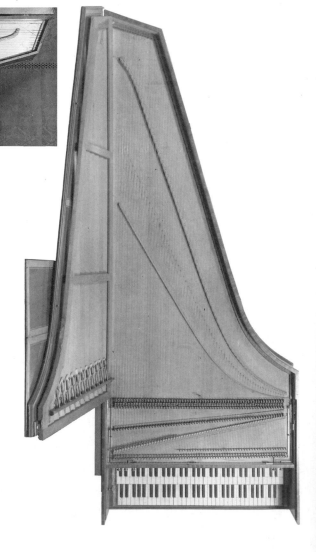

Below: Keyboard of a harpsichord made around 1725 by Thomas Hitchcock of London. The two manuals and three sets of strings allowed for changes in tone color, but these would only be made between movements, for neither did the music demand nor could the instrument make any change in registration in mid-performance.

Above: Soundboard of an English spinet made in 1770. This differed from a harpsichord in its size and in the placing of the keyboard at an angle to the strings, and it had only a single register. The spinet was still the principal keyboard instrument for domestic music-making, although the square piano was rapidly gaining popularity.

Right: Soundboard of a harpsichord made in London in 1782 by Burkat Shudi. Like many large concert harpsichords of this period the instrument has six stops, but it does not have the 'Venetian swell,' a device which was patented by Shudi in 1769 in an attempt to make the harpsichord capable of greater expressive variation.

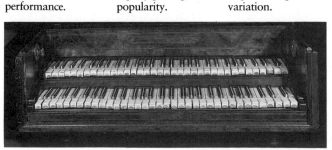

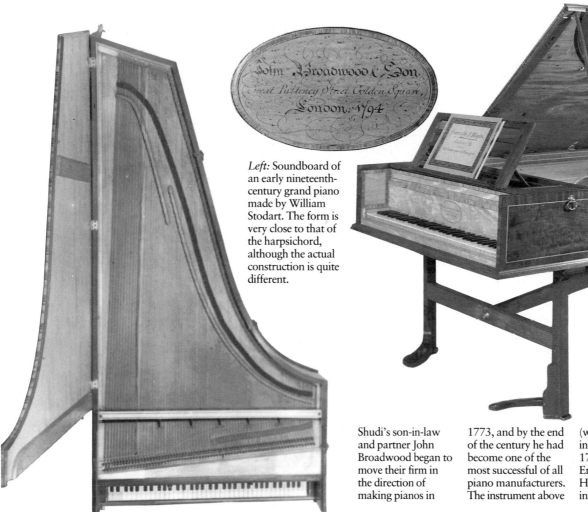

Left: Soundboard of an early nineteenth-century grand piano made by William Stodart. The form is very close to that of the harpsichord, although the actual construction is quite different.

Shudi's son-in-law and partner John Broadwood began to move their firm in the direction of making pianos in 1773, and by the end of the century he had become one of the most successful of all piano manufacturers. The instrument above (with a detail of its inlaid label), made in 1794, typifies the English pianos that Haydn got to know in London.

When Mozart wrote the Fantasia and Sonata in C minor (K.475 and K.457) dedicated to his pupil Therese von Trattner (*left*), he provided detailed instructions – unfortunately lost – for their performance, which must have given great insight into his attitude to the instrument. Something of the brilliance of his own improvisations can be imagined from the cadenzas he wrote out for his piano concertos. The examples below are for his A major Concerto (K.414), composed in the autumn of 1782.

Title-page and page with annotations for C. P. E. Bach's 1760 Sonatas 'for harpsichord' – almost certainly intended for the clavichord.

WOLFGANG AMADEUS MOZART

JULIAN RUSHTON

Opposite: Wolfgang Amadeus Mozart (1756-91) at the pianoforte in his apartment in Vienna; detail from an unfinished portrait by his brother-in-law Joseph Lange, probably painted in the years 1789 and 1790.

It was as a prodigy that Mozart first came to the attention of the public, and he may justifiably be considered in that light: not solely as an infant prodigy, but as the most prodigious talent ever to exercise itself in music. The time for such a phenomenon can never have been more propitious. Mozart was born into the heart of an age of musical internationalism, when even the previously impenetrable barriers separating French and Italian styles were being broken down, an age when the musical language of Europe was settling into patterns which could be assimilated in their totality.

Mozart possessed also a father who was prepared to abandon his own promising career as composer in order to cultivate the extraordinary gifts of his son. Leopold's advice, which forms a large part of a very remarkable family correspondence, may seem fussily protective, but he always had his son's interests at heart, and the young man's failure to win worldly success cannot be blamed on the father.

What makes Mozart eternally prodigious is the quality of his music, its richness of texture, its variety and its consistently high standard; in operas, its dramatic truth; in instrumental music its balance of lucidity and complexity, of form and expression; above all, to most listeners, its haunting beauty. Such perfection, paradoxically, can only be achieved by a marked lack of overt originality. Mozart's first manifestation of genius was the ability to copy – even to ape – and his right to be considered the most prodigious talent ever to exercise itself in music depends in part upon the conventionality of the language available to him, on his ability to manipulate a *lingua franca* of clearly understood terms with unmatched resourcefulness.

Mozart's supremacy also lies in his mastery of every available genre, whereas even the greatest composers are usually master of relatively few. In only two fields does Mozart's achievement seem comparatively slight: song, which scarcely existed then as a serious art-form, and to whose development some of his best work contributed; and sacred music, which was in any case going through a lean patch in the age of rationalism and in which Mozart's greatest works, the C minor Mass and the Requiem, are unfinished. In every other field Mozart may have peers, but he need yield to none.

Mozart's early life was dominated by travel, and by assimilation. The two went together; in provincial Salzburg, where his father was employed by the Prince-Archbishop, he could never have encountered such a profusion of musical styles. Of his first sixteen years, nearly seven were spent away from home, including one absence of over three years, and he was seldom at home for more than a few months. Nor were these periods used for recuperation, or assimilation of experience at leisure, for he entered regular, if ill-paid, employment at the court from an early age and had to produce both sacred and secular music at frequent intervals. It is small wonder that there is scant evidence of his interest in anything other than music.

The most important of young Mozart's journeys were the various forays to Vienna, of which the last became permanent; the two journeys through Germany to Paris, one as a prodigy, including a stay of over a year in England, the second as a twenty-one-year-old learning that the world now looked upon him with another face; and, perhaps most vital of all, the early visits to Italy. In Vienna he became acquainted with the capital of the empire in which he, like Haydn, was a provincial. In France he witnessed the most advanced of European societies, and in London he found a still more cosmopolitan capital and encountered Johann Christian, J. S. Bach's youngest son, whose training and predilection made him virtually an Italian composer. J. C. Bach was so much a major influence on Mozart that his own music today sounds Mozartian. In Italy Mozart came into direct contact with the fountainhead of his own musical language, the Italian opera, as well as the Italian academies which still maintained traditions of composition in strict or learned styles.

Salzburg, as a southern city of the Austrian domain, was much exposed to Italian culture; certainly it was not backward in assimilating recent trends in composition. From 1763 Salzburg was the home of Michael Haydn, who was among the foremost masters of advanced instrumental and church styles. From these various sources Mozart must have learned the tricks which he displayed in London, and it was not long after his return from there, aged eleven, that he was given the opportunity to compose the first act of a dramatic allegory, an oratorio for Lent called *Die Schuldigkeit des ersten Gebotes* (The obligation of the first commandment). The vocal and orchestral competence which this piece displays is developed in a Latin cantata,

Above: Title-page of Leopold Mozart's *School of Violin Playing*, published in his home town of Augsburg in the year of his son's birth.

Right: French print showing the Mozart family when Wolfgang was seven and his sister Nannerl eleven, at the time when their father was taking them round Europe to display their prodigious talent.

Far right: Title-page of Wolfgang's first published work (the two sonatas K.6 and K.7), completed when he was seven years old and published in Paris the same year with a dedication to the French Princess Victoire. Leopold took the engraver's plate to London the following year and had an English edition printed.

Apollo et Hyacinthus, composed between Easter and Trinity the same year (1767). The design of both works is essentially operatic; and although neither provided any occasion for that intricate penetration of character for which Mozart is rightly famous, they were valuable as a testing-ground for his sense of proportion in arias, and of the dramatic declamation of the recitatives.

Also in 1767 Gluck staged *Alceste*; the Mozarts attended a performance on a visit to Vienna in September. This was Mozart's second visit to the capital and included the first of many chagrins he experienced there. Leopold Mozart was reprimanded for being absent without leave and his salary was withheld. Then the *opera buffa* Mozart composed, *La Finta semplice*, was passed over by the theater management in favor of a revival of Piccinni's outstandingly successful *La Buona figliuola*. *La Finta semplice* is Mozart's first essay in Italian comic opera. Nothing in it could have justified a prediction that the composer would outstrip all his contemporaries in this genre; equally, nothing proclaims that the composer was still only a child.

Very much the same could be said of the early instrumental music. The earliest works, mainly for keyboard, are of childlike simplicity, but the London period (1765) saw a marked advance, perhaps through the encounter with J. C. Bach's sonatas (some of which Mozart arranged as piano concertos) and symphonies. The symphony at this time was essentially little different from an opera overture on the Italian model: a moderately fast movement, a slower lyrical movement, a high-spirited finale in a fast tempo. Such works could as well precede

an opera as occupy a lively opening or closing position in a concert. It was still many years before the word 'symphony' aroused public expectation of a work of high seriousness. Mozart learned to write symphonies in London as festive overtures, and this Italianate vigor remained with him even to his last symphony. The Viennese visit produced another half-dozen symphonies, one doubling as the overture to *La Finta semplice*. The time in Vienna was thus far from wasted and also included the performance of a short German-text opera, *Bastien und Bastienne*, in a private house in 1768. The première of *La Finta semplice* took place in Salzburg in May 1769. Doubtless Mozart's father had hoped to win fame and money by this work, and this provincial performance was hardly ideal; but at least the boy had the opportunity to see his characters fleshed out on the stage.

The next phase in Mozart's career, from 1770 to 1773, is governed by his three visits to Italy. On each of these he produced a dramatic work; and on the first and third, it was a full-scale *opera seria* for the prestigious theater at Milan. In Italy, where the education in the conservatories, notably those of Venice and Naples, was among the best in Europe, the boy Mozart was put through rigorous testing and duly admitted to the circles of learned musicians; he played at concerts and composed another half-dozen symphonies. But opera dominated the

scene and for the composer success in opera was the most lucrative, if hardly the most secure, means of gaining a livelihood.

Church music, too, was by no means moribund. The feat performed by Mozart in Rome in 1770 of taking down Allegri's *Miserere* from memory after a single hearing (as much a commentary on the simplicity of that beautiful work, as on the composer's abilities), is less important than his encounter with a tradition which extended back to the time of Palestrina but also included concerted church music in the modern (or 'rococo') style, with instrumental 'sinfonias' and florid solo vocal writing alternating with sober, seemingly archaic movements in the strict style. The mixture of austere and decorative styles is alive in Mozart's Salzburg church music (notably the Vesper psalms) and reaches its apogee in his unfinished C minor Mass.

In Rome Mozart received from the Pope the grandiose title of Knight of the Order of the

Golden Spur, and father and son traveled as far as Naples where they saw Jommelli's new opera *Armida*, which Mozart found old-fashioned and over-complicated. For his first opera composed in Italy, Mozart favored a more modern and simple idiom, and he took great care, as he was always to do, to suit his music to the singers, even when it necessitated rewriting whole arias. The opera, *Mitridate rè di Ponto*, was performed on 26 December 1770 and was well received, being given twenty-two times. Already, when the Mozarts set out for home in January 1771, a new opera was proposed for two years later; this was *Lucio Silla*. In the meantime Mozart wrote a *serenata* (*Ascanio in Alba*) for Milan later in 1771 and an oratorio, *La Betulia liberata*, on the story of Judith and Holofernes – the text by none other than the Caesarian poet of the imperial court in Vienna, Metastasio. This was commissioned for Padua, but there is no record of a performance. Soon afterwards came the

first of two Italian works written for Salzburg, *Il Sogno di Scipione* (May 1772).

None of these works compares in interest with *Lucio Silla*, which is undoubtedly a masterpiece of its genre. Yet the composer was not quite seventeen: in Köchel's catalogue of his works, which runs to over 600 items, *Lucio Silla* is only no.135. Much of it is simply a fine response to the conventional expectations of the time: arias of various characteristics exploring the generally stylized feelings of the persons involved in what is, in cold print, a pretty stilted drama. The characters are strikingly differentiated, however, and in certain scenes – those for the jealous, vengeful Giunia in particular – a note of emotional truth is struck which was the hallmark of the contemporary operatic reform.

• Instrumental music 1773-7 •

Up to the year of *Lucio Silla*, Mozart had composed remarkably little of what we now call 'chamber music.' The explanation is partly that, even at this stage in his career, he composed mainly on demand; but so fertile was his mind, and so intent his questing for musical knowledge, that he embarked from time to time upon compositions for which he had no commission. Such were, in all probability, the three-movement string quartets of the third Italian journey. These and the half-dozen or so more quartets written by the end of 1773, are among the few surviving works in which Mozart appears inexperienced.

Mozart is much more himself in his divertimenti, written for chamber-like groupings of strings or wind, or for small orchestras of varying sizes. Among the wind pieces, the listener should not be beguiled by the clarinets and cors anglais available in Italy; the musical strengths of the Salzburg works of 1773-7 are considerably greater despite their modest scoring for two each of oboes, horns and bassoons. Mozart's resourcefulness and understanding of these instruments was unequalled in his time. Although we appreciate his mastery most in later works, notably the operas and piano concertos, its foundations were laid in these pieces designed for the accompaniment of festivities. The string and orchestral divertimenti and serenades amount to over a dozen written for Salzburg between 1772 and 1779, after which Mozart wrote only one more, the famous *Eine kleine Nachtmusik*. The Salzburg works include the splendid 'Haffner' Serenade, in nine movements. The delectable *Serenata notturna*, however, has only three movements, with the strange scoring for solo quartet (with double-bass for the usual cello) and timpani as well as a string orchestra. Here is a Mozart already able to be elegant without being superficial; always ready with a piquant variation on the expected, yet never leading the innocent hearer into difficulties.

Above: Empress Maria Theresa and her husband Francis Stephen of Lorraine with their children in 1760. Leopold Mozart and his children were first received at court in October 1762. The Archduchess Maria Antonia, not yet seven years old, was very taken with the genius just one year her junior.

Left: Siegmund Christoph von Schrattenbach (1698-1771), Archbishop of Salzburg since 1753. Leopold Mozart had been engaged as a violinist in the court orchestra in 1743 and was appointed Vice-Kapellmeister in 1763. The Archbishop was an autocrat of the old school, but lenient, allowing Leopold complete latitude to travel with his brilliant young son and daughter. In 1769 Wolfgang became second Konzertmeister in the court orchestra, and after Schrattenbach's death he was constantly at odds with his successor, Archbishop Colloredo.

Above: Mozart in Paris, playing in the salon of the Prince de Conti in the summer of 1766. He is about to accompany the singer Pierre de Jélyotte, seen tuning his guitar.

The same years saw the composition of over twenty symphonies. Most of them seem no more relevant to the modern conception of symphony than do the serenades and *divertimenti*: they alternate serenity and vigor in the conventional proportions. Nevertheless, the forms and instrumentation are by no means without resource and variety. Mozart's orchestra could extend from two each of flutes, oboes, horns and trumpets, with timpani and strings (and probably a bassoon on the bass line as well), to the simple two oboes, two horns and strings; but three of the early symphonies use four horns. Some have three and some four movements, and a few go well beyond the engaging but straightforward appeal of the serenades and Italian overtures. Particularly remarkable is the Symphony in G minor of 1773, K.183 (no.25 in the usual numbering), sometimes called the 'little' G minor to distinguish it from no.40, but by no means a little work. Richness of sonority is obtained by independent scoring for two bassoons and by the four horn parts, two in one key and two in another to overcome the limited scale playable on the eighteenth-century

instrument. This work marks a considerable advance in Mozart's expressive capacities and it suggests yet again his quickness to perceive something in the musical air. Its vehemently driving rhythms, added to the rare use of the minor mode, directly recall some of Haydn's symphonies of the period of so-called 'Sturm und Drang.' The following year came another symphonic masterpiece, no.29 in A major, in which the rapidly maturing composer exhibits an equal subtlety and originality of invention with, here, no loss of charm and gracefulness.

As with chamber music proper, the absence of concertos in Mozart's early music is striking. It was only in the period after the third Italian journey that he really began to explore this medium; but when he did, it was with a thoroughness and artistic success which must surely have led him to recognize in himself a particular affinity for the form. The earliest Salzburg concertos, for piano and for bassoon, give little sense of the greatness to come. With the series of violin concertos – five were written in 1775, besides those embodied in various serenades – Mozart seems to develop in intelligence and

Left: Wolfgang and Nannerl painted in the court costumes they were given by the Empress in the fall of 1762. Wolfgang's had originally been made for the youngest of the imperial children Archduke Maximilian (later Archbishop of Cologne and a patron of Beethoven).

inventiveness from one to the next. The earlier ones are not without self-consciousness but the last three are altogether better, and it may be no accident that there is some involvement with dramatic music in this growth of assurance. The third, in G (K.216), uses a theme from the two-act opera *Il Rè pastore*, performed at the Archbishop's palace in April. But Mozart's training in *divertimenti* is also in evidence; the last violin concerto, in A (K.219), makes happy use of the kind of variety associated with such genres. The strict decorum of the older type of concerto reached in the earlier works is definitely broken here; the soloist enters in a fast movement with a slow operatic cantabile, a stroke which makes the concerto overtly dramatic and distinguishes the soloist markedly from the body of the orchestra as a separate kind of player, whereas in the baroque concerto he is first among equals. The finale changes time with an abruptness that would normally demand justification from a dramatic situation; a decorous minuet is split wide open by the rough 'Turkish' music, an early example of the popular genre Mozart was to use in *Die Entführung* and the Piano Sonata in A. At this stage in his career, Mozart could handle these contrasts with an impudent precision and balance, which make these clearly original works (the *Serenata notturna* is another such) among the most successful of the period. Later he would have no need of such devices.

Mozart's first masterpiece in this genre, however, was for his principal instrument. Expert as he was on strings, as a keyboard player he was among the greatest of the age. He is said to have particularly liked playing the organ, but as he never obtained a church appointment his opportunities for doing so were limited, and he left virtually no organ music. In his earlier years he probably played the harpsichord; most keyboard music at least until the mid-1770s was designed to be playable on that instrument. Nevertheless he rapidly inclined towards the pianoforte; and although his early keyboard concertos are surprisingly effective on the harpsichord, it is surely for the newer instrument that they were conceived.

The first great piano concerto is Mozart's in E flat, K.271, composed in 1777. The modest orchestra (two oboes, two horns, strings) is deployed to set off most effectively the alternation of limpid expressiveness and spicy brilliance in the solo part. It is noticeable that Mozart still uses an unorthodox device, one he never had need of again: the soloist joins in the enunciation of the opening theme, whereas in all the later concertos the principal ideas are exposed in an extended orchestral introduction. But in every other way – the profusion of ideas, their perfect integration into a single musical line of thought, the variety of restatement – K.271 is a mature concerto. The slow movement is a heart-rending elegy, in C minor, composed with complete assurance, as is the dispelling of shadows by the agility and high spirits of the finale.

Mozart's remaining works before his fateful journey to Paris in 1777 are mainly for the Church, and he resumed his duties in Salzburg, probably with rather little enthusiasm, in the period between his return from Paris and his definitive departure for Vienna. It may be convenient to summarize his activity as a religious composer here. He was asked to provide, for liturgical functions, several instrumental works (church sonatas), mainly for strings and organ; some add brass, but none (apart from K.278 and 329) has woodwind, which scarcely makes for a Mozartian sound, and a few use the organ as a solo rather than merely as a supporting or continuo instrument. They are not, to modern

Below: Spinet made by Scotti in 1753 on which Mozart played when he visited Milan in the 1770s.

ears, religious in feeling at all; and they may be considered a further proving-ground for the developing symphonist. In his litanies, Mass settings and Vespers, Mozart blends a more dignified style with a modern, operatic idiom. In 1779 and 1780 Mozart wrote two larger Masses in C major; they do not approach the symphonic power of Haydn's late Masses, but the broadly conceived design encloses choral and solo music in a measure of integration beyond that provided by the text.

Two operas preceded Mozart's journey to Paris: *Il Rè pastore*, a Metastasio text that seems not to have fired Mozart's imagination to its highest, and another *opera buffa*, *La Finta giardiniera*. This latter was not written for Salzburg; the commission came from Munich, where the opera was given three times in January 1775. It is uncertain who wrote the text, a drama of tangled love affairs which can only be resolved when the disguised Countess (the 'pretended gardening girl' of the title) reveals her identity. This is no farce but a work in the 'tearful' genre with only the scheming servant to recall the Italian *intermezzo* or anticipate *Figaro*. There are too many arias, too few ensembles, for the drama to move other than in jerks, and the long finales do little to restore this imbalance. It is impossible to take it seriously as drama, and the work survives by the charm and occasional intensities of Mozart's music; the wealth of craftsmanship and serious invention anticipate the use of the language of serious opera in the great comedies which followed.

One other dramatic work from this period merits a mention: the incidental music to the heroic drama by von Gebler, *Thamos, King of Egypt*. Mozart wrote far less of this kind of theater music than Beethoven, but *Thamos* is a magnificent example of this difficult genre. It consists of orchestral music, some of it with melodrama (speech heard in gaps between musical phrases, or over the music), and choruses, with the obligatory bass solo for the High Priest. The subject and the nobility of the musical style anticipate *Die Zauberflöte*.

• Paris: 1778 •

In Salzburg Mozart longed to spread his wings; and so his uneasy relationship with Archbishop Colloredo flared into open hostility. Mozart humbly petitioned to be allowed to travel; the Archbishop responded by dismissing the Mozarts, father and son. Eventually he confined himself to dismissing Wolfgang but forbidding Leopold to travel with him. For the first time, therefore, Mozart went away without his father. His mother left with him in 1777, their objective being Paris, where Leopold had been renewing old contacts to arouse interest in the visit.

It was not until the end of March 1778 that they reached Paris. One reason for this slow travel was Wolfgang's more realistic assessment of his own prospects. Leopold argued that

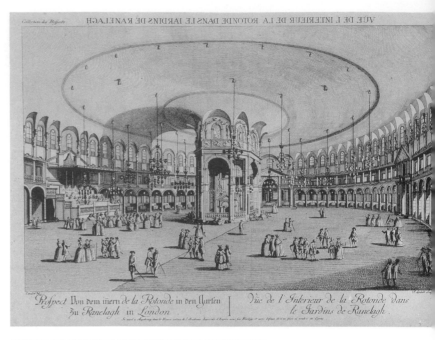

Above: The rotunda in Ranelagh Gardens in London. Wolfgang had played both harpsichord and organ at a charity concert given there on 29 June 1764.

Left: Motet (K.20) with English words, which Mozart wrote in London in July 1765. Leopold gave the manuscript to the British Museum together with a printed copy of the two violin sonatas first printed in Paris the previous year.

foreign musicians could make a fortune in Paris; the example of Gluck's success was to hand, and Piccinni had already arrived in Paris to compose *Roland*. Instrumental music also flourished, and a strong association existed with the Mannheim school. Mozart knew that his reputation as a prodigy was no passport to employment in so fashion-bound a capital and saw better prospects in Germany.

Accordingly, although receiving a stream of letters from Leopold urging him to hurry on, Mozart spent over a month in Munich and in Augsburg. He gave successful concerts which must have enhanced his confidence even if they could do little for his standing with a wider public. Like most men of genius, he had little doubt of his worth, and his reception by the musicians of Mannheim, where he arrived on 30 October, must have confirmed him in his feeling that this was the sort of environment in which he would flourish. He wrote several works for flute for a Dutch amateur, and doubtless plotted the *Sinfonia concertante* for the four Mannheim wind players who appeared regularly at the Parisian *Concert Spirituel*. He also began a set of violin sonatas, published in Paris as op.1 in 1778, and wrote two keyboard sonatas, K.309 and K.311.

Right: Padre Giovanni Battista Martini (1706-84). The Mozarts had arrived in Bologna from Milan on 24 March 1770, and two days later Wolfgang gave a concert which was attended by Padre Martini, with whom the composer studied during his three months in the city.

Below: Letter written from Milan on 18 December 1772 by Leopold Mozart to his wife (with a postscript by Wolfgang to his sister). It describes the preparations for Wolfgang's new opera *Lucio Silla* (K.135), which had its première eight days later.

In Mannheim Mozart encountered the Weber family and fell in love with one of the daughters, Aloysia, already a fine singer, for whom he at once wrote an aria. The visit to Mannheim was artistically fruitful, but there was no sign of a permanent position, and finally Mozart and his mother yielded to the bombardment of advice and exhortation coming from Salzburg and moved on to Paris.

If Paris did not make Mozart's fortune, fashion and Mozart's dislike of the place are mostly to blame. Joseph Legros, director of the *Concert Spirituel*, made no attempt to put on the *Sinfonia concertante* written for the four Mannheim wind players, but he did commission a symphony which became part of the repertoire of the concerts for a decade. The symphony is known as the 'Paris' (K.297) and is a grandiose piece using the largest orchestra Mozart had yet employed in a symphony. Mozart's letter about this symphony is very revealing of his attitude to public composition: 'Having observed that all last as well as first allegros begin here with

Right: The wedding in October 1771 of Archduke Ferdinand, Maria Theresa's third son and Governor of Lombardy, to Princess Maria Beatrice d'Este. Mozart composed his second opera, *Ascanio in Alba* (K.111), to celebrate the occasion, and his father used the opportunity to try to have his son taken on in the Archduke's service; but Maria Theresa advised against it, and the Mozarts returned to Salzburg.

all the instruments playing together and generally *unisono*, I began mine with two violins only, *piano* for the first eight bars followed instantly by a *forte*; the audience, as I expected, said "hush" at the soft beginning, and when they heard the *forte*, began at once to clap their hands. . . .' In the 'Paris' Symphony Mozart aimed to please, but not by simply copying the practices of other composers; he aimed at novelty, without completely overturning the legitimate expectations of his audience. This attitude is essentially that of the craftsman who is also a genius.

The months in Paris and Mannheim, though not particularly productive, witnessed Mozart growing up both humanly and musically. A work of the maturity and expressiveness of the Piano Concerto in E flat (K.271) had been a precocious exception; henceforth most of his works on such a scale are of equal quality. He experienced a new range of dramatic music in the wider world without his father's constant supervision; he witnessed his mother's death in a foreign capital and showed great maturity in the way he broke the news to his father, writing *after* her death a first letter mentioning that she was ill in order better to prepare him. Whether or not this loss inspired the A minor Sonata, K.310, is not certain, but this work is outstanding for its iron control of an almost unmatched emotional

Above: Opening of the 'Paris' Symphony (K.297) in Mozart's original manuscript. It was composed in June 1778 for Joseph Legros, the new director of the *Concert Spirituel*, and first performed in the Salle des Suisses in the Tuileries.

turbulence, explicit in the driving rhythms and harsh dissonance of its first movement.

Leopold was soon to summon his son home. The experiment had failed and, in August, a new prospect was opened up in Salzburg by the death of the court organist Adlgasser. On his return journey Mozart paused again at Mannheim although Leopold wrote almost frantically to point out that his appointment to the post of court organist and Konzertmeister was provisional and might not survive further delay. Mozart was staying with the Webers there, but Aloysia received him coolly; had he returned laden with fame from Paris it might have been different. He wrote of his misery, without making clear the cause, and lingered well into the new year. On 8 January he wrote, 'I swear to you on my honor that I cannot bear Salzburg.' Leopold then made it clear that not to return would be to break not only with the Salzburg court but also with himself. Cutting his losses, and abandoning hope of Aloysia, Mozart returned home, chastened but artistically hardened by yet further disappointments.

• Salzburg and Munich •

A few days later he successfully petitioned for appointment as court organist, a post he held for just over two years. This was a period of experiment and achievement, which culminated in 1780 with Mozart's first undoubted operatic masterpiece, *Idomeneo*. The experiments took place against a relatively uneventful background of routine duties, and they affected both instrumental and dramatic composition. In the wake of his Parisian experience, Mozart composed orchestral music with a new freedom and confidence, in which the barriers between genres, never hard and fast, seem unusually fluid for a time. The next symphony, K.318 in G major, consists only of a slow movement enclosed within a fast one, the form of an Italian overture. Three movements of the delightful 'Posthorn' Serenade exist as a symphony with slightly altered scoring; two others appear as a concerto. The blend of symphony and concerto known as *sinfonia concertante* preoccupied Mozart; besides two fascinating fragments of concertos for piano and violin, and for violin, viola and cello, there are two completed works, K.365, for two pianos, and K.364, the *Sinfonia concertante* for violin and viola, the greatest instrumental work of this period despite the two brilliant symphonies in B flat and in C major, K.319 and K.338. In this *Sinfonia concertante*, Mozart at last recaptured the quality of the piano concerto, K.271, in the same key. The viola is intended to tune its strings up a semitone so that increased tension provides a brilliance and penetration to match the violin. The antiphonal play of these two instruments had a particular appeal to Mozart and reappears in his great string quintets. Instead of the opening

Left: The Music Lesson, 1769, a painting by Jean-Honoré Fragonard of the seventeen-year-old Marie-Anne Gérard, whom he married later that year. Mozart had a number of pupils in Paris in 1778, including the daughter of the Duc de Guines, and he wrote his Flute and Harp Concerto (K.299) for her and her father.

Left: The Mozart family in the winter of 1780/1 painted by J. N. della Croce. Mozart's mother, whose portrait hangs on the wall, had died in Paris on 3 July 1778 after a short illness.

Right: The day his mother had died Mozart wrote to his father, daring only to say that she was gravely ill; at the same time he wrote this letter ('for you only') to a Salzburg friend, Abbé Bullinger, with all the sad news, asking him to tell Leopold: 'Mourn with me my friend! This has been the saddest day of my life – I am writing this at two o'clock in the morning. I have to tell you that my mother, my dear mother, is no more!'

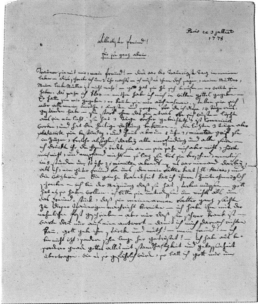

dramatic gesture of K.271, Mozart makes the maximum effect of delaying the soloists' entrance by bringing them in over the orchestral cadence; they float down from heaven, as it were, with a new melody, before beginning the business of decorating and developing the themes proposed by the orchestra.

Mozart's other area of experimentation was dramatic. He displayed a vigorous if short-lived interest in what is now usually called melodrama: speech with music. We know that Mozart intended to compose a *Semiramis* in this form, but if he did it is completely lost. However, his next operatic project, the unfinished *Zaïde*, employs melodrama; since it was in German it would not have had recitatives anyway. The source of the drama is called *Das Serail*; Mozart's next German opera was *Die Entführung aus dem Serail*. In some sense, therefore, the project was completed three years later, but Mozart did not use his earlier music again, and *Zaïde* remains a tantalizing fragment, complete enough to warrant performance, but impossible actually to reconstruct.

Everything else in this period is overshadowed by *Idomeneo*, the greatest of Mozart's serious operas. The history of its composition is illuminated by the exchange of letters between Mozart and his father, who conveyed the often very decisive ideas of the composer to the librettist Varesco, who was resident in Salzburg while Mozart was composing in the presence of the singers at Munich.

Idomeneo was not intended by Mozart as a reforming gesture; dogmatism of any kind would have seemed to him sterile. It is, however, remarkably close to the forms of contemporary French opera, which by 1780 meant Gluck, a few works by French composers and Piccinni. Like many of Piccinni's works, including *Roland* which Mozart had seen in 1778, *Idomeneo* is based on an old French libretto, reduced to three acts and adjusted to accommodate long arias. It differs even from so dramatically self-conscious a representative of the older forms as *Lucio Silla* in

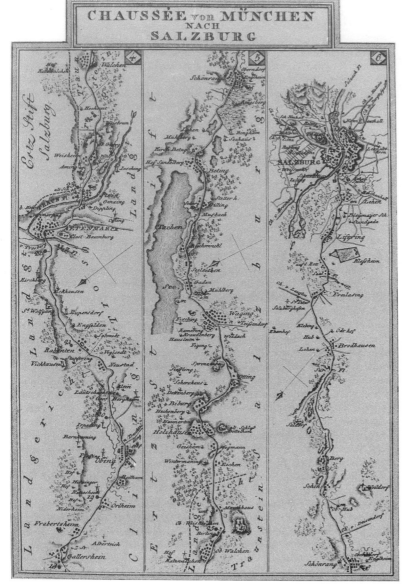

CHAUSSÉE VON MÜNCHEN NACH SALZBURG

expression is his foremost consideration. Mozart never excludes decoration in his arias and only intermittently aims at the 'naturalness' cultivated by many thinkers of the time. He is always artificial, in the best sense, and he takes beautiful singing, and the power of the best singer to execute difficult passages, as a legitimate extension of musical, and thence dramatic, expression.

Idomeneo contains magnificent choral writing, although there are none of the huge, repetitive structures of Gluck. The choral scene by the shore, when all seems set fair for Elektra's voyage home, is a delicious vignette; and when the monster emerges a few minutes later, the chorus of panic and accusation is of tremendous power. In the last act, the chorus deploring the ruin brought about by the monster is unforgettably poignant and maintains interest at a point when it might well have sagged, for it follows the most moving number of all, the justly famous quartet. Such ensembles had no place in the traditional *opera seria* and were not much used by Gluck, but for Mozart they were becoming a vehicle of the highest pathos. The quartet bears not the slightest resemblance to the ensembles of comedy; it is more like an aria for four voices, which seldom depart from each other in musical style, but in which the four persons come to life as much as in their solo utterances.

•Vienna: 1781-5•

After 1780 Mozart returned again to Salzburg only as a visitor. While he was in Munich the Prince-Archbishop had proceeded with his whole

Above: Road map of part of the route from Salzburg to Munich. Mozart had received a commission from Carl Theodor, Elector of Bavaria, to write an opera for the Munich carnival, and, with the Archbishop's grudging permission, he set out from Salzburg on 5 November 1780.

Right: Title-page of the libretto for *Idomeneo* (K.366), the opera Mozart wrote for Munich. The libretto was by Abbé Varesco, who had been court chaplain in Salzburg since 1766, and it was the subject of much anxious correspondence between Wolfgang and his father.

its use of chorus; the increase in orchestrated recitative (for which the experience of *Zaïde* was beneficial); and its continuity – from time to time Mozart deprived the singers of the normal occasion for applause by running the end of an aria into the next scene, a procedure which became common in Paris about this time. The musical style of *Idomeneo* is of outstanding richness, particularly in its orchestration. It was written for the old Mannheim orchestra, now at the court in Munich, but the sources of such a style are again French.

In one respect *Idomeneo* particularly recalls Gluck – its consistent adherence to dramatic truth. The language of late eighteenth-century music lends itself to frivolity and decorative note-spinning, but with only slight adjustments it is also capable of dramatic penetration unmatched by apparently more sophisticated styles. Mozart never subscribed to Gluck's opinion that music was the servant of poetry or, in opera, the equivalent of color in painting. For Mozart poetry was the obedient daughter of music, and in his adjustments to the libretto of *Idomeneo* the dramatic effect obtainable through musical

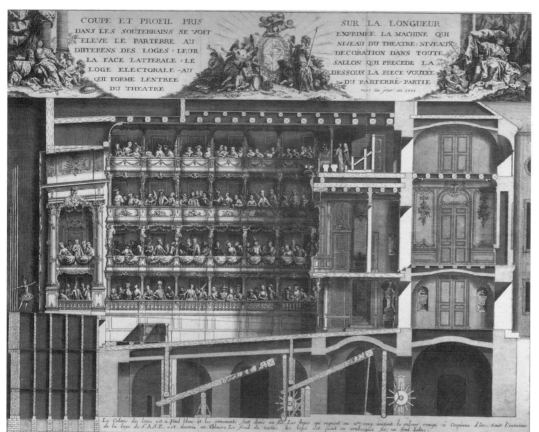

Above: Count Seeau (d.1799), intendant of the Residenz Theater in Munich since 1753, at the time of the production of *Idomeneo*. Despite his friendly attitude, Mozart was unable to obtain any court appointment from the Elector.

Above left: Cross-section of the Residenz Theater in Munich, where *Idomeneo* was first performed on 29 January 1781.

entourage to Vienna; Mozart joined him there in March 1781. Perhaps because the comparison between his status as a servant and the teeming life of the capital exasperated him, or because his achievement in composing a major opera for a major city was ignored by his master, Mozart chafed and finally rebelled. Whether or not he was literally kicked out, as he said, he left the Archbishop of Salzburg's service on 9 June 1781 and for the remaining ten years of his life was a freelance musician in Vienna, earning his living by teaching and composition. It was certainly not an easy life, but Mozart was not altogether unsuccessful. Neither he nor his wife, whom he married in August 1782, was particularly good at managing money, but nor did they ever want for the necessities of life. Certainly he would have been better off with steady employment. He had no rebellious preference for the difficulties of an independent life, and he was glad enough, in 1787, to be appointed court composer in place of Gluck (but at less than half the salary).

Mozart's wife need not be blamed for his hardships. She was loyal and did much to propagate his work after his death. She was frequently pregnant (but only two children survived into adulthood), and her health certainly cost Mozart anxiety as well as money; from the surviving correspondence it is she who might have been expected to die young (she lived until 1842). The younger sister of Aloysia Weber, Constanze Mozart was a member of a musically well-educated family and a good singer, if we may judge from what Mozart expected her to perform in his C minor Mass.

In the year before his marriage Mozart's chief concern was with his new opera, *Die Entführung aus dem Serail* (The Abduction from the Harem). *Die Entführung* may not be a very convincing piece of music-drama, but it will never lose its attractiveness. Never was Mozart's melody so beguiling, his instrumentation so luscious. The new Emperor Joseph II, whose intiative led to the commissioning of German operas, is said to have remarked, 'Too many notes, my dear Mozart,' and he continued to believe that Mozart wrote music difficult for the singers and heavily orchestrated. Incredible as this view seems now, it was true relative to the stylistic norm of the day, which was purely Italian. Mozart lavished a care and invention on the orchestra which inevitably made it a competing attraction to the voice; it begins to carry the dramatic message, as he observed in a letter to his father about Belmonte's second aria, 'O wie ängstlich': 'Would you like to know how I have expressed this, and even indicated his throbbing heart? By the two violins playing octaves . . . you feel the trembling – the faltering – you see how his throbbing breast begins to swell; this I have expressed by a *crescendo*. You hear the whispering and the sighing – which I have indicated by the first violins with mutes and a flute . . .' The passage gives valuable insight into the way Mozart conceived his theater music; within the controlling limits of acceptable musical style, he sought to register every nuance of dramatic expression, while writing 'expressly to suit Adamberger's voice.' His reply to the Emperor was 'Just as many notes as are wanted, your Majesty,' and few would now disagree.

Above: Three early illustrations of *Die Entfuhrüng aus dem Serail* (K.384) – the heroine Constanze (sung in the original production by Catarina Cavalieri), the hero Belmonte (sung by Valentin Adamberger), and the noble Pasha Selim (a speaking role) in his harem. Mozart had started work on the opera in July 1781, but the production was delayed, and in the end the Emperor had to intervene to ensure it was performed. Finally, it opened on 16 July 1782 and was a notable success, receiving sixteen performances in all during the year.

Die Entführung is filled with a richness of characterization quite unusual in this kind of opera, in which the slender plot is spun out by a variety of delays, and the inevitable happy ending is brought about by an act of clemency by the Pasha which nothing in the action has motivated; he, moreover, does not sing and thus has no musical personality. Constanze may posture like a heroine of *opera seria*, but she is far from being a cardboard heroine – consider her sorrow at her separation from Belmonte, her loving welcome, and her reproachful words when he dares to ask if her faith has wavered.

Framed in the merry sound of 'Turkish' music, with cymbal, drums and triangle, *Die Entführung* is a delightful rather than a profound work, but it showed the world what Mozart could do and vied in popularity with Gluck's *Pilgrims to Mecca*. Nevertheless, *Die Entführung* was first staged some nine months after it was scheduled, the kind of delay with which Mozart was already familiar. It was finally produced in July 1782, shortly before his marriage.

Other works of this period probably include the magnificent Partita (usually called Serenade) for twelve wind instruments and double-bass, K.361; the occasion for its composition is unknown. Here Mozart's unparalleled knowledge and love of wind instruments reaches its peak. He employs a wealth of forms and sonorities, working instruments in pairs or forming an operatic trio, in the slow movement, of oboe, clarinet and basset-horn against a murmuring background. The style is alternately sophisticated and rustic in the minuets, strangely expressive in the 'romanza' (a second slow movement enclosing a faster one), brilliant in the boisterous rondo. Two other wind works of the same period, the Serenades in C minor and E flat major, attain a greater symphonic breadth, although more modestly scored for an octet of oboes, clarinets, horns and bassoons. The E flat, K.375, has the amplitude normal for Mozart in that key, and the C minor, K.388, is so dark-hued for so much of its length as to belie its title 'Serenade.' Mozart later arranged it as a string quintet, a tribute to its intensity; in that form it cannot vie with the four masterpieces composed directly for that medium, but as wind music it remains unique.

As an act of thanksgiving for his marriage, Mozart vowed to compose a great Mass. He never finished it, partly, no doubt, because time did not allow work on projects with no immediate likelihood of performance or publication, but also perhaps because he found he did not wish to. The C minor Mass, had it been finished, would rank in musical weight and sheer length second only to Bach's Mass in B minor. Both are in the 'cantata' Mass form; sections of the text are composed for chorus, other sections as self-contained arias, which with Mozart inevitably acquire an operatic character. Perhaps in recognition of the dramatic nature of his musical thought, Mozart later arranged the music of the Kyrie and Gloria into an oratorio, *Davidde penitente*, but it is usually heard in its original form, with or without completion of the liturgical text by forced union with other Mozart Mass movements.

• String quartet and piano concerto •

With the completion by 1783 of the great wind serenades and two important symphonies, the 'Haffner' and 'Linz,' Mozart's main compositional activity for the next two years can be reduced to two genres: the piano concerto and the string quartet. He himself, of course, was busy with more than composition, and the piano concertos, of which fourteen appeared in the four years from March 1782 to March 1786, were composed for pupils as well as for himself. Teaching provided his main income at this time. He had gained a reputation as one of the world's finest keyboard players, partly through the famous contest with Clementi at the end of

Above: Constanze Mozart (1762-1842), painted in 1782 by Joseph Lange, the actor who had married her sister Aloysia.

Top right: Karl and Wolfgang, the Mozarts' two sons, painted when they were thirteen and six years old, well after their father's death.

1781. The latter, brought up as a harpsichordist, had developed a brilliant technique, but Mozart won the day by his greater sensibility and his powers of improvisation. Some taste of the latter may be gained from surviving piano music. The early Vienna years produced not only a group of sonatas but also various fantasias and variation sets. These include the Piano Sonatas in A (K.331, with its opening set of variations and final 'rondo alla turca'), and in C minor (K.457, a work of passionate intensity, remote from the galanteries of his teaching music). The sonata was published (as op.11), preceded by Mozart's greatest Fantasia (K.475), a work which challenges, by what one might consider almost an organic willfullness, the whole basis of eighteenth-century tonal organization; decorum is restored by a return to the opening, but only just.

This period also saw important works for violin and piano, notably the fine Sonata of 1784 (K.454), and for violin and viola, an unusual combination which Mozart apparently adopted to help out Michael Haydn, who was behindhand with a commission. The year 1784

also produced the superlative Quintet for piano and wind (K.452), which at the time Mozart considered 'the best work I have composed.' It has an important bearing on the later piano concertos, in which the writing for wind is so highly developed, but is not itself a miniature concerto; each wind player has a part perfectly adapted to his own instrumental capacities. The Mozartian miracle here is the blending of such a heterogeneous instrumental group, as it is later in the two great piano quartets of 1785 and 1786.

The Vienna piano concertos bring together all aspects of Mozart's greatest art into a synthesis, with considerable power to fascinate and delight. His ability to combine heterogeneous instruments harmoniously and derive the utmost variety from them; his brilliance and sensibility on the keyboard; his continual renewing of form, so that no two concertos are cut from the same pattern; his wit and dramatic sense of timing, awaiting, in the early Viennese years, fulfillment in Italian comic opera; his developed powers as a symphonist; his command of every style of the late eighteenth century – the military and hunting styles, the pastoral, the lyrical, the turbulent, the ornate – this form alone can accommodate every element. Delightful as they are, the Sonata for two pianos and the horn concertos, also written in this period, are relatively limited, and it is the greatest triumph of the Quintet, K.452, and the piano and string quartets that they are not overshadowed by this astonishing series of masterpieces.

The earliest Vienna concertos are modest works intended for publication; they can be performed without wind, as a quintet, and mark very little, if any, advance on the precocious K.271. Mozart described these works (K.413, 414, 415, in F, A and C) with some pride to his father as 'a happy medium between what is too easy and too difficult; they are very brilliant, pleasing to the ear, and natural, without being vapid.' He goes on to repeat his ideal conception of instrumental music, as delight for ear and intellect alike: 'There are passages here and there from which the connoisseurs alone can derive satisfaction; but these are written in such a way that the less learned cannot fail to be pleased, though without knowing why.'

Six concertos followed in 1784. Far from having exhausted the possibilities of the medium in this concentrated burst of activity, Mozart reaches the finale of the sixth concerto (in F, K.459) before introducing a new element – a friendly rondo-like beginning yields suddenly to a severe fugal exposition, and the alternation and integration of these elements makes a new and brilliant synthesis. The series of concertos began with the one in E flat, K.449, written for an accomplished pupil, Barbara Ployer; this is the first work written by Mozart into a personal catalogue of works which he maintained to the end of his life, and it may well be regarded as the first of the truly mature concertos. The next two concertos Mozart wrote for himself ('they make you sweat,' he remarked, with his usual frankness, to his father). The wind instruments here attain their *obbligato* role, especially in the two B flat Concertos (K.450 and 456), while the D major Concerto (K.451) is one of those in which the virtuosity of the pianist has to compete with the military clamor of trumpets and drums. This type recurs throughout Mozart's concertos, culminating in the so-called 'Coronation' Concerto, also in D major, (K.537, 1788), although the affection of the connoisseur may continue to be for the more intimate concertos, or those in which the weight of the trumpets and drums is offset by a minor tonality. K.453 in G is also intended for Ployer, and so is less difficult than the two preceding. Nevertheless,

its melodic invention is unmatched; its slow movement touches a new vein of intimate lyricism, and its finale ends with a hilarious coda which has all the panache, and the murmurs of dissent, of a confused operatic ensemble – the sextet in *Figaro* comes irresistibly to mind.

Mozart must have been longing, by now, to write another stage work. In the previous year he had made two abortive attempts to produce an Italian comic opera. One of these (*Lo Sposo deluso*) was to a text possibly by the best available librettist, Lorenzo da Ponte, but Mozart thought da Ponte was in league with Salieri, whose jealousy he feared, and turned instead to the librettist of *Idomeneo*. Varesco, however, had no original gift for comedy, and this work (*L'Oca del Cairo*) also exists only in fragments.

Between 1782 and 1785 Mozart composed six string quartets, his first for nearly ten years. They were published in 1785 with a dedication to Joseph Haydn in which Mozart begs his protection for his '"children," the fruit of long and laborious endeavor.' The condition of the autograph manuscripts confirms that this was no more than the truth. Few of his works took so long to compose as the six quartets, and few of his manuscripts show such evidence of compositional problems. Haydn's op.33 Quartets, published in 1782, were written, the composer claimed, in an entirely new manner. Mozart's six 'Haydn' quartets respond to op.33 as a mature artist; he had learned from the older master how to handle the ensemble as a quartet of equals, in which vital thematic activity could be divided subtly between the parts so that, at certain moments, one cannot say which instrument has the theme, which the accompaniment.

Above: Maria Cäcilia Weber (1727-93), mother of Aloysia and Constanze, who offered Mozart a place to live in Vienna, to make certain of securing him as her son-in-law.

Left: Petersplatz in Vienna, where the Webers lived on the third floor of the 'Eye of God' house, the second on the left. Mozart was taken in as a lodger at the beginning of May 1781 after he had rashly decided to quit the Archbishop's service. Despite his father's warnings, Frau Weber's plans came to fruition, and Wolfgang and Constanze were married on 4 August 1782.

But they remain pure Mozart and imitate few if any of the formal characteristics of op.33. For example, where Haydn usually composed short minuets, with eight-measure first sections, and in op.33 called them 'Scherzo,' Mozart maintained the steadier minuet character and extended the form; the first section, in the first quartet, is of forty measures.

The quartets are a rare example, for Mozart, of a complete set of six works, designed to set each other off by contrast. Whereas the six piano concertos of 1784 are a fortuitous grouping, with none in the minor and two in B flat, the quartets are all in different keys, with the single minor-key work lying second. The first, in G major (K.387), is at once lyrical in impulse and elaborate. Its first movement is made of a multiplicity of melodic ideas. Where Haydn tended to derive as much as possible from one or two motives, Mozart adds new thoughts throughout the first expository section; the most trivial of these may become the basis for the most extended development. Mozart also placed more emphasis on large-scale symmetry than Haydn, favoring a clear two-part form for his expansive, florid slow movements. The finale of K.387 is a *tour de force*: it contains two fugal subjects which are combined at their recapitulation, as well as music in his most brilliant style, ingeniously worked into a novel variant of the customary sonata form.

If the first quartet seems almost too ingenious, the second, in D minor (K.421), makes the chamber ensemble speak in the language of tragedy. The outer movements (of which the last is a set of variations) have a somber, veiled passion. In the first movement this results from a shifting harmonic foundation which the variations seem concerned to secure without mitigating its intensity. The quartet Mozart placed third, in B flat (K.458), is generally known from the lively first movement as 'The Hunt.' By contrast to K.421 it is all sweet naturalness, with an adagio of particular richness, a song from the *opera seria* transmuted into chamber music. The finale appears to be a conscious tribute to Haydn, its wit closer to broad comedy than was usual with Mozart.

The seriousness with which Mozart treated the quartet medium appears in the almost experimental nature of certain ideas. The finale of K.387 is a case in point, and so are the first movements of the fourth quartet, in E flat (K.428), and the sixth, in C (K.465). K.428 begins with a strange chromatic idea which Mozart strives to integrate into a flowing, moderate-speed movement – a Haydn tempo but not Haydnesque ideas. The slow movement is of haunting beauty, seeming to search for a lyrical melody and finding instead only fragments, one of which nearly anticipates the chromaticism of Wagner's *Tristan*. In K.465 the experiment is the slow introduction, which has led to a misleading nickname, 'The Dissonance.' Mozart was always prone to contrast darkness and light; his last opera is deeply concerned with this conflict. He prefaces K.465 with a harmonic mystery, a brief fantasia which anticipates Haydn's

Catarina Cavalieri

Valent: Adamberger

'Representation of Chaos' in its resolute refusal to define its own gravitational center. Mozart wrote much more dissonant music – the C minor Fugue for two pianos (K.426) for example – but few passages more disturbing in their harmonic implications. The rest of the quartet, like the supremely beautiful no.5 in A major (K.464), is harmonious, even sunny in disposition, but the C major is planned on a large scale whereas the A major revels in finely wrought detail.

The tally of great instrumental works completed before Mozart's next opera continues with the great piano concertos of 1785. The early part of the year produced two. The D

Top: Cavalieri (1761-1801) and Adamberger (1743-1804), the principal singers in *Die Entführung*. Adamberger became a close friend of the composer, and for Cavalieri Mozart later wrote the part of Donna Elvira in *Don Giovanni*.

Above: Playbill for the first performance of *Die Entführung aus dem Serail*, 16 July 1782.

Right: Page of musical sketches for a piano concerto, covered as well with calculations as to the length of individual numbers in *Die Entführung.* The sketches therefore date from 1782-3, the period of the piano concertos, K.413, 414 and 415, which Mozart published by subscription early in 1783.

minor Concerto (K.466) opens in a spirit of tragic unrest. This music is purely orchestral, so that Mozart was forced into another of his formal innovations, the entry of the soloist with a quite new melodic idea; the piano can make the orchestral material its own only by adding elaborate and expressive decoration. Mozart's interest in contrast reaches an almost disconcerting level in this concerto. After the complex turbulence of its first movement, its second is a limpid 'romanza' in which the main theme returns, rondo-fashion, to occupy most of the stage. The finale then begins with a rocketing theme on the piano and pursues its precipitous course until, as in the C minor wind Serenade and the later G minor Quintet, the work dissolves into a brilliant major-key conclusion. The C major Concerto (K.467) is more overtly brilliant, but many thematic and formal features make it the true twin of the D minor, and Mozart's resourcefulness in darkening the major mode with elements borrowed from the minor makes the first movement no less serious an affair. The slow movement unfolds an operatic *cantabile* over a gentle accompaniment, a breathtaking invention; and where some of his slow movements may seem, like that of the D minor concerto, to alternate material rather too symmetrically, this melody forms the whole basis of the extensions which follow. The finale is one of many brilliant rondo movements in which Mozart's continual inventiveness is no less remarkable than Haydn's.

The climax of this unparalleled series of concertos is in the three composed from December 1785 to March 1786, when Mozart was already involved with *Figaro.* The concertos are those in E flat (K.482), in A major (K.488) and C minor (K.491). Each is a unique masterpiece, yet also a culmination of a particular type of concerto. The E flat work is of the grand type, clearly defined by its ceremonial opening fanfare. In this and the A major Concerto the usual oboes are replaced by clarinets, imparting a warm glow to the orchestral sound; Mozart immediately displays his wind colors in solo passages which respond

to the opening gesture, where, in the early K.271, he used the piano solo to animate the opening period. For the soloist to enter with a new theme, and to be interrupted by the orchestral return to the opening, has now become almost normal, and in the expansive unfolding of ideas in this movement there is the confident stride of the composer for whom overt originality has become superfluous. As in K.271, Mozart turns to C minor for his slow movement, but the deathlike mood of the earlier work (or the *Sinfonia concertante* K.364) is replaced by lyrical pathos, and the structure resorts to the clear alternation of ideas of the D minor Concerto's romanza. Here, however, the first episode is scored entirely

Opposite: The Augarten in Vienna, a public park in the grounds of the Emperor's palace. In May 1782 Mozart gave the opening concert in a subscription series organized in the restaurant there by the impresario Philipp Jakob Martin.

Below: Ticket for a Mozart concert in Vienna.

Left: Poster for a concert by Mozart on 10 March 1785 at the Burgtheater announcing 'not only will he play a new Fortepiano concerto he has just completed [K.467 in C major], but he will also use an especially large pedal Forte piano for his improvisations.'

Above: Page of the catalogue of his own works that Mozart started in 1784. Listed here as numbers 1 to 5 are the three piano concertos in E flat, B flat and D (K.449, 450, 451), the quintet in E flat for piano and wind (K.452) and the piano concerto in G (K.453), all written between February and April that year.

for nine wind instruments, and the reprise of the main material is magnificently elaborated by the piano; after a second episode in C major, the second reprise takes on a new and sterner physiognomy, so that the simple structure only forms the background to a powerful sequence of varied moods. The finale begins with a hunting tune suitable for a horn concerto; but, again revealing this work as the mature composer's response to early forms like those of K.271, it reverts to a multi-sectional form. The hunt stops and an andantino, a kind of slow minuet, intervenes. Each phrase is given to the wind, then repeated by strings and piano. A mysterious transition leads to the resumption of the hunt and a brilliant conclusion.

The A major Concerto (K.488) is of the lyrical, intimate type, without trumpets and drums, so that the occasional martial figure in the first movement marks a climax within a lyrical development of ideas without breaking the mood. The orchestral melodies are so attractive that this time the soloist is content to play them over before proceeding to material of his own. So dependent is the discourse on melodic flow that the piano figuration, no less elaborate than usual, scarcely seems to be virtuosic at all; it is transmuted into melody. Mozart again chose the minor mode for his slow movement, but the continual flow of the movement's siciliano-like rhythm avoids sectionalization like that of K.482, and the use of a haunting refrain matches that of K.467 in eloquence. The rippling finale could stand as a type of Mozartian good spirits, at once mellow and brilliant.

The third of this wonderful triptych, and one of Mozart's most powerful works, is the Concerto in C minor. Its opening chromatic theme is not experimental (like that of the E flat Quartet) and it proves extremely versatile; in the first period Mozart seems prepared to confine himself to a single idea, as in the 'Haffner' Symphony. The soloist does not enter until the hundredth measure, but again proposes a new idea before the return of the first, which is immediately split among instrumental groups. The wind section is the largest Mozart ever used outside the opera house, with both oboes and clarinets, and the experience of writing wind serenades is put to the best possible use: in restating the piano's subsidiary theme in the first movement (one which first appears in the major, so that its

Don Giovanni (1787) derives from a variety of literary and popular sources which include at least one earlier libretto (Bertati's *The Stone Guest*, set by Gazzaniga in Venice early in 1787). *Così fan tutte* is claimed to have been based on fact. Da Ponte showed remarkable skill in translating and pruning for *Figaro*; improving and adding to an existing text in *Don Giovanni*; and in devising an original text for *Così*. Where comparison is closest, with Bertati's libretto, he can be seen to be immeasurably superior. Yet it is unlikely that we should take an interest if any other musician had set him to music, for no librettist can provide more than a skeleton for a music drama – the flesh, blood, and brains are those of the musician. It is not only Mozart's technical skill or invention which account for the superiority of these works over settings of da Ponte by other composers (Salieri, Martin y Soler, or Storace); it is his dramatic insight, his ability to create the finest distinctions of character and mood, his perfect timing.

Not the least remarkable aspect of *Figaro* is the manner in which the situations are directed by the librettist towards the ensembles, where

appearance in C minor heralds the end) and in whole episodes in the later movements. Mozart gathers his forces for a terrifying climax in the first movement; then, in a last masterstroke, avoids the usual closing uproar in favour of a whispered return to the main theme over a magical patina of piano figurations.

The slow movement appears at first to have something of the naïve directness of that of K.466. In fact, it is the complementary opposite of K.482, being in the major, but with a wind episode in the minor. The piano's decorated version of the latter is particularly eloquent, and the elaborate contrasts add to the depth of sentiment behind the deceptively simple melody when it returns. For the finale Mozart wrote one of his few sets of variations in the minor. These are powerful and cumulative, the usual glitter of decoration being replaced by a figuration whose speed does no damage to its expressive eloquence (compare the D minor String Quartet K.421). There is no relenting; major-key variations are followed by emphatic returns to the opening mood. After the cadence, however, the severity is mitigated by a closing section in a dance-like meter. In a convincing performance, the comparative sweetness of this section is the intensest pathos possible.

•The period of *Figaro* •

It was in 1785 that Mozart began the most fruitful collaboration of his career: apart from a one-act skit on singers and impresarios (*Der Schauspieldirektor*, 1786) Mozart's next three operas were composed to texts by Lorenzo da Ponte (1749-1838), who settled in Vienna when Venice had become too dangerous for him.

Le Nozze di Figaro (1786) is closely based on an expertly made play by Beaumarchais.

Above: Mozart's manuscript of the slow movement of the 'Dissonance' quartet in C (K.465) the last of the set dedicated to Haydn.

Mozart is able simultaneously to develop characterization and action. *Figaro* opens with a duet in which the most mundane activities are made musical: Figaro is measuring a room, Susanna is trying on a hat. At the end of the number we already feel we know them; we know, too, that Susanna is Figaro's equal in spirit and intelligence. Similarly, even if we did not know the dramatic situation exactly, we could tell that the duet between the Count and Susanna in Act III, although they are making an assignation, is not a love duet – and not merely because it is funny. The Count's opening plea and his subsequent expression of seeming contentment might pass for a lover's, but Susanna responds with a different musical intonation. At first, entirely collected, she answers by granting the assignation; but her response to his eloquent expression of joy is in a simple declamatory style, and when he asks her again and again if she will come she is only half-listening, for twice she answers

Joseph Haydn

Karl Ditter

Wolfg: Amade Mozart

'Yes' and 'No' when she means 'No' and 'Yes' and has hastily to correct herself.

Mozart had written several quite elaborate ensembles in earlier operas, but none of them has the dramatic cogency of most of the concerted pieces in the da Ponte operas. In *Figaro* a more elaborate example of the balance between character development, action development and the demands of the musical language itself is the Act III sextet. It has just been discovered that Marcellina, who had been hoping to marry Figaro, is his mother; the main obstacle to his marriage to Susanna is removed, and the Count, who wants Susanna himself, is temporarily thwarted. A careful analysis of the sextet would show that most of it follows principles of musical design, and that very little actually happens on stage. Nevertheless, the situation which emerged in the preceding recitative is not just extended; it only comes fully into focus when the sextet begins, because only here is the human consequence of the revelation of Figaro's parenthood explored. Marcellina's embrace, and Bartolo's slightly embarassed admission of paternity, are developed over a background of baffled mutters from the Count and the lawyer Curzio. At this point Susanna enters; she has money to buy Marcellina off. But she sees the embrace, is furious, and when Figaro prevents her from running off, she boxes his ears. All this takes no more time than it would in a play; and once more the action freezes, as the characters respond to this manifestation of her love for Figaro. The music, which has reached a climax of complexity, returns to the first key and melody as Marcellina begins to explain, and the irresistible comedy of Susanna's astonishment naturally leads to a symmetrical design as Figaro indicates each parent in turn and invites

the other to confirm the truth. Finally the characters sing together, four of them joyfully; the anger of the Count and Curzio occasionally bursts into the musical foreground.

In his finales to Acts II and IV Mozart was able to extend this kind of plan, in which musical and dramatic considerations reach a position of perfect harmony over enormous spans. It should not be thought that he invented these operatic forms which are now most closely associated with him; the extended finale in Italian comic opera was a good thirty years old. But Mozart brought to the finale the qualities of a symphonist. He had learned from Haydn how to engage in a witty musical discourse by development, combination, and reinterpretation of short, pliable motives, and this technique finds its apogee in the Act II finale of *Figaro*; the way in which the motives are tossed around the orchestra is not only witty in itself, but it allows the characters to get through a great many words without having to repeat them in order to satisfy the need for musical coherence. And in this Mozart was truly an inventor; continuous opera here received its strongest stimulus.

Figaro is also of particular interest for its realization in music of the tensions of social class. *Figaro* is as obviously about class as it is about sex, love and marriage; the Count's renunciation of the ancient *droit de seigneur*, and his wish nevertheless to retain it in practice, is the principal motivation of the plot, and Figaro's determination to resist and the Count's rage when he is frustrated are expressions of class as well as personal conflict. Such forthright expressions occur in arias; *Figaro*, despite its wealth of ensembles, also depends upon soliloquy. Figaro's 'Se vuol ballare, signor Contino' expresses his contempt for his social superior as much as the

In May 1784, the English composer Stephen Storace gave a quartet party for his friends, including the Irish singer Michael Kelly and the composer Giovanni Paisiello. The players were Haydn, first violin (*above left*), Carl Ditters von Dittersdorf, second violin (*center*), Mozart, viola (*right*) and J. B. Vanhal, cello. Kelly wrote in his *Reminiscences*: 'The players were tolerable; not one of them excelled on the instrument he played, but there was a little science among them. . . . '

271

Count's 'Vedrò, mentr' io sospiro' derives from his inborn belief in his right to do as he pleases. The poor Countess is left between the class to which she belongs (at least by marriage) and the servant class on whom she depends; she too has to explore her feelings in arias, as does Cherubino, more self-consciously, in 'Non so più,' or Figaro in his aria about cuckoldry in Act IV.

Figaro was a daring artistic gesture which nearly foundered on censorship and cabal; Beaumarchais's play was banned in Vienna, and the use of dancing in Act III, in a scene which furthers the drama by Susanna's conveying a note to the Count, gave an excuse to the author's enemies, for dancing in an opera was not normally permitted. Fortunately da Ponte seems to have enjoyed the favor of Joseph II, and *Figaro* was given in Vienna in May 1786, to be revived three years later. It was, however, in Prague late in 1786 that it created a veritable furor; its melodies were heard everywhere, Mozart reported with delight, and from that time Prague could boast of being the first city to appreciate Mozart at his true worth.

On this visit to Prague Mozart presented one of his greatest symphonies, the 'Prague' (no.38 in D major, K.504). In this work the wealth of invention and subtlety of musical discourse developed in recent quartets and piano concertos

find their first fulfillment in purely orchestral music. The symphony opens with a slow introduction which combines grandeur with harmonic mystery; the main allegro follows, beginning unobtrusively, the main theme passing imperceptibly from the lower instruments to the first violins. As in the 'Paris' Symphony, the *forte* withheld is all the more electrifying and contributes to the expansion of the form; this is among Mozart's longest first movements, and the slow movement and finale (there is no minuet) are its worthy sequel.

Although his life is now measured by the distance between operas, Mozart remained very active in instrumental music. In 1786 he wrote the delectable Trio for clarinet, viola and piano

Denkmal auf das Ende der Tranksteuer den 31 October 1783

(K.498), a fine Quartet (K.499 in D), and a Piano Trio (K.502). From this period also date the long and introspective Rondo in A minor for piano (K.511), in which Mozart's art of chromatic decoration reaches its apogee, and another splendid Piano Concerto (K.503, in C). But at this time interest in Mozart's public concerts was beginning to wane, and he turned to chamber music in the hope of making money through publication by subscription. In the early months of 1787 he composed two of his greatest chamber works, the String Quintets in C major and G minor (K.515 and 516), and made up half a normal set of six by his arrangement of the C minor wind Serenade.

Mozart had written only one earlier quintet, in 1773. There is, however, no sign of the problems he encountered with quartets. The quintets are as fine, and as contrasted, as the symphonies in the same keys of 1788. The C major Quintet begins with Mozart's longest first movement: below and above a gentle pulsation its arpeggio theme passes from cello to violin, covering four

octaves, and the temporal dimensions respond to this expansive use of musical space. The texture is carefully controlled by Mozart as he amplifies his design by passing material from a pair of violins to a pair of violas, reducing and varying his forces; the sound never cloys, even in the eloquent slow movements of both quintets, partly formed as a duet of equals between first violin and viola. The G minor Quintet is the dark shadow of its glowing companion; the pulsation of the opening is now restless and supports a fragmentary and uncertain melodic formation. Mozart is incomparable in this mood of somber agitation. Particularly remarkable is the finale, which has an introduction in the form of an operatic lament. The violin finally almost breaks into recitative, as Beethoven was to do in his late quartets; instead the cadence leads without preamble into a major-key finale of ample proportions.

In May 1787 Mozart heard of the death of his father in Salzburg after a period of illness. His reaction was curiously muted. He had written

of his feelings about the friendliness of death to his father, but his letters to his sister concern the disposition of the estate rather than their loss. His next completed works were the opposite of elegiac; they include that epitome of Mozartian grace, the serenade *Eine kleine Nachtmusik*, and a masterpiece of musical humor, combining buffoonery and subtle wit, the 'Musical Joke' (*Ein musikalischer Spass*). If this last may seem disrespectful in its jests at the expense of provincial composers, Leopold's fondness for such pieces should be remembered; this may even be a tribute. Mozart also wrote his last sonata for his father's instrument. His works for violin and piano had appeared sporadically of late, but it is possible to trace a growth, away from the old conception of a violin accompanying the piano, towards a duet of equals culminating in this beautiful A major work (K.526). The opening, in which the piano right hand and violin exchange material, is one sign of this; the haunting slow movement is another, based on a solemn piano line, no mere accompaniment, over which the violin spins its more ornate, but fragmentary, melody. The roles are then reversed, and their interlocking has a characteristic sensuous and intellectual fascination. Here too

Above: Illustration from an early edition (1785) of Beaumarchais's *La folle journée, ou Le Mariage de Figaro*, on which Mozart's opera was based. The scene is from the first act, where the Count discovers the page Cherubino, who from his hiding-place has overheard the Count's overtures to Susanna.

Left: Title-page and list of characters from the original libretto for Mozart's opera.

Sardi Bussany

Maria Piccinelli Mandini

Franz Bussani

Mich: Okelly

Left: Silhouettes of some of the singers in the original production of *Figaro*; from left to right: Paolo Stefano Mandini (Count), Luisa Laschi-Mombelli (Countess), Dorotea Sardi-Bussani (Cherubino), Maria Piccinelli-Mandini (Marcellina), Francesco Bussani (Bartolo and Antonio) and Michael Kelly (Basilio and Don Curzio).

Mozart inherited a form, and without a single revolutionary gesture transformed its essence from within.

• Don Giovanni •

The sonata was finished in August; the first performance of *Don Giovanni* was scheduled for 14 October, in Prague. Instead of composing it on the spot as usual, on this occasion Mozart must have sent plenty of music ahead of him, since he did not leave for Prague until 1 October. He did, of course, know most of the singers, from their performance in the Prague *Figaro*, and he probably had an eye on an immediate second production in Vienna. Some pieces were composed in Prague; the overture was as usual written last; some reports stated that it was splendidly sight-read at the first performance ('only a few notes fell under the table,' Mozart said). This, however, was not until the end of October for, as usual, the première was postponed. The opera was an enormous success in Prague, and more legends surround this period of Mozart's life than almost any other, partly because of the reputation the opera itself enjoyed in the nineteenth century.

Don Giovanni presents more problems for criticism than any of Mozart's works, and only *Die Zauberflöte* has generated an equally vast literature. *Don Giovanni* is the least satisfactory, and the most difficult to stage convincingly, of the da Ponte operas. It is wrong, however, to blame the librettist; its major flaw is the greatness of the music. Ostensibly a comic opera (as the subtitle '*dramma giocoso*' implies, although Mozart himself called it '*opera buffa*'), it begins with attempted rape and a fatal duel and ends with the principal character going unrepentant to Hell. The blend of farce and the supernatural is as old as the subject, of which the walking statue and comic servant are both integral parts. The music irretrievably shatters this comic mode; by rising fully to the awesome nature of the apparition, and by allowing the villainous Giovanni to acquire nobility in his deplorable refusal to repent, it opens ethical questions beyond the capacity of opera to resolve.

The social tensions are less important in *Don Giovanni* than in *Figaro*, although they appear in the bitterness of the peasant Masetto's resentment when Giovanni detaches him from his bride Zerlina. At one extraordinary moment, too, the banner of political freedom is waved: when the avengers arrive at Giovanni's party, he expresses their freedom to remain masked by the dangerously subversive phrase 'Viva la libertà,' taken up by the others with a gratuitous outburst of trumpets and drums.

Mozart rose fully to the challenge posed by his librettist with extraordinarily incisive musical characterization. His wronged Donna Anna and her lover Ottavio sing in the style of *opera seria*, whereas Donna Elvira, though not mad, as is sometimes suggested, lacks natural dignity and is prepared to harangue the naïve peasant-girl Zerlina; her musical style is correspondingly varied and flighty, but includes moments of tenderness, of which Giovanni is quite unworthy. Masetto is a bumpkin briefly endowed with irony; Leporello a cowardly servant, admiring and envying his master (as the music of the catalogue makes clear) and unable to tear himself away. Giovanni himself was raised by the nineteenth century, because of his defiance of Fate, into a Faustian hero. In sober reality he is a vicious playboy, a rake; but there is no sober reality here, and his essence, in Mozart's music, can hardly be grasped. We never learn to know

Below: Mozart's manuscript of Figaro's *cavatina* in Act I of the opera, in which he announces that he will call the tune if the Count wants to 'dance.'

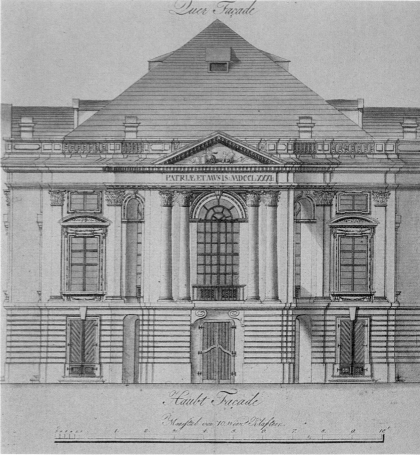

him as we do the others; he moves too fast, never pausing for more than a moment to contemplate his actions or think. He is an actor and a reactor, adapting his tone of voice for every situation, adjusting his style of seduction to meet each case, singing *buffo* with Leporello, even assuming nobility in his confrontations with the Commendatore. In this very lack of character lies the Mozartian characterization which has continued to fascinate commentators from Stendhal, E. T. A. Hoffman and Kierkegaard through Shaw to the present day.

In the final scene, in which after the statue has departed the other characters sort themselves out and sing the moral, Mozart returns us to normality, but normality is dullness compared with life when Giovanni is in our midst. In the stupendous music for the statue, which beggars description even as it compels our fascinated exploration, Mozart seems to threaten not only the conventions of comedy, but of classical balance and control. Its demonic, other-worldly quality retains its impact even today.

• Vienna: 1788-90 •

The early months of 1788 after Mozart's return from Prague, when he received Gluck's appointment, seem curiously flat and unproductive, although he wrote an appreciable amount of music, including some of his finest solo piano movements (the Adagio in B minor and movements for a Sonata in F), and a new Piano Concerto, the so-called 'Coronation' (K.537). His mind was on *Don Giovanni*; by April he had prepared the new version, with a different aria for Don Ottavio and an additional one for Elvira, as well as a duet for Zerlina and Leporello. This production was also postponed; the Emperor, who had commanded it, was away. Fourteen performances during the summer did not amount to a real success, and this must have been a considerable blow. Mozart, however, rose above disappointment and produced another series of instrumental masterpieces over the summer, the three last symphonies and the three last piano trios. The latter show the same kind of development as the violin sonatas, a growing independence of the string parts. In

this respect they are more 'advanced' even than the later masterpieces of Haydn in the medium, and were the models for the young Beethoven.

While chamber works were written with a view to publication (the trios came out in Vienna in 1788 as op.15), the origin of the symphonies of 1788 is somewhat obscure. It is not even certain which, if any, Mozart ever heard; there is a reference to a 'grand symphony' given in Frankfurt in September 1789, where he also

Top left: Design (1789) by Joseph Quaglio for the graveyard scene in *Don Giovanni* (K.527).

Above: Façade and section of the Estates Theater in Prague where *Don Giovanni* received its first performance on 29 October 1787.

movement. Mozart wrote two versions of this symphony: one using oboes for the principal wind solos, a drier, in some ways more intense version; the second adding clarinets and giving them the principal solos, a richer, more romantic sound, which is usually preferred.

The last symphony (K.551), which early acquired the nickname 'Jupiter,' also transcends its ancestry, which is the festive trumpet-and-drum type of C major symphony. Both these last two symphonies have extraordinarily beautiful slow movements and large, inventive minuets, but it is the outer movements which give them their character. Mozart's ability to combine different musical characters in a single thought is nowhere clearer than at the opening of the 'Jupiter': a stern call to action, a lyrical response, a fanfare. His next move is to combine these ideas with a decorative counter-melody in the wind, and as if that were not enough material, he introduces two completely fresh subsidiary themes. The contrast with Haydn's economy of means could hardly be greater. In the finale Mozart's profusion of invention takes another form; beginning gently enough – compare the 'Paris' Symphony – he introduces new material into the expected outburst of the whole orchestra. He then embarks on fugal treatment of his material, and eventually no fewer than five subjects are combined in a *tour de force* which also makes a brilliant conclusion.

In 1789 Mozart's thoughts almost certainly turned once more to opera. In the last two years

performed K.537. During 1788, still hoping for success with *Don Giovanni*, he turned his hand to the symphony in order to have works ready when the need arose; perhaps he was even contemplating a visit to London, where symphonies were in great demand. However, he declined an invitation to go there, and Haydn was left undisputed master of that profitable terrain.

The E flat symphony (K.543) is the only one with a slow introduction; the opening of the allegro, with its soft horn-call, is magical. A wealth of material, lyrically expansive or tautly argued, makes up a movement which could, with the 'Prague' Symphony, be considered a fitting end to Mozart's traditional symphonic writing; for the G minor and C major Symphonies virtually break the mold of the eighteenth-century symphony, the first by its unrelenting intensity of feeling, the second by its expanded scale and complexity of technique. This is especially so in the finales, where the utmost strain is imposed upon the listener used to a lighter conclusion (a convention still observed in the E flat Symphony, with its capricious monothematic finale).

In a minor-key work the composer can choose between a minor and a major ending. In the G minor Quintet, as has been observed, Mozart took the latter course. In the early G minor Symphony the finale is in the minor, but more energetic than pathetic. The finale of this symphony, however (K.550), whilst in the minor too, is nervous, electrical; if it conforms to type in being fast and rhythmically incisive, it transcends its models in its speed and intentness of

Above: Alabaster relief dated 1789 which again shows the graveyard scene in *Don Giovanni*

Opposite: Mozart's manuscript of Don Giovanni's serenade with mandolin accompaniment in Act III of the opera.

of his life he was to produce three, in strikingly different genres, and fulfilled to some extent his ambitions in serious opera and in German opera. The first commission, however, was for another comedy, stimulated not by *Don Giovanni* but by the revival of *Figaro* in August 1789. Mozart was beginning to acquire a wider reputation as an opera composer; early in 1789 he traveled to Berlin with Prince Karl Lichnowsky, where he may have heard *Die Entführung*. The popularity of the latter led the theater directors to

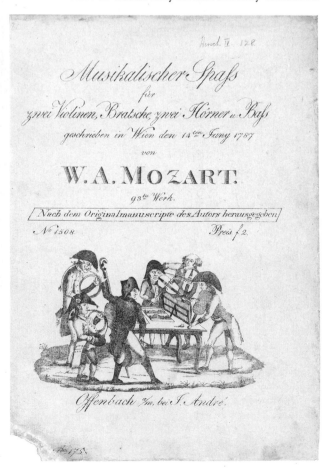

seek a successor, and they found it in German adaptations of *Don Giovanni* (none of them with Mozart's collaboration), which were given at eight centers before the end of 1789, though these versions were mostly appalling travesties, with spoken dialogue and new scenes added.

The visit to Berlin must have given Mozart hopes of preferment in the Prussian court. The King of Prussia, Frederick William II, was a cellist to whom Haydn had recently dedicated the six quartets op.50. Mozart began two quartets (in D, K.575, and in B flat, K.589); the hoped-for royal commission, however, never came, and K.589 was only finished in 1790, alongside Mozart's last quartet, in F (K.590). K.575 and K.589 concentrate particular attention on the cello, using it as a melodic instrument in the exposition of many principal themes. The result is another rethinking of quartet texture; the viola has to act as the lowest part, and the violins are often subordinate. The spare, attenuated sound is highly distinctive, and the compositional technique in these works, while wonderfully polished, is a good deal less intense than in the 'Haydn' quartets – or indeed in Haydn's own quartets. Some critics have suggested that a new stylistic phase was beginning in Mozart's music at this time, a 'late style,' which depended less on contrasts and modulations and more on the refined spinning of perfectly poised lines. One may well feel, however, that the fact of the King's being a cellist was a greater contributory cause to the color of these lovely quartets.

The Clarinet Quintet (K.581) was composed, as were most of Mozart's clarinet pieces, for Anton Stadler, and it is the masterpiece among the small group of chamber pieces with solo wind, just as the concerto written for Stadler in 1791 surpasses Mozart's other wind concertos. The Quintet achieves its own miraculous balance, between soloistic writing and true chamber music, an ensemble of equals. To this end Mozart exploits the singing register of the clarinet and also its lower register, with its power of blending; and he allows its brilliant figuration in the first movement to be translated to the strings in the central development. Only in the last movement, a set of variations, is the clarinet part intermittently virtuosic. The minuet is graced with two trios, one for strings only, the second a clarinet solo in rustic style. The slow movement is among Mozart's most perfect. Its

Above left: Playbill for the first performance of *Così fan Tutte* (K.588) on 26 January 1790 at the Vienna Burgtheater. The opera was repeated several times in the course of the year.

Above: Lorenzo da Ponte (1749-1838), who wrote the libretti for Mozart's three great Italian comic operas and also for his cantata *Davidde penitente.* Mozart owed this connection in part to Salieri, who had recommended da Ponte's appointment as theater poet for the new Italian opera in Vienna in 1783.

Left: Title-page of the first (posthumous) edition of Mozart's *Musical Joke* (K.522) written in 1787. A satire on clumsy composers, the work demonstrates, in negative, many of Mozart's ideas on composition. The manuscript of the work later belonged to Franz Schubert.

elegant melodic arch prolongs itself to a degree of almost painful beauty by the simplest means, and without departing (except at one interruption of the cadence) from a comparatively small range in the finest cantabile register of the instrument; vocal music becomes chamber music.

The opera of this period, performed just two years before Mozart's death, is *Così fan tutte*, or *The School of Lovers*. In this work Mozart's mastery of various types of ensemble is unsurpassed – homogeneous duets, argumentative trios, playful love duets, quintet and sextet finding their logical conclusion in two ample finales. He seems, moreover, to have developed the aria further as a vehicle for characterization; it is there that the listener learns to distinguish the personalities which break the symmetries of the two pairs of lovers. The plot is more traditional than its predecessors; there are no social tensions, and the tricking of each of the two girls into infidelity with the other's disguised lover has been seen as trivial and immoral. In truth, however, it is not only very funny (as well as intermittently farcical), but also very serious. Taking the conventions for what they are – that the disguise is impenetrable and that the action unfolds, like that of *Figaro* and *Don Giovanni*, within a single day – we can feel free to explore, with Mozart, the intricate situation of the lovers; Ferrando and Fiordiligi in particular, for his girl (Dorabella) falls easily for Guglielmo, while Fiordiligi fights her growing attraction towards Ferrando nearly to the end. What might appear heartless in the libretto becomes, sensitively realized, a situation of almost unbearable poignancy; the manner in which Ferrando breaks down Fiordiligi's resistance makes it almost impossible not to believe that he is now in love with her, and we are left to speculate, at the end, on the durability of the relationships once the men have returned to their original guise and their first loves.

• The last works: 1790-1 •

Così reached the stage on 26 January 1790, the day before Mozart's thirty-fourth birthday. The following months were curiously unproductive; it seems likely, therefore, since Mozart was neither ill nor traveling, that he worked on projects which can be dated only through their later completion. The performances of *Così* (ten in all) were interrupted by the death of Joseph II, who had on the whole been good to Mozart. The composer retained his small stipend from the court and, except for the period of mourning, continued to produce dances. He also completed his 'Prussian' Quartets and sold them, having no more hopes from Berlin. He had few pupils and had almost given up the idea of holding his own concerts. A hopeful visit to Frankfurt for the coronation of the new emperor led to no improvement in his prospects, and he bade farewell to Haydn, who was leaving for London, in a depressed condition. The end of 1790 and the early months of 1791 were again fully productive with instrumental music, and by then Mozart must have been at work on at least one of the operas produced in 1791. A serious opera for Prague, realized in the coronation opera *La Clemenza di Tito*, may have been mooted as early as 1789, and work on *Die Zauberflöte* was probably interrupted to complete *La Clemenza* when it was commissioned. At a concert in March Mozart played his final Piano Concerto, K.595 in B flat. He may also have planned to add three new string quintets to the still-unpublished works of 1787, to make a set of six. The Quintet in D (K.593) dates from late 1790, and that in E flat (K.614), his last chamber work, from April 1791. K.593 is unique among the quintets in having a slow introduction; still more unusual is the manner in which this solemn passage recurs at the end of the first movement, followed by the phrase with which the allegro began. Mozart's idiom is now so flexible that a beginning can be an ending. The E flat Quintet, on the other hand, begins with music in hunting vein, quite unusual for a first movement in that key. This movement and the skittish finale make the E flat Quintet a tribute to Haydn, whom Mozart never expected to see again. The slow movement is of the apparently artless romanza type, in contrast to its parallels in all the other quintets, for the D major follows the works of 1787 in the elaboration and warmth of its adagio, and in exploiting the contrasting register and timbre of the violas against the violins.

Marvellous as these works are, they cannot be said to represent a great advance on their earlier companions, and the same may be said of the last piano concerto. There is, however, about K.595 a gentleness which is a further

Left: Frederick William II, King of Prussia (1744-97), an excellent cellist, for whom Boccherini and Haydn among others wrote works. Mozart went to Berlin in 1789 while on a tour of Germany in the company of Prince Lichnowsky; he played for the Queen, and the King commissioned a set of piano sonatas for his daughter and six string quartets. It is reported that the King actually offered Mozart a position at the Prussian court, which he did not accept; in any event he fulfilled only part of the commission: one piano sonata (K.576) and the three 'Prussian' quartets (K.575, 589, 590) with their elaborate cello parts written with the King in mind.

manifestation of a 'late style,' beginning with the luminous texture of the 'Prussian' Quartets and continuing in the Clarinet Concerto K.622. The rustling start of K.595, a serene counterpart to that of the G minor Symphony, and the sweetness of its slow movement, are not altogether forgotten in the lively finale. For this, appropriately to the season of composition, Mozart used a recent little song about spring; but this concerto, like K.622, invites description more in terms of autumn. In the Clarinet Concerto the nature of the instrument requires a veiled orchestration, using flutes instead of oboes; the result, fully exploiting the solo instrument and especially its soft lower notes, is Mozart's most delicate pastel shading.

Mozart wrote a number of short works in 1791, including the remarkable pieces for mechanical organ. Feeling only distaste for the instrument, he characteristically responded by a far-ranging tonal and formal exploration, with magnificent results in the powerful, partly fugal fantasia, K.608. He also wrote a number of short vocal works, including his last songs and arias, and two Masonic cantatas, K.619 for solo soprano and piano, and K.623 for male chorus and orchestra, his last completed work. In June he composed the lovely *Ave verum corpus*, K.618, and in the summer he was commissioned to write the Requiem. No premonitions of death should be inferred from this turning to solemn and sacred matters, however, any more than from the mellow brilliance of the Clarinet Concerto, which derives from the soul of the instrument. Mozart was occasionally ill in 1791, but there was no indication that he was mortally afflicted, and his last letters are full of good spirits. The real tragedy is that he died just as recognition and a measure

of material success were on the horizon; financially his position seems to have been far better in 1791 than in the previous two years. Most of the stories of Mozart's last year are fanciful.

La Clemenza di Tito was started later than *Die Zauberflöte* but finished and performed earlier; indeed its final stages were so rushed that Mozart's pupil Süssmayr had to write the recitatives. *La Clemenza* is based on a libretto of 1734 by Metastasio, whom Mozart might be thought to have long outgrown, but, as he said, it was 'made into a proper opera' by Caterino Mazzolà, who reduced it to two acts, cut many arias, and inserted ensembles and a short concerted finale to Act I involving a considerable amount of action and spectacular stage effects (the burning of the Capitol). The result is not at all comparable to Mozart's comic operas; the ensembles are static, the finale in only two sections, getting slower not faster. The characters are given more vitality by Mozart than in most earlier settings of the libretto, but they remain two-dimensional.

Within these limitations, however, Mozart's music shows no sign of lack of care or interest in what he was doing. The orchestration is lighter than usual, but that was an aspect of *opera seria* style, and allows the full orchestra to make a great impact in the first finale. This statuesque style unashamedly depends for its dramatic as well as its musical effect on the persuasiveness of fine singing. Accordingly, the principal characters are permitted more extended arias.

Elegant, slender almost to a fault, *La Clemenza* defied its old-fashioned origins and was among Mozart's most widely performed works well into the next century. But it is, of course, *Die Zauberflöte* which is the true consummation of Mozart's operatic achievement, for it contains within it elements from almost every style he had ever cultivated. That it could do so, and that the mixture works, results from the nature of the subject-matter, which is both esoteric and direct; supernatural and straightforwardly human; serious and comic.

Above: Count Joseph Deym's 'Art Gallery' (or waxworks) in Vienna, for which Mozart was commissioned to write several pieces for mechanical organ in 1790 and 1791.

Below: Josepha Dussek (1754-1834), wife of the composer F. X. Dussek. They were among Mozart's most generous friends and owned the Villa Bertramka near Prague, where he completed *Don Giovanni* in 1787.

Josepha Duschek.

Left: A glass harmonica, the instrument invented by Benjamin Franklin for which Mozart wrote two works in the last year of his life (K.617 and K.356) for the blind virtuoso Marianne Kirchgässner.

Die Zauberflöte

The meaning of *Die Zauberflöte* is an inexhaustible subject for debate, but some of its sources are becoming less mysterious. There is no doubt that it has Masonic, and political, significance; love and understanding, tempered by severity and necessary discipline, are an image of an ideal society. That the leading part is given to a woman, Pamina, who is finally accepted as joint ruler of the Order, suggests something outside contemporary Masonic thought and quite overrules earlier denunciations of women in general and the Queen of Night in particular. The suggestion that Tamino represents Joseph II, the Queen Maria Theresa, the Order Freemasonry and its enemies the Catholic Church should not be dismissed, but such exterior meanings are of slight importance compared to the unfolding of the many-layered story.

Almost as inexhaustible are the arguments about the plot itself. It was long thought that the Queen was at first intended to be a sympathetic character and Sarastro the villain, but that their roles were exchanged in mid-composition. This is, however, an impossible story to believe, for Mozart would never have concerned himself only with the trivial adventure-story it implies. Clearly, the Queen must *appear* sympathetic at her first entrance because she has to convince the bemused Tamino; and Mozart did not omit to put a hard, even terrible, edge to this music or to make her attendant ladies disagreeably quarrelsome. Among other things, the moral is the danger of trusting only first impressions and being impervious to reason thereafter; it is Tamino's saving grace to perceive at once that the priestly order, which the Queen has described as the evil kidnappers of her child, is in fact benevolent, and to be convinced by the noble speech of the orator that Pamina is captive for the sake of her own virtue and wisdom.

The only problem of the actual mechanism of the plot is that it is the Queen who presents Tamino with the magic flute and Papageno, his 'everyman' companion and the opera's clown, with magic bells. But magic things respond only to the proper intentions of the user. The Queen is deceived in thinking that they would work for her; there is no evidence that they could work evil. More problematic are the three genii, who are offered by the Queen's ladies as guides to Tamino, but who turn out to be wholly on the side of good. Again, however, the delusion of the Queen explains the anomaly. Believing

Above: Procession for the coronation of Leopold II as King of Bohemia in Prague. Mozart had travelled to Frankfurt in 1790 for the Imperial coronation and was now trying desperately to get a good post at court. *La Clemenza di Tito* (K.621), performed on 6 September 1791 on the occasion of the Prague coronation, was commissioned by the Bohemian Estates, but it did not further Mozart's cause: the new Empress described the work as 'porcheria tedesca,' German trash.

Left: Design by Giorgio Fuentes for a new production in German of *La Clemenza di Tito* in Frankfurt in 1799. The scene is from the end of Act II, when the Emperor pardons the conspirators in the Senate House.

281

Left: Frontispiece to the original libretto of *Die Zauberflöte* (K.620), displaying a number of masonic symbols.

and depth of sonority. There is more extensive use than in Mozart's other operas of trombones and basset-horns, suited for solemnity, as well as special effects such as the solo flute and bells; but it is in the penetrating sweetness of quite normal instrumental groups, for instance in the lovely quintets, or the dangerous simplicity of the march (for flute, trombones and drums) during which Tamino and Pamina pass through fire and water, that Mozart achieves miracles out of nearly nothing – a seldom attained ideal of musical composition.

The musical styles, like the manner of writing for voices, cover every stage between extreme simplicity (the folk-like songs of Papageno; the march) and extreme elaboration (the Queen's music; the ensembles and finales). Dramatic recitative is used sparingly and with correspondingly greater force, notably in the first finale (the crucial dialogue of Tamino and the orator). To the vocal styles already mentioned must be added the Protestant chorale, treated in a fugal style, that inevitably recalls Bach. *Die Zauberflöte* is magical indeed in its power to assimilate so much without strain: Mozart's Italianate style, his German orientation, his most lyrical idiom and his penchant for the learned (the overture is another brilliant synthesis of fugue and sonata). This conflation (one can hardly call it synthesis) is perfectly in keeping with his dramatic intention, and is thus not at all disturbing; on the contrary it creates that universal quality which has made the work such an unending source of edification and delight.

Right: Schikaneder in the costume of Papageno, the bird-man, from the original libretto of the opera.

passionately in her own cause, she is both dangerous and vulnerable, for she calls genii to her aid who, as naturally beneficent beings, in fact aid the other side. The presence of the malicious Monostatos on Sarastro's staff is also a warning of the vulnerability even of societies founded upon reason; it is in order to deepen their own understanding of themselves, and so improve society, that Pamina is brought up by Sarastro and made joint ruler with Tamino in his stead.

It is not the text but Mozart's music which makes this interpretative speculation possible. His style ranges from the popular ditty of Papageno, through the more elevated vocal styles of the arias for Tamino and Pamina, to the most elaborately wrought vocal style in those of the Queen of Night, whose dizzy coloratura Mozart wrote for his sister-in-law Josepha Hofer. Somewhere between these extremes he found for Sarastro a style, direct and solemn yet not lacking in ornament, which Shaw declared was the only music fit for God to sing. The ensembles draw the characters together. The loveliest tribute to the union of man and wife is sung by the princess, Pamina, and birdman, Papageno. The variety of vocal color is enhanced by the three ladies of the Queen, alternately seductive, spiteful and tempestuous, and the three genii, whose music is so delicate that boys can sing it successfully even in an opera house. The chorus is not extensively deployed as it is, for instance, by Gluck, but its interventions are telling as well as providing a means of climax; Mozart's choral writing is simple when compared with that of Handel, on whose music he had worked so much, but it is of similar effectiveness. The orchestration wonderfully achieves lucidity

Above: Cover of one of the early editions of *Die Zauberflöte* in piano score, published in Bonn in 1793. In the vignette muses mourn by the funerary urn inscribed with Mozart's name.

Right: Emanuel Schikaneder (1751-1812), who had known Mozart since Salzburg days. He was a notable actor-manager, who had included Shakespeare and Lessing in his repertory, though now he is known only for his libretto – often criticized – for *Die Zauberflöte*.

Barely two months after the première, by which time the growing success of the work had become apparent, Mozart was dead. There is no reason to suppose that he died from anything other than natural causes. His health had never been strong, and he had suffered illnesses, exacerbated by hard work, a number of times in the last few years. No doubt he worked at the Requiem whenever he could, for the money from the commission was attractive; but the principal reason for his failure to recover from a severe attack of rheumatic fever was the condition of medicine at the time. Mozart took to his bed at the end of November and died on 5 December; he was buried two days later in circumstances which may seem mean to us now but which were consistent with his status and his widow's resources.

Mozart's last legacy was the unfinished Requiem, which Constanze caused to be completed, eventually, and after others had been asked, by Süssmayr. Mozart's pupil did not do the work justice; his orchestration is slovenly, and the music he composed – which includes the entire 'Sanctus–Benedictus–Osanna' sequence – is of mediocre quality. There are, however, some complete movements by Mozart, and several more are complete in their essence, needing only additional detail and instrumentation. It is possible that Süssmayr used sketches, although at least one has survived which he did not use. Sensibly enough, he repeated the music of the 'Kyrie eleison' at the end so that the work closes with authentic Mozart; this double fugue is, however, a relatively uninspired piece in a severe style. Even the authentic parts of the Requiem (like the C minor Mass, the only comparable work of Mozart's maturity) are too uneven for

Herr Emanuel Schikaneder.

us to believe that Mozart consciously planned this as his last will and testament. Like the C minor Mass, the Requiem is a magnificent torso, and modern attempts to retouch, or even to eliminate Süssmayr, are fully justifiable, even if they can never grant us what Mozart's death withheld.

JOSEPH HAYDN

PETER BROWN

Opposite: Franz Joseph Haydn (1732-1809) painted in 1785 by Christian Ludwig Seehas.

Joseph Haydn was born on the last day of March 1732 in the hamlet of Rohrau near the present border of Austria and Hungary. Rohrau was situated in the medieval fashion around the residence of Count Karl Anton Harrach, where Haydn's mother worked in the kitchen. His father, Mathias, who was a wheelwright by trade and village magistrate, made a respectable income. Little is known of Haydn's home life or his musical environment except that his father played the harp and sang. At a young age Joseph thoroughly knew his repertoire of songs. Such talents seemingly led Mathias to procure for Joseph an education beyond what Rohrau could offer, for at the age of six, 'Sepperl' was sent to Hainburg to enter the school operated by his cousin Johann Mathias Franck; here, in addition to music, he learned reading and writing.

Despite its limitations, Hainburg provided Haydn with his most decisive opportunity. The local parish priest, Anton Johann Palmb, was a friend of Johann Georg Reutter (1708-72), the newly appointed Kapellmeister of St Stephen's Cathedral, Vienna, and through the offices of Palmb, Reutter heard little 'Sepperl' sing. Having passed the audition with an accomplished trill rewarded by Reutter with some cherries, Haydn joined the choir school at St Stephen's.

Though Haydn was one of only six boy choristers, the total employ of the imperial musical establishment numbered some 140 musicians, who had to provide music for the chamber, theater and church, but it was the church music that formed the center of the young Haydn's experience. The normal celebration of the Mass might involve an orchestrally accompanied setting of the Ordinary with sections of the Proper set in the same manner or replaced by instrumental movements; for more festive days, solemn Mass would also be celebrated with trumpets and timpani in multiple choirs.

After nearly a decade at the Kapellhaus – where he was joined in 1745 by his brother Michael – Haydn's voice broke. No longer of any use to Reutter, who had to support the boys from his own accounts, Haydn was dismissed in November 1749 with three shirts, a coat and no money. Through a stroke of luck he was rescued from the wintry streets of Vienna by Johann Michael Spangler, a music teacher and tenor at the Michaelerkirche, who took him into his own small quarters. Haydn remained with Spangler, his wife and child for ten months at the most, until the birth of their daughter in September 1750.

When Haydn left the Spanglers he was totally independent for the first time in his life. It was probably within the next year that he considered entering the Servite Order and in the spring made the pilgrimage to the church at Mariazell. Upon his return to Vienna, Haydn received a loan of 150 Gulden from a market judge and began to earn his way by giving lessons. He also performed in the churches; he played the organ for the Chapel of the Brothers of Mercy in Leopoldstadt and for Count Haugwitz, in addition to singing in the choir at St Stephen's.

One evening Haydn serenaded the wife of the celebrated Hanswurst comic actor and impresario-director of the Kärntnertor Theater, Felix Kurz-Bernardon. Kurz-Bernardon himself wished to know who composed the music; the result was a commission for Haydn's first opera, *Der krumme Teufel*. Although censored, it was revived in the late 1750s under the title of *Der neue krumme Teufel. The Crooked Devil* was probably not the only music Haydn composed for Kurz-Bernardon; a collection of arias that were once a part of Kurz's repertoire survive without attributions.

With such fortunate strokes of fate, Haydn improved his position so that he was able to take a garret room in the Michaelerhaus. Here he made further important contacts; in the same house lived the imperial court poet Metastasio. Through him Haydn became the amanuensis and accompanist to the famous Italian composer and voice teacher Nicola Porpora, from whom he learned the 'true fundamentals of composition,' as well as Italian and singing.

Among Porpora's students was the mistress of Correr, the Venetian ambassador in Vienna. Correr spent his summers with his lady at the baths of Mannersdorf, and Porpora, together with Haydn, traveled with them to continue the lessons. During this time Haydn also accompanied Porpora at Prince Hildburghausen's in the presence of Gluck and Wagenseil. By the mid-1750s Porpora's accompanist became known to Karl Joseph Edler von Fürnberg, and as a result of Fürnberg's recommendation, Haydn was engaged as music director to Count Morzin around 1758-9.

No accounting of Haydn's responsibilities for Morzin exists. He taught keyboard and seemingly composed some symphonies (including

his first), *Tafelmusik* for wind instruments, as well as keyboard music. In about 1760 Morzin dismissed his musical establishment as a result of strained financial circumstances.

At some time during the 1750s Haydn resided with the wig-maker J. P. Keller, who had two daughters, Therese and Maria Anna. To the younger, Therese, Haydn developed a strong attachment, but she entered a convent in April 1755. Feeling a strong obligation to Keller for his generosity, Haydn agreed to marry the elder daughter, Maria Anna. The wedding took place on 26 November 1760 at St Stephen's. The marriage was an incompatible one; Maria Anna had little sympathy for Haydn's work and reportedly was an overly pious spendthrift.

Haydn's first works were written during his tenure at the Kapellhaus to liturgical texts . His early biographers refer variously to, a 'Mass for four-part chorus and sixteen-part orchestra,' 'a *Salve Regina* in twelve parts,' and 'a composition for sixteen parts.' Probably the first fully authenticated and extant composition is the *Missa Brevis* in F (Hob.XXI:1). Believed to have been composed in 1749, it owes much to the style of Reutter: the declamatory text setting, the figurative writing for the violins and what today would be regarded as faulty part-writing. Otherwise, it typifies the Viennese *Missa Brevis* with its compact Kyrie, telescoped texts in the Gloria and Credo, expansive treatment of the Benedictus and recapitulation of the Kyrie's music in the Agnus Dei.

If this early Mass owes something directly to Reutter, the style of some of the later vocal works reflects Haydn's studies with Porpora. Among these is the *Salve Regina* (Hob.XXIIIb: 1), which Haydn dated 1756, and the *Ave Regina* (Hob.XXIIIb:3). Both contain elaborate coloratura of the type Haydn may well have learned during the many voice lessons at which he was an accompanist for the Italian maestro.

The decade of the 1750s, however, is most significant for the instrumental works: music for keyboard in solo, ensemble and concerted settings for Haydn's own students; miscellaneous ensemble pieces for serenading; string quartets and trios for the Baron von Fürnberg; and symphonies, wind band music and additional keyboard compositions for Count Morzin.

Although Haydn's concerted keyboard music is the only instrumental genre of decidedly secondary historical importance, the solo sonatas for harpsichord or clavichord mark the end of a Viennese tradition that can be traced from Froberger to Wagenseil. While Wagenseil's divertimenti still reveal vestiges of the suite, all that remains in Haydn's are the minuets, which are often highlighted by *minore* trios of unusual expression. These divertimenti run the gamut from very small and simple works intended for the *Liebhaber* (amateur) to bigger sonatas suitable for the *Kenner* (connoisseur) – just what one would expect from a composer who depended so heavily on keyboard lessons for his livelihood.

Much the same could be said for the concertini, but not for the early keyboard trios, which are more uniform in their dimension and style. Here Haydn synthesizes two traditions: first the trio-sonata for two violins and *basso continuo* (the violin and the right hand of the keyboard form the treble; the left hand and cello, the bass), and second the texture of the accompanied sonata in which the violin doubles the keyboard or plays an otherwise secondary role. However, unlike other similar works of the time, the violin here is rarely optional.

The ten early string quartets (known from their unauthorized Parisian prints as op.1 and 2) are considered landmarks; they are the beginning of one of the most important genres in western art. Written, according to Haydn's own testimony, for the four performers (two violins, viola, and cello without *basso continuo*) available at Fürnberg's estate, these five-movement works use minuets for their second and fourth

Right: Popular theater in the Schottenplatz in Vienna, featuring Hanswurst (a local adaptation of Harlequin from the *commedia dell'arte*). In the background, left, is the town palace of the Harrach family, the local landowners at Rohrau, Haydn's birthplace.

movements, flanked by a combination of fast and slow movements. The initial and final fast movements are frequently of equal weight, while the slow movements, often arias for solo violin, provide the real center of gravity.

The quartets are only exceeded in importance by the symphonies, at this period in three or four movements. The weightier thoughts lie mainly in the initial fast and slow movements; the finales in 3/8 and 2/4 hold less interest. Their scorings are mostly for two oboes, two horns and strings, with occasional additions of a pair of *clarini* (trumpets) and timpani; Haydn probably intended the bassoon to double the bass when it was not scored separately. Even in these works one can find driving rhythms and scintillating effects, and by the late 1750s Haydn had mastered the symphonic idiom in a fashion unmatched by even his most gifted and famous contemporaries.

• Service with the Esterházys •

Haydn's entry into the service of the Esterházy family began officially on 1 May 1761, although he may have been in the Esterházy household before the signing of his contract. In addition to stipulating salary and demanding honorable personal and professional conduct, the Vice-kapellmeister's contract expected him to take charge of all musical activities save for those of the chapel, which remained under the direction of the aging and infirm Oberkapellmeister Werner; to compose music for the exclusive use of the Prince; to appear twice daily for instruction concerning musical performances; to care for the princely instruments; and to provide vocal instruction. The agreement further stated that if Haydn executed his obligations satisfactorily he could expect promotion to Kapellmeister.

The Esterházys were, by the second half of the eighteenth century, the most powerful of the Hungarian magnates, probably the wealthiest nobles in the Hapsburg domain, and, with the perilous decline in the imperial treasury, possibly financially more secure than the Empire itself. For several generations the family had had strong musical interests, and thus Haydn found himself in one of the most advantageous contemporary economic and musical environments. Prince Paul Anton, who had engaged Haydn, was in poor health and died in March 1762; he was succeeded by his younger brother Nicolaus, who was to hold the title of prince for some twenty-eight years. If anything, Nicolaus was a more avid enthusiast of music and theater than his older brother; from the mid-1760s to the mid-1770s his passion was chamber music with the baryton, an instrument from the gamba family, while from 1776 until his death it was the theater, both musical and dramatic.

Haydn's orchestra consisted of a flute, two oboes, one or two bassoons, two horns, five violins and violas (including Haydn), one cello, and one or two basses. It was this ensemble that he exploited so effectively in what are believed to be among his first works for Prince Esterházy, the three symphonies titled 'Le Matin' (no.6), 'Le Midi' (no.7) and 'Le Soir' (no.8). Each of these 'Tageszeiten' (Times of Day) Symphonies blends a variety of styles: operatic (instrumental recitative and/or aria), concertante (*tutti/solo* alternations), symphonic (sonata form) and characteristic (sunrise – introduction to 'Morning'; French overture – introduction to 'Noon'; storm – finale of 'Evening'). Here Haydn has utilized the orchestra not only in the standard combinations with trio and solo settings, but also in more surprising ones such as the bassoon and contrabass duet of Symphony no.6. Further concertante movements were also produced for Symphonies nos.36, 72 and 31.

Above: The walled city of Vienna in the mid-eighteenth century with the great spire of St Stephen's in the center.

Right: The exterior of St Stephen's cathedral. Haydn joined the cathedral *Kapelle* in 1740 after the Court Kapellmeister Georg von Reutter had heard his singing. In 1760, while in the service of Count Morzin in Vienna, Haydn was married in St Stephen's to Maria Anna Keller, whose sister Therese had been his first love but had taken the veil in 1756.

No.31, the 'Horn Signal,' and no.72 feature a quartet of virtuoso horns, which Haydn also employed in a related divertimento for violin, viola, bass, and horn quartet.

Among the most interesting of the early Esterházy symphonies is no.22, 'The Philosopher.' Since English horns replace the usual pair of oboes, this work has an unusual sound. It begins with a slow movement in which a *cantus firmus* styled theme is accompanied by a baroque eighth-note accompaniment; this symphony may well have been used for the liturgy. As in the 'Tageszeiten' Symphonies, an antiquated style is synthesized with a symphonic structure. One might expect this austere first movement to be followed by an equally serious contrapuntal one, but Haydn provides a straightforward allegro, follows with an aristocratic minuet and ends with a jesting folk-styled movement in 6/8 time.

Besides symphonies that featured the Esterházy musicians in consortium, Haydn also wrote concertos – one for flute, one for bassoon, two for horn, one for two horns, at least two for violin, several for cello and one for contrabass – but of these only one horn, one cello and two violin concertos dating from this period are extant and unquestionably authentic. In addition, probably for his own use, Haydn wrote one keyboard concerto (Hob.XVIII:3).

Die Metropolitankirche zum Heil. Stephan in Wien.   L'Eglise cathédrale de Saint Etienne à Vienne.

Despite the importance of the symphonies from this period, perhaps the most striking efforts are two keyboard pieces from *c*.1765: the *Capriccio* (Hob.XVII:1) and the *Twenty Variations* (Hob.XVII:2). The *Capriccio* juxtaposes a song of utmost harmonic simplicity, 'Acht Sauschneider müssen sein' (on the castration of a boar), with a series of extravagant modulatory gestures – most notably a central passage with a descending bass pattern derived from an old improvised formula discussed by C. P. E. Bach in his *Essay on the True Art of Playing Keyboard Instruments*, which Haydn bought *c*.1762. The *Variations* are on a minuet, which is reworked in a series of strophes that maintain their form only at the large dimension.

Within each strophe Haydn adjusts the punctuations in a most subtle manner. This, together with the transformation of the minuet into various characteristic types (for example, *polacca*, French overture, *gebunden*) and the architectural relationship of the variations, adds up to one of the great sets of the century.

The vocal works of the period include a series of ode-like pieces for the Prince and two operas: *Marchese* (1762), a comedy; and *Acide* (1762), a *festa teatrale*. *Marchese*, or *La Marchesa Nespola*, seems to have been written for Nicolaus's succession. It has a mixture of aria types ranging from those in 2/4 and 3/8, whose straightforward style belongs to the *opera buffa* and *intermezzo*, to those whose derivation is clearly

Right: Audience at the celebrations in Schönbrunn in October 1760 for the marriage of Maria Theresa's son, later Joseph II, to Isabella of Parma. The opera performed was Gluck's *Tetide* with a libretto by G. B. Migliavacca, who was later to provide the book for Haydn's first Italian opera, the *festa teatrale Acide*.

Left: A distant view of Eisenstadt around the time Haydn took up his appointment with the Esterházys.

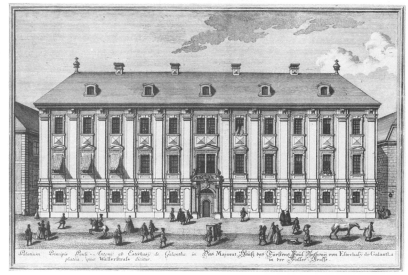

Above: The Esterházy town palace in the Wallnerstrasse in Vienna, where the Prince and his court spent the winter.

from the *opera seria*. *Acide* is more completely an *opera seria*; the plot is a familiar one, extended coloratura is more consistently used, the forms are predominantly *da capo* with extended ritornellos, and the arias are connected by both *secco* and accompanied recitatives. Three ode-like Italian cantatas (Hob.XXIVa:2, 3, 4), with texts by a resident poet, survive. In the style of *opera seria* with big ritornellos, elaborate vocal lines and *da capo* structures, each also requires a chorus. The two name-day cantatas have important solos for the harpsichord, which were presumably played by Haydn.

• Kapellmeister Haydn •

On 3 March 1766 Oberkapellmeister Werner died. Haydn was promoted to full Kapellmeister

as his initial contract had promised. About this time, the yearly routine of the Esterházy court also changed as Nicolaus's transformation of his modest hunting lodge Eszterháza into one of the most magnificent palaces in Europe reached a habitable state in 1766.

Of some 126 rooms, the castle was complemented by an enormous park that contained temples to the classical gods, a hermitage and a Chinese pavilion. Some of the musical entertainments took place within the halls of the castle, but the operas were given in two theaters: a small one for the German marionette operas and a larger one with a deep stage for the full-fledged Italian genres. In addition there was an inn as well as living quarters for the musicians; on one occasion in 1775 more than 1,300 guests were accommodated over several days.

It was for these *fêtes* that Eszterháza became legendary. Each celebration was provided with entertainment of the most lavish sort, including masked balls, hunts, fireworks, banquets, plays and operas often newly composed by Haydn for the occasion: *La Canterina*, *Lo Speziale*, *L'Infedeltà delusa*, *Philemon und Baucis* and *L'Incontro improvviso*. Haydn was also responsible for providing and/or directing the incidental music for plays and *Tafelmusik*, as well as music for the firework displays. In addition, he assumed responsibility for the chapel; the result was a series of liturgical works, which during the previous five years had been almost totally absent from his output.

That the Prince preferred Eszterháza to all his other residences also affected the lifestyle of his musicians, who had to leave their wives behind in Eisenstadt. Once when the Prince wished to extend his stay in Eszterháza by several weeks the musicians pleaded with Haydn to do something to prevent him. The composer had the

Right: Courtyard of Eszterháza Palace, the Hungarian Versailles, built by Prince Nicolaus when he inherited the title after his brother's death in 1762. Work started on a large scale in 1766 under the direction of Melchior Hefeles, and by 1768 the opera house and musicians' building were complete, though it was more than another fifteen years before the whole project was finished.

PROSPECT DER FÜRSTLICHEN HAUPT THOR   RESIDENZ ESZTERHAZ VON DEN GEGEN NORDEN.

Left: Baryton belonging to Prince Nicolaus Esterházy, carved with the head of a Hungarian Heyduck. The strings below the fingerboard not only reverberated in sympathy but could also be plucked with the thumb of the left hand. Haydn also learned to play the instrument, and his compositions include several works for baryton duet.

notion of writing a symphony (known as the 'Farewell,' no.45) in which one instrument after the other is silent, and each musician, as soon as his part was finished, was directed to put out his candle, pack up his music, and, with his instrument under his arm, go away. The Prince and the audience understood the meaning of this pantomime at once, and the next day came the order to depart from Eszterháza.

Even though the Esterházy court's respites in the imperial city were apparently very short, it was during this decade that Haydn consolidated his Viennese reputation: he was described in the 1766 *Wienerisches Diarium* as 'the darling of our nation,' he was commissioned to write a celebratory cantata for the monastery at Zwettl in 1768, the *Stabat Mater* of 1767 received Viennese performances in 1768 and 1771, and his opera *Lo Speziale* was staged at the Sumerau

palace in 1770. But perhaps the most musically prestigious event was a commission to compose the principal work, *Il Ritorno di Tobia*, for the 1775 concerts of the Tonkünstler-Sozietät, an organization founded in 1771 for the benefit of musicians' widows and orphans. In 1774 Haydn's first authorized publication finally appeared, six keyboard sonatas (Hob.XVI:21-6) dedicated to Nicolaus Esterházy and published by the Imperial printer, Kurzböck.

The instrumental works composed between *c*.1766 and *c*.1772 represent a turning point in Haydn's development. They are considered as a part of the musical 'Sturm und Drang,' a term borrowed from literary criticism. In nearly every genre of instrumental music, except those for baryton, one can sense that Haydn has placed aside the lighter style of his keyboard sonatas and string quartets of the 1750s and early 1760s and has considerably expanded the content of his symphonies.

If the keyboard sonatas from the second half of the decade are compared to the earlier ones, the transformation of this genre is nothing less than startling. Previously Haydn's sonatas derived from the established court style, as revealed in the works of Wagenseil, with their stereotyped melodies of short duration, harmonies of limited vocabulary and generally predictable events wrapped in the thinnest musical garb. From the mid- to late 1760s into the early 1770s the sonatas are of such substance that one can easily imagine them adumbrating those of Beethoven. Rather than being exclusively in major keys, now several are in minor; rather than containing movements of relatively short duration, now their length is considerably extended; rather than always including a minuet with trio, the minuet now may be omitted. An apex is reached with the Sonata in C minor (Hob.XVI:20), which begins with a carefully shaped melodic statement in two beautifully balanced phrases.

Left: Stage design (1762) by Girolamo Bon, who from 1759 worked for several years for the Esterházys as a stage designer at the theater in Eisenstadt. It is likely that he was the stage painter for some of Haydn's earliest operas.

Right: Portrait of Haydn by Ludwig Guttenbrunn, painted around 1770. Guttenbrunn also did decorative painting in the palace at Eszterháza – and became Frau Haydn's lover.

The rest of the first movement pits composed versus improvisatory and driving versus reposeful sections. Its slow movement is almost entirely underlined by moving eighth notes, recalling the baroque pattern found at the opening of Symphony no.22. For the triple-meter finale, Haydn provides not an elegant minuet but a movement of great energy cast in a sonata structure with two complementary recapitulations.

While the string quartets also reveal a decided break with those from the 1750s, they do have a stylistic affinity with contemporary Viennese works. But Haydn far exceeds the accomplishments of his colleagues. While their frequent use of fugal movements is often skillful, Haydn's may be seen as 'an exceptional device, a means of achieving individuality.' This is apparent from the three *sotto voce* fugues of op.20 which are on two, three, and four subjects.

The symphonies also include a series in the minor mode: nos.26 ('Lamentatione'), 39, 44 ('Trauer'), 45 ('Farewell'), 49 ('La Passione') and 52. Despite their esthetic similarities, each of their first movements lends to them an individual profile: no.26 uses the Lamentation chant (also in its second movement); no.39 is marked by driving surface rhythms interrupted by surprising pauses; no.44 is an unusually tight structure; no.45, after a stormy exposition, relaxes during the course of its development; no.49 commences with a slow movement; and no.52 exploits contrapuntal activity as a main feature of its development section. But Haydn also wrote symphonies in festive mood (no.48 in C major, 'Maria Theresa,' with its brilliant parts for high C horns) and in chamber style

(no.67 in F major, which is more delicately scored for two oboes, two horns and strings). Others were incidental music to plays given at Eszterháza; an example is the six-movement Symphony no.60 written for Regnard's *Il Distratto*, which became one of Haydn's most popular works. In addition to the above genres are nearly 200 trios and other works for the Prince's favorite instrument, the baryton.

Left: First page of the fugal finale of Haydn's quartet in F minor, op.20 no.5, written in 1772. Despite harking back to baroque forms (the fugue in particular), these works firmly established the string quartet as a cornerstone of the Viennese classical style.

Right: Prince Nicolaus I Esterházy (1714-90), 'the Magnificent,' Haydn's patron for nearly thirty years.

Haydn's liturgical works from the 1760s are also much more expansive. No longer restricting himself to setting the Mass text as a *Missa Brevis*, Haydn composed cantata Masses, in which nearly every line of the text generates a separate and complete section, as well as the *Missa Solemnis*, in which the five parts of the Mass Ordinary correspond to five musical movements in connected subsections. Of the two cantata Masses, the *Missa Cellensis* ('St Cecilia') is the more impressive with its big arias, vocal ensembles and well-developed fugues. The Masses of the 1770s are quite different in character, leaving behind the pretensions of the cantata Mass; the St Nicholas Mass of 1772 hovers between the dimension of the *Brevis* and *Solemnis* settings, while the *Little Organ Mass*, 'St Joannis de Deo,' returns with uncanny mastery to the *Missa Brevis*.

Among the remaining larger vocal works of this period are the *Stabat Mater* (1767), the *Applausus Cantata* (1768), the *Salve Regina* (1771) and *Il Ritorno di Tobia* (1775). Except for the *Salve Regina*, all hark back to the solo vocal orientation of *opera seria*, which peaks in the massive *da capo* arias of *Il Ritorno di Tobia*. The *Stabat Mater* was one of his most celebrated vocal works; the *Applausus Cantata* follows in the same tradition, but instead of the mournful minor keys and dark scoring with English horns, the major mode, fast tempos, and bright colors predominate. The *Salve Regina* is not unlike the *Little Organ Mass*, with its *obbligato* organ, the intimate character of its scoring for four solo voices, organ, and strings, and its hushed ending. *Il Ritorno di Tobia* is formed on the principles of the Metastasian libretto with recitatives both *secco* and accompanied, alternating with massive and often virtuoso arias, the role of the chorus being limited to only a few numbers.

Haydn also proved himself an accomplished composer of opera with the *dramme giocosi Lo Speziale* (1768), *Le Pescatrici* (1769-70) and *L'Incontro improvviso* (1775), the *burletta L'Infedeltà delusa* (1773) and the *intermezzo La Canterina* (1766), as well as operas in German for marionettes, of which only *Philemon und Baucis* survives. All of these operas belong to the lighter genres (the more elevated *opera*

seria was apparently not favored by the Prince) but even the two smallest works, *La Canterina* and *Philemon und Baucis*, contain a wealth of expression. *La Canterina*, a spoof on *opera seria*, uses in a parodistic fashion one cliché after another: overwrought accompanied recitative with orchestral interludes of unusual length and virtuoso arias with excessive text repetitions. If it was performed with some parts sung in falsetto, as has been suggested, the comedy could only have been enhanced. The opera for marionettes, *Philemon und Baucis*, on the other hand, achieves its touching effect through a total lack of sophistication both in plot and music; its arias are simply conceived in binary and strophic forms, while the finale uses the vaudeville pattern.

Above: Trompe l'oeil painting done in 1772 including a portrait of the cellist in the Esterházy orchestra, Joseph Weigl. He and Haydn were taken on in the same year and were close friends; as well as many elaborate cello parts, Haydn's Cello Concerto in C was written for Weigl around 1765.

Left: Frontispiece and list of characters for Haydn's opera *La Vera costanza*, first performed at Eszterháza in 1779, and again in a revised version in 1785.

• Growing Independence •

In 1776 Haydn's duties as Kapellmeister to Nicolaus Esterházy took a surprising turn; he became a conductor of what was to be one of the most active opera houses in Europe, with a season that occupied as many as ten months of the year and included some twelve to fifteen works. These operas were not only selected, prepared and coached, but also revised to suit the tastes of both Haydn and the Prince, as well as the abilities and resources of the Eszterháza troupe.

In the spring of 1779 Antonio Polzelli, a violinist, and his wife Luigia, a soprano, joined the Esterházy *Kapelle*. Neither was satisfactory; Antonio was sickly and Luigia's voice left much to be desired. Luigia, however, became Haydn's mistress, and it is believed that she bore him a son, named Aloysius Antonio Nicolaus, in 1783.

At the beginning of 1779 Haydn signed a new contract. Notable here is the absence of the requirement found in the May 1761 agreement that Haydn should compose music for the Prince alone and not permit his works to be distributed elsewhere without his consent. While this provision had already been *passé* for at least a decade, the fact that its deletion was now formalized allowed Haydn to publish his music more freely and widely.

Haydn invaded Vienna not only through printed publication; during those times of the year when the operatic schedule permitted, he was also present in some of the salons, where he was able to rub shoulders with the most important literary, musical and artistic personages in the imperial city. Haydn's desire to break away from the restrictions of Eszterháza is further confirmed by his attempts to broaden the distribution of his music beyond Vienna and its environs. A most telling example was the public relations campaign concerning the quartets of op.33. On 3 December 1781 three letters were sent out in which Haydn wrote that these quartets were 'written in a new and special manner, for I have not composed any for ten years.' This statement was taken by many commentators to mean that Haydn had embarked consciously on a new style and thus the year 1781 marked the advent of the so-called 'classic' era. During the next year Haydn apparently planned to go to London and even created three symphonies (nos.76, 77 and 78) for a trip that never materialized; Prince Esterházy probably could not bring himself to give his opera conductor a leave of absence. But Haydn continued to make further contacts with publishers abroad – Forster in London, Boyer in Paris and Bossler in Speyer.

In the end the campaign was eminently successful. Haydn was to receive commissions from France for nine symphonies (1785-6 and 1788), from Italy for nine *notturni* for the King of Naples (1786), and from Spain for a series of quartets (either lost or not completed), as well as *The Seven Last Words of Our Savior on the Cross* for the grotto service at Cádiz.

It was also during this decade that Haydn met Mozart. The first documented personal meeting was in January 1785, and communications between the two composers continued until Haydn left for London a year before Mozart's death. The musical influences between them were mutual, and similarities among the works of both composers exist, but it should be emphasized that both continued to represent stylistic poles in late eighteenth-century music: Mozart stressed contrast, Haydn continuity.

Much of Haydn's correspondence from this time concerns his business dealings with various publishers. Here one sees not the traditional image of 'Papa' Haydn, but rather a shrewd negotiator who is selling the same works to different publishers and exacting good prices for them. Another side of Haydn's personality emerges in the letters exchanged with Maria Anna von Genzinger, the wife of Prince Esterházy's Viennese doctor, whose home in the Schotten-Hof was a center of music-making.

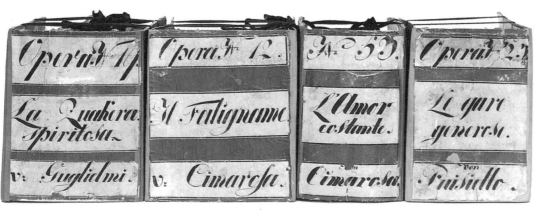

Left: Some of the folios in which the performing materials were kept for the operas Haydn directed at Eszterháza. Those shown here – by Guglielmi, Cimarosa and Paisiello – were performed (left to right): in 1787 with a revival the next year; in 1783, revived in 1784; in 1784; and in 1787 with revivals in each of the next three years.

Haydn's feelings for her were more than admiring, but her behavior toward him was reportedly friendly and full of respect. She was a fine keyboard player and it was for her that Haydn created the E flat Sonata (Hob.XVI:49), whose slow movement 'is somewhat difficult but full of feeling.'

In February 1790 Princess Maria Elisabeth, Nicolaus's wife, died; in early September Nicolaus himself became ill and by the end of the month he too was dead. His successor, Prince Anton, had little interest in music, and most of the musicians were given their salaries for September and dismissed. Eszterháza was closed and Haydn moved to Vienna. Although in 1776 Haydn had written that it was his desire to live and die as a Kapellmeister, the fifteen years of operatic drudgery had perhaps caused him to wish for greater independence; he could have taken a post with Prince Grassalkovics in Pressburg (Bratislava) or gone to Naples with King Ferdinand IV. But having heard of the death of Prince Esterházy, the German impresario and violinist resident in London, Johann Peter Salomon, traveled to Vienna to persuade Haydn to come to England.

On the evening of 14 December 1790 Haydn bade Mozart farewell. He began the new year by setting foot on English soil, initiating a series of experiences beyond the imagination of even the Esterházy Kapellmeister.

• Compositions 1776-90 •

Haydn's compositions of this period, with the exception of his own operas, seem to have been composed not so much with the Esterházy court in mind, but for a wider audience. They combine virtuosity and architecture with a popular idiom in the most sophisticated manner possible. The group of works which demonstrates this new posture most clearly is the six quartets of op.33 (1781). Comparison with op.20 from a decade earlier is interesting: the contrapuntal artifices are gone; rather than two quartets in the minor mode now there is only one; and the internal dance movements are now titled 'scherzo' rather than 'minuet.' Op.33 is pervaded by musical witticisms: no.5 begins with a punctuation rather than a statement; no.2 has the so-called 'Joke' finale, in which the phrase becomes so fragmented that one is no longer certain of its conclusion; and no.3 contains strong contrasts of high versus low in the scherzo as well as a teasing *presto* finale.

Op.50, 54, 55 and 64 are among Haydn's most adventurous products. The op.50 set was dedicated to the cello-playing Frederick William of Prussia. In no.6 Haydn exploits the purely coloristic possibilities of the medium in the second and fourth movements. The use of *bariolage* – the alternation of open and closed strings – in the finale earned for this quartet the subtitle 'Frog.' Except for the finale of op.50 no.4, for which Haydn wrote his last instrumental fugue, he otherwise consistently writes weighty first

Right: Cross-section of the opera house at Eszterháza, from a description of the palace published in 1784. Five years earlier the original theater had been virtually destroyed by firc, and this ncw building was opened in February 1781 with a performance of Haydn's own *La Fedeltà premiata.*

movements and finales full of energy. But even the finale of op.50 no.4 is handled more freely than the fugues of op.20. The third movements are again titled 'minuet,' but mainly marked *allegretto*, while the slow movements often synthesize refrain and variation forms by embellishing the returns.

Op.54 and 55 (1788) as well as op.64 (1790) were composed for the entrepreneur and one-time violinist at Eszterháza, Johann Tost, who it seems commissioned and collected quartets for his exclusive use. Here Haydn once again creates sophisticated virtuoso compositions which are notable for their harmonic language, texture and thematic concentration. Perhaps the most original of the 1788 group is op.54 no.2. The usual big first movement in sonata form is followed by one reminiscent of something from the Hungarian countryside, with its Bartókian

Above: Pietro Travaglia's set design ('mountains covered with snow') for Haydn's *Orlando paladino*, which was first performed in 1782. Travaglia was taken on at Eszterháza in 1777 and was chief designer for costumes and scenery for the opera as well as designer for the marionette theater. He was also responsible for lighting, for stage effects (lightning and fires) and for the illuminations of the palace itself.

parlando rubato style for the first violin, which leads directly to the minuet. The finale consists of two adagios framing a miniature presto in rondo style. Op.64 no.5, known as 'The Lark,' is deservedly famous for its 'soaring' solo violin in the initial movement, whose form harks back to the finale of the C minor Keyboard Sonata.

Unlike the quartets, the solo keyboard sonatas are concentrated not in the last half of the 1780s but during the decade from 1773/4 to 1783/4. There are four sets: the six sonatas (Hob.XVI: 21-6) dedicated to Prince Esterházy; six (Hob. XVI:27-32) distributed in 1776 through professional Viennese copyists; six (Hob.XVI:35-9, 20) published in 1780 by Artaria and dedicated to the Auenbrugger sisters; and three (Hob.XVI: 40-2) dedicated to Marie Hermenegild Esterházy, which were published in 1784 by Bossler. These are clearly not always recently composed works: the C minor Sonata dated 1771 was issued with the Auenbrugger set in 1780, and the first of the 1776 sonatas appears in a source that may date from the late 1760s. Furthermore, two of the Auenbrugger sonatas use the same theme, suggesting that they were composed over some length of time. At the end of the 1780s appear two single sonatas, one for Breitkopf (Hob.XVI:48) in C and another (Hob.XVI:49) in E flat for Maria Anna von Genzinger.

While the 1776 Sonatas begin to suggest the popular style that Haydn adopted in the op.33 quartets, this is not fully realized until the 1780 and 1784 sets. Among the former, the C and D major Sonatas (Hob.XVI:35 and 37), with their *con brio* first movements, come closest. This same spirit, but with greater elegance, pervades those dedicated to Marie Esterházy. Now, however, Haydn creates three miniature sonatas in two movements with emphasis on variation and rondo forms; even the traditional sonata form movement is absent from two of them. The sonata for Breitkopf follows in the footsteps of these Esterházy Sonatas – two movements without a sonata form – but on a much larger scale and architecturally more sophisticated. However, the Genzinger Sonata returns to the three-movement form with a weighty first movement followed by two movements deriving from the style of the Esterházy set.

Above: Göttweig Abbey, overlooking the Danube, where since the beginning of his career copies of Haydn's works had been collected, as in various other monasteries in Austria.

Below: A beautiful and costly harpsichord made in 1775 in London by Shudi and Broadwood and long believed to have been Haydn's, though it is now thought to be one that was ordered by Empress Maria Theresa. By this period Haydn's keyboard music was in fact being written almost entirely for the piano, although he would still often have directed the orchestra from the harpsichord.

One of the most interesting works for keyboard is the Fantasia in C major (Hob.XVII:4) of 1789 which was composed during a 'humorous hour.' Like the *Capriccio* of *c*.1765 (Hob. XVII:1), this work is fashioned out of an Austrian folksong, on this occasion 'D'Bäurin hat d'Katz verlor'n' (The farmer's wife has lost the cat). Haydn not only incorporates the tune as before, but also creates a quasi-programmatic composition with hunting motifs, quick changes in register to depict a leaping cat, unexpected pauses and chromatic retransitions. All of this is presented in a brilliant synthesis of rondo and sonata form.

In response to requests from both Artaria and London publishers, Haydn returned around 1784, after a break of more than two decades, to the keyboard trio. Apart from their scoring for violin, cello and keyboard, these have little in common with the earlier settings. All the vestiges of the trio-sonata are now done away with, and the accompanied style, in which the brunt of the material is carried by the keyboard, is almost exclusively used; the violin or flute either doubles the main line, accompanies it or is the principal voice, while the cello often follows the bass of the keyboard. This sort of disposition is in accordance with the sociology of eighteenth-century music making: keyboards were for the ladies, who had the leisure to practice a difficult keyboard part, and strings for the men.

From the mid-1770s until the early 1780s fewer symphonies were composed, and these too are more popular in style. Some are *pasticci*; for example, no.73, 'La Chasse,' incorporates an arrangement of Haydn's song 'Gegenliebe' for the second movement and employs the overture to *La Fedeltà premiata* for the finale.

Right: Miniature wax portrait of Mozart and Haydn made just after 1800.

Below: Goya's portrait (1795) of the Duke of Alba holding a book of 'Four Songs with Pianoforte Accompaniment' by Haydn. Haydn wrote his *Seven Last Words of Our Savior on the Cross* for performance during Lent in Cádiz Cathedral, probably in 1787, and his music was also known in Madrid, where, in the 1780s, he sent many works, both to the Benavente-Osuñas and to the Duke of Alba.

He had had two sets of twelve *Lieder* issued by Artaria in 1781 and 1784, and he wrote to the publisher that three songs 'have been set to music by Kapellmeister [Leopold] Hofmann, but between ourselves, miserably, and just because this braggart . . . tries to disgrace me every time with a certain high society, I have composed these very three songs to show this would-be high society the difference.'

Whatever esthetic reservations one may have concerning *pasticcio* symphonies, they are cancelled by those from 1785 to 1789: the 'Paris' Symphonies (nos.82-7), the symphonies for Tost (nos.88 and 89), and the ones for the Comte d'Ogny (nos.90-2). Of the 'Paris' works, half begin with a slow introduction, one of which uses the traditional French dotted rhythms; the slow movements are in a variety of styles from *gavotte* (no.85) and *siciliano* (no.84) to the *capriccio* (no.86); the trios of the minuets feature solo woodwinds; and the finales are very quick and often dance-derived. In addition, their melodic materials earned three of them special titles: no.82, 'The Bear' for its repeated heavy bass notes in the finale; no.83, 'The Hen' for the oboe's cackling in the first movement; and no.85, 'La Reine' as the slow movement was apparently a favorite of Marie-Antoinette. The 'Tost' Symphony in G major (no.88) presents in its first movement a display of thematic virtuosity which is exceeded by the contrapuntal complexity of the finale, while in the slow movement the entry of the trumpets and drums, absent from the first movement, was remarked upon. Of the d'Ogny symphonies the real *tour de force* is no.92. Here Haydn builds on the accomplishments of no.88 in architecture, counterpoint and the sheer energy of its first and final movements.

Although most of Haydn's *Lieder* cannot brook comparison with early nineteenth-century song, some are considerable achievements, for example, 'Trost unglücklicher Liebe,' with its 'strangely Schubertian' quality. Among the other vocal works of this period are cantatas and insertion arias, including a setting of *Arianna a Naxos* (1789) for voice and keyboard with alternating recitatives and arias.

Of Haydn's operas of this period, six survive: two *dramme giocosi*, *Il Mondo della luna* (1777) and *La Vera costanza* (1776-9); an *azione teatrale*, *L'Isola disabitata* (1779); a *dramma pastorale giocoso*, *La Fedeltà premiata* (1780-1); and two *dramme eroici*, *Orlando paladino* (1782) and *Armida* (1783-4). Except for *L'Isola disabitata*, with its Metastasian libretto set in a Gluckian fashion with only accompanied recitatives, all are viable stage works with many impressive moments.

Right: Maximilian Franz, the Emperor's youngest brother, who became Elector of Cologne. After Prince Nicolaus Esterházy's death in 1790, the whole musical establishment at Eszterháza was dismissed. Haydn was persuaded to go to London, and he broke his journey to visit the Elector, who received him with special favor and warmth.

• The English years •

Haydn was not prepared for the reception that he received upon his arrival in London, where he found himself an instant celebrity. During the 1790s London was the centre of musical activities in the entire civilized world; musicians flocked there from all over Europe and in particular from revolutionary France. Comparatively, Vienna was sleepy and provincial. Despite all this, English musical life was still dominated

Left: Frau Maria Anna von Genzinger (1750-93), the wife of a fashionable Viennese doctor, with whom Haydn carried on a correspondence from 1789 to 1793, which led to their very close friendship.

by the ghost of Handel, whose music struck Haydn as if he had been put back to the beginning of his studies.

The public concerts which Haydn attended as an honoured guest, as well as those at which he presided, were quite different in their content from those he knew in Vienna. The typical London concert given by Salomon was in two parts. In each would be found symphonic, concerted and instrumental chamber music, as well as vocal solos. The major work, a Haydn symphony, would be held in reserve until the second part to accommodate any latecomers.

Salomon's 1791 series began on 11 March and extended through early June with a performance every Friday. In addition to the subscription concerts, there would also be special benefit performances. When the season was over, Haydn's hectic pace took a brief respite, but in July, at the instigation of Dr Burney, he was given the doctor's degree by Oxford. This involved the presentation of three concerts; among the works performed was his most learned symphony, no.92 (1789), now forever dubbed the 'Oxford.'

During the rest of the year an active social life was continued and in his spare time Haydn gave lessons, counting among his pupils Rebecca Schröter, a widow with whom he had a lasting affair. But the main preoccupation must have been with new works for the next season. Although the death of Mozart in early December affected Haydn deeply, he could not afford to dwell on it; on 23 December his student Ignaz Pleyel arrived in London to work for Salomon's competitors, *The Professional Concert.*

The 1792 concerts should have been dominated by this rivalry, but the expected heat never seems to have materialized. Although Pleyel's works were well received, they do not seem to have caused the excitement that Haydn's generated.

The events of 1792 recapitulated those of 1791; only the details were different. The highlight of the season was Haydn's own benefit which took place on 3 May; its program seemingly included the Symphony no.97, the *Sinfonia concertante* in B flat, the Earthquake from *The Seven Last Words*, and an unidentified cantata. In June Haydn began his return journey to Vienna, and until he embarked for England again on 19 January 1794, he must have been attempting to complete some of the obligations for new compositions which the 1794/5 concerts required. In November 1792 Beethoven arrived in Vienna to 'receive the spirit of Mozart from Haydn's hands.' As is well known, Haydn, now the greatest living composer, and Beethoven, who in 1792 was considered a dapper young man with a streak of independence and a wealth of talent, did not get on in the way history might have wished, but it should not be misconstrued that they were on bad terms.

On 19 January 1794, Haydn departed for England with his faithful amanuensis Johann Elssler. Haydn had ready to take with him the fruits of the previous months: Symphony no.99, parts of symphonies nos.100 and 101, string

Above: Performers of a piano trio, a vignette from the cover of an edition (Artaria, 1798) of Haydn's trio no.23, which had been written in 1785.

Right: Drawing by George Dance of Johann Peter Salomon (1745-1815), the German-born violinist and impresario, who brought Haydn to London after the death of Prince Nicolaus.

quartets op. 71 and 74, and the F minor Variations for keyboard (Hob.XVII:6). They arrived in London in time for Salomon's first concert on 10 February.

He now had time to fulfill demands for new works beyond those required by Salomon. Many of these were for keyboard and/or voice; they included the Canzonettas, a series of piano trios, three solo keyboard sonatas, and various occasional works. Although some are cast in a big virtuoso style, they were essentially intended as music for private enjoyment.

During the off-season Haydn spent time composing and as a guest in residences outside of London and he also became a favorite of the Royal Family, who tried in 1795 to persuade him to remain in London and even offered a summer apartment at Windsor Castle.

The concerts of the 1795 season were reorganized. Salomon joined forces with the Opera, and the concerts, with Haydn's continued participation, moved to the King's Theatre. Here the same type of programs continued but with greater emphasis on vocal music. On 4 May 1795 occurred 'Dr Haydn's Night,' at which were performed the 'Military' Symphony no. 100, and the Symphony no.104, as well as the 'Scena di Berenice.' In mid-June Haydn made his last London appearance at a concert sponsored by the Prince of Wales. During the next six weeks he apparently completed some further works for the English public, settled with Salomon on the rights to six symphonies, and made a preliminary agreement to provide further works to Frederick Augustus Hyde. On 15 August Haydn left England forever. He arrived in Vienna in early September.

An accounting of Haydn's output while in England – which ranged from marches to *opera seria* – can be ascertained from a catalogue inscribed in the fourth London Notebook. Central to these years were the twelve London symphonies. Like those for Paris, each had special qualities that quickly endeared it to a wide spectrum of the musical public. For the amateur their witticisms caused only delight: the fortissimo bassoon intrusion in no.93, the 'Surprise' in no.94, the keyboard solo played by Haydn in no.98, the 'Turkish' music of no.100 ('Military'), the 'Clock' effect of no.101, the 'Drumroll' at the beginning of no.103, and

the use of popular tunes in nos.100 and 104. For the connoisseur, their overall technical perfection, consummate architecture, creative orchestration, tight motivic organization and incorporation of learned devices must have been a constant source of wonderment. Their total effect to a contemporary audience, regardless of the listeners' musical background, was that of 'grand' symphonies with a wealth of contrasting ideas.

Salomon's programs also contained string quartets. As a result Haydn to some degree revised his concept of the genre in op.71 and 74 from a style whose subtleties were meant for the performers seated at a quartet table to one that could be more easily grasped by an audience in a concert room. Most notable is that these quartets often begin with introductory hammerstrokes (several chords played loudly in full sonorities), whose purpose was to quiet the audience for the real beginning of the movement. The material which follows presents constantly changing textures and dynamics, cast in a brilliant style for the first violin. But this it not to say that their most telling effects are to be seen only in an exaggerated vocabulary. The slow movement of op.74 no.3, a chorale-like utterance with improvisatory flourishes for the first violin, contains one of the most extraordinary moments in quartet literature – a hushed and measured tremolo.

Haydn's keyboard music does not as a genre undergo such a stylistic change; rather, it was tailored to suit the performer for whom it was intended. For example, the two solo sonatas, Hob.XVI:50 and 52, he composed for Therese Jansen Bartolozzi, a student of Clementi and one of the finest pianists of the day, require a well

Left: J. M. W. Turner's watercolor of Oxford from the Meadows at the turn of the century. Haydn received an honorary doctorate from the University in 1791 at the instigation of Dr Burney. He gave three concerts, at one of which his symphony no.92 (the 'Oxford') was performed. Haydn wrote: 'I had to pay 1½ guineas for having the bells rung at Oxford in connection with my doctor's degree, and ½ a guinea for the robe. The trip cost 6 guineas.'

developed technique and a performer who can powerfully command the instrument. The F minor Variations (Hob.XVII:6), by contrast, intended for a different player and instrument, require many more delicate shadings. The trios however, were intended for publication, and the big virtuoso style does not seem to be as pervasive. In the most famous, Hob.XV:25, none of the movements uses the sonata form. It begins with a lyrical hybrid of rondo and variation, continues with another cantabile movement but in ternary form, and concludes with the ubiquitous 'Rondo in the Gypsies' Stile,' another of Haydn's excursions into an East European folk idiom.

Although there were other instrumental works, such as the trios for two flutes and cello, the adaptations of the *notturni* for the King of Naples, as well as dances and marches, there is also an impressive array of music with voice, including an *opera seria*, *L'Anima del filosofo*, known also as *Orfeo ed Euridice*. This was commissioned to be performed during Haydn's first season in London by Gallini's opera company at the King's Theatre, but the impresario's plans for a new theater ran into difficulty, and Haydn's opera never received a performance during his lifetime. Although an *opera seria*, it is totally unlike *Armida*, his last work of this type, and closer to the Gluckian reform opera with its stress on the chorus, accompanied recitative, and scenes that go beyond the recitative-aria sequence.

While there were other vocal works composed for the public concerts (including arias and the madrigal 'The Storm'), most of the rest was *Hausmusik*. Among these, the most significant were the fourteen Canzonettas, for which most of the texts were provided by Mrs John Hunter, the wife of the famed London surgeon. Here Haydn goes far beyond the songs published by Artaria during the 1780s; not only is the voice part independent of the keyboard, but the ex-

pression is deeper and dimension larger. Also belonging to this same tradition are the catches and glees, canons, *Dr Harington's Compliment*, and the arrangements of Scottish songs.

• Last years in Vienna •

When Haydn returned to Vienna, his activities centered on composing, public appearances and duties as Kapellmeister to the revitalized Esterházy musical establishment. He became an active member of the Tonkünstler-Sozietät in 1797, contributing substantially to concerts, and also gave public concerts of his own.

It was the Emperor's Hymn, 'Gott, erhalte Franz den Kaiser,' however, that contributed most substantially to Haydn's reputation in

Above: Hanover Square, London, in 1787, looking towards the south. The city's main concert hall, where the Salomon concerts were given, was the Hanover Square Rooms on the east side of the square.

Above: The Thames from the terrace of old Somerset House looking towards Westminster Abbey, a painting of Haydn's time attributed to Paul Sandby.

Left: Portrait of Haydn by Thomas Hardy, painted in 1791 when the composer was in London.

Vienna. Austria during this time was subject to threats from both within and without. Lorenz Leopold Haschka, who wrote the text, used the English 'God Save the King' as a model and Haydn created for it a simple but appropriately majestic setting. First performed at the Burgtheater on 12 February 1797 for the Emperor's birthday, it was an instant success.

Haydn also continued to maintain an active connection with publishers in England as well as throughout the continent. With the finalization of the 1796 contract with Frederick Augustus Hyde for some fifty-five compositions, Haydn's work schedule was full. Considering his established pace of composition, these obligations would have fully engaged him for about five years. Although Haydn never completed the terms of this agreement, he continued to do business with Sieber in Paris, renewed his association with Breitkopf in Leipzig and, of course, with Artaria in Vienna.

Under the new Prince Esterházy, Nicolaus II, Haydn's duties as Kapellmeister were merely a shadow of those of the hectic years under Nicolaus I. His main obligation was to compose a Mass for the nameday of Princess Marie Esterházy: six were completed from 1796 to 1802.

For string quartets, commissions were also forthcoming from the Viennese nobility. Op.76 (1796-7) was the result of a request from Count Joseph Erdödy, and in 1799 Haydn worked on a quartet series for Prince Franz Joseph Lobkowitz, of which only two were completed. Some believe that Haydn's failure to complete the series was a result of his confrontation with Beethoven as a composer. The fragment published as op.103 may have been intended as the third of the series but was later dedicated to Count Fries. With op.103 of 1803 Haydn bade farewell to his career as a composer by having a quotation from his song 'Der Greis' – 'Hin ist alle meine Kraft, alt und schwach bin ich' (All my strength is gone, I am old and weak) – engraved with the music. His compositional method had involved improvising at the keyboard and his memory was now unable to retain ideas long enough to transfer them to paper.

Whereas Haydn's output had previously stressed instrumental music, during this final phase of his creative career vocal music predominates. Only eleven major instrumental works were completed (a single keyboard trio, a trumpet concerto, the quartets op.76, 77 and 103), while for voices there are the three oratorios (*The Seven Last Words*, *The Creation* and *The Seasons*), the six Masses for Marie Esterházy, a setting of the *Te Deum*, part songs, canons and folksong arrangements.

Among the instrumental works, the op.76 and op.77 Quartets are Haydn's crowning achievements in the genre. In some ways they are stylistic successors to the London symphonies; they synthesize the learned and the popular and cast them in carefully calculated structures. Perhaps the best known of these works is op.76 no.3,

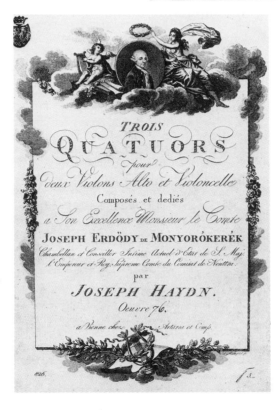

Above: Count Joseph Erdödy, who was the patron of Haydn's last complete set of string quartets (op.76), completed in 1797.

Top right: Haydn's manuscript of one version of his Austrian anthem 'Gott erhalte Franz den Kaiser.' The slow movement of the 'Emperor' Quartet (op.76 no.3) is a sublime set of variations on the theme. Four days before he died Haydn played the theme on the piano three times – the last music he performed.

Right: Title-page of three of Haydn's quartets dedicated to Count Erdödy (op.76 nos.4-6, issued by Artaria as op.76), published in 1799. Haydn thanked Artaria for the 'legible engraving and neat title page.' . . . 'Herr Count Joseph Erdödy wrote me many kind things, and thanked me for having made them available to the world at last.'

called the 'Emperor' because it uses the melody of 'Gott, erhalte Franz den Kaiser.'

Haydn's most successful concerto, the one for trumpet, was written not for the natural instrument but for one with keys which enabled it to play more than the notes of the overtone series. Composed in 1796 for the court trumpeter and inventor of the instrument, Anton Weidinger, in the opening movement it combines traditional fanfare-like material with chromatic passages idiomatic to Weidinger's invention. The slow movement is somewhat retrospective in style; it is a modified *siciliano*, but with a surprising change of key. The concerto concludes with a sparkling rondo.

Of the major vocal works, the first is Haydn's recasting of his instrumental version of *The Seven Last Words* for chorus, soloists and orchestra. Baron van Swieten based the text on Ramler's *Der Tod Jesu*, and Haydn essentially added choral and solo vocal sections to the original instrumental version. In addition, he composed choral prefaces in a harmonized chant style for each word and also added an austere interlude for winds.

The six Masses that Haydn composed for the nameday of Marie Esterházy essentially follow the outline of the *Missa Solemnis* in their larger form. Yet each has its own distinctive mark: the sounding of the trumpets and drums in the Agnus Dei of the *Missa in tempore belli*; the austerity of the orchestration of the 'Nelson' Mass scored originally only for trumpets, timpani and strings; the quotation from *The Creation* in the so-called *Schöpfungsmesse*; and the prominence of winds in the *Harmoniemesse*. Like Haydn's other late works, the Masses are synthetic works, but they combine not so much the popular with the learned as elevated and joyful *Affekte* (emotions) clothed in baroque and classic gestures.

With *The Creation* and *The Seasons* we come to the culmination of Haydn's work. Both were written to texts prepared by Baron Gottfried van Swieten, who reworked pre-existent material: for *The Creation* a libretto given to Haydn before he left England, and for *The Seasons* a poem by James Thomson. In *The Creation* the choruses serve not only to reflect and praise the process of creation, but also to provide columns upon which the oratorio's architecture rests, their grand style recalling that of Haydn's *Tobia* and *Missa Cellensis* as well as Handel and Purcell. The arias and ensembles reflect their texts by referring to characteristic styles that would have immediately underlined their meaning to an eighteenth-century audience; many of the arias bring to mind classic Viennese operatic idioms rather than the Handelian oratorio. However, Haydn's vivid portraits of natural phenomena and animals are reminiscent of Handel's *Israel in Egypt*, a work Haydn heard in England.

The oratorio begins not with the expected French or Italian overture, but with a profoundly original instrumental movement, 'The Representation of Chaos.' A study in controlled disorder, this musical painting utilizes elements of strict counterpoint and harmonic instability together with improvisatory gestures. These, combined with the minor mode, result in the perfect foil for the choral acclamation in the major, 'And there was LIGHT!' Gabriel's aria 'With verdure clad' is a pastoral text, which Haydn sets with appropriate music; the folk-like style of the openings is only briefly interrupted by coloratura, but here even the virtuosity seems leisurely and perfectly placed. With the universe in place, the first part closes with its most famous chorus of praise, 'The Heavens are Telling.'

The oratorio's second part is concerned with the creation of animal-kind, from the nightingale with its 'delightful notes' to the 'great whale.' It culminates with man and woman made in God's 'own image.' This final gesture of creation is reflected upon in Uriel's song 'In native worth and honor clad.' The text is in two parts; the first concerns itself with the physiognomy of man, the second with Adam and his 'fair and graceful spouse.' Haydn sets it in a binary structure; in the second part Uriel is joined by his own partner, an *obbligato* cello. The finale of Part II includes two powerful and parallel choruses on the text 'Achieved is the glorious work,' which frame a trio for Gabriel, Uriel and Raphael. The trio is distinguished from the choruses in every possible way: tempo, key, texture and sonority. Structured in sonata form, the exposition is scored for Gabriel and Uriel, while the development is for Raphael accompanied only by strings. The recapitulation brings together all three soloists as well as both winds and strings. The choruses, with their hammerstrokes alternating with polyphony, are Handelian in concept, but completely Haydnesque in their realization.

Above: Votive painting of the Bergkirche at Eisenstadt, where five of Haydn's late Masses received their first performances in fulfilment of his duty to provide a Mass each year for the name day of Princess Marie Hermenegild Esterházy.

Left: Title-page of the first full score of *The Seasons*, published by Breitkopf & Härtel in Leipzig in 1802.

The third part introduces Adam and Eve in a series of numbers, some with chorus, which bring to mind the German *Singspiel* as well as Italian opera of the 1790s. For the final number Haydn wrote perhaps his greatest chorus. Its main body is a complex exercise in polyphonic writing which is introduced by massive choral harmony. Especially notable here is the masterly and original way in which the orchestra doubles, complements and supplements the voices.

During the course of 1803, because of failing health, Haydn found it necessary to curtail his activities; on 26 December he conducted for the last time at a benefit concert which featured *The Seven Last Words*. In March 1808 he made his last appearance at a performance of *The Creation* celebrating his birthday; at this event touching homages were forthcoming from the nobility, Beethoven and other members of Vienna's musical élite. He died on 31 May 1809.

Left: Gottfried van Swieten (1734-1803), the imperial librarian, who collaborated with Haydn on a choral version of *The Seven Last Words* and then provided libretti for both *The Creation* and *The Seasons*. These contained extensive instructions to the composer as to how each section should be set, which wore down Haydn's patience during their collaboration.

Abel, Carl Friedrich (* Cöthen, 22 Dec. 1723; † London, 20 June 1787). German composer and viola da gamba player. Abel probably studied with his father and perhaps at Leipzig. After playing in the court orchestra at Dresden, he settled in London in 1759. In 1764 he both became a chamber musician to Queen Charlotte and joined with J. C. Bach in promoting a popular series of concerts in London. Their success encouraged the two musicians to have their own concert room built, in Hanover Square, and the concerts continued until Bach's death in 1782.

Abel's surviving works are almost entirely instrumental, including over 30 symphonies and a good deal of chamber music, as well as a small quantity of music for his own instrument, by then obsolescent. His concertos, some sixteen, are counted among his best works.

Adam de la Halle (* Arras, c.1245; † Naples, c.1288, or England, after 1306). French composer, trouvère and poet. Adam was one of the last and most important of a group of trouvères centered at Arras in northern France. After studying in Paris, he returned to Arras, but soon left for Italy in the service of Robert II, Count of Artois, and eventually joined the court of Charles of Anjou at Naples.

Adam excelled in monophonic jeux-partis and chansons, but also wrote many polyphonic works, mainly rondeaux, ballades and virelais, and the pastoral *Le Jeu de Robin et de Marion*. His musical and literary works encompass virtually every genre current in the late thirteenth century.

Albinoni, Tomaso Giovanni (* Venice, 14 June 1671; † Venice, 17 Jan. 1751). Italian composer. A member of a wealthy Venetian merchant family, he was trained privately in violin and voice and never sought a professional post. Albinoni's significance lies in his highly accomplished personal idiom. Aloof from new trends (even Vivaldi's), he made little contact with fellow-musicians, but cultivated eminent patrons. Of his 50 known operas only two survive

BIOGRAPHICAL DICTIONARY OF COMPOSERS

complete; his surviving cantatas suggest limited vocal individuality and a stereotyped approach – though his exceptional melodic gift and willingness to cultivate *galant* tastes ensured continuing operatic demand. The trio and solo sonatas (some 35 of each) and concertos (around 70) are more impressive. He favors a Corellian classical poise and vital contrapuntal textures within well tried frameworks, but achieves attractive results, notably in the idiomatic oboe concertos.

Albrechtsberger, Johann Georg (* Klosterneuburg, 3 Feb. 1736; † Vienna, 7 March 1809). Austrian composer, teacher, theorist and organist. He studied at Melk Abbey, 1749-54, and in Vienna. Appointed assistant to Leopold Hofmann at St Stephen's, he succeeded him as Kapellmeister in 1793 and remained at the cathedral until his death.

Remembered as Beethoven's counterpoint teacher (in 1794-5), Albrechtsberger was revered by Haydn and Mozart and was widely regarded as the finest organist of his time. His profound knowledge of older music influenced his own church compositions, which include 35 Masses. His secular works include symphonies, string quartets and sonatas, and among his voluminous keyboard works are many fugues. His textbooks on composition (1790) and figured bass (c.1791) were widely used and were translated into English and French.

Arcadelt, Jacques (* ?1505; † Paris, 1568). Composer, possibly of French or Flemish origin. He was probably in Florence in the 1530s and in Venice from 1537, where six volumes of his madrigals were printed (1539-44). He was in the service of Pope Paul III, from 1540 to 1551, and then worked for Charles of Lorraine in France until at least 1562.

Arcadelt wrote four Masses and several motets, but the bulk of his output was secular, and his madrigals in Italy and chansons in France enjoyed great popularity.

Arne, Thomas Augustine (* London, bapt. 28 May 1710; † London, 5 March 1778). English composer and violinist. Educated at Eton College and destined for a legal career, Arne persuaded his father to allow him to become a musician. In 1734 he was engaged at Drury Lane, where on 4 March 1738 he scored his first success with *Comus* (text adapted from Milton). Arne's masque *Alfred* (1740) contains the patriotic and popular 'Rule, Britannia.' In 1742-4 he was in Dublin, where his first oratorio, *The Death of Abel*, was performed. He received a D. Mus. degree at Oxford in 1759, continuing to compose for the London stage and also putting on oratorios during Lent, although his theater music suffered an eclipse during his later years.

Arne also wrote many songs for the London pleasure gardens. His other works include church music and six keyboard concertos, written for his gifted son Michael.

Bach, Carl Philipp Emanuel (* Weimar, 8 March 1714; † Hamburg, 14 Dec. 1788). German composer and theorist. He was the fifth son of J. S. Bach and his first wife Maria Barbara, and his musical instruction came entirely from his father, whose manuscripts and other material he preserved for posterity. In 1731 he began to study law at Leipzig, continuing at Frankfurt-an-der-Oder in 1734-8. During this time he started to compose, mainly keyboard and chamber music. In 1738 he became harpsichordist to Frederick of Prussia, and after the Prince became King (1740) Bach continued to serve him for nearly thirty years. He accompanied the flute-playing monarch, composed and wrote an important treatise, the *Essay on the True Art of Playing Keyboard Instruments*. In 1767 he succeeded Telemann as cantor and music director in Hamburg, providing music for the city churches, teaching, promoting public concerts and publishing his own music.

C. P. E. Bach's symphonies and concertos constitute an important transition from baroque to classical styles, but his most individual music is that for solo keyboard.

Bach, Johann Christian (* Leipzig, 5 Sept. 1735; † London, 1 Jan. 1782). German composer, the youngest son of J. S. Bach and his second wife, Anna Magdalena. After his father died in 1750, he lived with his half-brother Emanuel in Berlin, where he composed his earliest works, including some harpsichord concertos. In 1754 he went to Italy, studied with Padre Martini and in 1760 was made second organist at Milan Cathedral. He wrote operas for Turin and Naples, and in 1762 was invited to compose operas for London. There he collaborated with C. F. Abel in presenting the popular Bach-Abel concerts and in 1763-4 was music master to Queen Charlotte. He continued to write and adapt operas for the King's Theatre, and apart from brief visits to the continent (he wrote operas for Mannheim in 1772-4 and for Paris in 1779) he spent the rest of his life in London.

J. C. Bach is chiefly remembered for his symphonies, chamber works and keyboard concertos – which impressed and influenced the young Mozart, whom he befriended in London in 1764-5.

Bach, Johann Sebastian (* Eisenach, 21 Mar. 1685; † Leipzig, 28 July 1750). German composer and organist. See pp.161-83.

Benda, Jiři (Georg) (* Staré Benátky, bapt. 30 June 1722; † Köstritz, 6 Nov. 1795). Bohemian composer. One of a family of musicians, in 1742 he became a violinist in Frederick the Great's orchestra. As Kapellmeister in Gotha, from 1750, he wrote

operas and melodramas – a genre he pioneered in Germany. Benda retired in 1778 but continued to compose. As well as stage works, his output included church music, symphonies, concertos and instrumental compositions.

Biber, Heinrich Ignaz Franz von (* Wartenberg, bapt. 12 Aug. 1644; † Salzburg, 3 May 1704). Bohemian violinist and composer. At twenty he was violinist in the orchestra of the Prince-Bishop of Olomouc, but around 1670 he left for Salzburg, where he took on cathedral as well as court duties. By 1684 he was Kapellmeister, producing large- and small-scale ensemble music, operas and 'semi-operas' and sacred compositions, besides famous violin works.

Biber's outstanding historical and musical achievement lies in his pieces for solo violin; by reflecting his own extraordinary technique in his music, he widened the scope and expressive range of violin composition, using high positions, multiple stopping, elaborate figuration and even *scordatura*, notably in his celebrated 'Mystery' (or 'Rosary') Sonatas (*c*.1676, for cathedral presentation). He also used the device, with astonishing polyphonic effects, in trio-sonatas. Equal facility and imagination pervade much of his concerted and church music, which calls for unusual and often massive choral and orchestral forces.

Binchois, Gilles (* ?Mons, *c*.1400; † Soignies, 20 Sept. 1460). Franco-Flemish composer, one of the major musical figures of the first half of the fifteenth century. Little

is known of Binchois's life until 1419, when he became organist at the church of Sainte-Waudru in Mons. Later he served as a soldier in the occupying forces of the English Earl of Suffolk. By 1431 he had joined the chapel choir of Philip the Good, Duke of Burgundy, in whose service he remained for about thirty years. Binchois traveled little during his time in Burgundy, but he did meet his great contemporary Dufay in Mons in 1449, if not before. Both Dufay and Ockeghem wrote musical tributes on his death.

Despite his comparatively confined sphere of activity, Binchois was highly regarded by his contemporaries and was an important composer of both secular and sacred works. The latter include many Mass sections and several motets. The secular pieces are dominated by his rondeaux, a genre Binchois cultivated with assurance and melodic distinction.

Boccherini, Luigi (* Lucca, 19 Feb. 1743; † Madrid, 28 May 1805). Italian composer and cellist. He completed his training in Rome, and following a short stay in Vienna returned to Lucca as an orchestral player. In 1766 he left on a concert tour with a colleague from Lucca, the violinist Filippo Manfredi (1729-77), and the two earned a considerable reputation, especially in Paris. They finally arrived in Madrid, where in 1769 they found employment with the Spanish Infante, Don Luis.

Boccherini was forbidden to write music for anyone except Don Luis until the Infante's death in 1785, when he became chamber composer to the cello-playing Prince Frederick William of Prussia, but it seems likely that he continued to live in Madrid. After the death of Frederick William in 1797 his fortunes began to decline, and his last years were marred by family tragedies.

Central to Boccherini's output were more than 300 chamber works, including over 100 string quintets, mostly with two cellos, which he began writing in Spain. Other works include an opera and church music, and for the cello he wrote some ten concertos and more than 30 sonatas.

Bononcini, Giovanni (* Modena, 18 July 1670; † Vienna, 9 July 1747). Italian composer. Trained at Bologna, he was a member of the Accademia Filarmonica at fifteen, and by eighteen had published more than 70 trio-sonatas and orchestral *sinfonie* and had composed Masses and oratorios. His subsequent career was primarily operatic. At Rome (1692-7), Vienna (1698-1712), Rome again (1713-20) and London (1720-32) he enjoyed unusual prestige; he also worked in France and Portugal before retiring to Vienna.

Bononcini's *Camilla* (1696) was perhaps the most frequently performed or adapted opera of its day, and his flowing melodic style was extremely influential.

Buxtehude, Dietrich (* Bad Oldesloe, Holstein, *c*.1637; † Lübeck, 9 May 1707). German composer. In 1639 he went to Hälsingborg and in 1657 was appointed organist at the St Mary's church there. In 1660 he was appointed to the German church at Helsingør and then in 1668 succeeded Tunder as organist of the Marienkirche in Lübeck, where he remained for the rest of his life. His fame spread beyond Lübeck, and in 1699 Pachelbel dedicated his *Hexachordum Apollinis* to Buxtehude. In 1703 Handel (traveling with Mattheson), and two years later J. S. Bach, visited him – both chiefly with a view to succeeding him at the Marienkirche.

Buxtehude was the leading member of the Germano-Danish musical school that flourished during his lifetime, and his organ music was widely influential.

Byrd, William (* ?Lincoln, 1543; † Stondon Massey, Essex, 4 July 1623). English composer. He was a pupil of Tallis in London, and in 1563 was appointed organist and master of the choristers at Lincoln Cathedral. In 1572 he moved to London as a gentleman of the Chapel Royal, and three years later he and Tallis acquired a royal patent for publishing music.

As a Catholic, Byrd was fined for recusancy, but he continued to compose for the Roman rite and even published some of his music using the royal patent, which was his alone after Tallis's death. Byrd also wrote for the English church,

but he was a universal artist and in his long life contributed to most of the genres of his time, including keyboard and consort music, solo song and madrigal.

Cabezón, Antonio de (* Castrillo de Matajudíos, nr. Burgos, 1510; † Madrid, 26 March 1566). Spanish composer and organist, blind from early childhood. Some time after 1519 he went to live in Palencia and probably studied with the cathedral organist García de Baeza. In 1525 he moved to Toledo and the next year was appointed organist to Queen Isabella, continuing to serve the Spanish court until his death.

Cabezón was the leading Spanish composer of keyboard music in the sixteenth century, and his works influenced the many foreign musicians he met on his travels with Philip II.

Caccini, Giulio (* Rome or Tivoli, *c*.1545; † Florence, buried 10 Dec. 1618). Italian composer, singer and teacher. He studied in Rome and served the Medici in Florence, where he frequented the Camerata and later joined in creating some of the earliest Florentine operas. His music for *Euridice*, some already used by Peri, was printed in 1600, the year he succeeded Cavalieri as director of music to the Medici court.

Although remembered in connection with opera, Caccini's chief importance lies in his collection of songs, *Le nuove musiche* (1602), and its preface elaborating the new monody.

Caldara, Antonio (* Venice, *c*.1670; † Vienna, 28 Dec. 1736). Italian composer. A choirboy at St Mark's, Venice, and probably a pupil of Legrenzi, he was a singer at St Mark's until he was appointed director of music to the Duke of Mantua in 1699. In 1709-16 he was in Rome, and from then until his death he served the imperial court in Vienna, helping to introduce the new *galant* style.

Caldara's output includes many cantatas, some 100 operas and around 40 oratorios, but the dramatic quality of his music is marred in the later works by his increasingly *galant* fluency.

Campra, André (* Aix-en-Provence, bapt. 4 Dec. 1660; † Versailles, 29 June 1744). French composer. He trained in Aix as a musician and cleric and from 1681 was chaplain and director of music at Aix, Arles and Toulouse. Sent to Paris in 1694 for further study, he was soon made director of music at Notre Dame. But Campra became entranced by the theater; his earliest stage works (1697-9) were presented anonymously because of ecclesiastical disapproval, but in 1700 he resigned his cathedral position for one at the Paris Opéra. He gained royal attention and enjoyed theatrical successes, while still continuing to produce church music. In 1723 he succeeded de Lalande as co-director of the Chapelle Royale, and he became supervisor of the Académie Royale de Musique in 1730.

Campra's masterstroke was the creation of *opéra-ballet*, whose style dominated French theater music until Rameau; *L'Europe galante* (1697) and *Les Fêtes vénitiennes* (1710) were his finest examples.

Cannabich, Christian
(* Mannheim, bapt. 28 Dec. 1731; † Frankfurt-am-Main, 20 Jan. 1798). German composer, conductor and violinist. He was a pupil of Johann Stamitz at Mannheim and continued his studies with Jommelli in Rome. After Stamitz's death in 1757 Cannabich was made Maestro de' Concerti at Mannheim, and in 1774 he succeeded to Stamitz's former post as conductor of the Mannheim orchestra, which he trained to a very high standard of discipline and performance. In 1778 he moved with the Elector's court to Munich, where he spent the rest of his life.

Cannabich's music includes over 30 ballets, many symphonies and much chamber music, but he was admired most as an orchestral trainer; Mozart thought him the best conductor he had ever seen.

Carissimi, Giacomo
(* Marino, nr. Rome, bapt. 18 April 1605; † Rome, 12 Jan. 1674). Italian composer. He became succentor at Tivoli in 1624, choirmaster at Assisi Cathedral in 1628-9, and in 1630 choirmaster at S. Apollinario, Rome. By mid-century he enjoyed a reputation throughout Europe.

Carissimi is remembered for his contribution to the development of oratorio, for which he made the setting of the text in an immediately intelligible way of prime importance. He numbered Marc-Antoine Charpentier among his pupils, and influenced Cesti, Alessandro Scarlatti and Handel.

Cavalieri, Emilio de'
(* Rome, *c*.1550; † Rome, 11 March 1602). Italian composer, organist, singing teacher, choreographer and diplomat. From 1578 he was organist to the oratory of the Chiesa Nuova, Rome, and he came under the patronage of Cardinal

Ferdinando de' Medici. When the Cardinal succeeded as Grand Duke of Tuscany in 1587, he made Cavalieri superintendent of artists, craftsmen and musicians, responsible for staging the most lavish *intermedi* ever produced in Florence, for the wedding of Ferdinando and Christine of Lorraine in 1589. Cavalieri also produced pastorals with music and was employed on diplomatic missions to Rome. His sacred opera *La rappresentatione di anima e di corpo* was presented at the oratory of the Chiesa Nuova in 1600, and later that year he returned permanently to Rome.

Cavalli (Caletti-Bruni), Pier Francesco
(* Crema, 14 Feb. 1602; † Venice, 17 Jan. 1676). Italian composer. An organ pupil in Crema Cathedral, Caletti was able to go to Venice in 1616 thanks to the generosity of the Mayor of Crema, Federico Cavalli, whose name the boy took in gratitude. He joined the choir of St Mark's as a tenor, became a pupil of Monteverdi, and in 1640 second organist. Cavalli was also drawn to the theater and became a highly successful composer of operas. However, *Ercole amante*, commissioned in 1660 by Cardinal Mazarin to inaugurate the Tuileries theater in Paris, was beset with problems, and when finally performed in 1662 was not well received. Cavalli returned to Venice to devote himself to religious music, and in 1665 became first organist at St Mark's and choirmaster in 1668.

With Monteverdi, Cavalli ranks as the most significant exponent of early Venetian opera. He also wrote important ecclesiastical music, including the Requiem Mass for his own funeral.

Cesti, Antonio
(* Arezzo, bapt. 5 Aug. 1623; † Florence, 14 Oct. 1669). Italian composer and singer. He joined the Franciscan Order in 1637, and in 1643 became organist and later director of music at Volterra Cathedral; during this period he was also supported by the Medici family. In 1649 his first opera, *Orontea*, was performed in Venice, and from that time his career became centered on the theater. In 1652 he entered the service of Archduke Ferdinand Karl at Innsbruck and, apart from a short period in Rome, he remained at the archducal court there and later in Vienna, where his most famous opera, *Il pomo d'oro*, was produced in 1668. Cesti then returned to Italy, and he is listed as director of music at the Tuscan court in Florence in 1669.

Charpentier, Marc-Antoine
(* Paris, ?1645/50; † Paris, 24 Feb. 1704). French composer. He studied with Carissimi in Rome and from 1668 to 1688 served the Duchess of Guise; subsequently he worked for the Dauphin and the royal Duke of Orléans. He

collaborated with Molière (*Le Malade imaginaire*, 1673) and wrote a fine but unsuccessful tragic opera, *Médée* (1693), but he never gained a court post, probably because of Lully's intrigues. He thus had little scope for opera, and his dramatic talents were channeled into church works. He directed music at the leading Jesuit church in Paris from 1685, and from 1698 to his death was Maître at the Sainte Chapelle.

Charpentier was the most distinguished French religious composer of his era, and his output includes eleven Masses and numerous motets, psalms and oratorios, many of them extended works rich in texture, color and harmony, and contrapuntally resourceful; melodically he devised a distinctive style, imposing French embellishment and phrase-structure on a basically Italian idiom. His 30 or so theater pieces reveal wit and facility.

Ciconia, Johannes
(* Liège, ?*c*.1335; † Padua, Dec. 1411). Flemish composer and theorist. His date of birth has been put as late as *c*.1373, but it is known that he went to Padua around 1400 as a canon of the cathedral and Magister at the university and remained there until his death. Ciconia's music united elements of the French *Ars Nova* and the fourteenth-century Italian style. His secular music includes settings in both languages, and his Latin church music for Padua and Venice is influenced by both traditions.

Cimarosa, Domenico
(* Aversa, 17 Dec. 1749; † Venice, 11 Jan. 1801). Italian composer. He studied at the conservatory of S. Maria di Loreto in Naples, becoming a good singer, violinist and keyboard player. He also studied composition there. His first opera was produced in 1772, and he soon became widely known as an opera composer. In 1779 he became an organist at the Royal Chapel in Naples, and he was also appointed director of music at the Ospedaletto, one of the Venetian conservatories for girls.

In 1787 Cimarosa went to St Petersburg as director of music to Catherine II, remaining there for

four years. He then took up a similar appointment in Vienna, where his best-known opera, *Il Matrimonio segreto*, was performed in 1792. He returned to Italy the following year and was given the senior organist's post at Naples, but his republican sympathies led in 1779 to his imprisonment and very nearly to his execution. After his release he returned to Venice, where he died.

Clemens non Papa (Jacob Clement)
(* 1510/15; † 1555/6). Franco-Flemish composer. It is known only that he may have spent some early years in Paris, was succentor at Bruges Cathedral in 1544-5 and was employed for a short time at 's Hertogenbosch in 1550.

Clemens's music is among the finest composed during the early sixteenth century. As well as fifteen Masses, as many settings of the *Magnificat* and over 200 motets, he made three-part settings in Dutch of the psalms (*Souterliedekens*) for domestic use. French chansons figure largely among his secular works.

Clementi, Muzio
(* Rome, 23 Jan. 1752; † Worcestershire, 10 March 1832). English (Italian-born) composer. *See Volume II.*

Clérambault, Louis-Nicolas
(* Paris, 19 Dec. 1676; † Paris, 26 Oct. 1749). French organist and composer. A member of a Parisian musical dynasty in royal service since the fifteenth century, Clérambault became one of the greatest organists of his time, from 1719 holding posts simultaneously at Saint-Sulpice and the Jacobins in Paris and at the Royal School of Saint-Cyr at Versailles.

Clérambault's 1704 book of harpsichord pieces is in typical French style, while Italian elements are pronounced in his violin sonatas and trio-sonatas (*c*.1705). The two suites in his *Livre d'orgue* (1710) integrate Italian features into French idiom, but the ideal balance of national characteristics is found in his 25 cantatas (1710-26) – notably in *Orphée* – which are the finest French contribution to the genre. Clérambault's church music is sensitive but functional.

Corelli, Arcangelo (* Fusignano, 17 Feb. 1653; † Rome, 8 Jan. 1713). Italian composer and violinist. He was sent to Bologna in 1666, and aged only seventeen was admitted to the Accademia Filarmonica. By 1675 he was in Rome and by 1679 was established as chamber musician and composer to ex-Queen Christina of Sweden, dedicating his op. 1 trio-sonatas (1681) to her. By 1684 his main patron was Cardinal Pamphili, whose resident music director he became in 1687, and from 1690 he was employed by Cardinal Ottoboni. Though Corelli's four collections (twelve works in each) of trio-sonatas and the set of violin sonatas were published at roughly five-year intervals and his concertos only posthumously, it is clear that he was composing constantly. In 1706 (with Pasquini and A. Scarlatti) he was elected to the Accademia Arcadia; he led orchestras for Handel (1707-8), but retired to spend his last years revising his concertos.

The greatest violin teacher of his age, celebrated founder of new standards in orchestral playing, perfectionist composer, Corelli exerted unparalleled influence far into the eighteenth century, despite being almost exclusively an instrumental writer when opera was the trendsetter. His most significant achievement was the consolidation of the *concerto grosso* concept of alternating *tutti* and *concertino*, and while exploiting the agility of the violin he always exercised a restraint which made his art the acknowledged embodiment of its era's esthetic ideals.

Couperin, François ('le Grand') (* Paris, 10 Nov. 1668; † Paris, 11 Sept. 1733). French composer, harpsichordist and organist; the most important musical figure in France between Lully and Rameau. He was the most prominent member of a musical family which included his own daughter Marguerite-Antoinette, a gifted harpsichordist, his composer-uncle Louis and his father Charles. Aged ten, François inherited his deceased father's post at Saint-Gervais, Paris, where de Lalande was his guide until his eighteenth year. In 1689 he issued his first works (two capable 'organ Masses') and

in 1693 became court organist to Louis XIV; he was ennobled in 1696. From 1700 he was a court composer, producing chamber and sacred works, and from 1717 royal harpsichordist – which in practice he had been for a decade or more. His manual *L'Art de toucher le clavecin* (1716) is an invaluable insight into technique and style.

Couperin worked in restricted fields, having no opportunity to develop operatic or orchestral idioms; his finest achievement are his 27 harpsichord suites (four books: 1713, 1717, 1722, 1730). Almost all their pieces, he declared, were inspired by people, events or ideas he encountered; they form an intimate portrait gallery and a microcosm of intellectual and everyday life projected through a refined, individual, essentially French synthesis of rococo and baroque elements. *See pp. 151-4.*

Dittersdorf, Carl Ditters von (* Vienna, 2 Nov. 1739; † Pilgram [Pelhřimov], Bohemia, 24 Oct. 1799). Austrian composer and violinist. From 1751 he played the violin and studied composition in the household of the Prince of Sachsen-Hildburghausen, and in 1761 entered the service of Count Durazzo; there he met Gluck, with whom he visited Italy. He held posts as Kapellmeister to the Bishops of Grosswardein (Oradia) (1765-9) and Breslau (Wroclaw) (1770-95), but maintained contact with Viennese musical circles, receiving commissions for symphonies, operas and oratorios. His best-known opera, the *Singspiel Doctor und Apotheker*, was first performed in 1786.

Dittersdorf introduced important innovations into the *Singspiel*, and his symphonies (around 120) include some notable for their programmatic content. He also wrote chamber music and four oratorios.

Dowland, John (* ?London, 1563; † London, buried 20 Feb. 1626). English composer and lutenist. He was in the service of Sir Henry Cobham and went with him in 1580 to Paris, where he converted to the Roman church. Having been refused a post as lutenist to Queen Elizabeth in 1594, he left England and traveled to Germany and then Italy. Here he exposed a plot by exiles against the life of the Queen and returned home, but was

again refused a court post and in 1598 left for Denmark, where he became lutenist to King Christian IV. Despite the King's generosity, Dowland ran into debt and was dismissed in 1606. He returned to London and was finally made lutenist to James I in 1612.

Dowland was the greatest songwriter of his day and one of the finest in the history of English music, earning a particular reputation for melancholy pieces.

Dufay, Guillaume (* nr. Cambrai, c.1400; † Cambrai, 27 Nov. 1474). French composer. After singing at Cambrai Cathedral from 1409, Dufay went to Italy, working for the Malatesta family at Pesaro. He moved to Bologna and in 1428 became a singer in the papal choir in Rome. Granted leave of absence in 1433-5, he visited the court of the Duke of Savoy as well as his homeland. He accompanied Pope Eugene IV when he went to Florence in 1435 and composed a motet for the dedication of the new dome of the Cathedral (1436). After a period in the service of the Duke of Savoy, he finally returned to Cambrai.

Dufay was one of the most versatile of fifteenth-century composers, and with his Masses, motets, hymns, chansons and Italian songs he forms a bridge between the Middle Ages and the Renaissance, doing much to mold Renaissance musical language. *See pp. 38-40.*

Dunstable, John (* c.1390; † London, 24 Dec. 1453). English composer. Little is known of his life. He may have been in the service of the Duke of Bedford and perhaps journeyed with him to France in 1422-35. An epitaph describes him as an astrologer and mathematician as well as a musician, and astronomical treatises survive which are probably in his hand.

Dunstable's surviving works are mostly sacred and include Mass sections and several motets. He was the most eminent of an influential group of English composers active during his time and had a marked effect on developments on the Continent (where most of his extant compositions are preserved).

Durante, Francesco (* Frattamaggiore, 31 Mar. 1684; † Naples, 30 Sept. 1755). Italian composer. He studied in Naples and then probably in Rome. In 1728 he became principal music master of the Poveri di Gesù Cristo conservatory in Naples and in the 1740s of the S. Maria di Loreto and S. Onofrio conservatories there, establishing high standards at all three. His prolific output makes him the most considerable Italian church music composer of the late Baroque, and he was a gifted and influential teacher, counting Pergolesi, Traetta and Piccinni among his pupils.

Dussek, Jan Ladislav (* Čáslav, 12 Feb. 1760; † Saint-Germain-en-Laye or Paris, 20 March 1812). Bohemian pianist and composer. *See Volume II.*

Festa, Costanzo (* c.1490; † Rome, 10 April 1545). Italian composer and singer. He was in the service of the Duchess of Francavilla on Ischia and in 1517 joined the papal choir, remaining in Rome for the rest of his life. Festa composed church music (four Masses, twelve *Magnificat* settings and many motets) and was one of the first and most influential of the Italian madrigalists, ranking as the most important Italian composer between the periods of Josquin and Palestrina.

Frescobaldi, Girolamo (* Ferrara, ?15 Sept. 1583; † Rome, 1 March 1643). Italian composer and organist. He studied with the Ferrara organist Luzzaschi and shortly after 1600 went to Rome. In 1607 he was appointed organist of S. Maria in Trastevere, and the following year of St Peter's. He held posts in Mantua (1615) and Florence (1628-34), but returned to Rome and to St Peter's for the rest of his life.

Frescobaldi wrote church music and many madrigals, but he owed his high reputation to his keyboard works, published in thirteen volumes between 1608 and 1645, and he was, with Sweelinck, the most influential keyboard composer of his age.

Fux, Johann Joseph (* Hirtenfeld, Styria, 1660; † Vienna, 13 Feb. 1741). Austrian composer and music theorist. After a period spent in the service of the Archbishop-Primate of Hungary, Fux was appointed court composer in Vienna in 1698. He was sent to Rome for further study with Pasquini and on his return combined court duties with the post of organist at St Stephen's Cathedral, becoming court Kapellmeister in 1715.

An influential teacher, his *Gradus ad Parnassum* (1725) codified compositional principles for musical training throughout the classical era. His compositions include abundant church music, operas, and numerous suites and trio-sonatas.

Gabrieli, Andrea (* Venice, c.1510; † Venice, 1586) and **Giovanni** (* Venice, c.1555; † Venice, Aug. 1612). Venetian organists and composers. Andrea was a singer at St Mark's, Venice, and in 1557 became organist at S. Geremia there before entering the service of Duke Albrecht v of Bavaria in Munich. He was made second organist at St Mark's in 1566 and first organist in 1585. Giovanni, his nephew, also worked for Duke Albrecht v and in 1585 became an organist at St Mark's.

Both Gabrielis wrote Masses, motets, madrigals and instrumental pieces, and they were chiefly responsible for developing the polychoral style of church music.

Galuppi, Baldassare (* Burano, nr. Venice, 18 Oct. 1706; † Venice 3 Jan. 1785). Venetian composer. Galuppi studied music with his father and Antonio Lotti and from 1740 to 1751 was director of music at the Ospedale dei Mendicanti in Venice, for whom he wrote church music and oratorios. He held other church appointments in Venice, including director of music at St Mark's (from 1762), but also won fame as an opera composer, spending years in London (1741-3) and St Petersburg (1765-8), where he was also director of music at the court chapel.

Galuppi wrote about 100 operas, and from 1749 his collaboration with the librettist Carlo Goldoni produced the comic operas which constitute a landmark in the genre. He was also important both as a keyboard composer and in the development from operatic *sinfonia* to concert symphony.

Gassmann, Florian (* Brüx [now Most], 3 May 1729; † Vienna, 20 Jan. 1774). Bohemian composer. Gassmann's first known opera was produced in Venice in 1757, and in 1763 he was invited to succeed Gluck as court composer in Vienna, where he founded the Tonkünstler-Sozietät and in 1772 became court Kapellmeister. Although known chiefly for his operas, he also wrote symphonies and chamber music, including over 30 string quartets.

Geminiani, Francesco (* Lucca, bapt. 5 Dec. 1687; † Dublin, 17 Sept. 1762). Italian violinist, composer and theorist. Geminiani trained with Corelli (violin) and A. Scarlatti (composition), becoming a violin virtuoso. Following theater posts in Lucca and Naples, he moved in 1714 to London and in middle life traveled extensively in Europe.

His compositions, which bear witness to the influence of Corelli, are decidedly passionate, dramatic and virtuosic and comprise violin and cello sonatas, trio-sonatas for flute and violin, and *concerti grossi*. His several theoretical treatises, in particular *The Art of Playing on the Violin* (1751), were highly influential.

Gesualdo, Carlo, Prince of Venosa (* ?Naples, c.1561; † Gesualdo, Avellino, 8 Sept. 1613). Italian nobleman and composer. In 1586, he married his cousin but in 1590 murdered her and her lover. Four years later he married Leonora d'Este and spent some time in Ferrara. He also formed his own musical establishment at Gesualdo, where from about 1600 he spent most of his time.

Gesualdo's choice of madrigal texts and the highly charged, often chromatic, music in which he clothed them reflect the melancholia and emotional instability to which he was prone. His other works include motets and instrumental music.

Gibbons, Orlando (* Oxford, 1583; † Canterbury, 5 June 1625). English composer and organist. Gibbons was a choirboy and student at King's College, Cambridge, where he received his B. Mus. in 1606. By then he had moved to London, where he joined the Chapel Royal, becoming senior organist and securing other royal appointments. In 1623 he was made organist of Westminster Abbey. He wrote some fine anthems and memorable madrigals and was a master of organ music and the instrumental fantasia.

Gluck, Christoph Willibald (* Erasbach, 2 July 1714; † Vienna, 15 Nov. 1787). German composer. See pp.237-47.

Gossec, François-Joseph (* Vergnies, Hainaut, 17 Jan. 1734; † Passy, nr. Paris, 16 Feb. 1829). French composer. Gossec moved to Paris in 1751, where Rameau secured for him a post in the orchestra of La Pouplinière. In 1762 he became director of the Prince de Condé's theater at Chantilly and in 1769 founded the *Concert des Amateurs* in Paris, remaining its director until 1773, when he became co-director of the *Concert Spirituel*. He was also employed at the Opéra until 1789 and directed the new Ecole Royale de Chant, but after the Revolution he turned increasingly to teaching.

Gossec was a pioneer of the symphony in France and an important composer of opera. He also wrote church music, oratorios, chamber works and pieces celebrating the Revolution, many for outdoor performance with massed voices and orchestra.

Graun, Carl Heinrich (* Wahrenbrück, c.1703; † Berlin, 8 Aug. 1759). German composer. The youngest of three musical brothers, he was a tenor at the Brunswick opera and Vicekapellmeister there before joining his brother Johann Gottlieb in the service of Crown Prince Frederick at Ruppin in 1735. When Frederick became King (1740), C. H. Graun was made court Kapellmeister and charged with the revival of opera in Berlin.

He himself wrote at least 26 operas – though his most famous work is the Passion oratorio *Der Tod Jesu*, 1755 – and both brothers shared a role in the development of the pre-classical symphony and concerto.

Grétry, André (* Liège, 8 Feb. 1741; † Paris, 24 Sept. 1813). French composer. He won a scholarship to Rome in 1761 and six years later, encouraged by Voltaire, moved to Paris. Here he inaugurated a series of *opéras comiques*, much admired for their tunefulness, adroit characterization and the strength of their ensembles, which established him as a leading composer in the genre until the Revolution.

Grétry's other works include songs (some with Revolutionary texts) and a small quantity of instrumental and church music.

Guerrero, Francisco (* Seville, ?4 Oct. 1528; † Seville, 8 Nov. 1599). Spanish composer. Guerrero sang in Seville Cathedral choir from 1542 to 1546, when he became *maestro de capilla* of Jaén Cathedral. In 1549 he was offered a singing post at Seville Cathedral, where he became associate *maestro* in 1551 and *maestro* in 1574. He traveled frequently and widely, and his works, which include a number of secular pieces as well as the more usual sacred compositions, were nearly all published outside Spain.

Handel, George Frideric (* Halle, 23 Feb. 1685; † London, 14 Apr. 1759). German (naturalized English) composer. See pp.189-207.

Hasse, Johann Adolf (* Bergedorf, nr. Hamburg, bapt. 25 Mar. 1699; † Venice, 16 Dec. 1783). German composer. Hasse was employed as an opera singer at Hamburg and Brunswick before going to study in Naples with Alessandro Scarlatti. From 1731 to 1763 he was Kapellmeister to the Elector of Saxony in Dresden, although he made frequent visits abroad to consolidate his reputation as a composer of *opera seria*. After the Elector's death he spent ten years in Vienna, where his long collaboration with Metastasio ended with *Ruggiero* (1771). He retired to Venice, where he wrote church music for the Ospedale degli Incurabili and some cantatas.

Hasse was the most esteemed and highly paid composer of his time, admired by both J. S. Bach and Mozart. Besides *opere serie*, he composed cantatas, concertos, instrumental and keyboard sonatas and much sacred music.

Haydn, Joseph (* Rohrau, 31 Mar. 1732; † Vienna, 31 May 1809). Austrian composer. See pp.285-303.

Haydn, Michael (* Rohrau, bapt. 14 Sept. 1737; † Salzburg, 10 Aug. 1806). Austrian composer. Like his elder brother Joseph, Haydn was a chorister at St Stephen's Cathedral in Vienna. He was appointed Kapellmeister to the Bishop of Grosswardein (Oradia) in Hungary in 1757 and five years later moved to Salzburg as Konzertmeister to Archbishop Schrattenbach. He spent the rest of his life in Salzburg, where he was friendly with Mozart, whom he succeeded as cathedral organist.

Although he wrote numerous symphonies, divertimenti and string quartets, his best works are to be found among his 30-odd Masses and other sacred pieces.

Hiller, Johann Adam (* Wendisch-Ossig, nr. Görlitz, 25 Dec. 1728; † Leipzig, 16 June 1804). German composer and writer on music. He entered Leipzig University as a law student in 1751 and took an active part in the musical life of the city. In 1763 he was put in charge of the Grosses Conzert, in 1775 founded the Musikübende Gesellschaft, and from 1781 directed the Gewandhaus Conzert which succeeded it. He did much to revitalize orchestral playing in the city and also founded a singing school. In 1785-9 he held posts in Mitau and Breslau (Wrocław), but returned to Leipzig, becoming cantor of St Thomas's.

Although during this last period Hiller wrote some church music, his greatest contribution as a composer was to help establish the German *Singspiel*.

Holzbauer, Ignaz (* Vienna, 17 Sept. 1711; † Mannheim, 7 Apr. 1783). Austrian composer. Holzbauer became Kapellmeister to Count Rottal of Holešov in Moravia in the early 1730s and in 1737 was appointed musical director of the Viennese court theater. After a long journey in Italy and two years as Oberkapellmeister at Stuttgart, he was made Kapellmeister to Elector Carl Theodor at Mannheim.

Holzbauer's principal works were his operas, although little of their music has survived. He also wrote some 60 symphonies as well as oratorios and chamber music.

Hummel, Johann Nepomuk (* Pressburg [Bratislava], 14 Nov. 1778; † Weimar, 17 Oct. 1837). Austrian pianist, composer, and teacher. *See Volume II.*

Isaac, Heinrich (* Flanders, c.1450; † Florence, 26 Mar. 1517). Flemish composer. Isaac served Lorenzo de' Medici as a singer in Florence but in 1492 left Italy to enter the service of Emperor Maximilian I, becoming his court composer in 1497.

Isaac was a prolific composer, his works including songs in French, Italian and German, some 40 Masses and many motets, as well as the cycle of Mass Propers, *Choralis constantinus* (1508-9). His influence on German music was enormous, as both composer and teacher.

Janequin, Clément (* Châtelleraut, c.1485; † Paris, 1558). French composer. After almost twenty years in the service of Lancelot du Fau, vicar-general of Bordeaux and later Bishop of Luçon, Janequin entered the priesthood in 1523,

serving as canon or curate in several churches in the Bordeaux area. He was for a short time master of the choirboys at Auch Cathedral and from 1534 to 1537 *maître de chapelle* at Angers. In 1549 he moved to Paris as a university student and later found employment at court as a singer and then composer.

Although Janequin wrote a small quantity of liturgical music (three Masses and a few motets), his greatest talent was as a composer of descriptive French chansons, notable for their picturesque word-painting.

Jommelli, Niccolò (* Aversa, 10 Sept. 1714; † Naples, 25 Aug. 1774). Italian composer. Jommelli trained in Naples, where his first opera was produced in 1737. Four years later he went to Bologna, where he started a lifelong friendship with Padre Martini. He soon became known for his operas and oratorios, and in 1743 was made musical director of the Ospedale degli Incurabili in Venice. In 1754 he was appointed Oberkapellmeister at the French-influenced court of Duke Carl Eugen in Stuttgart, although he continued to compose for Italian theaters, and in 1769, after returning to Naples, he entered into an agreement with the Portuguese King José I to provide operas and church music for his court in Lisbon.

Jommelli wrote over 80 operas, in which he modified Metastasian *opera seria* to make it less singer-dominated and dramatically more viable. The orchestral and structural innovations of his operatic *sinfonie* were extremely influential on the Mannheim school of symphonic composers.

Josquin Despres (* ?Saint-Quentin, c.1440; † Condé-sur-l'Escaut, 27 Aug. 1521). Franco-Flemish composer. Josquin was a singer in Milan Cathedral from 1459 to 1474 and then in the private chapel of Galeazzo Maria Sforza. In 1476 he entered the service of Cardinal Ascanio Sforza, whom he accompanied to Rome, where he was a member of the papal choir from 1486 to 1494. In 1503 he was director of music at the Este court in Ferrara, and towards the end of his life he returned home to France.

Josquin was the central musical figure of the early Renaissance, and his sensitivity to the moods of

his texts and the expressiveness of his compositions – some 20 Masses, 100 motets and 80 secular works are extant – set him apart as a pioneer in his day.

Keiser, Reinhard (* Teuchern, nr. Weissenfels, bapt. 12 Jan. 1674; † Hamburg, 12 Sept. 1739). German composer. Keiser studied in Leipzig with Kuhnau and in 1692 was appointed to the ducal chapel at Brunswick, where in 1693 he produced the first of the 100 or so stage works which established him as the central figure in German baroque opera. In 1695 he moved to the Hamburg Opera, and although he was official director only from 1703 to 1707, he was the Opera's driving artistic force until the last decade of his life.

Keiser's operas to German texts established a native school independent of Italian fashions. His other surviving compositions include cantatas and serenatas as well as a series of Passions.

Kozeluch, Leopold (* Velvary, 26 June, 1747; † Vienna, 7 May 1818). Bohemian pianist, teacher and composer. Kozeluch moved to Vienna in 1778, where he became a successful teacher and pianist, and in 1782 founded his own music-publishing business. Ten years later he received a court appointment from Franz II, which he retained until his death.

Kozeluch's music is largely for piano, including 49 sonatas, over 20 concertos and numerous piano trios, as well as symphonies and six operas.

Kuhnau, Johann (* Geising, 6 Apr. 1660; † Leipzig, 5 June 1722). German composer, keyboard player, music theorist, scholar, writer and lawyer. Kuhnau began legal studies in Leipzig in 1682 and from 1684 was also organist at St Thomas's. From 1688 he practiced law and in 1701 became cantor at St Thomas's, establishing himself as a major force in German music.

None of Kuhnau's theater music survives, and only about one-third of his 75 German cantatas, although these, like his keyboard music, are highly accomplished, anticipating many

of Bach's features. Among his writings are translations, legal dissertations and a satirical novel on contemporary musical life.

Lalande, Michel-Richard de (* Paris, 15 Dec. 1657; † Versailles, 18 June 1726). French composer, organist and harpsichordist. De Lalande's skill as a keyboard player brought him aristocratic pupils and organist's posts – notably at Saint-Gervais until 1686 as locum for the young François Couperin. Between 1683 and 1722 he exerted a growing influence on the Chapelle Royale, becoming director of the *musique de la chambre* in 1695 and royal composer in 1709.

De Lalande was the only great French church-music specialist of his day. Apart from secular ballets and pastorals, he wrote more than 70 Latin *grands motets*, which represent a synthesis of the most effective expressive means available at the time.

Landini, Francesco (* Fiesole or Florence, c.1325; † Florence, 2 Sept. 1397). Florentine composer, poet, organist, singer and instrument-maker. Landini went blind during childhood. Renowned for his powers of musical memory and skill at improvisation, he was organist at the monastery of S. Trinità in Florence in 1361 and at the church of S. Lorenzo from 1365 until his death.

Landini was the most important and one of the most prolific composers of the Italian *Ars Nova*. His extant compositions are almost all secular, mostly ballate.

La Rue, Pierre de (* ?Tournai, c.1460; † Courtrai, 20 Nov. 1518). Flemish singer and composer. La Rue sang as a tenor at Siena Cathedral and from 1489 to 1492 in the cathedral choir at 's Hertogenbosch. Between 1492 and his retirement in 1516 he held posts with Maximilian I, Philip the Fair, Margaret of Austria and Archduke Karl.

La Rue was one of the leading composers of the Josquin period in Flanders. As might be expected, his compositions include many French chansons, but the best of his music is to be found in his motets and some 30 Masses.

Lassus, Roland de (* Mons, 1532; † Munich, 14 June 1594). Franco-Flemish singer and composer. Lassus entered the service of Ferrante Gonzaga when he was about twelve and visited Mantua (1547-9), Sicily and Naples before spending a year in 1553 as director of music at St John Lateran in Rome. In 1556 he joined the Munich court of Duke Albrecht V as a tenor, becoming director of music in 1563 and remaining in Munich for the rest of his life, apart from the frequent travels his post entailed.

Lassus was one of the most prolific and versatile composers of the High Renaissance. He excelled in every branch of vocal music, sacred and secular, his numerous compositions including French, German and Italian polyphonic songs, about 60 Masses, four Passions, over 100 *Magnificat* settings and about 500 motets, which are generally regarded as his finest works.

Lawes, Henry (* Dinton, Wiltshire, 5 Jan. 1596; † London, 21 Oct. 1662) and **William** (* Salisbury, bapt. 1 May 1602; † Chester, 24 Sept. 1645). English composers. Henry became a gentleman of the Chapel Royal in 1626 and in 1631 was appointed one of the King's musicians for the lute and voices. During the Commonwealth period (1649-60) he taught the viol and singing until the restoration of his post by Charles II. He was the leading English songwriter of the mid-seventeenth century.

William joined his brother as one of the King's musicians for lute and voices in 1635, but was killed while fighting with the royalist troops in the Civil War. Despite his early death, he was more prolific than his brother and was the principal English composer of dramatic music before Purcell, while also writing distinguished instrumental works.

Leclair, Jean-Marie the Elder (* Lyons, 10 May 1697; † Paris, 22 Oct. 1764) French violinist and composer. The eldest of a whole family of musical children, he was regarded as the founder of the French school of violin playing. His music, with the exception of one extant opera, is predominantly instrumental, and his twelve concertos constitute the only notable French contribution to the baroque concerto repertory.

Legrenzi, Giovanni (* Clusone, nr. Bergamo, bapt. 12 Aug. 1626; † Venice, 27 May 1690). Italian organist, teacher and composer. From 1645 Legrenzi was organist at the principal church in Bergamo, where he was also ordained. He became director of music at the Ferrara Accademia in 1656 and moved to Venice c.1671, holding appointments at S. Maria della Fava (1677) and St Mark's (1681). Here he became director of music in 1685, building up the choir and orchestra to record size and impressive standards, and also organizing concerts, which earned him wide prestige.

Legrenzi is a key figure in the establishment of late baroque style. He expanded harmonic resources and tonal design and developed fugal writing, thematic character, extension techniques and rhythmic impetus. His major sacred works, numerous chamber and orchestral pieces and operas had an enormous influence on the next generation of composers.

Le Jeune, Claude (* Valenciennes, 1528/30; † Paris, buried 26 Sept. 1600). French Protestant composer, also known as Claudin. Le Jeune was master of the choirboys to François, Duke of Anjou, from 1580 to 1584, but from 1589 spent seven years at La Rochelle as a Protestant refugee. He returned to Paris in 1596 as composer of chamber music to Henri IV. His main compositions were psalms, chansons, madrigals and airs, the last embodying the techniques of *musique mesurée à*

l'antique formulated by Jean Antoine de Baïf, of whose Academy Le Jeune was a member.

Leo, Leonardo (* S. Vito degli Schiavi [now de Normanni], 5 Aug. 1694; † Naples, 31 Oct. 1744). Italian teacher and composer. Leo studied at the Naples conservatory of S. Maria della Pietà and held several appointments at the Royal Chapel there. From 1714, he produced a steady stream of *opere serie*, becoming a leading national figure, and when, c.1725, he temporarily lost supremacy to Vinci and Hasse, he turned to comic opera with equal success. Leo was also renowned as an oratorio writer and reformer of church music, helping to free it of operatic superficialities. His pupils included Piccinni and Jommelli.

Léonin (fl. Paris, c.1160-90). Composer of organum. Léonin is credited with having compiled the *Magnus liber* of organum in use at Notre Dame in Paris.

Locatelli, Pietro Antonio (* Bergamo, 3 Sept. 1695; † Amsterdam, 30 Mar. 1764). Italian composer and violinist. After studying in Rome from 1711, he became a protégé of Cardinal Ottoboni and of the imperial governor of Mantua, where a flexible appointment allowed for travel as a concert virtuoso. In 1729 he settled permanently in Amsterdam, where he became involved with teaching, amateur music-making, publishing and the importation of Italian strings.

Locatelli was an influential performer, particularly admired in *cantabile* playing, and his travels brought his progressive style wide notice. Essentially an instrumental composer, he wrote many *sinfonie*, concertos, and sonatas, of which the twelve violin sonatas (1737) are notably original in design.

Lully, Jean Baptiste (**Giovanni Battista Lulli**) (* Florence, 28 Nov. 1632; † Paris, 22 Mar. 1687) French composer, dancer, violinist and instrumentalist of Italian birth. At fourteen Lully was page to Mlle de Montpensier, cousin of Louis XIV; he became a violinist in her private orchestra and an accomplished dancer in the ballets and masques she sponsored, and took part in royal entertainments. From his appointment in 1653 as court composer of ballet music, his facility and influence grew rapidly, and in 1656 he took charge of the royal orchestras, transforming their capabilities and ensemble techniques. By 1662 he was master of music to the royal family. Collaborations with Thomas Corneille and Molière (from 1664) were followed by royal monopolies to produce opera, train performers, control copyright and manage the royal theater. With the contributions of his librettist, Quinault, and of

choreographers, engineers and designers, he mounted masterful productions of *opéra-ballets* and *comédies-ballets*. Once the mood of the King and court became more serious after 1683, Lully tactfully mixed the composition of religious and theatrical works.

Although he also wrote ballets, comedies and religious motets, the *tragédies lyriques* Lully composed between 1673 and 1686, including *Alceste* (1674), *Psyché* (1678) and *Amadis* (1684), are his greatest achievement, and by alternating a new kind of declamatory or lyrical recitative with airs or ensembles he created a lasting French operatic style. *See pp.139-41.*

Machaut, Guillaume de (* ?Rheims, c.1300; † ?Rheims, 13 Apr. 1377). French composer and poet. He served as secretary to John of Luxemburg, King of Bohemia, until 1346, but remained in contact with Rheims, becoming a canon of the cathedral in 1333.

Machaut was the principal representative of the *Ars Nova* in France, and his music is remarkable for its quantity, quality and range. It is predominantly secular and includes many monophonic songs in the trouvère tradition, but Machaut turned increasingly to polyphonic settings, including ballades, rondeaux and motets (mostly secular) in two to four parts. His most famous composition, however, is sacred, the *Messe de Notre Dame* – the earliest known polyphonic setting of the entire Ordinary of the Mass by one composer.

Marais, Marin (* Paris, 31 May 1656; † Paris, 15 Aug. 1728). French composer and bass viol player. Marais studied bass viol with the virtuoso Sainte-Colombe and composition with Lully. For some fifty years (1676-1725) he held royal posts as an instrumental player, and he was internationally famous as a composer and revered as a teacher.

Marais's compositions include over 600 works for his own instrument, involving important technical innovations, as well as trio-sonatas and four operas.

Marcello, Alessandro (* Venice, 1684; † Venice, 1750). Venetian philosopher, poet, painter and composer. The son of a senator, he was a fine violinist and capable singer, but his many other interests left him little time for composition. Nevertheless, his small output was distinguished enough to gain him election to Rome's Accademia Arcadia and to prompt publications in Augsburg and Amsterdam as well as in Italy.

All his works show an intriguing tendency towards harmonic and tonal experiment, and each tends to be individually characterized, as can be heard in the renowned oboe concerto in D minor, transcribed for keyboard by J. S. Bach.

Marcello, Benedetto (* Venice, 24 July/1 Aug. 1686; † Brescia, 24/25 July 1739). Venetian statesman, composer, poet and theorist. Although, like his brother Alessandro, ostensibly an amateur musician, Benedetto, who was a pupil of Gasparini, was a prolific composer. He was a member of both the Accademia

Filarmonica in Bologna and the Accademia Arcadia in Rome.

His instrumental music shows the influence of Vivaldi (whom he satirized as an operatic composer), and while only a handful of short stage works by Benedetto survive, in many of his 400 (mainly solo) cantatas dramatic feeling is strikingly prominent. His more conservative church music includes Masses, oratorios and motets, as well as 50 cantata-style settings of Italian psalm-paraphrases (1724-6), which brought him wide recognition.

Marenzio, Luca (* Coccaglio, nr. Brescia, 1553/4; † Rome, 22 Aug. 1599). Italian composer and singer. He probably studied with Giovanni Contino, director of music at Brescia Cathedral, then went to Rome, remaining there to the end of his life, apart from a brief post in Florence (1588-9) and a visit to Poland (1595-8).

Marenzio was one of the most prolific and wide-ranging madrigalists of the late sixteenth century, and his reputation has been sustained by his twenty books of madrigals published between 1580 and 1599. His sacred motets are fewer in number and are still little known.

Martini, Padre Giovanni Battista (* Bologna, 24 April 1706; † Bologna, 3 Aug 1784). Italian composer, teacher and writer. He studied with his father and later with G. A. Perti, and in 1729 he became a priest. From 1725 for most of his life he served as director of music at the church of S. Francesco, rarely leaving his native city.

His compositions embrace almost every contemporary genre, and include music in the *stile antico* as well as in an up-to-date *galant* style. His writings include an influential treatise on counterpoint, an unfinished history of music and some 6,000 letters. He was much sought after as a teacher, his numerous pupils including J. C. Bach, Grétry, Jommelli and Mozart.

Mattheson, Johann (* Hamburg, 28 Sept. 1681; † Hamburg, 17 Apr. 1764). German composer, critic, musical journalist, lexicographer and theorist. By the age of thirteen Mattheson was studying composition and seven instruments and was already a singer at the Opera. Working with Kusser and Keiser, he conducted rehearsals, had four operas mounted by 1705 and at the same time became a virtuoso organist, enjoying a mutually fruitful friendship with the young Handel. At twenty-five he became secretary to the English Ambassador at Hamburg, by 1715 he was musical director of Hamburg Cathedral, and from 1719 he was also Kapellmeister to the Holstein court – all concurrent with his diplomatic career. Between 1728

and 1735 his hearing failed, making practical music impossible, but he continued to produce his theoretical works.

Almost all Mattheson's works in manuscript perished in World War II, although one oratorio and one opera survive. The keyboard and flute pieces issued in his lifetime show him adept in both Italian and French idioms, a marked melodic flair betraying the singer and opera-composer.

Méhul, Etienne-Nicolas (* Givet, Ardennes, 22 June 1763; † Paris, 18 Oct. 1817). French composer. *See Volume II.*

Milán, Luis de (* c.1500; † c.1561). Spanish vihuela player, composer and writer. Milán spent most of his life in Valencia, though he may have visited Italy, and he almost certainly spent some time in Portugal, since his most important book *El maestro* (Valencia, 1536), a didactic work containing forty fantasies for the vihuela and much other music, was dedicated to King João III.

Mondonville, Jean-Joseph Cassanéa de (* Narbonne, bapt. 25 Dec. 1711; † Belleville, 8 Oct. 1772). French composer and violinist. The son of a church organist at Narbonne, he was in Paris by 1733, and his appearances as a soloist at the *Concert Spirituel* met with much acclaim. He took up his first post at court in 1739.

Mondonville composed operas, one of which (*Titon et l'Aurore*, 1753) added fuel to the *Querelle des Bouffons*, but his most important works are his motets and violin sonatas.

Monn [Mann], Matthias Georg (* Vienna, 9 Apr. 1717; † Vienna, 3 Oct. 1750). Austrian composer and organist. He was a chorister at Klosterneuburg monastery in 1731-2 and later became organist at the Vienna Karlskirche.

In his short life Monn played an important part, along with Wagenseil, in establishing the early Viennese school of symphonic composers. He wrote 21 symphonies (one of which was the earliest in four movements with a minuet as the third movement) and several concertos, including a particularly fine one for cello. The chamber music, which includes six string quartets, is rather more conservative in style.

Monsigny, Pierre-Alexandre (* Fauquembergues, nr. St Omer, 17 Oct. 1729; † Paris, 14 Jan 1817). French composer. He studied in Paris with Pietro Gianotti (d.1765), composing a number of successful operas, and in 1768 entered the service of the Duke of Orléans. The following year *Le Déserteur* was produced, one of the earliest and best examples of sentimental comedy known as *opéra comique larmoyant* and one of several on which he collaborated with the gifted playwright Michel-Jean Sedaine (1719-97).

After *Félix* (1777) he went into retirement, living another forty years but writing no more operas.

Monte, Philippe de (* Mechlin [Mechelen], 1521; † Prague, 4 July 1603). Flemish composer. He probably sang in the choir of St Rombaut's, Mechlin, and he is known to have worked in Naples (1542-51), Antwerp (1554) and England (1554-5). He was appointed court Kapellmeister to Emperor Maximilian II in Vienna in 1568 and continued to serve the imperial house in Vienna and Prague until his death.

Monte wrote about 40 Masses and more than 200 motets, but his achievements in church music are dwarfed by his madrigals, which number more than 1,100, most of them published in 34 books between 1554 and 1600.

Montéclair, Michel Pignolet de (* Andelot, Haute-Marne, bapt. 4 Dec. 1667; † Aumont, 22 Sept. 1737). French composer, theorist and teacher. A choirboy at Langres Cathedral, Montéclair also visited Italy with the Prince de Vaudémont. From c.1698 to his death he was basse de violon player and continuo director at the Paris Opéra, helping to introduce the contrabass into French orchestras. A fine teacher, he wrote a pioneering violin *Méthode* for children.

Musically Montéclair was important to the era betweeen Lully and Rameau. His opera *Jephté* (1732) demonstrated that composers might make increased technical demands on performers, and his precise and imaginative instrumental coloring points forward to Rameau. He also wrote three suites for wind and strings and twenty notable cantatas.

Monteverdi, Claudio (* Cremona, bapt. 15 May 1567; † Venice, 29 Nov. 1643). Italian composer. Monteverdi was a pupil at the cathedral school in Cremona, published his first compositions at the age of sixteen, and in 1589 entered the service of Vincenzo Gonzaga at Mantua. Initially a string player, in 1601 he became director of the Duke's private music for both chapel and chamber music. After the death of the Duke in 1612, Monteverdi left Mantua and, after a brief spell in Milan, was appointed director of music at St Mark's, Venice.

Monteverdi was clearly the foremost composer of the early baroque period in Italy, and although only three of his operas have survived, there are nine volumes of his madrigals, and three collections of sacred music, which contain three Masses, his Vespers, psalms and motets. *See pp.74-5, 80-86, 91-2.*

Morales, Cristóbal de (* Seville, *c.*1500; † ?Marchena, betw. 4 Sept. and 7 Oct. 1553). Spanish composer. He probably studied with Pedro Fernández de Castilleja (*c.*1485-1574), *maestro de capilla* at Seville Cathedral, and was himself *maestro de capilla* at Avila Cathedral (1526) and at Plasencia (1528) before leaving for Italy in 1530, where he joined the papal choir in Rome in September 1535. In 1540 his first book of Masses was printed in Venice, but in 1545 he returned to Spain, working at Toledo, Marchena and Málaga.

Morales wrote chiefly for the church, anticipating with his austere outlook the style and spirit of the Counter-Reformation.

Morley, Thomas (* Norwich, 1577/8; † London, early Oct. 1602). English composer, editor, theorist and organist. He was probably a choirboy at Norwich Cathedral and may have studied with Byrd in London. In 1583 he was appointed organist and master of the choristers at Norwich Cathedral, remaining there until 1587. He took a B. Mus. degree at Oxford the following year and by 1589 had been appointed organist at St Paul's Cathedral in London. In 1592 he was made a gentleman of the Chapel Royal. In 1598 he was granted the patent for printing music which had previously

belonged to Byrd, but by then most of his madrigals and church music had already been published.

By grafting the Italian shoot onto native stock, Morley became the most influential figure in the brief but brilliant flowering of the Elizabethan madrigal.

Mozart, Wolfgang Amadeus (* Salzburg, 27 Jan. 1756; † Vienna, 5 Dec. 1791). Austrian composer. *See pp.253-83.*

Muffat, Georg (* Megève, Savoy, bapt. 1 June 1653; † Passau, 23 Feb. 1704). German composer and organist of French birth.

Muffat trained in Paris (1663-9) and became organist and chamber musician to the Archbishop of Salzburg. In 1681/2 he was in Rome, studying with Pasquini, but by 1690 he had left Salzburg to become Kapellmeister in Passau.

Unique in having worked with both Corelli and Lully, Muffat brought their styles to Germany, absorbing them into his own idiom – demanding Italian practice in his concertos and French methods in his fifteen *Florilegium* suites. His flexible approach to forms reaches its peak in his organ toccatas and variations (1690).

Mysliveček, Josef (* Prague, 9 Mar. 1737; † Rome, 4 Feb. 1781). Bohemian composer. He became a miller, like his father, but also studied music. In 1763 he left for Venice where he studied with Giovanni Pescetti (*c.*1704-66), and his first opera *Medea* was performed at Parma the following year. Its success brought him other commissions, and in 1772 he visited Vienna and Munich, but soon returned to Italy, where his music was more appreciated. However, after 1779 his style was overtaken by changes in taste, and his last works met with failure. He died in poverty and neglect.

Mysliveček grafted a natural melodic gift onto an international operatic style and cultivated it where the artistic and material rewards were greatest. As well as operas he wrote oratorios, symphonies and chamber music, and his keyboard sonatas earned the commendation of Mozart.

Obrecht, Jacob (* ?Bergen op Zoom, 22 Nov. *c.*1450; † Ferrara, 1505). Netherlands composer. In 1476 he was made choirmaster at Utrecht and later worked at Bergen op Zoom, at Cambrai, at St Donation, Bruges, and at Antwerp. He spent two periods at the Este court in Ferrara, in 1488 and 1504-5.

Obrecht's most important works are his Masses, of which he is known to have written at least 29. His other works are mainly motets, both sacred and secular, many of the latter settings of Dutch texts.

Ockeghem, Johannes (* *c.*1410; † ?Tours, 6 Feb. 1497). Franco-Flemish composer. He may have studied with Binchois, but certainly

he was a singer at Notre Dame in Antwerp in 1443-4, and shortly afterwards entered the service of Charles I, Duke of Bourbon. From 1451 he was attached to the Chapelle Royale of France. His travels to Spain and Italy brought him in contact with leading musicians of his day.

Ockeghem's Masses, motets and chansons are admired both for their contrapuntal ingenuity and for their expressiveness.

Pachelbel, Johann (* Nuremberg, bapt. 1 Sept. 1653; † Nuremberg, buried 9 Mar. 1706). German composer and organist. He studied voice, organ and composition, but could not afford university studies and from 1670 filled organist's posts in Regensburg, St Stephen's Cathedral, Vienna, and Eisenach. In 1678 he obtained a major post in Erfurt, by which time his organ playing was exceptional and his composing style mature as a result of contact with Kerll and with Italian works. His reputation as performer, teacher and composer spread rapidly. A short unsettled period involving posts at Stuttgart and Gotha (1690-95) ended with his return to Nuremberg.

Pachelbel's most celebrated music is for organ, comprising some 150 chorale-based compositions and *Magnificat* fugues for liturgical use, as well as variation sets and toccatas.

Paisiello, Giovanni (* Rocca-forzata, nr. Taranto, 9 May 1740; † Naples, 5 June 1816). Italian composer. He studied in Naples, and in 1764 his first opera was produced at Bologna. He quickly became famous at Naples as a composer of comic opera and in 1776 was appointed *maestro di cappella* to Catherine II at St Petersburg. He returned to Naples in 1784 and entered the service of Ferdinand IV, but after the revolution of 1799 was suspended until 1801. The following year he became director of chapel music to Napoleon, but remained in France barely two years. When in 1806 Napoleon's brother Joseph ousted Ferdinand IV, Paisiello became director of music, but Ferdinand returned in 1815, and Paisiello died in disgrace.

Paisiello was a gifted opera composer, *Il barbiere di Siviglia*

(1782) and *Nina* (1789) being particularly admired, and he also wrote oratorios and church music, as well as a few instrumental compositions.

Palestrina, Giovanni Pierluigi da (* probably at Palestrina, 1525/6; † Rome, 2 Feb. 1594). Italian composer. He was a choirboy at S. Maria Maggiore in Rome, and in 1554 was appointed organist at Palestrina Cathedral. When the Bishop of Palestrina became Pope Julius III (1550), Palestrina was made *maestro* of the Cappella Giulia at St Peter's, the next year.

In 1554 his first book of Masses was published, with a dedication to the Pope, and in 1555 he was admitted to the Pope's official chapel, the Cappella Sistina. After Julius's death, Palestrina left the chapel and became director of music at St John Lateran (1555-60) and at S. Maria Maggiore (1561-6). Between 1567 and 1571 he was in the service of Cardinal Ippolito d'Este, taught at the Seminario Romano and wrote music for the Gonzaga court at Mantua. In 1571 he returned as *maestro* to the Cappella Giulia.

The purity and mastery of Palestrina's polyphony made his music, especially his Masses, a model of all that was perfect in late Renaissance style.

Pepusch, Johann Cristoph (* Berlin, 1667; † London, 20 July 1752). German-born English composer, teacher and theorist.

Having worked for twenty years at the Prussian Court, he moved to Holland in 1700 and settled in London in 1703/4, becoming a leading figure in English musical life. He was music director to the Duke of Chandos at Cannons, and he arranged the music for Gay's

The Beggar's Opera. He took Italian models for his chamber music and English cantatas, while incorporating Germanic contrapuntal elements. Of his 100 or so instrumental sonatas, the five sets for violin, though influenced by Corelli, are individual works in a wide range of keys.

Pergolesi, Giovanni Battista (* Iesi, Marche, 4 Jan. 1710; † Pozzuoli, nr. Naples, 16 Mar. 1736). Trained initially by local musicians, Pergolesi was sent in about 1722 to the conservatory of the Poveri di Gesù Cristo at Naples, where in return for his services as vocalist and violinist he paid no fees. From 1732 he held appointments in Naples, but he died at the age of twenty-six.

No other composer has achieved so much of permanent value in a public career of barely four years, but many works were (and still are) misattributed to him. His only authentic compositions are one sacred opera, four *opere serie*, two *intermezzi*, two *commedie musicali*, six chamber cantatas, two fine Masses, a handful of other sacred works and a small quantity of instrumental music. Apart from his celebrated *Stabat Mater*, it was his sparkling *buffo* style that ensured lasting fame, in works such as the *commedia Lo Frate 'nnamorato* (1732) and the *intermezzo La Serva padrona* (1733) – still the center of Parisian operatic storms in 1752.

Peri, Jacopo (* Rome, 20 Aug. 1561; † Florence, 12 Aug. 1633). Italian composer, singer and instrumentalist. In 1579 Peri was appointed organist at the Badia, Florence, and in 1586 (or earlier) a singer at S. Giovanni Battista. From 1588 until his death he served as singer and composer at the Medici court. He wrote the music for Rinuccini's pastoral drama *Dafne*, performed in 1598, and in 1600 his *Euridice*, the earliest opera for which complete music has survived, was staged. Peri continued writing dramatic works and solo songs for Mantua and Florence, though the evidence of his contemporaries suggests that he was more gifted as a singer than as a composer.

Pérotin (fl. Paris, *c.*1200). French composer of organum, discantus and conductus. Pérotin was active in Paris and is almost as obscure a figure as his predecessor Léonin. He was associated with Notre Dame, Paris, and perhaps also St Germain-l'Auxerrois there. He is said to have revised the *Magnus liber* of organum (attributed to Léonin) in use at Notre Dame.

Perti, Giacomo Antonio (* Bologna, 6 June 1661; † Bologna, 10 Apr. 1756). Italian composer. He was admitted to the Accademia Filarmonica in 1681 and held various Bolognese posts before becoming director of music

at S. Petronio (1696), a position he retained until his death.

Perti was the dominant personality of the later Bologna school, and his 21 operas were widely successful. He also wrote some 200 chamber cantatas, 28 Masses, 20 oratorios and about 150 large-scale psalms and motets.

Philidor, François-André Danican (* Dreux, 7 Sept. 1726; † London, 31 Aug. 1795). French composer and world-famous chess player. The most distinguished member of a musical family that had been in royal service for two generations, he was a choirboy in the Chapelle Royale at Versailles and studied under Campra. His extensive travels to play chess gave him a more cosmopolitan outlook than other French composers of his generation.

Philidor wrote 25 operas, including *Tom Jones* (1765), based on Fielding's novel, and *Ernelinde* (1767), considered his finest work. His half-brother Anne was the founder of the *Concert Spirituel* in 1725.

Piccinni, Niccolò (* Bari, 16 Jan. 1728; † Passy, nr. Paris, 7 May 1800). Italian opera composer. He studied with Durante in Naples, where his first opera, a comedy, was performed in 1754. As well as writing operas for major Italian centers, he held posts as organist at Naples Cathedral and at the Royal Chapel and also taught singing. In Rome his most famous opera *La Cecchina, ossia La buona figliuola* (1760), to a libretto by Goldoni, was a wild success, but in the 1770s the fickle Roman public transferred their favors to Anfossi and towards the end of 1776 Piccinni left for Paris. Here he was soon caught up in the pamphlet controversy over rival

versions of *Iphigénie en Tauride*, his own and that by Gluck. Piccinni's opera (1781), although not without merit, was unable to compete with Gluck's masterpiece of two years earlier. He returned to Naples in 1791, but went back in 1798 to Paris, where he died.

Pleyel, Ignaz Joseph (* Ruppersthal, Austria, 18 June 1757; † Paris, 14 Nov. 1831). Austrian composer, music publisher and piano-maker. Pleyel was apprenticed to Haydn at Eisenstadt, and his first opera, for marionettes, was given at Eszterháza in 1776. After spending a number of years in Italy, during which time he wrote an opera for Naples, he became assistant to F. X. Richter at Strasbourg Cathedral, succeeding him as Kapellmeister in 1789. After the Revolution Pleyel spent six months in London (Dec. 1791-May 1792) directing the *Professional Concert* in rivalry with Salomon. In 1795 he settled in Paris, where he founded an important music-publishing firm and, in 1807, also started trading as a piano-manufacturer. During the rest of his life composition took second place to these new interests. His son Camille (1788-1855) succeeded him in the firm.

Pleyel's compositions include 40 symphonies, several concertos and a vast body of chamber music.

Porpora, Nicola Antonio (* Naples, 17 Aug. 1686; † Naples, 3 Mar. 1768). Neapolitan composer and singing teacher. Although trained locally, he had risen by 1715 to be head of vocal and composition studies at the Naples conservatory of S. Onofrio, but only after collaboration with Domenico Scarlatti (1718) did he become internationally famous. Between 1726 and 1747 he was director of music at the Ospedale degli Incurabili in Venice and at the conservatory of S. Maria di Loreto in Naples, and from 1733 to 1736 he headed the rival opera company to Handel's in London. In 1747 he moved to Dresden, becoming court Kapellmeister (with Hasse). Retiring to Vienna in 1752-3, he acquired the young Haydn as pupil, assistant and valet. In 1760 he returned to

academic posts in Naples, where he died impoverished.

As well as operas and cantatas Porpora wrote effective church music, attractive violin and trio-sonatas and some concertos.

Praetorius, Michael (* Creuzburg an der Werra, nr. Eisenach, 15 Feb. ?1571; † Wolfenbüttel, 15 Feb. 1621). German composer, theorist and organist. After working at Frankfurt-an-der-Oder, in 1592 he became was organist and later Kapellmeister at Wolfenbüttel. He stayed there until 1620, but traveled widely, spending two and a half years in Dresden, where he met Heinrich Schütz and became acquainted with the most recent Italian music, and was employed at Magdeburg, Halle, Sondershausen, Kassel and elsewhere.

Praetorius was an important composer of church music, much of it based on Lutheran chorales. He was also the author of the *Syntagma musicum*, one of the most comprehensive of all seventeenth-century treatises on music.

Purcell, Henry (* London, 1659; † London, 21 Nov. 1695). English organist and composer. *See pp.156-9*

Rameau, Jean-Philippe (* Dijon, bapt. 25 Sept. 1683; † Paris, 12 Sept. 1764). French composer and theorist. Having studied in Milan, his early career was as an organist, and not until he was forty did he permanently forsake the provinces for Paris. Though he had written keyboard pieces, motets and secular cantatas, his compositions were little known; however, his theoretical writings now brought him fame as a leading, if controversial, musical thinker. He held no permanent organ post in Paris until 1732, but issued further keyboard volumes (1724, 1728), worked on light theatrical sketches, and became director of the private orchestra of the financier-patron La Pouplinière, who encouraged him to compose his first opera, *Hippolyte et Aricie* (1733). Belatedly he had found his most stimulating creative outlet, and he composed almost 30 stage works. Despite fierce criticism, the operas brought Rameau public success, royal commissions and elevation to the nobility. He produced *comédies* and ballets as well as *tragédies lyriques*, while his keyboard works, many of them short *genre* pieces, foreshadow his dramatic accomplishment. *See pp.143-4, 154-5.*

Reichardt, Johann Friedrich (* Königsberg [Kaliningrad], 25 Nov. 1752; † Giebichenstein, nr. Halle, 27 June 1814). German composer and writer on music. *See Volume II.*

Richter, Franz Xaver (* 1 Dec. 1709; † Strasbourg, 12 Sept. 1789). German composer and singer of Moravian-Bohemian descent. After working in Kempten, he moved in the mid-1740s to Mannheim, where he sang bass and may have played violin. He composed symphonies, church music and oratorios, but became increasingly dissatisfied with the Mannheim style and in 1769 left to become Kapellmeister at Strasbourg Cathedral, where he remained until his death.

Trained in the Fux tradition, Richter cultivated a more conservative and contrapuntal style than his contemporaries at Mannheim, to be seen in his symphonies, sonatas, church music and oratorios.

Rore, Cipriano de (* ?Mechelen, 1515/16; † Parma, Sept. 1565). Flemish composer. Rore seems to have been in Venice in the 1540s, since his first books of madrigals (1542) and motets (1544) were published there by Gardano. He was director of music at the ducal court in Ferrara (*c.*1545-59), working subsequently in Brussels and Parma. In 1563 he succeeded Willaert as director of music at St Mark's, Venice, though he soon returned to Parma.

Rore was the first great composer to concentrate chiefly on madrigal writing, but he also composed some fine church music, including five Masses.

Rosetti, Francesco Antonio (Franz Anton Rösler) (* Leitmeritz, [Litoměřice], *c.*1750; † Ludwigslust, 30 June 1792. Bohemian

composer and contrabass player. He finished his Jesuit training in 1773, but renounced his vows and took up employment with the Prince of Oettingen-Wallerstein as a contrabass player and later Kapellmeister, composing works for the prince's famous wind band. In 1789 he left to become Kapellmeister to the Duke of Mecklenburg-Schwerin.

Rosetti's music combines personal wit and charm with the grace of the early classical style and the contrapuntal strength of the late Baroque. His works include symphonies, concertos, instrumental music, oratorios and a Requiem.

Rousseau, Jean-Jacques (* Geneva, 28 June 1712; † Ermenonville, 2 July 1778). Swiss philosopher, author and composer. Largely self-taught, Rosseau left Geneva in 1728 and was for a time flautist and singer at Annecy Cathedral. In the early 1740s he composed operas in Lyon and Paris with little success, and in 1743 went to Venice as secretary to the French ambassador. He returned to Paris and continued his operatic ventures, but only with *Le Devin du village* in 1752 did he achieve popular acclaim.

Although composition came second to Rousseau's literary and philosophical work, he initiated a new type of French opera and also developed the melodrama.

Salieri, Antonio (* Legnago, 18 Aug. 1750; † Vienna, 7 May 1825). Italian composer and teacher, mainly resident in Vienna. Orphaned in 1765, Salieri studied in Venice with Giovanni Pescetti, going the following year to Vienna with Gassmann, who taught him counterpoint. During the 1770s he had several operas performed at the Burgtheater, succeeding Gassmann in 1774 as court composer and director of the opera. In 1788 he became Kapellmeister, a post he held for thirty-six years. He scored many operatic successes in Italy and Paris, but gave up composing large-scale works after 1804, although he continued to participate in the musical life of Vienna and was much sought after as a teacher. His pupils included Beethoven, Schubert, Hummel and Liszt.

Sammartini, Giovanni Battista (* ?Milan, 1700 or 1701; † Milan, 15 Jan. 1775). Milanese composer. In 1728 he became director of music to the Congregation of the Santissimo Entierro in Milan. During the 1730s Sammartini became widely known outside Milan, mainly through his symphonies, which circulated in both printed editions and manuscript copies. He also composed a great deal and was in demand as a teacher, his most notable pupil being Gluck. As Milan's most distinguished musician, he came into contact with many foreign visitors, including J. C. Bach and Mozart.

While most of his Italian contemporaries excelled as vocal composers, Sammartini's three operas are of little interest, and he is important as a protagonist of the early classical style in symphony.

Sarti, Giuseppe (* Faenza, bapt. 1 Dec. 1729; † Berlin, 28 July 1802). Italian composer. Sarti studied under Padre Martini in Bologna and became organist at Faenza Cathedral in 1748, director of the theater in 1752 and in 1753 wrote his first opera. In 1775 he went to Copenhagen as Kapellmeister to King Frederick V and wrote operas in both Danish and Italian. After twenty years he returned to Italy and in 1779 became director of music at Milan Cathedral. He continued to write operas and in 1784 succeeded Paisiello at St Petersburg, where he collaborated on one of the earliest Russian operas.

Scarlatti, Alessandro (* Palermo, 2 May 1660; † Naples, 22 Oct. 1725). Italian composer noted especially for his operas and cantatas. At the age of twelve Scarlatti went to study in Rome and then entered the service of ex-Queen Christina of Sweden and the cardinals Pamphili and Ottoboni. In 1684 he went to Naples, where he remained for the rest of his life, apart from a brief spell between 1702 and 1707. He traveled extensively from there, however, to supervise productions of his operas. *See pp.124-7.*

Scarlatti, Domenico (* Naples, 26 Oct. 1685; † Madrid, 23 July 1757). Italian composer, keyboard teacher and performer. At sixteen

Scarlatti was his father Alessandro's assistant organist and composer in the Royal Chapel, Naples, and from 1705 to 1719 he worked mainly in Rome, writing church music and operas, perhaps under the psychological domination of his father, which he finally countered by a writ of independence (1717). In 1719 he assumed church and court appointments at Lisbon, and in 1729 moved to Spain as harpsichordist and (probably) court music organizer to his pupil, Princess Maria Barbara of Portugal.

Few of his vocal works survive, and neither they nor his 17 orchestral *sinfonie* are remarkable. But in Iberia he wrote 550 keyboard sonatas which reveal creative powers and musical sensitivity of the highest level, and which are remarkably advanced in technique and idiom, pointing openly to the classical age.

Scheidt, Samuel (* Halle, bapt. 3 Nov. 1587; † Halle, 24 Mar. 1654). German composer and organist. Scheidt became organist at the Moritzkirche in Halle in 1603 and in 1608 went to spend a year in Amsterdam to study with Sweelinck. He returned to Halle, becoming Kapellmeister (1620) and, briefly, director of town music (1628-30). His later years were spent in teaching and composition.

Scheidt published instrumental dance music and motets, but his chief compositions were for the keyboard, contained in his *Tabulatura nova*, and his vocal *Geistliche Concerte*.

Schein, Johann Hermann (* Grünhain, nr. Zwickau, 20 Jan. 1586; † Leipzig, 19 Nov. 1630). German composer. Schein was a choirboy in the Dresden court chapel in 1599 and studied law in Leipzig. After a year as Kapellmeister at Weimar, he became cantor at St Thomas's, Leipzig.

Schein's many compositions include German songs, Latin and German motets, spiritual madrigals (*Konzerte*), dance suites and chorale harmonizations, as well as secular concertato pieces. He was instrumental in developing the *geistliches Konzert*, in which he combined a modern Italian declamatory style with Lutheran chorale melodies in a remarkable way.

Schütz, Heinrich (* Köstritz, Thuringia, ?14 Oct. 1585; † Dresden, 6 Nov. 1672). German composer. Schütz went to Venice in 1609 and studied with Giovanni Gabrieli until 1612. On his return he was court organist in Kassel, and then in 1617 Kapellmeister in Dresden. He returned to Venice in 1628, to familiarize himself with the new music of Monteverdi and Grandi, and there were also visits to Copenhagen in 1633-5 and 1642. He retired soon after 1650.

Schütz played a central role in the creation and development of early baroque style in Germany, bringing to it what he absorbed on his two visits to Italy. Apart from early Italian madrigals and a lost opera, *Dafne*, all his surviving output is sacred music. His three late Passions, in an archaic style, continued a German tradition which can be traced through to J. S. Bach. *See also pp.98-100.*

Senfl, Ludwig (* ?Basle, c.1486; † Munich, 1542/3). Swiss composer active in Germany. As a choirboy in Vienna, Senfl was taught by Isaac. He studied for the priesthood and had a living at Basle Cathedral but was still employed at court. After a period in Italy he returned to the court chapel in Vienna, and succeeded Isaac as court composer. It was not until 1523 that Senfl found a permanent post in Munich, where he remained until his death. He resigned his clerical status in 1529. Lutheran sentiments are embodied in the pieces he wrote between 1526 and 1540, though his other music was mainly for the Roman rite, including seven Masses and numerous Latin motets.

Sermisy, Claudin de (* c.1490; † Paris, 13 Oct. 1562). French composer often known as Claudin. He was a cleric at the Sainte Chapelle, Paris, and a singer in the personal chapel of King Louis XII, taking charge in 1532. Sermisy was one of the greatest masters of the French chanson, of which he left about 175 examples. He also wrote some excellent church music, including a dozen Masses, a Passion, several *Magnificat* settings and many motets.

Stamitz, Carl (* Mannheim, bapt. 8 May 1745; † Jena, 9 Nov. 1801). German composer and violinist of Bohemian origin. He received his musical training from his father

Johann and from other musicians at Mannheim, but left when he was twenty-five. During the 1770s he was in Paris, but after that held no permanent post until 1795, when he was appointed Kapellmeister and teacher of music at Jena University. Like his father, he made an important contribution to the early classical symphony and wrote numerous *symphonies concertantes* for Paris as well as many concertos and chamber works.

Stamitz, Johann (* Německý Brod [now Havlíčkův Brod], bapt. 19 June 1717; † Mannheim, buried 30 Mar. 1757). Bohemian violinist, composer and teacher. He joined the Mannheim orchestra as a violinist c.1741, and was the principal violinist by 1743. Further promotion brought him the post of Konzertmeister and, in 1750, director of instrumental music.

Stamitz trained his orchestra to a remarkable pitch of excellence, and the symphonies he composed for it are very important in the early history of the genre, establishing the four-movement form used by Haydn and his contemporaries.

Stradella, Alessandro (* ?Nepi, nr. Viterbo, 1638/9; † Genoa, 25 Feb. 1682). Italian composer. Stradella worked for Christina of Sweden as singer and composer. Though always in demand as a composer of oratorios, operas and dramatic works, he was forced out of Rome (1677) because of his scandalous life, working in Venice, Turin and Genoa.

A celebrated vocal composer, Stradella is significant in the development of baroque style. Relatively few dramatic works survive, but there are some 200 cantatas and large quantities of church music. His instrumental compositions include excellent trio- and solo violin sonatas.

Sweelinck, Jan Pieterszoon (* Deventer, ?May 1562; † Amsterdam, 16 Oct. 1621). Netherlandish composer, organist and teacher. His father, Peter Swybbertszoon, was organist at the Oude Kerk, Amsterdam, from about 1564, and from about 1577 Sweelinck held the same post for the rest of his life. Much admired as an organist and teacher, he almost single-handedly created the school of Dutch and north German organists.

The largest part of Sweelinck's output consists of sacred vocal music, though little was intended for church use, since Amsterdam was a Calvinist stronghold, but his organ music gave the decisive impetus to the German school.

Tallis, Thomas (* c.1505; † Greenwich, 23 Nov. 1585). English composer. Organist of the Benedictine Priory of Dover in 1532 and then of St Mary-at-Hill, London, in 1537, Tallis moved to Waltham Abbey the following year. In 1540 he went as a lay clerk to Canterbury Cathedral and in 1542 became a gentleman of the Chapel Royal, remaining a member of the royal household for the rest of his life.

In 1575 Byrd and Tallis were granted a patent from Queen Elizabeth I to print and publish music. Like Byrd, Tallis wrote church music for both Catholic and Anglican rites and, as a practicing organist, made an important contribution to the repertory of early English keyboard music.

Tartini, Giuseppe (* Pirano, Istria, 8 Apr. 1692; † Padua, 26 Feb. 1770). Italian composer, violinist, teacher and theorist. Tartini studied music largely independently. By 1714 he was in the Ancona opera orchestra and by 1720 was orchestral director at the basilica of St Anthony in Padua. A flexible contract enabled him to travel; he was frequently in Venice, and in Prague in 1723-6. He made the Padua orchestra outstanding, and for forty years from c.1727 directed a violin school which drew gifted students from all over Europe and ensured the dissemination of his advanced technical principles, exemplified in the renowned 'Devil's Trill' sonata. In 1740 injury restricted his playing, and after 1750 he composed little, preferring to concentrate on theoretical studies, but in the thirty years from 1720 he wrote some 150 violin concertos, many other concertos and *sinfonie*, some 200 sonatas and other pieces for violin and about 30 sacred items.

Telemann, Georg Philipp (* Magdeburg, 14 Mar. 1681; † Hamburg, 25 June 1767). German composer. Telemann was

a precocious, largely self-taught musician. He went to Leipzig to study law, but turned increasingly to music and finally abandoned law to direct the Leipzig Opera and found the Collegium Musicum. From 1708 to 1712 he was at the court in Eisenach, where he met J. S. Bach. After nearly ten years in Frankfurt-am-Main he moved in 1721 to Hamburg as cantor of the Gymnasium Johanneum and music director of the city's principal churches, remaining there until his death.

Telemann was a prolific composer, writing in every current musical form, including operas, oratorios and cantatas as well as keyboard, orchestral and instrumental works. He was also active in organizing concerts and as a writer and publisher.

Tomkins, Thomas (* St Davids, Pembrokeshire, 1572; † Martin Hussingtree, Worcestershire, buried 9 June 1656). British composer. His father was organist and choirmaster at St Davids Cathedral. He studied with Byrd in London, and became instructor to the choirboys of Worcester Cathedral in 1596. By 1621 he was a gentleman of the Chapel Royal, and in that year he was appointed one of the Chapel Royal organists, though retaining his Worcester appointment.

Services and anthems for the Anglican rite make up the bulk of Tomkins's compositions, but he also wrote notable madrigals, consort and keyboard music.

Torelli, Giuseppe (* Verona, 22 Apr. 1658; † Bologna, 8 Feb. 1709). Italian composer. Torelli seems to have been director of music at Imola Cathedral before moving to Bologna, where he was elected as violinist to the Accademia Filarmonica in 1684 and promoted to composer c.1692. By 1686 he had become a member of the *cappella* of S. Petronio, frequently performing elsewhere in northern Italy. When the orchestra was disbanded he worked in Germany and Austria, and served the Margrave of Brandenburg as violinist, composer and musical director, rejoining the re-formed S. Petronio orchestra after 1701.

As chief representative of the Bologna school, Torelli was a major force in the development of the concerto. His surviving work is almost entirely instrumental, including some 80 concertos.

Traetta, Tommaso (* Bitonto, nr. Bari, 30 Mar. 1727; † Venice, 6 April 1779). Italian composer. Traetta studied at Naples and in 1758 was appointed director of music at Parma, where he tried to unite French *tragédie lyrique* with Neapolitan *opera seria*. He received commissions from Mannheim and Vienna, and in 1765, when interest in opera declined in Parma, he moved to Venice. Three years later he went to St Petersburg as music director to Catherine II. Ill health forced him to leave in 1775, and in 1777 he returned to Venice.

Except for church music and an oratorio, Traetta wrote almost entirely for the stage, including over 40 full-length operas, some of which influenced Gluck; others were in turn influenced by Gluck's reform operas.

Tunder, Franz (* Burg, Fehmarn Island, 1614; † Lübeck, 5 Nov. 1667). German composer. In 1614 he was appointed to the Marienkirche in Lübeck, where he founded the famous recitals, or *Abendmusiken*. Tunder is significant not only for his contribution to the organist's repertoire with his *Preludes* – that combine the techniques of fugue and toccata – and his chorales, but also as a composer of solo motets and choral cantatas.

Vanhal, Johann Baptist (* Nové Nechanice, Bohemia, 12 May 1739; † Vienna, 20 Aug. 1813). Bohemian composer and music teacher. He studied with local teachers and between 1757 and 1760 held minor appointments as organist and choirmaster. His violin playing and some of his music attracted the interest of Countess Schaffgotsch, who sent him to Vienna to study with Dittersdorf. Between 1769 and 1771 he was in Italy. A post in Dresden had to be turned down because of mental illness, and Vanhal never again held a permanent position, but made a living by composing and teaching. From 1780 he lived in Vienna.

The works for which Vanhal is remembered are the symphonies, of which over 70 are extant, and he also wrote a vast quantity of chamber works, the string quartets being of particular interest.

Viadana, Lodovico Grossi da (* Viadana, nr. Parma, *c*.1560; † Gualtieri, 2 May 1627). Italian composer. He became a friar and held a number of church musical posts. His historic importance lies in his introduction into sacred polyphony of a *basso seguente* part for organ, an important step in the introduction of *basso continuo* and the development of the solo motet.

Victoria, Tomás Luis de (* Avila, 1548; † Madrid, 20 Aug. 1611). Spanish composer. Victoria sang as a choirboy in Avila Cathedral and in 1563-5 enrolled in the German College in Rome as a singer, coming into contact with the music of Palestrina. Between 1569 and about 1574 he was a singer and organist at S. Maria di Monserrato in Rome, and then director of music at the German College until 1576/7. In 1575 he was made a priest. He left Rome to become chaplain to the Dowager Empress Maria at the Monasterio de las Descalzas de S. Clara in Madrid, where he was chaplain and choirmaster and later organist.

Victoria composed only sacred music, most of which was published during his lifetime. His twenty Masses are among the finest examples of Renaissance church music, and his Office for Holy Week has a drama and poignancy rarely equalled during the sixteenth century.

Vitry, Philippe de (* Paris, 31 Oct 1291; † Paris, 9 June 1361). French philosopher, mathematician, scholar and musician. He studied at the Sorbonne in Paris and was made Bishop of Meaux in 1351.

Vitry's treatise *Ars Nova*, dating from about 1322-3, lent its title to a new range of musical expression that characterized the fourteenth century, and initiated far-reaching developments in the notation of musical rhythms. Of his own music only about a dozen motets survive.

Vivaldi, Antonio (* Venice, 4 Mar. 1678; † Vienna, 28 July 1741). Italian composer. His father, Giovanni Battista, a violinist at St Mark's, was his principal teacher. Suffering ill-health all of his life, Antonio surmounted disability and undertook a hectic musical career as performer, teacher, composer and operatic entrepreneur. From 1703 (when he was ordained priest) he held teaching positions with the Ospedale della Pietà, making its gifted orchestra of women one of Europe's most brilliant ensembles and a force in the spread of his fame and ideas. Only in 1738, when Venetian popularity had deserted him, did the Pietà authorities discard him. He traveled to Amsterdam that year, and in 1740 to Vienna hoping to renew his fortunes, but he died there impoverished.

Vivaldi wrote 40 operas and over 50 solo motets and psalms, but it was in instrumental music that he excelled, producing some 60 *concerti grossi*, over 400 solo, double and multiple concertos and nearly 100 solo, trio and mixed sonatas. *See pp.113-5, 128-30.*

Wagenseil, Georg Christoph (* Vienna, 29 Jan. 1715; † Vienna, 1 Mar. 1777). Austrian composer, keyboard player and teacher. When Wagenseil was twenty his musical gifts attracted the notice

of J. J. Fux, who taught him for three years and recommended him for the post of court composer, which he held until his death.

Wagenseil's early compositions were mainly sacred, followed by operas for the Viennese court in the years up to 1750, but his reputation rests on his symphonies, concertos and other instrumental works composed in the latter part of his career.

Weelkes, Thomas (* ?Elsted, Sussex, ?25 Oct. 1576; † London, buried 1 Dec. 1623). English composer. Weelkes was a gifted madrigalist and a major composer of English church music, most of whose rather checkered career was spent at Chichester Cathedral.

His madrigals are noted for their contrapuntal mastery, expressive word-painting, and harmonic boldness. His church music, no less accomplished, includes about 50 anthems and several services.

Wert, Giaches de (* ?Weert, nr. Antwerp, 1535; † Mantua, 6 May 1596). Flemish composer working in Italy. Wert went to Avellino, near Naples, as a child and from 1553 or 1558 was at Novellara in the service of Count Alfonso Gonzaga. In about 1565 he was appointed director of music to the Mantuan court, where he remained until his death, though traveling widely and also establishing ties with the Este court at Ferrara.

Wert was particularly admired for his madrigals, which are progressive in style and in some ways anticipate the new music of Monteverdi, who may have been his pupil.

Wilbye, John (* Diss, Norfolk, bapt. 7 Mar. 1574; † Colchester, 1638). English composer. By 1598 he had become a musician at Hengrave Hall, near Bury St Edmunds, where he remained for about thirty years. Wilbye published only two sets of madrigals (in 1598 and 1609), but they are regarded as perhaps the finest by any Englishman.

Willaert, Adrian (* Bruges or Roulaers, *c*.1490; † Venice, 17 Dec. 1562). Flemish composer and teacher, active in Italy. He studied law in Paris and took music lessons with Mouton. From July 1515, or earlier, he was at Ferrara, and traveled to Hungary

in 1517. In 1519 he returned to Ferrara, and in 1520 became a singer in the ducal chapel. He moved to Milan in 1525 and two years later to Venice, as director of music at St Mark's, where he remained until his death. His pupils there included Zarlino, Rore and Andrea Gabrieli.

Willaert's music includes numerous sacred compositions for St Mark's, as well as important contributions to the French chanson and the Italian madrigal.

Zelenka, Jan (* Lounovice, 16 Oct. 1679; † Dresden, 22 Dec. 1745). Bohemian composer. He received general and musical education in Prague, finding work there until in 1710 he became a contrabass player in the Dresden court orchestra. He studied with Fux in Vienna (1715) and Lotti in Venice (1717), returning to Dresden in 1719, where in 1735 he acquired the post of 'church composer.'

Zelenka's highly individualistic idiom no doubt militated against general favor, although he was clearly admired by discerning contemporaries. The bulk of his output was religious music, including three oratorios, a sacred opera about St Wenceslas and twelve Masses, as well as many smaller works.

INDEX

PICTURE CREDITS